THE DEADLY EMBRACE

By the same authors

OPERATION LUCY
COLONEL Z – A SECRET LIFE

ANTHONY READ
and
DAVID FISHER

THE DEADLY EMBRACE

Hitler, Stalin and the Nazi-Soviet Pact
1939–1941

W·W·NORTON & COMPANY
New York   London

To Rosemary and Barbara,
with love and gratitude

Printed in the United States of America.

Library of Congress Cataloging-in-Publication Data

Read, Anthony.
The deadly embrace: Hitler, Stalin, and the Nazi-Soviet Pact,
1939-1941 / Anthony Read and David Fisher.
p. cm.
Bibliography: p.
Includes index.
1. World War, 1939-1945—Diplomatic history. 2. Germany.
Treaties, etc. Soviet Union, 1939 Aug. 23. 3. Germany—Foreign
relations—Soviet Union. 4. Soviet Union—Foreign relations—
Germany. I. Fisher, David, 1929 Apr. 13- II. Title.
D749.5.R8R43 1988
940.53′2—dc19   88-18123

ISBN 0-393-02528-4

W. W. Norton & Company, Inc., 500 Fifth Avenue, New York, N.Y. 10110
W. W. Norton & Company Ltd., 37 Great Russell Street, London WC1B 3NU
1 2 3 4 5 6 7 8 9 0

CONTENTS

LIST OF ILLUSTRATIONS

LIST OF MAPS

ACKNOWLEDGEMENTS

A comprehensive list of those who helped us in interviews and correspondence is printed elsewhere in this book, but we must record our special gratitude to Hans 'Johnnie' von Herwarth, for pointing us in the right direction at the outset and for opening so many doors; his wife Elisabeth 'Pussi' von Herwarth, whose vivid personal memories brought the pre-war diplomatic community of Moscow to life for us; to Walter and Eva Schmid, whose warm hospitality, detailed knowledge and enthusiasm helped to sustain us in our long researches; to Dr Karl Schnurre, for so patiently answering so many questions both grand and trivial about his part in the events described in this book; to the late Sir Hugh Greene, for allowing us to use not only his professional despatches but also his private letters to his mother; to Professor John Erickson, for his usual firm but lively guidance; to Professor Anthony Upton and Professor Geoffrey Hosking for their wise counsel and advice on Finland and the Soviet Union respectively; to Dr Ingeborg Fleischhauer, for her hospitality and advice; to the late Sir Conrad Collier, for sharing his memories of the military mission to Moscow and its personalities; to Alexei Nikiforov, for his efforts on our behalf in arranging our visit to Moscow; to Richard Schulze-Kossens, for welcoming us into his home and giving us so much information about his time as adjutant, first to Ribbentrop and then to Hitler; to the late Albrecht Graf von der Schulenburg and his family, for receiving us so warmly in the castle restored by Ambassador von der Schulenburg and for providing us with memories and documents concerning him; to Lasse Lehtinen for his help in organising our trip to Finland; to Johann Nykopp, for spending so much time in guiding us through the Winter War and for helping to make our stay in Finland so memorable; to Dr Erich Sommer, for his hospitality, good advice and a wealth of fascinating information; and to Bundespräsident Richard von Weizsäcker, for finding space in his crowded presidential schedule to receive us and spend so much time talking to us about the subject of this book and particularly about his late father. To all of these, and to all those who gave us their time and attention so generously, we offer our grateful thanks.

As always, we are grateful to the librarians and staff of the several libraries and archives which have helped us in obtaining documents, books and other research material. These include: the Foreign Office Library, London; the Federal German Foreign Office Archives, Bonn; the National Archives, Washington; the Bundesarchiv, Koblenz; the Sikorski Institute, London; the Imperial War Museum, London; the London Library; the New York Public Library; Berkshire County Library, Maidenhead and Slough; Buckinghamshire County Library, Burnham.

We received help and advice from the embassies in London of the Soviet Union, the Federal Republic of Germany, Bulgaria, Finland, Romania and Yugoslavia, for which we thank them all.

For invaluable assistance with research and translation we thank Andrew Wiseman, Frank Hilton and Patrick Hinchy. For coping with the enormous task of word processing and managing to remain not only cheerful but also immensely enthusiastic, we are doubly grateful to Angela Cassidy of Syntax Wordprocessing.

We are deeply indebted to our editors and publishers, notably to Donald Lamm and Starling Lawrence of W. W. Norton & Company for yanking us firmly back on to the track whenever we began to stray, and to Alan Brooke and Roland Philipps of Michael Joseph. We sincerely hope we have repaid them with a finished book that is worthy of their patience and constant encouragement. In this area, we must also mention our agents, Julian Bach in New York and Murray Pollinger in London, for their unfailing support – and give special thanks to Julian Bach for suggesting the subject of this book in the first place.

Finally, but by no means least, we must pay tribute to the amazing forbearance of our wives, Rosemary Read and Barbara Fisher, during the long haul of research and writing. For five years *The Deadly Embrace* has dominated all our lives, and without their support, the task we undertook in 1982 might well have proved impossible – as at times it appeared to be. Any success which this book achieves will belong to them as much as it does to us.

*

We gratefully acknowledge the following publishers and copyright holders for permission to use quotations from the books listed: Cassell PLC: 1940: *The Second World War* by Winston S. Churchill; Century Hutchinson Limited: *The Last Attempt* by Birger Dahlerus, *Mein Kampf* by Adolf Hitler, trs. Ralph Manheim (UK rights), *Who Helped Hitler?* and *Memoirs of a Soviet Ambassador* by Ivan Maisky (UK rights); Don Congdon Associates Inc.: *Berlin Diary* by

William L. Shirer; Collins: *Against Two Evils* by Hans von Herwarth with Frederick Starr, *Child of the Revolution* by Wolfgang Leonhard; Curtis Brown: *An Opposing Man* by Ernst Fischer; André Deutsch Limited: *Home and Abroad* by Lord Strang; Doubleday & Company, Inc.: *The Ciano Diaries*, edited by Hugh Gibson; Victor Gollancz Limited: *Under Two Dictators* by Margarete Buber, *Memoirs* by Ernst von Weizsäcker; Greenwood Press: *Home and Abroad* by Lord Strang (USA rights); Hamish Hamilton Limited: *The Goebbels Diaries* edited by Fred Taylor; William Heinemann Limited: *Hitler's Interpreter* by Paul Schmidt; Her Majesty's Stationery Office: Cabinet Papers, *Documents on British Foreign Policy*, *Documents on German Foreign Policy*; Houghton Mifflin Inc.: *Duel for Europe* by John Scott, *Mein Kampf* by Adolf Hitler, trs. Ralph Manheim (USA rights); Albert Langer Georg Müller: *Das Memorandum* by Erich F. Sommer; Macmillan Publishers Limited: *An Army in Exile* by Lieutenant-General W. Anders; Progress Publishers: *History in the Making* by Valentin Berezhkov, Judy Piatkus (Publishers) Limited: *Liliana's Journal* by Liliana Zuker-Bujanowska; Putnam Publishing Group: *The Goebbels Diaries* edited by Fred Taylor (USA rights); The Royal Institute of International Affairs: *Hitler's Speeches* edited by N. H. Baynes; Raymond Savage Limited: *Failure of a Mission* by Sir Nevile Henderson; Souvenir Press Limited: *Stalin and His Generals* edited by Seweryn Bialer; The USSR Copyright Agency (VAAP): *Who Helped Hitler?* and *Memoirs of a Soviet Ambassador* by Ivan Maisky (USA rights), *Memoirs* by Georgi Zhukov; A. P. Watt Limited: *Only One Year* and *Twenty Letters to a Friend* by Svetlana Alliluyeva; George Weidenfeld & Nicolson Limited: *Witness to History* by Charles E. Bohlen, *Inside the Third Reich* by Albert Speer, *Inside Hitler's Headquarters* by Walter Warlimont.

In a very few cases, in spite of making every effort, we have been unable to trace the copyright holders of material from which we have made quotations. To these, and to anyone we may have inadvertently missed, we offer our apologies and our thanks.

Anthony Read
David Fisher
November 1987

PRINCIPAL PERSONALITIES

GERMAN

ADOLF HITLER Führer and Chancellor of Germany 1933–45 (committed suicide, 30 April 1945)

JOACHIM VON RIBBENTROP Foreign Minister 1938–45 (hanged at Nuremberg, 16 October 1946)

FIELD MARSHAL WALTHER VON BRAUCHITSCH Army Commander-in-Chief 1938–December 1941 (retired after severe heart attack; died in British captivity, 1948)

VICE-ADMIRAL WILHELM CANARIS Chief of the Abwehr, the OKW intelligence service, 1935–44 (hanged by the Nazis, April 1945, for complicity in assassination attempt on Hitler)

DR JOSEPH GOEBBELS Minister of Propaganda 1933–45 (committed suicide in Hitler's bunker, 30 April 1945)

REICHSMARSCHALL HERMANN GÖRING Minister for Air 1933–45, President of Reichstag, Luftwaffe Commander-in-Chief 1935–45, Head of Four Year Plan (committed suicide at Nuremberg, 1946)

GENERAL HEINZ GUDERIAN Panzer commander, inventor of *Blitzkrieg*

COLONEL-GENERAL FRANZ HALDER Army Chief of Staff 1938–42 (imprisoned in concentration camp for anti-Hitler activities, rescued from execution 4 May 1945 by US troops)

HANS 'JOHNNIE' VON HERWARTH Second secretary, German embassy in Moscow 1931–39 (escaped detection as member of the assassination plot against Hitler, 20 July 1944; first ambassador in London for German Federal Republic, 1955–61, head of Presidential Office, Bonn, 1961–5, ambassador in Rome 1965–9)

RUDOLF HESS Deputy Führer until flight to Britain, 1941 (sentenced to life imprisonment at Nuremberg; died in captivity, 1987)

WALTHER HEWEL Ribbentrop's personal liaison man with Hitler 1938–45

LIEUTENANT-GENERAL ALFRED JODL Chief of operations staff, OKW, 1939–45, Hitler's closest military adviser (hanged at Nuremberg, 16 October 1946)

GRAND ADMIRAL ERICH RAEDER Navy Commander-in-Chief 1935–43 (sentenced to life imprisonment at Nuremberg; died in captivity, 1960)

PAUL OTTO SCHMIDT Chief interpreter, Foreign Ministry, 1923–45, head of secretariat 1935–45

DR KARL SCHNURRE Head of Eastern Europe section, Foreign Ministry economic policy department, principal economic negotiator 1938–45

COUNT FRIEDRICH WERNER VON DER SCHULENBURG Ambassador in Moscow 1934–41 (executed by Nazis for complicity in 20 July assassination plot, 1944)

MAJOR-GENERAL WALTER WARLIMONT Deputy to Jodl in OKW 1939–45

BARON ERNST VON WEIZSÄCKER State Secretary in the Foreign Ministry 1938–43; ambassador to the Holy See 1943–45 (tried and acquitted at Nuremberg; released 1949; died 1951)

SOVIET

JOSEF V. STALIN General Secretary of the Communist Party of the Soviet Union 1922–53, Chairman of the Council of People's Commissars (Prime Minister) 1941–53 (died of cerebral haemorrhage, 5 March 1953)

VYACHESLAV M. MOLOTOV Chairman of the Council of People's Commissars (Prime Minister) 1930–41, Foreign Commissar 1939–49 (expelled from Communist Party 1964, reinstated July 1984; died peacefully 8 November 1986, aged 96)

GEORGI A. ASTAKHOV Counsellor of embassy, Berlin, 1938–41 (died in Soviet prison camp at Komi, late 1941)

EVGENY BABARIN Deputy head of Soviet trade delegation in Berlin 1938–41

VALENTIN M. BEREZHKOV Interpreter for Molotov on November 1940 visit to Berlin; first secretary, Berlin embassy, December 1940–June 1941

VLADIMIR G. DEKANOZOV Ambassador to Berlin 1940–41, previously head of foreign affairs for NKVD and Deputy Foreign Commissar (purged December 1953 and executed)

LIEUTENANT-GENERAL (later Marshal) FILLIP I. GOLIKOV Stalin's intelligence chief 1940–41

ADMIRAL NIKOLAI G. KUZNETSOV Naval Commissar 1939–53

MAXIM M. LITVINOV Foreign Commissar 1930–39, chief of foreign affairs information, Central Committee of CPSU, 1939–41; ambassador to Washington 1941–3

IVAN M. MAISKY Ambassador to London 1932–43

ALEXEI MEREKALOV Ambassador to Berlin 1938–9

ANASTAS I. MIKOYAN Trade Commissar 1926–64 (President of the Soviet Union, 1964–5; died peacefully in retirement, October 1978)

VLADIMIR P. POTEMKIN Deputy Foreign Commissar 1937–45

MARSHAL BORIS S. SHAPOSHNIKOV Army Chief of Staff 1937–40, 1941–2

MARSHAL SEMEN K. TIMOSHENKO Defence Commissar 1940–1

MARSHAL KLIMENT Y. VOROSHILOV Defence Commissar 1926–40 (President of the Soviet Union 1953–60; died peacefully in retirement, 3 December 1969)

ANDREI Y. VYSHINSKY First Deputy Foreign Commissar 1940–6 (Soviet representative at UN, 1946–54; died peacefully 1954)

ALEXANDER S. YAKOVLEV Leading aircraft designer, Deputy Commissar for the Aircraft Industry 1940 onwards

ANDREI A. ZHDANOV Secretary Leningrad Communist Party, member of Politburo, Chairman of Foreign Affairs Commisssion, President of Naval Soviet (died 1948)

GENERAL (later Marshal) GEORGI K. ZHUKOV Chief of Staff January–July 1941, the Soviet Union's most successful and most decorated commander (Defence Minister 1955–7; died peacefully in retirement 1974)

BRITISH

NEVILLE CHAMBERLAIN Prime Minister 1937–40

WINSTON CHURCHILL First Lord of the Admiralty 1939–40, Prime Minister 1940–45

ANTHONY EDEN Minister of War May–December 1940, Foreign Secretary 1935–38, December 1940–45

VISCOUNT (later EARL) HALIFAX Foreign Secretary 1938–40, ambassador to Washington 1940–45

ADMIRAL THE HON. REGINALD PLUNKETT-ERNLE-ERLE-DRAX, ADC to King George VI, leader of Allied military mission to Moscow 1939

SIR NEVILE HENDERSON Ambassador to Berlin 1937–9

ROBERT HUDSON Secretary to Department of Overseas Trade 1937–40

GENERAL (later Field Marshal Lord) SIR EDMUND IRONSIDE Inspector-General of Overseas Forces 1939, Chief of the Imperial General Staff 1939–May 1940, Commander-in-Chief Home Forces May-July 1940

SIR WILLIAM SEEDS Ambassador to Moscow 1939–41

WILLIAM STRANG Head of Central Department, Foreign Office

SIR HORACE WILSON Chief Industrial Adviser to Chamberlain

FRENCH

EDOUARD DALADIER Prime Minister April 1938–March 1940
PAUL REYNAUD Prime Minister May–June 1940
GEORGES BONNET Foreign Minister April 1938–September 1939
CAPTAIN ANDRÉ BEAUFRE Assistant to air force representative in military mission to Moscow, 1939
ROBERT COULONDRE Ambassador to Moscow 1936–October 1938, to Berlin November 1938–September 1939
GENERAL JOSEPH DOUMENC Leader of French delegation in military mission to Moscow, 1939
PAUL NAGGIAR Ambassador to Moscow 1939–41

ITALIAN

BENITO MUSSOLINI Founder of the Fascist party, head of government and Prime Minister 1922–43
COUNT GALEAZZO CIANO Foreign Minister 1936–February 1943, son-in-law of Mussolini (executed for attempting to overthrow Mussolini, 1943)
BERNARDO ATTOLICO Ambassador to Berlin 1935–May 1940

FINNISH

MARSHAL CARL GUSTAV VON MANNERHEIM Commander-in-Chief 1939–44 (President 1944–6)
ELJAS ERKKO Foreign Minister 1938–9
JUHO PAASIKIVI Leader of delegation to Moscow, 1939 (Prime Minister 1918, 1944–6, President 1946–56)
VÄINÖ TANNER Finance Minister 1938–9, Foreign Minister 1939–41

JAPANESE

YOSUKE MATSUOKA Foreign Minister July 1940–July 1941
GENERAL HIROSHI OSHIMA Military attaché in Berlin 1936–8, ambassador November 1938–October 1939, February 1941–May 1945

POLISH

COLONEL JOSEF BECK Foreign Minister 1932–September 1939
MARSHAL EDWARD SMIGLY-RYDZ Inspector-General of the army, 1936–9
JOSEF LIPSKI Ambassador to Berlin 1934–9
COUNT EDWARD RACZYNSKI Ambassador to London 1934–45 (later President of government-in-exile)

SWEDISH

BIRGER DAHLERUS Swedish businessman, friend of Göring, unofficial emissary to London 1939

SWISS

CARL J. BURCKHARDT League of Nations High Commissioner in Danzig 1937–9

THE DEADLY EMBRACE

Prologue

'THE BIGGEST FRONT LINE IN HISTORY'

Josef Vissarionovich Djugashvili, better known as Stalin, absolute ruler of the Union of Soviet Socialist Republics, left his office in the Kremlin earlier than usual during the night of 21–22 June 1941. Normally, he worked in the long Cabinet room in the Praesidium building, with its green-baize-covered conference table in the centre, and the stern eyes of Lenin, Marx and Engels staring out from their portraits on the oak-panelled walls, until about 5 am. As the first light of day glimmered on the golden onion domes of the cathedrals opposite his window and coloured the rosy red bricks of the crenellated outer walls of the ancient city within a city, he could regularly be found at his cluttered desk, cocooned in smoke from the dark 'Herzegovina Flor' cigarettes which he smoked constantly, sometimes broken up into tobacco for his English Dunhill pipe. But that night, of all nights, he finished work well before 2 am, and after clearing one or two outstanding items with his secretary, A. N. Poskrebyshev, walked along the corridor from room number one, took the little, red-carpeted, gilt elevator down one floor to ground level, and left the building.

Settled in the back of his black armoured limousine, he was whisked away through the still warm, sleeping streets and out of Moscow. He had rarely slept in his apartment in the Kremlin since his wife committed suicide there in 1932, and he apparently saw no reason to make this night an exception. The motorcade surrounding his car, controlled by his personal security chief, the huge, square-shouldered NKVD General Nikolai Vlasik, drove as always down the middle of the road at full speed. It covered the twenty miles to Kuntsevo, then a small village in the pine and birch forests to the east of Moscow, in well under half an hour. There, it turned left off the broad, dark highway on to a side road, past a security barrier manned by armed guards in a clump of young fir trees, and on through a gate, also heavily guarded, into the driveway of a

single-storey, rambling white house set amidst gardens and terraces.
This was Stalin's dacha *Blizhny* – the name simply means 'nearby', to
distinguish the place from his other houses, which were all further away
from Moscow. It was not a grand house, certainly no palace. Stalin's
daughter, Svetlana, always remembers it with affection: in summer the
roof was a vast sun deck where she loved to run and play as a child.
Blizhny was a wonderful house for children. Stalin had had it designed
to his own specifications in 1934, but since then he had changed it
continuously, having rooms knocked together, rooms divided, new
rooms built on, even whole floors added and removed again. Stalin was
never satisfied with any house for long. All his homes, but *Blizhny* in
particular, were in a permanent state of structural flux, like a colony of
amoeba.

In spite of his obsession with building and rebuilding, however, Stalin
personally lived almost entirely in one room of the house at Kuntsevo,
the dining room. He slept on a sofa there, with the various telephones
that kept him in touch with the outside world lined up on a low table
beside it. Stalin always slept on sofas, never in a bed; when he did stay in
the Kremlin, he used a couch in a small office beyond the Cabinet room.
The other furnishings of the *Blizhny* dining room were simple: a
sideboard, several chairs and a large table which was usually piled high
with documents, books and newspapers. When dining alone, he had one
end cleared and ate there. Only when he was entertaining people –
members of the Politburo, the Soviet Union's inner Cabinet, or
particularly favoured visiting dignitaries – was the whole table cleared,
and its front half set with all kinds of Russian and Georgian dishes on
warmed silver platters.

On 22 June there was no one to entertain, so Stalin retired early. He
was fast asleep on his sofa soon after 2.30 am, seemingly untroubled by
the cares of the world.

The great majority of the Soviet population, both civil and military, was
also sleeping peacefully that night, except in the northern cities like
Leningrad, where thousands still promenaded happily through the
streets, celebrating the whitest of the 'white nights', the summer solstice,
when the sun barely dipped below the horizon. Despite the ominous
rumours which seeped in from the outside world, few were concerned
about the threat of war, for had not Stalin himself assured the nation
there would be no German invasion? Indeed, he had specifically
forbidden the Red Army to take more than the most tentative
precautions against possible incursions by German troops. Whatever
happened, he had ordered, Soviet frontier forces must not allow
themselves to be provoked into firing at the Germans: under no
circumstances was Hitler to be given the opportunity of branding the
Soviets as aggressors.

The evening of 21 June had therefore been almost exactly like any other summer Saturday, even in the frontier districts. Free from the fear of attack, the troops relaxed and enjoyed the warm sunny weather. Most senior officers were at home with their families, or at their clubs, or watching shows in garrison theatres or cinemas. Very few indeed were aware that they were in fact sitting on an immense powder keg – and that the fuse had already been lit.

On the other side of the Soviet Union's 930-mile-long western frontier with Germany, German-occupied Poland and Romania, and for a further 800 miles with Finland in the north, the picture was very different. As the brief darkness of the shortest night of the year descended, a mighty invasion force moved stealthily forward into the positions from which it was to attack at dawn. In forest clearings, amid cornfields and pastures, in the long grasses of river banks where the croaking of thousands upon thousands of amorous bullfrogs imprinted itself for ever on the memories of the waiting men, German officers assembled their troops and began giving them their final orders, prefaced by the reading of a proclamation from their Führer, Adolf Hitler.

'Soldiers of the eastern front' – Hitler's words echoed through companies and regiments, batteries and squadrons – 'an assembly of strength on a size and scale such as the world has never seen is now complete. Allied with Finnish divisions, our comrades are standing side by side with the victor of Narvik on the shores of the Arctic Ocean in the north. German soldiers under the command of the conqueror of Norway, and the Finnish heroes of freedom under their own marshal, are protecting Finland. On the eastern front, you stand. In Romania, on the banks of the Pruth, on the Danube, down to the shores of the Black Sea, German and Romanian troops are standing united under the head of state, Antonescu.' This was, Hitler declared, 'the biggest front line in history', and it was about to go into action, 'to save our entire European civilisation and culture' from the threat of bolshevism.

Between the Baltic and the Black Sea, the German forces were arranged in three massive army groups, comprising seven armies, four Panzer groups and three air fleets. Poised on the frontiers, waiting for dawn to break, were no fewer than 3,200,000 men – 148 divisions, including nineteen Panzer divisions and twelve motorised infantry divisions, with 600,000 trucks, 750,000 horses, 3,580 armoured fighting vehicles, 7,184 artillery pieces and 1,830 aircraft. It was indeed an awesome array of force – by comparison, the Allied invasion of Normandy on 6 June 1944 landed a first wave of six seaborne divisions and three airborne, a grand total of nine divisions containing some 75,000 British and Canadian troops and 57,000 Americans, along a front of less than fifty miles, as opposed to one of nearly 1,000.

It would clearly have been impossible to conceal the presence of such a vast force. Hitler had been assembling it since shortly after the beginning of the year, and by mid-May, when most units were in their preliminary positions, no fewer than 19,500 special trains had rolled eastwards from Germany, all clearly visible from the ground and from the air. There had been a hiatus in the build-up for a few weeks in March and April, when Hitler had been forced to withdraw some of the troops in order to crush Yugoslavia and Greece, but by returning them to the regions bordering the Soviet Union as soon as they had finished in the Balkans, he had made both their presence and their purpose even more obvious. To Winston Churchill, in London, these German troop movements 'illuminated the scene like a lightning flash', removing any doubts he may have had about Hitler's intentions. But their significance did not seem to have been appreciated by Stalin.

The Soviet leader had in fact been kept fully informed of the German build-up. He had been deluged with warnings for several months, from his own intelligence sources and from friendly foreign governments, notably the British and American. He had been told repeatedly that Hitler planned to attack him, and had even been given the correct date and time. Churchill had sent him, both directly and through clandestine channels which he thought the suspicious Stalin might accept more readily, the complete German order of battle and Hitler's plan of attack, obtained through Enigma intercepts. Stalin had chosen to ignore them all.

The last warnings were still pouring into the Kremlin during that fateful Saturday night and Sunday morning, as the final hours before the attack slipped away. From frontier guards along the entire border came reports of increased activity on the German side: they could hear engines being revved, the clink of equipment and the unmistakable screech and clatter of tank tracks. From London, Soviet Ambassador Ivan Maisky sent a message saying he had been called back from a weekend in the country to be told by Sir Stafford Cripps, the British ambassador to Moscow who was then in London for consultations, that the British government had reliable information that Hitler intended to attack the Soviet Union next day. A similar message came from the military attachés at the Soviet embassy in Berlin, though the ambassador there had told his staff to forget it and prepare for a Sunday picnic.

Still Stalin brushed the warnings aside. When a German deserter left his unit and crossed the lines specifically to alert the Soviets after hearing the orders for the attack, the Soviet leader dismissed the story as a German provocation. By that time, the Soviet Defence Commissar, Marshal Semen Timoshenko, and the Red Army's Chief of Staff, General Georgi Zhukov, were taking the reports seriously: they begged Stalin to allow them to put their frontier forces on full alert, and to issue live ammunition. But he refused. All he would agree to was a watered-down directive stating that it was thought the Germans might stage attacks in order to incite Soviet troops to fight, but that such provocations were to be resisted.

When Zhukov called him at 12.30 am on the Sunday morning, to report that a second German deserter had swum the river Pruth to bring a repetition of the warning, Stalin ordered the man to be shot, 'for his disinformation'. It was shortly after this that he left his office and went home, to sleep. He was still convinced that the threatening attitude of the German forces was nothing more than a ploy by Hitler to blackmail him into giving political and economic concessions.

Stalin was awakened shortly after 3.45 am by General Vlasik, who told him Zhukov was on the telephone from Moscow, demanding to speak to him. Sleepily, he lifted the receiver. At the other end, the Chief of Staff was agitated.

'The Germans are bombing our towns!' he shouted.

Stalin was silent, deeply shocked. Zhukov repeated his message, and went on to list reports of air raids on towns and cities, ports, harbours, airfields, rail junctions, from Sevastopol in the deep south to Tallinn in the north.

'I reported the situation,' Zhukov wrote later, 'and requested permission to order our troops to start fighting back. Stalin was silent. The only thing I could hear was the sound of his breathing. "Do you understand me?" I asked. There was silence again.'

Incredibly, Stalin still refused to believe that this was really war. He did not give Zhukov the authorisation he wanted, for the Red Army and Air Force to fight back. Instead, he called a meeting of the Politburo to discuss what was happening and what should be done. As he was being driven back to the Kremlin, the dawn sky along the western frontier of his empire, 350 miles away, was torn apart by gigantic flashes of artificial lightning and the ground beneath shuddered to the roar of man-made thunder, as the German artillery opened up its massive barrage. By the time he reached his office, German ground forces had crossed the frontiers to begin the actual invasion. But still he refused to believe what was happening, as garbled reports rained in.

The chaos and confusion among nearly all the Soviet frontier forces was compounded by the fact that undercover units from the Germans' Special Regiment 800, which had been operating behind the Soviet lines wearing Red Army uniforms for some days, had cut the telephone cables on which they depended for most of their communications. German aircraft had completed the task of disruption by destroying radio stations and signals centres, along with railway tracks and junctions, bombing them with a pinpoint accuracy made possible by months of aerial reconnaissance and photography which they had never bothered to conceal or deny. The bombers encountered little resistance anywhere.

So unprepared were the Soviets that few of the vital bridges across the broad rivers that form much of the frontier were mined with demolition charges, and those that were remained unblown. They were all captured intact by the Germans, either by force or by trickery – in several cases, German guards simply called their Soviet opposite numbers into the centre of the bridge, as though to talk, and then gunned them down; in other places German squads were hidden in rail wagons, under fake loads of gravel or other freight cargo, leaping out from cover and overpowering the guards after rolling across to the Soviet side. At zero hour, 3.15 am Central European Time, German armour was able to pour unhindered across the bridges.

Elsewhere, infantry and other units crossed the rivers in rubber dinghies or flat-bottomed boats, accompanied in many places by specially prepared submersible tanks, in the face of only rifle and light weapon fire from the Soviet border guards. They had no serious obstacles to overcome, since Stalin had forbidden the construction of any permanent defences or fortifications for fear they might upset Hitler!

On Soviet airfields, which had also been thoroughly reconnoitred by the Luftwaffe, few aircraft were either camouflaged or under cover. Most were neatly positioned, in full parade formation, ideally displayed for destruction. Many were actually pegged down to the ground, so that they could not easily be moved, and very few were either armed or fuelled. This was the normal condition in Soviet fields, to prevent pilots deciding either to abscond or to pose an armed threat to the regime. For the same reason, ammunition for the Red Army was kept under separate control, well away from the weapons it was intended for. The result was that when the Germans swooped down from the skies, not only were the Soviet planes sitting ducks, they were also unable to take off to defend themselves or their bases. By noon on 22 June, the Germans had destroyed some 1,200 Soviet aircraft, at least 800 of them on the ground. Within forty-eight hours, the number had reached 2,000, and the Red Air Force in the west was wiped out as a fighting force.

Like the attack itself, the sheer size of the catastrophe unleashed on the Soviet Union that day was unparalleled in history. It was to take the Soviet Union four long years of savage fighting to avenge Hitler's treacherous blow. The cost was enormous: at least twenty million Soviet citizens died in the war, a further twenty-five million were mutilated or crippled, and huge areas of the country were laid waste. Out of every hundred young Soviet soldiers who went to the front, only three survived physically unharmed to the end. It was a terrible price to pay for the blindness of one man, Josef Stalin, to the insatiable greed of one other, Adolf Hitler.

* * *

Unlike the other countries which Hitler had attacked since September 1939, the Soviet Union was, at least on paper, militarily stronger than Nazi Germany. Official Soviet figures give the size of the Red Army in June 1941 as 5,373,000 men, armed with over 67,000 field guns and mortars, 1,861 tanks, and over 2,700 combat aircraft 'of new types', plus even larger numbers of outdated, but still serviceable, older models. Of these forces, no fewer than 170 divisions with a total strength of 2,680,000 men, armed with 37,500 guns and mortars (Soviet figures do not differentiate between the two types of weapon), 1,475 tanks and 1,540 modern combat aircraft, were stationed in the western frontier districts. Bearing in mind the old military dictum strictly adhered to by Allied commanders of the day such as General Bernard Montgomery, that a numerical superiority of 3:1 is necessary to ensure the success of an attack, the Red Army should have had no difficulty in holding off the Wehrmacht, had it been prepared. The fact that it was not prepared, in spite of all the warnings that were given, must in the end be laid at the door of Josef Stalin.

'Stalin was so afraid of war,' Nikita S. Khrushchev, then first secretary of the Communist Party in the Ukraine, wrote in his memoirs, 'that even when the Germans tried to take us by surprise ... [he] convinced himself that Hitler would keep his word and wouldn't really attack us.' A good many of Khrushchev's pronouncements need to be taken with large doses of salt: he was always prepared to bend or stretch the facts in order to make a point, and the point he was constantly trying to make after he came to power was to denigrate everything about his predecessor. But in this case, there is undoubtedly a great deal of truth in what he says.

Why, then, was Stalin so afraid of war? Why was he willing, against all evidence and experience, to trust Hitler? What was the word which he believed Hitler would keep? Khrushchev himself supplies part of the answer to the first question. He says Stalin 'had obviously lost all confidence in the ability of our army to put up a fight', and claims that after the fall of France in 1940, Stalin had told him: 'Hitler is sure to beat our brains in.'

The answers to the other questions lie in the complex personal attitudes of the two dictators to each other, and in the deadly embrace into which they entered when their Foreign Ministers signed a non-aggression pact on their behalf in Moscow on 23 August 1939 – an embrace which could only end in the total destruction of one of them.

1

'THE ROAD OF THE TEUTONIC KNIGHTS'

Hitler and Stalin never met. Many commentators and historians have speculated on the possibility that had they done so they would have reached an understanding, and the war between their countries might have been avoided. Such wishful thinking ignores the fact that both men were prisoners of the systems which they had themselves created, prisoners of their own totalitarian philosophies, prisoners, too, of history.

The animosity between Germany and Russia stretches back over the centuries to a time before either of them existed as a nation. It is rooted in the rivalry between the two dominant racial groups in the central and eastern European landmass: Teutons and Slavs. When the early Slavs swept westwards as far as the river Elbe in the fifth century AD, it was a Teutonic tribe, the Goths, who gave them their name by calling them '*Slavan*', meaning silent. The Slavs, for their part, called the Teutonic tribes '*Niemcy*', meaning mute. For much of the time since then, communication between the two groups has been a dialogue of the deaf, if not the dumb.

Despite sometimes long periods of quiescence, the basic antagonism between the two races continued over the centuries from pre-history to modern days. During this time, the Teutons developed an unshakeable belief in their innate superiority; they were convinced they were the sole fount of all civilisation in the region. The inferior Slavs were incapable on their own of building cities, forming states or creating true culture: everything they had which was worthwhile had been achieved by or with the help of Germans.

The Germans had carried their culture with them when they pushed out to the east, sometimes peacefully, sometimes by force. The Teutonic Knights conquered Prussia and Lithuania by the sword; German merchants had brought trade, prosperity and stability to the Baltic;

German administrators had helped the tsars to run their empire; German settlers had developed the agriculture of great areas of Russia as far east as the Volga. During the nineteenth century there were literally millions of Germans farming Russian land – even at the end of the century, when their numbers had declined considerably, there were still some 1,800,000 ethnic Germans, *Volksdeutsche*, living in Russia outside the Baltic provinces. For the most part, they made no attempt to assimilate, but remained proudly and obstinately German, generally living in closed communities.

Along with their contempt for what they regarded as a backward people, however, the German nation also had a constant fear of being overrun by them. By the beginning of the twentieth century, tsarist Russia had a population of 170 million, while Germany had only 65 million, and the gap was growing wider all the time, for the Slav birthrate was three times that of the Germans'. Hitler himself called them 'an inferior race that breed like vermin'. With no natural frontiers, and therefore no physical barriers in the central landmass, the threat they posed seemed very real.

Otto von Bismarck, who united the German states into one nation in 1871, based his foreign policy on maintaining an understanding with Russia. But this was rooted in fear rather than friendship, expediency rather than expectancy. Kaiser Wilhelm II, who removed Bismarck from office in 1890, did not understand the 'Iron Chancellor's' policies, and allowed the relationship to sour. As a result, in 1914, Germany was faced with a war on two fronts, and although the Russians lived up to the poor estimation of their military capabilities, the effort needed to defeat them was a major factor in Germany's eventual downfall. Had the Russians been stronger, they could have swept across the plains and descended on Berlin like a horde of modern-day Mongols while the bulk of the German army was locked in combat with the French and British. The nightmare would have come true. As it was, it remained to haunt the German generals with the dread that no matter how much they despised the Russians, one day, inevitably, through sheer force of numbers they would be strong enough.

When tsarist Russia became the Soviet Union, the fear of bolshevism was added to the old radical anxieties. Although the military threat had collapsed, at least for the moment, there was now the danger that a weakened Germany could be fatally infected with this bacillus from the east. In 1917, though, the immediate need to remove Russia from the war far outweighed such worries, and the Germans even played their part in assisting the Bolshviks by allowing Lenin to return home across their territory.

The German leaders, however, had no intention of allowing Lenin and his associates to enjoy the fruits of their bloody revolution. Their intention was to take the opportunity of splitting up the old Russian empire into smaller, and therefore weaker, parts. Indeed, they eagerly signed a separate peace treaty in early February 1918 with the Ukraine, which, with active German encouragement, had already declared its independence. After finally signing a peace treaty with the Soviet government at Brest-Litovsk in March 1918, the Germans went on to recognise the independence of Georgia, and the Kaiser sent a message to the leader of the Don Cossacks outlining his plans for the 'ultimate partitioning of Russia into four independent states: the Ukraine, the Union of the South-East, Central Russia and Siberia', together with puppet grand duchies to be set up in the Baltic states.

The most important individual part of this plan was the Ukraine, which was to come completely under German economic control. Germany had entered the war in the West prepared only for a short campaign. When the armies became bogged down in the trenches, and the short campaign developed into a long war of grinding attrition, stocks of food and raw materials soon began to run short as the Allies, with the British Royal Navy controlling the seas, imposed a blockade which stopped fresh supplies getting through. The Ukraine, with its fertile black soil, its coal and iron mines, became a vital goal for the Germans: once they had it in their grasp, they could not be starved into submission.

As it happened, the collapse of Russia and the peace with the Ukraine came too late to save Germany, for the Allies had gained an even greater boost with the entry of the United States of America into the war. But the lesson was not lost on the German leaders, then or in the future. Least of all was it lost on Adolf Hitler.

When he wrote his testament, *Mein Kampf*, in 1924, Hitler castigated the government of the Second Reich for leading Germany into what he saw as a pointless war with the West, and declared: 'If land was desired in Europe, it could be obtained by and large only at the expense of Russia, and this meant that the new Reich must again set itself on the march along the road of the Teutonic knights of old, to obtain by the German sword sod for the German plough and daily bread for the nation.'

The insistence with which Hitler returned time after time in *Mein Kampf* to land and the plough illustrates the one great obsession which dominated all his thought and all his actions: ensuring the survival and the ultimate triumph of the 'Aryan' race. To achieve this, he had to provide it with '*Lebensraum*'. The word '*Lebensraum*', which occurred so frequently in Nazi philosophy, translates literally as 'living space', and certainly space was important to Germany at that time. Hitler claimed in *Mein Kampf*: 'Germany has an annual increase in population of nearly 900,000 souls. The difficulty of feeding this army of new citizens must grow greater from year to year and ultimately end in catastrophe, unless ways and means are found in time to forestall the danger of starvation and misery.' But the doctrine represented by *Lebensraum* was far more complex than the avoidance of overcrowding and the provision of food. Encompassing a mystical union of a race and the soil for which its blood has been spilt – '*Blut und Boden*' – it was burned into the German soul long before Hitler hijacked it as a cardinal principle of National Socialism.

The need for *Lebensraum* was not simply to provide food for a growing population, but actually to enable that population to grow. 'The duty of the foreign policy of a national state,' Hitler wrote, 'is to ensure the existence of the race included in that state by keeping a natural and healthy proportion between the numbers and the increase of the nation and the size and quality of the land in which they dwell. Nothing but sufficient space on the earth ensures freedom of existence to a nation. In this way only can the German nation defend herself as a world power.'

There was a valuable corollary in seeking this space in the east: the Slavs, Hitler maintained, were able to breed at three times the rate of the Germans because of the immense area they had to live in – by seizing and colonising much of that area, the Germans would not only increase their own rate of growth, but would also reduce that of the Slavs.

Truth and honesty had no place whatsoever in Hitler's dealings with other men: he regularly contradicted himself when talking of his intentions, telling everyone only what they wanted to hear or what he wanted them to believe at that particular moment – which has always been the bane of scholars and historians trying to assess exactly what he was about. But among the falsehoods and the vacillations, there is one constant, one overriding imperative: the determination to create his pure master race and to provide the conditions and the territory in which it could flourish. Ultimately, every major act of policy from the time he came into power was directed to this end. There were three great phases: first, the purification of the race by driving out or eliminating the Jews and other undesirables; second, the unification of the race under one banner through the creation of the Greater German Reich, incorporating those who were initially outside its frontiers in Austria, Czechoslovakia and Poland; and finally the drive into new lands to be colonised by them, to house and feed them and their descendants for the next thousand years. Everything else was of secondary importance. Hitler's only reason for going to war with Britain and France in 1939 was that they interfered with his plans by trying to stop him marching into Poland – the first, essential, stride on his way to the Soviet Union in general and the Ukraine in particular.

Stalin could hardly have been unaware of Hitler's designs on his empire. The Soviet leader was a completely political animal, given to detailed analysis of other leaders' words and deeds – though he did tend to overestimate his opponents' powers of logic, crediting such men as British Prime Minister Neville Chamberlain and French Minister President Édouard Daladier with machiavellian abilities equal to his own, when for much of the time they were only capable of muddling through from one crisis to the next. In failing to realise that Hitler worked on intuition and emotion rather than hard logic, however, Stalin made what was probably the most serious mistake of his career.

He had certainly read *Mein Kampf* in Russian translation, and must therefore have been familiar with passages such as this (the italics are Hitler's in the original): *'We take up where we broke off 600 years ago. We stop the endless German movement to the south and west, and turn our gaze towards the land in the east. At long last we break off the colonial and commercial policy of the pre-war period and shift to the soil policy of the future.* If we speak of soil in Europe today, we can primarily have in mind only *Russia* and her vassal border states . . . This colossal empire in the east is ripe for dissolution. And the end of Jewish domination in Russia will also be the end of Russia as a state. We have been chosen by Fate to be the witnesses of a catastrophe which will be the strongest confirmation of the soundness of the nationalist theory of race.'

Given that he knew all this, it seems strange that Stalin should have chosen to sign first a non-aggression pact and then a treaty of friendship with such a man as Hitler – especially when that man also wrote: *'You do not make pacts with anyone whose sole interest is the destruction of his partner.'* (Again, the italics are Hitler's.) But in truth, Stalin had little or no choice in 1939, for while Hitler had made Nazi Germany the best-equipped, most efficient and most feared military power in the world, Stalin himself had all but destroyed the Red Army as an effective fighting force with savage purges during 1937–8. Terrified that the army and its officers would be able to challenge his leadership and perhaps even mount an armed revolt against him, he had instigated the arrests of most of the generals and senior officers on charges of 'espionage and treason to the Fatherland'.

The floodgates were opened for the military purges on 11 June 1937 with the execution of Marshal M. N. Tukhachevsky, the most brilliant commander in the Red Army and probably the only man who could then have posed a personal threat to Stalin's position, plus seven leading generals. At the same time as the announcement of the sentences – which had already been carried out – Defence Commissar Kliment Voroshilov issued an order to all military districts demanding that any suspect persons should be immediately denounced.

The references to Tukhachevsky and his fellow victims in Voroshilov's order are most revealing in the light they throw on Stalin's fears: 'The ultimate objective of the traitors was the annihilation of the Soviet regime at any cost and by all means. They strove for the overthrow of the workers' and peasants' government and had made preparations for murdering the leaders of the party and the government. They expected help from the fascist circles of a foreign country and, in return, would have been prepared to hand over the Soviet Ukraine.'

The orgy of killings released by Voroshilov's order quickly reached horrifying proportions. Accurate figures are, of course, impossible to obtain, but most reliable estimates place the number of men who were either shot or sent to labour camps at around 35,000. At least half of the army's entire officer strength was removed, including three out of the five marshals, thirteen out of fifteen army commanders, 220 out of 406 brigade commanders, seventy-five of the eighty members of the supreme military council, including every single commander of a military district, and all eleven vice-commissars of war. The remnants were inexperienced, disorganised and completely demoralised, and the modernisation and mechanisation programmes, which had been progressing well, were utterly shattered.

At the same time, the Soviet Union's political and administrative leadership had also been devastated by Stalin's civil purges. Present-day Soviet historian Roy Medvedev believes the number of those summarily shot was between 400,000 and 500,000, and that the total number of victims during the years 1936–9 was some 4·5 million. Like the armed forces, the national and local governments – and the economy which they controlled – were clearly in no fit state to face up to a rampant Nazi Germany.

Stalin was thus left with three options in resisting Hitler's desire to destroy the Soviet Union and colonise her most fertile regions with his own people. The first was to sacrifice the Ukraine and allow Hitler to occupy it virtually unopposed, in the hope that he would then be satisfied. The second was to seek help elsewhere, by forming military alliances, especially with the Western Powers, against Germany. The third was to try to deflect Hitler from his purpose, even if only temporarily, by offering him friendship and the supplies of food and raw materials which he needed, without his having to fight for them. Coupled with this last option would be help in obtaining territory elsewhere.

The first option was obviously out of the question and was not even worth considering. The other two would therefore have to be pursued, simultaneously if possible.

In spite of all their personal, ideological and historic reasons for enmity, Hitler and Stalin had good, practical reasons for co-operation, if not for actual friendship. Indeed, there were excellent precedents for such a policy. Bismarck had followed this line with tsarist Russia, and in the infant – though hardly tender – years of the Soviet Union, the two nations had been literally forced into each other's arms by the hostility of the rest of the world. For when the victors of the first world war set out to create a brave new Europe at the Paris Peace Conference in 1919, they turned Germany and Communist Russia into twin outcasts.

With the demise of the other continental empires, Austro-Hungarian and Ottoman, Germany was left to carry the entire responsibility for the war. The Western Powers, led by France, were determined to make her pay for it in every possible way, stripping the Germans of territory, colonies, weapons, most of their remaining wealth and all of their dignity. As for the Russians, they were blamed for capitulating and making a separate peace with Germany at Brest-Litovsk – though Lenin had since denounced that treaty and was busily trying to reclaim those parts of the tsars' empire which had seceded with German help. At the same time, the Germans were blamed by the Allies for aiding and abetting the Bolsheviks and thus assisting in the hated Russian Revolution, which the democracies were then trying to suppress by sending in troops to intervene against the Reds in the Civil War that was raging throughout Russia.

In such circumstances, it is hardly surprising that the two countries should have turned to each other for the only support either was likely to find. And while there were vast differences between their regimes, they did have many things in common. The most significant, both then and over the next two decades, was their shared resentment of the Treaty of Versailles, particularly where this involved the boundaries of new states. Both lost heavily, and nowhere more so than in the reborn Poland, which was largely carved out of Germany in the west and the old Russia in the east, taking not only territory but also people from each. Both were agreed that the new Poland had no right to exist – but the Poles made quite sure of the Russians' continuing hatred by invading the Ukraine on 25 April 1920, capturing Kiev, the capital, on 6 May. They were only driven out a month later and forced to retreat to Warsaw by a Red Army brilliantly commanded by Tukhachevsky, the man Stalin was to execute in 1937.

The young German republic, which had earlier refused to join an economic blockade against Russia, now prepared to join her in destroying Poland. But before General von Seeckt, Commander-in-Chief of the new German army, the Reichswehr, could put his plans into operation, the Poles, aided by the French, staged a successful counter-attack. The Russians were defeated, and for the second time in three years were forced to sue for peace on extremely unfavourable terms. The Polish price was a further 40,000 square miles of territory to the east of the Curzon Line, the frontier decided on by the Allies, plus the whole of the Ukrainian province of eastern Galicia. In the process, they gained some six million Ukrainians. It was a settlement which was to rankle with the Soviets for the next eighteen years.

With the Germans also feeling bitter over the loss of large areas of Prussia and the ancient Hanseatic seaport of Danzig, plus the separation of East Prussia from the rest of Germany by a corridor of land giving Poland access to the Baltic Sea, it could only be a matter of time before one or both of Poland's once powerful neighbours decided to seek revenge, and to take back what they saw as rightfully theirs. This common interest helped to unite Germany and the Soviet Union. They established full diplomatic relations in May 1921, but even before then, Lenin had proposed a collaboration between the Red Army and the Reichswehr, a suggestion that was welcomed by Seeckt with the comment: 'Poland must disappear!' In 1922, when the Allies tried to play them off against each other, they took the world by surprise by signing a pact, at Rapallo in Italy.

For the next ten years both countries were happy to continue their marriage of expedience. In 1926, they signed a pact of friendship and neutrality, and as Stalin emerged as Lenin's successor, having ruthlessly outmanoeuvred all the other apparently better qualified contenders, he made no attempt to change his policy. Trade between them prospered and the Soviet Union helped Germany to get round the restrictions placed on her armed forces by providing not only military schools and training grounds but also factories in which the Germans could build new generations of aircraft and armaments. In return, the Germans opened their staff colleges to Red Army officers, most of whom had only been NCOs in the tsarist forces, where they could learn the higher arts of strategy, logistics and administration.

Everything changed abruptly, however, when Hitler came to power at the end of January 1933. Although both regimes continued to protest their desire for continuing good relations – and in fact the 1926 friendship treaty was renewed in May 1933 – Soviet–German trade during the first half of that year was almost halved. At the same time, the Reichswehr moved out of its secret bases in the Soviet Union. The days of trust and collaboration were over.

With true Marxist pragmatism, Stalin at first welcomed Hitler's accession, reasoning that he could not last long and that his inevitable fall would clear the way for a communist take-over. Indeed, he even ordered that members of the KPD, the German Communist Party, should vote for the Nazis and not for the Social Democrats in the first and last free elections of the Hitler era on 5 March 1933. But as the thirties progressed, Stalin's fears and suspicions grew – though some observers believed that he viewed many of the Nazi dictator's actions with a certain amount of admiration. Hitler's 'Night of the Long Knives', for example, when he eliminated all potential threats from inside the Nazi Party with between 100 and 200 brutal murders (the exact figure has never been established) on the night of 30 June to 1 July 1934, is often considered to have been the model for Stalin's own purges.

The seeds of Stalin's policy of pursuing his twin options to protect the

Soviet Union against Germany were sown at this time. On the one hand, he sought to establish good relations with the Nazis, losing no opportunity to point out how well Moscow got along with other right-wing governments, notably those of Turkey and Italy where the communist parties were completely banned. 'We don't care if you shoot your German communists!' declared Maxim Litvinov, the Soviet Foreign Commissar. At the same time, however, Litvinov, on Stalin's behalf, was vigorously pursuing other alliances, a policy which he labelled 'collective security'.

Litvinov was an urbane and sophisticated statesman of great charm and ability, a short, plump man who wore well-cut suits, wide-brimmed panama hats in summer and rakish fur caps in winter, and whose pince-nez glasses always sported an elegant black ribbon. He had held his current position since 1930, but his experience in foreign affairs stretched back over many years. He had travelled widely, had lived in England – where he had been arrested and gaoled for passing banknotes stolen in 1907 during a bank raid masterminded by Stalin himself in Tbilisi, Georgia – and even had an English wife. He had been exchanged in 1918 for a British secret agent arrested in Moscow, one of the first deals of its kind in modern times. He was also a Jew, which was one more reason why he was not inclined to look kindly upon Hitler and his regime. As long as he was Foreign Commissar, the option of friendship with Germany would always come second, as it clearly did at that time with Stalin.

In trying to establish a defensive line of buffer states between the Soviet Union and Germany, Stalin was even prepared to swallow his pride and overlook the grievances he had with these regimes. He signed extended non-aggression pacts with the former tsarist provinces of Estonia and Latvia, which had seceded at the end of the first world war, though this meant continued recognition of their independence. He signed similar pacts with Poland and Romania, though this meant formally accepting the new frontiers which Poland had gained by force, and acknowledging the loss of the Ukrainian province of Bessarabia to Romania, which had seized it in 1919.

Looking further west, Stalin aligned himself with France by signing a pact of mutual assistance with Czechoslovakia, in which the Soviet Union promised to come to the aid of the smaller nation should she be attacked – but only if the French did so first. And later that year, in September 1934, he made a complete about-face by taking the Soviet Union into the League of Nations, an organisation which he had always professed to despise, and then supporting the French in their efforts to develop an all-embracing Eastern European pact, in which all the nations in the region would guarantee not to attack each other. The attempt failed when not only the Germans but also the Poles flatly refused to take part.

Collective security depended for its effectiveness not only on the Western Powers preferring to join forces with the Soviet Union against Hitler, but also on their being prepared to take effective action. European responses to the moves made by Hitler and his friends, notably Benito Mussolini, fascist dictator of Italy, piled doubt upon doubt that they would ever do any such thing.

When Hitler in his first months as Chancellor took Germany out of the international disarmament conference and then out of the League of Nations, Britain and France remained silent. They did nothing, either, in early 1935, when he took back the heavy industrial region of the Saar, on Germany's south-western border with France, which had been detached from Germany in 1919 to be administered by the League of Nations. And when, on 16 March, he denounced the disarmament clauses of the Versailles treaty and restored universal military service in Germany, they made indignant protests, but again did nothing. Their reaction to Mussolini's invasion of Ethiopia that year was exactly the same – a great deal of noise but no action.

Soviet hopes for Anglo-French involvement in collective security rose when both the future British Foreign Secretary, Anthony Eden, and his French counterpart, Pierre Laval, visited Moscow for talks in April and May 1935 respectively. The French even signed a mutual assistance pact with the Soviet Union – but significantly the drafting of the military agreement needed to make any assistance effective was postponed until later, and in fact was never completed.

A year after this, on 7 March 1936, Hitler made his boldest move yet, testing the Allies to the limit by sending German troops into the Rhineland, which had been declared a demilitarised zone in 1919. Since this placed his growing army to the west of the Rhine and immediately alongside the border with France, even Hitler's own generals believed the French could not possibly ignore it, but were bound to react violently. Hitler himself was apprehensive enough to order that the occupation was to be aborted at the first sign of opposition from the French army on land or the British Royal Navy around German ports. In the event, neither made any such move. Appeasement had become the rule.

Soviet–German relations sank to a new low during 1936. When the Spanish Civil War broke out in July, they found themselves actively assisting different sides. Britain and France, meanwhile, carefully avoided getting involved, thus demonstrating once again the lack of conviction with which they opposed fascism. At the Nazi Party rally in Nuremberg in September, Hitler announced to 160,000 supporters crammed into the immense stadium the start of a four-year plan for economic self-sufficiency, and of a new crusade against bolshevism and the powers of disorder. Confirming the statements he had made twelve years earlier in *Mein Kampf*, he told his wildly enthusiastic audience: 'If I had the Ural Mountains with their incalculable store of treasures and raw materials, Siberia with its vast forests, and the Ukraine with its tremendous wheatfields, Germany and the National Socialist leadership would swim in plenty!' Ominous words to Soviet ears.

In October, Hitler increased his strength by concluding a formal alliance with Italy, telling the thirty-four-year-old Count Galeazzo Ciano, Mussolini's son-in-law and newly appointed Foreign Minister, that the Germans and Italians should unite in an 'invincible coalition' against bolshevism and the Western democracies. In a speech in Milan five days later, 1 November, Mussolini gave the link-up a name when he declared: 'This vertical line between Rome and Berlin is not a partition but rather an axis around which can revolve all those European states with a will to collaboration and peace.'

On 14 November 1936 Hitler tore up yet another part of the Versailles treaty, by renouncing international controls over the rivers Rhine, Elbe, Oder and Danube, calling the arrangement 'intolerable'. Yet again, nothing but futile protests came from the West. And eleven days later, completing the pressures that had been building up during the year, he signed an Anti-Comintern Pact with Japan, with the object of curbing Soviet political activities abroad. A secret clause in the pact barred either partner from making any political agreement with the Soviet Union, and provided for consultation on joint action should either become involved in a war with her.

For Stalin, the Anti-Comintern Pact was a cause for grave concern even without the secret clause: he had been having trouble for some time with Japanese forces making incursions along the disputed border between Siberia and Japanese-occupied Manchuria. Any alliance between Hitler and Japan raised the dread prospect for the Soviet Union of a war on two fronts, with the Germans in the west and the Japanese – old adversaries of Russia – in the Far East. The prospect was not improved when Italy joined the pact the following year.

In 1938, with Hitler becoming more confident, more arrogant and more aggressive every day and the Red Army in total disarray at the height of the purges, Stalin had good cause to be nervous. Although the German dictator still held a deep grudge against France as the chief instigator of the hated Versailles settlement, the remilitarisation of the Rhineland marked his last stated objective in the west. His territorial ambitions now lay entirely in the east, marking out a path which led directly towards the Soviet Union. Clearly, it was time for Stalin to increase his efforts to achieve one or both of his protective options. He was to discover very quickly, however, that there were formidable obstacles in either direction.

2

'MY POOR FRIEND, WHAT HAVE YOU DONE?'

1938 was Hitler's *annus mirabilis*, the wonderful year when everything went his way. While Stalin was enmeshed in the terrors which he had himself unleashed on the Soviet people, Hitler marched on from strength to strength, dominating every other international leader and forcing them to dance to his tune.

He began the year by completing the Nazi revolution as he eliminated the last traces of opposition to his personal rule. On 4 February, he called his Cabinet together for the last time, to set the seal on his final take-over of power. They were required to give formal approval to a decree beginning: 'From now on I personally take over the command of the entire armed forces.'

He then dismissed Field Marshal Werner von Blomberg, War Minister and Commander-in-Chief of all the armed forces, and General Werner von Fritsch, Commander-in-Chief of the army, on trumped-up charges – Blomberg for having married a so-called prostitute, Fritsch on a totally false charge of homosexuality. Both were officers of the old school, honourable and conservative, with little sympathy for Nazi ideology or morality. With them into enforced retirement went sixteen top generals who had shown a marked lack of enthusiasm for the Nazi regime.

Hitler replaced Fritsch as commander of the army with General Walther von Brauchitsch, an equally honourable but more pliant soldier, who could be guaranteed to do as he was told. But instead of simply replacing Blomberg, Hitler abolished the War Ministry and in its place created a new body, the High Command of the Armed Forces, the OKW, *Oberkommando der Wehrmacht*. He himself took over as Commander-in-Chief – he was already the supreme commander, of course, as head of state, but his new role gave him a more direct control, making him the complete war lord. As chief of the OKW, he appointed

General Wilhelm Keitel, a tall, broad-shouldered man with a square face, pale eyes, grey hair brushed straight back and a neatly trimmed moustache. With a monocle firmly screwed into one eye, the stiff-backed Keitel looked every inch the traditional Prussian officer, though he came, in fact, from a strongly anti-Prussian family of landed gentry in Brunswick.

Keitel was a dedicated admirer of the Führer – after first meeting him in July 1933, he spoke enthusiastically about him to his wife, who wrote to her mother saying he had told her: 'His eyes were fabulous, and how the man could speak . . . !' During his interrogation at the Nuremberg trials in August 1945, Keitel made no bones about his commitment: 'From the bottom of my heart I was a loyal shield-bearer for Adolf Hitler; my political convictions were National Socialist.'

With the sycophant Keitel heading the OKW, the weak Brauchitsch in charge of the army and his own faithful deputy, Hermann Göring, commanding the air force, Hitler's grip on his armed forces were now secure. He could be certain they would follow whatever course he chose, and would pose no threat to his person.

On the economic front, he had dismissed the old financial wizard, Dr Hjalmar Schacht, from his position as Economics Minister and Plenipotentiary for War Economy at the beginning of December 1937. Schacht, although he had wrought many wonders for Hitler and the party in the past, was now issuing too many Cassandra-like warnings about the perilous state of the economy and the impossible cost of Hitler's plans. He was also ambitious, and had even told French Ambassador André François-Poncet that he hoped to succeed Hitler, 'should things go ill with the Führer'. Now, Hitler announced a permanent replacement in the form of Walther Funk, a servile party hack who had once been editor of the financial newspaper, the *Berliner Börsenzeitung*, and had acted as go-between raising funds from rich businessmen. William Shirer, then Berlin correspondent for CBS Radio, describes Funk as 'a greasy, shifty-eyed, paunchy little man' whose face reminded him of a frog.

To complete the events of that fateful Saturday, Hitler also secured total compliance in the field of foreign affairs by dismissing his Foreign Minister, Baron Konstantin von Neurath, and the ambassadors in Rome, Tokyo and Vienna. Neurath, like Blomberg and Fritsch, was a conservative who had been appointed by Field Marshal von Hindenburg, Hitler's predecessor as President of the German Republic, to help curb the worst Nazi excesses. In his place, Hitler appointed Joachim von Ribbentrop, who was then serving as a disastrous ambassador in London, where he had earned himself the nickname 'Herr Brickendrop' from the British Foreign Office, because of his undiplomatic be-haviour.

The new Foreign Minister of Germany, who was to play a central part in Hitler's dealings with Stalin, was forty-four years old at the time of his appointment. He stood about five feet ten inches tall, and was quite handsome in a fleshy sort of way, but with cold, metallic eyes. He was intensely ambitious and hard-working but not particularly intelligent, and was totally under the domination of two people – his wife and Hitler.

Ribbentrop – his use of the aristocratic prefix 'von' was extremely dubious, since he had acquired it by having himself 'adopted', as an adult, by a distant relative who was entitled to it – had served as an officer in the 12th Hussars, a good Prussian cavalry regiment, during the first world war. In the twenties, between enjoying himself as a man about town and pursuing his favourite pastime of foxtrotting at tea dances and night clubs, he built up a thriving export–import business in wines and spirits and married Annelies Henkell, heiress to the famous sparkling wine firm of that name, despite strong opposition from her father. Although the marriage was a success, Henkell *père* steadfastly refused to offer a partnership or indeed any place in the firm to Ribbentrop, whom he always considered an adventurer.

Ribbentrop first met Hitler in August 1932, when the Führer was already an established political figure. He was asked by friends to act as an intermediary between the then Chancellor, Franz von Papen, whom he knew, and Hitler, who had retired to his mountain home above the little Bavarian town of Berchtesgaden in a fit of pique after being offered only the Vice-Chancellorship. Like General Keitel, Ribbentrop was immediately won over. He came away from the meeting convinced that only Hitler and the Nazis could save Germany. Next day, he joined the party.

The initial talks arranged by Ribbentrop were a failure, but a few months later he was able to bring the principals together again, and this time a deal was struck which gave Hitler what he wanted. This second set of secret talks, which involved Hitler, Papen, Göring, SS chief Himmler, SA chief Röhm, and President Hindenburg's son, Oscar, took place in Ribbentrop's villa in the fashionable Berlin suburb of Dahlem. Virtually every day from Thursday, 10 January 1933, right through to Sunday, 29 January, Ribbentrop sent his own car to bring Papen discreetly to the house, while Hitler had his car driven into the Ribbentrops' garage so that he could enter unseen through the garden at the rear.

Hitler was appointed Chancellor of Germany on 30 January. As Ribbentrop watched the immense torchlight procession of the Nazi columns turning the Wilhelmstrasse into a river of fire that night, he was almost overwhelmed by the spectacle. 'I prayed fervently,' he wrote later, 'that this new government might prevent chaos in our Reich and lead Germany back to a respected place among the nations of the world.'

Aware of his ignorance in the field of foreign affairs, Hitler soon began calling regularly on the Ribbentrops for dinner, retiring after the meals to the study to talk. Ribbentrop was one of the few leading members of the party with any experience of life in other countries: he had been to school in France and Britain, spoke both languages fluently, and as a youth had spent the four years before 1914 in Canada, earning a living in a variety of small-time jobs. He could therefore claim to know something of North America. Now, he made frequent trips to London and Paris, selling his wines. Hitler asked him to report to him personally after each visit, with his impressions of the two countries, an arrangement which soon developed into a more formal, full-time appointment.

Hitler was deeply suspicious of the conservatives in the Foreign Ministry, with their high ideals and 'outdated' sense of honour. He could not rely on them to be sufficiently ruthless in pursuing his policies, and the advice he received from their experts was not always what he wanted to hear. He felt that he needed his own advisers, his own diplomatic intelligence service which would owe its allegiance solely to him, a service which would not be afraid of dirty work, untrammelled by the niceties which governed the activities of the 'good old *Auswärtiges Amt*', as the Foreign Ministry was known to its traditionalist staff. Ribbentrop, a polished cosmopolitan when compared with the ignorant provincialism of most leading Nazis, was the obvious choice to head such a service.

In late 1933, Ribbentrop was appointed Hitler's Ambassador-at-Large and given the building which had housed the former Prussian Prime Minister's office at 63 Wilhelmstrasse, immediately opposite the long, buff-painted, three-storey building of the Foreign Ministry at No. 76. Here he set up the Büro Ribbentrop, an alternative, 'black' Foreign Ministry, from which he established himself as the party's unchallenged expert on foreign affairs. He continued to run the Büro even while he was ambassador in London from 1936 onwards, dealing directly with Hitler over the head of Neurath, the official Foreign Minister, and even negotiating the Anti-Comintern Pact from the London embassy.

When he appointed Ribbentrop as Foreign Minister, on 4 February 1938, Hitler must have felt he had removed the last vestige of independence from the Foreign Ministry. Ribbentrop was so besotted by him, so dependent on his thinking and his opinions, that if Hitler was displeased with him he went sick and took to his bed. Those who worked under him recall that he never had any original ideas of his own, and never questioned his master's. He was adept at listening with great patience to Hitler's interminable monologues, remembering what he had said and storing every word for the future, to be trotted out as 'advice' when Hitler asked for it.

*   *   *

NORWAY

FINLAND

SWEDEN

Leningrad

Tallinn

ESTONIA

L.Peipus

Tartu

Baltic Sea

Windau
(Ventspiels)

Riga

LATVIA

Moscow

DENMARK

Liepaja

Memel

LITHUANIA

Kaunas

Belo-
Russia

Gdynia

Danzig

Konigsberg

Vilna
(Vilnius)

Minsk

USSR

Berlin

East
Prussia

Vistula

Bialystock

Warsaw

Brest-
Litovsk

Pripet-
Marshes

GERMANY

POLAND

Lublin

Kiev

Kharkov

Prague

PROT. OF
BOHEMIA-MORAVIA
(March '39)

Cracow

Galicia

Lvov

Ukraine

SLOVAKIA

Bukovina

AUSTRIA

(March '39)

HUNGARY

Bessarabia

RUMANIA

Sevastopol

Black Sea

0   100   200 Miles

0   200   400 Kilometres

With compliant puppets in charge of the country's armed forces, finances and foreign affairs, the way was now clear for Hitler to set out in earnest along his road to destiny in the east. From now on, there would be no one in any position of authority in Germany to restrain him, no one prepared to tell him that any of his plans were impossible.

Within a week of making the new appointments, Hitler called the Chancellor of Austria, the forty-one-year-old Dr Kurt von Schuschnigg, to the Berghof, his mountainside house above Berchtesgaden, and presented him with an ultimatum demanding in effect that he hand over power to the Austrian Nazi Party, and merge his country's economy with Germany's. On 12 March, after a month of unremitting pressure, he sent his troops to march unopposed into Austria, and the following day announced the '*Anschluss*', or union, of the two countries.

Austria had ceased to exist as an independent state without a shot being fired; the rest of the world had not raised a finger to help. Indeed, at the very moment the news of the Nazi invasion of Austria reached British Prime Minister Neville Chamberlain, he was entertaining Ribbentrop and his wife to a farewell lunch at 10 Downing Street. Winston Churchill, who was one of the sixteen or so people present, records how the message from the Foreign Office was given to Chamberlain halfway through lunch, and that although the Prime Minister appeared to be slightly preoccupied for a few moments, 'the meal proceeded without the slightest interruption.' The closest Chamberlain came to remonstrating with Ribbentrop was over coffee in the drawing room afterwards, when the Ribbentrops insisted on hanging on 'for nearly half an hour, engaging their host and hostess in voluble conversation'; eventually, Chamberlain brought himself to say, 'I am sorry I have to go now to attend to urgent business.'

Neville Chamberlain had been Prime Minister of Great Britain for almost a year. Aged sixty-eight, he was a lean, stringy man, with a beaky nose and heavy moustache. His scrawny neck emerging from the stiff winged collars he always wore gave him the air of a half-starved turtle. Although he came from a famous political family – his father and brother had both held high office – he had been elected to Parliament only at the age of forty-nine, after many years in business. Since then, he had held several Cabinet posts, including that of Chancellor of the Exchequer, all of which he had fulfilled with efficiency rather than distinction. As a domestic politician he had many admirable qualities, but as a world statesman at a time of grave crisis he was totally out of his depth.

William Strang, who was to play an important role in Allied negotiations with Moscow in 1939 and who eventually became Permanent Under-Secretary at the Foreign Office, later wrote: 'It can fairly be said of Neville Chamberlain that he was not well versed in foreign affairs, that he had no touch for a diplomatic situation, that he did not fully realise what it was he was doing, and that his naive confidence in his own judgement and power of persuasion and achievement was misplaced. 'Strang summed up Chamberlain's approach to the subject coolly and without rancour, despite the frustration, and even desperation, which he must have felt at the time, but which he concealed like the dedicated civil servant he was. 'His mind was dominated,' Strang said, 'by two thoughts. The first was hatred of war so deep that he would think that heavy sacrifices would be justified in order to avoid it. The second was the belief that the German and Italian dictators were men whose word could be relied on; that it was possible to come to agreements with them which could transform the international situation for the better and give peace to Europe; and that by his personal influence with them he could hope to bring such agreements about.'

The trust which Chamberlain had in Hitler and Mussolini did not extend to Stalin and the Soviet government. As a good Birmingham businessman he had an abiding hatred of communism in any form, which inevitably coloured all his dealings with the Soviet Union. His reluctance to come to any agreement with Stalin, coupled with his eagerness to do so with Hitler, was to be a major factor in the events of the next eighteen months.

The pattern was set within a week of the Austrian *Anschluss*. There could be no doubt that after Austria Hitler's next target was Czechoslovakia, starting with the three million Germans living in the Sudetenland, a horseshoe-shaped region encompassing the country's entire western frontiers and including the sophisticated modern fortifications which had been constructed to defend the young republic from attack. Encouraged by the Nazis, the Sudeten Germans had been agitating for some time for their 'return' to the Fatherland and after Hitler's triumphant success with Austria he immediately began whipping up pressure on Czechoslovakia to surrender them and their territory to him. With the Sudetenland gone, Czechoslovakia would be stripped of its defences and it would only be a matter of time before Hitler gobbled up the rest of the country, which in its turn would become another stepping stone to the east.

This would be a most disturbing development for Stalin, and he was quick to sound the alarm. On 17 March, Litvinov called on Britain, France and the United States to join with the Soviet Union in formulating collective action against Hitler. The response, to say the least, was cool. The Americans were still determined not to be drawn into any European conflicts; the French were preoccupied with their latest internal political crisis; Chamberlain was terrified of upsetting Hitler, and dismissed the whole idea as impracticable. 'You only have to look at the map,' he wrote in a letter to his sister on 20 March, 'to see that nothing that France or we could do could possibly save Czecho-slovakia from being overrun by the Germans, if they wanted to do it. I have therefore abandoned any idea of giving guarantees to Czecho-slovakia, or to the French in connection with her obligations to that country.'

Four days later, on 24 March, Chamberlain made his reply public in a speech to the House of Commons: 'His Majesty's government are of the opinion that the indirect but none the less inevitable consequence of such action as is proposed by the Soviet government would be to aggravate the tendency towards the establishment of exclusive groups of nations, which must in the view of His Majesty's government be inimical to the prospects of European peace.'

Encouraged by the British attitude, Hitler proceeded with his plans. On 21 April, the day after his forty-ninth birthday, he summoned General Keitel and ordered him to update the plans for an invasion of Czechoslovakia, codenamed Operation Green, which had originally been drawn up nearly a year before. 'As always,' Keitel recorded in his memoirs, 'he spoke his thoughts out loud to me in a little speech: the problem would have to be solved some time, not only because of the way in which the Czech government was oppressing the German population living there but because of the strategically impossible situation that would develop should the time ever come for the big reckoning with the East, and by that he meant not just the Poles but particularly the Bolsheviks.' Unable to accuse the Czechs of harbouring aggressive intentions towards Germany, Hitler was forced to use the Soviet Union as his excuse for mounting a pre-emptive strike – his standard justification for every invasion. Western Czechoslovakia, he told Keitel, 'would act as a springboard for the Red Army and Air Force, and in no time at all the enemy could be at the gates of Dresden and in the heart of the Reich'.

Shortly afterwards, he ordered a speeding-up of the construction of fortifications in the 'West Wall', the 'Siegfried Line', along the border with France. Transferring responsibility from army engineers to Dr Fritz Todt, the Inspector-General of Roadbuilding, he decreed that 10,000 concrete structures ranging from massive forts to small bunkers were to be completed within eighteen months, with 5,000 bunkers to be ready by the autumn of 1938. Since these were all essentially defensive structures, this implied all too clearly that he had no intention at that time of mounting any attacks in the West, but was concerned only with protecting his rear while moving in the other direction.

The Czechs, however, were not inclined to give in to him without a fight. Their army, though small, was highly efficient and particularly well equipped – the Czech arms industry, led by the giant Skoda works, produced some of the most modern and effective weapons in the world, and was itself one of the prizes Hitler sought. When news was obtained by their excellent intelligence system of Hitler's plans, on the very day Keitel delivered the draft directive to him at the Berghof, the Czech government immediately ordered a partial mobilisation of their army. Faced with this, and with intense pressure from Britain, France and the Soviet Union, Hitler was forced to back down and to deny that he had ever had any intention of attacking: at that stage he was nowhere near ready and had barely even started preparing the ground wth propaganda and carefully staged incidents. For several days he nursed his rage at being humiliated in such a way, then flew back to Berlin to assemble his service chiefs and senior ministers in the Chancellery on 28 May. In a three-hour speech about his plans for the future, he told them: 'It is my unshakeable resolve that Czechoslovakia shall be wiped off the map of Europe.' He did not give a firm date for the start of Operation Green, but all the preparations were to be completed by 1 October.

Througout the summer of 1938 Hitler kept up the pressure on Czechoslovakia, turning the screw tighter and tighter, fomenting trouble with the Sudeten Germans over grievances and atrocities, both real and imagined. He made speech after speech vilifying the Czechs and their leaders. German troops were massed on the borders, under the deliberately transparent cover of summer exercises. Every minor incident was blown up out of all proportion.

Again, the British response was disappointing to say the least: they warned the Czechs that they should be prepared to make concessions to Germany, and could only expect British support if they were prepared to listen to reason. And when on 22 July the British ambassador in Berlin, Sir Nevile Henderson, proposed that Britain should join with France, Germany and Italy – but not Czechoslovakia – in a four-power conference to produce a settlement, Chamberlain rejected the idea because, as Henderson himself recorded, 'it would be difficult to exclude other powers from participating in such a conference'. The 'other powers', of course, meant the Soviet Union. Instead, Chamberlain sent a former President of the Board of Trade, Lord Runciman, to Czechoslovakia to investigate the problem and to mediate between the Czechs and the Sudeten Germans: in other words, to make the Czechs see sense.

With the temperature of the crisis soaring towards boiling point in September, Britain and France studiously avoided all the Soviet efforts to form a united front against Hitler. As the month progressed, they issued a stream of contradictory statements, on the one hand affirming their determination to fight on behalf of the Czechs, and on the other hedging frantically and claiming that the Sudeten issue need not necessarily be a *casus belli*. The Czechs, meanwhile, under Western pressure, offered concession after concession, meeting at least ninety per cent of the demands against them – but every time a settlement seemed possible, the Germans invented some new pretext for breaking off the talks.

The Soviets continued to stress their willingness to aid the Czechs, calling on the French on 2 September to arrange a conference between their general staffs to work out the necessary measures for military co-operation, and raising the matter in the League of Nations. At the same time, Stalin sent word to Czech President Eduard Beneš via the general secretary of the Czech Communist Party, Klement Gottwald, telling him the Soviet Union was ready to provide military assistance in the event of a German attack even if the French did not do so. On that same day, Hitler set 27 September as the date for his invasion of Czechoslovakia.

By the middle of the month, the crisis had developed to a point where it seemed to be out of control. After a speech by Hitler to the Nazi Party rally at Nuremberg on 13 September, rioting erupted in the Sudetenland and the Czech government declared martial law. Two days later an anxious Chamberlain, accompanied by his chief political adviser, Sir Horace Wilson – a civil servant with even less experience of foreign affairs than himself – boarded an aeroplane for the first time in his life and flew to meet Hitler at the Berghof. There, Hitler treated him to a lecture, laid out his minimum demands and graciously promised not to begin hostilities until Chamberlain had had a chance to consult his Cabinet and his allies. French Premier Daladier and Foreign Minister Bonnet visited London to discuss the situation, and the two governments accepted Hitler's demands for the cession of all territory with a German-speaking majority population.

The Czechs appeared to have no option but to agree to this, since it was now obvious that neither Britain nor France was prepared to come to the rescue. The Soviets had started massing troops in the Ukraine – thirty infantry and ten cavalry divisions, one tank corps, three tank brigades and twelve air brigades were already along the frontier with Poland and there were another thirty infantry and ten cavalry divisions in a state of readiness – but they had no common frontiers with Germany or Czechoslovakia and could not march against the Germans without permission from Poland or Romania to cross their territory. There seemed little hope of such permission being granted, for the Poles and Romanians, who had both seized Russian territory in 1919 and 1920, were understandably nervous at allowing the Red Army inside their frontiers.

In fact, the Romanians did agree to allow Soviet aircraft bound for Czechoslovakia to overfly their territory, and at the beginning of September some twenty Soviet bombers flew to join the Czech air force, the first of a total of sixty which the Soviets had promised. By 15 September, the Romanians had withdrawn their objections to the passage of troops by the rail line across the Carpathian mountains.

The Poles, however, were a very different case. They were already lining up with Germany to demand territory from the Czechs, and were moving their own troops up to the border with the northern Czech region of Teschen, or Cieszyn as they knew it, which was rich in iron and coal and which had a minority Polish population. Litvinov was quick to warn the Poles that if they attempted to take Teschen by force the Soviet Union would consider her non-aggression pact with Poland as being annulled, and would then be free to take appropriate action in support of the Czechs. Haughty as ever, the Poles chose to ignore the Soviet threat, and continued with their claims.

On 21 September, Litvinov addressed the Assembly of the League of Nations in Geneva. He reminded everyone that after the Austrian *Anschluss* the Soviet Union had proposed that the other European powers should join her in establishing a system of collective security, 'which, if carried out, could have saved us from the alarm which all the world now feels for the fate of Czechoslovakia'. He went on to reiterate his earlier declarations that his country would stand by its obligations to the Czechs, and was ready to start general staff talks immediately with the French. Two days later, he suggested to the British representatives at Geneva, R. A. Butler and Lord De La Warr, that there should be an immediate conference of Britain, France and the Soviet Union, to decide on joint action. The Britons promised to report his suggestion to London at once – and that was the last that was heard of it, or of his statements to the League.

'It is indeed astonishing,' Winston Churchill wrote later in his account of those eventful days, 'that this public and unqualified declaration by one of the greatest powers concerned should not have played its part in Mr Chamberlain's negotiations, or in the French conduct of the crisis.' Astonishing it may have been, but by then Chamberlain was already back in Germany, this time at Bad Godesberg on the Rhine, to report to Hitler that all his demands had been agreed.

Chamberlain was convinced that he had solved the problem and could now finalise the details of a peaceful hand-over of the Sudetenland. But as always, he had misjudged Hitler, whose response was to renege on his earlier promises and make new and bigger demands, together with an ultimatum: he would attack if Czechoslovakia did not turn over even larger areas by 1 October. In a state of shock, Chamberlain retired to his hotel to consider the new situation, but next day met Hitler again. Buttressed by the German dictator's assurance that the Sudetenland really did represent the last of his territorial ambitions in Europe and that he had no wish to include in the Reich people of other races than German, Chamberlain gave way again and promised to try to persuade the Czechs.

For the next seven days, the world was in a turmoil of tensions and uncertainty. War seemed inevitable. The Czech army had mobilised while Chamberlain was still at Godesberg with Hitler. The British mobilised the Royal Navy, while the French began a partial mobilisation of their army and called up several categories of reservists. The Soviets also mobilised their fleet, in addition to continuing to build up their army and air forces on the frontiers – a fact which escaped the attention of most Western commentators. From across the Atlantic, President Roosevelt sent a stream of telegrams urging peace on everyone.

The diplomats and politicians argued and quarrelled among themselves. In London, Churchill led a group of MPs – Conservatives like himself, who were out of the government and out of sympathy with Chamberlain and his fellow appeasers – in calling for the inclusion of the Soviet Union. The best they could get out of the government, however, was an anodyne communiqué from the Foreign Office stating that if Hitler attacked Czechoslovakia, 'France will be bound to come to her assistance, and Great Britain *and Russia* will certainly stand by France.' Next day, Chamberlain repudiated the Foreign Office statement, saying: 'We cannot in all circumstances undertake to involve the whole British Empire in war simply on [Czechoslovakia's] account.' He then sent a message to Hitler and Mussolini proposing a conference with Czechoslovakia, Germany, France, Britain and Italy. The Soviet Union was deliberately excluded. 'It would only have complicated things,' Sir Horace Wilson later told journalist and author Leonard Mosley. 'You can't trust the Russians, anyway. They've always been tricky.'

Mussolini urged Hitler to accept Chamberlain's proposal, saying: 'I feel certain you can get all the essentials without war and without delay,' and so the conference took place in the recently completed Führer Building in Munich, on 29 September. The Czechs were not allowed to take part, but were relegated to a side room, to await news of their fate. It came at 2 o'clock on the morning of 30 September: they were to evacuate the whole of the Sudeten region, including all their border fortifications, starting on 1 October. They were to be out by the 10th, 'without any existing installations having been destroyed'. Everything was to be left behind – not only military arms and equipment but also all personal belongings: civilians would be allowed only the clothes they stood up in. They had to leave homes, furniture, household goods, the family horses and cows, everything. There would be no compensation paid by Germany, either to the Czech government or to individuals.

The Munich agreement has gone down in history as a byword for shortsightedness, betrayal and cowardice, a triumph for appeasement and the policies of peace at any price. It undoubtedly opened the door to the second world war, by handing Hitler a bloodless victory where in all probability, had the Czechs and their supporters chosen to fight, he would have suffered a bloody defeat. That, of course, must remain as supposition. What is certain is that Czechoslovakia under German domination was turned into a dagger pointing east towards the heart of the Soviet Union. Because of this, Stalin would be forced to take action to protect his country. Because of the behaviour of the Western Powers, both towards the Soviet Union and Nazi Germany, he would also be forced to reassess his policies.

Winston Churchill summed up the result of the attitude of Britain and France towards the Soviets during the Munich crisis pithily and succinctly: 'The Soviet offer was in effect ignored,' he wrote. 'They were not brought into the scale against Hitler, and were treated with an indifference – not to say disdain – which left a mark in Stalin's mind. Events took their course as if Soviet Russia did not exist. For this we afterwards paid dearly.'

The direction in which Stalin's mind inevitably turned was signalled shortly after Munich by the Soviet Vice-Commissar for Foreign Affairs, Vladimir Potemkin. 'My poor friend, what have you done?' he asked French ambassador to Moscow Robert Coulondre. 'For us I see no other outcome but a fourth partition of Poland.' Potemkin's meaning was unmistakable: there was only one country with whom the Soviet Union could divide Poland, and that country was Germany.

3

'THE ONE AND ONLY COLONEL BECK'

In the immediate aftermath of Munich, Hitler and Stalin both turned their attention to Poland. Stalin, as Potemkin's remark to Coulondre showed, saw the division of Poland as a means of bribing Hitler away from his designs on the Soviet Union, and of establishing some sort of *rapprochement* with Germany. Hitler, however, had other plans for the Poles at that time: he hoped to use their hatred of the Russians to make them his willing accomplices in obtaining the Ukraine. Once he had achieved this, he foresaw no difficulty in dealing with the Poles at his leisure, turning them into vassals of Germany.

Hitler had started the softening-up process for Poland at Munich, by helping her obtain Teschen without opposition. There had been some friction when the Poles went further than agreed and occupied the important rail junction of Oderberg (known to the Poles as Bogumin and to the Czechs as Bohumin) on the extreme north-eastern tip of the region, which had a large German element in its population. Göring had been all for throwing the Poles out, believing the town was important to his economic plans, but Hitler had intervened personally, making a present of Oderberg to Poland. He had followed this up by having Ribbentrop invite Polish Ambassador Lipski to lunch at the Grand Hotel in Berchtesgaden on 24 October, for a friendly chat.

Unlike his master, Ribbentrop was very fond of good food and wine. The lunch was lavish and went on for three hours, during which the German Foreign Minister floated Hitler's ideas for closer co-operation, stressing that what he was saying was in the strictest confidence and nothing should be put down on paper. Lipski, he said, should report it to Polish Foreign Minister Josef Beck in person, by word of mouth only. He also asked Lipski to give Beck an invitation to visit him, adding unctuously, 'Our Polish friends have a standing invitation to visit Germany.'

'It is time,' Ribbentrop went on, 'to arrive at a general settlement of all possible points of friction between Germany and Poland.' He then went on to present a list of proposals which were indeed sweeping, and which did appear to cover all outstanding problems.

There were many possible sources of friction between Germany and Poland, but the most obvious was the free city of Danzig, or Gdansk as the Poles called it. Marshal Pilsudski, the architect of modern Poland and her first President, always said he regarded Danzig as the touchstone of Polish–German relations, an infallible indicator of danger or calm. This ancient port was German in almost every way, including the nationality of most of its inhabitants. However, it occupied the mouth of the Vistula, Poland's only major river, was a vital outlet to the sea for Poland's trade, and its hinterland as a port was entirely Polish.

The Allied statesmen redrawing the map of Europe in 1919 had wanted to give Danzig to the new Polish state. But Lloyd George, the British Prime Minister, had foreseen the problems inherent in that and had managed to restrain his colleagues. They had taken Danzig away from Germany, but instead of giving it to the Poles had made it a free city, under the control of the League of Nations. At the same time, they had given Poland a strip of territory to the west of Danzig, to provide her with a short but important coastline. The trouble was, that strip of land, the 'Polish Corridor', separated the German province of East Prussia from the rest of the Reich; the only way for Germans to get there, apart from flying or going by sea, was by crossing Polish territory. Of all the many retributions exacted from Germany by the victors of the first world war, none was more bitterly resented than the loss of Danzig and the Polish Corridor. Germans of all classes and creeds dreamed of the day when their brothers and sisters in Danzig would be reunited with them.

Inevitably, Danzig figured large in Ribbentrop's proposals to Lipski: the 'reversion' of the Free State of Danzig to the German Reich was the first item on his list. 'Danzig,' he said, 'was German, had always been German and would always remain German.' But he was careful not to press the matter too hard. He reminded Lipski that the Führer had waived all claims to the South Tyrol, another area which had been reallocated in 1919, because he wanted a complete settlement with Italy, although for Hitler himself, as an Austrian, the South Tyrol was a much more emotive subject than the essentially Prussian claim to Danzig and the Corridor. Ribbentrop also indicated to Lipski that Hitler was working on 'a clear arrangement' with France and had waived all claims to Alsace-Lorraine. In fact, Ribbentrop was then preparing a non-aggression pact with France, which was signed in December.

Ribbentrop explained to Lipski that Hitler wanted a similar agreement with Poland, as part of Germany's policy of establishing good relations with her neighbours – of course, he did not mention Austria or Czechoslovakia in this context. The smile on the face of the tiger did not slip when he went on to say he did not want an answer there and then, but was taking a long-term view: 'One has to think in terms of centuries,' he proclaimed. Then he began to dangle his bait. 'One should not exclude a certain reciprocity in these matters,' he said – a typical Ribbentrop pomposity meaning simply that they might be able to do a deal.

The deal the Germans had in mind was that in return for Danzig they would recognise and guarantee Poland's western frontiers, including the Corridor itself. All Hitler wanted in addition to the city was an extra-territorial autobahn and multi-track railroad across the Corridor, belonging to Germany, to link East Prussia to the rest of the Reich. He was prepared to give Poland a similar road and railroad through Danzig, and a free port there, and a guaranteed market for her goods in the Danzig area. As an added incentive, Germany was prepared to extend the 1934 non-aggression pact with Poland from ten to twenty-five years.

On the face of it, the proposals were extremely generous. But the hook showed through when Ribbentrop had suggested that as part of the package Poland should join the Anti-Comintern Pact, hinting fairly broadly that in return Poland could have part of Ruthenia, otherwise known as the Carpatho-Ukraine, the extreme eastern region of Czechoslovakia. The fact that Ruthenia was not yet Germany's property to dispose of was not even considered.

Hitler's generosity was viewed with some alarm in Warsaw. The new Poland, 150,000 square miles of mainly fertile land occupied by 33 million argumentative but industrious people, was a partial rebirth of the state which had died and disappeared from the map of Europe in 1795, partitioned for the third time since 1772 between Russia, Prussia and Austria. Although the Poles liked to delude themselves into believing they were a great power, they could hardly fail to be aware of the two resentful giants on either side of them, each of whom would be capable of overwhelming them by sheer weight of numbers. If, God forbid, they ever joined forces against her, Poland would be crushed as surely as a grain of wheat between two millstones.

The main plank of Polish foreign policy was to remain on good terms with both neighbours, but never to become aligned with one against the other – if that happened, not only would Poland be in danger of being swallowed by the one she had chosen, but the other would feel threatened and might attack in self-defence. The Poles labelled their policy 'maintaining equilibrium': by the end of 1938, it began to look more like trying to keep one's balance on a tightrope in a hurricane.

The man who bore the main responsibility for keeping his country on the tightrope – and who could therefore be said to hold the future of the world in his hands for several vital months in 1939 – was Colonel Josef Beck, the Foreign Minister. In 1938 Beck was forty-four years old, a tall, lean man with aquiline features, his thinning black hair brushed straight back and plastered down on his scalp. From certain angles, he looked not unlike Noël Coward. From others, he resembled a marabou stork, with hunched shoulders and prominent, beak-like nose. He liked to dress elegantly, even sharply, but had a weakness for teddy-bear fur coats, in which he looked decidedly raffish.

He also had several other, more serious shortcomings, one of which was a very weak head. He claimed not to drink while he was working – but a Foreign Minister is very rarely not working, and a great deal of that work takes place during receptions, dinners and lunches. For Beck, these were constant sources of danger: a couple of glasses of wine and he was gone, in that state of aggressive touchiness which marks the habitual drunk. Count Edward Raczynski, then ambassador in London and now President of the Polish government-in-exile, recalls that at a formal dinner at the British Foreign Office in November 1936, Beck fell out so violently with Montagu Norman, the Governor of the Bank of England, that an embarrassed Raczynski only just managed to restrain him from using his fists.

When Beck entertained Duff Cooper, the British First Lord of the Admiralty, and his wife, Lady Diana, during an official visit to Danzig and Gdynia in August 1938, Lady Diana believed he was never once sober. She recorded in her diary that he spent most of his time telling her, over and over again in his sketchy French, that he was 'the one and only Colonel Beck', that he had fought in fifteen wars and the medal ribbons he wore were all equivalent to the Victoria Cross. In fact, one of them was Poland's highest decoration for bravery, the Virtuti Militari Cross, won in 1916 as a young artillery lieutenant. But to Lady Diana, Beck was 'nothing but an Ancient Pistol and a very weak and tipsy Pistol at that, repeating himself with the persistence of a cuckoo and waving his tail with peacock vanity'. She regarded him as such a concentrated bore that she and the other ladies in the party took him on in shifts, smiling bravely as they danced with him while he 'tangled their toes and pinched their thighs'.

Beck's diplomatic career had had a very shaky start. In 1922 he had been sent to Paris as Poland's first military attaché there. Gathering information is one of the legitimate functions of a military attaché, but Beck's interpretation of this role was far too broad. French security service archives tell how he was soon in trouble for stealing secret documents from the desk of a French general. This might have been forgotten or forgiven, if he had not then been caught taking bribes from the Germans to obtain French military secrets for them. He was expelled from France in double quick time.

Despite his clumsiness in Paris, Beck was well qualified for spying. He had worked as a secret agent during the Polish struggle for independence, and had also been the army's intelligence chief during the 1920 war with Russia. In any case, he was soon back in official service, promoted to lieutenant-colonel and appointed to the general staff.

The main reason why Beck was able not only to survive but also to prosper was that he was the protégé of Poland's great hero, Marshal Josef Pilsudski. Pilsudski was the Charles de Gaulle of modern Poland, its saviour, indeed almost its creator. He had led the fight for freedom during the first world war, setting out against Russia in 1914 with an army of 170 men against an empire of 130 million. When the fight was won – admittedly with the help of the Germans, the Allies and Lenin – he became the new country's first head of state. It was he who went to war with the Soviet Union in 1920, giving the Bolshevik colossus a very bloody nose.

Like de Gaulle in France a quarter century later, Pilsudski resigned when a new constitution denied him real power in 1922. He was not a believer in parliamentary democracy, describing the Polish Seym as 'the house of prostitutes'. 'I am a strong man,' he proclaimed, 'and I like to decide all matters by myself.' When Pilsudski stepped out of the spotlight it was, again like de Gaulle, only to wait in the wings for his cue to return to centre stage. The cue came three and a half years later, when the country was in such a mess that the situation looked hopeless. The republic's fifteenth government since 1918 was in deep trouble: inflation was raging out of control; law and order were breaking down; unemployment was rocketing; the out-of-work rioted. Pilsudski called on the army – his army. On 12 May 1926 he marched into Warsaw at the head of his troops. After two days of fighting, he entered the parliament chamber to demand the resignation of the government. Standing alongside him, gun in hand, was his young chief of staff, Josef Beck.

From that point on, Beck's rise was assured. He continued as Pilsudski's right-hand man for another four years, then was made Vice-Premier and Minister Without Portfolio. On 2 November 1932, he became Foreign Minister.

Beck's first achievement in his new role was to sign a three-year non-aggression pact with the Soviet Union on 27 November 1932, after which, in order to maintain the all-important equilibrium, he turned his attentions to Germany, and the new regime which took power at the beginning of 1933. To his delight, he found Hitler quite different from his predecessors, all of whom had regarded Poland with undisguised hostility. Hitler was more than willing to be friends – at least on paper. On 27 January 1934, he signed a non-aggression pact with Poland. Beck was overjoyed. But Pilsudski had no illusions about their western neighbour: 'Poland has been changed,' he commented drily, 'from Germany's hors d'oeuvre to her dessert.'

The Polish pact was Hitler's first major success in foreign affairs and over the next few years he was not to forget that Beck had been the first foreign statesman to give him proper recognition and to do business with him. Meanwhile, to prove there was no favouritism, Beck had immediately set out for Moscow on an official visit. The German pact was for ten years; by May he had persuaded the Soviets to extend their pact with Poland by the same amount.

Buoyant with success, Beck was now convinced of his own brilliance and importance, believing he was already a world-class international statesman. His delusions of grandeur both for himself and for his country were to grow, fertilised by copious doses of alcohol, at an alarming rate over the next five years.

When Pilsudski died in 1935, there was no one left in Poland who could control or even seriously question Beck. Although there was an elected national assembly, it had little or no power. Three men effectively ruled the country as the dead dictator's successors: President Ignacy Moscicki, a former professor of chemistry and close friend of the old marshal; Commander-in-Chief of the armed forces Marshal Edward Smigly-Rydz (his original name was simply Rydz, but his cover name during his days as a freedom fighter had been 'Smigly', meaning speedy or nippy, and he chose to hang on to it), who had been Pilsudski's closest lieutenant; and Beck himself. Moscicki was a quiet, weak man, easily dominated. Smigly-Rydz knew absolutely nothing about foreign affairs, and in any case preferred to concentrate on keeping an iron grip on the country's interior.

This left Beck free to indulge his own whims and his own interpretation of the foreign policy bequeathed to him by his former mentor, a freedom which he exploited to its full extent.

Hitler's suggestion that Poland should join the Anti-Comintern Pact – in effect, joining Germany, Italy and Japan in an alliance against the Soviet Union – created a serious predicament for Beck. While the offer was extremely flattering – as, of course, it was meant to be, implying that Hitler recognised Poland as a major power – it would clearly destroy the policy of equilibrium, and therefore could not be accepted. However, Beck could not afford to offend Hitler by an outright refusal. He chose therefore to make no response either way, leaving the offer hanging in the air, and to make use of Germany's friendly approach by trying to arrange for Ribbentrop to pay an official visit to Warsaw. By this, he would gain political kudos among the smaller nations of Eastern Europe, reinforcing Poland's claims to be regarded as their leader.

In the meantime, Beck needed to repair his fences with the Soviet Union after Munich and the Teschen affair, which had led to a marked cooling of relations. Despite the threat to tear up his non-aggression pact with Poland if she invaded Teschen, Stalin had taken no further action: since there had been no fighting, but only an agreed handing-over of the disputed territory, in line with the German acquisition of the Sudetenland, there had been no call for Soviet intervention. With Teschen safely in his grasp, Beck hurried to restore the Soviet connection, instructing his ambassador in Moscow, Waclaw Grzybowski, to assure the Soviet Foreign Commissariat of his friendship. Stalin, anxious now to do everything in his power to keep Poland out of Germany's grip, was happy to accept Beck's assurances. On 26 November, he reaffirmed the non-aggression pact, and suggested that the two countries should start talks immediately for a trade agreement.

As 1938 drew to a close, the wooing of Poland gathered pace, with Hitler and Stalin continuing – gently at first – to push their suits. So, when the Poles seemed to be dragging their heels over the proposed trade agreement, Litvinov called Ambassador Grzybowski to see him and offered some advice: the Poles should speed up the trade negotiations, he said, in order 'to forestall German intrigues'. And when Beck sent a message to Ribbentrop saying he was spending Christmas and New Year in Monte Carlo and could stop off on his way home on 5 or 6 January for a chat about the Nazi Foreign Minister's official visit to Warsaw he found himself invited to call not at the Wilhemstrasse in Berlin, but at Berchtesgaden, to take tea with the Führer himself.

When Beck met his *chef de cabinet* Count Michal Lubienski and his ambassador to Germany, Josef Lipski, in Munich, none of them seemed to realise the fateful significance of the journey they were about to take. To Beck, the meeting with Hitler was just one more move in a chess game which he hoped could be played indefinitely, with no checkmate at the end. The special train carried them out of the Bavarian capital and away east on the 120–kilometre journey into the snow-covered mountains. At Berchtesgaden they were met at the grandiose railway station, its bulk incongruously large for a small alpine town, and whisked away in a Mercedes to the Berghof.

Hilter, flanked by Ribbentrop and Count Hans Adolf von Moltke, who had travelled from his post as ambassador in Warsaw to be present at the meeting, greeted Beck and his party on the broad flight of steps leading up to the front door. The Berghof was Hitler's own property, built around a cottage, Haus Wachenfeld, which he had bought with his royalties from *Mein Kampf* and various magazine articles written under a pseudonym for the American Hearst Press. He liked to regard visitors as his personal guests, standing on the steps to welcome them as they stepped from their cars, a habit which had almost caused an incident the year before, when British Foreign Minister Lord Halifax, seeing only a pair of black-clad legs and patent-leather pumps as he climbed out of the car, had mistaken him for a servant and had been about to hand him his hat until saved by a discreetly whispered warning.

Hitler had designed the new building himself, using a drawing board and instruments borrowed from his favourite young architect, Albert Speer. It was unremarkable to look at, a white-walled, three-storey main block with a longer, lower wing forming an L. The roof had the typical overhanging eaves of a mountain chalet, and the smaller windows had shutters painted with bold diagonal stripes.

The new house was built around the old one, and this caused considerable problems: the entrance hall was cramped; the overall ground plan was impractical – Speer reckoned it would have been graded D by any professor of architecture – but it was Hitler's own, and he was fond of it. His greatest pride was the huge picture window in the great salon, which could be raised and lowered automatically at the push of a button. The only trouble was that Hitler had put the garage immediately beneath it, so when the window was lowered it let in the smell of gasoline, oil and exhaust fumes. However, the view from it was magnificent, looking out across the valley, over Berchtesgaden and Salzburg, and to the Untersberg mountain, inside which the legendary Emperor Barbarossa is reputed to have been sleeping for the past 1,000 years, with 5,000 of his men, waiting for the moment when he will emerge and save Germany in her hour of need, restoring her former glories.

Hitler led his guests into the spacious, sixty-foot-long salon, with its deep red carpet, red marble fireplace, and coffered ceiling. He beamed as they admired the wonderful view, then settled down with them in armchairs around a circular, glass-topped table in front of the window, flanked by a precious Gobelin tapestry depicting a French hunting scene. Ever the attentive host, he ordered tea to be brought, and smiled graciously at Beck. Paul Schmidt, the official German interpreter, hovered discreetly at the Führer's elbow, translating the small talk as they readied themselves for business. Ambassador Lipski translated for Beck.

The conversation got off to a good start, with Beck emphasising his desire for good relations with Germany. He reminded Hitler that Poland had stood by Germany during the Sudeten crisis, supporting the German actions against Czechoslovakia. Hitler acknowledged this, but did not pursue the subject. He did not remind Beck that any debt owed by Germany to Poland had been more than repaid by the virtual gift of Teschen, including the town of Oderberg. Instead, he turned to the proposals made by Ribbentrop at his lunch with Lipski on 24 October, going immediately to the real purpose behind them, making it perfectly clear that he was asking Poland to become Germany's ally against the Soviet Union.

'Regardless of whether Russia was bolshevik or tsarist,' he told Beck, 'Germany's attitude towards her would always be one of the greatest caution.' Poland was a valuable buffer. 'Purely from a military point of view,' he went on, 'the existence of a strong Polish army means a considerable easing of Germany's position. The divisions which Poland stations at the Russian frontier save Germany just so much additional military expenditure.'

Hitler was placing his cards on the table, face up. His next play was another clear signal: he began talking about the Ukraine. Of course, he lied, Germany had no interest in the Ukraine, despite the rumours of German aims in that direction, which had been promoted by the world press. Nobody had anything to fear from Germany in that region; it was a matter of indifference to him what the countries that were interested in it did there.

When he finally got round to the question of Danzig and the Corridor, Hitler was sweet reason personified. There might, he suggested with great sincerity, be a way of reaching a settlement along entirely new lines: perhaps the city could be brought into the German political community again in accordance with the wishes of its people, but remain with Poland economically. It might, he thought, be possible to create 'a new organism', a corporation to operate the city as a form of condominium between Poland and Germany. Whatever happened, Poland's interests would have to be fully protected. And whatever happened, he assured Beck, there would be no *fait accompli* over Danzig.

On the Corridor, Hitler was even more conciliatory. Although it was a difficult psychological problem for Germany, it was, he said, 'completely absurd to want to deprive Poland of her outlet to the sea. If Poland were bottled up like that, she might, in view of the tension that would arise, be described as a loaded revolver whose trigger might be pulled at any minute.' Here too, Hitler thought, they could do justice to both sides by using entirely new methods, but since any compromise would be very hard for the German people to swallow, only Hitler himself could pull it off.

Having made his main play, Hitler moved on to talk about the Jewish problem, where he again thought Poland and Germany had a common interest. In many ways he was right, of course. For many years there had been outbreaks of sporadic violence in Poland against Jews; their homes and businesses had been smashed or daubed with slogans; they were forced to emigrate in droves. By the beginning of 1939, more Jews had left Poland than had fled Germany – well over 400,000. But they still made up nearly ten per cent of Poland's population, and in Warsaw the proportion was twenty-eight per cent. In the autumn of 1938, indeed, there had been quarrels between Germany and Poland over the number of Polish Jews who actually chose to live in the Reich – and the Polish government had suggested expelling Jews from Europe to Madagascar long before the Nazis in Germany took up the idea. Now Hitler chose to ignore the tensions of a few weeks before: as part of his wooing, a little sympathy over a shared problem had to be good tactics.

To round off his long discourse, Hitler made sure Beck really got the point of what he was offering by turning to the subject of Germany's lost colonies. If only the Western Powers had shown more understanding, Hitler might have been able to make a territory available in Africa where he could have settled both German and Polish Jews. But the Allies had not understood, any more than they understood that Germany desperately needed colonies to feed her fast-growing population.

There was the final signal: the need for *Lebensraum*, for vast areas of fertile land. Exactly the sort of land to be found to the east, in the Soviet Ukraine – and since Poland had always had its eyes on part of the Ukraine, too, what could be more logical and natural than a joint campaign to prise the Ukraine from the Soviet Union and split it between them?

Beck listened, and understood. But he refused to be drawn. Instead of taking up Hitler's suggestions, he turned to another question, Ruthenia, or the Carpatho-Ukraine, the reward Ribbentrop had offered Poland as an inducement to join the Anti-Comintern Pact. This was the poorest and most remote section of the polyglot Czechoslovakian state, a triangular mountainous territory at the extreme east of the country, populated by Ukrainians. While Czechoslovakia was being carved up, Beck wanted this territory to be given to Hungary, to whom it had belonged in the days of the Habsburgs. This would then give Hungary and Poland a common frontier, and enable them to act together in fulfilling one of his greatest dreams: a 'third Europe' block, with Romania and hopefully Lithuania, Yugoslavia and Bulgaria, stretching from the Baltic to the Black Sea and the Adriatic, aligned to neither Germany nor Russia. Naturally, in Beck's vision of this unlikely alliance, Poland would be the dominant partner, as befitted its status as an independent Great Power. Beck's complaint at the moment was that in spite of his constant urging, and even though they had already been given a large part of it after Munich, the Hungarians could not be persuaded to seize the rest of Ruthenia.

Teatime at the Berghof ended with Beck promising to think over the Danzig problems 'at leisure', avoiding saying anything at all about Hitler's other points, and assuring the Führer that Poland would 'remain true to the line followed since 1934'. He then took his leave, and travelled back to his hotel in Munich, well pleased with himself for standing firm and refusing to be bought.

Hitler saw his guests off, then stomped back into the house. He was not so pleased with Beck's performance. In fact, his patience was very close to breaking point. It was stretched still thinner next day, the last day of his vacation at the Berghof, when Ribbentrop reported to him on his further conversation with Beck at the Vier Jahreszeiten Hotel on Maximilianstrasse, in the heart of old Munich.

One of Ribbentrop's prime characteristics was an ability to persist to the point of offensiveness in trying to get his own way. 'I often saw him keep at it so long without the least regard for tact or politeness, that the other side gave in through sheer exhaustion,' his chief interpreter, Paul Schmidt, recalled. So, when Hitler wanted to make sure the Polish Foreign Minister had not failed to grasp the full meaning of what he had said at the Berghof, he sent Ribbentrop to see him.

Amid the splendid rococo elegance of the Vier Jahreszeiten, Ribbentrop hammered away at Beck for an hour and a half, spelling out Hitler's message again, word by word, more clearly and more insistently. But Beck was having none of it. To Ribbentrop's astonishment he told him: 'Today, for the first time, I am pessimistic. Particularly in regard to the Danzig question as it was raised by the Chancellor, I see no possibility whatever of agreement.'

When Ribbentrop again invited Beck to join the Anti-Comintern Pact, the Pole was still evasive. If Poland entered into a political treaty of that nature with Germany, he argued, then she would not be able to maintain the 'peaceful, neighbourly relations with Russia which were necessary to her security'. Since the whole idea of Hitler's proposal was for Poland to join forces with Germany in attacking the Soviet Union, this must have seemed a rather academic point to Ribbentrop. However, Beck was not quite through: although he did not want to do anything to provoke the Soviets he did not want to offend Germany either. He therefore went on, desperately trying to avoid a flat rejection of Hitler's offer, to assure Ribbentrop that Poland's policy 'might be capable of developing in the direction Germany sought, in the future'.

Even the prospect of the Ukraine could not tempt Beck to climb down from his tightrope. Ribbentrop craftily reminded him of Marshal Pilsudski's ambitions in that direction. Had the Poles given up those aspirations? At this, the official record says, Beck laughed. Yes, he agreed, under Pilsudski in 1920 the Poles had actually taken Kiev, the capital of the Ukraine. And yes, there was no doubt those aspirations were still alive. But he still did not accept the offer.

Ribbentrop refused to let Beck off the hook. He accepted the long-standing invitation to pay an official visit to Warsaw that winter, but in return, extracted a promise from Beck that he would think seriously about a deal. In the meantime, their ambassadors would carry on negotiating.

On that note they parted. Ribbentrop took his gloomy report to Hitler, Beck returned to Warsaw, to start preparing for Ribbentrop's visit and to inform Moscicki and Smigly-Rydz what was happening. His account of his conversations with Hitler and Ribbentrop was not nearly as pessimistic as might have been expected after his statements at the Vier Jahreszeiten. His interview with Hitler might be the decisive moment in Polish–German relations, he told his colleagues, but since Hitler had not demanded an immediate answer, it should be possible to avoid an open break. They could go on talking, and playing for time.

Beck had, however, decided he must hedge his bets even more. He would start working to achieve closer relations with Britain and France. France was technically the new Poland's oldest ally, bound by a treaty signed in 1921, but it had become little more than a paper alliance. French attitudes to affairs in Central Europe were by no means always in line with Poland's, but if things did go disastrously wrong with Germany, France was the only power on the Continent which could offer any tangible help. France, however, would not do anything without British support, therefore Beck would have to court both nations simultaneously.

This would take time, of course, and meanwhile Hitler was waiting. With the approval of his fellow junta members, Beck proposed they should try to do something about the Danzig problem. When the meeting was over, he ordered Michal Lubienski, his *chef de cabinet*, to talk to German Ambassador Moltke about a possible compromise solution. Moltke, who had of course been present at the Berghof meeting with Hitler, must have been surprised at the suggestion put to him by Lubienski: it was for the League of Nations mandate on Danzig to be abolished and replaced by a joint Polish–German condominium. What Beck was proposing as his radical new approach was almost exactly what Hitler himself had suggested, and which had prompted Beck to say he saw no hope of reaching agreement!

4

'A NEW ERA IN GERMAN–SOVIET RELATIONS'

When Hitler's special train drew into Berlin on Sunday morning, 8 January 1939, there was an air of expectancy in the city. It was a bright day, crisp with the dry cold of Central Europe in mid-winter. In the city's biggest park, the Tiergarten, people were skating on the frozen ponds and lagoons. There was still evidence in the streets of the terrible night of 9 November, barely two months earlier, when Nazi thugs had rampaged through the city and the entire country, in an orgy of destruction and terror against the Jews in Germany's first organised pogrom since the Middle Ages. Crystal Night, they called it, because of the broken glass from the windows of shops, houses and synagogues. But there had been more than glass broken. The official figures showed that ninety-one Jews had been killed by the mobs, and another thirty-six seriously injured; 814 shops and 171 private homes had been destroyed, and 191 synagogues put to the torch. But those were only the official figures, as admitted by the Nazi government. The truth was considerably worse.

The glass had been swept up, the dead and dying cleared away, but the scars remained, in boarded-up shops and gutted buildings. Hitler drove past them without a second glance. He could hardly wait to get to the Reich Chancellery.

At the end of January 1938, he had asked his young architect, Albert Speer, to build him a new Chancellery adjoining the existing one, which he had described in 1933 as being 'only fit for a soap company'. He had given Speer a free hand, and the whole of Voss Strasse, running from Wilhelmplatz. Cost was no object, as long as the result was sufficiently grand, but he would have less than a year, from start to finish – the building was to be complete in every respect by 9 January 1939.

In his memoirs, Speer recalls how Hitler arrived at the new Chancellery in an excited mood, expecting to find the place filled with frantic workmen putting the finishing touches to the building, removing scaffolding, sweeping up dust and rubbish, unrolling carpets, hanging paintings, swarming everywhere like disturbed ants. What he found astonished him: there was not a single workman in sight. Everything was in place, completely ready. He could have sat down there and then at the huge desk in his impressive new study and started work.

Deeply impressed, Hitler learned that Speer had had the building ready forty-eight hours ahead of the 'impossible' completion date. With great satisfaction he walked through the marble halls, inspecting and approving. During his very first conversation with Speer about the project, he had told the architect: 'I need grand halls and salons which will make an impression on people, especially the smaller dignitaries.' Now, looking at the finished product, he acknowledged that Speer had done him proud.

Everything about the new building was on a grand scale. The Voss Strasse frontage stretched for a quarter mile of yellow stucco and grey stone. Huge square stone columns framed the main entrance, where visitors drove through great gates into a court of honour. An outside staircase led them into a reception room; from there they could pass through double doors almost seventeen feet high and flanked by gilded bronze and stone eagles, each clutching a swastika in its claws, and on into a large hall with floor and walls clad in gold and grey mosaic tiles. From this Mosaic Hall a flight of steps led up to a circular chamber with a high, domed ceiling, and from there, the visitor passed into a magnificent gallery lined with red marble pillars. At 480 feet, the Marble Gallery was twice as long as the Hall of Mirrors at Versailles, a fact which gave Hitler particular pleasure. Beyond the gallery was a great hall for state receptions. The whole concourse of rooms was some 725 feet of rich materials and colours, flamboyant, ostentatious, brash even, but highly effective.

'On the long walk from the entrance to the reception hall,' Hitler had crowed delightedly when Speer first showed him the plans, 'they'll get a taste of the power and grandeur of the German Reich!'

Speer recalls that he had been worried about the polished marble floors, which he was reluctant to cover with a runner, but which he feared might be dangerous. Hitler dismissed these fears contemptuously. 'It's exactly right,' he said. 'Diplomats should have practice in moving on a slippery surface.'

If the marble halls met with Hitler's approval, the study which Speer had designed for him, opening off the gallery, sent him into positive ecstasies of delight. He was particularly thrilled by an inlay on the desk, representing a sword half drawn from its sheath. 'Good, good,' he chuckled. 'When the diplomats sitting in front of me at this desk see that, they'll learn to shiver and shake.'

The study was a vast room, intended for public use and for housing meetings. As a private study, Hitler retained his cosier room in the old Chancellery building, where he also continued to live, but the new study was eminently suitable for impressing visitors. A huge, pastel-coloured carpet covered the floor, ornate chandeliers hung from the gilded ceiling, and over the four doors from the room Speer had placed gilded panels decorated with pictures of the four Virtues: Wisdom, Prudence, Fortitude and Justice. On the front of the desk, beneath the inlay of the sword, were three heads, one of them of Medusa, complete with snakes writhing on her head. In front of the window, a large table, made of the familiar red marble, stood ready for conferences.

In addition to the public rooms, the new Chancellery contained some 400 offices, housing civil servants and the party organisation. The new building was connected to the old one by a corridor and a large dining room. It had taken 4,500 workers, toiling round the clock in shifts, to meet Hitler's deadline of 9 January. There had been only one mishap: a few days before completion, when the furnishings and decorations were being installed, workmen had dropped the marble bust of Bismarck which had stood in the old Chancellery for decades. The famous bust of the first Chancellor of modern Germany, the man who had unified the individual states into one Reich, had broken off at the neck. Had Hitler heard of it, he would undoubtedly have seen it as a bad omen: he was fond of telling the story of how the Reich eagle had toppled from the post office building at the start of the first world war, presaging disaster. Speer had saved the day by having sculptor Arno Breker make an exact copy, which they had 'aged' by steeping it in cold tea.

The deception over Bismarck's bust worked. Hitler was completely unaware of any bad portents as he took possession of his new headquarters. He was relieved to be back in his own Berlin home, after many weeks as a guest in Joseph Goebbels's house at Schwanenwerder, near Potsdam. His elation was slightly dampened, however, by the first piece of business he found waiting for him: a memo from Hjalmar Schacht, the man he had dismissed as Economics Minister a year before but who was still president of the Reichsbank, signed not only by Schacht himself but also by every other director. The bankers were giving Hitler the sternest warning about what his vast spending programmes were doing to the German economy. The cost of rearmament, they cautioned, was dragging the country to the brink of ruin, the stability of the currency was threatened, and if he did not call a halt immediately, the Third Reich would soon be bankrupt.

Hitler read the memo, and put it aside. Schacht might be the 'Old Wizard' of German finance, the man who had saved the currency and the economy in 1924, and who had been first to sign the petition to President Hindenburg in 1933 calling for Hitler to be appointed Chancellor. He might be the man who had financed the Nazi Party's final election after the Reichstag fire. But he was not indispensable.

Hitler had no doubt whatever about his own ability to control internal affairs; he could deal with Schacht and the bankers in his own good time. For the moment, he was more concerned with international affairs, and what he was going to do about Beck's obstinate refusal to play his game. There was still a chance that the Poles might see sense. Ribbentrop's official visit to Warsaw must be arranged for the earliest possible moment, so that he could make one final attempt at persuading them. But the prospects were not bright, and it was time to start making alternative plans.

The direction in which Hitler's alternative plans might go was signalled next day, when Soviet Ambassador Alexei Merekalov called at the German Foreign Ministry to talk to Emil Wiehl, director of the economic policy department. Merekalov was a pale, colourless individual who, like most but by no means all Soviet ambassadors, did only as he was told and never dared to show any personal initiative. The fact that he had asked for a meeting indicated that Stalin wanted it. The message he brought was that the Soviet Union was prepared to resume the credit negotiations which had broken down in March 1938. Indeed, he went even further, informing Wiehl 'of the Soviet Union's desire to bring a new era in German–Soviet relations'. That the ambassador himself was dealing with the matter proved how serious the Soviets were.

Trade is a natural barometer of relations between countries, and the figures for trade between the Soviet Union and Germany are particularly revealing. Throughout most of the twenties, Germany had been the Soviet Union's chief ally, and trade between them had flourished. In 1928, Germany was taking almost twenty-nine per cent of total Soviet exports, including a far higher proportion of their manganese ore, timber, oil, flax and furs. In the other direction, Germany was supplying a similar percentage of total Soviet imports, mainly in machinery, which was most important to Germany since there were at that time few other markets open. By the time Hitler came to power, Germany was supplying an amazing 46·5 per cent of the Soviet Union's total imports. But that was the high water mark, and as the Nazis increased their grip on Germany, so the tide of trade fell dramatically. Within two years, Germany's share of Soviet imports had dropped to a mere nine per cent, and even though new agreements were made things did not improve as the thirties progressed. In spite of Germany's almost unlimited need for the raw materials which the Soviet Union could supply, German imports during 1938 barely totalled 50 million Reichsmarks, where a few years before they had been counted in hundreds of millions. And they were still dropping: for the first quarter of 1939 there would be only 6 million Reichsmarks' worth.

For Hermann Göring, as head of the Four Year Plan, the situation was coming perilously close to disaster. As early as 8 February 1938, in a secret lecture in Berlin, he had told senior officers of the armed forces and high officials of the War Industries Department that Germany's economic position was so critical that the completion of the Four Year Plan seemed hardly possible. The only way out of the difficulties, he had said, was the immediate annexation of Austria and the conquering of Czechoslovakia, which would also bring Hungary and the Balkans under German economic dictatorship, providing enough foodstuffs, war materials and added military strength to prevent defeat in war by blockade on the high seas.

During the first few months of 1938, the army had received only one third of its iron and steel quotas for the manufacture of munitions. Many military construction projects were lying half finished because of steel shortages. The giant Krupp concern was falling far behind schedule in producing guns, tanks and weaponry: production of trench mortars, for example, for which there was capacity for 200 a month, was reaching barely thirty. The army was involved in continuous fights with the party over the use of steel for construction projects. No one quibbled over Hitler's own schemes, such as the new Chancellery, but the building of new youth hostels came under attack, and when no less than 300 tons of precious steel was used to construct grandstands, shelters and flagpoles for Mussolini's visit to Berlin, the army protested bitterly.

As a result of these shortages, the military programme was falling behind. In the early part of 1938, Hitler was persuading the world to believe that he had thirteen complete army corps, comprising thirty-nine fully equipped divisions. In fact, there were only thirty-two divisions, many of which were far short of their full strength of artillery.

Food supplies, too, were under pressure during 1938. Germany tried to buy meat from Argentina on credit, and was refused. To compensate, and to cover the situation, stocks of canned goods held in government reserve had to be released in increasing quantities.

The *Anschluss* with Austria, bringing Germany her iron mountains, metallurgical industry, overflowing granaries and two million potential soldiers and workers helped to ease the problem, temporarily. The Sudetenland, too, was making its contribution, and when Hitler finally completed his plan for occupying Czechoslovakia there would be even more useful gains in materials, manpower and the excellent arms and aircraft with which the Czechs had equipped their forces, plus the resources of the great Skoda works.

All this, however, was not sufficient to fulfil Germany's needs if she was to continue with Hitler's full rearmament programme. The only answer – apart from the unthinkable alternative of abandoning every-thing Hitler held dear – lay in the east. For months, Göring nagged at the Foreign Ministry, demanding that they persuade the Soviets to talk. But it seemed that the political situation always prevented it. The negotiations which had been started early in 1938 had been abruptly halted by the *Anchluss*; throughout the late spring and summer, Germany's aggressive intentions towards Czechoslovakia had kept the Soviets away; and Munich appeared to have upset Stalin even more, despite Hitler's protestations that the Sudetenland marked the limit of his ambitions.

Early in October 1938, however, the German embassy in Moscow realised that the Soviet attitude towards them was changing. Stalin had been more upset by the British and French at Munich than by Germany. He had kept noticeably silent while Poland seized Teschen and had refrained from saying or doing anything against Germany.

A jubilant Counsellor Werner von Tippelskirch reported to Berlin at that time that the anti-German, pro-Western policy of Litvinov had suffered a complete fiasco, and that he would have to go. The time could be right, he suggested, for a new economic agreement. A few days later, Count Friedrich Werner von der Schulenburg, the distinguished ambassador in Moscow, informed the Foreign Ministry that he intended approaching Molotov, the Soviet Prime Minister, to try to settle the questions which were disturbing Soviet–German relations.

The Foreign Ministry did not need more urging. Within a few days, its brilliant young economic troubleshooter, Karl Schnurre, was asking Ribbentrop for approval to start discussions with the Soviet trade delegation in Berlin, though he was not hopeful of success. The trouble was, he said, German industry always fell down on delivery of the finished goods which the Soviets needed as payment for any raw materials they sent to Germany.

In spite of Schnurre's doubts, Ribbentrop said yes. Schnurre called a meeting of German officials from other departments and from the Ministry of Economics. They met on 1 December, sorted out their internal differences, and by 22 December were sitting down with the Soviet deputy trade representative, Skossyrev, in the absence of his chief, Davydov, who was sick in Moscow.

The Germans started with a bold, simple statement: they wanted to 'undertake a general clearing-up, then start with a clean slate'. Schnurre went on to make the firm proposal: a new credit agreement, under which 200 million Reichsmarks' worth of German exports would go to the USSR over the next two years, to be covered by Soviet deliveries of raw materials to the value of 100 million Reichsmarks a year, 'materials which are very important to us but in the export of which the Russians would otherwise have no interest'.

Skossyrev listened attentively, but remained non-committal, then went away to report. Over Christmas and the New Year there had been no response from Moscow. Now, on 11 January, Ambassador Merekalov brought Stalin's reply. It sounded good – in fact, it sounded almost too good: the Soviet government wanted the talks to start immediately, and in Moscow. In vain, Wiehl tried to dissuade him. The last talks had taken place in Berlin, he said. All the more reason why they should now be in Moscow, Merekalov replied. But the German delegation couldn't leave Berlin at the moment, as they were involved with other negotiations, Wiehl countered. That was not the Soviets' problem, Merekalov insisted, digging in his heels. If the Germans refused to go to Moscow, it would, at the very least, make negotiations more difficult.

The Soviets wanted the talks in Moscow because that would show the world how much value the Third Reich placed on its relations with the Soviet Union. The German Foreign Ministry was reluctant to present Stalin with such a propaganda coup, but there was little they could do about it: Germany needed Soviet raw materials so badly they dared not risk doing anything which might interfere with negotiations. Wiehl promised he would look into the matter and give Merekalov an answer as quickly as possible. As it happened, however, Merekalov was to receive the first official response direct from Hitler himself, the very next day.

As noon approached on 12 January, the ambassadors, ministers and chargés d'affaires drove through the great gates of the new Chancellery, climbed the stairs to the entrance hall, then made their way through Speer's amazing galleries to the great reception room. The whole of the Diplomatic Corps was present for Hitler's annual New Year reception – though Britain's ambassador, Sir Neville Henderson, was still in London, recovering from an operation for cancer, and was represented by the first secretary, Sir George Ogilvie-Forbes. They were all duly impressed by the magnificence of the new building.

Behind the doors of his study, Hitler waited for the clock to strike noon. He listened with satisfaction to the sounds of the diplomats gathering, and to the band greeting each of them with a roll of drums or a full military salute, depending on his status. Unusually for such an occasion, Hitler was wearing his brown party tunic, adorned only by the Reich eagle emblem on his left arm and his Iron Cross, first class, on his breast.

The clock struck, Hitler nodded to his adjutants and stepped forward as they swung open the doors. Past the assembled guests, drawn up in a semi-circle in strict order of precedence, he moved, hands clasped before him, with the strange, crab-like gait he always used on such occasions. He stopped under the two great crystal chandeliers, so that he would have sufficient light to read his speech without wearing his glasses, and prepared to meet the diplomats as they stepped forward, shaking hands with each in turn, and exchanging a brief greeting.

Everything proceeded normally, and formally. Then Alexei Merekalov stood before him. Hitler shook hands – and began a conversation. All over the room, diplomatic eyebrows raised, and stayed raised as Hitler continued chatting for several minutes – some reports say the conversation lasted nearly three quarters of an hour. The last time Hitler had met Merekalov, at a dinner in the autumn, he had conspicuously snubbed him. When the Soviet ambassador had visited the Berghof in July, he had given orders that there was to be no guard of honour, though the Egyptian minister who had preceded Merekalov had been greeted with full ceremony. Now, the Führer was making a point of bestowing his favour on the Russian in the most public way. It was clearly a signal, and in the world of diplomacy such signals are regarded very seriously. But what exactly did Hitler's signal mean? And what was he saying that was so important?

There is no known official record in either German or Soviet archives of what Hitler actually said to Merekalov that day, but soon afterwards press reports, almost certainly inspired by Moscow, began circulating saying that Hitler had agreed to talks with the Soviet Union, and that he had asked Merekalov to inform Stalin 'that Germany entertained no designs on the Ukraine at the present time'.

The mention of the Ukraine was particularly significant, for in Rome that morning Neville Chamberlain, paying a friendly official visit to Mussolini in spite of the fact that the Italians were regularly attacking British ships sailing to Spain, had naively asked the Duce whether Hitler had ambitions in the Ukraine, Poland or the Soviet Union. German activities, he had said, seemed to indicate an attack in that direction, and were keeping the whole of Europe in a state of nervous anticipation. Mussolini had denied any such intentions on Hitler's part, saying his armament was for purely defensive purposes and he needed a long period of peace to assimilate his new territories into the Reich, and promptly had the conversation reported to Berlin. Hitler, seeing the capital to be made from Chamberlain's gauche question, arranged for it to be passed on to Moscow – indeed, it may even have formed part of his conversation with Merekalov.

The story which reached Stalin, however, had been subtly doctored, to reinforce his belief that the Western Powers were conspiring to incite Hitler to attack him. Litvinov told Polish ambassador Grzybowski that he 'had received information from a reliable source, that in his conversations in Rome Chamberlain had sought to raise the Ukrainian question, allowing it to be understood that Britain would not view German aspirations in this direction with disfavour'. Litvinov's deputy, Potemkin, repeated the same story to Italian Ambassador Rossi on 5 April, an indication of how seriously the Soviets were taking it.

To Stalin's suspicious mind, the report was further proof of the duplicity of the British, who had deliberately excluded him from Munich, and who were now clearly trying to turn Germany and the Soviet Union against each other by sowing the seeds of distrust between them. It was, in his view, unthinkable that the leader of the world's greatest empire was simply not clever enough, not devious enough and not ruthless enough to conceive such a plan. Assuming that was the British intention, Stalin had to consider the best defence against it. One of the possibilities, one way of spiking the Western democracies' guns, would be to come to an understanding with Hitler.

5

'CHESTNUTS OUT OF THE FIRE'

Although he had made such a public show of bestowing his favour on Alexei Merekalov at the New Year's reception, Hitler's interest in the Soviet Union during the early months of 1939 was still principally as a source of vital raw materials. With Germany on the verge of bankruptcy and almost totally devoid of foreign currency, a barter deal with the Soviets was the only way he could get them, but, for the moment at least, he was not prepared to go further than that in establishing any sort of relationship. As late as 7 February, Ribbentrop – who, of course, always voiced Hitler's thoughts and never his own – could tell the French ambassador that German foreign policy consisted of trying to regain lost colonies, and fighting communism. 'Towards the Soviets, we will remain adamant,' he said. 'We will never come to an understanding with Bolshevik Russia.'

On the economic front, however, practical necessity outweighed political scruples, and on 20 January – the same day, incidentally, that Hitler finally dismissed Hjalmar Schacht as president of the Reichsbank for warning him that his rearmament programme was ruining the country – Merekalov was told Germany agreed that talks on a new credit agreement should be held in Moscow. They would be sending Karl Schnurre, head of the Eastern Europe section of the Foreign Ministry's economic policy department, the man who had been leading the talks in Berlin for the renewal of the 1938 trade agreement.

Schnurre, then forty years old, was one of the rising stars of the Foreign Ministry. A good-looking, beefy man, just over six feet tall, with receding sandy hair and a rather prominent nose, he had great vitality and enjoyed the good life. Walter Schmid, who went on to a distinguished diplomatic career himself and who was then his assistant, recalls that as a rule Schnurre did not like to be in his office before about 10 am, but that when the job demanded he would work day and night without pause or complaint. Related by marriage to both Ribbentrop and the German ambassador in Moscow, Count von der Schulenburg, Schnurre was a lawyer with the qualifications to be a judge. He had practised international law, specialising in the scientific field, and had worked for some time in London before joining the Foreign Ministry in 1929. His rise had been rapid: by 1936 he was the youngest man ever to hold the rank of counsellor in the German foreign service, and was promoted to minister in 1939. Urbane and sociable, he was liked and respected by everyone, and was an excellent choice for the role he was to play at the heart of all negotiations with the Soviets.

The plan was for Schnurre to travel to Moscow in secret at the end of January, from Warsaw, where he had business already planned. As a cover, he was to accompany Schulenburg, who was then on leave in Germany and who would meet him in Warsaw: since the two men were known to be personal friends of long standing, it would seem perfectly natural for Schnurre to go with him for a few days' 'vacation'. In this way, Ribbentrop no doubt hoped to deny the Soviet Union the chance of making political capital out of the visit, at the same time avoiding alarm to Germany's allies by being seen to approach the Soviets.

Schnurre's stay in Warsaw happened to overlap with Ribbentrop's official visit, which started on 25 January, to coincide with the fifth anniversary of the 1934 non-aggression pact. Beck had spent five years trying to arrange this German return of the official visit he had himself then made to Berlin, and he meant to make the most of it with grand receptions, dinners and much-publicised high-level meetings, starting on the first evening with a magnificent banquet in the ballroom of the Brühl Palace, which housed the Foreign Ministry.

Peter Kleist, the Büro Ribbentrop's expert on Eastern Europe, who was part of the Foreign Minister's large retinue, was very struck by this building, and by the contrasts embodied in it, which were somehow typical of Poland at that time. 'The rich beauty of the exterior had been preserved unaltered,' he wrote in his account of the visit. 'Inside, it was fitted up with the most daring innovations of Parisian internal design of the twenties, but coarsened a little to be in keeping with Polish style. In the large entrance hall on the ground floor the visitor had a shock when he saw a huge statue, well over life size, the marble of which shimmered under a deep bowl reflector like white sugar. The first impression was so devastating that I do not know to this day whether it represented Mother Polonia or Marshal Pilsudski. The reception rooms on the first floor were resplendent in bright, definite tones – a dazzling white, a gleaming sky-blue or a rich ox-blood red, on which the lovely old paintings paled into dull splotches of colour.'

It was against this setting that Ribbentrop made a long speech emphasising Polish–German friendship as 'an essential element in German foreign policy'. 'The political foresight, and the principles of true statesmanship, which induced both sides to take the momentous decision of 1934,' he declaimed, 'provide a guarantee that all the other problems arising in the course of the future evolution of events will also be solved in the same spirit, with due respect and understanding of the rightful interests of both sides . . .' It was against the same setting – for Beck lived in an apartment decorated in a similar ultra-modern style immediately below the ballroom – that Ribbentrop hammered away at him in their private discussions, still trying desperately to persuade him to join the Anti-Comintern Pact and to join Germany in marching against the Soviet Union.

Beck somehow managed to duck the question yet again. Though, according to Ribbentrop's own account, he made no secret of the fact that Poland had aspirations directed towards the Soviet Ukraine and a connection with the Black Sea, he was still not prepared to risk his treasured equilibrium. Even when Ribbentrop increased the stakes by offering him Slovakia – an ominous confirmation of Hitler's next move – as payment for throwing in his lot with Germany, he still would not commit himself.

There was one area, however, where Beck was only too ready to make a decisive statement: that area was Danzig and the Corridor, and the statement was a decisive no. Under pressure from his fellow junta members, he had now backed down from his earlier suggestion of a special arrangement for the Free City, along the lines of Hitler's proposal.

Already in a thoroughly bad mood because of his failure to win Beck's support, Ribbentrop soon had reason to be positively furious. Halfway through his crowded schedule, while hurriedly changing into formal dress at the Palac Blanca, where he was staying, ready for a meeting with President Moscicki, he learned that the London *Daily Mail* and most of the French papers that day were carrying sensational reports that a large German delegation with over thirty leading economic experts headed by Schnurre was on its way to Moscow, where it would work out a comprehensive programme of German–Soviet co-operation.

Ribbentrop exploded. 'At a time when I am trying to establish the principle of co-operation between Germany and Poland against the Soviet Union on behalf of the Führer,' he roared, 'this scandalous and upsetting news is like a stab in the back. Schnurre must return to Berlin at once!'

Schnurre protested vigorously, but it was no use. Ribbentrop refused to budge. Schulenberg was forced to return alone to Moscow, where he had the thankless task of trying to explain to a disbelieving Soviet government that the change of plan was not meant as a rebuff to them, but was caused by sudden, urgent business requiring Schnurre's attention in Berlin: the economic negotiations would be carried on by the embassy. Despite Schulenburg's efforts at reassurance, however, the damage had been done. Although the negotiations did go ahead, progress over the next four weeks was slow and uncertain, aggravated by impossible Soviet demands not only for machinery and finished goods but also for armaments and military equipment.

Where the offending press reports originated remains a mystery – but Schulenberg for one had few doubts. In a letter to Ernst von Weizsäcker, State Secretary in the Foreign Ministry, he laid the blame squarely at the door of 'interested parties' who stood to benefit by continuing antagonism between Germany and the Soviet Union, and who saw 'something "suspicious" if we import so much as a little timber, manganese and petroleum from the Soviet Union'.

'I am sorry,' he continued, 'but I must express the suspicion that in the case of Schnurre's journey our Polish friends are the chief culprits. Herr Schnurre was forced to tell them about his journey to Moscow; they obviously gave the cue to the French press. It is striking that my Polish colleague here [in Moscow] knew almost before we did that Herr Schnurre was not coming here. Be that as it may, the statements of the French press have achieved their aim: they have put a spoke in our wheel.'

Whether or not Beck had any hand in torpedoing the Soviet–German talks, he was certainly striking out in a new direction: on the same day that he rejected Ribbentrop's latest advances, he contacted the British ambassador in Warsaw to begin making arrangements for the visit to London. He no longer had any faith in France's commitment to come to Poland's aid if she were attacked; he needed to enlist the support of Britain, too – if only to apply the required pressure on France to fulfil her treaty obligations. Within a short time, the visit was agreed. It would take place at the beginning of April, a piece of timing that was to prove particularly fateful.

Stalin was undoubtedly upset by the cancellation of Schnurre's journey – Peter Kleist wrote that Georgi Astakhov, counsellor in the Soviet embassy in Berlin, 'said to me reproachfully that we had arranged Schnurre's trip and sent out the press report about a large economic delegation merely in order to snub the Soviets in front of the whole world by the recall of Schnurre'. But the gall of Munich, the blatant cold-shouldering of the Soviet Union by France and Britain, was far more bitter to Stalin and he was prepared to continue trying for an understanding with Germany. In his curious way of avoiding the direct approach but making his wishes and intentions known obliquely, by signals, he took a leaf out of the Poles' book and made use of the Western press to let Hitler know what he was thinking. It was a method which had the added advantage that the signal could be seen at the same time by Britain and France as a warning of what he might do if they failed to respond to his advances.

On 27 January, an article appeared in the London *News Chronicle* by its diplomatic correspondent, Vernon Bartlett forecasting a deal between the Soviet Union and Germany. Bartlett was known to have very close connections with Ivan Maisky, the Soviet ambassador, who regularly used him as a channel for Soviet news and views. In his article, which was reproduced in full and without comment in *Pravda* next day, he pointed out that the British and French governments had deliberately ignored the Soviet Union, while the Germans and Poles had initiated the trade negotiations which were then in progress. 'At present,' the article went on, 'the Soviet government evidently has no intention of giving any help to Great Britain and France if the latter come into conflict with Germany and Italy. The USSR intends to conclude agreements with its neighbours on the condition that it be left in peace. From the point of view of the Soviet government, there is no great difference between the positions of the British and French governments on the one hand and the German and Italian on the other, which would justify serious sacrifices in the defence of Western democracy.'

Bartlett concluded by saying that it would be unwise to consider the present differences between Moscow and Berlin as an insurmountable factor in international politics. By reprinting the story in *Pravda*, the official organ of the party, Stalin was not only underlining his message to Hitler and the Western leaders. He was also beginning the process of preparing his own people for a possible change, should it prove necessary.

The first possible sign of reciprocation from Hitler came almost immediately, in his speech on 30 January to celebrate the sixth anniversary of his accession to power. For the first time, the speech included no attack on communism or on the Soviet Union, an omission which could not have been accidental, and which could be read as at least a tentative step towards *rapprochement*. The speech also showed, however, that Hitler had not yet given up hope of winning the Poles over to his side: it also contained a noticeably warm reference to the friendship between Germany and Poland, which Hitler described, somewhat optimistically if not ironically, as 'one of the reassuring factors in the political life of Europe'. This did not, however, stop the Poles signing their trade agreement with the Soviet Union on 19 February.

As far as Britain was concerned, there were apparently genuine efforts to improve relations with the Soviet Union over the next few weeks – indeed, Chamberlain had given Foreign Secretary Lord Halifax specific approval to pursue such a course. On 20 February, Halifax dined at the Soviet embassy in London, and this was followed nine days later by a visit from Chamberlain himself, accompanied by four other Cabinet ministers, the first by a British Prime Minister since the Revolution in 1917. Arrangements were also made for Robert Hudson, Parliamentary Under-Secretary to the Department of Overseas Trade, to go to

Moscow in March to discuss increased trade, but there was still no apparent inclination to join the Soviets in any form of collective security.

Stalin's need of an understanding with one side or the other became more pressing in February, as the barrier of Central European states between his country and Germany crumbled. Hitler stepped up the political and propaganda campaign against Czechoslovakia: it was obvious that it was now only a matter of time, and not a great deal of time at that, before he made his move against her. New governments in Romania and Yugoslavia were openly pro-German, and were making arms deals with Hitler. On 24 February Hungary joined the Anti-Comintern Pact, and the Bulgarians expressed their willingness to follow suit. At about the same time, the four nations which made up the Balkan Entente – Romania, Yugoslavia, Turkey and Greece – agreed that Germany's drive to the east, the historic *Drang nach Osten*, 'was a natural phenomenon which would increase in strength to the extent that colonial questions were left unsolved. The Balkans must meet this impetus, however, by co-operating closely with Germany, especially in the economic field.'

By the beginning of March, with the German–Soviet credit negotiations grinding to a halt and the announcement that a high-powered British trade delegation was to go to Berlin, the situation for Stalin was looking bleak. In his keynote speech to the Eighteenth Congress of the Soviet Communist Party on 10 March, Stalin declared that the Soviet Union would go to the assistance of the victims of aggression who were fighting for their independence. But this was not the most important part of the long speech. As far as international relations were concerned, much of what Stalin had to say was only repeating and underlining earlier statements of policy and belief. He castigated Germany, Italy and Japan for their aggressive acts, but blamed Britain, France and the USA for appeasing them with concession after concession. Noting that the Western Powers combined were 'unquestionably stronger than the fascist states, both economically and militarily', he accused them of rejecting the policy of collective security, and taking up a position of non-intervention. He charged them with being afraid that another world war would lead to 'the victory of the revolution in one or several countries', just as the first imperalist world war had led to its victory in Russia.

Non-intervention, he claimed, was merely a cover for actively encouraging the aggressors: 'Not to hinder Japan, say, from embroiling herself in a war with China, or better still with the Soviet Union; not to hinder Germany, say, from enmeshing herself in European affairs, from embroiling herself in a war with the Soviet Union; to allow them to weaken and exhaust one another; and then, when they have become weak enough, to appear on the scene with fresh strength, to appear, of course, "in the interests of peace", and to dictate conditions to the enfeebled belligerents. Cheap and easy!'

The speech contained clear and significant messages to both the Western democracies and to Hitler. To the West, he directed a warning: 'Far be it from me to moralise on the policy of non-intervention, to talk of treason, treachery and so on. It would be naive to preach morals to people who recognise no human morality. Politics are politics, as the old, case-hardened bourgeois diplomats say. It must be remarked, however, that the big and dangerous political game started by the supporters of the policy of non-intervention may end in a serious blow for them.'

To Hitler, he offered an invitation, both openly and through further half-veiled signals. 'The foreign policy of the Soviet Union is clear and explicit,' he said. 'We stand for peace and the strengthening of business relations with all countries. That is our position; and we shall adhere to this position as long as these countries maintain like relations with the Soviet Union and as long as they make no attempt to trespass on the interests of our country.' Echoing the *News Chronicle* article, he stressed that there were no insurmountable differences between the Soviet Union and Germany apart from their ideological disagreements, and no visible grounds for conflict.

As he came to the end of this part of his speech, Stalin summed up what he described as the tasks of the party in the sphere of foreign policy. Three of the four tasks he listed were concerned with the conventional aims of strengthening 'international bonds of friendship with the working peoples of all countries', building up the Red Army and Navy, and continuing the pursuit of peace. The fourth was a final signal to Hitler and the West, in a phrase which was to become one of the most quoted of all Stalin's utterances. It was: 'To be cautious and not allow our country to be drawn into conflicts by warmongers who are accustomed to have others pull the chestnuts out of the fire for them.'

Besides being both pointed and memorable, Stalin's chestnuts were undoubtedly calculated to strike a chord with Hitler, for in *Mein Kampf* – which Stalin had studied carefully in translation – Hitler had said while writing of British attempts to reach an understanding with Germany at the turn of the century: 'The Germans were upset by the idea of "having to pull England's chestnuts out of the fire for her" – as though there could ever be an alliance on any other basis than a mutual business deal.'

Hitler gave no sign of recognising Stalin's signal. His attention was heavily occupied elsewhere at that moment, for the long-running Czech crisis, which he had kept simmering since Munich, was finally starting to boil over. In October 1938, Slovakia had been given autonomy within a confederated state – its name changed to a hyphenated Czecho-Slovakia – along with Bohemia and Moravia, 'Czechia', to the west and Ruthenia, the Carpatho-Ukraine, in the east. Since then it had become the focus of German moves to continue the general destabilisation, its government aligning itself at every turn with Germany. Now, German-fanned separatist agitation flared in both Slovakia and Ruthenia, and the national government in Prague was forced to take action. On 6 March, President Hacha dismissed the pro-Nazi government of Ruthenia. On 10 March, he did the same to the autonomous Slovak government. Hitler suddenly had the opportunity he needed to complete the plans for the annexation of the Czech lands which Munich had so inconveniently interrupted.

Within five days, it was all over. The Slovaks were bullied into an immediate announcement of their independence, German troops were hurriedly moved to the Czech frontiers, and when President Hacha travelled to Berlin to see Hitler in the early hours of 15 March, he was presented with an ultimatum that was particularly brutal, even for the Nazis. He was told that German troops were in position on three sides of his frontiers, the order for them to invade in four hours' time had already been given, and the only way Hacha could serve his country now was by accepting that it was to be incorporated into the Greater German Reich. Any resistance would only result in the annihilation of Czecho-Slovakia, starting with the bombing of Prague.

Hacha, who was a frail, elderly man with a weak heart, collapsed and had to be revived with an intravenous amphetamine injection by Hitler's physician, Dr Theo Morell, before he could be harried into signing his country's death warrant, a statement Hitler had already had prepared for him, saying that 'he confidently placed the fate of the Czech people and country in the hands of the Führer of the German Reich'.

Immediately Hacha had signed, Hitler rushed from the room and into the adjoining office, where his two secretaries, Christa Schröder and Johanna Wolf, were waiting. Schröder later recalled that his face was transfigured as he threw out his arms to them and cried: 'Children! Kiss me! Quickly! Hacha has just signed. It is the greatest triumph of my life! I shall go down in history as the greatest German!'

At 6 am, as a spring blizzard swept across Central Europe, German troops crossed the frontiers and sped towards Prague, unopposed. Hitler and his entourage followed in his special train later that morning as far as the border. 'From the frontier onwards we drove in a long convoy of motor cars along the broad road to Prague,' Keitel wrote later. 'Very shortly we came across the marching columns of our army. It was very cold and wintry, there were snow drifts and black ice, and the mobile columns with their trucks and guns had to overcome the most formidable obstacles to their progress, particularly when our convoy wanted to overtake them.

'We reached the outskirts of Prague as dusk was falling, simultaneously with the first troop units, and escorted by a mobile company we drove down the Hradschin to where we were to be billeted. A cold supper was bought for us in the town as we had brought nothing with us: cold Prague ham, bread rolls, butter, cheese, fruit and Pilsener beer; it is the only time I ever saw Hitler drinking a tiny glass of beer. It tasted wonderful to us.'

Hitler and his chief aides were, in fact, 'billeted' in the Czech Presidential Palace, the ancient seat of the kings of Bohemia, Hradschin Castle. When Hacha arrived back there several hours later – his train having been held up in Germany to allow Hitler time to install himself – he was dismayed to find himself driven not to the front door but to the servants' entrance at the rear, a move which symbolised the position the Czechs were to have from now on, in what had been their own land.

Hitler proclaimed from the castle that Czechoslovakia no longer existed. The provinces of Bohemia and Moravia were now German protectorates; Slovakia was an independent state, though also under German protection; Ruthenia's independence, announced on 14 March, had lasted just twenty-four hours, before Hungary marched in and swallowed it, as a gift from Hitler to please the Poles, giving them the common frontier they had wanted with the Hungarians. Hitler had every justification, as he stood on the balcony of the castle on 15 March, for feeling pleased with himself, a feeling which was no doubt increased when an aide brought confirmation that neither Britain nor France had started to mobilise.

In fact, both the British and French governments were busy excusing themselves from doing anything to support Czechoslovakia, the state which they had offered to guarantee at Munich. In Paris, according to William Shirer, who was visiting the city at that time, there was complete apathy over Hitler's latest coup. Bonnet told the Foreign Affairs committee that the Munich guarantee 'had not yet become effective', and that France was therefore under no obligation to do anything. In London, Chamberlain's excuse to the Cabinet and to the House of Commons was that since Czechoslovakia had ceased to exist, there was no longer any point in British promises to guarantee her frontiers.

Stalin said nothing. While Hitler was clearly not interested in responding to his signals, the Western Powers were once again demonstrating that they could not be relied on to offer any resistance to German aggression. Their passivity could still be interpreted as encouraging Hitler to move eastwards with their blessing. As German troops continued to pour into Bohemia and Moravia, and on into Slovakia in response to a request from the new government there for German protection, the Soviet Union seemed to be completely alone.

When Chamberlain announced the occupation of Czechoslovakia to the House of Commons on 15 March, he was still trying to handle Hitler with the softest of kid gloves. To the total amazement of MPs of all parties, not least his own, he even refused to associate himself with any 'charges of breaches of faith' on the part of the Nazi leader, and declared that he would not be deflected from his course by what had happened. 'We will continue to pursue our policy of appeasement,' he promised.

Such statements must have been sweet music to Hitler's ears – and confirmed Stalin's deepest suspicions. But within two days, on the eve of his seventieth birthday, the British Prime Minister had made such an astonishing change of tack that the whole situation was turned completely on its head. Back on his old home ground inside Birmingham's solid, classically pillared Town Hall, he surprised everyone by ditching the speech he had prepared on domestic issues, and launching into a savage attack on Hitler, angrily listing all the personal assurances that now lay in tatters. At the time of Munich, he had described the Czech crisis, in a BBC radio broadcast, as 'a quarrel in a far-away country between people of whom we know nothing'. On the evening of Friday, 17 March 1939, he suddenly found he knew – and cared – a great deal.

'Who can fail to feel his heart go out in sympathy to the proud, brave people who have so suddenly been subjected to this invasion, whose liberties are curtailed, whose national independence is gone?' he asked. 'Now we are told that this seizure of territory has been necessitated by disturbances in Czechoslovakia . . . If they were disorders, were they not fomented from without?' Indignant, hurt, outraged, he lashed out at Hitler with all the venom of a spurned suitor. Finally, it seemed, the scales had fallen from his eyes as he voiced the questions which others had been asking for years: 'Is this the last attack upon a small state, or is it to be followed by another? Is this, in fact, a step in the direction of an attempt to dominate the world by force?'

Chamberlain's abrupt change of heart had been brought about mainly by his politician's instinct for survival. After his calm acceptance of the rape of Czechoslovakia in the House of Commons on the Wednesday, the surge of discontent was so great, not only among opposition MPs and troublesome Tories like Winston Churchill and Anthony Eden but also among those who had always been his staunchest supporters, that he was in imminent danger of being unseated. Press reaction next day was unanimously violent, and it was soon clear that the mood of the country had swung against him, too. The millions who had cheered his return from Munich promising 'peace for our time' were now rejecting the policy of appeasement which they had genuinely supported. If Chamberlain did not disown that policy now, they – and the Conservative Party – would disown him. The realisation of this danger was undoubtedly the main reason why, during the two-hour train journey from London to Birmingham that afternoon, he tore up his prepared speech on social problems in Britain and hurriedly prepared the notes from which he could extemporise a new one.

Among the many defectors in the government's own circle, perhaps the most surprising and certainly the most significant was Edward Frederick Lindley Wood, the first Earl of Halifax, whose name was being mooted as replacement Prime Minister. Halifax, six feet five inches tall, with a cadaverous head and a congenitally withered, handless left arm, was a quiet, amiable and intensely honest man, a devout high Anglican Christian, who had been Viceroy of India from 1926 to 1931. He had become Foreign Secretary in February 1938, after Chamberlain had engineered the resignation of the brilliant but independently minded Eden. Eden had been a bitter opponent of the fascist dictators and of the appeasement which he believed pandered to them and encouraged them; with Halifax, Chamberlain had had no such difficulties – until now. He had always been the Prime Minister's most loyal and obedient servant, but he had finally been unable to swallow Hitler's latest excesses.

It was Halifax who brought Chamberlain news on 17 March, before he set out for Birmingham, which gave him a second and equally urgent reason for changing course. The news came from Viorel Virgil Tilea, the Romanian minister in London, who had called on Halifax at the Foreign Office that morning in a state of great agitation. Tilea told Halifax that the Germans had given his country an ultimatum: they were demanding a monopoly on Romanian exports, and restrictions on Romanian industrial production for the sake of German interests. He believed Romania was next on Hitler's list, and that an invasion might take place within the next few days, since Germany had far more troops in Czechoslovakia than she needed.

This alarming information came at the same time as reports from Berlin and Paris describing Hitler's preparations for war – the British ambassador in France sent a note which he had typed himself, saying, 'Hitler's personal wish . . . is to make war on Great Britain before June or July' – and rumours that he might launch a surprise attack on the British fleet, coupled with other warnings that Mussolini was about to follow Hitler's lead and occupy Albania or try to grab territory from France in North Africa. Everywhere, tensions ran high as the scare stories multiplied.

In fact, Tilea's alarms about German moves against Romania were completely false. Within twenty-four hours Romanian Foreign Minister Grigore Gafencu had sent an urgent message to Halifax saying Tilea had misrepresented the situation. He assured Britain that the negotiations that were going on with Germany were 'on completely normal lines, as between equals', and that he had given Tilea 'a tremendous head washing'. There was no ultimatum, no immediate threat to Romania's independence.

The denial came too late, however. For once, Chamberlain and Halifax had acted swiftly, and telegrams had already been sent out to

Poland, Turkey, Greece, Yugoslavia and France to sound out their governments about joint action against Germany. A similar message was also sent to Moscow, where Ambassador Sir William Seeds was asked to find out whether the Soviet Union would be prepared to give active help to Romania.

6

'I'LL COOK THEM A STEW THAT THEY'LL CHOKE ON'

The second half of March passed in a confused frenzy as the various nations involved struggled to come to terms with the situation. Only the Soviet Union appeared to follow a consistent line from the start, when Stalin seized the opportunity offered by Chamberlain's volte-face and replied to the British approach with what his ambassador in London, Ivan Maisky, described as phenomenal speed. That same evening, Saturday, 18 March, he proposed an immediate conference, preferably in Bucharest, with Britain, France, the Soviet Union, Turkey, Poland and Romania, to decide on concerted action to stop Hitler.

The British response was disappointing, to say the least: Halifax told Maisky Britain could not spare a 'responsible minister' to go to such a conference, and in any case the government believed it would be 'dangerous' to hold one without being sure of its success in advance. To soften the blow a little, Halifax said the British and French were discussing an alternative idea, since they 'fully realised the need for urgent action'.

Two days later, they announced their alternative proposal. It was for Britain, France, the Soviet Union and Poland to make a joint declaration, pledging to consult each other immediately there was any threat to the independence of any European state. Again, the Soviet response was swift: Litvinov told Seeds in Moscow next day that although they regarded such a declaration as inadequate, they were ready to sign it as soon as France and Poland did. The French gave a firm yes. The Poles, inevitably, refused to sign anything which involved the Soviet Union, on the grounds that this would anger Hitler. After further pressure from London, Beck agreed that he would sign if the agreement was kept secret. This, of course, would nullify its whole purpose and by this time, in any case, Litvinov had already announced Soviet willingness to the press.

While Halifax was trying to convince Ambassador Raczynski in London that Poland's only chance was to join Britain, France and the Soviet Union in an alliance against Germany, Ribbentrop was trying to persuade Ambassador Lipski in Berlin that the Poles must align themselves with Germany against the Soviets, and that they must make up their minds quickly.

Lipski's meeting with Ribbentrop was heated and somewhat acerbic. The Pole complained bitterly of German pressure, particularly in sending troops into Slovakia to 'protect' her – presumably against Poland. He pointed out that Poland had a special interest in Slovakia, since the Slovaks were 'related linguistically' to the Poles. Ribbentrop in turn complained of Polish press attacks and anti-German demonstrations, particularly by Polish students in Danzig. Waving the carrot and the stick at the same time, he repeated German offers to give Poland Slovakia and a share in the Ukraine, in exchange for Danzig and the extra-territorial road and rail links across the Corridor, then warned that Hitler's patience was wearing thin, and that he wanted to see Beck in Berlin very soon to settle matters once and for all.

While all the diplomatic shuffling was going on, Hitler struck again, swiftly and effectively. The victim this time was not Romania, as everyone had expected, but Lithuania, and the prize Hitler sought was the ancient Baltic port of Memel, known to the Lithuanians as Klaipeda. Memel, together with a strip of territory running along the border with East Prussia, was another piece of Germany that had been removed at Versailles in 1919, and which Hitler had been determined to reclaim. On 20 March, while the rest of the world was still reeling from the shock of his Czech invasion only five days previously, he had presented Lithuania with an ultimatum demanding the immediate cession of Memel and its hinterland. Without waiting for an answer, he had then embarked on the battleship *Deutschland*, to sail into Memel at the head of a German naval squadron and personally take possession of the city for the Reich.

Because of the Polish Corridor, the only way to get to Memel, without the unthinkable humiliation of having to ask Polish permission to cross her territory, was by sea. Hitler was a poor sailor, and the weather was rough; he was violently seasick for the whole of the three-day voyage. His temper was not improved by the fact that the Lithuanians had the temerity to resist his demands for most of that time, while they cried for help to the British, French and Polish military attachés in Berlin. They did not appeal to the ambassadors, whom they considered too pro-Nazi, or to the Soviets – Lithuania had won independence from Russia only at the end of the first world war and was still understandably nervous of her former rulers even without the menace of bolshevism. But no one was interested. Alone and friendless, the Lithuanians finally capitulated at 1.30 am on Wednesday, 23 March, after Ribbentrop had warned that the German warships would shoot their way in.

Hitler, looking pale and drawn after his ordeal at sea, rode into Memel at the head of his troops at 2.30 pm that afternoon, delivered the usual rousing speech welcoming the population back 'into an even mightier Germany', and made a tour of the city before flying back to Berlin with another bloodless triumph to his credit, the second within a week, both taking him ever nearer the Soviet frontiers.

This was a development that could not please Stalin: if the cession of the Memel region were to herald the swallowing of the rest of Lithuania, as the Sudetenland had led on to the rest of Czechoslovakia, the domino effect might include the other two Baltic states, Latvia and Estonia, which bordered on the Soviet Union. Once in possession of those prime launch pads, Hitler would pose a direct threat, particularly to Leningrad. On 28 March, Litvinov sent a warning to the Latvian and Estonian governments, saying the Soviets would not tolerate any concessions from them to Germany. The Soviet Union was determined to protect their independence against Germany, by force if necessary, whether they liked it or not.

If the seizure of Memel was disturbing to Stalin, to the Poles it came as a very nasty shock indeed. Not only was Memel on their doorstep, but it bore a remarkable resemblance to Danzig, which was now obviously the next item on Hitler's menu. In fact, he confidently expected the Poles to be reasonable and accede to his demands without the need of force. Although he recognised that Beck would have problems persuading his people to accept a voluntary surrender, he believed, as he told General Brauchitsch, that 'a *fait accompli* by us would help them to a solution'. He even prepared a detailed plan to sail to Danzig on the *Deutschland*, as he had to Memel, arriving with virtually the whole German battle fleet behind him and going ashore in a torpedo boat to make his triumphal entry into the city. With the stumbling block of Danzig removed, he was convinced the Poles would join him on his crusade against the Soviet Union.

The Polish reaction, however, finally killed Hitler's hopes. While the Romanians signified their willingness to go along with Germany by signing a far-reaching trade agreement the day after the seizure of Memel, the Poles mobilised their forces and started moving troops towards the Free City. Brusquely rejecting all the offers made in Ribbentrop's last message, Beck warned that if Hitler persisted in his demands it would mean war. When the German ambassador in Warsaw, Moltke, protested 'You want to negotiate at the point of a bayonet!' Beck shot back, 'That is your own method!'

Next day, Hitler asked General Brauchitsch to start drawing up plans for an invasion of Poland, to be codenamed 'Operation White'. Although he told the army commander he did not intend to act immediately but would wait until the time was exactly right, he left no doubts as to his determination. 'I will then knock Poland out so completely,' he said, 'that she will not need to be taken into account politically for many decades to come.'

Although Beck was finally standing up to Hitler, he still refused to accept any links with the Soviet Union. Chamberlain began to realise that if he could not have both Poland and the Soviet Union in the same alliance, he would have to choose between them. After toying with the idea of a two-tier arrangement – a public alliance with France and the Soviet Union, and a secret one with Poland alone – he chose Poland.

Halifax told the American ambassador to Britain, Joseph Kennedy, that the British felt Poland was much more valuable to them, because the latest information on the Soviets showed 'their air force to be very weak and old and of short range, their army very poor and their industrial backing for the army frightful, and the most they could expect from Russia, if Russia wanted to be of help, would be that they might send some ammunition to Poland in the event of trouble'.

Chamberlain had personal doubts, too, as he showed in a letter to his sister next day. 'I must confess,' he wrote, 'to the very most profound distrust of Russia. I have no belief whatever in her ability to maintain an effective offensive, even if she wanted to. And I distrust her motives, which seem to me to have little connection with our ideas of liberty, and to be concerned only with getting everyone else by the ears. Moreover, she is both hated and suspected by many of the smaller states, notably by Poland, Romania, and Finland.'

The frantic search for international agreements against Hitler had been triggered by false reports of an impending attack on Romania. Now, a new panic was set off in the British government by a false report that Germany was about to invade Poland at any moment. There had been a spate of rumours from various sources, including the American embassy and the British military attaché in Berlin, but on 29 March Ian Colvin, Berlin correspondent for the *News Chronicle*, had got hold of the fact that Hitler had asked Brauchitsch to start planning an attack; he had not been told, however, that this was for some time in the future. The report was uncorroborated, but it was good enough for Chamberlain in his new mood of defiance: he immediately sent a message to Beck offering to guarantee Poland unconditionally. Beck, as he himself said later, 'accepted between two flicks of ash from my cigarette', and at 2 pm on 31 March, after consulting France and rather belatedly informing Ivan Maisky, Chamberlain announced the guarantee to an enthusiastic House of Commons.

On 3 April, Beck arrived in London for the official visit which had been arranged back in January, and proceeded to negotiate a more formal alliance, in which Britain would support Poland if Germany attempted to undermine her independence economically or in any other way. 'In the event of other action by Germany which clearly threatened Polish independence, and was of such a nature that the Polish government considered it vital to resist with their national forces,' the agreement continued, 'His Majesty's Government would at once come to the help of Poland.' The new all-embracing guarantee was announced on 6 April. The treaty ratifying the alliance was to be signed later, after various detailed points had been settled. Beck returned to Warsaw delighted with his diplomatic triumph, as well he might be: Chamberlain had given him a blank cheque, to write as and when he chose.

There was much criticism of the way in which Chamberlain had now placed the decision on whether and when Britain went to war in the hands of such an unstable character as Beck. But the world saw now that Britain was at last prepared to stand up and fight. And when Mussolini invaded Albania the very next day, 7 April, thus posing a threat to the remainder of the Balkans, the British and French quickly offered similar guarantees to Romania and Greece.

The new guarantees obviously impressed Stalin, and on 14 April he sent Maisky to see Halifax, to tell him that 'in view of British interest in the fate of Greece or Romania, the Soviet government are prepared to take part in giving assistance to Romania'. Halifax responded by asking his own ambassador in Moscow, Seeds, to approach Litvinov and ask if he was prepared to issue a declaration over Romania, and perhaps even over Poland. When word came from the Berlin embassy later that day that 'the German government are contemplating securing the return of Danzig to the Reich by Herr Hitler's birthday, 20 April', Halifax immediately sent off a second telegram asking if the Soviets would make a declaration that 'in the event of any act of aggression against any European neighbour of the Soviet Union, which was resisted by the country concerned, the assistance of the Soviet government would be available'.

Chamberlain had thus made another abrupt about-turn: only days after rejecting the Soviet Union in favour of Poland, he had now decided Soviet help was vital and urgent. His request marked the beginning of serious negotiations between the Western allies and the Soviet Union: Stalin's first option was suddenly open again.

In fact, as Stalin was soon to realise, his other option – that of protecting his country by reaching an understanding with Hitler – was also revived by the British and French guarantees to the Poles. Hitler, if he was to attack Poland and thus run the risk of an Anglo-French attack on his rear, would need to remove the added threat of a simultaneous attack from the Soviets. While he was still not convinced that such a threat was serious enough to warrant so drastic a measure as coming to terms with Stalin, Hitler was clearly prepared to start exploring the possibilities.

The news of the British guarantee on 31 March had thrown Hitler into one of his wildest rages. Admiral Canaris, the chief of the Abwehr, the German secret intelligence service, told his associates that when he reported it to him, the Führer had flown into a passion. 'With features distorted by fury,' he said, 'he had stormed up and down his room, pounded his fists on the marble table-top and spewed forth a series of savage imprecations. Then, his eyes flashing with an uncanny light, he had ground out the venomous threat: "I'll cook them a stew that they'll choke on!" '

Next day, speaking at Wilhelmshaven after launching the new battleship *Tirpitz*, he castigated the Western allies and warned: 'When they say in other countries that they will arm and keep on arming more and more, I can tell those statesmen only this – me, you will never tire! I am determined to continue on this road.' One statement more than any other, however, seemed to be directed at Stalin's ears: 'He who pulls the chestnuts out of the fire for these powers must realise he will burn his fingers . . .'

On 3 April, the draft directive for Operation White was ready. It called for the annihilation of Polish forces, the removal of any threat from this direction for ever, and the incorporation of the Free State of Danzig within the Reich. 'Preparations,' the directive laid down, 'must be made in such a way that the operation can be carried out at any time from 1 September 1939 onwards.' As for the Soviet Union: 'Intervention by Russia, if she were in a position to intervene, cannot be expected to be of any use to Poland, because this would mean Poland's destruction by bolshevism.'

Hitler set in motion his first direct, if tentative, move towards an understanding with Stalin on Good Friday, 7 April, as Mussolini's troops were marching into Albania. On that day, Ribbentrop telephoned from his castle at Fuschl, near Salzburg, to tell the Eastern European expert on his personal staff, Peter Kleist, to start improving his relations with the Soviet diplomats in Berlin. Kleist was told nothing more and, as he recorded in his memoirs, was left in some bewilderment, wondering whether Hitler was really about to change his foreign policy, set aside his ideological principles, and 'try out, just this once, something that appeared impossible'. It did not seem likely. What did seem a possibility was that 'Poland was about to have the screws put on her in an attempt to force a solution of the frontier problems'.

Kleist managed to get himself invited to tea a few days later in the faded splendour of the former Kurland Palace in the Unter den Linden which now housed the Soviet embassy. His host was the embassy's counsellor, Georgi Astakhov, a tall, thin young Don Cossack with a sparse goatee beard, a career diplomat who was the real power in the embassy. He was almost certainly one of Stalin's own men, for unlike most Soviet diplomats he seemed to enjoy a great deal of freedom in what he said and did. Kleist was immediately impressed by the fact that Astakhov received him and his companion, an expert in Eastern economic affairs, alone – something which even high-ranking Soviet officials could not normally do.

Astakhov, who spoke German fluently, had obviously been fully briefed for this teatime chat. After a short discussion on French Impressionist painting, on which he proved to be very knowledgeable, he turned to the question of Soviet–German relations and began explaining 'how absurd it was for Germany and the Soviets to fight each other over "ideological subtleties" instead of making grand policy side by side, as they had done so often in history'.

'A statesman must be able to jump over his own shadow,' he said. 'Why don't we decide in favour of a common policy, instead of tearing off each other's heads, which would only serve the interests of some third party?'

When Kleist replied that the 'ideological subtleties' had become important realities which stood in the way of any *rapprochement*, Astakhov 'swept this aside with an easy movement of his hand. He said that Stalin and Hitler were men who created that reality and did not let themselves be dominated by it.'

These had to be Stalin's own words – no Soviet diplomat, however trusted, would dare voice such opinions on his own initiative. Kleist hurried back to his office to prepare a report on his 'sensational conversation', but when he gave it to Ribbentrop, the Foreign Minister seemed alarmed that the talk had gone so far, so quickly.

'For the moment avoid any contact with Astakhov,' he ordered. 'I do not think the Führer would wish that conversation to be continued.'

Within a few days of Astakhov's teatime chat with Kleist, Stalin began pursuing both his options simultaneously and in earnest. On 17 April, Ambassador Merekalov called on State Secretary Ernst von Weizsäcker at the Foreign Ministry for the first time since his appointment to Berlin in June 1938. The official reason for the visit was to ask whether arms contracts which the Czech Skoda works had with the Soviet Union would still be fulfilled. Merekalov admitted that the material involved was not particularly important, but stressed that this was a test case, which would show just how serious Germany was about increasing trade with the Soviet Union. From this, he moved on to talk about the current political situation, and the real reason he was there – German–Soviet relations. Finally, he steered the conversation towards the message he had to give. It bore a close resemblance to what Astakhov had said to Kleist: ideological differences need not come between their two countries; as far as the Soviet Union was concerned there was no reason why she should not live with Germany on a normal footing, and 'from normal, relations could get better and better'.

Hitler's response to this latest indication of Stalin's willingness to come to terms was another deafening silence: he could not yet bring himself to grasp the Soviet leader's outstretched hand. For the moment, the only sign of softening in his attitude came some ten days later, when he authorised the Foreign Ministry to help obtain the release of seven Soviet seamen who had been held prisoner in Spain since 1936, and to organise their return to the Soviet Union in exchange for Italians held prisoner there.

There was silence, too, from London and Paris on the Soviet reply to the British proposals of 14 April for the Soviet Union to make a sweeping, and entirely unilateral, declaration that she would come to the help of any neighbouring state that was attacked. Not surprisingly, such a single-handed guarantee did not appeal to Stalin, and on 17 April he made his own proposals for a three-power pact. After stating that this would be for the protection of countries menaced by fascist aggression the official Soviet account says: 'The Soviet government added that the agreement which it proposed could be embodied in three acts: in the first place an agreement between the three powers for mutual assistance; in the second place the conclusion between them of a military convention which would give real strength to the mutual assistance pact, and finally a guarantee by the three powers to all states between the Baltic and the Black Sea.' In other words, Stalin was now proposing a full-scale military and political alliance covering the whole of northern and eastern Europe.

Such a positive move went far beyond what Chamberlain was prepared to accept, in spite of vehement and growing pressure from public, press and Parliament for just such an alliance. The Foreign Office had its own view, summed up by Permanent Under-Secretary Cadogan in a memorandum on 19 April: 'This Russian proposal is extremely inconvenient. We have to balance the advantage of a paper commitment by Russia to join in a war on one side, against the disadvantage of associating ourselves openly with Russia.' Chamberlain still thought the Soviets were of little use except as the only possible supplier of *matériel* to Poland. He dismissed Stalin's proposal in those terms: 'It cannot be pretended,' he told the Foreign Policy Committee, 'that such an alliance is necessary in order that the smaller countries of Eastern Europe should be furnished with munitions.'

For three weeks, the British government stalled, using its disagreements with the French and the Poles as an excuse. The French government, while agreeing that Stalin's proposal went too far, wanted a three-power mutual assistance pact, under which all partners would be obliged to go to the assistance of any other which was at war as a result of fulfilling its obligations to Eastern European countries. This, however, could still involve the Soviet Union coming to the aid of Poland, and the Poles continued to reject such a possibility out of hand.

The anti-appeasement lobby in Parliament, led by Winston Churchill, pressed the government to accept the Soviet offer. Churchill, who believed both at the time and in retrospect that a grand alliance would have halted Hitler and probably averted war, commented: 'Above all, time must not be lost. Ten or twelve days have already passed since the Russian offer was made. The British people ... have a right, in conjunction with the French Republic, to call upon Poland not to place obstacles in the way of a common cause. Not only must the full co-operation of Russia be accepted, but the three Baltic states, Lithuania, Latvia and Estonia, must also be brought into the association ... There is no means of maintaining an eastern front against Nazi aggression without the active aid of Russia. Russian interests are deeply concerned in preventing Herr Hitler's designs on Eastern Europe.'

The government was unmoved by such urgings. Halifax thought: 'A tripartite pact on the lines proposed would make war inevitable.' Another voice in the Cabinet, that of Malcolm MacDonald, said, in stark contrast to Churchill's insistence that time must not be lost: 'We do not wish to give offence to Russia – it would be a serious matter if Russia were neutral and supplying Germany with food and raw materials. Would it not be possible to keep negotiations continuing for some further period, in the hope of finding a compromise?'

By the time this discussion took place, however, the situation had moved on. On 27 April, Chamberlain had reluctantly agreed to introduce conscription in Britain, for the first time ever during peace. Hitler's reaction had been swift: the following day, in what was to be his last major speech in peacetime, he addressed the Reichstag in the ornate Kroll Opera House which it had used since its own building had been burned down in 1933, and denounced first the Anglo-German Naval Treaty and then the German–Polish non-aggression pact. He charged Britain with a 'policy of encirclement' against Germany, and Poland with violating the pact by the recent agreement with Britain which 'under certain circumstances would compel Poland to take military action against Germany'.

The speech lasted two hours, and was one of the longest ever made by Hitler in public. He devoted much of that time to ridiculing Roosevelt in a bitingly sarcastic reply to a long message from the US President sent on 15 April, asking for an assurance that he would not attack or invade a list of thirty-one countries ranging from Finland and the Baltic states in the north to Palestine, Egypt and Iran in the south. But in all the two hours of speaking, Hitler did not direct one word of criticism or abuse against the Soviet Union. Since such attacks had been a feature of almost every major speech of his career, it was a significant omission, and one that was noted in Moscow.

Maxim Litvinov was never a member of the Politburo, the inner Cabinet which governed party and state under Stalin, in spite of his high office. However, at the annual May Day parade in Moscow's Red Square he always had a place on the rostrum on top of Lenin's tomb with the leading members of the communist hierarchy. May Day, 1939, was no exception – but this time one thing was different from other years: whenever he caught Stalin's eye as the massive parades churned past, the party secretary pointedly looked the other way. For a man with so much experience of reading the signs in politicians' behaviour, it was not difficult for Litvinov to divine that something was wrong.

Ivy Litvinov, his English-born wife, later told friends in London that as they made their way home afterwards he told her he had a bad feeling. 'And I have heard rumours from the wives,' she replied.

'They are changing their policy,' he said. 'I knew it would happen.'

Ivy had no doubts where to lay the blame for a Soviet move from the uphill path towards collective security which her husband had trodden for so long: 'Damn that fool Chamberlain!' she spat.

Two days later, Litvinov's fears proved correct. After another fruitless meeting with Sir William Seeds in the morning, he kept an appointment with Stalin in the late afternoon. Stalin told him, quite gently, that he was being replaced as Foreign Commissar by Vyacheslav Molotov, the Chairman of the Council of People's Commissars – in other words the Prime Minister – of the USSR.

'It's all over,' Litvinov recorded in his diary that night. 'I have been fired like a maid caught stealing . . . without so much as a day's notice.'

In fact, Litvinov was let down remarkably gently. Stalin and Molotov told him the Politburo was not blaming him for anything, but felt it was time for a change. He would be found a new job worthy of his talents and experience – as indeed he was, being retained as an adviser to the Foreign Commissariat, where he also helped train a new generation of diplomats before being sent to Washington, as ambassador to the USA, in 1941. Some time earlier, Stalin had told him, 'Whatever may happen, Papasha, I will not let you down.' For once, Stalin was as good as his word.

The removal of Litvinov, a Jew and the arch-advocate of an alliance with the Western Powers, was the strongest signal Stalin could possibly give to Hitler that he was open to offers, short of a direct proposal – which he would not make, for fear of receiving a humiliating rebuff. In any case, he was not yet sure enough of the Nazi dictator to risk losing his western option by frightening off the British and French, as he would surely do if he were seen to be making definite overtures to Germany. That way, he could end up losing both options, finding himself totally isolated once more.

The opportunity of making sure Hitler had got the message came only one day after the news was made public, when Schnurre asked Astakhov to call on him for the answer on the Skoda arms contract. In Schnurre's pleasant, sunny room in the Foreign Ministry building, tastefully furnished with beautiful furniture from the time of Bismarck, the two men greeted each other warmly. Schnurre opened by saying his government had agreed to fulfil the contract, and had already given instructions to Skoda to deliver the arms to the Soviets. Astakhov was delighted: it was not the material side of the question that counted, he stressed, but the principle, the sign of German goodwill. Now, he wanted to know, did the Germans intend to restart the economic negotiations which had broken down in February, after Schnurre's aborted trip to Moscow? Schnurre could not answer this – there were too many problems still to be resolved, he told the Soviet diplomat.

With the ground cleared, Astakhov broached the big subject: would the dismissal of Litvinov lead to a change in Germany's attitude to the Soviet Union? Molotov, he pointed out, might not be a specialist in foreign affairs, but because of his position at the very top of the Soviet tree – only Stalin was above him – he would have tremendous importance in future foreign policy.

Astakhov made sure there could be no doubts in German minds that the replacement of Litvinov was a deliberate move in their direction. He need not have worried: Hitler had read Stalin's signal correctly. 'It struck me like a cannonball,' he later told his generals. 'Litvinov's dismissal was decisive.' He had already ordered Schulenburg and his military attaché in Moscow, Lieutenant-General Ernst Köstring, to come to Germany immediately to discuss the significance of the change and to talk about a possible deal with Stalin. He had also ordered Propaganda Minister Joseph Goebbels to instruct German newspaper editors to stop all attacks on the Soviet Union, until further notice.

As it happened, Schulenberg was then in Teheran, representing Germany at the wedding of the Iranian Crown Prince, and Köstring was travelling somewhere in the Amur region of eastern Siberia, so neither of them was able to answer Hitler's call. In their place, the embassy's commercial counsellor, Gustav Hilger, hurried back home.

Hilger was a fairly tall, thin man in his mid-forties, with pale skin, prominent cheekbones and dark, sunken eyes behind thick glasses. He and his wife were both completely bilingual, having been born in Russia – indeed, he even spoke German with a slight Russian accent. He had been in business in Moscow before the first world war, had joined the embassy immediately Germany recognised the USSR, and had stayed there ever since. He was therefore extremely experienced in all matters Soviet, and could think and act like a Russian – Karl Schnurre recalls that watching Hilger and Andrei Vyshinsky, then a rising young official, in discussion was like seeing a fireworks display, so energetic were their gestures.

Hilger had never met either Hitler or Ribbentrop before, and was not very impressed by either of them. Ribbentrop, he wroter later, struck him immediately as: 'A man who occupied a responsible position for which he had neither talent, knowledge nor experience, and he himself knew or sensed this very well . . . At the same time he sought to hide his feelings of inferiority by an arrogance that often seemed unbearable.'

As for Hitler, Hilger recalled that when he arrived at the Berghof with Ribbentrop, after a hair-raising drive round the mountain roads from Salzburg, the Führer 'approached us slowly, gazing at us with strangely shifty, cunning eyes. Neither then nor during later meetings with Hitler did I feel anything of the hypnotising effect that has been attributed to him. At the sight of his small stature, the funny forelock that hung in his face, and that ridiculous small moustache, I felt only indifference, which in the following hours changed into physical revulsion produced by the fact that he was constantly chewing his fingernails.'

Hilger's reference to fingernails is a revealing sign of Hitler's condition at that time. In fact, he was never known to bite his nails – a habit that was considered particularly odious in Germany. What Hilger actually witnessed was the compulsive nibbling or gnawing at the tips of the fingers themselves which doctors recognise as a classic symptom of amphetamine abuse. In Hitler this was the result of Dr Morell's wonder injections: he was giving the Führer daily shots, backed up by so-called 'multi-vitamin' tablets, or methamphetamine – the same drugs which had revived the ailing Czech President Hacha after he had collapsed on 15 March. The fact that Hitler was more or less constantly high on amphetamines, coupled with his growing intoxication with his own success, must have had a significant effect on his behaviour during those critical months of mid-1939.

It was some time after the appointed time of 1 pm – for Ribbentrop had slept late in his castle at Fuschl – when he and Hilger sat down with Hitler at the round table before the famous picture window in the Berghof's grand salon. With them were General Keitel and Karl Schnurre, who had been summoned from Berlin, and Walther Hewel, Ribbentrop's liaison man in Hitler's personal circle, a friend of the Führer who had been with him in Landsberg Prison after Hitler's failed attempt at a putsch in Munich in 1923. Hewel was an intelligent, good-looking bachelor of thirty-five, a pleasant and approachable young man. The night before, he had chatted to Hilger about the forthcoming meeting, reassuring him that he had nothing to be nervous about. 'Don't worry about it at all,' he had said. 'I bet he won't let you get a word in edgewise. Instead, he'll do all the talking himself, and then he'll end the session before you've had a chance to make any comments.'

For once, Hewel was wrong. For the most part Hitler was content to ask questions, and then to listen carefully while Hilger answered at length. The first question was what reasons Stalin might have had for dismissing Litvinov. Hilger told him he believed it was because Litvinov had pressed for an understanding with Britain and France, while Stalin thought the Western Powers simply wanted to have the Soviet Union pull the chestnuts out of the fire for them. Hitler said nothing, but glanced at Ribbentrop with a look that showed this made sense to him.

The next question was the big one: did Hilger believe that Stalin might, under certain circumstances, be ready for an understanding with Germany? Hilger says he was tempted to give Hitler a résumé of German–Soviet relations since 1933, reminding him of the number of times Stalin and his government had, in the early years of the Nazi regime, expressed a wish to maintain the old, friendly relationship. But he restrained himself, and merely reminded him of the speech of 10 March. Both Hitler and Ribbentrop purported not to remember what Stalin had said, and made Hilger repeat the relevant passage about there being no visible grounds for conflict between the two countries.

For the rest of the meeting, Hitler made Hilger tell him 'how things looked in Russia', leaning forward and listening with eager attention, while he spoke of Stalin's efforts to build up his country, of the growing success of Soviet industrialisation and the strengthening of national consciousness. When Hilger had finished, he expected the Führer to say something about his own views on German–Soviet relations. But instead, he was dismissed 'with a few formal words of thanks'.

When Hilger had gone, Hitler turned to Ribbentrop, thoughtfully. He had not been pleased by what he had heard in the last part of the meeting. 'That Hilger is a bit of a Russian himself, now, of course,' he said, and then went on: 'One possibility is that he has fallen victim to Soviet propaganda. In that case, his description of conditions in the Soviet Union is worthless. But if he is right, then we have no time to lose in taking measures to prevent any further consolidation of Soviet power.'

For the next week, he did nothing about it, however. On 17 May, Astakhov called on Schnurre again in Berlin, ostensibly to talk about the position of the Soviet Trade Commission in Prague. But he quickly moved on to talk about the real issue, commenting that he had been very pleased to note the change that had taken place in the attitude of the German press to the Soviet Union – the reporting had suddenly become fair and objective, and he had even seen pictures in a Rhineland newspaper of Soviet industrial installations. He hoped this was permanent. Once again, Schnurre recorded, he reiterated that there 'were no conflicts in foreign policy between Germany and the Soviet

Union and that therefore there was no reason for any enmity between the two countries'. Certainly, he went on, there was a distinct feeling in the Soviet Union of being menaced by Germany – but this could easily be put right, and Moscow's mistrust wiped out. When Schnurre asked about the Anglo-Soviet negotiations, Astakhov dismissed them scornfully. The way things stood at the moment, he said, 'the result desired by Britain would hardly materialise.'

Schnurre wasted no time in reporting this latest advance. Schulenburg, who had arrived in Munich direct from his stay in Iran for talks about the new situation, was given instructions by Ribbentrop to reopen the economic talks. He flew back to Moscow immediately, and on 20 May went to see Molotov for the first time in his role as Foreign Commissar.

7

'HIS SMILE OF SIBERIAN WINTER'

Vyacheslav Mikhailovich Molotov was Stalin's man in every sense of the word. He had been his deputy, his henchman and often his mouthpiece since 1922, when he had been replaced by Stalin himself as executive secretary of the party's Central Committee, a position which the Georgian quickly converted into his power base as General Secretary. The two had first met before the Revolution, when Molotov was secretary to the editorial board of *Pravda*, the party newspaper which he had helped to establish; since then, he had given Stalin unwavering support for over twenty years as he intrigued, manoeuvred and murdered his way to dictatorship. Through all those years, Molotov was content to follow Stalin's lead: he was never a man of action but always an administrator, never seemed to have any ideas of his own, and never took a decision without consulting his master first.

Molotov was born on 9 March 1890, to well-to-do bourgeois parents. His real name was Scriabin – he was the nephew of the famous composer Alexander Scriabin, and briefly studied music himself before his immersion in politics – but took the pseudonym 'Molotov', meaning 'The Hammer', in 1912, at about the same time that Josef Djugashvili started calling himself 'Stalin', which means 'Man of Steel'. He had joined the Bolsheviks in 1906, had been arrested and sent into a two-year exile in 1909 before going to St Petersburg to enrol at the Polytechnic, where he became the organiser of a group of Bolshevik students.

At the beginning of 1912, he became a journalist, joining the staff of *Zvezda* (*The Star*), which led to his playing a leading part in setting up the new party organ, *Pravda* (*Truth*). In 1916, after escaping from the last of several further periods of imprisonment and exile, he became a member of the newly formed Central Committee in St Petersburg. From then on, he was always at or near the heart of party affairs, and in 1930, because of his unswerving loyalty to Stalin, was made Chairman of the Council of People's Commissars – the official head of the Soviet government.

A man of average height and nondescript colouring, always soberly dressed in a neat grey suit and stiff white collar, rimless pince-nez glasses on his stubby nose, short arms held stiffly at his sides, Molotov looked the epitome of the faceless bureaucrat. Of all the many descriptions of him, none can ever surpass that given by Churchill, who met him many times during and after the war: 'Vyacheslav Molotov was a man of outstanding ability and cold-blooded ruthlessness . . . His cannon-ball head, black moustache, and comprehending eyes, his slab face, his verbal adroitness and imperturbable demeanour, were appropriate manifestations of his qualities and skill . . . I have never seen a human being who more perfectly represented the modern conception of a robot . . . His smile of Siberian winter, his carefully measured and often wise words, his affable demeanour, combined to make him the perfect agent of Soviet policy in a deadly world.'

Apart from the message to Hitler embodied in the dismissal of Litvinov – it was carefully concealed from the German leader, both by his own diplomats and by the Soviets, that the new Foreign Commissar had a Jewish wife – the appointment of Molotov signified to the world at large that at this critical time the Soviet Union was determined to place the conduct of foreign affairs in the hands of one of the inner circle. Since Molotov was Stalin's creature, it meant in fact that Stalin himself was taking direct personal charge of the execution as well as the formulation of policy. But for the diplomats who had to deal with the Kremlin, the change did nothing to ease their task, as Sir William Seeds discovered on 9 May, when he finally delivered the British reply to the Soviet proposals of 17 April.

After much huffing and puffing, and a great deal of toing and froing between London and Paris, to say nothing of Warsaw, Chamberlain had rejected the Soviet call for a triple alliance. In its place, he again suggested a declaration. The new proposal was only a slight modification of the original British idea. Now they were asking the Soviets to give an undertaking that if Britain and France found themselves at war as a result of the guarantees they had given to Poland and Romania, the Soviet Union would come to the rescue, when asked, in a manner and on terms which might then be agreed. Not surprisingly, Stalin and Molotov found this vague, one-sided but open-ended proposition completely unsatisfactory.

On 15 May, Molotov called Seeds to the Foreign Commissariat. It was the first time the ambassador had dealt with the Soviet Premier directly, and he found the contrast with his predecessor striking. Litvinov knew and understood the Western mind and the Western world, and although, as William Strang put it, 'he could be both sharp and stubborn', he was always willing to argue. Seeds later said that if a difficult point arose when dealing with Litvinov, he could 'by an expressive cocking of his eye sometimes bring an answering grin to Litvinov's face and a common, if tacit, understanding'. Such finessing was impossible with Molotov: 'One had to say exactly what one meant, neither more nor less, and to say it over and over again in the same words.'

Seeds found it impossible to convince Molotov that the latest British proposal was not really one-sided, and in any case would involve the Soviet Union only when Britain and France were already at war with Germany. For Molotov this was simply not good enough, and he proceeded to reiterate the Soviet proposals for a military and political alliance which would guarantee the Soviet Union herself, as well as all the countries between her and Germany 'from the Baltic to the Black Sea'. What was more, he insisted that all the ways in which the three states would provide military help should be spelled out and agreed in every detail.

Dissatisfaction with the British and French attitude must certainly have been an important factor in persuading Stalin to send Astakhov to see Schnurre in Berlin on 17 May. Another factor was that on 13 May German agitators had started attacking Polish property and harassing Polish citizens in Danzig, and an orchestrated campaign had begun for the reunification of the city with the Reich. Coupled with the appearance of stories in the German press of supposed atrocities being committed against Germans in Poland itself, this looked very much like Hitler's propaganda build-up before the inevitable attack on Poland.

Clearly, time was running short for Stalin to achieve a protective alliance. The urgency for this was fuelled still further by events some 4,000 miles away from the European trouble spots. For while Hitler was still only posing a potential threat to the Soviet Union's western frontiers, her Far-Eastern border was already under attack by Germany's Anti-Comintern partner Japan. Fierce fighting broke out on the frontiers with Manchuria and Mongolia on 15 May, the latest clash in a conflict that had been dragging on for years but which now promised to explode into something more serious.

With no way of knowing how this undeclared war with the Japanese would develop, Stalin was faced with the nightmare of having to fight on two fronts, dividing his ill-prepared forces between the two extremes of his huge empire. Already, he had been forced to commit at least twenty-four divisions of his best troops to the Far East, with 1,900 tanks, 2,000 aircraft and between 350,000 and 450,000 men. In the Kwantung Army, as the Japanese forces in Manchuria were known, they had as an opponent one of the world's most feared fighting machines, case-hardened in the furnace of many years of war. The Soviet newspaper

Red Fleet estimated its numbers at 250,000, with 600 tanks, 1,000 guns and 450 planes, plus a further 80,000 men in the puppet Manchukuo (Manchurian) army, officered by 10,000 Japanese 'instructors'.

Contention between Japan and Russia had been acute since the turn of the century. At its root was a curious echo of the issue which caused the threat from Hitler's Germany: Japan was over-populated and under-nourished. Every square metre of arable land, much of it of poor quality, was already under cultivation. More than two thirds of all farms were smaller than two and a quarter acres, and even with all the traditional ingenuity of the Japanese peasant farmer, food production was of necessity limited. The situation was further complicated by the fact that Japan lacked both raw materials to supply her industries and – at that time, at least – overseas markets to absorb her manufactured goods.

For a solution to their country's problems, many Japanese looked to the mainland of Asia, and in particular to Manchuria, in much the same way that Hitler and many of his countrymen looked to the Ukraine. They saw in the expanses of Manchuria both a larder and a *Lebensraum* for their excess population. Manchurian mineral wealth would fuel Japanese industry, while the native population, enlarged by the influx of Japanese settlers, would provide an ever-growing market for her cotton and rayon fabrics and other manufactured goods. Without Manchuria, they believed, Japanese expansion was doomed.

The northernmost province of China, Manchuria covered an area of some 380,000 square miles, roughly the size of France and Germany combined. It was the most industrialised and also the richest in terms of natural resources, with large reserves of coal, iron, gold, magnesium and oil shale. It shared frontiers with Korea, Mongolia – and Russia. And it was in Manchuria that the long-running conflict between Russia and Japan started.

Manchuria's potential had been first developed by the Russians, between 1895 and 1905. They persuaded the Chinese administration to allow them to build a railway line, which they called the Chinese Eastern Railway, through Manchuria via the city of Harbin. This gave them a shorter, more direct route between Vladivostok and the Lake Baikal region of Siberia. Later, they leased from the Chinese the tip of the Liaotung peninsula, known as the Kwantung promontory, and built a further rail link from Harbin to Port Arthur and Dairen, both situated on the promontory, which thus became Russia's only warm-water ports in the Far East, Vladivostok being ice-bound in winter. But all this was swept away between 1904 and 1905.

On the night of 8–9 February 1904, Japanese destroyers and torpedo boats, with lights blacked out, slid into Port Arthur harbour, where the Imperial Russian Navy's Far-Eastern Fleet rode peacefully at anchor. They attacked with torpedoes, hitting two battleships and a cruiser. The

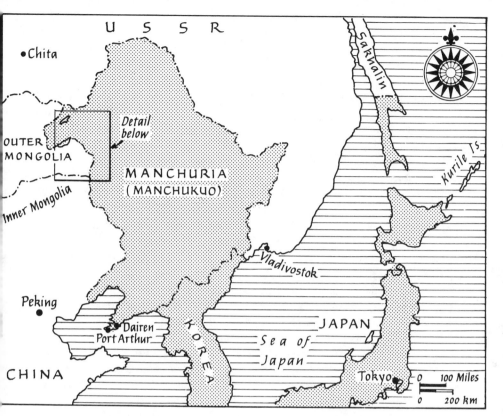

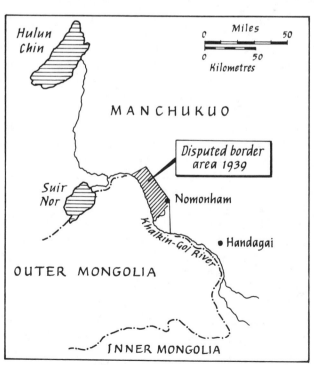

destruction would have been greater, but many of the torpedoes either missed their targets, or failed to explode – not surprisingly, perhaps, since this was the first time the weapon had been used in naval warfare. Having crippled the Russian fleet, Japan declared war the following day.

International reaction had been surprising. *The Times* of London even described the Japanese attack as 'an act of daring . . . destined to take a place of honour in naval annals'. It was a reaction which Stalin did not forget when assessing Western attitudes thirty-five years later.

The Russo-Japanese War had been a disaster for Russia, and she had been forced to sue for peace in 1905. President Theodore Roosevelt was invited to act as mediator, and under his auspices the Treaty of Portsmouth was concluded in the autumn of that year. The terms were humiliating for Russia. She had to agree to the division of Manchuria into two areas of interest, the northern where she would still be paramount, the southern where Japan would hold sway. Port Arthur and the Liaotung peninsula, and the Chinese Eastern Railway as far as Changchun, were taken over by the Japanese. Russia was also forced to surrender the southern part of Sakhalin Island, thus considerably extending Japanese fishing and mineral rights.

From that point on, the relationship with Japan in the Far East was a constant aggravation, a grumbling appendix always threatening to erupt into something more serious than a niggling pain. In 1918, with Russia wasted by war and ravaged by revolution, Japan readily accepted an American invitation to send about 7,000 troops into Siberia as her contribution to the combined Allied Intervention Forces against the Reds. However, the Japanese were suspicious of US territorial ambitions in south Manchuria and in eastern Siberia, where they had ambitions of their own. Instead of a mere 7,000 men, they sent nearly ten times that number, and also proceeded to conclude a series of agreements with China to co-ordinate military and political action for joint operations against Siberia.

As the Allied Intervention faltered and faded, the British, French and US governments withdrew their forces from Russia with varying degrees of relief. The American forces were all gone by early 1920. But the Japanese stayed on. They continued to occupy part of eastern Siberia until as late as 25 October 1922, when they finally pulled out of Vladivostok, and they did not give up their occupation of the northern half of Sakhalin Island until three years after that – by which time they were back in northern Manchuria. One reason why Lenin's armies had been unable to eject the Japanese in 1920 must have sounded an ominous note for Stalin in 1939: it was because they were at war in the west, with Poland.

In 1923, the Japanese formulated a new imperial defence policy, which identified Russia as the most likely future enemy – the USA was named as the next potential foe after Russia – and Manchuria as the most likely battlefield.

In spite of this, Stalin had persisted during the remainder of the decade in seeking an understanding with Japan. The two nations signed a treaty in January 1925 which ostensibly 'normalised' relations in the Far East, and at the Fourteenth Party Congress at the end of that year, Stalin declared: 'We have no interests that lead to our relations with Japan becoming strained. Our interests lie in the direction of *rapprochement* between our country and Japan.'

The Japanese, however, refused to comply with Stalin's hopeful thesis. They opposed the Soviet Union at every turn, particularly in China, where Stalin unexpectedly chose to give Soviet support to Chiang Kai-shek in the monumental upheavals which were rending that ancient empire. Stalin's daughter, Svetlana, has described her father as 'an oriental'. Undoubtedly, his attitude of Soviet aspirations and obligations in the east followed the 'Asiatic view', which implied pursuing the aim of Soviet primacy on the mainland of Asia. However softly he may have spoken to the Japanese, he could never persuade them to ignore this challenge to their own interest and ambitions.

By the beginning of the thirties, the friction between the two powers had begun to escalate, with the formation of a Soviet Special Far Eastern Army, while the Japanese worked out a detailed war plan which stressed the sudden surprise blow as a vital element in Japan's strategy. The first step towards this strategy was to secure Manchuria as a base for operations against the Soviets.

In September 1931, the Kwantung Army, acting independently and in spite of ineffectual protests from its own government in Tokyo, overthrew Chinese rule in Manchuria. The following year, they established a puppet state, which they renamed Manchukuo ('Manchuland'), installing the last Manchu emperor, Hsuan T'ung, as putative head of the Manchukuo government. Their aim was ultimately to set him on the Dragon Throne in Peking, with the whole of northern China as a Japanese dependency.

The Japanese army's tendency to act independently of its own government added considerably to Stalin's dilemma in dealing with the Far-Eastern problem. There was no guarantee that the Kwantung Army would abide by any decision reached by the politicians in Tokyo – indeed, the reverse was often more likely. What would have been regarded as rank insubordination in any other society was accepted in Japan as '*gekokoju*', a peculiarly Japanese concept meaning 'rule of the higher by the lower'. The expression was originally employed in medieval times to describe the disobedience of provincial lords who defied the authority of the *shogun*, or generalissimo; over the centuries, it came to be regarded as almost legitimate conduct on the part of juniors, as long as it was obviously committed for the greater glory of the nation.

There were two rebellious factions active in the Japanese army in the 1930s. Both were ultra-nationalistic and both regarded Western capitalism and Soviet communism with equal abhorrence, believing the Orient must be saved from all such pernicious Western influences, from whatever source. One faction wanted to set up a military dictatorship, and believed war with the Soviet Union was necessary and inevitable. Occupation of Manchuria was the first step in their strategy. The other advocated a form of National Socialism along Nazi German lines, and wished to maintain friendly relations with the Soviets – for the time being. For them, China and South-East Asia were to be the prime areas for Japanese expansion, once Manchuria had been secured. For both factions, however, the acquisition of Manchuria and the establishment of its borders was the first priority.

Acquisition, however, proved to be much easier than demarcation of Manchuria's frontiers. In many places, the border was not clearly defined; frontier markers had disappeared, or had simply never existed. Some of the treaties defining the border dated from as far back as the eighteenth century and were drafted in several different languages, frequently with serious divergencies between the various texts. There was no problem with Korea, or with China. But Manchuria's other frontiers were with the Soviet Union and with the former Outer Mongolia, which was now the Mongolian People's Republic, the Soviet Union's only satellite and only ally – in fact, the only other communist state in the world at that time. Any encroachment on Mongolia would be regarded by Stalin as an attack on the Soviet Union itself.

The situation was like an open powder barrel at a fireworks party. Mutual paranoia between Japan and the Soviets made any frontier incident seem more sinister than it really was: the burning-off of grassland by one side or the other to clear the ground for observation posts, the emergence of a fresh sandbank in the middle of a river, an error in map-reading by a military patrol – all could lead to an exchange of fire. In consequence, both sides began to reinforce their frontier units.

From 1932 onwards, both the Soviets and the Japanese were reporting between eighty and a hundred border infringements each year. These were not confined to any one area, but were widely dispersed along the entire frontier, and with more and more troops ready to retalitate on either side, each incident became magnified. In 1935, in Mongolia, tanks and aircraft were used for the first time. In 1936, after another series of minor clashes, the Soviets sent motorised units to the Mongolian border and, fearing Japanese pressure on the Trans-Siberian Railway where it ran through 'the throat of Far Eastern Russia' along the corridor between the sea and the Manchurian border to Vladivostok, they also began to reinforce their troops in the Maritime Provinces. On 12 March 1936, Stalin regularised his troops' position in

Mongolia, and sounded a warning to the Japanese, with a protocol on mutual assistance between Mongolia and the USSR. The build-up of forces, however, continued on both sides, as arguments over remote and barren areas of territory flared into bloody, full-scale battles, in 1937 on the Amur river and in the summer of 1938 near Lake Khasan.

By the spring of 1939, although there had been no more major clashes, the tension had increased to breaking point. During the first week of May, a troop of Mongolian cavalry on patrol in a disputed area on the Khalkin-Gol river, some twenty miles from the Manchurian village of Nomonhan, was attacked by units of the Japanese 23rd Division. This minor skirmish escalated rapidly over the next few days, with Soviet troops being drawn in to support their Mongolian friends, and the Japanese pressing forward strongly in an effort to test the Soviet will, taking advantage of Stalin's preoccupation with European affairs.

By the end of the month, after a great deal of savage fighting, the Japanese had been forced to withdraw, and seemed content for the moment to let the matter rest. Stalin, however, could no longer afford such luxury, for the Japanese could choose to strike again at any time. If the situation were allowed to get out of hand, it would seriously weaken the Soviet ability to resist any attack by Hitler in the west. Even the threat of a major conflict in the Far East would affect his negotiating position both with Hitler and with Britain and France. Conversely, as long as he had no protective agreements in the west, Stalin would be unable to commit all his strength to fighting a full-scale war with the Japanese – a fact which would surely not have escaped the attention of the Japanese themselves. His first priority in the east, therefore, was to settle matters as quickly as possible by wiping out the Japanese threat once and for all. While dealing with this, he could be vulnerable to attack from the west, and therefore either an early accommodation with Hitler or a military alliance with the democracies would be a great relief.

Despite the pressure on him to reach a quick agreement, Stalin was still deeply suspicious of both sets of potential allies, and continued to do his best to play them off against each other. When Schulenburg called on Molotov at the Foreign Commissariat on 20 May, he found the new Commissar infuriatingly cautious. The meeting was conducted in French, the language of diplomacy, since Molotov had told the German ambassador not to bring an interpreter as he would be providing one. Molotov himself spoke no foreign languages. The young man concerned, Schulenburg reported afterwards, translated from French into Russian very correctly but very slowly, so that the conversation dragged on for over an hour though little was actually said and even less accomplished. At the end, Schulenburg was still not clear what Molotov actually wanted, and on his way out of the building called on Vladimir Potemkin, the skilled professional who had stayed on as Vice-Commissar, to ask if he could either enlighten him or find out for him.

What did emerge from Molotov was that he and Stalin were still upset over the cancellation of Schnurre's visit at the end of January, and the subsequent failure of the talks. They suspected that Hitler did not seriously want to reopen trade negotiations but was playing some sort of game – perhaps trying to upset the talks with the Western Powers. Molotov insisted that he was interested only in restarting economic negotiations if the necessary 'political basis' had been established first. This appeared to be a clear signal inviting the Germans to enter into a political alliance – or at least to enter the race for one against Britain and France. But when Schulenburg tried to pin Molotov down on what sort of political agreement he was looking for, the Soviet Premier refused to be drawn. The nature of the 'political basis', he said, 'was something both governments would have to think about'.

Although, as Stalin well knew, Germany badly needed Soviet raw materials, Hitler was still not prepared to make a first move towards a full-scale pact. It was not yet urgent for him: he did not intend making his move against Poland for at least another three months, and in that time it was possible there might be developments which would make such a distasteful deal with the devil unnecessary. Ribbentrop, for his part, was hoping to draw the Japanese into the full military alliance which he was then concluding with Italy – the 'Pact of Steel' as they called it was signed on 22 May – and he was naturally afraid they would be offended and perhaps frightened away by a German understanding with the Soviets. Both Schulenburg and Weizsäcker feared they were simply being used by Stalin to put pressure on the British and French to come to terms – though in fact this was something both men would welcome as a curb on Hitler's military ambitions. The response from Berlin was therefore an instruction for Schulenburg to 'sit tight and wait and see if the Soviet Russians will speak more openly.'

It is ironic that the two officials primarily responsible for carrying out the policies laid down by Hitler and Ribbentrop for dealing with Stalin were both staunch anti-Nazis. Both Weizsäcker and Schulenburg did their best to encourage the West to come to an understanding with the Soviet Union before Hitler did, since they both knew this was probably the only way he might be dissuaded from starting a war. But since both were loyal German patriots and also men of the old school whose code of honour made it impossible for them not to carry out their duties to the best of their abilities, they found themselves unwilling but efficient tools of the dictator they hated.

Baron Ernst von Weizsäcker was a short, rather square man, fifty-seven years old, with severely cut white hair and erect carriage, a pink complexion and clear blue eyes. He had originally been a career naval officer, but after twenty years' service had transferred to the Foreign Ministry when the Imperial Navy was disbanded after the first world war. He had become State Secretary in 1938 after a period as head of the ministry's political department, having previously served in Switzerland, Denmark and Norway. Like many members of the German resistance at that time, Weizsäcker tried to work from within to thwart Hitler's plans and eventually, he hoped, to help remove him from power. From mid-1938 onwards, he did his best to warn the British and French what was going on, both discreetly through their diplomats in Berlin and also through supporters in the German embassy in London.

Count Friedrich Werner von der Schulenburg, born in 1875 the son of a Prussian officer, also became a member of the anti-Hitler resistance movement, and in fact would be executed in 1944 for his part in the 20 July assassination attempt in that year. Schulenburg was everyone's idea of the perfect, old-world gentleman, both in manners and appearance. He was an attractive, elegant man, tall, with silver hair clipped short around a balding pate, eyes twinkling with good humour, and a luxuriant white moustache. In 1939, he was the doyen of the Diplomatic Corps in Moscow, having served there since 1934, following periods as ambassador in Romania and Iran. He was universally liked, respected and admired, both by his fellow diplomats from all countries, and by the Soviet government, who were delighted to have a true aristocrat serving there. By his own staff, he was worshipped as a wise and warm father figure.

During the early years of his career he had served as a consul in tsarist Russia from 1907 until 1914, and had always remained a firm Russophile, like almost every member of the staff of his embassy. He had long been dedicated to the improvement of relations between the Soviet Union and Germany, and spent a great deal of time and energy trying to convince Hitler that friendship and co-operation with the Soviet Union was his best policy.

Since he believed until it was too late that war between Germany and the Soviet Union could be avoided by the genuine *rapprochement* which he sought to bring about, Schulenburg did not follow the example of his friends in Berlin and London and pass information to the West warning them of the dangers of a Nazi–Soviet pact. However, his personal assistant, a bright young second secretary called Hans von Herwarth, more than made up for this by feeding vital information to his friend in the American embassy, Charles E. 'Chip' Bohlen.

Hans-Heinrich Herwarth von Bittenfeld, to give him his full name, was generally known simply as 'Johnnie', a nickname he had gained in early childhood from an English friend of his grandmother. A slim, pixie-faced young man aged thirty-four, with thick glasses and a mass of dark hair combed straight back, he was one of the most popular members of the Moscow diplomatic community in the thirties. With his vivacious young wife, Elisabeth – known to everyone as 'Pussi' – he was always at the centre of diplomatic social life.

Among the younger set, much of this social life revolved around the country house, or dacha, rented by the Americans some twenty kilometres to the south of Moscow. There they would meet regularly to play tennis, ride out from the dacha's stables, chat, and enjoy the plentiful supplies of food and drink contributed by the different nationalities who made up what they called their 'Mutual Admiration Society' – wines, beer and sausages from the Germans, Scotch whisky from the British, and more wine from the Italians. It was in this relaxed and informal atmosphere that Johnnie Herwarth took Chip Bohlen aside on 16 May 1939 and told him something was afoot. For the moment, he was not sure where it was heading, but all the signs were that there could soon be a marked change in the German approach to the Soviet Union. When Schulenburg returned from Berlin three days later with his oral instructions from Ribbentrop to sound out the Soviets, Herwarth reported everything to Bohlen again, asking him to pass it on to Washington.

Bohlen knew Herwarth to be a convinced anti-Nazi, though naturally he was guarded in what he said publicly. 'He was noted,' Bohlen wrote of him later, 'for the frankness and freedom with which he discussed international problems ... In the Western diplomatic contingent in Moscow, he had a high reputation as an intelligent and forthright man.' But Bohlen at the time could not understand why his friend was giving him, a representative of a country which was unfriendly towards Germany, such sensitive secret information.

In fact, Herwarth was another member of the resistance organisation along with the Kordt brothers, Admiral Canaris, other senior officials and military men. Like them, he was dedicated to bringing about the overthrow of Hitler. Like them, he was determined to do all in his power to thwart the dictator's war plans, and had since before the Munich crisis been passing information to his British, French and Italian friends in the Mutual Admiration Society in the hope of opening the eyes of their leaders back home, and so persuading them to act more resolutely.

The Italian approach, which Herwarth had followed through his friend Guido Relli, proved to be ineffective, as well as dangerous, and so was soon dropped. The British, first through Fitzroy Maclean and then through his successor Armin Dew, and the French through Baron Gontran de Juniac, did not seem to be doing much good, but were valuable as back-up to the efforts of Theo Kordt in London. And when the British and French finally entered into serious negotiations with the Soviets, Herwarth found it impossible to continue feeding them directly and so concentrated all his efforts on Chip Bohlen and the United States, knowing the Western allies would be informed through Washington.

Bohlen faithfully reported everything his friend told him, but this was not passed on to the British and French until later that summer, when it began to look more certain that Hitler and Stalin really could be about to do a deal. In late May, however, such a possibility seemed to be growing more remote – particularly when the British suddenly changed tack.

8

'NITWITS AND
NINCOMPOOPS'

When Halifax returned to London on 23 May, after long, hard talks with
the French in Paris and with Ivan Maisky in Geneva, where the Soviet
ambassador had been chairing the League of Nations Council, he was
persuaded at last that the Allies needed an agreement with the Soviets
before Hitler beat them to it. Maisky had convinced him that Stalin
would not accept any compromise over his demand for a mutual
assistance pact coupled with a detailed military agreement and
guarantees for all the states bordering the Soviet Union. It would have to
be that or nothing.

Halifax brought his new policy to the Cabinet in London next
morning. Chamberlain still had his doubts. 'As my colleagues will be
aware from the attitude which I have hitherto adopted,' he told his
ministers, 'I view anything in the nature of an alliance with Russia with
considerable misgivings, I have some distrust of Russia's reliability and
some doubt of her capacity to help us.' Nevertheless, to everyone's
surprise, he supported Halifax and said he thought Britain should now
go ahead.

Important new instructions were flashed to Seeds in Moscow, telling
him that the government was 'now disposed to agree that effective co-
operation between Soviet, French and British governments against
aggression in Europe might be based on a system of guarantees, in
conformity with the principles of the League of Nations'. That same
afternoon, Chamberlain made a statement in the House of Commons
which at last gave some satisfaction to those members, led as always by
Churchill, Eden and Lloyd George, who in a heated debate five days
earlier had roasted him for failing to make an alliance with the Soviets. 'I
have every reason to hope,' Chamberlain now told the House, 'that as a
result of proposals which His Majesty's government are now in a

position to make on the main questions arising, it will be found possible to reach full agreement at an early date.'

Chamberlain did not tell the House of his personal misgivings, nor that the same Cabinet meeting which had authorised his optimistic public statement had also agreed that he should go on trying to conciliate Hitler – 'the positive side of our policy', as he called it.

Chamberlain's confident announcement was enough to make Hitler draw back from his own approach to Moscow: if the British and French really were on the point of reaching an agreement, then he could only expect a humiliating rebuff. Weizsäcker summed up the situation as seen from Berlin in a letter to Schulenburg. Although there were undoubtedly areas where the Germans could disrupt and slow down the Allied talks, he wrote, it would not be easy to prevent an Anglo-French–Soviet agreement. 'The probability of success was always assessed here as quite limited, so one had to weigh up whether very frank language in Moscow instead of being helpful, might not be rather harmful and perhaps even call forth a peal of Tartar laughter.'

Over the next few days, however, the Tartar laughter seemed to be directed more against the West than against Germany. When Sir William Seeds and his French counterpart, the newly appointed ambassador, Paul-Emile Naggiar, presented the new proposals to Molotov in the form of a draft treaty, they confidently expected him to welcome them with open arms. They believed, as did their governments, that they had fulfilled all the Soviet demands: that the new offer was exactly the pact the Soviets had asked for. They were to be swiftly disillusioned.

Molotov received the two ambassadors not in the Foreign Commissariat but in his office alongside Stalin's in the Kremlin. This was a large, rather gloomy room, with figured walnut panelling to a height of about five feet, and cream-painted walls above that. Molotov sat at a large desk, made from the same walnut as the panelling, in the right-hand corner of the room. Perhaps the most notable thing about the desk was that it stood on a raised dais several inches high, while visitors were relegated to small chairs on the lower level, like suppliants at the feet of the Soviet Prime Minister.

Molotov wasted no time in telling them he did not like the draft treaty – his personal reaction, he said, was negative. He had the impression, he continued, that 'Great Britain and France wanted to continue the conversations ad infinitum, but were not interested in obtaining concrete results'. Seeds was dismayed by this, and asked Molotov to explain. The answer lay in Britain's reference to the League of Nations, which inevitably meant interminable delays, endless fine words and paper resolutions. Seeds was shocked by what he took to be a deliberate misreading of the draft: certainly there was a reference to the League – but only to its spirit and principles. Molotov, however, refused point-blank to accept this, insisting doggedly that the Allies intended following the League's 'procedure'.

Like Schulenburg a week earlier, Seeds was discovering that Molotov's negotiating technique left a great deal to be desired. 'He seemed,' Seeds reported, 'to be either blindly acting on instructions or else capable of misunderstanding.'

Four days later, in his first speech to the Supreme Soviet as Foreign Commissar, Molotov lambasted the Western democracies for their hesitation and accused them of not taking the negotiations seriously. Significantly, he quoted Stalin's famous 'chestnuts' warning from the Eighteenth Congress in March. While he accepted that the latest Anglo-French proposals marked a step forward, he criticised them for the references to the League of Nations, and more strongly, because they did not include specific guarantees to 'three of the Soviet Union's north-western neighbours' (Latvia, Estonia and Finland). He made no mention of the fact that all those neighbours had vehemently rejected any suggestion of outside guarantees and had even gone so far as to state that they would regard any uninvited military assistance as an unfriendly act.

While all this was depressing enough for the democracies, the rest of the speech proved to be even worse. Not only did Molotov pointedly avoid all criticism of Germany, but he also went out of his way to signal that the door was still open to her. He drew attention to the fact that the Anti-Comintern alliance between Italy and Germany had now become, under the Pact of Steel, quite clearly directed against the West and not against the Soviet Union. And he said it was now quite possible that the economic negotiations with Germany could be restarted.

Stalin, however, was still not prepared to let go of the Anglo-French option, and on 2 June Molotov presented the Allied ambassadors with a revised draft treaty. Gone was all reference to the League of Nations; gone was any mention of the need for any of the smaller countries, which were now named as Belgium, Greece, Turkey, Romania, Poland, Latvia, Estonia and Finland, to agree to be helped. One possible concession was the acceptance of the Western proposal that the three powers should help each other if any of them got into war through defending other states. There was to be a military pact to take effect at the same time, and an agreement that none of the three nations would conclude a separate peace in the event of war.

The new proposals raised several fresh problems, which needed to be settled by proper negotiation, and after much heartsearching and discussion the British government decided they must start serious talks. Halifax called Seeds home to be briefed, but unfortunately the ambassador, who was already a sick man suffering from cancer, was taken ill and confined to bed with a high temperature. William Strang, head of the Foreign Office's Central Department, which dealt with

German and Eastern European affairs, was the government's leading expert on the subject; he was on a fact-finding mission in Warsaw at the time, and had already been ordered to fly home immediately. When he arrived, he was told he would be going to Moscow to help Seeds negotiate the treaty.

Strang, a rather dry, bespectacled man, was not in fact sent to conduct the negotiations, but only to assist Seeds. He was an excellent choice for this role, having served for three years, from 1930 to 1933, as counsellor in the Moscow embassy. He also had the dubious distinction of having accompanied Chamberlain to Berchtesgaden, Bad Godesberg and Munich. The Soviets knew him and respected him – but were nevertheless deeply offended by his selection. Chamberlain, after all, had gone to Germany himself, and to send a comparatively minor Foreign Office official, no matter how skilled, to Moscow was taken as a slight. The fact that he was not actually intended to conduct the negotiations was ignored as a matter of mere semantics.

Molotov had instructed Maisky to ask Halifax if he would go himself, in order to complete the negotiations and sign the pact on the spot. But when the ambassador called on him and put the question, Halifax was non-committal and, according to Maisky's account, merely promised to bear the invitation in mind. Halifax, in his report of the conversation, says he told Maisky: 'While nothing, of course, would give me greater pleasure, I do not feel that it is possible for me at present to absent myself from London.' Either way, the opportunity was lost. Anthony Eden, who as a former Foreign Secretary and League of Nations minister had considerable international standing and was well known and liked in Moscow, had offered his services, but Chamberlain refused even to consider sending him. Strang left London on 12 June, accompanied by his assistant, Frank Roberts, a dynamic young man of great personal charm who was to become ambassador in both Moscow and Bonn in the 1960s. Flying via Stockholm, they arrived in Moscow in the early morning of 14 June. The first meeting with Molotov was held next day.

Throughout the first half of June, while the British were steeling themselves to start serious negotiations with the Soviets, the German diplomats watched and waited, still frustrated by Hitler's order to mark time. Hilger and Schulenburg kept in touch, very cautiously and quietly, with Mikoyan and Potemkin respectively, before Schulenburg returned to Berlin for a few days to report on the situation as he saw it. Schnurre champed at the bit, eager to get on with the business of negotiating the trade deals which he was sure he could win. On the international front, Hitler moved to counter the Anglo-French–Soviet talks about guaranteeing the Baltic states by himself signing non-aggression pacts first with Denmark and then, on 7 June, with Estonia and Latvia. But in general, activity between Germany and the Soviet Union was virtually at a standstill.

Hitler, it seemed, was still hoping for some sort of understanding with Britain. From 1 to 5 June, Prince Paul, Regent of Yugoslavia, and his wife, Princess Olga, were his guests in Berlin, and he wasted no opportunity of trying to impress them with his reasonableness. Olga was the sister-in-law of the Duke of Kent, younger brother of King George VI, and thus represented a useful connection with London. The couple were welcomed to Berlin with a great military parade through the heart of the city, and a banquet in the Chancellery, followed by a performance of *Die Meistersinger* in the Prussian State Opera House – during which the princess noted that Hitler listened with his eyes closed, 'as if he were in a trance'. He entertained them alone twice, once to lunch and once to tea, turning on the charm for all he was worth.

Weizsäcker recorded that Hitler, 'who on official occasions was often stiff as a post towards his female guests, overwhelmed the princess with small attentions, showed her the rooms and objets d'art, and when she referred to the fact that it was nearly midnight, and spoke of going, he answered her like a lover: "Happy people have no clocks." ' The princess later told the US minister in Belgrade that when the talk turned to children, tears came to Hitler's eyes, which she described as 'remarkable, clear blue and honest looking'. He told her, she said, that he had a dual personality: his true character was that of an artist and architect, but fate had decreed that he should also be a politician, a military man, and the builder of a new Germany; as a man of simple tastes, he would prefer to live in a small house with no luxury whatsoever, but was forced to live in a large palace surrounded by a certain amount of pomp and ceremony.

But perhaps the most important part of Hitler's conversations with Princess Olga was that in which he told her he could not understand why he was so misunderstood in England, and that he wished relations between Great Britain and Germany might be restored. In this, at least, he was speaking the truth: a little over a week before, at a conference of his military chiefs in his study in the Chancellery on 23 May, he had been at pains to stress that he did not seek war in the West, but was really concerned only with gaining *Lebensraum* in the east, and that, to begin with, Poland must be isolated. General Halder, the army Chief of Staff, recalled later that Hitler had assured his generals that he would keep Britain and France out of Operation White, saying: 'I would have to be a complete idiot to slide into a world war – like those morons of 1914 – over the lousy Polish Corridor.'

The first positive move towards a full German–Soviet pact came from Stalin on 14 June, when Strang had just arrived in Moscow. He made it, however, in a typically indirect and guarded way: Astakhov called on

Parvan Dragonov, the Bulgarian minister in Berlin, for no apparent reason, and proceeded to talk for two hours about German–Soviet relations. It gradually became clear to the bewildered Bulgarian, who hardly knew Astakhov, that the Soviet chargé d'affaires wanted him to pass on what he said to the Wilhelmstrasse. What the message boiled down to was that the Soviets were trying to make up their minds which of three courses to follow: 'The conclusion of the pact with England and France, a further dilatory treatment of the pact negotiations, or a *rapprochement* with Germany.' Of the three possibilities, Astakhov said, the Soviet government preferred the last, which need not involve ideological considerations. 'If Germany would declare that she would not attack the Soviet Union,' he went on, 'or better still that she would conclude a non-aggression pact with her, the Soviet Union would probably refrain from concluding a treaty with England.'

Dragonov hurried to deliver this bombshell next day to the Wilhelmstrasse, where its importance was duly recognised. Ribbentrop was particularly impressed, and the very next day told the Japanese ambassador to Rome, Toshio Shiratori, then in Berlin on a visit, that since Japan had not accepted Germany's invitation to join the Pact of Steel, 'Germany would now conclude a non-aggression pact with Russia.'

Hitler, however, remained unmoved. He did give approval for Schnurre to go to Moscow with full plenipotentiary powers, to reopen the trade talks, but when Hilger suggested this to Soviet Trade Commissar Mikoyan, the Soviet response was guarded, to say the least. Mikoyan made no secret of the fact that he still did not trust the Germans. He was afraid they only wanted to send Schnurre to Moscow in order to make political capital and to disrupt the Anglo-French talks – and that once these had broken down, they would stop their own negotiations, just as they had done in January and February. Stalin was now looking for some larger and more positive gesture from the Germans.

Though both the Western Powers and the Soviets feared he might attack Poland at any moment, Hitler knew he still had two months to play with. On 15 June, while the Bulgarian envoy was deliverying Astakhov's message in Berlin, at the Berghof General Brauchitsch was delivering to Hitler the army's operational plan for the invasion of Poland, which laid down 20 August as the date for the deployment of the Wehrmacht to begin. 'All preparations must be completed by that date,' it stated. On 17 June, Goebbels made a speech in Danzig itself, savagely attacking the Poles, and Nazi activity in the Free City was stepped up, though still under tight control from Berlin. On 22 June, the OKW presented its overall plan for Operation White, and the next day this was discussed by the Reich Defence Council under the direction of Göring. The OKW plan was all-embracing and finely detailed. It called for total military and civil mobilisation, with seven million men drafted into the armed services and concentration camp inmates to be used as forced labour.

On 29 June, Stalin made yet another signal that he was open to offers. One of his closest associates, Andrei Zhdanov, chairman of the Supreme Soviet's Foreign Affairs Committee, published an article in *Pravda* under the headline 'British and French Governments Do Not Want a Treaty on the Basis of Equality for the Soviet Union'. As Schulenburg's deputy Tippelskirch reported, 'The article was undoubtedly written on orders from above,' though Zhdanov claimed that the views expressed were entirely his own – as if such a thing were possible in the Soviet Union at that time.

Zhdanov's article could be read as an invitation to Hitler, or as an effort to put further pressure on the Western democracies. Either way, Hitler had little to lose by holding back. If the Allies did respond positively enough to conclude a pact, he would avoid the humiliation of that 'peal of Tartar laughter'. And if Stalin really did want a deal with Germany instead, keeping him waiting could only improve Hitler's bargaining position, like a prospective customer walking away from a desperate merchant in an eastern bazaar. The same day the article appeared, Hitler ordered a complete stop to all economic as well as political negotiations with the Soviet Union.

There was, in fact, good reason for Zhdanov's article to be pursuing both purposes at the same time, for the Anglo-French talks seemed to have reached stalemate a whole week earlier, after four fairly fruitless meetings. The situation was not helped by the lack of the technical back-up which high-level negotiators normally expect. 'In most other countries,' Strang wrote, 'there would be, side by side with the formal contacts between the heads of delegations, informal discussions between the respective experts by which the way would be cleared for removing misapprehensions or reaching compromises. Such informal contacts are not possible here.'

The meetings were held in Molotov's office, where he sat at his desk on the raised dais while the others sat in a semi-circle below him, Seeds on the left, Strang next to him, then Naggiar, and finally Potemkin, the Vice-Commissar, who acted as interpreter, translating from English and French into Russian, and from Russian into French, as the others spoke in their own languages. Although there was a conference table over on the left of the room, there was never any suggestion that it should be used, so all except Molotov had to balance their papers on their knees and make notes as best they could. Neither Molotov nor Potemkin made any notes, in fact, but Molotov, according to Strang, 'fiddled from time to time with what I took to be a switch under the desk-top at his left hand, and I assumed that this was relaying those parts of our talk which he wished to have taken down for record'.

There was one other significant feature of the discussions in Molotov's room. 'Behind the table on our left front,' Strang noted, 'was an always open door which I found faintly disturbing, as though there was somebody listening.' Strang's feeling was correct, for as Schulenburg was later to discover, the listener was Stalin himself, who made a habit of keeping an ear on his Prime Minister's meetings in this way. Small wonder, then, that Molotov should never step out of line by so much as one word during negotiations.

The first session was entirely taken up by the Allied response to the Soviet draft treaty of 2 June. This was not very promising, for they still did not wish to list the states to be guaranteed, holding that they could not impose this on independent nations who did not want it. Instead, they suggested that this could be taken care of by the three powers agreeing to come to the aid of any one of their number which found itself at war as a result of a guarantee it had given to a smaller state, with that state's consent. There was no need, the Allies contended, actually to name the countries concerned. This arrangement would cover the five nations which the Western Powers had already guaranteed – Belgium, Greece, Turkey, Romania and Poland – but did nothing for the Baltic states and Finland, which the Soviets wanted included in the treaty, or Holland and Switzerland, which the Allies wanted. For these countries, none of which were prepared to accept any guarantee, the Allies proposed a complicated arrangement: the three powers would agree to consult each other if any one of them considered its own security was endangered by a threat to the independence or neutrality of any other European country – again without naming names; if the other two powers agreed that the danger was real, and the first power was involved in a war as a result, then they would provide help.

As far as the other two clauses in the Soviet draft were concerned, the Western reaction was equally negative. They did not want to hold up the signing of the political treaty to coincide with a detailed military agreement, nor to undertake that they would not sign any separate armistice or peace treaty. Molotov, after subjecting Strang to an intense barrage of questions, said he was disappointed, but would reserve comment for the moment and give an answer later.

The next meeting, two days later, was extremly short. When Strang and the ambassadors entered Molotov's office, they found his expression grim, and his words, once they had settled themselves on their low chairs like schoolchildren before a teacher, were as harsh as his face.

'You will remember,' he said, 'that on 2 June the government of the USSR handed to you, as representatives of Great Britain and France, a draft treaty which, it was suggested, should be signed by all three governments. I need not remind you of its details. The special delegate from the British government brought me the reply of your governments, and it was a rejection.'

Strang interrupted. What he had brought, he said, was not a rejection, but suggestions for improving the Soviet draft. However, the British and French could not agree to any treaty that involved interfering in the internal affairs of another state.

'It was a rejection,' Molotov repeated. 'As to the proposals which the British delegate brought with him, I said at the time that they seemed most disappointing to me, but that I would think about them. I have now thought about them. If you think that the Soviet government is likely to accept these proposals, then you must think we are nitwits and nincompoops!'

He paused to allow Potemkin to translate, watching the faces of the three Westerners as he did so. The Vice-Commissar spoke, as usual, in French, until the last three words. These were in English, emphasised to match the vehemence with which the Soviet Premier had uttered the original Russian.

'If His Majesty's government, and the French government treat the Soviet government as nitwits and nincompoops,' Molotov went on, 'then I myself can afford to smile. But I cannot guarantee that everyone will take so calm a view. The guarantees to the Baltic states are indispensable, and your refusal to afford them would place the Soviet government in a humiliating position. Unless, therefore, you can do in respect of Latvia, Estonia and Finland what you are asking the Soviet government to do in respect of your five client states (Belgium, Greece, Turkey, Romania and Poland), it would be better to drop the whole idea of giving guarantees in respect of other states and to confine the treaty to a straight agreement of mutual assistance to come into force only in the case of a direct attack by an aggressor on the territory of the three powers.'

Having delivered his broadside, Molotov stood up, said that was all, handed over the written version of his reply, then marched quickly out of the room through the ever-open door.

Back in London, Halifax was not particularly depressed over the outcome so far, feeling that Molotov's reaction was based on a misunderstanding of the Anglo-French position. But as usual, Halifax underestimated Molotov and Stalin. When Strang and the two ambassadors delivered his new message to the Kremlin, suggesting that all the difficulties could be smoothed out by simply omitting the names of the states to be protected, the answer was a categorical 'No'. All eight of the states originally listed must be named, and all three powers must undertake to defend them. Holland and Switzerland, with whom the Soviets had no diplomatic relations, were not even mentioned. Molotov also produced a new condition: the military guarantees to be given to the Soviet government by the Allies must be spelled out in exact detail, in advance. The new proposals from London, Molotov stated coldly, 'did not represent any progress', but nevertheless he would submit them to the Soviet government.

'The Soviet government', who had doubtless been listening to every word from the next room, did not take long to prepare his reply. It was short and to the point, and Molotov handed it over, in writing, next day: 'In view of the fact that these proposals constitute a repetition of previous proposals made by England and France, which, as already stated, have met with serious objections on the part of the Soviet government, the latter have come to the conclusion that these proposals must be rejected as unacceptable.'

Halifax was staggered by this outright rejection. 'You are doubtless as bewildered as I am by the attitude of M. Molotov,' he cabled Seeds next night. 'The position as I see it is that we have declared ourselves ready to give him the substance of everything he requires.' To Maisky, whom he saw two days later on Friday, 23 June, the British Foreign Secretary was indignant. He asked him 'point-blank' whether the Soviet government really wanted a treaty at all. 'Throughout the negotiations,' he complained, 'the Soviet government has not budged an inch and we have made all the advances and concessions. Saying "no" to everything is not my idea of negotiation. It has a striking resemblance to Nazi methods of dealing with international questions.'

For several days, the British and French struggled with the problem of what to do next, aided by detailed explanations from Seeds and Strang of why the Soviets, distrustful of the Allies, wanted to have them bound by precise obligations, and why the last draft fell short in Soviet eyes. It was during this time that Zhdanov wrote his *Pravda* article. Eventually, on 1 July, Strang and the ambassadors were able to present new concessions – supposedly final ones.

For a while, everything looked hopeful again: when Seeds suggested that the list of states might be contained in an agreed but unpublished protocol to the agreement, Molotov said he thought the Soviet government would be willing to agree to this. He still insisted that Holland and Switzerland could not be included in the list, but indicated that he might be able to do a deal over this in return for some 'compensation', such as if Poland and Turkey could be persuaded to sign mutual assistance pacts with the Soviet Union. At last, there seemed to be real negotiations, and real progress. Then Molotov suddenly produced a fresh demand, in the shape of a two-word phrase that was to prove fatal to the talks: 'indirect aggression'. As an example, he cited the case of Czech President Hacha, who had been bullied and intimidated into signing away his country's independence in March.

For two and a half weeks, the three powers argued over the definition of indirect aggression, and whether or not it should be included in the treaty as a reason for their going to the assistance of any victim. Most of the potential victims, meanwhile, continued to protest that they did not want to be helped against their will, and that they would themselves resist any such attempt. While the term was defined and redefined, the suspicions which the two parties had of each other became more and more evident.

Molotov insisted that the treaty should cover situations where nations were coerced without the direct threat of force. This was too much for the British to swallow. They felt it gave the Soviets a licence to interfere in the governments of other countries – a dangerous precept which could itself be described as indirect aggression. They therefore held firm to the belief that there were two basic requirements: the victim must be acting against their will under threat of force, and their actions must involve abandoning their independence or neutrality.

Molotov for his part refused to budge over the inclusion of 'without threat of force', and also insisted that a definition must be included in the body of the treaty itself. By the tenth meeting, on 17 July, the negotiations were on the point of collapse, for in addition to digging in his heels over indirect aggression, he was now demanding that the political and military agreements must be agreed and signed simultaneously. 'In the Soviet conception', he told the Western representatives, 'there would not be two agreements, but a single political–military agreement . . . on this point there should be no misunderstandings.' Unless Britain and France agreed, he added, there could be no point in continuing.

9

'THE BIGGEST BRIBE IN HISTORY'

After nearly three weeks of suspense, Hitler's policy of stopping all negotiations with the Soviet Union paid off. On 18 July, while Strang and the two Allied ambassadors fretted in Moscow, the Soviet deputy trade representative in Berlin, Evgeny Babarin, and two of his aides arrived at the Wilhemstrasse to see Schnurre. 'I have a message from the Commissariat for Foreign Affairs,' Babarin announced, 'which I hope will give the government of the Third Reich as much pleasure as it does me.' His hope was well founded: the message was that the Soviet government wanted him to discuss the proposals which had already been made for an economic agreement, and to 'clarify' a few points. If the clarification was satisfactory, he was empowered to sign the treaty in Berlin.

Schnurre was astonished by the directness of Babarin's approach, and by the sudden switch of approach and venue. Previously, Mikoyan himself had insisted that all negotiations must be held in Moscow. Why the change? Babarin waved the question aside. It was of no importance, and could always be settled later, he said. The main thing was for them to deal with the few outstanding points.

Schnurre, in fact, did not need Babarin to explain the significance of the Soviets' change of heart, especially since they also appeared to have withdrawn their objection to restarting economic talks before a political agreement had been settled. Clearly, the talks Babarin was offering were for real, not for show. If the negotiations were held in Berlin, with Babarin representing the Soviet Union, they could be kept quiet. If they were in Moscow, Mikoyan himself would have to be involved, there would inevitably be wide publicity, and the whole world would know something was going on. For a simple trade deal, that would hardly matter – but this was no simple trade deal. Both sides knew the stakes in this particular game were much higher.

Negotiating in Berlin would usually be a long and laborious process: before they agreed to even the smallest detail, the Soviets would normally have to refer it back to Moscow. Yet here was Babarin not only claiming he had the authority to sign, but also holding out the prospect of important concessions right from the start.

In offering the trade deal Germany so badly needed, Stalin was making his boldest move yet towards inviting Hitler to approach him for a full-scale pact. He had already stated his terms for such a pact a week earlier, in his usual oblique way: he had had Maisky feed a story to one of his friends on the London *News Chronicle*, the paper which he had used to 'forecast' a Nazi–Soviet deal on 27 January. On 11 July it carried an article by A. J. Cummings which stated, entirely erroneously:

Unofficially and indirectly Hitler has made the following proposals to Moscow:
(1) Freedom of action for Germany in Eastern Europe involving no threat against Russia or the Ukraine.
(2) Partition of Poland.
(3) Freedom of action for Russia, with full German support, in Asia and the Far East.
(4) Germany's withdrawal of co-operation with Japan – that is, dropping Japan from the Axis.
(5) Political Russo-German Alliance along these lines.
    The proposals mark the third German attempt in the present year to buy off Russia. The two approaches in the early months of the year were curtly rejected. The latest effort signifies to the full Hitler's fear of the consequences of a close British–French–Russian line-up against aggression.

After commenting on the sudden lack of anti-Soviet propaganda in the German press, and pointing out how Goebbels could use the controlled media to make an alliance with the Soviets seem 'quite proper', the article concluded with a warning:

THE ONE CERTAINTY
It should be in the power of the British Government to torpedo this alluring plan tomorrow. Yet there are Conservatives in high places who do not want the British Pact with Russia. The *Daily Express* says the Pact is like an egg which is addled.
    If there is one certainty in an uncertain world it is that failure to come to an agreement with Russia will make war almost as inevitable as death – war in circumstances of grave peril to the British Empire.

It would be hard to find a better example of Stalin's regular practice of flying kites by planting carefully calculated stories in the Western press, stories which he could then deny indignantly in public. But in this case, there was no denial, not even for the sake of form. It would be hard, too, to find a better example of his attempts to play both sides simultaneously. While letting Hitler know that a pact with Germany was possible on the terms suggested, the article was also making the point to the British that it was entirely up to them to prevent it, by reaching a quick agreement with the Soviet Union themselves.

Stalin was not the only one playing a double game: the Germans and British, and to a lesser extent the French, too, were doing exactly the same. Fortified by the Cabinet's approval for his pursuit of 'the positive side' of his policies, Neville Chamberlain still clung to his dream of a conciliation with Hitler. His heart had never been with Seeds and Strang in Moscow – even while they were chipping hopelessly away at the granite block that was Molotov, he was searching desperately for some understanding with the Germans that would let him out of the rash promises he had made to the Poles, and relieve him of the need for any sort of agreement with the Kremlin.

Of course, he was well aware that any approaches he made must be strictly secret. In addition to the effect it would have on Moscow, it would be more than his political life was worth at home to be seen making up to Hitler again. He had an election to fight that year, and had already decided on his platform: 'Safeguarding World Peace with Chamberlain'. Appeasement was now a tainted policy: if it ever got out that he was negotiating with the Nazis, there would be such an outcry that he would have no chance of pulling off any agreement. His only hope was to present it as a *fait accompli*. Then, surely, it would be hailed as a triumph, his reputation would be restored, and he would sweep to victory in the November elections to enjoy another five years in power.

From Berlin, Ambassador Henderson had suggested that Chamberlain could simply write to Hitler. He even drafted a letter for him: 'It is quite clear that confidence and tranquillity can only be restored in Europe by means of Anglo-German co-operation. To this end, His Majesty's government will be ready to discuss with the German government all such problems as limitations of armaments, trade barriers, raw materials, *Lebensraum*, and eventually colonies, provided you, Herr Reichskanzler, are willing on your part definitely to reassure me of your pacific intentions.'

Chamberlain turned the letter down flat. It was not that it offered Hitler everything he wanted in return for nothing more than a vague promise to be a good boy; it was simply too risky, politically. Hitler might publish it (how Goebbels and Ribbentrop would love to crow!) or the Germans might leak it not only to Chamberlain's opponents in Britain but also to the French, the Poles and the Soviets. If there were to be any chance of success, no one must know what was going on – not the

French, not the British Parliament, not even the Cabinet. And certainly not the Foreign Office. The matter would have to be handled entirely by Chamberlain himself, through his trusted amanuensis, Sir Horace Wilson.

A discreet invitation was passed to Berlin. On 17 July, Helmut Wohlthat, Göring's commissioner for the Four Year Plan, arrived in London, ostensibly to represent Germany at the International Whaling Conference which was just about to begin, in reality to talk with Wilson and Robert Hudson, Secretary of the Department of Overseas Trade. Like Stalin, Chamberlain was hoping to woo Hitler through his pocket, with an offer of an economic deal.

Wohlthat was an ideal choice as the German go-between: he reported directly to Göring, who was sympathetic to Britain, and was always travelling around on official business of one sort or another. The last time he had been in London, on 6–7 June, he had been attending a meeting of the Intergovernmental Committee on Jewish Emigration, the body set up to deal with the problems caused for Nazi Germany by the enforced exodus of Jews. He had met Wilson on that visit, at the Mayfair house of the Duke of Westminster, Britain's richest man and biggest property owner apart from the Crown. They had got on well.

This time, Wilson invited him to his own London home in Kensington, well away from his office at 10 Downing Street. Wohlthat arrived at 3.15 in the afternoon and was given tea. Wilson told him Chamberlain had personally approved the location, and impressed the need for secrecy: 'You have Mr Chamberlain's political future in your hands,' he warned. 'If this leaks out, there will be a great scandal and Mr Chamberlain will be forced to resign.' He then went on to say he wanted to speak to him 'as to one who is a colleague and a friend'.

Their first talk lasted an hour and a quarter. For most of that time they were discussing a long memorandum which Wilson and Chamberlain had written together, an astonishing document outlining proposals for the closest alliance imaginable between the two countries. It covered political, military and economic areas: Britain's guarantees to Poland and Romania would be ditched as 'superfluous'; Danzig would be relegated to being no more than a minor problem; industrial and economic co-operation between Europe's two greatest industrial nations would bring about 'an unprecedented economic boom' throughout the world.

There was a plan for what was described as a 'colonial condominium' in Africa: 'a large, integrated territory, which would embrace the greater part of tropical and sub-tropical Africa. Togoland, Nigeria, the Cameroons, the Congo, Kenya, Tanganyika (German East Africa), Portuguese and Spanish West and East Africa and Northern Rhodesia might be included. In this territory, the production of raw materials and food, the investment of capital goods, foreign trade and currency, transport, administration, police and military control could be uniformly organised.' Although the other European colonial powers would be involved, Britain and Germany would be in control.

In view of the contents of the memorandum, it is small wonder that Wilson and Chamberlain wanted the talks kept secret, particularly from France and Italy.

By a supreme irony, at precisely the time Wilson was talking to Wohlthat, seeking ways to dump Poland, General Edmund 'Tiny' Ironside was talking to Beck and Smigly-Rydz in Warsaw. What he was telling them, on instructions from Chamberlain, was that Poland 'could rely absolutely on Great Britain'.

Ironside was one of the most remarkable generals in the British army. He was a huge man, both physically and mentally, six feet four inches tall, an interpreter in fifteen languages and at fifty-nine still full of vigour. He was the original for John Buchan's fictional hero Richard Hannay and his own life had been almost as colourful. It had included commanding the Allied expedition in Archangel during the Intervention. Throughout his career, he had been in constant trouble with his superiors for his independent and often unconventional attitudes but somehow had managed to survive and become one of Britain's most senior generals.

In July 1939 he had just been recalled from a spell as Governor to Gibraltar, to become Inspector-General of Overseas Forces. He had been promised another post in the event of war: he was to be Commander-in-Chief of the British Expeditionary Force.

When the Prime Minister and Halifax briefed Ironside for his visit to Poland, at Downing Street on 10 July, he had startled them by saying how pleased he was to see that Chamberlain no longer had any belief in Hitler's promises. He went on to say that he had met Hitler, and wasn't sure whether he 'blew up spontaneously, or whether he did it to impress'. Chamberlain said he thought it was spontaneous. Ironside countered that in that case there was more danger of war and when Chamberlain disagreed, proceeded to argue with him, forcefully.

But the real disagreement came over the Soviet Union. When Chamberlain asked Ironside's opinion about coming to an agreement with the Russians, Ironside's answer was unequivocal: 'Though it is much against the grain, it is the only thing we can do.'

'The only thing we cannot do!' Chamberlain ejaculated immediately. Two days later, he was singing a different tune in Cabinet. 'On the whole,' he told his ministers, 'I am disposed to think the Soviet government intends to make an agreement with us, but it is probably in no hurry to do so.'

It took a whole week from his briefing to get Ironside on board an aircraft for Warsaw, on his urgent mission to find out what Beck and

Smigly-Rydz intended to do. As the days dragged by, Ironside became more and more impatient – in the end, he drafted his own instructions, which he then got Halifax and War Minister Leslie Hore-Belisha to sign.

'They are all dreamers and thinkers and cannot turn them into orders,' he confided angrily to his diary. 'Unpractical creatures. Not a good augury for war.'

In Warsaw, he watched manoeuvres and displays by the Polish army and air force, and discussed plans with Smigly-Rydz and his staff. He was most impressed by the troops, and by the immense efforts the Poles were making to prepare themselves for war, but was appalled by their planning, and by the arms and equipment he saw. The sight of mounted cavalry charging across open ground may have been romantic and stirring, but it belonged to another age. There had been no proper winters and little snow for the past three years, and 1939 had been exceptionally rainless. The whole country was baked hard; marshes and rivers, Poland's only natural barriers on which she depended for protection, had dried out, creating perfect conditions for the German Panzers to sweep through at full speed. The few tin cans the Poles had for tanks would stand little more chance against them than the cavalrymen with their lances. The brave and dashing pilots of the air force had to fly hopelessly out-of-date aircraft, which Hitler's Messerschmitts and Focke Wulfs would shoot out of the sky as easily as falcons stooping on defenceless pigeons.

Deeply depressed, Ironside fumed at the British delays in bringing in the Soviets, and at the Polish reluctance to accept their help. For the moment, however, all he could do was cable back to London urging the government to give the Poles more money to pay for arms, with fewer strings attached. Time, he reminded Halifax, was short. In fact, a Polish delegation had been in London for several days, begging for a loan of £50 million. So far, the Cabinet had demurred. Sir John Simon, Chancellor of the Exchequer, thought Britain might do something, as long as France contributed, too, but nothing had been decided: Simon was more concerned with inflation in Poland, and the state of the zloty.

The matter was discussed in Cabinet again a week later, on 26 July. Halifax did not even mention Ironside's message. The ministers agreed to give Poland export credits of £8 million, to be spent in Britain, but there would be no direct loan. Simon declared he was 'not disposed to give Poland gold, which Poland would store in vaults in Warsaw and make the basis for further expansion of her paper currency'.

Wohlthat had returned to Wilson's house at 5.30 pm on 20 July, for his assignation with Overseas Trade Secretary Robert Hudson. This time, the talk was about money. Chamberlain was essentially a conventional businessman: his family background, in addition to producing famous politicians, was firmly rooted in Birmingham trade. Wilson's civil service background had also been concerned with business: he had made his name at the Board of Trade as a negotiator with trades union leaders. Both believed with complete sincerity that money is truly what makes the world go around. They had tried all the methods of conventional diplomacy on Hitler, and got nowhere; now they felt it was time to ignore the professional diplomats and follow their own instincts.

Hudson had been told to dangle money in front of the Germans, and he proceeded to do just that. Britain would settle Germany's international debts, provide loans for the German Reichsbank, restore the link between the European capital markets, settle the south-east Europe currency and debt questions – and so the list went on. The total amount offered came to around £1 billion – a far cry from the paltry £8 million offered as a credit to Poland. An enemy, it seemed, was worth over 125 times more than an ally.

Hermann Göring was particularly well represented in London that Thursday afternoon. While one of his men was talking to Hudson, another of his secret envoys was with Halifax.

Birger Dahlerus, a Swedish businessman who had been a close personal friend of Göring for many years, had volunteered to act as an intermediary between him and Britain, a country where he had lived and worked for some time during his youth. He was deeply attached to Britain and the British, and was horrified at the thought that they could soon be at war with Germany, which he also loved. He was convinced that the whole thing was a misunderstanding, particularly on the part of Hitler, who did not seem to realise that the British government would keep its word to go to war over Poland. Dahlerus believed he could convince Hitler of this by bringing to Germany a group of his British business friends – men who had no part in government but who could speak for the people. Göring, with Hitler's approval, gave his consent for Dahlerus to arrange a meeting, which he himself would attend on behalf of the Third Reich, and on the strength of this, Dahlerus had arranged to see Halifax.

The British Foreign Secretary was showing interest in the Swede's suggestion. 'An open discussion,' he agreed, 'free of all restraint, between leading Englishmen and members of the German government could be of great use at this moment. But I must explain that the British government does not want to be directly involved and will not send any of its members to the conference.'

Dahlerus patiently explained that this was exactly what he was proposing: there must be no politicians involved from the British end. Halifax nodded his bony head approvingly and continued, in his best dry manner: 'We will be interested to receive a detailed account of the results from the Englishmen who take part in the talks. If they prove to be of a positive nature, this meeting ought to pave the way for a future conference between authorised delegates. It could take place in Holland or Sweden.'

When it came to conferences with the Germans, Halifax was still the eternal optimist. His attitude to the Soviet talks was very different. He was inclined to agree with the diplomatic correspondent of *The Times*, who had described them the day before as 'a depressing subject, which even lacked the excitement of the hunt'. That same day, he had reported to the Cabinet that he thought the Moscow negotiations might collapse.

'This will not cause me very great anxiety,' he had said, 'since I feel that, whatever formal agreement is signed, the Soviet government will probably take such action as best suits them if war breaks out.'

In France, Foreign Minister Bonnet and Premier Daladier were also afraid the talks might collapse, but their reaction was markedly different from the British. They had sent a frantic message begging for the negotiations to be continued 'no matter what the price', and urging the British government to agree to the Soviet formula. Halifax calmly ignored their pleas.

Halifax's blasé unconcern was matched only by his blindness to danger signals. He had gone on to tell his Cabinet colleagues: 'It seems that discussions of some kind are proceeding between the German government and the Soviet government. It is impossible to assess their real value, but it seems likely that these discussions relate to industrial matters.'

Chamberlain had joined his Foreign Secretary in dismissing the significance of the intelligence reports, saying, 'I cannot bring myself to believe that a real alliance between Russia and Germany is possible.'

William Strang had no such delusions about the possibility of the Soviet Union and Germany getting together: for him it was a nightmare which was daily coming closer and closer to reality. The previous day had been a holiday, in honour of sport and physical culture. Throughout the country there had been parades and displays, the biggest, naturally, in Red Square, Moscow. For five hours, athletes and gymnasts had marched and pranced and twirled; a vast kaleidoscope of colours had folded and unfolded in the mass displays so beloved by the Soviets, while martial music had blared from bands and loudspeakers.

For the whole five hours, Stalin had stood on the reviewing dais on top of the Lenin Mausoleum, along with Molotov, Kaganovich, Voroshilov, Andreyev, Kalinin, Mikoyan and the rest of the Politburo, all looking relaxed and enjoying the spectacle. And in pride of place on the diplomats' stand, immediately to the right of the Mausoleum, had been Count Friedrich von der Schulenburg.

Schulenburg's two teenage nephews were staying with him for their summer vacation, and he had taken them to the parade, as a treat. The boys had been as interested in the men on the dais as they were in the parade – it would be quite something to tell their friends back at school that they had seen Stalin and stood quite close to him. Their uncle had pointed out other people to them, including the bespectacled man with the long thin nose further along their stand. The man had nodded back in a reserved but not unfriendly way.

'That's Mr Strang,' Schulenburg had told them. 'The British negotiator.'

Albrecht and Christian had looked at the tight lips and close-clipped moustache. They saw a typical bureaucrat, a faceless man who could not compare with their warm, sparkling uncle. They were not impressed, and quickly turned their attention back to the more charismatic figure of Stalin.

Schulenburg was surprised to see Alexei Merekalov, the ambassador to Berlin who had been in Moscow for some time now, on the diplomats' stand with his family. The two men greeted each other cautiously.

'When will you be returning to Berlin?' Schulenburg asked, casually.

Merekalov's reply was almost too quick.

'Oh, I still have leave for the whole of August.'

'Then you will be in Berlin at the beginning of September?'

'Perhaps.'

Gustav Hilger, who had joined them, asked the Russian why, if he was staying in Moscow, he had not accepted the invitation Schulenburg had sent him for the German embassy's summer reception. Merekalov answered evasively.

'As a matter of fact, I am not on duty at present.'

The two Germans exchanged glances – to them, it all sounded suspicious. Merekalov had obviously not fallen from grace or he would not have been on the diplomats' stand, but there was a strong rumour that Molotov was planning to replace all heads of mission who had been appointed by Litvinov. If Merekalov were to be replaced would that herald a change of policy towards Germany?

Strang could not have failed to notice the conversation, even if he could not hear what was being said. He, too, was aware of the rumours, and wondered what Merekalov's continuing presence in Moscow meant. But for the moment, he could only speculate and try to enjoy the show.

With the parades over, it was back to business for Strang – or at least it should have been. But without fresh instructions he could do nothing. Sitting in his stifling room in the British embassy he stared across the brown waters and concrete banks of the Moscow river at the golden domes and stucco palaces of the Kremlin. It was time to take stock of the situation, time to write to his masters in London pointing out a few home truths.

He took a pile of paper, unscrewed his fountain pen and began. He

wrote not to Halifax or even to Cadogan, but for the more sympathetic
eyes of his friend Sir Orme Sargent, the Deputy Under-Secretary at the
Foreign Office. Partly the letter was a cry for help: 'Molotov does not
become any easier to deal with as the weeks pass,' it opened. '. . . On the
whole, negotiations have been a humiliating experience. Time after time
we have taken up a position and a week later we have abandoned it; and
we have had the feeling that Molotov was convinced from the beginning
that we should be forced to abandon it.

'This was, I think, inevitable,' he continued. 'It is we, not the Russians,
who took the initiative in starting negotiations. Our need for an
agreement is more immediate than theirs. Unlike them, we have
assumed obligations which we may be obliged to fulfil any day; and some
of the obligations we have undertaken are of benefit to the Soviet Union
since they protect a good part of their western frontier. Having
committed ourselves to these obligations, we have no other policy open
to us than that of building up the Peace Front. The Russians have, in the
last resort, at least two alternative policies, namely, the policy of
isolation, and the policy of accommodation with Germany.'

Strang understood the situation very well. He also, in complete
contrast to the politicians in London, understood the Russians. He was
convinced that they wanted an agreement with Britain and France. 'But,'
he pointed out, 'we must remember that the conclusion of a close
political and military alliance with the two capitalist Powers would be
something quite new in their foreign policy. These negotiations are as
much an adventure for them as they are for us. If we do not trust them,
they equally do not trust us. They are not, fundamentally, a friendly
Power; but they, like us, are driven to this course by force of necessity. If
we are in two minds about the wisdom of what we are doing, so are they.
It is possible that there are differences of opinion in the Kremlin about
it, and it is this uneasiness on both sides which is making the
negotiations so difficult . . .

'Their distrust and suspicion of us have not diminished during the
negotiations, nor, I think, has their respect for us increased . . . We
should perhaps have been wiser to pay the Soviet price for this
agreement at an earlier stage, since we are not in a good position to
bargain and since, as the international situation deteriorates, the Soviet
price is likely to rise. We could probably have got a better agreement by
closing quickly with the substance of the Soviet draft of the 2nd June than
we shall get today.'

As a brutally honest and penetrating assessment, Strang's letter would
have been impossible to better. For page after page he wrote, calmly and
professionally, displaying the clarity of thought which was later to take
him to the top as Permanent Under-Secretary. He urged that his
government should agree immediately to military talks, and stressed the
urgency and the importance again. 'A break would create bad feeling,'

he wrote. 'It would encourage the Germans to act. It might drive the Soviet Union into isolation, or into composition with Germany.'

Strang showed the finished letter to Seeds, who endorsed it wholeheartedly. Then he sent it winging back to London in that day's diplomatic bag.

On Saturday morning, 22 July, the citizens of the Soviet Union and Britain were both greeted by press headlines about secret negotiations. Four days earlier in Berlin, Babarin had indicated to Schnurre that the Soviets wanted their talks kept quiet; now, the entire Soviet press was trumpeting the news on its front pages that talks had begun. The reason was to be found on the front pages of the British papers, which carried the story of Chamberlain's offer of a loan to Germany: 'The biggest bribe in history', it was called.

The story of Hudson's meeting with Wohlthat had been leaked to French intelligence the day before. Daladier and Bonnet had been furious and had seen to it that the British press was informed. And of course the story had reached Moscow in double-quick time – 'Smiling Maisky' had many good friends in Fleet Street, and they were not slow in feeding him this juicy information even before their papers went to press. Stalin's immediate response had been to order the publication of the news about Soviet–German talks, as another clear warning that if the Allies did not stop vacillating he would make a deal with Hitler instead.

Fortunately for Chamberlain, the French and British had only got part of the story – they had not found out about the political proposals made by Wilson. He could therefore contain the damage, claiming that the press stories were wild exaggerations and distortions, blown up out of all proportion. He could stand up in the House of Commons – with Halifax doing the same in the Lords – and state with absolute truth that the Cabinet had known nothing about it. He could not deny that Wohlthat had met Hudson, but he could play down the significance of the meeting.

'I do not see any harm in this particular conversation,' he told the Commons. 'It was a personal conversation between my friend and an official of the German side. The mischief, if mischief there was, was in the disclosure of the conversation to the newspapers.'

In fact, it had been Hudson himself who had leaked the information to the French, as his way of sabotaging Chamberlain's latest appeasement strategems. He later admitted this when questioned about the leak by the *Daily Express* and the *News Chronicle*. However, he had not been party to Wilson's conversations, so had not been able to alert the French or the press about the political component of the bribe. As a result, Chamberlain was able to use the financial revelations as a smokescreen to hide the more important – and explosive – political proposals. While the furore was raging about the money, his opponents in Parliament and elsewhere were far too busy shouting about it to imagine there could be anything else.

While the British and Russian newspapers were both full of stories about negotiations of one sort or another with Germany, the French journals were more concerned with the stalemate in Moscow in the Anglo-French–Soviet talks. Bonnet and Daladier were dismayed by the British government's refusal to respond to their pleas. In desperation, they decided to use the press to lean on Chamberlain. Bonnet briefed the political correspondents, and the stories duly appeared. The British, they chorused in Paris and London, were dragging their heels and obstructing the French wish to reach agreement with the Soviet Union.

Halifax, Chamberlain and Wilson, however, steadfastly refused to be hustled. They were determined to go at their own pace, eagerly seizing any excuse for delay. Halifax cabled Seeds in Moscow: 'There have been press reports in Paris and London to the effect that French government are prepared to meet M. Molotov at all points and have been urging His Majesty's government in vain to fall into line. If subject is raised you may inform your French colleague that we have every reason to believe that leakage is from French sources.'

Far from being prepared to 'meet Molotov at all points', Halifax was considering calling a halt to the whole proceedings. 'If faced by the alternative of a limited treaty or a complete breakdown,' he asked Seeds, 'do you think M. Molotov would become more amenable to argument, or would he cheerfully accept the prospect of an immediate breakdown?' He was thinking of recalling Strang, 'so as to be able to say that the discussions had not broken down but had only been suspended'.

Seeds and Strang were horrified. Seeds cabled back to Halifax that he and Naggiar had drafted an alternative formula, and thought they could find an acceptable definition of 'indirect aggression'. Could he have approval before his meeting with Molotov next day? This time it was Halifax who was horrified. He hurriedly cabled his reply: 'I cannot give you definite decision in time. In no circumstances should you commit HMG without further instructions.'

If London, Paris and Moscow were buzzing with activity on that hectic summer Saturday, Berlin was equally busy. For a start, the German newspapers were making their own contribution to the international confusion, proclaiming that the Nazi government believed Chamberlain would give in over Danzig, and that 'England would exercise sufficient influence upon Poland' to prevent armed resistance by the Poles. 'The political barometer is 100 per cent against war,' an unnamed German official spokesman was quoted as saying, by the Exchange Telegraph correspondent. That same spokesman went on to say that 'such influence by Britain might be the more effective if the Anglo-Soviet negotiations were to fail'.

There were now less than six weeks until the planned start date for Operation White: according to the OKW plan, Hitler had twenty-five days left before the final deadline for his decision. He could not afford to put off a deal with Stalin any longer. When Ribbentrop telephoned from Fuschl with the latest situation reports, he told him to instruct the Foreign Ministry to take off the brakes.

At noon, Weizsäcker cabled Schulenburg, telling him, 'As far as the purely political aspect of our conversations with the Russians is concerned, we regard the period of waiting stipulated for you in our telegram No. 134 (30 June) as having expired.' Germany wanted an agreement as soon as possible; in Berlin they would be acting 'in a markedly forthcoming manner' and in Moscow Schulenburg was to 'pick up the threads again'.

Having told Ribbentrop what he wanted from the Foreign Ministry, Hitler then telephoned the Navy High Command and ordered the admirals to be ready at short notice to send the cruiser *Nürnberg* to Danzig. He did not say why the ship was to go. That would be explained later. The *Nürnberg* was an elderly ship, but she had a formidable array of heavy guns, which could provide powerful artillery support when the fighting started.

For Hitler, the countdown had begun.

10

DINNER AT EWEST'S

Monday, 24 July, was Navy Day in the Soviet Union, and once against Moscow was *en fête*. There were parades of rowing boats, sailing boats and motor launches on the Moscow–Volga Canal, plus demonstrations of all kinds of water sport. The highlight of the day was a group parachute drop into the canal from low-flying aircraft.

Naval Commissar Nikolai G. Kuznetsov made a speech about the growing strength of the Soviet navy, claiming it now had more submarines than any other nation – more than Germany and Japan combined. He also announced great plans for the shipbuilding industry: the government, he said, envisaged the Soviet Union 'occupying one of the leading positions in the world in the number and tonnage of shipping launched annually by 1942 or 1943'. To the shipping world, it sounded like wishful thinking – Soviet yards' capacity was so limited they were still having to look abroad for help. Indeed Molotov's brother-in-law had recently started negotiating, through the Soviet–American trading company which he ran, for America to build them a battleship in a deal worth between sixty and a hundred million dollars, calling for a duplicate ship to be built at the same time in a Russian yard, with American technical help.

In the Kremlin, Stalin and Molotov had other things on their minds, however. The previous day, while the people of Moscow had enjoyed a restful Sunday strolling in the summer sunshine or travelling out to the country to pick early mushrooms, Molotov had received Strang and the two ambassadors in his office. As usual, he had shown no sign of feeling the heat, either from the weather or from the international situation.

For a while, the meeting had followed the depressingly familiar pattern: Naggiar had said little; Seeds and Strang had obeyed instructions, splitting hairs, arguing over words, continuing to press for a definition of 'indirect aggression'. Their government, they said, was prepared to accept the Soviet demand that the political and military agreements should come into force simultaneously, but still wanted the political side settled before starting military talks. There were, they maintained, important points of principle involved.

Molotov heard them out, then coldly told them to stop wasting time. 'I do not think,' he lectured them, 'that these questions will raise insuperable difficulties. I am convinced that our three governments can find a formula that will satisfy us all.'

Seeds tried to argue again: the British government, he said, insisted on definitions. Molotov directed a basilisk stare through his pince-nez and repeated his assertion: there were no insuperable difficulties.

'You are wasting time,' he rasped. 'It is essential that there should be no further delay about opening military conversations. *I* insist the military discussions begin immediately.'

Ironside, safely back in London from Warsaw, rose at 6 that Monday morning and was in Whitehall early. He had an urgent meeting with the Minister of War, Leslie Hore-Belisha, at the War Office. He had not yet had time to write his report, but Belisha wanted to hear his reactions to his visit to Poland. Did he think the world war was coming? Ironside said he thought it was. Was it coming this year? Probably, but who could tell.

The War Minister then pulled down a wall map of Europe: he managed to find Poland on it, but that seemed to be about as far as his knowledge of the country went. Ironside was appalled by his ignorance. He was even more appalled when it dawned on him that Belisha was, as he put it in his diary, 'getting a few ideas out of him' for a meeting that morning of the Committee of Imperial Defence, called to discuss Poland. Since none of its members knew anything about the subject, it would have made sense to have Tiny Ironside there, but the thought apparently never occurred to any of them. The meeting went ahead without him.

Two hundred yards away from the War Office, in Downing Street, Chamberlain and Halifax were considering Seeds's report on the previous day's meeting in Moscow. The ambassador said he was not optimistic about the possibilities of success in military talks, but felt they could have some value. 'To begin with them now,' he suggested, 'would give a healthy shock to the Axis Powers.'

Chamberlain wavered. Should he send a military mission? And if he did, whom should he choose to lead it? Ironside was the obvious man for the job: the Soviet press had reported favourably on his visit to Warsaw, his reputation was good in Europe – indeed Strang had already hinted that the Soviets would be very pleased if he were chosen. But could Ironside be trusted to do what Chamberlain wanted? He was vociferously enthusiastic about making an alliance with the Soviet Union, but did that count for him, or against him? The whole thing needed very careful thought.

To help with this difficult decision, Chamberlain sent for the holders of the other two great offices of state, Sir Samuel Hoare, the Home Secretary, and Sir John Simon, Chancellor of the Exchequer, to join him and Halifax in their deliberations. Together, the five ministers agreed that, while they could delay the choice of a leader, they had no option but to consent at once to sending a mission. To refuse would be to cut off all negotiations with the Soviets and possible drive them into the arms of the Germans. Without consulting the rest of the Cabinet, Chamberlain authorised Halifax to send instructions to Seeds telling him to inform Molotov that military talks could start immediately.

At the full Cabinet meeting next day, the reaction was considerably less than enthusiastic. Some of the other ministers were decidedly uneasy, fearing Britain would be put in a weak position if they told the Soviet Union military secrets before a pact was signed. Halifax argued that sending the mission would have 'a good effect on world opinion', but the doubters continued to doubt. It was a ludicrous concern – there were no secret plans for anyone to divulge. Indeed, Ironside was at that very moment exploding with rage in the War Office as he discovered just how unprepared the army was – the only military secret the Russians might learn was how weak Britain's forces really were.

Eventually, the meeting found a solution which satisfied everyone: the mission should be sent, but 'our representative should be instructed to proceed very slowly with the conversations until a political pact had been concluded.'

When Halifax called Maisky to the Foreign Office to inform him officially of the decision to send a military mission, the first question the ambassador asked was straight to the point.

'Tell me, Lord Halifax,' he asked, 'when in your opinion can these negotiations begin?'

Halifax pondered. He tilted his angular frame back in his chair and stared thoughtfully at the ornate ceiling.

'We shall need at least a week or ten days to do all the preliminary work,' he eventually replied.

In his memoir of the occasion, Maisky recalls how he realised that on that basis the talks could not possibly begin for two weeks. His heart began to sink.

'And have the members of your mission for the military negotiations already been selected?' he asked.

'No, not yet,' came the calm reply. 'We shall do this in the next few days. We think the most convenient place for the military talks would be Paris, but as the Soviet government has expressed a wish that they should be conducted in Moscow, we are ready to meet there.'

Maisky was alarmed at the lack of urgency in every tired word. He tried to make Halifax realise the importance of the talks, and to influence the choice of leader, which would be vital.

'Even if you, Lord Halifax, did not go to Moscow in June,' he urged, 'let today, at any rate, the chief representative of Britain be some really prominent and active military figure.' This, he emphasised, 'would be valuable for the negotiations themselves. It might somewhat cool the aggressive ardour of Hitler. It would be evidence of a serious attitude to the tripartite pact on the part of Britain if even now, on the very threshold of war, there took place some change for the better in the attitude of its ruling group.'

Halifax's reactions did not fill Maisky with confidence. For once, the ambassador was not smiling. But he did not give up – he called Arthur Greenwood, deputy leader of the Labour Party, whom he knew well, and asked him to tell Chamberlain that the Soviet government hoped to see a very prominent military man at the head of the British delegation. Oddly, he did not mention Ironside, the name that seemed to be on everyone's lips, but said the Soviets' favourite would be General Gort, Chief of the Imperial General Staff.

Greenwood did as he was asked. In reply, Chamberlain wrote to him saying that unfortunately the government could not send Lord Gort to Moscow, 'as he was too much required at the moment in London'. However, he said, the delegation would be headed instead by 'someone who would command the necessary respect of the Soviet government'.

While the rest of the world leaders were in turmoil, agonising over Hitler's next move, the Führer himself calmly started his annual pilgrimage to Bayreuth, where he would take a holiday from affairs of state in a ten-day orgy of Wagner. He arrived on 25 July, to stay, as always, in the spacious wing which Winifred Wagner had had specially built for him on to her home, Haus Wahnfried, where he could relax with a few carefully chosen guests.

The statuesque, matronly Winifred was, in fact, half English, having been born in Hastings on 23 June 1897, the daughter of a British journalist and his German wife. She had married the composer's son, Siegfried, in 1915, and had been widowed in 1930. One of Hitler's most fervent worshippers from his earliest days in politics, she had sent him food parcels, books of poetry, pencils, ink, erasers, and even the paper on which he had written *Mein Kampf*, when he was in prison in 1923–4. Her devotion had never wavered and Hitler accepted it gratefully, affording her a very special place in the movement, and in his affections. He confided many times to his closest associates that if ever he decided to marry for reasons of state, it would be to Winifred Wagner – in addition to his affection and gratitude, the idea of linking the names Hitler and Wagner held immense attraction for him.

For fifteen years he had made regular visits to the Wagner family. The four children called him 'Uncle Wolf', though it was rumoured their father had not approved of him. Before 1933, he always went incognito to Bayreuth – calling himself 'Bandmaster Wolf' – in order to avoid embarrassing the organisers of the festival, but after he came to power he became its official patron, making Bormann provide hundreds of thousands of marks from party funds every year to ensure the festival productions were the glory of the German opera season. Thanks largely to him, the festival became internationally successful, Winifred Wagner became rich and famous, and Bayreuth became the music capital of Germany, if not of Europe.

For Hitler, besotted with Wagner's music and ideas since his youth, it was the fulfilment of a wild dream. Music had always occupied a special place in his life: as a boy, he had sung in the choir at the local Benedictine monastery in Lambach and he could still sing the Mozart masses from memory; his knowledge of Wagner's operas was phenomenal – he had seen *Die Meistersinger* no less than forty times!

In 1939, the Bayreuth Festival was offering *The Flying Dutchman*, *Parsifal*, *Tristan und Isolde* and, of course, the entire *Ring* cycle. Hitler was looking forward to it with great pleasure. He tried, as far as was possible, to forget politics during his visits to Bayreuth, treating his time there not merely as a holiday but also as a period of recharging his energies, drawing fresh inspiration from the works of his idol.

This year, however, he could not stop the real world intruding – he had hardly been there one day when Ribbentrop telephoned to report two developments which could affect the decision to make a positive move towards the Soviet Union.

The first of these was a visit by Astakhov to Weizsäcker the day before. He had brought an invitation for two Germans, a scientist and a member of the Ministry of Agriculture, to spend ten days in Moscow as guests of the Society for Cultural Relations with Foreign Countries, at the first All-Union Agricultural Show, which was due to open on 1 August. Astakhov had explained that this was intended to help re-establish cultural relations between Germany and the Soviet Union – he and his government had been most gratified when he had been invited to the opening by Hitler of the Exhibition of German Art in Munich ten days before.

'It would certainly do no harm,' he had told Weizsäcker, 'if a contribution were made towards improving our relations in general by means of a number of small gestures.'

Having established that the Soviets were ready to better relations, Astakhov had gone on to discuss the Anglo-Japanese negotiations then taking place in Tokyo. For some time, the Japanese had been running a vicious campaign against the British in China. They had bombed British ships on the Yangtze river, and organised anti-British riots in Chinese cities, while their occupation forces had physically assaulted British men and women, beating and stripping them naked on the streets. The Japanese price for stopping the humiliations was that Britain should renounce any support for China, recognise Japan's occupation, and instruct all British citizens not to do or say anything against them. Chamberlain's reaction to all this had been typical: after the briefest of negotiations, the British government were kow-towing.

Astakhov had seemed to derive great pleasure from this. Moscow, he had said pointedly, would not be impressed by the British retreat.

After this latest piece of encouragement from Moscow, Ribbentrop's second report was a grave disappointment. He had just received Italian Ambassador Bernardo Attolico and his counsellor, Massimo Magistrati, brother-in-law of Foreign Minister Ciano, who had come to discuss a proposed meeting between Hitler and Mussolini, scheduled for 4 August at the Brenner Pass. Hitler had never been particularly keen on the meeting, and Ribbentrop knew he would be even less so when he heard what Attolico had had to say. The Italians were trying to wriggle out of their obligations to support Germany in the event of war, proposing another Munich, another compromise, another watering-down of Hitler's ambitions.

Ribbentrop had got rid of the Italians as quickly as he could, assuring them that, like Italy, Germany was determined to avoid war for as long as possible. Amazingly, they had appeared to believe him. Now he wanted to discuss the implications of the Italian backsliding with Hitler, and to get the Führer's orders for this next move.

Germany's principal allies were becoming less enthusiastic and less trustworthy every day. Even the Hungarians had just written to say that although they would adhere absolutely to the Axis, they could not, 'on moral grounds', take armed action against Poland. With Italy, too, reluctant to enter any fray, the Germans would have to make other arrangements to safeguard themselves.

Ribbentrop considered it was extremely doubtful whether Britain and France would actually fight when Germany invaded Poland – but no one could be entirely sure. The French had an army of 800,000 men, as many as Germany's. With the main strength of the Wehrmacht committed to the east, they just might summon up enough courage to attack the German rear. The West Wall should hold them, at least for as long as it would take to smash the Poles with a *Blitzkrieg*, a lightning war. But if the Soviet Union were to join forces with Poland, Britain and France, the situation would be drastically changed: the lightning war would become prolonged; Germany would be in serious trouble.

The various messages Ribbentrop had received in the last few days from the Foreign Ministry and his own intelligence sources were worrying. He had believed the British and French were hopelessly bogged down in their political talks with the Russians, but now it seemed they were getting a second wind. The news that they were finally about to start military negotiations was frankly alarming. If someone like

Ironside were sent to Moscow, there was every possibility he would cut through the formalities and reach an agreement quickly. Since the signals from the Soviets were becoming more and more positive, perhaps the time was right for Germany to make a bold move. Hitler listened, considered, then gave his approval.

Since time was of the essence, Ribbentrop needed to put his plan into motion immediately. As soon as he had finished talking to Hitler, he called the Wilhelmstrasse in Berlin and spoke to Karl Schnurre, ordering him to drop everything and fly to Salzburg at once, for a secret briefing at Schloss Fuschl.

The beautiful old castle on the edge of Lake Fuschl, a few miles from Salzburg, was the latest of many real estate prizes which Ribbentrop had collected since the Nazis came to power. It was the ancestral home of an Austrian nobleman, Gustav von Remnitz, a strong advocate of Austrian independence, whom Ribbentrop had persuaded Himmler to arrest and throw into Dachau concentration camp after the *Anschluss*. He had then taken the place over, complete with all its contents, having Frau von Remnitz and her young son evicted in the middle of the night by storm-troopers. Ribbentrop, in fact, had had his eyes on the castle and its owner for some time, ever since Remnitz had snubbed him by refusing to invite him to the dinners which he held there every year for distinguished foreign visitors to the Salzburg Festival. Now, the Foreign Minister used it as his base whenever Hitler was staying at the Berghof, which was within about half an hour's drive – he had a neurotic need to be close to his Führer at all times, following him about the country when necessary.

In these beautiful surroundings, with the blue lake and picturesque mountains as a backdrop, Schnurre listened as Ribbentrop gave him his instructions. There was a great deal to be said, and everything had to be stated precisely and understood precisely. Even though he knew only too well of the Foreign Minister's unorthodox methods, Schnurre was astonished to learn that he had been chosen as the man to make the vital first move towards an all-embracing deal with the Soviets, bypassing Weizsäcker and the rest of the Foreign Ministry hierarchy, ignoring Schulenburg and the embassy in Moscow. Ribbentrop, who had clearly been preparing for such a moment for some time, insisted on going over and over every last detail, telling Schnurre the exact words he was to use. When he had finished, he sent him back to Berlin, ordering him to keep what he had been told strictly secret, even within the Foreign Ministry itself.

Schnurre did not trust Ribbentrop, however, and was not prepared to follow his unwritten and unrecorded instructions without covering himself in some way. If things went wrong, he did not want to find himself taking all the blame – in any case, as a loyal member of the

Foreign Ministry he did not like the idea of going behind the back of the State Secretary. The first thing he did on arriving back in Berlin, therefore, was to report everything to Weizsäcker, a man he did trust, and respect. Weizsäcker appreciated Schnurre's problem, and assured him of his support. He told him to go ahead, but added one piece of advice: 'You need a witness. Take someone with you.'

Schnurre agreed. He called on Otto Bräutigam, a counsellor in the Political Department who dealt with Soviet affairs, and asked him if he was free next evening. Bräutigam replied that he was sorry, but he already had an engagement. Schnurre could not tell him how important the invitation was, so he had to look elsewhere. He chose his assistant, a young man who had been in the Foreign Ministry only since October 1938, Walter Schmid. Schmid, at twenty-four one of the youngest and most junior attachés in the entire services, was delighted to be invited out to dinner by his boss, and accepted immediately.

So did the other two guests: they were Georgi Astakhov and Evgeny Babarin.

Schnurre and Schmid met Astakhov and Babarin for dinner at 9 the next evening, Wednesday, 26 June. Schnurre had been allowed by Ribbentrop to choose the location himself, and had settled on Ewest's, a small, old-established restaurant with a good atmosphere, in a quiet side street near the Wilhelmplatz. Ewest's had been used by Foreign Ministry officials for generations – 'Steak Holstein', a dish consisting of a fillet steak with a fried egg on top, had been created there for Friedrich von Holstein, principal adviser on foreign affairs to the Kaisers from the time of Bismarck until the first world war. It was also a favourite haunt of officers in the Abwehr, and had a reputation for discretion, which recommended it to Schnurre, though Schmid recalls that he was still worried it might be bugged – not by the Soviets, but by the Gestapo.

The decor was in quiet good taste – simple cream walls, heavy drapes and a few pleasant pictures on the walls – and the lighting was generally low. Schnurre had reserved a small private room on the ground floor at the rear, and had ordered the meal with care: hors d'oeuvres followed by cold poached salmon from the Rhine, washed down with plentiful supplies of the best Rhine wines. Schnurre recalls that the food, in fact, was not particularly good: 'German cuisine at that time had not yet started to improve,' he says with a wry smile. They were attended by a single waiter in a black tuxedo, who left immediately he had served the main course. The dinner was a civilised affair – both Schnurre and Schmid were polished young men from good families, and the Soviet diplomats were men of the world who knew how to conduct themselves well, especially Astakhov, who was urbane, independent, and a considerable *bon viveur*. Babarin was a much less impressive character.

Everything about him was very ordinary, Schnurre recalls: middle-aged, middle height, mousey colouring, lacking all imagination and initiative in negotiations. But he was pleasant enough company at the dinner table.

During the meal, the conversation was confined to social chit-chat and small talk – neither Schnurre nor Schmid can recall anything that was said. But when they had finished eating they moved away from the dining table to easy chairs around a low coffee table in the corner of the room, attacked the brandy bottle with gusto, and began on the serious business of the evening. Schnurre had told the young Schmid to keep his end up during the meal, but then to stay quiet and say nothing, leaving all the talking to him. He did not tell him anything in advance about the subject to be discussed, only that it was extremely important. So when he started telling Astakhov what he had been instructed to say, Schmid found it difficult not to sit open-mouthed as he realised its explosive nature.

Astakhov and Babarin, however, did not seem to be at all thrown, and took up the conversation in a lively and interested way, as Schnurre went through the various topics given to him by Ribbentrop. Astakhov spoke of the way Germany and the Soviet Union had collaborated in the past and of their common interests in foreign policy. Schnurre took his cue; such close collaboration, he said, could be achieved again, if the Soviet Union wanted it. He envisaged three stages. First, re-establishment of economic ties, through the trade and credit treaty they were already discussing. Second, normalising and improving general relations, which would include respecting each other's achievements and interests in the press, and working on public opinion. Astakhov's invitation to the Day of German Art in Munich, and his response in inviting German delegates to visit the Moscow Agricultural Exhibition, came under this heading. The third stage – and here he paused, because this was the nub of the whole discussion – was the full re-establishment of good political relations, either on the lines of the old Berlin Treaty of 1926, or a new arrangement which took account of the vital political interests of both countries.

So, it was out: Schnurre was suggesting a new political treaty. The Russians smiled encouragingly. Schnurre went on. This third stage, he said, appeared to him to be attainable, because 'there was no problem between the two countries anywhere from the Baltic to the Black Sea, and to the Far East, which could not be solved. No problem at all.'

It was an enormous claim, but Schnurre made it with complete confidence. To back it up, he added that in spite of their different ideologies, National Socialist Germany, fascist Italy and the Soviet Union had one thing in common: opposition to the capitalist democracies. It would, he said, be paradoxical for the Soviet Union as a socialist state to want to align itself with the Western democracies.

The Soviet representatives both agreed with what Schnurre had said, but Astakhov pointed out that although *rapprochement* was in the vital interests of both countries, the tempo might well be only slow and gradual – after all, the Soviet Union had felt threatened by Germany, especially since Munich. Moscow might find it difficult to believe in a shift of German policy towards her. It would take time.

This was the danger point: Ribbentrop had stressed in his instructions that time was short. Schnurre assured Astakhov that Germany's policy in the east had changed completely since the previous September – there could be no question now of her threatening the Soviet Union. He repeated that he envisaged a far-reaching arrangement of mutual interests with due consideration for vital Russian problems. However, this possibility would disappear the moment the Soviet Union signed a treaty with Britain, and aligned herself against Germany. What could Britain offer Russia? At best, participation in a European war, and the hostility of Germany, hardly a desirable end for Russia, surely?

What could Germany offer? Neutrality and keeping out of a possible European conflict, and, if Moscow wished, a German–Soviet understanding on mutual interests which, just as in former times, would work to the advantage of both countries – in other words, the carving-up of Europe between them.

The offer had been made. The main purpose of the dinner party had been achieved. The atmosphere became more relaxed, and more and more friendly. The conversation developed into a detailed discussion of all the possible points of conflict. The wine may have been flowing, the protestations of friendship may have been coming thick and fast, but Schnurre and the two Russians were all highly skilled professionals. They discussed everything from the Baltic to the Black Sea, and included the Far East and Japan, too. What were Germany's aims and intentions in Finland, the Baltic States, Romania? Did the Soviet Union not realise that the Anti-Comintern Pact was directed not against them, but against the Western Powers? What about Galicia and the Ukraine, did Germany have no ambitions there? Was Germany's friendship with Japan – whose troops were at that moment fighting Soviet troops in Outer Mongolia – really not aimed against the Soviet Union? The questions came thick and fast. Schnurre had answers for them all.

Astakhov asserted that Danzig would return to the Reich 'in one way or another', and that the Corridor question would also have to be solved somehow in favour of the Reich. But why, he asked as the discussion deepened, had National Socialism sought the antagonism of the Soviet Union in the field of foreign policy? In Moscow they had never quite been able to understand this. It was a penetrating and fundamental question, but Schnurre fielded it like a master. Ah, he said, that was something in the past, before the change that had occurred in Soviet bolshevism in recent years. That had been when the Nazis were fighting the German Communist Party, which was dependent on Moscow and was only a tool of the Comintern, the Communist International, which controlled local parties throughout the world. But now, the German Communist Party had been eradicated, and the Comintern was less important than the Politburo, the Soviet party's own inner Cabinet, which was conducting quite a different policy.

Schnurre was warming to his theme now. With complete seriousness he told his guests that 'the amalgamation of bolshevism with the national history of Russia, which found expression in the glorification of great Russian men and deeds' – he cited the Battle of Poltava, Peter the Great, the Battle of Lake Peipus, Alexander Nevski – had indeed in some measure changed the international face of bolshevism as the Germans saw it. This was particularly so since Stalin had postponed world revolution 'to the Greek calends' – that is indefinitely! Because of this, he concluded, the German government saw possibilities today which they had not seen earlier, provided, he added quickly, that there was no attempt made to conduct any form of communist propaganda in Germany.

The talk went on, through more and more brandy and cigars, until about 12.30 am. By then, not only had they dealt with all the political points, but they had discussed the trade and credit treaty in great detail. Schnurre never believed in wasting time, or an opportunity – his capacity for work was enormous, and it was matched by Astakhov and Babarin.

As they left, Astakhov promised to report what had been said to Moscow, telling Schnurre and Schmid how valuable the conversation had been to him. He had one final question before they parted.

'If a high-ranking Soviet personage,' he asked, 'discussed these questions with a high-ranking German personage, would the German put forward similar views?'

Schnurre's long face broke into a broad smile.

'Oh, yes,' he replied. 'Certainly.'

And on that note they walked out into the balmy Berlin night.

11

'A QUICK FAILURE, OR A SLOW ONE?'

Hitler was delighted by Schnurre's report of the positive way Astakhov had reacted to his proposals during the dinner party at Ewest's. He ordered that total secrecy must be maintained at all costs, until the time was right. To help camouflage his interest in the east, while Stalin considered his offer, he would divert attention in the opposite direction by leaving Bayreuth and visiting the West Wall, accompanied by Ribbentrop and Keitel. They would spend the weekend ostentatiously inspecting progress on construction of the fortifications which he had himself designed. There were times when even Wagner had to take second place.

For Chamberlain, meanwhile, it was the approaches to Germany that had to be kept secret, and the dealings with the Soviet Union that could be used as a smokescreen. Even here, however, he was showing a strange hesitancy: the British press on the morning of Thursday, 27 July, was full of confused reports on the military mission to Moscow, reflecting the government's indecision.

For twenty-four hours statements, counter-statements, denials and, as the *Daily Worker* put it, 'plain lies' had been pouring out of Downing Street and the Foreign Office. Early the previous morning, the news had been issued from No. 10 that British staff officers were to leave for Moscow 'within ten days'. By mid-afternoon, however, the Foreign Office was denying everything – such statements, it said, were 'premature and mischievous' – and Chamberlain rose in the House of Commons to disclaim the story which had originated from his own office. 'Everything depends,' he said, 'on the next conversations between the British and French representatives in Moscow and M. Molotov, the Soviet Premier.'

This was strange behaviour from the Prime Minister, since he had already officially confirmed the decision to Maisky and the French.

Perhaps one explanation was his continuing unwillingness to let the public into his confidence: the public were responding that day with an organised campaign of lobbying their Members of Parliament, demanding that the House should not rise for the summer recess until the Soviet pact was signed, a demand which Chamberlain chose to ignore.

In the Foreign Office, the Finnish minister, G. A. Gripenberg, was adding to the government's worries over the negotiations. He had called on Rab Butler, the Parliamentary Under-Secretary, whom he knew well, seeking reassurance. Gripenberg admired and trusted Butler, regarding the thirty-six-year-old intellectual as 'looming a head higher' than most other leading politicians.

Like his government back in Helsinki, Gripenberg was deeply worried. There were rumours flying around that Germany was about to do a deal with the Soviet Union, in which she would concede Finland and the Baltic states to the Soviets, though the Germans had denied this, calling the rumours 'propaganda fairy tales'. At the same time, it was well known that Britain was hoping to make a pact with the Soviet Union which might include the dreaded question of indirect aggression. As it was defined at present, almost anything that happened in Finnish political life could be interpreted as an indirect attack on the country's independence, which would justify the Soviet Union's intervention. Naturally, the Finns were alarmed at this prospect.

Butler replied in the same way as he had to the Swedish ambassador, who had spoken to him on Finland's behalf the day before. The British government, he said, would not approve any agreement that would conflict with Finland's interests as a neutral country.

'If we had abandoned Finland,' he said, 'the treaty would have been signed long ago.'

In any case, he told Gripenberg, the subject of indirect aggression had been shunted into the background for the time being. In spite of the press confusion, negotiations for a military agreement were about to begin.

The military negotiations, in fact, were occupying Chamberlain, Halifax and Wilson over in No. 10 at that moment. After a great deal of thought, they had found the solution to the knotty problem of who was to lead the mission to Moscow.

Admiral the Honourable Sir Reginald Aylmer Ranfurly Plunkett-Ernle-Erle-Drax, RN, was the very model of an admiral in His Britannic Majesty's Royal Navy, both in manner and in appearance. He looked and behaved like an illustration from a boys' adventure story of the thirties: he was tall, lean and elegant, with silvery hair, blue eyes, clean-cut manly features and a firm jaw; he spoke slowly and carefully, and cleared his throat a great deal by way of punctuation. To most foreigners, and many of his own countrymen, he represented all the traditions of England, in the highest degree.

He had been born in 1880 as plain Reginald Plunkett, the second son of John William Plunkett, heir to the Irish title Baron of Dunsany – his elder brother, who became the eighteenth Lord Dunsany, was a popular and witty writer of plays and fantasy stories. He changed his name by royal licence: after his mother's death, Captain Reginald Plunkett, RN, became at a stroke Captain Reginald Plunkett-Ernle-Erle-Drax. Ernle was his mother's first name, Erle was the first owner of Charborough, the beautiful seventeenth-century Dorset mansion which Reginald inherited from her; Drax was a later owner of the house. It is as Admiral Drax that he is now remembered.

He was promoted admiral in 1936 and on 1 April 1939 was made principal naval aide-de-camp to His Majesty King George VI. He was within a month of his sixtieth birthday when he received an urgent telephone call at Charborough from the Admiralty. Would he catch the first train to London? The Chief of Naval Staff wished to see him. The atmosphere in London on Friday, 28 July, was heavy with the threat of war. The headlines in *The Times* were ominous: 100,000 territorial soldiers under canvas in the New Forest . . . gas masks to be distributed to civilians . . . employers liable to heavy fines if they failed to provide air-raid shelters and ARP training for their staffs. One curious item which might have appealed to Drax, with its presaging of future technological developments, was a report on John Logie Baird's new television system, which he had demonstrated the previous day by televising a photograph of King George VI in 'natural' colour.

Drax made his way to the old Admiralty building in Whitehall and called on Admiral Sir Dudley Pound, as requested, in his dark, wood-panelled room. There, with Lord Nelson's good eye staring down at him from the portrait over the fireplace, Drax learned that he had been chosen to lead the combined British Military Mission to Moscow. They were to leave as soon as possible.

Drax was an unlikely choice. He had a reputation in the navy as an unorthodox thinker – intellectually, he was said to stand out from his brother officers – but it is hard to see how his previous experience fitted him for the job. However, Chamberlain had decided, no doubt for his own reasons, that Drax was exactly what he wanted. The representatives of the other services were to be Major-General T. G. G. Heywood for the army, and Air Marshal Sir Charles Stuart Burnett representing the Royal Air Force.

The Joint Planning Sub-Committee was hard at work, Drax was told, preparing the draft of his instructions, but it would not be ready before the weekend. All being well, the three Deputy Chiefs of Staff would approve it on Monday morning, ready for a meeting of the Committee of Imperial Defence in the afternoon.

* * *

Back in his own room at the Admiralty, Drax had an unexpected visitor, a short, stocky man wearing the smile of a benign uncle and a bowler hat which was too small for him, jammed on top of his head. His handshake was gentle. Only the dark, watchful eyes betrayed the toughness of his character. Drax knew him well, and called him by his nickname, 'Quex'.

Quex was in fact Admiral Sir Hugh Sinclair, otherwise 'C', the legendary chief of the Secret Service. He had come not to encourage the unlikely diplomat in his mission to Moscow but to point out the difficulties and problems that lay ahead. He began, in his deceptively gentle voice, by describing what had happened so far in the political talks.

'When they started,' he said, 'the Russians were here and the British were here.'

He held his hands about eighteen inches apart.

'Now, the Russians are here, and the British are here.'

His right hand, representing Russia, stayed still; his left hand, representing Britain, moved across to within two inches of the right. Drax gained the impression that Quex disapproved of the British flexibility towards the Soviet Union, which was hardly surprising: he had always regarded the Bolsheviks as the prime target for his organisation's activities, ever since he had taken over as 'C' in 1923. Only very recently had he been forced to start directing his agents against Nazi Germany.

As the conversation continued, it was clear to Drax that certain members of the government were not optimistic about the outcome of any negotiations with the Bolsheviks.

'It's an infernal shame,' Quex sympathised, 'that they should send you out to Moscow to try to clear up the mess that has been made there by the politicians.'

This was the first indication he had, Drax recalled later, that the political dimension was not quite as straightforward as he had believed. Everyone else, including the British press and politicians, appeared to think that the Russians, however unorthodox and difficult they might be, were eager to reach a satisfactory agreement with the British and French. They, in their turn, were supposed to be keen to stop Hitler. Now Quex was questioning this comfortable scenario, adding an entirely new dimension to his mission.

Across the Channel, as night fell in Paris, German Ambassador Count Johannes von Welczeck was receiving news from his spies that the French, too, had decided on the leader of their military mission. He was to be General Joseph Edward Doumenc, General Commanding the 1st Region, which comprised the *Départements* of Nord and Pas-de-Calais.

Although Doumenc was sixty years old, he was the youngest general in the French army. Like Heywood, the British army representative, he was an artilleryman. He was also an expert on tank warfare whose ideas had greatly influenced the young Charles de Gaulle. In the great war he had organised transport, been Deputy Chief of the General Staff under Weygand, and commanded the French 1st Division in the front line in Lille. As a product of the École Polytechnique, he was regarded as a brilliant soldier and an original military thinker.

Welczeck's spies also told him that the French government was very optimistic: they believed they could achieve both political and military treaties with the Soviets, and that the political talks were now making good progress. The ambassador had the information coded and cabled to Berlin immediately. It arrived in the Foreign Ministry at midnight.

Weizsäcker called Ribbentrop next day at Saarbrücken, during a break from the inspection of the West Wall, and gave him the report from Paris, together with the latest news from London and a message from Italy. Mussolini said he still favoured a conference on Danzig, but did not mind putting off doing anything about it for a while. He understood Hitler's problem, he said: the Führer wanted peaceful development, but had not yet made up his mind how to take the first step.

Peaceful development, in fact, was the last thing on Hitler's mind. What was concerning him was that the clock was ticking away towards the deadline for Operation White, and although it was now three days since the dinner party at Ewest's, there had been no response from Moscow. Ribbentrop had already telephoned Schnurre that morning to ask if he had heard anything – from the time he had called Schnurre to Fuschl right through until the pact was finally signed, he spoke to him at least once every day. The suspense was becoming unbearable for Hitler. It was time to stop holding back. He told Ribbentrop he wanted a pact with Stalin, and he wanted it signed within fourteen days.

A special courier was flown to Moscow with detailed instructions for Schulenburg – they were considered too secret and too delicate to be sent by wire, even in code. He also took him a copy of Schnurre's report on the dinner at Ewest's with a request that the ambassador should find out if there had been any response in Moscow to the proposals made to Astakhov. If he had an opportunity of talking to Molotov, he could sound him out personally and could also put the same ideas himself. If Molotov was receptive, Schulenburg could go further: he could put the generalised ideas expressed by Schnurre into more concrete form, and make firm proposals. In particular, he could offer the Soviet Union deals on Poland and the Baltic states.

Even while Schulenburg was digesting this staggering message, the impatient Ribbentrop was wiring another: 'Please report by telegram the date and time of your next interview with Molotov as soon as it is fixed. We are anxious for an early interview.'

* * *

Added pressure for a quick pact was again coming from Danzig, which could now be clearly seen as the detonator which would set off a much greater explosion. Hitler had told his Nazi Party Gauleiter in the city, Albert Forster, to keep things as calm as possible until he gave the order for action. Now, however, there was a danger of the situation running out of control.

Under the terms of the Treaty of Versailles, Danzig, although a free city, came under Polish customs control, an imposition that had always galled the predominantly German Danzigers. For some time, the Nazis had been harassing Polish frontier guards and customs officers, intensifying their hate campaign as the Poles steadily increased the number of officers in a vain attempt to stem the flow of smuggled German arms into the city. There had been more and more incidents as the summer of 1939 progressed. The Danzig police force, which was entirely German, had been increased from 3,000 to 4,000, supposedly to deal with these incidents, and 'to meet the menace of the Polish army'.

Beck threatened economic reprisals if the harassments continued. He told Arthur Greiser, President of the Danzig Senate, that he would ban imports to Poland of Danzig herrings and margarine, valuable revenue earners for the Free City. Greiser's response on Saturday, 29 July, was to announce that Danzig no longer recognised the Polish border guards or customs officers. He demanded their immediate withdrawal.

Greiser's note to Marjan Chodacki, the Polish diplomatic representative, was so offensive that Chodacki did not dare send it to Beck, but made a carefully worded report, giving the gist of it. But no matter how diplomatically he tried to wrap Greiser's demands, the implications were clear: by getting rid of Polish customs authority, the Nazis would be tearing up what remained of the Treaty of Versailles itself – and that would mean war.

Izvestia and *Pravda* observed the twenty-fifth anniversary of Russia's involvement in the first world war on Monday, 31 July, with articles and editorials. *Izvestia* made a great point of relating it to the present day, producing another clear signal to the Western democracies.

'The USSR,' it stated, 'has always stood for the establishment of a genuine peace front capable of halting the further development of fascist aggression, a peace front erected on a basis of full reciprocity, full equality, and honest, sincere and resolute repudiation of the fatal policy of "non-intervention".'

Was all this just empty rhetoric? Or was it a public plea to the British and French?

In the House of Commons that afternoon, Chamberlain at last confirmed that the mission would be leaving for Moscow, 'possibly this week', and gave the names of the three chosen officers. Maisky, looking down from the diplomats' gallery of the House, was immediately suspicious – in seven years as Soviet ambassador, he had never before heard Drax's name. When he checked up on him, he was not reassured. 'Even had one wished,' he stated later, 'it would have been difficult to find a candidate more unsuited to conduct negotiations with the USSR than this elderly British admiral.'

He was not much happier about the other members of the mission. In Maisky's opinion, Burnett and Heywood 'did not rise above the average level of the leading personnel in the British land forces'. If the three were absent from Whitehall for any length of time, it would not inconvenience the War Office, Air Ministry or Admiralty. Maisky concluded that the British intended to stay in Moscow 'indefinitely', a conclusion which seemed to be borne out by Chamberlain's statements in the angry debate which followed his announcement.

Chamberlain's opponents from all sides of the House waded in with violent criticism when he could not give them any information about progress in the political talks. Sir Archibald Sinclair, leader of the Liberals, spoke for many in both House and country when he expressed the fear that Chamberlain might try to pull off another appeasement coup while Parliament was dispersed for the summer recess. He demanded that 'a person of the highest political rank' should be sent to Moscow at once, plus an assurance from Chamberlain that he would not hold any conversations, official or unofficial, with the German or Italian governments without informing the other allies. Sinclair also wanted a definite declaration from the Prime Minister, drawing the line at aggression in Danzig, the Far East, or anywhere else.

From Chamberlain's own Conservative benches, Anthony Eden led the call for someone to be sent to Moscow with sufficient authority to deal direct with the Soviet government. Hugh Dalton, for the Labour Party, pressed again for Halifax himself to go to Moscow, or for a senior member of the Soviet government to be invited to London.

Chamberlain remained totally deaf to their pleas. Completely unperturbed, he reminded Members that it had taken six months to negotiate the Anglo-Japanese Alliance in 1903. The Anglo-French *Entente Cordiale* in 1904 had taken nine months. The Anglo-Russian Entente of 1907 had taken no less than fifteen months.

'The present negotiations with the USSR,' he said with a patronising smile, 'have been going on only four and a half months. What do you expect?'

As he finished, there was an enormous clap of thunder overhead. Lightning flashed. The heavens opened in a tremendous downpour. Within minutes, the ancient Westminster Hall alongside the chamber of the House of Commons was flooded with eighteen inches of water. It would be hard to imagine a more fitting comment on the proceedings.

*   *   *

In Paris, Prime Minister Daladier announced who was to accompany Doumenc to Moscow: the other members of the French mission were to be General Valin of the air force, and Captain de Corvette Willaume of the navy. The Soviet ambassador, Yakov Suritz, was hardly more impressed with them than Maisky was with the British team. They were all narrow specialists, he complained, obviously being sent for the purpose of discovering 'the conditions of our army'.

Oddly enough, the German military attachés in London thought much the same. Dirksen had reported to Berlin that there was 'a surprising scepticism' in British military circles about the mission. 'It is impossible,' he wrote in his airgram, 'to brush aside the impression that, on the British side, the talks are being conducted mainly to obtain for once a picture of the real fighting strength of the Soviet army . . . *None* of the three representatives of the services has had a training which specially qualifies him to negotiate on operational measures. All three gentlemen, however, are combatant officers, who consequently have a particularly well-trained eye for the fighting value of a unit and its equipment.'

In spite of the urgency of Ribbentrop's messages, Schulenburg could not get to talk to Molotov until after 1 August. The Soviet Prime Minister had an important domestic arrangement: he was at the opening of the first All-Union Agricultural Exhibition at Pashkinskoyi, a suburb of Moscow. Agriculture has always been vitally important to Russia, and the big show was a major event. There was no way Molotov and the rest of the Politburo could simply pay a courtesy visit – they had to see everything, though it would take all day.

The exhibition was built in the heart of pinewoods, its pavilions set among 17,000 specially planted trees. The site included villages from the past and present, carefully constructed to highlight the advantages of life in the modern socialist state. At its centre, 'Collective Farms Square' was bigger than Red Square itself. Around a large pool, bordered by a carpet of flowers, were pavilions housing some 80,000 exhibits showing the achievements of agriculture in the eleven Union republics. But the most important area was undoubtedly 'Mechanisation Square': it contained a monumental statue of Stalin, eighty-two feet high.

With such a counter-attraction, the diplomats in Moscow could do nothing but wait.

In Berlin, however, Astakhov had news, albeit unofficial. Because of Ribbentrop's obsession with secrecy within the Foreign Ministry itself, Schnurre had taken to meeting the Soviet chargé in the Tiergarten, where they would stroll along leafy paths discussing the situation informally, off the record. Only when there was a major advance did Astakhov come to the Wilhelmstrasse for an officially recorded meeting.

It was among the flowers and lakes of the Berlin park, therefore, amidst playing children and nodding elders, that on the morning of 1 August Astakhov told Schnurre that Molotov was interested in a political agreement. There were three conditions: anti-Soviet propaganda in the German press and radio must cease; there should be a new credit agreement; and the first two points must be settled before any political talks could begin. Schnurre assured him there would be no problems on any of these and on that note they parted.

Later in the day, Babarin called on Schnurre at his office. Calling himself 'Moscow's postman', he brought the latest Soviet proposals on the trade pact, which Schnurre was delighted to see contained further concessions on the essential elements of raw materials deliveries and interest payments. He was now convinced that they would be able to complete the agreement.

That day, Germany's annual air exercises began, the biggest ever held. At night, Berlin was blacked out, and searchlights probed the sky as 'raiders' tested the city's defences. The military and air attachés in the British embassy watched with interest, and some alarm. They had noticed recently that reservists were being called up for training, and not returning to their jobs. Everywhere, the signs of preparation for war were becoming more and more obvious.

Nevile Henderson had just returned to Berlin after an abortive trip to Bayreuth, where he had gone in the hope of contriving an informal, 'accidental' meeting with Hitler. He still believed he could persuade the German leader to recognise the inherent goodwill of the British government, particularly if he could catch him at a time when he was relaxing at the opera. Henderson could talk about Wagner with reasonable confidence: 'Though absolutely unmusical,' he admitted, 'I like Wagner.' As a student in Dresden, he had learnt by heart all the *leitmotifs* of *The Ring*. He had never forgotten them. More recently, he had seen the entire cycle twice in Berlin.

The trip had been a disaster from start to finish. His car broke down on the way there, and when he arrived, he found his quarry was away inspecting the West Wall. Winifred Wagner had taken pity on him and invited him to lunch – but it had been in Hitler's absence. And when Hitler did return, on the last day of Henderson's visit, he had studiously ignored him. The best Henderson had been able to manage was a distant glimpse of him in the opera house that night. He had to console himself with the pleasure of seeing a marvellous performance of *Die Walküre*.

Now, back in Berlin again, he sat down at his desk to write to London. Like many of his letters, this one was addressed privately to Halifax. 'My views in an official form might be embarrassing to you,' he wrote. 'I live on the other side of the Rhine, British internal politics are not my affair and if I may see too much of the other man's view, in England one may well see too little.'

Hitler's deliberate snub in refusing to see him had not diminished Henderson's regard for him. He believed the Poles should hand over Danzig, and that they were largely to blame for the threat of war. 'I regard it as essential,' he told Halifax, 'that the Poles, in their own ultimate interests, should be persuaded to be reasonable.' With so much pro-German advice from one of his most senior ambassadors, as well as from Wilson and Chamberlain himself, it is small wonder that Halifax was not inclined to woo the Soviet Union with very great ardour.

On that damp Tuesday in London, Halifax was concerning himself with the practicalities of the military mission. The Foreign Policy Committee met that morning under his chairmanship. High on the agenda was the question of actually getting the mission to Moscow.

Halifax had asked the French if they had any preferences and they had replied that they would most like to go by rail, since General Doumenc 'did not appear attracted' to the idea of flying. Under normal circumstances, the trip could certainly have been made by train, via Berlin and Warsaw – but these were far from normal circumstances. Halifax had consulted Henderson, who thought it would be 'unnecessarily provocative' for the mission to travel across Germany.

In spite of Doumenc's lack of enthusiasm, the idea of flying was discussed. No British or French commercial airline flew a regular route to the USSR, however, and it appeared that the only civil aircraft available were two old 'Hannibals' – which would have to land in Germany according to air regulations. In any case, another regulation forbade serving officers flying over Germany, and there was some question as to whether Soviet aviation fuel would be suitable for capitalist machines.

Sunderland flying boats could reach the Soviet Union via Denmark, flying outside territorial waters. But the British and French would each be taking about twenty advisers and assistants. It would take six or eight Sunderlands to carry the whole party, Lord Chatfield told the committee, and the aircraft were 'urgently required for Fleet exercises'. Wellington bombers could be made available, but they would mean a dreadfully uncomfortable journey, so it looked as though the mission would have to go by sea. Of course, that meant the journey would take longer, delaying the start of talks, but Chamberlain, when he was told, did not seem to mind.

'I do not think,' he said, 'that a difference of two days in the date of arrival will be very important.'

Molotov's reaction to the news was very different. Strang and the two ambassadors called on him on the Wednesday morning and gave him the names of the officers who would be coming, and the projected date for their arrival. He made no verbal comment – he did not need to. While Seeds read out the list, Molotov sat on his dais and stared frigidly over their heads, his contempt so obvious that Strang felt acutely embarrassed and wanted to look away.

Once Seeds had finished, Molotov launched into a biting attack on the British government. Why, he demanded, had R. A. Butler grossly misrepresented Soviet attitudes? He insisted that Butler, when winding up Monday's stormy debate in the House of Commons, had said the Soviet government wished to infringe the independence of the Baltic states, and that Britain's refusal to agree to this was the main reason for the delays in negotiation. This was not true, Molotov snapped. The Soviet Union in fact wished to guarantee that independence. What had caused the delays was the Soviet Union's insistence that the formula for 'indirect aggression' should leave no loophole for any aggressor to risk an attempt on the independence of the Baltic states.

Seeds desperately tried to explain that Butler had said nothing new, and made no accusations. But it was too late: Molotov refused to be placated.

'It is a gross misinterpretation of what we have in mind,' he lectured, shaking his finger at them. 'You appear to be deliberately misunderstanding us. Do you not trust the Soviet Union? Do you not think we are interested in security too? It is a grave mistake. In time, you will realise how great a mistake it is to distrust the government of the USSR.'

With that, he stood up abruptly and marched out through the open door into the next room. Strang and the two ambassadors left in a state of shock, completely exhausted. The fact that their talks had reached stalemate came not as a disappointment but as a relief – at least they could take a break now.

'Thank God,' said Naggiar as they drove out of the Kremlin, 'that fellow Molotov will not be taking part in the military negotiations!'

The report of Butler's speech had appeared that morning in *Izvestia*. It said exactly the same as Molotov had said to Seeds and Strang. Schulenburg, in the Soviet embassy, read it with delight as a clear signal that in spite of the forthcoming military talks, all was far from well in the Anglo-French negotiations. He picked up the telephone and put in a call to the Kremlin, to arrange a meeting with Molotov.

It was yet another rainy day in London. The members of the military mission assembled in the morning for a further briefing in Gwydyr House. After lunch, they squelched their way down Whitehall to the House of Lords for a conference with Halifax, Lord Chatfield, Minister for Defence Co-ordination, the three service ministers and assorted officers and officials. By now, the instructions for the mission had been printed in full, making a document about an inch thick, and these were explained at some length.

At the end of the conference, Halifax asked if everything was now clear. Recalling his chat with Quex Sinclair, Drax himself had a pertinent question.

'Suppose the whole exercise turns out to be a failure?' he asked. 'Suppose the British, French and Russians fail to find sufficient common ground to sign a military convention – which God forbid – would you prefer a quick failure, or a slow one? A quick conclusion and a prompt withdrawal would be more dignified, but there is the question of the weather in Poland to consider. Snow in October could make the prospect of a military campaign unattractive if not totally impracticable as far as the German army is concerned.'

There was a short but impressive silence. Then Halifax gave his reply: 'On the whole,' he said, 'it would be preferable to draw out the negotiations as long as possible.'

12

'FROM THE BALTIC TO THE BLACK SEA'

The attitude in Berlin now was very different. Schnurre wrote to Schulenburg on Wednesday, 2 August, telling him that 'the problem of Russia is being dealt with here with *extreme urgency*.' Ribbentrop, he said, was constantly exchanging views with Hitler. He wanted results as soon as possible, 'not only on the negative side (disturbing the British negotiations) but also on the positive side (an understanding with us)'.

Ribbentrop himself was back at his desk in the Foreign Ministry. The visit to the West Wall had not been a success – Hitler had been dismayed to see how far behind schedule the fortifications were. Since they were nowhere near ready to keep out anybody, he would have to rely on bluff, as he had done so often before, to persuade the French and everyone else that Germany was as strong as he claimed.

This made the need for an agreement with the Soviet Union even more urgent. When Astakhov called at the Wilhelmstrasse to see Weizsäcker that afternoon, Ribbentrop's hopes rose. When it turned out that he was there only to talk about the German delegates to the Agricultural Exhibition, the suspense became too much. The Foreign Minister, as casually as he could manage, invited him into his room for a chat, during which he clumsily contrived to give Astakhov the impression that he was in no hurry. Everything depended, he said, on Moscow, since Germany was favourably disposed to the Soviet Union. If Moscow took a negative attitude, the Germans would know where they stood and how to act. But if Moscow reacted positively – and here he paused, as he prepared to drop in the key phrase: 'There is no problem from the Baltic to the Black Sea that could not be solved between the two of us.'

Astakhov recognised Ribbentrop's new theme song instantly, but he was still bemused by the German Foreign Minister's ham-fisted attempts to sound casual. What exactly did he mean? he asked.

'There is room for the two of us on the Baltic,' Ribbentrop told him. 'Russian interests there by no means need to clash with ours.'

Astakhov tried again to pin him down to something more precise, but soon realised he was getting nowhere. He switched the conversation to Poland, asking what were Germany's intentions there.

'As far as Poland is concerned,' Ribbentrop replied, 'we're watching further developments attentively, and ice cold. In the event of Polish provocation, we will settle accounts with them in the space of a week.' He then proceeded, as he later informed Schulenburg, to 'drop a gentle hint at our coming to an understanding with Russia on the fate of Poland'. Astakhov pressed on, trying to get Ribbentrop to say something more definite. All he managed to get, however, was an assurance that Ribbentrop would be prepared to make his offers more concrete as soon as the Soviet government told him officially they were interested in a deal with Germany.

Still bewildered by his meeting with Ribbentrop, Astakhov called Schnurre early next morning and arranged a meeting, arriving in Schnurre's office at 12.30. First, they talked about the trade negotiations. Schnurre proposed that they should include a political element in the preamble to any agreement, or failing this in a secret protocol, an idea which Astakhov liked. Then the Soviet chargé turned to his meeting with Ribbentrop. Most of what the Foreign Minister had said tied in with what Schnurre had previously told him, but there was one puzzling aspect: Schnurre had stressed the urgency of the situation, but Ribbentrop did not seem to care about time.

Schnurre sighed and tried to explain. Never mind what Ribbentrop had said, he told the Russian, they really did want to get things moving in the next few days; Schulenburg, who was seeing Molotov later that day, had been told everything, and would confirm it all to the Soviet Premier. Because of the time element, however, the real talking would be better done in Berlin. Astakhov agreed. Assuring Schnurre that he was keeping their talks strictly secret and not even telling anybody in his own embassy, he said he was dealing direct with Molotov. He would telegraph this latest information to him immediately.

While the Germans were speeding up their efforts to reach an agreement with the Soviet Union, Halifax was considering Seeds's agonised message describing the last meeting with Molotov and asking for instructions. His reply was short and to the point: 'I shall not be replying in any detail to urgent points dealt with in your telegram for some days.' He was busy preparing to go north to his estate in Yorkshire – there were only nine days left before the shooting season started and there was a great deal to be attended to.

Chamberlain was also packing his bags, though he would not leave until the next day for his fishing trip in Scotland. The House of

Commons was being troublesome again: Churchill and Greenwood, having failed to get the start of the recess changed from 4 August, were now trying to get the date of reassembly brought forward. They wanted the House to return on 21 August instead of the amazingly distant 3 October which the government had decreed. Churchill spoke with his usual vigour: was this the moment, he demanded, for Parliament to separate for two whole months? It would be quite wrong, he went on, 'for the government to say to the house, "Begone! Run off and play. Take your masks with you. Do not worry about public affairs. Leave them to the gifted and experienced ministers," who, after all, so far as our defences are concerned, landed us where we were landed in September of last year, and who, after all – I make all allowances for the many difficulties – have brought us in foreign policy at this moment to the point where we have guaranteed Poland and Romania, after having lost Czechoslovakia, and not having gained Russia.'

But it was no use. Chamberlain cracked the party whip and declared that a vote for an early return would be a vote of no confidence in his leadership. The motion failed – to the great relief of Henderson in Berlin, who commented: 'The proceedings in Parliament do not help the temperature in Europe to fall and to my mind that is what is above all needed at this moment.'

What Chamberlain still thought was needed at that moment was an agreement with Hitler, which would be as close an alliance as the Anglo-French *Entente Cordiale*. Horace Wilson, acting on the Prime Minister's orders, invited German Ambassador Dirksen to call at his house, asking him to come on foot in order to avoid attracting attention.

Sitting comfortably in flowered chintz-covered armchairs in the quiet Kensington drawing room, Wilson repeated the offer of a deal which he had proposed to Wohlthat a few days before. What Chamberlain was offering, he said, was a 'full-bodied political world partnership' between Britain and Germany. If Hitler agreed the terms, then Britain would put pressure on the Poles over Danzig and the Corridor. Germany would get what she wanted, and Britain would be freed from her guarantee to Poland.

As Chamberlain's holiday was about to begin, Hitler's was ending. He had watched the final performance of *Götterdämmerung* the previous night. Before he left, however, there was one piece of private business to be attended to. He had invited his old schoolfriend, August Kubizek, to the festival, but had not yet spoken to him. Kubizek had been his closest companion – perhaps the only really close friend he ever had – during his days in Linz and Vienna, but they had not seen each other since Hitler had walked out of their shared room in September 1908, without leaving a message. An SS man was sent to escort Kubizek to Haus Wahnfried. When they stood face to face again, Hitler grasped

Kubizek's right hand in both of his. Kubizek could hardly speak. They ate lunch together with Winifred Wagner and as they talked over old times, Kubizek reminded Hitler of a certain November night in 1906, when the two of them had watched Wagner's early opera, *Rienzi*, in Linz.

Hitler's face lit up. He turned to Winifred and told her, 'That was when it all began!' His eyes sparkled as he recalled the whole story for her. He had been electrified by the opera, he said, the tale of an unknown young notary in fourteenth-century Rome, who had risen from the midst of the oppressed plebs, rallied and roused them and led them to liberty, becoming dictator of the city. He and Kubizek had left the opera house long after midnight to walk the deserted streets in a state of euphoria. On a hill outside the town, Hitler's emotions had overflowed. He had suddenly seized Kubizek's hands and declared that one day he would lead his own people out of subjugation, to the pinnacles of freedom. Sending his friend home, he had spent the night in the open, alone with his dreams. The fire that had started in his soul that night, he said, had never left him – it burned as brightly as though it were only yesterday.

After lunch, Hitler signed a pile of postcard photographs which Kubizek had brought for people back home in Austria, then he carefully removed his reading glasses and led his former friend out into the garden, to stand beside Wagner's tomb.

'I am happy,' he told him, 'that we have met once more on this spot, which has always been the most venerable place for both of us.'

That afternoon, filled with the emotional charge of ten days of Wagner topped off with such a potent reminder of the roots of his ambition, Hitler left Bayreuth. He drove south to Nuremberg, to inspect the arena and the preparations for the annual party rally, which was due to start in a month's time and which he had decreed was to be called this year 'The Party Day of Peace'. But there were now only nine days to the deadline for his decision on the invasion of Poland, and war.

At 8.30 that evening, Schulenburg and Hilger were shown in to Molotov's room in the Kremlin. To their surprise, the Soviet Premier greeted them warmly, the stony reserve was gone, and in its place was a friendly openness. They talked easily and frankly together for a full hour and a half.

Schulenburg started by saying the economic talks seemed to be going well in Berlin, and his government expected an early conclusion. Then he confirmed what Schnurre had told Astakhov at Ewest's. He finished, as instructed, with the key phrase: 'From the Baltic to the Black Sea there are no problems between Germany and the Soviet Union which cannot be solved.'

Molotov reacted cautiously. He agreed that an economic agreement was likely and said he was pleased with the start that had been made on resuming cultural relations. But he was less certain about a political deal. He reminded Schulenburg about the Anti-Comintern Pact, about Germany's support for Japan, and about the way the Soviet Union had been excluded from Munich. These showed, he said, that it was the fault of Germany, not the Soviet Union, that political relations had deteriorated so badly.

For a while, they fenced with each other, an art in which they were both highly skilled. Schulenburg hinted at a deal over the Baltic states; Molotov showed interest, and asked if that included Lithuania. He showed even more interest when Schulenburg talked about coming to an understanding about Poland, and said he would inform his government.

It had been a quite successful meeting. Schulenburg left convinced that the Soviet government wanted improved relations with Germany, but still believing they were determined to sign a pact with Britain and France, even though it might take some time. He knew he had made a good impression on Molotov, but he also knew it would take more than good impressions to swing Stalin to Germany's side.

Having completed his tour of the Nuremberg arena on 4 August, Hitler drove down the autobahn to Munich. In his private apartment there, he freshened up after his journey, changed into a dark blue suit, and received General Keitel and his staff officer Major Bernhard von Lossberg in the cavernous drawing room.

Although the apartment was dark and gloomy, Hitler had a great affection for it – it had been his home longer than any of his other residences. He had first moved in to the second floor of the big stone building on the corner of Prinzregentenplatz in September 1929, renting it from a merchant called Hugo Schühle. He needed room for his growing library, he said. There should certainly have been enough space, for it had nine rooms, plus two kitchens, two storage rooms and two bathrooms – a marked improvement on his previous home, a tiny two-roomed apartment on Thierschstrasse, handy for the *Völkischer Beobachter* printing works. Over the years, he had gradually acquired other parts of the building – in 1935 he bought the other apartment on the second floor, and knocked the two into one – and now he personally owned the whole place. His adjutants were housed on the floor beneath him, and his RSD, Reich Security Service, guard was in the left-hand apartment on the ground floor. There were fourteen RSD men permanently assigned to guard duties at 16 Prinzregentenplatz, working in two shifts of seven men including one permanently stationed on the roof.

The furniture and decoration of the apartment were severe and monumental. On the floor was thick, dull red carpet. Illumination was mainly from tall standard lamps. On the walls were paintings – none of them modern, of course – which he had bought with his book royalties, all by German artists, interspersed with prints of Palladian architecture. In his study, to give him strength and inspiration, was an Albrecht Dürer engraving of 'The Knight, Death and the Devil'.

At one end of the hallway there was a permanently locked room. This was where Hitler's niece and lover, Geli Raubal, had shot herself in 1931. Hitler kept it, as he did her room at the Berghof, exactly as she had left it.

Keitel and Lossberg had brought the final timetable for 'White': the invasion of Poland was set for 25 August, exactly three weeks ahead. The OKW planners reckoned that was the latest safe date – after that, there was a danger that the rains which normally came in mid-September would bog down the Panzers in a sea of mud and also hamper Luftwaffe operations.

Hitler invited his guests to make themselves comfortable in easy chairs while he explained to them exactly why he had to deal with the Poles then. He was affable and relaxed, and Lossberg was surprised to hear him lapse into his native Austrian dialect. It was all the fault of Chamberlain and the British, he told them: if they had not given Beck their stupid guarantees, the Poles would not be resisting so strongly. As it was, the British and French were too far behind Germany in rearming their forces to be able to give Poland any real help – even if they truly wanted to. The result would be the same as in March, when the Wehrmacht had marched into Prague.

'The gentlemen in London and Paris won't undertake anything against us this time, either,' he said. Then his voice changed into the familiar, strident tones. 'I will see to that. This Polish conflict will never, never, never result in a European war!'

Early on Friday, 4 August, Quex Sinclair called on Admiral Drax again. He suggested that in view of the importance and great difficulty of the forthcoming work of the mission, it might be desirable if Drax had a chat with the Prime Minister before sailing to Russia next day. The invitation obviously came from Chamberlain himself. It was typical of his fondness for backstairs politics that he should bypass his own Foreign Secretary and secretly brief the official emissary.

As it happened, Drax could not go to Downing Street until late afternoon – he had two official engagements to fulfil before then, the first with Ivan Maisky. Maisky had decided to give a luncheon for the members of the military mission in the Soviet embassy at 13 Kensington Palace Gardens, a wonderfully Gothic Victorian pile, complete with turrets and castellations, set back from the wide, tree-lined private road known to Londoners as 'Millionaires' Row'. 'However disappointed I was in the composition of the mission,' he wrote later, 'diplomatic politeness required such a gesture on my part. Moreover, I wanted to have a personal talk with the delegates.'

The luncheon was held in the former conservatory of the embassy, a glass construction at the rear of the building. It looked out on the left towards the Peter Pan statue in Kensington Gardens, and on the right to the grounds of Queen Victoria's birthplace, London's most elegant royal palace, where news of the eighteen-year-old princess's accession to the throne had been brought to her in the middle of the night in 1837.

Unfortunately, the French would not arrive in London until that afternoon, so Maisky had to make do with Drax, Heywood and Burnett. From the Soviet side there were the military, naval and air attachés and senior members of the Trade Delegation. Drax, as the senior guest, was placed on Maisky's right. Over coffee, the ambassador turned to him. 'Tell me, Admiral,' he asked, 'when are you leaving for Moscow?'

'It has not yet been finally decided, but in the next few days.'

'You are flying, of course? There is not much time. The situation in Europe is very tense.'

'Oh, no,' Drax replied, calmly. 'There are about forty of us in the two delegations, if you count the technical staff. And we have a lot of baggage. It would not be convenient to go by plane.'

'Well, if it isn't suitable by plane,' Maisky continued, 'I hope you are going to the Soviet Union in one of your fast cruisers. It would be very much in style and very impressive: military delegations on a warship. And it would not take much time from London to Leningrad.'

Drax started to look sour.

'No,' he said, 'a cruiser wouldn't be suitable either. If we were to go by cruiser, it would mean depriving a couple of dozen of its officers of their cabins. Why should we put people to such inconvenience? No, we won't be going by cruiser.'

'But in that event,' Maisky asked, 'perhaps you will take one of your fast-going commercial vessels? I repeat this is a very urgent moment. You ought to be in Moscow as quickly as possible!'

Drax was obviously unwilling to continue the conversation any further. He replied with utter finality: 'Really, I can't tell you definitely. The Board of Trade is organising the transport. Everything is in its hands. I don't know what is going to happen.'

What was going to happen, in fact, was that the missions were to depart the very next day from Tilbury, on board an elderly cargo and passenger steamer called the *City of Exeter*. In early August, passenger ships were in short supply – it was the best the Board of Trade could manage in the time.

After the luncheon in the Soviet conservatory, with the rain falling depressingly on the glass, Drax took his team to Victoria Station, to meet their French colleagues off the boat train. The Frenchmen had left Paris that morning to grave predictions in the press. The newspaper *Ordre*, which was generally accepted as having close contacts with military circles, declared on its front page that 'competent circles in Paris seem to expect a German initiative which would oblige the French government to take widespread mobilisation steps in the second half of August'. The French general staff, it appeared, were openly predicting that Hitler would be on the move with fresh aggressions within the next three weeks. The French Prime Minister, the Radical Socialist Édouard Daladier, agreed with his general staff. His briefing of Doumenc had been very much to the point.

Like so much of the politics of France during the thirties, Daladier's political stance was confusing – the labels no longer matched the contents of the packets. Although he called himself a Radical, he was anti-communist and anti-leftist; at the same time, like most of his party, he was also anti-fascist and feared the dictators on France's eastern frontiers. Yet both he and his party starved the French army of money for rearmaments and reorganisation.

Daladier came from good peasant stock. He was the second son of a baker from the small town of Carpentras, near Orange, in Provence. A clever child, he won a scholarship at the age of ten to a secondary school in Lyons, and from then on he never looked back. Like so many clever children from poor families, in a desperate search for social standing he turned to teaching as a profession. But politics attracted him, too, and in 1912 he was elected mayor of his home town.

Called up at the beginning of 1914, he spent the next four years in the trenches, where he rose from the ranks to become captain of a company. He was mentioned in despatches several times and was also awarded the Cross of the Legion of Honour. More to the point, he survived the holocaust of Verdun, where in a few short weeks he saw the flower of the French army destroyed and a little later, at Châlons, experienced at first hand the effects of a gas attack. Although he escaped with no lasting physical damage, the whole experience left him with a profound horror of war and a belief that nothing was worth slaughter on such a scale.

In 1919, at the age of thirty-five, he was elected to the Chamber of Deputies, and soon people in the Radical Party were talking of him as a potential minister. Indeed, over the next few years he held several ministerial appointments, including that of Minister for War. In 1933 he was invited to form his first government, and thus joined that curious barn dance of French pre-war politics, when governments rose and fell and political parties changed partners with almost monotonous frequency.

Oddly enough, Daladier's great historical hero was not a Frenchman, not Napoleon or Louis XIV, but a Dutchman – William of Orange, sometimes called 'The Silent'. Daladier admired his style and seems to have tried to model himself on the man. 'He never spoke but in earnest,' he once said, 'thus avoiding the disillusions that inevitably follow easy popularities. He had an intense inner life, by which he gained the strength to dominate the anger of men and the changes of fortune.' Alas, Daladier the history teacher was never able to live up to his hero.

Well-meaning, intelligent and – unusually for French politicians of the period – totally incorruptible, Daladier always promised more than he was capable of delivering. Many of his contemporaries regarded him as the strong man of French politics, calling him 'The Bull from the Vaucluse' – the electoral district he represented. But, as an unkind political enemy put it, he was a bull 'with the horns of a snail'.

Daladier was not a man who inspired admiration, particularly among the foreign press. 'A velvet hand in an iron glove' and 'a dirty man with a cigarette stuck to his lower lip, stinking of absinthe' were just two of the less than flattering views held of him. Harold Nicolson, the English writer and diplomat, described him as looking 'like a drunken peasant', and it is true that after the death of his wife he turned to the bottle more and more for consolation. His real failing, however, was an inability or unwillingness to make decisions.

Daladier remains a curiously grey and forlorn figure, like the Dutch boy with his finger in the dyke. Politically and by personal inclination he was a man of the wavering centre, the elected representative of the 'don't knows', who felt they could rely on him not to know either and to react accordingly.

Yet Daladier was at least clear on one matter: above all, he saw the desperate necessity of a political and military agreement with the USSR. His instructions to General Doumenc were a model of clarity: 'Bring us back an accord – at any price.' Anything, even a pact with the devil himself, would be better than a second world war. Doumenc had no doubt as to what his government expected of him, and he was determined to make every effort to achieve the goal.

Drax and Quex Sinclair saw Chamberlain at 4.30 that afternoon at 10 Downing Street, having settled the Frenchmen in their hotel. They found him worried and uneasy. The Russian situation had got out of hand, he felt. Ever since Munich, both Churchill and Lloyd George had been putting pressure on him in Parliament and in the country, wanting him to come to an accord with the USSR, simply as a means of constraining Hitler's territorial ambitions. Like the French, they wanted to fence Germany in with pacts. But a pact with Russia was the last thing Chamberlain actually wanted. He still did not trust the Russians, nor did he believe – as he had told the Foreign Policy Committee – that the Soviet government really desired an agreement. The House of Commons, he complained to Drax, had pushed him further than he wished to go. It was on that note that the British mission was sent to Moscow.

* * *

In his room in the Foreign Office overlooking St James's Park, Halifax also briefed a British delegation that day, the six businessmen, led by Charles F. Spencer, who were going to Germany to talk to Göring, as arranged by Birger Dahlerus. They, too, would be leaving next day, each man travelling separately and secretly by different routes to Hamburg, where Dahlerus would meet them. Halifax's briefing was more enthusiastic than the Prime Minister's to Drax. He told Spencer the line they should follow: although Britain would stand by the guarantee to Poland, and would go to war if necessary, the British government was still more than willing to talk and to listen.

In Britain it was the start of the August Bank Holiday weekend. At last, the rain had stopped and the sun was shining for the first time in weeks. After an early lunch, the British and French delegations made their way to Cannon Street station, where a specially chartered LNER train waited to take them to Tilbury Docks. Among those on the platform to see them off was Ivan Maisky. With his ready smile flashing at the battery of cameras, he looked for all the world like a successful Jewish banker seeing his family off on their holidays.

The train left at 2.50 pm. A little over half an hour before, the Imperial Airways flying boat *Caribou* had taken off from Southampton Water, on the inaugural flight of the new British transatlantic airmail service. After mid-air refuelling above Foynes, Eire, the flying boat was due to complete the 2,370 mile flight to Newfoundland at 11.0 am local time next day. It would then fly on to Montreal and New York. Even after a three-day stopover in New York, the *Caribou* would be back in Southampton before the military mission reached Moscow.

From Cannon Street to Tilbury is a little over twenty miles. The normal travelling time is about half an hour, but because of the bank holiday, crowds of Londoners were making their way to the seaside resorts on the Essex coast and extra trains had been laid on to cope with the additional traffic. Delays were inevitable, and inevitably the VIPs' train was delayed. They arrived at Tilbury at 4.30 pm, over an hour later than expected, where they were greeted by yet more cameras, yet more pressmen.

But the saga of set-backs was not yet over. It had been agreed with the Russians that the mission would arrive in Leningrad on Wednesday, 9 August, to catch the train to Moscow. When Drax checked this schedule with the master of the *City of Exeter*, Captain Radcliffe, he was horrified to learn that because the vessel was only capable of a maximum speed of thirteen knots, there was little chance of reaching Leningrad before 10 August.

13

SLOW BOAT TO MOSCOW

With the political talks between Britain, France and the Soviet Union firmly aground and unlikely to be floated again for some time, there seemed little point in Strang's staying on in Moscow. Claiming that a great deal of work had accumulated for him in London, he made his farewells and packed his bags over the weekend of 5 and 6 August. On the morning of Monday, 7 August, he and Frank Roberts climbed aboard the regular Swedish airliner, a twelve-seater, three-engined JU 52, for the seven-hour flight to Stockholm via Riga.

The next morning they flew on to London. As their aircraft sped southwards, it crossed the route of the *City of Exeter*, steaming slowly north – indeed, had they looked out of the window at the right moment, they might even have been able to see the grey hull, white superstructure and tall, single smokestack ringed in black, white and buff, of the elderly vessel carrying the military mission across the still, calm waters.

The *City of Exeter* was not a large ship, but she was comfortable and solid. The five-day voyage from Tilbury to Leningrad passed uneventfully, giving the two delegations a chance to get to know each other. One of the French party, Captain André Beaufre, wrote later that life aboard was 'very agreeable, punctuated by copious repasts of curry, served by Indian stewards in turbans'.

Beaufre also recorded his impressions of the senior British officers. In spite of his bluff, beefy appearance – another observer likened him to 'a monocled John Bull' – Major-General Heywood impressed Beaufre favourably. He described him as 'extremely diplomatic and able', and said 'he possessed all the finer points required in the diplomatic art of negotiation and he played a considerable role in the discussions.' As far as the French were concerned, Heywood enjoyed the inestimable advantage of having been born in France and of speaking perfect French. Some of them remembered him, too, from his four years as military attaché in Paris.

They were less sure of Air Marshal Sir Charles Burnett. Beaufre thought him 'a traditional figure . . . the military type made popular in France by Colonel Bramble [the hero of a novel by André Maurois] and found also in hunting prints. He never agreed to any proposition that was put forward until he understood it thoroughly, and this occasionally took some time.'

For Admiral Drax, however, Beaufre reserved his most lyrical description. He admired him as a man, seeing in him a perfect English officer and gentleman *sans peur, sans reproche*, and wrote about him with a kind of awed disbelief, as though he were a medieval cathedral made fragile by the depredations of death-watch beetle, which might collapse at any moment.

But Beaufre's comments on this perfect English gentleman's ability to lead the British delegation were decidedly double-edged: 'Not very quick on the uptake because of his scrupulous mind, he possessed utter intellectual honesty and the will to negotiate with the Soviets in all frankness, but was baffled by the complexities of the task which had been thrust upon him.'

The French were not encouraged by the British approach on tactics. They were alarmed by reading the British delegation's instructions, contained in the inch-thick document presented to Drax in London, which according to Beaufre 'examined every facet of the problem without producing any ideas as to directive'. These bore out precisely what Halifax had told Drax. 'It was recommended,' wrote Beaufre, 'that we should proceed only with the utmost prudence, never pass over any information, bear in mind constantly that German–Soviet collusion was possible, and above all to spin out the negotiations as long as we could. It appears that the British had no illusions as to the outcome of the conversations which they were about to open, and that they were above all anxious to gain time.'

The only member of either delegation who had any experience of the Soviet Union, or who spoke any Russian, was Burnett's RAF aide, Group Captain (later Air Marshal Sir Conrad) Collier. Collier had been in Archangel in 1919–20, during the Allied Intervention, when he had found himself governing an area the size of England and Wales and had developed an abiding affection for the country and its people. He had also been air attaché in Moscow from 1934 to 1937, and spoke the language fluently. Schulenburg noted with interest that Collier was among the delegation, describing him approvingly as 'a very sober and quiet man [who] knows Soviet conditions well'.

Unfortunately for the Allies, Drax did not attach as much importance to Collier's experience and expertise as did the German ambassador. Collier recalls how the admiral insisted on twice-daily conferences during the voyage, to discuss agendas and tactics, and even to produce a draft text which could provide a basis for the possible Anglo-French–Soviet military treaty.

The shipboard conferences were held in what was normally the children's playroom, a venue which Collier considered very apt. In his opinion, the whole business was a waste of time, and everyone would have been much better employed playing deck tennis and enjoying the glorious weather. Collier knew the Russians. He liked them, but had no illusions that they were easy to negotiate with, or that they could be diverted from their objective by diplomatic casuistries. They had invited the British and French to Moscow to discuss what the Russians wanted to discuss, and not what Drax and Doumenc thought they should.

In the event, Collier was proved right: none of the work done on board the *City of Exeter* bore fruit in Moscow, and the draft treaty never even saw the light of day. But the delegates did find time to enjoy some deck tennis. They even organised a tournament, which was eventually won by Admiral Drax himself, defeating the ship's first officer in a closely contested final.

The sea was as calm as a lake, mirroring the pale, clear Nordic sky, when the port of Kronstadt appeared on the *City of Exeter*'s starboard bow at 8.30 pm on Wednesday 9 August. Soon, the ship was surrounded by a flotilla of small Soviet craft, which shepherded her towards the opening of the long canal leading to Leningrad. At 1 o'clock the following morning, after their last curry dinner, the two delegations – the British senior officers in full mess kit – leaned on the ship's rail and watched the business of docking, and the start of unloading their nine tons of baggage. There were no excited crowds on the Leningrad quayside, only a few expressionless Russian soldiers in green caps.

Before landing, the delegations burned most of their notes. Their few remaining papers, including the draft treaty, were locked in a steel box and placed in the charge of two Royal Marines. Quex Sinclair had impressed on Drax the importance of security, and he was taking no chances. The Russians, he believed, were masters of espionage and from now on the delegates must expect their every move to be closely watched.

The reception for the mission in Leningrad, Schulenburg was pleased to note, was 'on a small scale'. There was no guard of honour when they disembarked next morning, to be met by the Chief of Staff of the Leningrad Military District, General Chibisov, accompanied by a handful of Soviet military officers, and the French and British military attachés. They spent the day sightseeing in Leningrad, then boarded the Red Arrow overnight express for Moscow, where they arrived next morning.

When they left the comfortable old train, its coach roofs peppered with pointed chimneys like a string of venerable chicken houses, they were again accorded no grand welcome. No band played, no guard of honour saluted. They were left to tramp the dusty length of the open wooden platform of Moscow's Leningrad station without escort, led by Drax in a knee-length admiral's frock coat, his medals and decorations glinting on his breast, stepping out at a brisk pace to the front hall of the station. There, they were treated to a desultory greeting from the Deputy Chief of the Soviet General Staff, Lieutenant-General Smorodinov, several lesser Soviet officers, Chief of Protocol Barkov, junior staff from the British and French embassies, and, for some odd reason, the Turkish military attaché, Lieutenant-Colonel Türkmen. The British and French ambassadors, following the rule of protocol for such occasions, waited at their respective embassies.

The fact that there was no guard of honour, and 'no high-ranking military personages', was reported to Berlin by Schulenburg at 5.20 that afternoon. To him, the scale of the initial reception was highly significant, boding well for his hopes of a German deal with Stalin.

It had been a busy day for Schulenburg – the report was his third signal to Berlin that afternoon. He had first been able to send what appeared to be extremely valuable information on the British line for the talks, thoughtfully passed to the Germans by the Italian military attaché, who had discussed it in great detail with Firebrace, his British opposite number. According to this, the main British argument would be that in the coming war Germany would do nothing in the West, but that German troops would overrun Poland in one or two months, and would then be on the Soviet frontier. At this point, Hitler would offer the Western Powers a separate peace, in return for a free hand to advance in the east. If the Soviet Union did not make a pact now with Britain and France for protection against German attack, it would be too late.

Equally valuable to Ribbentrop and Hitler was the information in Schulenburg's second signal. This said that American travellers on the Trans-Siberian railway all talked of seeing war material and troops being transported eastwards from the Urals towards the fighting on the Mongolian–Manchurian border. From this, the American, and also the Japanese, embassies deduced that Soviet reinforcements for further battles against the Japanese were being drawn from the western Siberian and eastern European areas, and that therefore Stalin did not expect trouble on his western front. To Schulenburg, and indeed to his leaders back home, this could be taken as yet another indication that Stalin was seriously interested in a deal with them.

The British and French delegations quickly settled into their quarters in Moscow – Drax stayed at the embassy with Sir William Seeds and his wife, the other delegates were accommodated in various diplomats' apartments, and at a hotel nearby. Group Captain Collier was lucky enough to be able to take over his own old apartment, where he had lived during his time as air attaché, and to have his chief, Air Marshal Burnett, in with him. There, he would at least be able to advise Burnett in depth, and perhaps exert a little influence.

In the afternoon, while Schulenburg was drafting his messages to Berlin, Ambassadors Seeds and Naggiar took Drax and Doumenc to the Kremlin to be received by Molotov and his Vice-Commissar for Foreign Affairs, Vladimir Potemkin. The meeting was stiff and formal, a matter of protocol rather than pleasure. Molotov said little, and his visitors were glad to leave as quickly as decency allowed. They moved on to the Defence Commissariat, where the welcome was much warmer from the Commissar, Marshal Voroshilov, and his Chief of Staff, General Boris Shaposhnikov, a former tsarist officer whose lectures while head of the Frunze Military Academy were said to have been attended by Stalin and Molotov. According to Seeds, Voroshilov, whom he had not met before, 'gave a most favourable impression, both of friendliness and energy. He seemed really pleased to meet the mission.' Voroshilov would be heading the Soviet delegation to the talks, and it was agreed that the first session should begin at the Spiridonovka Palace in the Kremlin the following day.

Marshal Kliment Yefremovich Voroshilov was one of the six most important figures in the entire USSR. He had been appointed Commissar for War in November 1925, and elected to the Politburo in early 1926. His title had been changed to Commissar for Defence in 1934. He was a personal friend of Stalin – if 'friend' is the right word to describe anyone close to the Party Secretary. Certainly, they went hunting together, took holidays together at Sochi on the Black Sea, and were frequently seen in each other's company.

Born in 1881 in the Ukraine, the son of a retired railway track worker and a washerwoman, Voroshilov came from a poor and illiterate family. At the age of eight he started work as a herdsboy, and seems to have spent only two terms at primary school, where he learned to read and write. This lack of a formal education was carried through into his military career, for although he rose to become one of the first marshals of the Red Army, he never received any conventional military training. Unlike many other senior officers, he had never served in the tsarist army, and as a result was often looked down on by the likes of Marshal Tukhachevsky, who once loftily observed that Voroshilov was 'not very clever, but he has at least the virtue of not trying to be clever'.

Unlike Tukhachevsky, Voroshilov survived the purges during the 1936–8 period. Although he does not appear to have been responsible for actually drawing up the lists of those officers to be arrested and shot, he certainly signed them, along with Stalin and Yezhov, then head of the GPU (which later became the KGB). One of the first to die was

Tukhachevsky – Voroshilov may well have found a certain grim pleasure in signing his death warrant.

Voroshilov's military reputation was based less on his ability as a strategist than on his legendary bravery under fire during the Civil War. Indeed, during the late 1920s, something of a personality cult grew up around him, and he was hailed as the archetypal 'worker-commander'. It says much for his talent for survival that this did not bring the wrath of Stalin on his head, although it was said he spent more time posing in the studio of Stalin's 'court' painter Gerasimov than he did attending to his job as commissar.

The delegates of the Anglo-French mission found him correct and businesslike in negotiations, and whatever his limitations may have been as a soldier, he dominated the conference, proving to be an adept tactician and a master of procedural matters. When they mingled socially, they found him charming and extremely good company, in spite of the language difficulties. It was his social face which most of the delegates saw first, for that same evening he was hosting a banquet in their honour, at the Spiridonovka.

The great banqueting room of the Spiridonovka, a former tsarist palace, was impressive. It was a vast room decorated in mock Gothic style with a fireplace large enough to burn whole trees and an oak-beamed roof that had been modelled on Westminster Hall in London. The banqueting table, laid for fifty people, was shaped in a horseshoe, laden with linen, crystal and silver all bearing the arms of the Tsar.

The Russians, to a man, looked resplendent: Voroshilov and his aides were dressed in white, and Marshal Budenny, an ex-tsarist cavalryman and the only other Soviet marshal to survive the purges, completed his outfit with a magnificent pair of high white boots. As though seeking to make up for the low-key welcome in Leningrad and at the railway station in Moscow, Voroshilov had wheeled out an impressive array of military big guns. In addition to Shaposhnikov and Budenny, who was commander of the Moscow Military District, there were, of course, the other members of the official Soviet delegation: Admiral N. G. Kuznetsov, People's Commissar for the Navy, General Loktionov, Commander-in-Chief of the Air Force, and Lieutenant-General Smorodinov, Deputy Chief of the General Staff, plus Generals Kovalev, commander of the Belorussian Military District, and Timoshenko, commander of the Kiev Military District.

In all, the banquet lasted three hours. The food was superb and the consumption of vodka heroic in a seemingly endless succession of friendly toasts. Afterwards, everyone moved to the music room, for a concert by violinists, singers, acrobats and conjurers. The entertainment proved to be remarkable not only for the outstanding talent of the various soloists but also for the oddity of their dress: one female violinist with close-cropped hair appeared to be wearing a tennis dress. As they staggered back to their quarters in the small hours of the morning, the Anglo-French delegates were heartened by the warmth of the reception they had received, and were lulled into a general feeling of optimism. But if they thought the talks were going to be easy, they were in for a very rude awakening next day.

14

MILITARY SECRETS IN A SMOKE-FILLED ROOM

The first session of the military talks started promptly at 10.30 am on Saturday, 12 August. The three delegations took their seats around a huge oblong table with no particular order of precedence, and a whole crowd of secretaries was brought in to take notes in Russian, English and French. With Voroshilov as chairman, a timetable and procedures were quickly agreed: meetings would be held twice daily, from 10.30 to 12.30 in the mornings and from 5.30 to 7 in the afternoons; the three heads of mission would take it in turn to chair the conference, beginning with Voroshilov, followed by Drax and then Doumenc. As a gesture of goodwill, Voroshilov offered to sit all day if necessary, to help speed things along. It all seemed an excellent beginning, pleasantly informal and generally optimistic. But the atmosphere soon began to deteriorate.

The heat was sweltering. It was to stay that way for the next two weeks, which put the British and French at a distinct disadvantage. They had come prepared for a cool Moscow summer, not for the temperatures in the high seventies and eighties which were common to the whole of Central Europe that year. So, while the Soviet delegates wore crisp white cotton, the Allied officers sweated in their heavy woollens, a contrast which epitomised much of what was to follow.

For Drax, there was even worse discomfort. Voroshilov quickly lit up a strong, black *papirosa* cigarette, and most of the other delegates immediately followed suit. Poor Drax had a weak throat. At the best of times he was constantly having to clear it; in the heavy smoke which soon filled the conference chamber he found himself coughing almost continuously. When he heard what Voroshilov had to say next, however, his coughing reached a crescendo in a nervous attempt to cover his embarrassment.

The Soviet marshal rose and read out a document which stated that his mission had 'the power to sign military agreements for the maintenance of peace and against aggression'. Then he invited the other heads to present their credentials. General Doumenc produced orders signed by Prime Minister Daladier, which confirmed that he had authority to negotiate on all military matters. The phrasing was slightly ambiguous, but it satisfied Voroshilov. But Drax had no written credentials at all, nothing on paper explaining his orders or indicating that he had any authority to negotiate, never mind sign, on behalf of His Majesty's government.

It was a bad moment. To the Russians, Drax's lack of authority indicated a lack of seriousness in the British approach to the negotiations. Drax tried to pass it off by saying that his mission would hardly have been sent if it did not have the power to act, and that if it were convenient to transfer the negotiations to London he was sure he would be given full powers on paper. Voroshilov drily replied, amid general laughter, that 'bringing papers to Moscow was easier than taking such a large company to London'.

Doumenc helped save the day by explaining that as far as Britain and France were concerned, military missions did not negotiate treaties: they merely advised and recommended points of agreement to their governments. But the Russians could rest assured that they would press on and work hard. Drax undertook to wire London for something to be sent out by airmail – a document did turn up nine days later, on 21 August, but by then it was only of academic interest – and after conferring with Shaposhnikov, Voroshilov agreed to continue the discussion. Following a cold lunch in the same magnificent banqueting hall where they had dined the night before, the delegations got down to work.

Voroshilov, having already stamped his personality on the conference, wasted no time in coming to the point. The political negotiations were not going well, he declared, precisely because of the absence of positive thinking. He did not intend that the military negotiations should be similarly afflicted.

'We need to know from the start,' he said, 'the plans which have been made by Great Britain and France with Poland and Turkey and so on.' He proposed that each mission in turn should reveal its country's military strength and the plans they had made to tackle the Nazi menace.

Drax was appalled: instead of having time to manoeuvre he had been hustled straight away into a corner. He protested that now was not the moment for concrete discussions. Surely, the first thing to be done was to agree upon general principles.

'What principles?' Voroshilov demanded.

Drax itemised them: '(a) to resist aggression; (b) to maintain communications by land and sea with the Soviet Union; (c) to build up a solid and durable line of defence in the east, as had been done in the west.' Conrad Collier found it hard to resist a sardonic smile at this last

reference to what he thought of as the 'Imaginot Line', but he need not
have been concerned. Voroshilov ignored it, sweeping aside Drax's
attempt to deflect him into a long discussion.

'Principles, principles!' his reply came back, staccato. 'We don't want
principles, we want facts. How many tanks have you got? How many
ships? How many aircraft?'

Drax was completely floored.

'As Voroshilov was adamant on this,' he wrote ruefully in his memoir
of the conference, 'we agreed to end the session so that the Allied
delegations could consider what reply should be given to the marshal's
demands.'

The problem facing the Allies was one of trust. Neither delegation
could rid itself of the suspicion that the Russians might be making use of
them to improve their own bargaining power with Hitler: that they might
even have deliberately organised this conference in order to get the
Allies' military secrets and pass them on to the Germans. For Drax there
was the added problem that his instructions specifically forbade his
discussing such things. However, after lengthy discussions they agreed
to go ahead. Doumenc would speak first, giving 'a very general
description of French army plans for the Western Front, including data
such as total available French divisions, tanks, etc. in round numbers'.
Doumenc's instructions, unlike Drax's, made it clear that he was to
answer Soviet questions. In any case he was sure the German High
Command already knew the figures, so he would be giving away no real
secrets.

The conference, as all conferences do, quickly fell into a regular pattern.
Each morning, the Allied delegates arrived at the Spiridonovka shortly
before 10.30, and each morning the Soviet guards failed to salute them –
a source of great irritation to Admiral Drax. They then entered a large
hall where they hung their caps and signed the attendance register, like
children arriving at school. From there they passed into the conference
room, which was invariably hot and stuffy. The long conference table
ran down the centre of the room. The British and French sat on one
side of it, and the Russians on the other.

Two rooms next to the conference room had been allocated to the
Allies for their private discussion, but Drax – remembering Quex
Sinclair's dire warnings – was suspicious of the profusion of electric
wiring in the rooms, and feared they were bugged. As a result, the
delegates used the garden if they wanted to talk, though Drax wondered
how bug-free that was: there seemed, he thought, to be 'a super-
abundance' of wiring to power the few exterior lights.

The security arrangements at the Spiridonovka were another
inhibiting feature of the place. Armed sentries were placed at intervals of
a few yards along the garden wall, with orders to keep out of sight. So

when the delegates walked up and down the paths, they were met by the sight of large Russian soldiers trying to make themselves invisible behind the slender trunks of the few ornamental trees. Once, when Drax strolled as far as the end of the garden, two plainclothed NKVD men suddenly emerged from a large clump of bushes, trying unsuccessfully to look like gardeners.

The Allied officers' mistrust of the Soviet system was not helped by their observation of life in Moscow. One of the attachés at the British embassy related a chilling tale when he returned from a brief journey outside the city. He told how he had stopped at a level crossing to allow a train to pass. The train consisted of about twenty wooden wagons like cattle trucks, each wagon featureless apart from one small barred window measuring about a foot square, set high up on the side. As he watched them pass, he was astonished to see the faces of people pressed against the bars and realised what it was – another trainload of enemies of the state on their way to the gulags.

In the conference room, what Beaufre described as 'this comedy of laying military secrets on the table' continued. While everyone tried to appear sincere, the figures they gave were, according to Beaufre, 'usually misleading and generally exaggerated'. They certainly were in the British case. Drawing on his experience with the Russians, Group Captain Collier advised his chief to multiply the true number of British first-line aircraft by a factor of three. 'They'll divide any figure you quote by three anyway,' he told Air Marshal Burnett.

Collier's advice was taken – but when General Heywood gave his figures for the British army, the Russians reacted with shocked disbelief, not because they were so large, but because they were so small. How could a major power like Britain offer only sixteen divisions 'ready for service in the early stages of war', to be followed by a further sixteen some unspecified time later? Voroshilov thought he must have misheard. He pressed Heywood to repeat his statement and to say exactly how many divisions Britain could field immediately. The result was even worse: Heywood told him Britain only had four infantry divisions and one armoured division ready for action in Europe.

Had Voroshilov known the true state of the British army, he would probably have called off the conference on the spot. Back in London, that same day, Ironside was discovering that all he would have at his disposal was a 1st Corps of two divisions, and that would need twenty-four days to assemble overseas. The rest was 'all in the air'. The single armoured division listed by Heywood in Moscow could not be counted: its tanks were not suitable for war in Europe. By 1 September, Ironside could have another corps of two modified divisions, though this would still need thirty-three days for assembly. It would be four months after that before two more Territorial divisions could be ready to make the two corps up to full strength, and yet another month before a further four divisions of Territorials could be available. As Ironside noted angrily in his diary, heavily underlining the first sentence for added emphasis, 'This is a terrible result after all these years of preparation. We have indeed to look to a long war.'

Of course, the estimates Heywood gave to Voroshilov failed to take into account possible reinforcements from the empire and the dominions. He did not mention Australian, Canadian, New Zealand and South African contingents, to say nothing of the Indian army, all of which would have helped swell the 'derisory figure', and might have helped persuade the Russians that Britain was an ally worth having.

For the RAF, Burnett put up a much more impressive show – Collier was pleased to note that his chief was following his suggestion and lying enthusiastically. He claimed that the RAF already possessed over 3,000 modern fighting aircraft, and described large numbers of non-existent schools for pilots and aircraft mechanics.

On the sea, Drax had no need to lie or even to exaggerate. As an island, Britain had never needed a large army to protect herself or her lifelines to her far-flung empire. Her main source of strength lay in her navy. The Royal Navy in 1939 was still the world's most powerful and was certainly capable of imposing a blockade on Germany's ports which could starve her into submission – as long as she could not obtain supplies via other routes. But starvation is a slow death, and what was needed against Hitler's Germany was the means to deliver a mortal blow swiftly and effectively, before the Panzer divisions and dive bombers could build up the lethal momentum of *Blitzkrieg*.

The French, as a major land power, helped redress the balance by offering an army of 110 divisions, excluding anti-aircraft and coastal defence forces and troops in Africa. To this number, Doumenc added about 200,000 refugee soldiers from Republican Spain – a figure the Russians knew to be exaggerated – who had asked to be incorporated into the French army. He also claimed some 4,000 modern tanks and 3,000 pieces of heavy artillery, while General Valin, for the French air force, claimed 2,000 first-line aircraft, of which he said about two thirds were modern types.

When it came to the Russians' turn to detail their forces and describe their plans on the fourth day of the conference, they began by giving the Red Army's mobilisation plans for Europe. Over a period of between eight and twenty days, they said, they would be able to put into the field in Europe no fewer than 120 infantry and sixteen cavalry divisions, 5,000 heavy guns, 9–10,000 tanks and 5–5,000 fighting aircraft.

The Soviet figures were an impressive proof of military might – if they could be believed. Collier and the service attachés advised their superiors to take them with several tablespoons of salt: like the Allied claims, they were meant to impress. They also had grave doubts whether the Soviet transport system could cope with such numbers, even if they should be forthcoming.

Even allowing for optimism, exaggeration and transport problems, however, it was evident that the three powers could yield joint forces which, numerically at least, were far more powerful than the combined forces of Germany and Italy. A genuinely concerted effort, free from other conditions, would certainly have been enough to deter and possibly even to defeat Hitler's armies. Unfortunately, there were other conditions, and some of them appeared to be insuperable.

Voroshilov and Shaposhnikov explained that the Soviet forces they had described would be deployed in various ways depending on what action Germany took. The marshal considered the three most likely scenarios: first, if Germany attacked France; second, if Germany attacked Poland and Romania; third, if Germany attacked the USSR through the Baltic states and Finland. In each case, the Russians wished to lay down precise guarantees as to the proportion of troops each country would be expected to deploy. In the event of an attack on France, for example, he suggested the Soviet Union would guarantee to field an army equal to seventy per cent of the combined Anglo-French forces committed on the Western Front.

In the light of subsequent events, the third scenario was to assume great importance; it also harked back to the political talks, and the issue which had caused them to be suspended. 'With a view to protecting the independence of the Baltic states and Finland,' as they put it, the Russians insisted that the British and French governments must obtain permission from the states involved for the temporary use of, among others, bases on the Aaland Islands in the Gulf of Bothnia, and Hangko, the Finnish port at the mouth of the Gulf of Finland. The Soviet fleet would co-operate with the British and French navies in the Baltic, and they would wish to use the bases once the British and French had taken them over – a convenient way for the Soviet Union to acquire important bases through someone else's efforts.

The Baltic scenario provided a prophetic glimpse of future Soviet actions. But the other two scenarios were of more immediate importance, for they both highlighted the obstruction which would prevent any meaningful agreement between the Soviet Union and the Western Powers. Any Soviet assistance to France, or to Poland and Romania, depended entirely on the Poles and Romanians agreeing to the passage of Soviet land and air forces across their territory, since the Soviet Union had no common frontier with either France or Germany. Would the Romanians, and more particularly the Poles, agree?

The Polish question had been raised on the first full day of the conference, Sunday, 13 August, when Voroshilov had asked if there was a treaty between France and Poland stipulating the forces the French were to put in the field and the action to be taken, in the event of hostilities. Doumenc had replied rather evasively that if Poland were attacked France would fight, and vice versa. The Russians then asked for details of the strength of Polish forces and how they would operate. Doumenc was forced to admit that he had no information on this, but he understood that Poland would fight with all her strength.

When Doumenc tried to turn the question back on to the Russians by asking the Soviet delegation to describe what action they would take, Voroshilov wasted no time in reminding the Allies of the geographical position of his country, and invited them to explain what they expected of the Soviet Union in the event of a German invasion of Poland. The next day, Monday, 14 August, he returned to the subject, more insistently.

'Yesterday, I asked General Doumenc the following question,' he began. 'What part do the present missions, or the general staffs of France and Britain, consider the Soviet Union should play in war against an aggressor, if he attacks France and Britain, if he attacks Poland or Romania, or Poland and Romania together, and if he attacks Turkey?'

'General Gamelin holds the view,' Doumenc began in reply, 'and I as his subordinate share it, that our initial task is for each party to hold firm on its own front and group all its forces on that front. As regards the countries referred to earlier, we consider that it is their duty to defend their own territory. But we will extend help to them when they ask for it.'

'But what if they do not ask for it?' Voroshilov demanded.

Doumenc tried to evade the question. 'We know that they are in need of assistance,' he said.

For Voroshilov, that was not good enough.

If Poland and Romania failed to ask for this assistance in good time, it would mean only one thing – 'that they have put up their hands, that they have surrendered'. In that case, he wanted to know, what would the Allied reaction be? What would the French do?

Doumenc was forced to admit that his government would probably pull its army back, retreating into the laager to shelter behind Collier's 'Imaginot Line'.

Drax tried to come to the rescue of his French colleague, dismissing Soviet fears of Polish and Romanian surrender as groundless. 'After all,' he said, 'if a man is drowning in a river and another man says he is ready and willing to throw him a lifebelt, will he decline to ask for it?'

It was Shaposhnikov who took up Drax's metaphor. 'The trouble with lifebelts,' he countered, 'is that they need to be to hand: they need to be ready for immediate use. Otherwise, the victim drowns.'

Doumenc replied that he was confident the Poles and Romanians 'would implore the marshal to support them', and Drax added that he thought it 'inconceivable' that they should do anything else. Unfortunately, Drax did not stop there. He went on to say that 'if they did not ask for help when necessary and allow themselves to be overrun, it may be expected that they would become German provinces'. It was hardly the best form of diplomacy to remind the Russians of the one thing they wished to avoid at all costs: the presence of Nazi troops on the Soviet Union's own frontiers. But Drax blundered on with the argument he had put to the French during the voyage, no doubt in one of the sessions in the children's playroom of the *City of Exeter*, and which the French had begged him never to mention in front of the Russians. After a prolonged fit of coughing, he told Voroshilov: 'Don't forget that Poland, if she is on her own, may be crushed in two weeks.'

In the event, Drax's estimate of the strength of the Polish army proved substantially correct. But it must have come as a shock to the Russians to hear it from the head of the British military mission. It meant that even if the Poles did agree to Soviet help, the chances were that the Wehrmacht would be on the Soviet frontier before the Red Army could mobilise. If the Russians needed any incentive to avoid signing a treaty with the Allies, Drax had just handed one to them on a plate.

Voroshilov made a great play of taking a special note of Drax's statement, and then returned to the attack, hammering away again at the central issue and demanding a direct answer to his questions: 'Do the French and British general staffs think that the Soviet land forces will be admitted to Polish territory in order to make direct contact with the enemy in case Poland is attacked? Is it proposed to allow Soviet troops across Romanian territory if the aggressor attacks Romania?'

The instructions Drax had received were precise, if unhelpful, on this subject: 'If the Russians propose that the British and French governments should communicate to the Polish, Romanian or Baltic states proposals involving co-operation with the Soviet government or general staff, the delegation should not commit themselves but refer home.' However, these instructions did give the mission a way out of the immediate difficulty, and Drax and Doumenc took it. Poland and Romania, they protested, were sovereign states and it was for those countries themselves to agree whether or not they would allow Soviet forces to cross their territory. It was, therefore, a political and not a military question. 'However, if the marshal specially wishes it,' they conceded, 'we are prepared to refer to London and Paris to ask if our governments would be willing to [approach] the Polish and Romanian governments.' The answer would, of course, depend on whether the USSR was an ally of Great Britain and France. If the marshal wished to avoid wasting precious time, they proposed, 'let us assume that the answer (to the Polish question) will be "Yes", and our conference can then usefully continue.'

It was a neat ploy and it stopped Voroshilov in his tracks. He asked for a ten-minute recess. The Allies thankfully made their way out into the fresh air of the garden. There, Drax turned pessimistically to Doumenc. 'I think our mission is finished,' he told him.

An hour later, however, the Russians returned to the table, presumably having consulted Stalin himself. They agreed that it was a political rather than a military question, but it had to be put and answered. In the meantime the conference could continue. To wind up the day's proceedings, Voroshilov had a written statement to read out. It covered all the points so far discussed, and ended on an ominous note: 'The Soviet military mission expresses its regret at the absence of an exact answer on the part of the British and French missions to the question raised about the right of passage of Soviet armed forces over Polish and Romanian territory. The Soviet military mission considers that without a positive solution of this question the whole present attempt to conclude a military convention between France, Britain and the Soviet Union is, in its opinion, doomed to failure.' That night, Doumenc sent off a telegram to his government in Paris, with a copy to London, explaining the Soviet position and asking for further instructions. He and the French ambassador strongly advised that General Valin, the French air force representative, should be secretly sent to Warsaw to persuade the Polish general staff to allow the Franco-British delegations to negotiate on the Polish question without officially involving the Polish government.

The French government refused, though Valin was eminently suitable for the task of talking to the Poles, since he had been air attaché in Warsaw and had many friends in the military establishment there. Doumenc then proposed that the present military attaché in Warsaw, General Musse, should come to Moscow to be briefed. Again, he was refused. On the British side, there was silence, though Drax's instructions to go slowly were changed on 15 August and he was told to support Doumenc in seeking a positive conclusion 'as soon as possible'. Nothing was said, however, about the Polish problem. Such decisions were made more difficult to obtain by the fact that there was no one in authority left in London. The shooting season had begun in Britain on 12 August, the 'glorious twelfth', and Halifax was occupied on his Yorkshire estate, shooting grouse and organising local cricket matches. Chamberlain was fishing in the Scottish highlands. Even Horace Wilson was at his seaside home in Bournemouth on the south coast, relaxing in the sunshine which had appeared at last over England.

The military missions struggled on, waiting impatiently for the news which never came. By the fifth day of the conference, Wednesday, 16 August, Voroshilov was proposing an adjournment until the Allies could produce definite answers to his questions. It took all Doumenc's powers of persuasion to induce him to continue, assuring him that there was at least a reasonable chance that favourable replies would come from London and Paris.

In London, in increasing desperation at the government's dilatoriness, the Foreign Office turned to the Deputy Chiefs of Staff for a military assessment of the consequences of failure in Moscow. They obliged with a statement that was as clear as it was unequivocal: 'If the Russians are to collaborate in resisting German aggression against Poland or Romania they can only do so effectively on Polish or Romanian soil . . . We suggest that it is now necessary to present this unpalatable truth with absolute frankness both to the Poles and the Romanians . . . If the negotiations with Russia break down, a Russo-German *rapprochement* may take place of which the probable consequence will be that Russia and Germany decide to share the spoils and concert in a new partition of the Eastern European states.'

On Thursday, 17 August, after six days of fruitless discussion, Voroshilov's patience finally ran out, and he declared that the conference must now adjourn until the Polish and Romanian governments had made their position clear regarding the Soviet request for passage for their troops. Drax objected, pointing out that in the event of an adjournment both the British and French governments would have to issue a statement to the world's press, giving the reasons. How were they to avoid giving the impression that negotiations had broken down irrevocably? Voroshilov's response was simple: 'Tell the press nothing,' he advised. He was, however, prepared to make a concession for the sake of appearances: the conference would reconvene on Monday, 21 August.

On that note, the delegates returned to their quarters. Both Drax and Doumenc sent messages back to their capitals. Drax wrote a depressing letter to Lord Chatfield. 'We . . . have not yet found a single point on which we can reach a definite agreement,' he wrote. He reported that Voroshilov had become increasingly pessimistic and was now convinced that a European war was inevitable. He said he now believed the USSR no longer had any desire to sign a military agreement or any treaty with anybody, but wished only to remain neutral in the coming war. The Russians planned, he thought, to sit on the sidelines and watch while the other Europeans cut each other's throats.

Unlike Drax, Doumenc was still determined to fight on. His message again badgered his government to act. 'It is now essential,' he cabled Paris, 'if discussions are to continue, for me to be able to give an affirmative reply to the question which has been put.' Again unlike Drax, he was not content to sit and wait for a response: he decided to take positive action to influence events. On his own authority, and in the greatest secrecy, he sent Beaufre, the most junior but perhaps the most persuasive member of his mission, to Warsaw.

Beaufre's brief was to make contact with the officers of the Polish general staff, in the hope that he might be able to convince them to persuade their government to accommodate the Soviet request. Even if Beaufre failed, however, Doumenc would be able to show the Russians that the Allies were doing everything they could to save the conference. In that way, he might win more time for Britain and France to reach some kind of political understanding with the Soviet Union.

Beaufre left Moscow that same evening by train, ostensibly bound for Paris, rolling out of the Belorussian station in an ornate *wagon-lit* to the accompaniment of airs from Bizet's *Carmen*, then very popular in the USSR, echoing from the station's loudspeakers. When he reached the Polish frontier, he was alarmed to find some twenty or more Western travellers stranded on the Russian side, where they had been kept for days by the Soviet officials, waiting for authorisation to cross. To his relief, Beaufre experienced no such delay. His diplomatic passport was stamped with almost indecent haste and he was soon in a Polish train on his way to Warsaw. Twenty-four hours after leaving Moscow, he alighted at a suburban station, where he was picked up by an unmarked car and driven swiftly to the French embassy. There, he found a formal dinner party was in progress and he was left to kick his heels until after midnight before he could speak to Ambassador Noël and his military attaché, General Musse.

Noël and Musse were profoundly pessimistic about their chances of persuading their host government to allow Soviet troops on to Polish soil. They felt the Poles were bound to regard any such request with the gravest suspicion, seeing it as a Russian plot to take back the territory which Marshal Pilsudski had conquered in 1921. Noël feared that any attempt by the French to put pressure on the Poles would succeed only in driving them into the arms of Germany – after all, had not Pilsudski himself concluded a non-aggression pact with Hitler in 1934? And there was a further consideration. As Musse prophetically observed, 'How do you know that the Russians themselves have not got an understanding with Germany?'

Beaufre explained that his brief was to find some way of enabling the Allies to continue the negotiations in Moscow. If Doumenc and Drax could hold on for another month, the likelihood of war starting that year would be considerably reduced. Appreciating this, General Musse agreed to approach his friend General Stackiewicz, Chief of the Polish General Staff, while Noël sought an urgent meeting with Colonel Beck.

Back in Moscow, meanwhile, the two delegations received clear signs that their mission was already doomed. Friday, 18 August, was Soviet Air Day and they were all given invitations to the annual air show at the Chkalov Aero Club on Tushino airfield. What they were not given was official transport, nor did any of the Soviet negotiators offer to accompany them. Although relations outside the conference room had become extremely cordial between the members of the three delegations, 'partly as a result of two banquets and the consumption of much vodka', the goodwill obviously did not extend to being seen fraternising in public.

All foreign embassies, however, were given special passes for their cars, so there should have been no trouble getting to the show. But Tushino airfield lay nearly fifteen miles outside the city, and the road was jammed with cars crawling along nose to tail at no more than ten miles an hour. The only way to make faster progress was to pull out and drive on the wrong side of the road, which Drax noticed Soviet official cars doing. When the British and French drivers attempted to follow suit, however, they were waved angrily back into line by the sentries posted along the route. They flourished their passes at the soldiers, but their documents did not seem to carry the same authority as those held by Soviet officials – or, as Drax remarked with great indignation, by members of the German embassy staff, who were also allowed to sweep past, ignoring traffic regulations.

Eventually, after over an hour's slow driving, the entourage reached the airfield. They found it packed with thousands of Muscovites making the most of the glorious weather and preparing to enjoy the flying displays. Just before the show was due to start, a large black limousine with dark green windows, accompanied by a heavily armed escort, sped into the field. The door opened and Stalin emerged, a small, wary figure, followed by his daughter Svetlana. They watched the flying from the grandstand, surrounded by members of the Politburo and senior officers of the armed forces and their wives, a vista of brightly coloured dresses and smart white uniforms. The British and French officers had a balcony to themselves – a privilege which kept them safely isolated from the other spectators – while they enjoyed what *The Times* correspondent described as 'a well-earned day off'.

There were signs that the heat wave was about to break. From time to time, violent summer storms interrupted the flying, but none was serious enough to stop the show completely. It began with a flypast of some two hundred bombers in formation, followed by fighter planes performing aerobatics. One group of three planes flew round the airfield upside down. An autogyro – an early form of rotary-winged aircraft, forerunner of the helicopter – and an airship put in an appearance. After a display of precision bombing, in which a dummy factory was comprehensively destroyed, eleven gliders arrived over the field towed by a single large aircraft, slipped their tow and manoeuvred in formation before landing in a long spiral. For good measure, six of the gliders also performed aerobatics. Finally, there was a simultaneous jump of fifty parachute troops from three large transport aircraft. It was the first time Admiral

Drax had seen the use of either gliders or parachute troops. He was impressed.

After the show, the delegates' cars crawled slowly back to Moscow, where they were greeted with the news that Germany had signed a military treaty with Slovakia, by which the Germans 'assumed the military protection' of Slovak territory. In order to provide this 'protection' Hitler had ordered huge contingents of troops into the country, where they would be perfectly poised for an attack on Poland. Within the next two weeks, no fewer than thirty-one of the fifty divisions which Hitler was to unleash against Poland would take up their start positions there. The death agony of Czechoslovakia was finally over, the Munich agreement laid to rest.

The British embassy staff also had another piece of news, though at first sight it appeared to be less momentous: the old Austrian legation at 6 Myortvy Pereulok, 'Death Lane' – which had, of course, been taken over by Nazi Germany after the *Anschluss* – was being given a fresh coat of paint. The Russians, it seemed, were expecting an important visitor to stay there.

15

'THE MARK OF DEATH IS STAMPED UPON THE POLISH ARMY'S FACE'

Saturday, 19 August, passed in an agony of suspense for Doumenc, waiting for news from Beaufre in Warsaw. Would the Poles finally see sense and accept the only lifeline which could rescue them from their mortal danger? Or would they remain blinkered by a pride which, however gallant, seemed to blind them to all reason? The outcome of the Allied talks in Moscow depended, he knew, on their response. What he did not know was that there was now another, even more pertinent question: was it already too late for any Polish decision to make any difference? During the two weeks in which the Allied negotiators had been steaming slowly to Leningrad and then struggling in their sticky conference room with Voroshilov, the Germans had been advancing unseen and were now all but poised to grab the prize.

The first indication that the Soviets were prepared to regard them as serious contenders had come, in fact, at the very moment when the British and French missions were finishing their early lunch in London on Saturday, 5 August. As Drax, Doumenc and their entourages prepared to leave for Cannon Street station, Astakhov arrived in Schnurre's office in Berlin. He brought welcome news from Molotov, who had spent the previous day discussing the German proposals with Stalin and the Politburo: the Soviet government was prepared to talk. They still wanted the credit agreement signed first, Astakhov said, but would regard this as 'the first important stage of a complete understanding'.

Schnurre was a little surprised. His impression of the last meeting between Molotov and Schulenburg was that it had been too much concerned with the past, with raking up old quarrels and grievances.

'We shall have to stop doing this if we want to discuss the future,' he told the Russian.

Astakhov smiled. 'Ah,' he said, 'but remember, this is the first time Molotov has ever discussed these matters. From information received, I have the impression that the conversation ended on a positive note.'

Astakhov told Schnurre that Molotov's attitude represented a significant step forward, and that he regarded the questions to be discussed between Germany and the Soviet Union as 'urgent and serious'. He, Astakhov, would be at the German government's disposal at any time.

The breakthrough came at exactly the right time for Hitler. Only the previous day he had decided to go all out for a pact with Stalin, and had telephoned instructions on this to Berlin during the night. His reasons are quite clear: the events of the last few days in Danzig had finally convinced him that he could not intimidate the Poles with his threats, any more than he had been able earlier to win them over with his blandishments. They would not give up the Free City without a fight.

His ambassador in Warsaw, Hans-Adolf von Moltke, confirmed his conclusions in two messages to Berlin on 5 and 6 August, when he said there was now 'hardly any doubt' that Poland would fight. And Marshal Smigly-Rydz himself confirmed it beyond all question on 6 August in Cracow, when he addressed a parade of veterans commemorating the start of Pilsudski's campaign to free Poland from the Russians twenty-five years before. 'No one is going to infringe Poland's rights and interests,' he declared to a wildly cheering crowd. 'Anyone who attempts to do so will be repelled by force! No one is going to take Danzig away from us – she has been united with Poland for centuries, and she will stay united!'

This suited Hitler's purposes admirably. He needed Danzig as a pretext for war with Poland, and he needed a war with Poland in order to continue his eastward drive for German *Lebensraum*. The British and French might or might not go to war on Poland's behalf if Hitler attacked her. But even if they did, there would be little they could do to prevent a German *Blitzkrieg* from overwhelming Poland probably before the French could complete their mobilisation and certainly before the British could get their meagre army across the Channel.

But Hitler still did not think the Allies would go to war. All his intelligence reports indicated that the French did not have the stomach for it, and he had every reason to believe that Chamberlain's bold words were nothing more than hollow rhetoric, meant to satisfy the British Parliament. In the end, he was sure, the British Prime Minister would capitulate again. The sub-text of Chamberlain's utterances in public, surely, lay in the approaches and offers made to Germany in secret – indeed, Weizsäcker noted on 6 August: 'Underground feelers from

Chamberlain towards a compromise (via Horace Wilson) prove that a dialogue with Britain could be got going if we wish.'

That day, too, the British businessmen led by Charles Spencer were assembling secretly in Hamburg, ready to be driven north by Birger Dahlerus in a convoy of Mercedes limousines flying the Swedish flag, to talk to Göring at Bredstedt.

Hitler, therefore, could feel reasonably confident that he had nothing to fear from the West, a confidence that was boosted continuously by the advice he received from his Foreign Minister. 'Ribbentrop is guaranteeing,' Weizsäcker recorded in his diary, 'that the British and French will remain neutral provided we deal annihilating blows to Poland in the first three days. He thinks this is certain.'

The principal danger to Hitler's plans appeared to come not from the West but from the Soviet Union. Until he received Molotov's message of 5 August, it seemed the best he could hope for was that Stalin might be content to stand on the sidelines, and wait to see what damage the Germans sustained. As late as 4 August, he issued a naval directive saying: 'Russia's attitude is uncertain, though at first it can be assumed that she will remain neutral but with a definite bias towards the Western Powers and Poland.'

On 5 August, that assessment suddenly changed. Evidently Stalin was unimpressed by the composition of the Anglo-French mission and by the length of time it was taking them to get to Leningrad, and was now prepared to consider the German alternative. If he could be bought off, then Hitler would not have to face the prospect of fighting the Soviet Union – at least not yet and not over Poland. Deprived of Soviet support, the Allies should then lose what little enthusiasm they might have had for fighting Poland's battles, leaving Hitler with the limited campaign he wanted, and for which his armed forces were best suited and equipped.

Throughout Germany, the harvest was now in full swing. If the Polish war was to begin as planned on 26 August – that is, immediately after the completion of harvesting and before the start of the autumn rains in the east – then Hitler's preparations would have to shift into higher gear. While he continued moving troops into East Prussia, 'for summer exercises', he also had to start whipping up the German people, providing justification, no matter how spurious, for an attack on Poland. Over the next few days his machinery for creating propaganda and provocations, already tried and tested with Austria and Czechoslovakia, swung into well-oiled motion.

First, the German press was unmuzzled. After months of subdued comment, violent headlines complained about Polish 'aggression'. William Shirer, returning to Berlin from a vacation in Switzerland, noted in his diary: 'Whereas all the rest of the world considers that the peace is about to be broken by Germany, that it is Germany that is threatening to attack Poland over Danzig, here in Germany, in the world the local newspapers create, the very reverse is being maintained . . . What the Nazi papers are proclaiming is this: that it is Poland which is disturbing the peace of Europe; Poland which is threatening Germany with armed invasion, and so forth. This is the Germany of last September, when the heat was turned on Czechoslovakia.'

Der Führer, the daily paper of Karlsruhe, was typical of the popular Nazi press. 'WARSAW THREATENS BOMBARDMENT OF DANZIG! UNBELIEVABLE AGITATION OF POLISH ARCH-MADNESS', it proclaimed. Even the *Börsen Zeitung*, Berlin's normally staid equivalent of the *Wall Street Journal* or the *Financial Times*, carried a banner headline 'POLAND? LOOK OUT!', adding for good measure, 'ANSWER TO POLAND, RUNNING AMOK AGAINST PEACE AND RIGHT IN EUROPE!'

Inevitably, the Polish press replied in kind, complaining loudly of 'German guns pointing at Danzig'. The Cracow *Czas*, normally a moderate conservative paper, trumpeted, 'Let the Nazis try to effect a *fait accompli* in Danzig, and Polish guns will speak!'

The Polish complaints undoubtedly had more merit – though perhaps less effect in a nation where only two million people read any kind of newspaper and whole villages were without a single radio set – but this did not prevent Hitler from flying into one of his rages when he saw them. When Otto Dietrich, his press chief, brought a bundle of Polish press clippings to him in his study at the Berghof, he tore them from his hands and threw them on the floor. Rounding on Dietrich he demanded more anti-Polish stories in the German papers, stories about atrocities committed by Poles against innocent Germans, stories about corruption in Warsaw, stories that would discredit the Poles and open German eyes to their true nature as he saw it, a bastard race unfit to have its own country.

On 7 August, Hitler personally summoned Gauleiter Forster from Danzig, sending his aeroplane to bring him to the Berghof for new instructions. The last time Forster had received instructions, he had been told to keep things cool, to say the Führer was looking for *détente*, and to control hotheads like the Senate President, Arthur Greiser, who might easily go too far too soon. Now, the picture had changed. Hitler told him his patience with the Poles had reached its limit. He briefed him in detail on the way he was to handle things from now on, and on the speech he was to make when he returned. He was to speak of Danzig as a purely German state and emphasise its right to return to the fatherland. He was to lay the entire blame for the present situation on the Poles and do all he could to stir up popular feeling against them. Afterwards he was to fly to Nuremberg and make similar speeches throughout southern Germany, so that those in the south would no longer regard the question of Danzig as a purely Prussian concern.

When he had briefed Forster, Hitler ordered Ambassador von Moltke to be brought back from Warsaw to Berlin, where he was to stay until further notice. He was to have no contact with his embassy, or with any Polish authorities. The German Foreign Office, too, was to avoid all contact with the Poles, and no one was to make any comment about the reasons for von Moltke's departure. In his absence, the German embassy in Warsaw was ordered to confine itself to receiving any Polish communications without comment and passing them on to Berlin. It was also to collect every story from the Polish press which could possibly be used as propaganda.

Count Istvan Czaky, the Hungarian Foreign Minister, got the full force of Hitler's vilification of Poland when he called on him at the Berghof at 3 pm on Tuesday, 8 August. The Hungarians had made the mistake of telling Hitler in two letters that although they would 'stand by' Germany in the event of a German–Polish conflict, they could not join in. Hitler had been furious: the Hungarian attitude did not merely represent cowardice and ingratitude, it was also an insult to Germany to suggest that she needed outside assistance in dealing with the Poles. No one had asked Hungary to fight.

The misunderstanding made the Hungarians feel decidedly nervous, fearing they had offended Hitler, and the visit by their Foreign Minister was intended to mollify him. But Czaky was astonished and somewhat shaken to find himself facing a tirade lasting one hour and forty minutes, during which Hitler paced back and forth in front of the great window in the salon, waving his fist in front of Czaky's face at particularly emotional moments.

'Have they gone mad in Warsaw?' he cried. 'The Poles are obviously incapable of realistic thinking either in the military or in the political field. They are labouring under a dangerous delusion about their own strength. Their illusions about the strength of the German army are incomprehensible!'

Poland presented no military problem whatever for Germany. 'The mark of death is already stamped upon the Polish army's face,' he proclaimed. 'We are reckoning, from the start, on a war on two fronts, which, if it comes, will be conducted with lightning speed. We will destroy not only the Polish army but also the Polish state!'

Hitler laid out his thinking before Czaky as though convincing himself of its rightness. Before long, he was trying out his response to Polish provocations. The German people, he declared, were now much more anti-Polish than they had been anti-Czech, for the Poles had not only seized what had formerly been German territory but had also behaved in the most bestial manner towards innocent Germans. There was a piece of news, he said, which he had not dared to publish, for fear of the uproar it would cause: some Germans in Poland had actually been castrated! At moments of crisis, it seemed Hitler had an obsession with castration – he always demanded stories about it in the press when a propaganda campaign was reaching its peak. No doubt he saw it as a guaranteed method of inflaming his people in general and his soldiers in particular.

Hitler's assessment of the Soviet position in the impending war was the most rational part of his tirade to Czaky. The Soviet government, he said, apparently wished to bind themselves to no one. They would not fight against Germany. Few senior Red Army officers had survived Stalin's purges, and those newly promoted were as yet untested in complex military operations. Moreover, it was well known that the Red Army fatally lacked mobility. In any case, 'the Soviets would not repeat the Tsar's mistake and bleed to death for Britain.' What they would try to do was to 'enrich themselves, possibly at the expense of the Baltic states or Poland, without engaging in any military action themselves'.

In spite of the way he dismissed the very idea of help from the Hungarians, there is no doubt they could have been useful to Hitler in his Polish campaign. Thanks to his generosity in giving them the Carpatho-Ukraine, they now enjoyed a common frontier with Poland, across which they could invade, drawing off Polish forces from defence against the main German attack. However, as Czaky informed him, 'Our national honour does not allow us to fight against Poland.'

The Hungarian defection served to highlight the fact that Hitler's allies were proving a grave disappointment to him at this crucial time. The smaller nations, such as Bulgaria, simply wanted him to provide them with large quantities of modern arms which he could ill afford. The stronger countries, Italy and Japan, were also failing to come up to scratch, displaying a marked reluctance to get involved in what they rightly feared could turn into a general conflict.

Hitler had wanted the Italians to keep the French occupied by attacking them in the south and tying up their forces there. But not even the prospect of recovering Nice and Corsica was enough to tempt Mussolini; he realised only too well that his painless victory in Albania was unlikely to be repeated against the French, and he had cried off. He had asked for the postponement of the meeting which had been arranged for himself and Hitler at the Brenner Pass to discuss war plans. Instead, in the morning of 7 August, the day before Hitler met Czaky, Mussolini had sent word with his ambassador in Berlin, Bernardo Attolico, that he would rather wait until he knew the outcome of the Anglo-French talks with the Russians before doing anything. In the meantime, could his son-in-law, Foreign Minister Count Galeazzo Ciano, come and talk to Ribbentrop about the political situation?

The Japanese, meanwhile, were busy arguing among themselves about the proposed military alliance with Germany, and were signally failing to come to any decision. It took all the wiles of War Minister General Itagaki, backed by the army, even to get the five principal Japanese ministers together on 8 August in Tokyo. He demanded that talks should be restarted with the Axis powers. The Ministers of Finance, Marine and Foreign Affairs all refused, and the Minister President, Baron Hiranuma, sat on the fence. Admittedly, the Japanese were engaging the Russians in Mongolia, but this was still on a relatively small scale and there were no plans to escalate the conflict, or to start fighting the British and French in the Far East.

The lack of support from his existing friends made it still more imperative for Hitler to look to Stalin for reassurance that the Soviet Union would not respond to his invasion of Poland by declaring war on him. He ordered Ribbentrop to step up his efforts for a quick agreement.

On 8 August, Ribbentrop had Schnurre fly down from Berlin for a briefing at Schloss Fuschl, bringing with him General Köstring, the military attaché from Moscow, who was back in Germany on leave. They discussed tactics at some length, and Schnurre left with instructions to call Astakhov to the Wilhelmstrasse for more detailed talks. In Moscow, meanwhile, as though realising what was in Hitler's mind, Stalin was writing a letter to Svetlana, who was on vacation at his villa at Sochi, on the Black Sea.

'Hello, my little housekeeper!' he wrote, using the language of the private game he and his daughter played. 'I got both of your letters. I'm glad you haven't forgotten your little papa. I couldn't answer you right away. I was busy. I hear you weren't alone at Ritsa [a mountain lake resort near Sochi] and that you had a young man with you. Well, there's nothing wrong with that. Ritsa is nice, especially if you have a young man along, my little sparrow.

'When do you mean to set out for Moscow? Isn't it time? I think so. Come to Moscow by 25 August, or even the 20th. Write me what you think of this. I don't plan to come south this year. I'm busy. I can't get away. My health? I'm well. My spirits are good. I miss you a bit, but you'll be coming soon.

'I give you a big hug, my little sparrow.'

In fact, as we have seen, Svetlana was back in Moscow well before 20 August, for she was there in time to accompany him to the air show on 18 August. She realised that when he said he was busy it was something of an understatement, and like a good daughter anywhere, she hurried home to look after her 'little papa'.

Having sent Forster back to Danzig and Schnurre back to Berlin, Hitler evidently felt that he could spare the time for a short break while awaiting the next developments. He spent Wednesday, 9 August, in Salzburg, attending the music festival there, looking confident and relaxed.

16

'SOMETHING TO THINK ABOUT'

'I believe we have really given the Soviets something to think about,' Schulenburg wrote from Moscow on 7 August. However, unlike Astakhov, who had been optimistic about Molotov's reactions, Schulenburg was not so sanguine about the prospects of an early settlement. 'At every word and at every step,' he continued, 'one can sense the great distrust of us. We have known for a long time that this is so. The unfortunate part of it is that the mistrust of such people is very easily kindled but can only be allayed slowly and with difficulty.'

Schulenburg went on to report a prime example of the Soviets' suspicious nature: Molotov had taken the Latvians and Estonians to task for signing non-aggression treaties with Germany, insisting that these represented a leaning towards Germany and against the Soviet Union. He refused to budge from this line, even though they pointed out that they already had similar treaties with the Soviet Union. Bearing this in mind, Schulenburg had been quick to reject a suggestion from the Estonian minister that Germany might like to guarantee the independence of the Baltic states as she had done with Belgium. He did not think, he said, that the Soviets would like it.

The letter reached the Wilhelmstrasse on 9 August, and Schnurre telephoned 'the interesting parts of it' through to Ribbentrop at Fuschl that evening. The Foreign Minister was not dismayed by his ambassador's doubts. His confidence remained unshaken: only he and the Führer knew how far they were prepared to go in buying off the Soviets. In any case, Ribbentrop had nothing but contempt for the slow and stately measure of the traditional diplomatic minuet with its carefully regulated steps; the Nazis were, after all, a revolutionary organisation and as such were committed to getting rid of old bourgeois conventions. They could, therefore, move swiftly, directly and decisively when it suited them, untrammelled by old-fashioned niceties of behaviour. What counted at

French Premier Edouard Daladier
(*left*), the inevitable Gauloise
between his fingers, leaves
10 Downing Street with his Foreign
Minister Georges Bonnet after
agreeing concessions to Hitler

Naïvely optimistic as ever, British
Prime Minister Neville Chamberlain
prepares to fly out of Heston on
22 September 1938 to meet Hitler at
Bad Godesberg. His *éminence grise*,
Sir Horace Wilson, is on his right

ABOVE The 'good old Auswärtiges
Amt' on Berlin's Wilhelmstrasse, hub
of negotiations for the pact.

RIGHT Hitler discusses plans for the
new chancellery with architect Albert
Speer. Even in the midst of war, he
pushed ahead with his grandiose
dreams of rebuilding Berlin and
other cities

OPPOSITE PAGE:
TOP Teatime at the Hotel Dreesen,
beside the Rhine at Bad Godesberg –
and Hitler's face clearly reveals his
boredom. On the right, Ambassador
Sir Neville Henderson looks equally
wearied, but interpreter Paul
Schmidt remains alert

BELOW Entering the Sudetenland in
triumph, Hitler is greeted
rapturously by newly-annexed young
subjects

TOP Visiting Rome in January 1939, Halifax and Chamberlain, here sandwiched between Foreign Minister Galeazzo Ciano and Benito Mussolini, are completely taken in by the carefully staged welcome

BELOW Polish Foreign Minister Jozef Beck has every reason to feel pleased as he arrives at Victoria Station, London, on 3 April 1939, to receive Britain's 'blank cheque' guarantee

OPPOSITE Soviet sports clubs parade before Stalin in Red Square, Moscow, on 19 July 1939. William Strang and Count Schulenburg watched from the diplomats stand, to the right of Lenin's Tomb

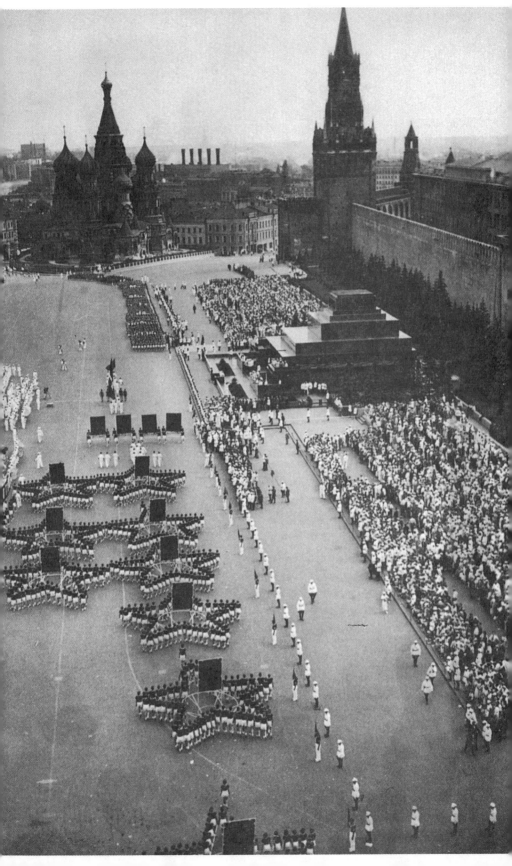

ABOVE Karl Schnurre, the Germans'
ace economic negotiator, used by
Ribbentrop to prepare the ground
for the non-aggression pact

TOP RIGHT Marshall Kliment
Voroshilov, Soviet Defence
Commissar, Stalin's most loyal and
adoring servant – until the débâcle
of the Winter War with Finland

RIGHT Stalin and Molotov, the
world's most formidable double act,
adept at playing hard man and soft
man in negotiations

OPPOSITE PAGE:
TOP Admiral Drax (*right*) and
General Doumenc (*left*) lead the
Allied military mission along the
open platform of Moscow's
Leningrad Station on their arrival in
the Soviet capital

BELOW: Naval Commissar Nikolai G.
Kuznetsov stressed the dangers of
the Seaborne threat to Leningrad
and Kronstadt

Hans and Elisabeth – otherwise known as 'Johnnie' and 'Pussi' – von Herwarth. A staunch anti-Nazi, later a member of the conspiracy which tried to assassinate Hitler, Herwarth did his best to warn the Allies of the coming pact and its implications

Ribbentrop (*left*) arrives in Moscow on 23 August 1939 and is greeted by Ambassador Friedrich Werner von der Schulenburg (*right*). Between them in the background are Gustav Hilger and Richard Schulze

that moment for Ribbentrop was not what the conservative Schulenburg thought, but the fact that both Astakhov and Babarin were meeting Schnurre next day, to talk business.

Schnurre's meeting with Astakhov lasted about an hour, from 11 am till noon. It started amicably, with the subject of the German representatives who were to go to the Moscow Agricultural Exhibition. Now named as Herr Moritz, Herr Meyer and Count Grote, these three men had become symbols of good intent between the two nations, and Schnurre was happy to be able to tell Astakhov they would be leaving for Moscow on Saturday. Astakhov, smiling, promptly invited them, along with Schnurre and Martin Schliep, head of the Foreign Office Political Department's Eastern Europe division, to lunch at the Soviet embassy next day. Schliep's inclusion was an acknowledgement by both sides that the talks were now moving from trade to politics.

Having laid down this marker, the two diplomats got down to serious business. The meeting swiftly developed into a sounding-out operation, with each side trying to persuade the other to make the first firm offer, like two farmers starting to haggle over a fat cow, each reluctant to come out with a starting figure.

Schnurre assured Astakhov that German interests in Poland were strictly limited, and that there was no need for them to clash with Soviet interests; that if it did prove necessary to settle the Polish problem by force of arms, Germany was willing 'to enter upon a large-scale adjustment of mutual interests with Moscow'. If Molotov would let them know what he considered were basic Soviet interests, they could then 'discuss concrete problems'.

Astakhov replied that he had no instructions to discuss either Poland or the Anglo-French negotiations – then went on to discuss both in considerable detail. On the negotiations, he reminded Schnurre that they had started at a time when there had been no indications that Germany was willing to come to an understanding with the Soviet Union. The Soviets, he said, had entered into them without much enthusiasm, but they had felt they had to protect themselves against Germany, and had to accept help where it was offered. Schnurre affected to be shocked by this, and quickly responded that if the only reason for negotiations with the Allies was fear of Germany then the Germans were prepared to give the Soviets every assurance they wanted. He drew Astakhov's attention to the essential difference between the German position and that of the British: the Germans actually had something concrete to offer – trade plus territory in Poland, once it was conquered – while Britain had not. British support, he pointed out, could never become effective in Eastern Europe.

Astakhov acknowledged the argument, and the reference to the coming Anglo-French military talks. 'But one cannot simply break off something which was begun for well-considered reasons. However, in my opinion the outcome of the negotiations is uncertain and it is quite possible that my government likewise considers the question to be completely open. Our conversation today, with those we have already had, will surely have an effect on their thinking.'

This was the first positive sign that German efforts to drive a wedge between the British and French and the Soviets were succeeding. Its timing could hardly have been better, coming on the very day when Admiral Drax and his party landed in Leningrad. On the question of the price to be paid, however, Astakhov was less forthcoming. Although he was prepared on his own initiative to talk about Poland in some detail, he doubted whether he would get any firm reply from Moscow on 'this massive problem'.

'At this stage of the conversations,' he told Schnurre, 'it is like putting the cart before the horse.' Then he promptly turned the question back on the Germans: what were *their* aims and ambitions in Poland? Were there likely to be any decisions in the next few days?

Now it was Schnurre's turn to avoid giving a straight answer, for he had no authority as yet to make the opening bid. The stand-off could only be broken at a much higher level, as everyone well knew. Astakhov promised to report back to Molotov; in the meantime, Babarin would call on Schnurre that afternoon to continue discussing the trade and credit agreement.

On 10 August, as the Anglo-French mission was arriving in Moscow, Colonel Beck in Warsaw demanded to see the German ambassador, and was most put out when told that Moltke was still in Berlin. Rather than receive someone of lesser status, he delegated the job with bad grace to his Under-Secretary of State.

Beck's move was the expected reaction to a significant turn of the screw over Danzig, which Hitler and Ribbentrop had applied the previous day. While Schnurre had been talking to Astakhov, Weizsäcker had had the Polish chargé d'affaires standing before his desk while he read out the text of a note dictated to him at 11.15 pm on 8 August by Ribbentrop. This was in response to the ultimatum from the Polish government to the Danzig Senate, and was itself an ultimatum. Any repetition of such demands, or any more threats, it stated, would lead to an aggravation of German–Polish relations which would be entirely the fault of the Polish government. The Reich government disclaimed all responsibility for the consequences. When he had finished, and while the chargé d'affaires was still trying desperately to take down what he had said, Weizsäcker, obeying Ribbentrop's orders to the letter, had him shown out immediately, refusing to allow him to say anything, even unofficially.

In itself, the note meant little. What mattered was the way in which it was delivered and the fact that this was the first time the German government had not channelled its views through its puppets in the Danzig Senate, but had replied directly to the Poles. This marked a distinct escalation of tension, placing the German and Polish governments in confrontation with each other not merely over rights of access but over the internal affairs of the Free City itself.

The Polish reaction was even better than Hitler could have hoped for. Beck's message was quite unlike anything he had ever received from someone he was threatening. Sarcastic, arrogant and belligerent in tone, it noted 'with extreme surprise' the statement given to the chargé in Berlin. 'The Polish government,' it said, 'will continue to react as hitherto to any attempt by the Free City authorities to impair the rights and interest which Poland enjoys in Danzig under her agreements, and will do so by such means and measures as they alone may deem appropriate . . . they will regard any future intervention by the German government as an act of aggression.' It was perfect fuel for the fire Hitler was busily stoking.

In Danzig, meanwhile, Forster went ahead and made his speech, as coached by Hitler, to a highly receptive Nazi gathering. Their next rally, he declared to the wildly cheering crowd, would take place after Danzig's annexation by the Reich. At the same time, in Düsseldorf, Colonel General Walther von Brauchitsch, Commander-in-Chief of the army, was addressing munitions workers, winding them up to be ready for 'the final sacrifice which might be necessary for the preservation of our nation'.

There was encouragement for Hitler in two reports received that day from Schulenburg on the poor prospects for Anglo-French success in their negotiations. One pointed up the difficulties over guarantees to the Baltic states, the other repeated a conversation between the Polish and Italian ambassadors in Moscow, in which the Pole reasserted his country's refusal, under any circumstances, even to consider allowing Soviet troops or aircraft on to or across its territory. This was good news indeed for Germany, as also was a signal from Ambassador Dirksen in London, reporting on his farewell meeting with Halifax before returning to Germany on leave. The British Foreign Secretary had reiterated his government's willingness to talk and reluctance to fight; he had promised that Britain was prepared to go 'a long way' to meet German wishes.

Also on 10 August, the chief of the Abwehr (the German Secret Service), Admiral Wilhelm Canaris, was flown to Salzburg for a conference with OKW Chief of Staff Colonel General Wilhelm Keitel and Hitler's personal OKW adjutant, the forty-four-year-old Lieutenant-Colonel Rudolf Schmundt. After discussing plans for sabotage and subversion operations behind Polish lines during Operation White, the admiral drove to Schloss Fuschl to receive other orders from Ribbentrop, on behalf of Hitler. These were for a very different type of operation, one which would be organised not by Canaris and the Abwehr but by Himmler and the SD, the SS security service. Canaris's part in it was to be confined to providing, from the Abwehr's stocks, 150 Polish army uniforms and assorted Polish small arms.

Reinhardt Heydrich, the head of the SD, had given the codename 'Canned Goods' to the operation. It provided Hitler with what he was looking for – a 'provocation' which would give him the final excuse for a war with Poland. What made it particularly attractive was that it could be staged at precisely the moment chosen by Hitler, since it did not rely on the Poles doing anything. The operation consisted of two separate but co-ordinated incidents, both of which involved the use of condemned men from concentration camps – the actual 'canned goods' – together with special SS squads masquerading as Polish troops.

The first incident was to be led by one of the SD's brightest intellectual gangsters, thirty-nine-year-old Alfred Helmut Naujocks, who had studied engineering at Kiel University, joined the SS in 1931 and had been a member of the SD since its inception in 1934. He specialised in undercover assignments such as disposing of enemies of the Nazis both in Germany and elsewhere, and running arms and explosives into Czechoslovakia during the build-up for the German invasion. After the war, in one of several sworn affidavits for the Nuremberg Tribunal, he recalled his instructions for 'Canned Goods'.

'On or about 10 August 1939,' Naujocks recorded, 'the chief of the SD, Heydrich, personally ordered me to simulate an attack on a radio station near Gleiwitz, near the Polish border, and to make it appear that the attacking force consisted of Poles. Heydrich said: "Practical proof of these attacks by the Poles is needed for the foreign press as well as for German propaganda."

'My instructions were to seize the radio station and to hold it long enough to permit a Polish-speaking German who would be put at my disposal to broadcast a speech in Polish. Heydrich told me that this speech should state that the time had come for fighting between Germans and Poles.'

The second incident was more complex and even more provocative. In this, a group of Polish-speaking troops, also wearing Canaris's uniforms and using the weapons he was to supply, was to attack and seize a German customs post near Hochlinden, engaging SS troops in a mock battle. Genuine Polish troops garrisoned just across the border at Rybnik would be ordered into the fight by a Polish officer who had just defected to Germany.

In both cases, there were to be 'Polish' bodies – which was where the concentration camp prisoners came in. They were to be supplied by Heinrich Müller, chief of the Gestapo. As Naujocks said in his affidavit: 'Müller stated that he had twelve to thirteen condemned criminals who were to be dressed in Polish uniforms and left dead on the ground at the scene of the incident, to show they had been killed during the attack. For this purpose, they were to be given lethal injections by a doctor employed by Heydrich. They were then also to be given gunshot wounds. After the incident, members of the press and other persons were to be taken to the spot.' Naturally, the corpses would all have Polish army passbooks in their pockets, to confirm their identities, in addition to their uniforms and weapons.

Heydrich was proud of his scheme. In his briefing to Naujocks he said: 'Up to now, the idea was mine and I've prepared this without the Führer's knowledge. But now the Führer has endorsed the plan.' The enthusiasm with which Hitler did so can be judged from what he said to Professor Carl Burckhardt next day, when the League of Nations High Commissioner flew from Danzig to see him, at his urgent request.

Burckhardt was an important figure in Hitler's plans, and the Nazi leader gave him suitably privileged treatment. He sent his own brand-new Focke Wulf 200 Condor aircraft, *Immelmann III*, to collect him from Danzig and fly him in the utmost comfort to Salzburg. From there a Mercedes was waiting to whisk him not to the Berghof but to the even more exclusive pavilion perched on the 6,017-foot-high summit of the nearby Kehlstein mountain, conceived and built by Martin Bormann as a gift from the party to the Führer for his fiftieth birthday on 20 April 1939. Three thousand workers, some German, some Italians supplied by Mussolini as a gesture of friendship, but mostly slave labourers, had toiled unceasingly to complete the project in only 390 days and nights.

It was, by any standards, a remarkable feat of engineering and construction, a fitting monument to the arrogant confidence of Nazi Germany at the time. 'To the builders of the Third Reich,' it proclaimed, 'nothing is impossible.' It was also, by any standard, a remarkable folly, costing over 30 million Reichsmarks, the equivalent now of some 90 million US dollars, to little practical purpose.

Even the approach to the Kehlstein house was staggering: it was reached by four miles of specially built roadway, clinging to the sheer sides of the mountain, winding its tortuous path through five tunnels and countless bends to end abruptly at 5,500 feet before an immense portal with two electrically operated bronze doors, twenty feet high and set into the rock face of the mountain like the entrance to Valhalla.

Beyond the great doors constantly guarded by SS sentries, a high, arched tunnel lined with dressed granite and illuminated by heavy copper lanterns led four hundred feet to a circular hall, glistening with moisture, in the heart of the mountain. From this hall a heated elevator, lined with Venetian mirrors to help soothe Hitler's claustrophobia, climbed silently and smoothly a further four hundred feet to the building itself. The elevator was a two-tier affair, with the lower part used for goods or, when the occasion demanded, for persons of lower ranks or importance.

The building itself was a simply designed structure, its massively thick walls constructed of sandstone and pinkish-coloured granite. The focus of the whole place was the principal room, at the eastern end. This was semi-circular, some thirty feet across, with a heavily beamed ceiling, its walls lined with rough-hewn Unterberg marble and pierced by five picture windows to make the most of the magnificent view. Its one interior wall was dominated by a great open fireplace of dark red polished marble, a birthday present to Hitler from Mussolini. In the centre of the room a circular table some ten feet in diameter was surrounded by a number of comfortable armchairs upholstered in rich floral brocade. Other armchairs, settees and smaller tables were placed around the walls and in front of the fireplace. The floor was covered by a huge oriental carpet, a gift from the Japanese Emperor Hirohito.

The other rooms, which were panelled in elm or pine, included a dining room, a tea room, a study, a duty room for the SS guards and a modern electric kitchen. A large cellar contained supply and machinery rooms, one of which housed an eight-cylinder 300-hp MAN diesel U-boat engine to provide emergency power in the event of a failure of the electricity supply from Berchtesgaden.

The house was protected by a six-foot fence erected around the entire summit. The tunnel, house and elevator were further protected by concealed remote-controlled gas capsules, with gas masks for guards and occupants kept ready in special containers.

Perched on its rocky crag, the Kehlstein house was a visible symbol of Hitler's grandiose fantasies, his image of himself made concrete in granite and marble. The fact that it was conceived and executed by Martin Bormann in no way detracts from this, for the steward could never have completed the task without his master's approval.

At first, Hitler was delighted with his new toy. Building and architecture were his abiding passions. Bormann could not have thought of a better and more appropriate birthday present. In the three or four months after its completion, in September 1938, the Führer visited it nearly every day he was at the Berghof.

It was French Ambassador André François-Poncet who gave the house the name by which it became best known: he described it as being like the nest of an eagle, and the description stuck. To Hitler it remained the Kehlstein house. To the rest of the world it became for ever 'The Eagle's Nest'.

As the novelty wore off, Hitler became disenchanted with his eyrie. He felt claustrophobic riding in the elevator in the heart of the mountain, and developed a fear that lightning might strike and travel down the cables. At the top, he suffered palpitations and shortness of breath, due to the sudden change in altitude. In the summer of 1939, however, he was still sufficiently pleased with it to use it for entertaining specially favoured guests whom he wanted to impress. On 11 August, he was clearly determined to impress his Swiss visitor, knowing that Burckhardt was the best choice as mediator with the Allies, should it become possible or necessary to attempt another Munich settlement.

As always when he had a captive audience, Hitler could not resist giving a performance. Burckhardt had to endure two and a half hours of Hitler monologue, largely following the same script as that used for the Hungarian Foreign Minister three days before. But Burckhardt thought Hitler showed signs of fear and nervousness, as well as looking older and greyer than when he had last seen him. There were some variations on the Czaky performance – the Polish plans now 'far exceeded all the visions of Alexander and Napoleon' – but for the most part the essence was the same.

'If there's the slightest provocation, I will shatter Poland without warning into so many pieces there'll be nothing left to pick up,' he shouted. 'Do you hear me?'

Burckhardt nodded, alarmed. 'Very well, Herr Chancellor. I realise that would mean a general war.'

'So be it,' Hitler replied, 'agitated and almost appealingly' according to Burckhardt. He set his face in an expression of mixed pain and anger. 'If I have to wage war, I would rather do it today than tomorrow. I will not conduct it like Wilhelm II, who always had scruples of conscience before waging total warfare. I will fight relentlessly to the bitter end.'

After tea, however, Hitler's mood and direction changed abruptly, as he moved on to the second act of his drama. The bellicose tone vanished, and was replaced by sweet reason and a desire for peace.

'All this eternal talk of war is nonsense. It is driving the nations insane,' he said, quietly. 'What is the real question? Only that Germany needs grain and timber. I need space in the east in order to have wheat; I need a colony for timber, just one. We can manage then. Our crops have been excellent in 1938 and this year. But one of these days the soil will have had enough and it will go on strike like a body that has been doped. What then? I cannot have my people suffering hunger. Wouldn't I be better leaving two million on the battlefield than losing even more from hunger? We know what it is like to die from hunger.

'I have no romantic aspirations,' he continued, still calm and reasonable, 'no appetite for domination. Above all, I want nothing from the West, not today and not tomorrow. I want nothing from the thickly settled regions of the world. There I am seeking nothing – once and for all, absolutely nothing. All the ideas that people ascribe to me are inventions. But I must have a free hand in the east.'

Outside the circular room, the sun was setting, colouring the mountain peaks into a fantastic operatic backdrop. Hitler led Burckhardt outside on to the terrace.

'How happy I am when I am here,' he said, gesturing expansively at the scenery all around. 'I have worked enough. Now it is time to rest. I would be happy to stay here and take up painting – I am an artist, you know.'

Having drawn attention to the setting, Hitler started on his grand finale, opening on a note of humanity and personal concern as he advised Burckhardt to send his children away from Danzig, back to Switzerland.

'I have been glad to see you. You come from a world which is strange to me, but you have worked for a peaceful solution,' he said with great sincerity, before moving on smoothly to the real point: 'I have great sympathy for another man – Lord Halifax. They have said much ill of him to me since, but my first impressions still hold good: I thought he was a man who saw things on a grand scale and who wanted a peaceful solution. I hope to meet with him some time; I want to live in peace with Britain. If they will give me freedom in the east, I will happily conclude a pact with the British and guarantee their possessions all around the world.'

'Wouldn't it be better for you to talk about this directly with a British representative?' Burckhardt asked.

'The language is too big a barrier,' Hitler replied. He paused, then brightened. 'But perhaps we could find some German-speaking Englishman? I am told General Ironside speaks fluent German.'

'May I tell them that you have such a wish?'

'Yes,' Hitler replied eagerly. 'Couldn't you go to London yourself? If we want to avoid a catastrophe we must not lose any time.'

Burckhardt was staggered by this odd suggestion. There were times when Hitler's penchant for unorthodox diplomacy bordered on the bizarre: why should Hitler need to use someone like him when Germany and Britain still enjoyed full diplomatic relations? However, before returning to Danzig, Burckhardt flew to his home in Basle, Switzerland, called the British and French ministers from Berne, and duly passed on the information. What he did not tell them, however, was Hitler's final statement – partly because he did not fully appreciate its significance.

'Everything I am doing is directed against Russia,' he had said in parting. 'If the West is too obtuse to grasp this, then I shall be forced to come to terms with the Russians and turn against the West first. After that I will direct my entire strength against the USSR. I need the Ukraine, so that nobody can ever starve us out again, as they did in the last war.' It was one of the very few occasions when Hitler told a foreign politician the truth.

In Moscow, at about the time Hitler was saying his farewells to Burckhardt, fourteen men were gathering for a meeting in Stalin's office. They took their seats around the green-baize table to the left of the door, under the gaze of Lenin and Marx, staring down from their portraits on the cream-painted walls. Alongside the two socialist leaders, however, were two other pictures, stiff chromolithographs like those one would expect to find in any provincial office, in identical carved wooden frames. These were portraits of military heroes from pre-Revolutionary days. Prince Alexander Suvorov and Mikhail Kutuzov, who led the Tsar's armies against Napoleon: when it came to choosing heroes, nationalism played as important a part as political dogma. The same tenet could be applied to the deliberations of the Politburo, as its members approached the main business of the meeting – to lay down guidelines for Voroshilov in the talks with the Anglo-French missions, which were due to begin next day.

Voroshilov had already prepared a paper in which he made a scathing attack on the Allies' vagueness and incompetence. Now that he had actually met Drax and Doumenc, shortly before the Politburo session, his earlier doubts had been reinforced. He would, of course, show the Anglo-French mission the full warmth of traditional Russian hospitality at the banquet that evening, but he wanted the guidance of his fellow members as to how seriously he should pursue an agreement.

It was an interesting question, for the Soviets now found themselves in a most gratifying position: after so many years as the lepers of the international scene, they were now being propositioned by all and sundry. Astakhov's latest report from Berlin, on his meeting with Schnurre the previous day, told how Hitler was virtually inviting them to name their own price. To Stalin, this was a most welcome and timely change of fortune, and one which he was determined to exploit to the full. On the best way of achieving this object, he was, as always, ready to listen to the views of the Politburo before making final decisions though, as always, those decisions would be his alone.

No one could doubt that Hitler now intended to invade Poland, and that that invasion was imminent – the signs were all far too clear. The great danger for the Soviet Union was that Hitler was likely to crush the Poles swiftly and decisively, ending up with his armies on the Soviet border. Now, however, Molotov was able to say that the Germans were indicating that they were prepared to carve up Poland in a new partition which would both return those parts of the Russian empire that had been snatched by Pilsudski in 1921, and the same time provide a buffer state between Germany and the USSR.

Stalin asked whether the Germans could be pinned down on this question if he agreed to their requests for political talks. Molotov answered that he was sure they could: they were now in a great hurry. Stalin considered this, and pointed out to the meeting how untrustworthy he believed the Western Powers to be; they were weak and uncertain, and he did not believe they would fight.

Backing up Stalin's view, Molotov told the meeting he had evidence that the democracies were holding secret negotiations with the Germans which could lead to another Munich. He listed the conversations Wohlthat had had in London, and the talks which were still going on – though he thought they were in Denmark rather than in German Schleswig-Holstein – between the British businessmen and Göring. This led him to the conclusion that the British would not honour their guarantees to Poland, but would come round to an understanding with Germany.

'But,' asked Stalin, 'what if they do not?'

Molotov turned to the others round the table. 'That,' he said, 'is for the Politburo to decide.'

The Politburo, however, under Stalin's direction, chose not to decide anything for the moment. In Stalin's view, the urgency lay entirely with the other parties. It was the Germans who wanted to be free to attack Poland, and the Allies who had given her their guarantees. The Marxist approach to such a situation is quite clear: one must always try to keep two options open, and delay until the last possible moment the choice between them. In that way, the maximum advantage can be wrung from any negotiations.

Voroshilov would open the military talks with the Allies next day, in all seriousness. Molotov could let the Germans know that he was prepared to open political talks with them, also in all seriousness. Whoever could offer the best deal for the Soviet Union would win.

17

'WE WANT WAR'

In the late afternoon of Saturday, 12 August, Walther Hewel hurried into the salon of the Berghof, carrying two sheets of paper. At the circular table by the picture window, Ribbentrop sat listening in a bored manner as Hitler held forth to Italian Foreign Minister Count Galeazzo Ciano. Hewel moved swiftly across the thick red carpet to whisper in his ear. Ribbentrop was suddenly alert. He sat up, glanced at the papers, then turned to the Führer, daring to interrupt him in mid-flow. Hitler listened with growing interest as Ribbentrop, in his turn, whispered urgently. He then rose and, pausing only to excuse himself to Ciano, left the room with his Foreign Minister and Hewel.

When they returned a few minutes later, Hitler's previously sombre mood had completely changed. The displeasure which he had manifested to the Italian was replaced with smiling affability as he suggested they leave the rest of their talks until next morning. He invited Ciano to accompany him to the Kehlstein house for tea, while the light was still good enough for them to enjoy the view. Poor Ciano was forced to accept, albeit with obvious lack of enthusiasm – he hated heights and disliked tea – since Hitler was clearly intent on celebrating the news he had just received: two messages, Ribbentrop explained, one from Moscow, the other from Tokyo.

'The Russian government,' Hitler announced, 'has agreed to open political negotiations, and has asked for a minister to be sent.'

He paused, waiting for some comment, perhaps even for applause. But Ciano remained silent, convinced the 'messages' were nothing more than a typically theatrical device, part of Hitler's attempt to inveigle Italy into a disastrous military partnership.

Ciano may well have been right, at least in part: the only message from Tokyo at that time had been received the day before and had not brought favourable news, but had listed the problems the Japanese War Minister was having in trying to persuade his colleagues in government to support Germany. Significantly, Hitler and Ribbentrop made no effort to tell Ciano what was in this message, no doubt hoping he would assume it offered Japan's backing.

The other message was in fact a teleprint from Schnurre in Berlin, but here Hitler was only slightly stretching the truth in what he told Ciano. Schnurre reported that Astakhov had called on him that morning, on instructions from Molotov, to say that the Soviets were interested in 'a discussion of the individual groups of questions that had been raised before'. 'Besides the pending economic questions,' he had said, 'these were, *inter alia*, press questions, cultural collaboration, the Polish question and the question of the old German–Soviet political treaties.'

This was exactly what Hitler had been longing to hear – though, at this point, celebrations were to prove premature. There was still a long way to go, and the Soviets, once they had realised just how desperately he needed this agreement with them, did not propose to make things easy. They were in a position to dictate the pace of the negotiations, and they were in no hurry. Indeed, Molotov instructed Astakhov to stress that discussions could only proceed '*by degrees*', one stage at a time. He also proposed that any talks should be held in Moscow, rather than in Berlin. And despite what Hitler told Ciano, he had not asked for a minister to be sent out, but had played down the importance of the talks by saying he would leave open the question of whether they should be left to the German ambassador or to someone – he did not specify whom – to be sent out from Berlin.

It was, nevertheless, the all-important breakthrough for Hitler, and even if Ciano did not totally accept it, it was enough to leave him almost literally speechless. The trip to the mountain-top eyrie completed the process: as Hitler waxed loquacious on the grandeur of the scenery, Ciano could only sit and shiver disconsolately. That night, he telephoned his father-in-law in Rome: 'The position is serious.' From Italy's point of view it certainly was. A pact between the USSR and Germany would considerably reduce Mussolini's ability to influence events. Free from the threat of Soviet retaliation when he invaded Poland, Hitler would no longer need to pander to the fears of his southern ally. Any moderating influence which Mussolini might have been able to exert would have vanished, leaving Italy vulnerable to the whims of her Axis partner. Ciano could see his country being dragged into a war she was not ready to fight and did not really want.

The sole purpose of Ciano's visit to Germany, replacing as it did the projected meeting between Hitler and Mussolini, was to try to persuade the Nazi leader to call off the attack on Poland and allow Mussolini to set up an international peace conference – as he had done at Munich the year before – to discuss the problem of Danzig and the Corridor.

'The Duce is anxious,' Ciano confided in his diary the day before he left Rome, 'that I prove to the Germans, by documentary evidence, that the outbreak of war at this time would be madness.'

Interestingly, in the same entry, he recorded that the Japanese ambassador in Rome had told him Tokyo had decided to adhere to the alliance. He doubted if this was true, but feared that if it were it could 'make Germany more arrogant and encourage her to rush along a path of intransigence and thus bring the crisis to the boiling point as concerns the Danzig problem'. He also noted that the 'conversations with Moscow are as yet inconclusive'. It was almost as though Hitler had read that diary entry, so conclusively did he demolish Ciano's hopes with the two pieces of paper which were produced at the Berghof.

At the resumption of talks next morning, Ciano had, as the interpreter Paul Schmidt put it, 'folded up like a jack-knife'. When Hitler proclaimed: 'I am unshakeably convinced that neither England nor France will embark upon a general war,' he did not try to contradict him, or to continue pressing Mussolini's conviction that any offensive in Poland would inevitably develop into a general war throughout Europe. Instead, he could only mutter feebly: 'You have been proved right so often before when we others held the opposite view that I think it very possible that this time, too, you see things more clearly than we do.'

Ciano's visit had been a disaster from the very start. He had spent the first day, Friday, 11 August, at Fuschl and Salzburg with Ribbentrop, where the atmosphere had been icy. The two men disliked each other intensely: Ciano thought Ribbentrop was a pompous dullard who lied continuously; like Hitler, Ribbentrop despised Ciano as 'a brilliantined dandy' addicted to womanising and heavy drinking. The ten hours they spent in political discussion that day did nothing to reduce their antipathy. By the time they sat down to dinner, which Ribbentrop had arranged at the Weisse Rossl, the famous White Horse Inn at St Wolfgang, where 'a jolly folk festival' was in progress, they had nothing left to say. While the zithers twanged and the dancers clapped and yodelled in the background, the two Foreign Ministers ate in glacial silence, neither uttering a word to the other.

Ciano's distrust of Ribbentrop was so great that he ordered the crew of his aircraft to stay with it in the hangar at Salzburg airfield all night, fearing sabotage. And when he discussed the day's conversations with Ambassador Attolico and Counsellor Magistrati from the Berlin embassy, he insisted on doing it in the bathroom with all the taps running to foil the bugs which he was sure had been planted in his room.

During the day, Ciano complained to his diary, Ribbentrop had been evasive when asked for particulars about German plans. 'His conscience bothers him,' he noted. 'He has lied too many times about German intentions towards Poland not to feel uneasy now about what he must tell me and what they are getting ready to do.' But if Ribbentrop had been reluctant to discuss details, he apparently had no such inhibitions about revealing general intentions.

'Well, Ribbentrop,' Ciano had asked as they walked in the garden at

Fuschl before lunch, 'what do you want? The Corridor or Danzig?'

'Not that any more,' Ribbentrop had replied, gazing at him with his 'cold metallic eyes'. 'We want war!'

Over lunch, Ribbentrop had continued to pour scorn on Italian fears. He had insisted on making an extravagant bet with Ciano: if England and France stayed neutral, as Ribbentrop maintained they would, Ciano would give him a painting by an Italian old master; if, on the other hand, they intervened, and there was general war, then Ribbentrop would give Ciano a collection of antique German armour. In spite of the fact that the bet was made in front of several witnesses, however, Ribbentrop never honoured it.

Ciano's visit to Hitler at the Berghof next day, which ended so dramatically with the arrival of the two messages, was stage-managed from the start in order to exert every ounce of pressure on the Italian. As an opener, Hitler did not follow his normal custom of greeting his visitors on the front steps, but had Ciano, Attolico and Magistrati shown directly into the salon, where they 'discovered' him standing at the table spread with strategic maps, apparently immersed in military matters. He greeted them warmly, then proceeded to deprive Ciano of his supporters by stating that what he had to say was for his ears alone. Ringing a bell, he summoned Martin Bormann to take the two diplomats away and 'entertain them'.

Ribbentrop, who had accompanied them, naturally stayed in the room, and Ciano was not pleased to see that there were also not one but two interpreters. In addition to Paul Schmidt, there was also a young man whom he knew only too well: Eugen Dollmann, whose usual occupation was as a Gestapo agent attached to the Rome embassy, where he specialised in compiling incriminating dossiers on the private lives and indiscretions of Italian ministers – including, of course, Ciano himself, whose indiscretions were legion.

As soon as Attolico and Magistrati had gone, Hitler launched into a great lecture on the strength of Germany's defences on all frontiers, using the maps to illustrate his points to the startled Ciano, heaping derision on the British, French and Polish forces. Germany, he declared, was impregnable to attack from any direction. But he was soon making it clear that he was set on invading Poland, and that he expected Italy's support.

As always when making such proposals, he offered Italy an inducement, a reward for her friendship. In this case, it was to be Yugoslavia. If Italy provided cover for Germany by invading France during the attack on Poland, then Germany would reciprocate by helping Italy to occupy her Balkan neighbour.

Turning to Danzig, Hitler set about convincing Ciano that it was impossible for him to yield, for it was not only material interests which were at stake but also powerful emotional attachments: Danzig was 'an ancient German city, the Nuremberg of the north, which aroused sentimental feelings in every German'.

'Imagine Trieste in Yugoslav hands,' he implored Ciano, 'and a strong Italian minority on Yugoslav soil being treated with brutal force. It could hardly be assumed that Italy would tolerate that for long.'

In spite of the power of Hitler's eloquence, and the fact that he had allowed Ribbentrop to browbeat him into silence the day before, Ciano stood up to Hitler manfully. He countered his arguments with force and wit, and when they broke for lunch he had the temerity to poke fun at the floral decorations on the table, which had been arranged by Eva Braun, Hitler's mistress. The lady herself was nowhere to be seen, having been banished to her room by Hitler before the guests arrived: he did not want any distractions, and he may even have been a little jealous, for Eva made no secret of the fact that she found Ciano most attractive. She had to content herself with peeping from behind her bedroom curtains as the Italians arrived – but not so discreetly that they did not notice her. She took snapshots of them with a camera fitted with a telephoto lens. When she pasted these into her album, she captioned a shot of them at the entrance, glancing curiously up to her window: 'Up there there's something forbidden to behold – me!'

During the afternoon session, Ciano continued to press Hitler, complaining that he had not kept Italy informed of the gravity of the situation. He accused Hitler of misleading Mussolini. Italian plans had always been made on the assumption that there would not be a general war for two or even three years, by which time they would be ready. At the moment, however, they were in no position to fight, and would much prefer to try to obtain a peaceful solution of the Danzig problem, through an international conference. Indeed, he made so much of Italian reluctance that at one point Ribbentrop, exasperated, exclaimed: 'We don't need you anyway!' To this, Ciano snapped back: 'The future will show.'

As the meeting progressed, it became more and more clear that while Hitler was determined to go to war, the Italians were equally determined not to. Hitler trotted out the usual arguments about the Polish weather forcing him to invade soon: 'From September to May, Poland is one vast swamp and completely unsuitable for any military operations,' he claimed. Poland could occupy Danzig in October, as she probably intended to do, he said, knowing that Germany could do nothing about it, since he would naturally never bomb and destroy the city. He began to rant about the Poles, claiming that they were intent on taking the whole of East Prussia and advancing as far as Berlin.

'It is unbearable,' he shouted, 'for a Great Power to have to tolerate perpetually such a hostile neighbour only 150 kilometres from her capital. I am therefore determined to make use of the next act of political provocation – be it in the form of an ultimatum, brutal maltreatment of Germans in Poland, an attempt to starve Danzig out, an entry of Polish troops into Danzig territory, or anything of that kind – to attack Poland within forty-eight hours and solve the problem that way.'

'When is such an operation against Poland to be expected?' Ciano wanted to know, 'since Italy will naturally have to be prepared for all eventualities.'

'In the present circumstances,' Hitler replied, 'a move against Poland must be expected at any moment.' The deadline was the end of August.

It was at this fortuitous point that Hewel entered with the two messages, bringing the day's business to a close. Before setting out for the Kehlstein house, however, Hitler and Ribbentrop spelled out for Ciano exactly what the Russian move meant.

Ribbentrop opened. The Russians, he said, were fully informed of Germany's intentions towards Poland. On orders from the Führer, he had personally told the Russian chargé d'affaires what they wanted. Hitler then took over, with a familiar and well-tried refrain: in his opinion, the Russians would not be prepared to pull the Western Powers' chestnuts out of the fire. Stalin could be in danger just as much from a victorious as from a defeated Russian army. If the Red Army were defeated because of what was perceived to be the result of Stalin's purges, then Soviet senior officers might well turn on their inquisitor in either vengeance or self-defence. If, on the other hand, the army returned victorious, then they would tell themselves they had won in spite of Stalin, and might feel strong enough to overthrow him. Either way, Stalin would be the loser.

Of course, Hitler said, the Soviets were determined to exact a price for their co-operation with the Third Reich. But as far as Hitler could see, their principal aim was merely to extend Soviet access to the Baltic via Latvia and Estonia – a modest enough demand in all conscience. As for the Poles, Hitler did not believe that the Russians would ever intervene on their behalf – they 'thoroughly detested' them. And as for the Anglo-French military mission, he could not take this seriously. The only reason for sending it, he declared, was to cover up the disastrous state reached in the political negotiations.

Hitler's performance had two principal aims: first, to frighten the Italians and bring them to heel; second, to frighten the Allies and sow doubts in their minds, since he knew anything said to Ciano would inevitably find its way to the British Foreign Office.

After a brief second meeting from 11.30 to 12 on Sunday morning, 13 August, when Hitler repeated much of what he had said the day before, Ciano flew out of Salzburg that afternoon. 'I return to Rome,' he wrote in his diary, 'completely disgusted with the Germans, with their leader, with their way of doing things. They have betrayed us and lied to us. Now they are dragging us into an adventure which we have not wanted and which might compromise the regime and the country as a whole.' He claimed to have advised Mussolini to refuse to support Germany in a war. Whether he did or not must be open to question – it is generally accepted that he doctored his diaries while awaiting execution in 1943 – but what is certain is that Hitler had judged Mussolini accurately. The promise of German backing for an Italian occupation of Yugoslavia was too tempting for him to resist, and he announced, 'Honour compels me to march with Germany.'

Despite this, after his meetings with Ciano, Hitler could have had few illusions about the reliability of Italy as a partner. Nevertheless he cynically exploited their position in the communiqué issued after the talks. Ciano had come with a prepared statement saying that, while resisting the Allies' attempts at encirclement, Italy and Germany were in complete agreement that the problems facing Europe could all be settled 'through normal diplomatic negotiations'. Ciano's draft reaffirmed 'the peaceful intentions' of the two governments. But Hitler would have none of this, and it was eventually decided, after much discussion, that there would be no communiqué. Less than two hours after Ciano's departure, however, one was issued by the German press service, the DNB, saying that the talks had covered all the problems of the day, with particular reference to Danzig, and that there had been 'one hundred per cent agreement'. Not a single problem, it stated, had been left in suspense, and there would be no further meetings because there was no need for any.

The Italians were furious. Attolico accused the Germans of acting in bad faith, and leaked the details of Hitler's war plans to British Ambassador Henderson. He considered the communiqué a machiavellian move to bind Italy to Germany after the attack on Poland, and begged Mussolini to be firm with Hitler and demand that he fulfil the provisions in the Pact of Steel, which allowed a month's grace for the settlement of disputes such as Danzig through diplomatic channels. But it was to no avail; his pleas went unheard. It would have made little difference if Mussolini had acted on them, for Hitler had come to realise, finally, that Italy was likely to be more of a liability than an asset. This made a deal with the Soviet Union utterly vital to his plans, and he ordered Ribbentrop to pull out all the stops to get one.

In view of the time factor, with only two days to his latest date for a firm decision to invade Poland, and less than two weeks till the planned date for the attack itself, it seemed an impossible task. The Allies, after all, had been negotiating with the Soviets for months already. But to Hitler and Ribbentrop it was a perfect opportunity to demonstrate what could be achieved by their new-style diplomacy, cutting across all the old conventions. Ribbentrop called Schnurre on the Sunday evening, and told him to prepare to go to Moscow, with Dr Hans Frank, Minister without Portfolio in the Reich Cabinet and director of the Nazi Party legal office (later to be Governor-General of German-occupied Poland). Schnurre was to let Astakhov know immediately that he and Frank would be going as soon as it could be arranged.

On Monday, 14 August, Hitler's plans and preparations moved into overdrive; both in Germany and the Soviet Union this was a day of vital decisions. In Moscow, however, as the Anglo-French mission approached the crisis in their third day of negotiations, with the increasingly impatient Voroshilov demanding answers on Poland and Romania, Schulenburg sat down in his study and began to write a letter to Weizsäcker. Unaware of the desperate and highly unorthodox measures that Hitler was prepared to take in order to meet his impossible timetable, the veteran ambassador continued to urge caution. 'I am still of the opinion,' he wrote, 'that any hasty measure in the matter of our relations with the Soviet Union should be avoided; it will always be harmful.'

Schulenburg was worried about the instructions he had received to attend the Nuremberg party rally. Like all other German diplomats, he had been ordered to wear the new grey uniform which Ribbentrop had designed, and this meant he would have to spend at least three days in Berlin for fittings and for buying the various accessories needed. This, he told Weizsäcker, would entail his leaving Moscow by 26 August at the very latest. It was an ironic choice of date: Schulenburg simply could not envisage negotiations for a pact with the Soviet Union being in any advanced stage by then, still less that it should be the very day set by Hitler for the invasion of Poland, with everything already wrapped up. Schulenburg's concern was that he might not be available to deal with Molotov.

'Certainly, I am the person who can best and most easily carry on conversations with M. Molotov,' he continued. 'This strange man and difficult character has now grown accustomed to me and in conversations with me has to a large extent abandoned the reserve which is otherwise always evident. Any new man would have to start from scratch.'

With great circumspection, he asked Weizsäcker to let him know which should take precedence, his role in handling Molotov, or his attendance at the party rally. Not even as respected and senior a figure as Count von der Schulenburg dared allow any hint of disloyalty to the Nazis to be set against his name in 1939.

It was not until 5 that afternoon that Schulenburg received information from Schnurre about his conversation with Astakhov, but this contained nothing to change his opinions, stressing as it did Molotov's insistence on proceeding 'by degrees'. By that time, however, there was already another message on the wire to him, from Weizsäcker. This arrived fifty-three minutes after Schnurre's, and was short, direct, but somewhat cryptic: 'Please arrange for an interview with Molotov tomorrow, Tuesday, 15 August. Instructions on the statement to be made to Molotov follow by telegram. Please telegram the time of your reception by Molotov.'

Hilger telephoned the Kremlin at 6.26 pm, and spoke to Molotov's secretary, who promised an early reply.

Both Schulenburg and Weizsäcker had to wait several hours before they were told the purpose of the meeting with Molotov. Ribbentrop was busy drafting his message, but he could not send it without Hitler's approval, and Hitler was occupied at the Berghof for most of the day with his Commanders-in-Chief. He had summoned Brauchitsch, Göring and Raeder for a military conference, along with Halder, Canaris and Dr Todt, the engineer of the West Wall. The OKW's deadline for a decision to go ahead with Operation White was next day, but Hitler had already made up his mind. The invasion was on.

Like all Hitler 'conferences', the meeting took the form of a lecture by the Führer. Brauchitsch never opened his mouth to speak during the entire day; Raeder added nothing; Göring limited himself to agreeing with his chief. Not one of them questioned Hitler's intention to lead the country into war.

'The great drama,' he told them, 'is now approaching its climax. Success, either politically or militarily, cannot be had without taking risks.' However, he was convinced that Britain and France would not fight. France he dismissed out of hand as being too demoralised. As for Britain: 'She has no leaders of real calibre. The men I got to know at Munich are not the kind to start a new world war . . . England will not allow herself to blunder into a war which will last for years – not even England has the money nowadays to fight a world war. What should England fight for? You don't get yourself killed for an ally.'

Poland, therefore, could be taken on alone. The proof that England would not support her, in spite of all the big talk, was that she would not give the Poles money to buy arms. If the British had been serious, they would have given the Poles more than a beggarly £8-million loan, and the Poles would have been considerably more insolent. All that Hitler required from the army and the Luftwaffe was that they should show the world that Poland was doomed within the first few days of the attack. Once that was achieved, they could take their time in finishing her off – six weeks or two months, even, it would not matter. No one would come to the rescue: not the British, and certanly not the Russians. 'A lost war is as dangerous to Stalin as a victorious army.'

Without giving the generals any specific details, he aroused their expectations by hinting at what was to come. He spoke of the trade negotiations, and said he was considering whether 'a political negotiator should go to Moscow, and whether this should be a prominent figure'. The Russians understood the need for the destruction of Poland. Their interests were limited at most to the Baltic states. Hitler was 'inclined to meet them halfway' in a 'delimitation of spheres of interest'.

If Hitler was still considering who should go to Moscow, it did not take him long to decide. Immediately the generals had left him, he spoke to Ribbentrop and approved the message to be sent to Moscow. It was despatched from the Wilhemstrasse at 10.53 pm, and received by Schulenburg at 4.40 on the morning of 15 August.

Like any message composed by Ribbentrop, the telegram was long and woolly. For six lengthy paragraphs it rambled on about there being no basic conflict between Germany and Russia, reiterating what had already been said by Schnurre at Ewest's and in other conversations and messages, and repeating the now familiar phrase 'from the Baltic to the Black Sea . . .' It held out the promise, once again, of a deal covering the Baltic states, Poland and the south-east, and painted the Western democracies as the villains of the hour, 'the implacable enemies of both Nationalist Socialist Germany and Soviet Russia', trying to drive Russia into war against Germany.

Then, suddenly, it came to the point: both sides wanted an understanding, but normal diplomatic channels were too slow. Ribbentrop himself was therefore prepared 'to make a short visit to Moscow in order, in the name of the Führer, to set forth the Führer's views to M. Stalin'.

With their consistent refusal to send anyone of real authority or standing to Moscow, the British and French had been snubbing the Russians for months. By proposing to go himself, without even waiting for the Soviets to ask, Ribbentrop was proving beyond all doubt that the Germans were serious. What was more, he was at the same time acknowledging Stalin's position, something the West had never done. It was an inspired piece of flattery from Hitler, displaying his intuitive understanding of Stalin's character.

For some reason, Ribbentrop instructed Schulenburg not to give Molotov the message in writing, but to read it out to him verbatim, since he wanted it 'to reach M. Stalin in as exact a form as possible'. If he had the chance, he was to ask for an audience with Stalin, so that he could read it out directly to him, too. A meeting with Stalin, as well as Molotov, would be a condition for Ribbentrop's making the trip to Moscow.

It was not until the next morning that Schulenburg received an answer to his request for an appointment with Molotov. The Soviet Premier would see him at 8 o'clock that evening: aware of the Germans' hurry, he naturally wanted to make them wait just long enough to keep them on the boil. He had, in any case, been unable to get back to them the previous evening; there had been another meeting of the Politburo.

Stalin had called the meeting to discuss Voroshilov's report on the proceedings so far in the Anglo-French talks, a report which was equally damning of both the abilities and the intentions of the Allied delegates. So, while Doumenc was frantically drafting his telegram to Paris begging for permission to apply pressure on Poland, the Soviet Politburo was hearing that the democracies could not be trusted. They obviously preferred Poland to the Soviet Union, Stalin said, and Nazi Germany to them both. The British, he told his colleagues, were still secretly meeting the Germans, no doubt hoping to frighten them into making an agreement by pretending to negotiate seriously with the Soviet Union. Stalin was tired of the deception; it was time for the Allies to face the consequences of their bad faith. The Soviet Union would begin political negotiations with Germany.

The Anglo-French talks would continue. It would be good strategy in dealing with the Germans to have them still going on as an apparently viable alternative. Voroshilov, who was not present at the meeting, need not be told what had been decided: no doubt Stalin thought he would make a better job of stringing the Allies along if he continued to believe in what he was doing. Besides, there was always the chance of a miracle. Even at one minute to midnight, the Allies might suddenly come to their senses, Poland might finally succumb to reason, or the German offer might collapse for some unpredictable reason. Stalin, as always, wanted to keep both options open, but from that moment on, the order of preference changed: the Germans were now the favourites; the Allies were relegated to the fall-back position.

18

'HOW DO THINGS STAND WITH THE IDEA OF A NON-AGGRESSION PACT?'

By the time Schulenburg arrived at the Kremlin on 15 August to deliver Ribbentrop's proposals, events in Germany had moved forward with remarkable speed. Following their conference with Hitler, the Commanders-in-Chief had started issuing their orders for the count-down to Operation White. Plans were put in hand to move army headquarters to Zossen, south of Berlin, where it would be nearer the action when war began. Advance mobilisation orders were given to the railways to prepare for the immense task of moving men and *matériel*. The pocket battleships *Graf Spee* and *Deutschland* were prepared to sail for their battle stations in the Atlantic, along with twenty-one U-boats. And Brauchitsch called up a quarter of a million men for the armies of the West, just in case France should decide to do anything foolish. This, however, seemed most unlikely: Winston Churchill, who was visiting the Maginot Line that day as a guest of French General Georges, was struck by 'the complete acceptance of the defensive which dominated my most responsible hosts'. To Churchill's eyes, the French no longer had 'the life thrust to mount a great offensive'.

In Berlin, both the British and French ambassadors had called at the Wilhelmstrasse during the day. They had been seeking some sort of reassurance, but the State Secretary had been able to offer them no comfort, only continued warnings of the mounting danger. Although he was an opponent of Hitler's aims and a committed fighter for peace, Weizsäcker was a patriotic German who despised the Poles and deeply resented their actions and attitudes. While he had given up reading the German press, so disgusted was he with its biased and bombastic rantings, he was keenly aware of what was really going on in Poland: by no means all the atrocity stories were false, and indeed there were genuine provocations from the Polish side. Weizsäcker had an even lower regard for Beck and Smigly-Rydz than he did for Ribbentrop and Hitler.

'It was therefore my task,' he wrote in his memoirs, 'to make it clear to the English that their promise of aid to the Poles had the effect of a blank cheque; the decision as to whether war was to be unleashed had been placed in the hands of the irresponsible and subordinate authorities of a foreign country.' In his office on 15 August, he lectured first Henderson and then Coulondre about their countries' promises and guarantees, which were encouraging the Poles to ever-greater acts of insolent bravado.

He also did his best to warn the Allies of the progress that was being made by Ribbentrop in his dealings with Molotov. Inhibited both by his honour as a German and the need for caution – Weizsäcker, of course, knew only too well how many telephone calls were tapped, diplomatic messages intercepted and deciphered, and conversations recorded through hidden microphones – he did not dare to speak directly. He hinted strongly, however, telling Henderson that he believed the Soviet Union would offer Poland only the most negligible assistance and would, in fact, join in sharing the spoils with Germany.

Henderson duly passed the message back to London, but without any great conviction. He might have been more convinced of Hitler's determination had Weizsäcker told him about another order which had come from the Berghof that day: Hitler had secretly cancelled both the Nuremberg party 'Day of Peace' rally and the Tannenberg anniversary celebrations, planned for 27 August, which were still providing a useful cover for the movement of troops into East Prussia.

The supposed object of all this activity, the Free City of Danzig, remained amazingly calm, its inhabitants blindly confident that the Führer would achieve their return to the Reich without bloodshed – after all, both Austria and Czechoslovakia had turned out to be wars of flowers, and they saw no reason why things should be any different for them. Unlike Hitler, however, most Danzigers saw little need for urgency. They wanted to keep the Polish trade on which they depended for their very existence, and so were prepared to wait for a deal which would guarantee this.

Making the most of the warm, sultry weather, during the daytime they crowded on to the beaches of Zoppot, part of Danzig territory and the Baltic's leading summer resort. At night, they packed into the casino. In between they filled the cafés and beer gardens, knocking back the powerful local schnapps, called 'Danziger Goldwasser' because it had tiny golden particles floating in it. Their faces showed little sign of tension. William Shirer, visiting the city then for CBS News, commented in his diary that there was more drunkenness in Danzig than he had seen anywhere outside America.

Certainly, the city had become highly militarised, with German army vehicles – bearing Danzig number plates – charging through the streets, and the leading hotels filled with German officers. There seemed to be little effort to conceal the great quantities of weapons, including machine guns, anti-tank, anti-aircraft and light artillery pieces, which were brought in at night across the Nogat river from East Prussia. Most of these arms were made in Czechoslovakia, products of the great Skoda works, a fact which served to remind outside observers of the similarities between the situation in Danzig and that which had existed in the Sudetenland a year before. But despite this, and the tank traps and log barriers on the roads leading in from Poland, the general atmosphere stayed relaxed.

'I have more and more the feeling,' Shirer noted, 'that Danzig is not the issue and I'm wasting my time here. The issue is the independence of Poland or German domination of it.'

In Moscow, the German embassy was ablaze with lights that evening. The strains of an orchestra drifted through the open windows on to the drab Russian streets, as limousines deposited elegant men in white ties and tails and women in jewels and long gowns, under the awning at the front door. Inside, they drank, ate canapés and caviar, and raised their voices in the brittle chatter of the diplomatic corps at play. The embassy was giving its summer ball, always one of the highlights of the season, and the attendance was as full as ever, despite the international tension.

One person, however, was conspicuous by his absence, and this quickly became the principal topic of conversation. Where, the diplomats speculated, was their host, Count von der Schulenburg? His secretary, Johnnie Herwarth, greeted his particular friends as they arrived, took them aside, and told them privately that Schulenburg was with Molotov, having received important instructions from Berlin.

First to receive this news was Bartholomeo Migone, first secretary of the Italian embassy, whom Herwarth had been using to pass information to Rome. Then, at about 10 o'clock, Chip Bohlen, second secretary of the US embassy, arrived with his wife and two visitors, Carmel Offie, the confidential secretary to William J. Bullitt, US ambassador to France, and Joseph P. Kennedy Junior, son of the ambassador to Britain and elder brother of the future president. Herwarth told Bohlen he had not seen the message himself, yet, but he understood the instructions went a long way towards meeting Soviet wishes. He promised to let him know more when Schulenburg returned. Bohlen fully appreciated the importance of what Herwarth was saying, and waiting impatiently for further news.

'I was greatly excited,' he recalled later. 'I remember thinking that a momentous event was taking place at the Kremlin while I was eating pâté de foie gras and drinking champagne at the German embassy. I whiled away the time by dancing, conversing and drinking. I watched my drinks because I wanted a clear head in order to obtain, to remember, and to transmit the information to Washington.'

It was an hour and a half later before Schulenburg appeared, looking his usual urbane, smiling self, and giving, as Bohlen put it, 'no indication that he had just pulled off one of the greatest coups in diplomatic history'. Bohlen's assessment was slightly premature, but the meeting had indeed gone well. Molotov had been open and friendly, and had had a secretary take down every word of Ribbentrop's message, assuring the ambassador that it would all reach Stalin 'in as exact a form as possible'. What Schulenburg had told him was so important, he said, that he could not give him an answer immediately, but must report to his government first. However, he promised that he would let him know very soon.

Unusually forthcoming, Molotov said he was now convinced that Germany was serious in wanting improved relations with the Soviet Union. He welcomed the suggestion that Ribbentrop might come to Moscow, but was careful to insist there would have to be adequate preparation. He repeated no less than three times that he was not interested in receiving Ribbentrop simply in order to 'exchange opinions'. What he wanted were results, in the form of concrete decisions. Revelling in having the Germans as suppliants, he began naming his terms. First, Germany must use her influence on Japan to improve Japanese relations with the Soviet Union and to restrain her from creating further border incidents. Second, there must be more progress in the economic talks which had been dragging on for so long. Then, having disposed of these two points, Molotov finally came right out with the real question.

'Also,' he asked, 'how do things stand with the idea of a non-aggression pact? Are the German government sympathetically inclined to the idea, or has the matter not yet been discussed in detail?'

Schulenburg was so impressed by the directness of Molotov's approach that he made a special point of stating in his report that these were his exact words. But Molotov had not finished yet. He went on: 'It is very important for the Soviet government, in connection with the intended trip of the Foreign Minister to Moscow, to obtain an answer to the question of whether the German government is prepared to conclude a non-aggression pact or something similar with the Soviet Union. On an earlier occasion, there was mention of the possibility of "a resurrection and revival of earlier treaties".'

Schulenburg hurriedly assured him that the Germans really were considering a new order of things. Hardly daring to believe what he had heard, he asked if Molotov really meant that this was what he would discuss with Ribbentrop in Moscow. Was he raising the subject now in order that Schulenburg could prepare his Foreign Minister? Molotov nodded. Of course, he would have to come back to Schulenburg with an official reply, he said, but he appreciated the need for haste. He repeated that there must, however, be adequate preparation – in other words, he wanted everyone to be quite clear what they were going to agree before Ribbentrop set out for Moscow. Schulenburg should tell his government this.

Johnnie Herwarth despatched Schulenburg's telegram, briefly outlining what Molotov had said, at 2.48 on the morning of 16 August, while the guests in the embassy were still dancing happily. A few minutes later, he sought out Chip Bohlen and took him into a corner. There, his voice masked from eavesdroppers by the sound of the band, he told the American its contents, and asked him to come to the embassy next day, when he would give him all the details of the meeting. He also told Migone, in the hope not only that it would reach the British that way, but that it might also spur Mussolini on to fresh efforts at restraining Hitler. Migone's messages had little impact, however, since the Italians already knew what was going on through Admiral Canaris, who had been busily feeding the Italian military attaché in Berlin, and also of course through Hitler and Ribbentrop themselves, in their talks with Ciano. None of it did any good.

When Bohlen arrived in Herwarth's office next afternoon, he found the young German second secretary in a deeply depressed state. Herwarth knew he could do nothing more towards preventing the disaster of war. Saddened and sickened, he had asked Schulenburg to release him from his duties. He had lost his faith in diplomacy as a weapon for peace, and now wished to take what he saw as the only honourable course left to him by joining the army. His last diplomatic duty would be to act as Schulenburg's special courier to Berlin, delivering the detailed report of the meeting with Molotov. Speaking quietly and quickly in a low voice, he told Bohlen the exact contents of the report and begged him to pass them on in the hope that, even at this late stage, someone might take heed.

Bohlen sent off a long coded telegram to Washington that same day, giving precise details of all that had been said between Schulenburg and Molotov. American Ambassador Steinhardt did not think it would be proper for him to tell the British and French in Moscow – for one thing, this would obviously increase the risk of exposing Herwarth, which no one wanted – but Bohlen gave a pretty broad hint to the State Department, concluding his telegram: 'I have every reason to believe that the Soviet government has not in connection with the present negotiations informed the French and British governments of these developments in its relationship with Germany.'

Steinhardt was able to pursue the question of the German negotiations himself, when he paid a courtesy call on Molotov that evening. He got short shrift from the Soviet Premier, however, especially when he had the temerity to warn him about the dangers of an alliance with Germany. Molotov denied that the Soviet Union had any such intention, and said his government attached great importance to the Anglo-French negotiations, which were still continuing. These, he said, were aimed at specific mutual obligations to counteract aggression, and much had already been achieved. Although the outcome depended as much on others as it did on the Soviet Union, he fully expected the negotiations to be successful.

Bohlen's telegram was received with some scepticism in Washington, where no one could believe that the Bolsheviks would ever make a deal with the Nazis. Nevertheless, the hint about the British and French being kept in the dark was picked up, and Under-Secretary of State Sumner Welles called in their ambassadors and told them what was in the report. The information reached London and Paris on the Friday morning, 18 August, by which time, of course, the military talks had already been adjourned.

The French, when they heard, increased their pressure on the Poles. The British seem to have ignored the clear warning that a non-aggression pact between Germany and the Soviet Union was now not only possible but imminent. Halifax, indeed, remained blissfully unaware of the true state of affairs, and had actually just sent instructions to Seeds in Moscow saying: 'Now that the military talks are in progress, it is desirable that the discussions on outstanding political points should be continued.' Evidently, Halifax still did not consider the position serious enough to warrant his making any direct, personal intervention. Far from suggesting that he might go to Moscow, he did not even intend leaving the annual cricket week on his Yorkshire estate to go to London.

If Halifax did not take the news from Moscow seriously, Ribbentrop most certainly did. He had spent a sleepless night at Fuschl, waiting by the teleprinter and calling Berlin no less than four times to ask if anything had arrived. When Schulenburg's first report was telephoned through from the Wilhelmstrasse at 6.40 am, he fell upon it eagerly, then called for his car and drove to the Berghof. Molotov's message represented such a triumph that he wanted to deliver it to Hitler in person. Unfortunately, the Führer had also been up most of the night, in his normal fashion, and was now sound asleep. It was unthinkable for anyone to disturb him – Ribbentrop would have to wait until he awoke.

Fuming with frustration, the Foreign Minister paced the floor of the salon for nearly three hours. He spent some of the time conferring with Dr Friedrich Gaus, director of the Foreign Office's legal department, the man responsible for drawing up treaties. Together, they composed possible replies to Molotov, and drafts for a pact. But until Hitler woke at nearly midday, there was nothing positive they could do.

At last, the Führer appeared. He was as delighted as Ribbentrop by the report from Moscow, and proposed that the two of them, plus Gaus, should spend a working lunch discussing the implications and preparing a suitable reply. In the meantime, a message was sent to Schulenburg ordering him to arrange another meeting with Molotov immediately, detailed instructions for which would follow 'within the hour'. By 2.30 pm, Hitler was satisfied with what he and Ribbentrop had written, and the text was put on the teleprinter to Berlin marked: 'This telegram should be given at once to State Secretary von Weizsäcker personally, who is requested to arrange for the telegram to be despatched to Moscow immediately.' It was enciphered and ready for transmission by 4 pm, only fifteen minutes after the first order had gone on the wire, but it was 1 am Moscow time on 17 August before it was received and deciphered.

The message was simple and to the point: the Germans accepted all the Soviet proposals and were in a hurry to settle everything. They were prepared to sign a non-aggression pact which would be undenounceable for a period of twenty-five years. They agreed to a joint guarantee of the Baltic states. And they would use their influence on the Japanese. Because the situation with Poland could explode at any moment – Schulenburg was told to stress that Germany was determined not to endure Polish provocation indefinitely – Ribbentrop was prepared to fly to Moscow at any time from Friday, 18 August, not only to discuss everything of interest to the two countries but also to sign the treaties. Once again, Schulenburg was instructed to read out the message word for word, and to ask for a response from Stalin immediately. Confidentially, Ribbentrop told him he wanted to make the trip either at the end of that week or the beginning of the week following.

Unfortunately, the order to arrange a meeting had not reached Schulenburg himself until 11 pm, so he had to wait until next morning before he could act upon it. Worse, for Hitler's and Ribbentrop's nerves, there was no point in even trying to reach Molotov until after 10 am, for he was never in his office before then, and often did not arrive until noon if the previous night's dinner with Stalin had been a heavy one.

By lunchtime in Germany, with no word from Moscow, Ribbentrop was frantically cabling and telephoning Schulenburg, demanding to know what was happening and asking at what time the ambassador had actually requested an interview. It made no difference, of course: Molotov was determined to extract every ounce of psychological advantage and was being infuriatingly casual. He took three hours to return Schulenburg's call, and when he did it was to offer him an appointment at the regular time of 8 that evening, just as though they were only expecting to discuss routine matters. As a result, there was no chance of Ribbentrop receiving a reply of any sort before Friday, never mind being able to fly out to Moscow that day. He and Hitler would simply have to restrain their impatience as best they could.

There was both comfort and torment for them in a report they received from the press department at the Wilhelmstrasse, however. On the Wednesday morning, Georgi Astakhov and his press attaché, Andrei Smirnov, had given an interview to Joe Barnes, until recently the *New York Herald Tribune* correspondent in Moscow and now its man in Berlin. The Soviet government, Astakhov told Barnes, now believed Hitler would win Danzig without having to go to war. The British and French would not stand by their agreements with Poland; Chamberlain and Bonnet, neither of whom was trusted by the Soviets, would stage another Munich. Because of this, the Soviets were drawing out the Anglo-French negotiations as long as possible, playing for time. When Hitler did succeed in Danzig, his prestige would soar and the smaller countries of Eastern Europe and the Danube basin would do whatever he wanted them to, realising that they could not expect any more protection from the Allies than Czechoslovakia had received the year before. Germany would then be able to rest on her laurels for a time, and the Soviet Union would be able to start political discussions with her.

Astakhov was obviously obeying instructions from Moscow in talking to Barnes. He could certainly not have spoken as he did without authority, and it was equally obvious that the information was intended to reach both the Americans and the Germans. It was good for Hitler to know that the Soviets were openly predicting his success, but the implications that a political agreement would have to wait until after he had taken Danzig must have been extremely alarming.

The British, however, still seemed to be seeking a conciliation with Germany. Following the discussions between Göring and the British businessmen led by Charles Spencer, there was now another Englishman in Berlin talking about terms for a possible settlement with Germany, along much the same lines as those proposed to Wohlthat by Sir Horace Wilson. Charles Roden Buxton was a Quaker and a former Labour MP. Although he was careful to stress that his proposals were purely his personal suggestions, made as a private individual with no authority from anyone, Ribbentrop's research department said that he knew Chamberlain and Halifax and was 'very closely associated with Butler' (of the Foreign Office). The German Foreign Minister was convinced, therefore, that 'Buxton would not be making such proposals without a certain degree of approval from his government'. Once more, a naive amateur, well-meaning but seeking peace at any price, was undermining the official efforts to make Hitler believe that Britain really would go to war for Poland.

As Hitler waited for Stalin's response, the machinery which he had set in motion for Operation White continued to build up momentum. During the day on 17 August, he gave his authorisation for the attacks on the Gleiwitz radio station and Hochlinden customs post, and for a specially trained commando of fifty Abwehr men to seize the 300-yard-long railway tunnel at Jablunka, on the main line from Vienna to Warsaw. German intelligence had confirmed that the Poles had planted demolition charges in the twin tunnel, and if they managed to detonate them it would seriously hinder the advance into Poland of the German 14th Army, which was already being deployed in Slovakia under the command of General Wilhelm List.

While railroads and tunnels were important in the mountainous southern front, in the north it was rivers that formed the main obstacles. Hitler became personally obsessed with the problem of securing the two strategic bridges, each nearly a mile long, which crossed the Vistula at Dirschau, leading from Danzig territory into Poland. Again, the Poles had planted demolition charges, which the Germans could clearly see. Hitler spent hours studying aerial photographs and models of the bridges, devising plan after plan. During the afternoon of 17 August, this was a welcome diversion from the nerve-racking suspense of waiting for word from Moscow. Eventually, he settled on a dive-bomber attack, coinciding with the arrival of storm-troopers and sappers aboard a disguised train. Hitler personally briefed Lieutenant-Colonel Gerhardt Medem, who was to command the operation.

There was always the possibility that the Dirschau operation might fail, even though it had been planned by the Führer himself, so the army was also to move up pontoons to provide an emergency crossing. When the Poles protested at such overt moves on Danzig soil, Hitler had Weizsäcker respond: 'Danzig is doing nothing more than defending herself against her "protector".' At the same time, the elderly battleship *Schleswig-Holstein* was ordered to sail to Danzig on a 'courtesy visit'. Although she was too old for naval warfare, the *Schleswig-Holstein* possessed a formidable array of guns, which would be used to bombard the Westerplatte, the strip of land commanding the entrance to the harbour at Danzig, where the Poles had set up an illegal stronghold.

Hitler was also able to occupy himself with other aspects of the build-up, in particular with the process of whipping up emotions in Germany. The Poles had begun taking security measures against their indigenous German population, and inevitably there were violent protests. On the afternoon of 17 August Hitler was gratified to receive a telegram from some of them: 'Thousands of German men and women in eastern Upper Silesia have for days been suffering the most brutal maltreatment by the Poles. Yesterday and today, hundreds of German men and women were arrested, manhandled and deported. Many of our comrades have been beaten up beyond recognition. In our dire distress we appeal to our Führer to help and protect us.'

Hitler had a copy of the telegram sent to the Wilhelmstrasse, with instructions that it was to be held ready for publication in the press at the right moment, and that in the meantime Weizsäcker was to use his discretion in revealing the contents of the telegram to foreign diplomats. While the telegram was not to be published yet, there was no embargo on reporting the events themselves, though these were treated very selectively. The day before, a Polish soldier had been shot on the Danzig frontier, with the result that Polish troops had been ordered to shoot on sight anyone crossing the border. The Nazi press, however, did not print this. It was too busy: 'Mass deportations of Germans to Poland's interior!' screamed the headlines in Goebbels's *Völkischer Beobachter*.

The sun was just beginning its descent towards the western horizon, tinting Red Square an even deeper shade of rose, as Schulenburg made his way across it that Thursday evening. At exactly 8 pm he presented himself at Molotov's office, where he was received with courtesy and warmth. Molotov listened attentively as he followed his instructions and read out Ribbentrop's latest message. As before, a secretary took down every word as it was translated into Russian. Then, totally ignoring what had been said, Molotov told him he could now give him the Soviet government's response to the message of 15 August.

Stalin, Molotov emphasised, was following the conversations with great interest, was informed of all the details, and was in complete agreement with him – a slightly roundabout way of saying that Stalin was personally in charge and was telling Molotov exactly what to say. Having established that, he then proceeded, as though mimicking the German approach, to read out a long-winded prepared statement, starting with several paragraphs reprimanding the Germans for all their hostile acts and statements in the past, particularly the Anti-Comintern Pact, into which they had enticed Japan. It was entirely Germany's fault that the Soviet Union had been forced to try to organise a defensive front against her threatened aggression.

But if the German government was truly changing its policy and wanted to be friends, the Soviet government was prepared to do the same. After all, said Molotov, without a hint of irony, 'the principle of the peaceful co-existence of different political systems represents a long-established principle of the foreign policy of the Soviet Union.' Everything necessary for establishing friendly relations on a practical basis was already at hand, he claimed.

The first step must be to settle the trade and credit agreement. After that, they could conclude either a non-aggression pact or a reaffirmation of the 1926 neutrality pact, whichever Germany preferred. The Soviet Union did not mind which. But in either case there must be a special protocol agreed at the same time and forming an integral part of the pact, laying down 'the interests of the contracting parties in this or that question of foreign policy'. This special protocol, Molotov added, his prepared statement now at an end, must include all the German promises made in Ribbentrop's last message.

'What about Ribbentrop's visit to Moscow?' Schulenburg asked.

'The Soviet government are very gratified by this proposal,' Molotov replied. 'Sending such an eminent politician and statesman proves how serious the Germans are. This is a noteworthy contrast to the English, who, in the person of Strang, sent only an official of second-class rank.'

But the Soviets were not to be hurried. They did not like all the publicity attached to such a visit, Molotov said. They preferred 'to do practical work, without much fuss'. And in any case, he reiterated, such a visit needed thorough preparation.

Schulenburg argued that if Ribbentrop came to Moscow, the 'practical goal' could be reached more quickly. But Molotov was not to be moved. The Soviet government, he said, preferred the other way. First, there had to be a trade agreement, then they could think about the other. But what about the new message which he had just delivered? Schulenburg asked. What was Molotov's reaction to that? Did it change anything? No, said Molotov. All the essentials were already there, in the statement he had just made. He handed Schulenburg a copy of the text. If the Germans wanted, they could start drafting a pact, together with the protocol he had mentioned. The Soviets would do the same.

'Very well,' Schulenburg replied. 'I will report these proposals to my government. But it might become necessary to have more exact information about the wishes of the Soviet government with regard to the protocol.'

Like Astakhov in Berlin, Molotov refused to be drawn on the question of how much he wanted. Still keeping to the Soviet line of 'how much are you offering', his only response was to ask for the German drafts 'as soon as possible'.

Schulenburg's report on the meeting arrived at the Wilhelmstrasse at 9 am on Friday, 18 August, and was immediately put on the teleprinter to Fuschl. Without waiting for Hitler's reaction, Ribbentrop called Schnurre and told him to have the trade and credit agreement wrapped up that day. It was not an impossible task, since Schnurre and the Soviet trade delegates had been talking for several months already. All that remained to be settled were minor details, and with Hitler now ready to agree to anything the Soviets asked, there was no reason why these should take any time at all. Astakhov and Babarin were waiting for Schnurre's call. By the time Hitler rose from his bed in the Berghof to find Ribbentrop waiting for him again, a final negotiating meeting had been arranged for that afternoon.

By early evening, the complete text of the trade treaty had been agreed. It was a complex document, allowing the Soviet Union to buy capital goods such as machinery and machine tools, construction and scientific equipment, chemical plant, ships and vehicles, to the value of 200 million Reichsmarks over a two-year period. In order to pay for them, the Soviet Union would export to Germany equivalent values of raw materials, semi-finished products, oil, grain, timber, ores, phosphates and so on. Only one small question of wording had caused any problem during the discussions, and both sides had been happy to remove this for settlement later, rather than allow it to hold up the rest of the agreement.

Delighted and relieved, Schnurre proposed that they should meet at noon next day, for the actual signature of the treaty. Somewhat ominously, the Russians started hedging: they might have to refer back to Moscow for approval before they could sign anything, even though they had obtained everything they wanted.

Like Molotov's deliberate lack of response to the suggestion that Ribbentrop should go to Moscow that weekend, this latest example of Soviet awkwardness was obviously a negotiating ploy, intended to put pressure on Hitler to raise the stakes. It was frustrating, infuriating even, but Hitler remained convinced that if he offered a big enough bribe he would win. The only question was, could he now do it in time? In mid-afternoon he had Ribbentrop send off another 'most urgent' telegram to Schulenburg, telling him that further instructions were being prepared. They would reach him during the night, and in the meantime he was to arrange another interview with Molotov for the Saturday, doing everything in his power to be received during the morning. Time was now so critical that the loss of even half a day, should Molotov offer the usual evening appointment, could be catastrophic.

As it happened, it was Soviet Air Day in Moscow. As we have seen, Molotov and all the other Soviet leaders, including Stalin himself, were at the air show. Schulenburg's secretary noted in the margin of the telegram that it would be impossible even to ask for an appointment until 8 am German time next morning – 10 am Moscow time – and that Molotov would probably not be in his office for another two hours after that.

Meanwhile, the countdown to war continued inexorably. The British ambassador, Henderson, called on Weizsäcker in Berlin, ostensibly to tell him he would be flying to Salzburg for the motor-cycle races on 22 August, and tried once again to convince him that Britain would fight for Poland. But even as he sat in Weizsäcker's office in the Wilhelmstrasse, Hitler's 'A' movement, consisting of some 220 train-loads of troops and military equipment, was starting to roll eastwards.

19

'WITH THE RUSSIANS, WE LOSE OUR SOUL'

Saturday, 19 August, was one of the most decisive days in Hitler's life. It was also one of the most testing, as Stalin and Molotov went on playing their game of cat and mouse almost beyond the limits of his endurance. By evening, his nerves were in tatters, and his courtiers were becoming concerned for his health. Even a week earlier, the strain had been showing. Admiral Canaris, after his trip south to discuss covert operations at the start of the war, had told his fellow anti-Nazi, Erich Kordt: 'Emile [his nickname for Hitler] is going through a crisis. The courtiers cringe every time he comes out of a room.' According to Canaris, Hitler's mood had been switching violently between loud rage against Poland and long silences when he would sit, hands on stomach, brooding 'like a grim, grey bird'. Now, waiting for word from the Soviets, the tension was even worse, and the state of his temper and of his intestines showed it all too clearly.

He could find some relief by issuing orders. The U-boats and pocket battleships which were already on stand-by were to sail for their war stations – the submarines to be deployed aggressively to the north and south of the British Isles, the *Deutschland* athwart shipping lanes in the North Atlantic, and the *Graf Spee* off the Brazilian coast. He still did not believe he would have to use them, but it was a sensible precaution to have them in place, in spite of Ribbentrop's latest assurances.

While he refused to see or hear Ambassador Herbert von Dirksen, freshly returned from London with dire warnings of Britain's resolve to fight if need be, Ribbentrop was pleased to show Hitler a report from his personal research office which, perhaps not surprisingly, supported Ribbentrop's own view. This pointed out that although foreign journalists in Berlin were understandably nervous, with some French correspondents already packing up and going home, no Britons had left. One British journalist 'of good repute', just back from London, had told neutral correspondents that Chamberlain and Halifax did not really want war with Germany and could be expected 'to do their utmost to avoid a conflict with her'. This, unlike Dirksen's Cassandra-like alarums, was exactly what Ribbentrop wanted to hear.

The news from other quarters, however, was less reassuring. Schnurre reported that Babarin had telephoned him at noon, the time he was due to sign the trade and credit agreement, to say he and Astakhov wanted to talk to him again 'on a few unimportant matters'. Half an hour later, the Russians had called again, with 'some irrelevant formal questions', which he had answered immediately. When he asked if they had heard anything from Moscow, they said they did not yet have any definite news, but hoped to hear at any moment. They would call him again at 1.30, to let him know whether the signing could take place that day.

Throughout the afternoon, the Soviets continued giving Schnurre – and through him, Hitler and Ribbentrop – a hard time. When they called at 1.30, as promised, it was only to say that they had still not heard anything, and would ring again at 4 o'clock. At 4, the news was that they would not be able to sign that day, but wanted another meeting, for 'further discussions', at 10 am on Monday. Schnurre was not optimistic. 'The Russians' delay and temporisation in signing,' he said in his teleprinter message to Ribbentrop, 'has no longer anything to do with the economic and credit treaty. The reasons put forward by the Russians are transparent pretexts. It is obvious that they have received from Moscow, for political reasons, instructions to delay the conclusion of the treaty. In these circumstances, I doubt whether the Russians will be ready to sign on Monday.'

As the minutes and then the hours ticked away, Hitler must have been at a loss to understand why Stalin and Molotov were suddenly blowing so cold again when he had agreed to give them everything they wanted. There was no explanation and little comfort from Moscow. The only message received from Schulenburg during that long afternoon was about a Tass denial, printed in that day's *Pravda*, of stories which had appeared in various Polish newspapers. These said the Soviet talks with the Anglo-French mission were in trouble because of Soviet demands for military support in the event of a war in the Far East. Tass described the stories as 'pure invention from beginning to end'. 'The differences of opinion which did in fact exist,' it said, 'were over entirely different matters.'

The public admission that there were problems with the Anglo-French talks could be significant. But in itself it was not enough to satisfy Hitler's desperate need. And as if to emphasise his predicament, there was unwelcome news from Danzig, too: Poland was suddenly being reasonable. This, of course, did not suit Hitler's plans at all. He was relying on the Poles running true to form and reacting to his pressures strongly enough to give him the excuse to attack. Forster, through the Danzig Senate, had demanded the withdrawal of about twelve Polish customs officers. To his astonishment, the Poles seemed ready to agree. Forster now wanted Hitler's approval to increase the pressure again: he would demand the withdrawal not of twelve officers but of fifty, and immediately. If the Poles still gave way and agreed, then he would go on upping the ante, increasing the demands 'so as to make agreement impossible'. Hitler gave his consent, but reminded his Gauleiter that whatever he did, he must make sure the Poles could still be blamed when the negotiations failed.

In Moscow, meanwhile, Molotov had agreed to see Schulenburg at 2 pm, an early appointment which seemed to bode well. The ambassador had received his full instructions at 5.45 that morning, and so had had plenty of time to digest them. The general tone of Ribbentrop's telegram was so frantic it bordered on hysteria, and Schulenburg must have been relieved that this time he was not ordered to read it out, word by word, but simply to press for a rapid response and to counter any fresh objections which Molotov might raise, all in his own way.

The Germans, Ribbentrop said, had fulfilled every condition imposed by the Soviets, including agreeing the text of the trade and credit treaty, and so were now ready to move swiftly on to Molotov's second stage. They were willing to agree to the spheres of interest suggested by the Soviet Union, but the details would have to be settled orally, in face-to-face discussions. Ribbentrop stressed that when he came to Moscow, he would have the full authority of the Führer to agree and sign anything. 'Please emphasise,' he told Schulenburg with unusual courtesy, 'that German foreign policy has today reached a historic turning point.'

Having disposed of the rhetoric, the German Foreign Minister turned to the Soviet suggestion that he might start drafting the text for a pact. In sharp contrast with the rest of the telegram, this section was uncharacteristically concise and direct. No doubt Hitler had provided the wording himself: 'As far as the non-aggression pact is concerned, it seems to us to be so simple as to require no long preparation. We have in mind here the following three points, which I would ask you to read to M. Molotov but not to hand to him. Article 1: The German Reich and the USSR will in no event resort to war, or to any other use of force, with respect to each other. Article 2: This treaty shall enter into force immediately upon signature, and shall be valid and not liable to denunciation thereafter for a term of twenty-five years.' The third of Ribbentrop's 'three points' never appeared – if there ever was one, it was omitted in the final text.

Molotov was singularly unimpressed by Ribbentrop's and Hitler's idea of a simple pact: this was not the Soviet way of doing things.

Reverting to his most schoolmasterly manner, he lectured Schulenburg on what was expected. If Germany did not know how to draft such a pact, then they could use as a model any of the numerous non-aggression pacts which the Soviet Union had concluded with other countries – Poland, Latvia, Estonia, it did not matter which. The German government, he added sarcastically, could pick the one that seemed most suitable. And what about the secret protocol? This was a very serious question, and the Soviet Union expected Germany to be specific about what was to go into it. It was not good enough for Ribbentrop to brush it aside, airily suggesting that everything could be settled at a face-to-face meeting.

By now, Molotov's lecture was turning into a dressing-down, as he became increasingly acid. 'The attitude of the Soviet Union towards treaties which they conclude,' he snapped, 'is a very serious one. We respect the obligations which we undertake, and we expect the same of the other parties to these treaties.'

If Schulenburg had been optimistic about the meeting, he must have changed his mind by now. Nevertheless, he persisted for an hour in trying to break down the barrier which the Soviet statesman had so unexpectedly re-erected. Again and again, using every ounce of his diplomatic skills, he tried to convince Molotov that he should receive Ribbentrop quickly. At every attempt he met a solid stone wall. Of course the Soviet Union appreciated the reasons why Ribbentrop wanted to come to Moscow, Molotov acknowledged. But at the moment it was not possible to fix the time of such a visit, even approximately, since it was still essential to make thorough preparations. In any case, he added, they had not even taken the first step – the economic agreement had not yet been signed. First, that must be signed and published. Then, when it had achieved its effect abroad, they could start talking about the non-aggression pact and its protocol. Those were the views of the Soviet government, and there was nothing more to add.

Schulenburg trailed back despondently to the embassy, baffled by this latest switch in the Soviet attitude, and no doubt torn between his professional duty to succeed in carrying out his government's wishes, and the flickering hope, as an individual who hated everything the Nazis were doing to his country, that the plans for a pact would fail. He had hardly reached his room, however, when he received a telephone call from the Kremlin: Molotov wanted to see him again in an hour's time, at 4.30 pm.

The change in Molotov was remarkable when Schulenburg arrived for the second meeting. This time, the Soviet Premier was affable and charming, full of apologies for putting him to the trouble of having to return so quickly, though he made no mention of his earlier coldness. He explained that after the previous meeting he had reported 'to the Soviet government' and had been instructed to hand over the Soviet draft for a pact, which he now did. Smiling warmly, he said Ribbentrop could come to Moscow about a week after the signing of the economic treaty. That meant that if the treaty were signed the next day, Ribbentrop could arrive in Moscow on 26 or 27 August. Schulenburg, taking advantage of Molotov's good mood, tried to persuade him to make it sooner, but in spite of the smiles, the Russian was as firm as ever on this point.

Back in the Berghof, Hitler waited in his study with Ribbentrop, in a fever of anxiety. His stomach, knotted with tension, was giving him hell and he pressed one hand to it constantly while with the other he ate apple after apple – a regular habit when he was particularly nervous – spitting out the pips and dropping the cores on the floor. In the hallway and the salon, his staff conversed in low whispers, afraid that the slightest disturbance would provoke their leader's anger. At 7.10 pm precisely, Hitler's buzzer suddenly broke the hush. Friedrich Gaus, the treaty expert, leapt to his feet and hurried into the study, where he found Hitler and Ribbentrop crouched over the teleprinter as it rattled out Schulenburg's report, which they had all been waiting for. It was a brief communication, barely two paragraphs long. A full account would follow later.

Hitler, Gaus recalled, threw his hands in the air in triumph, and started to laugh. Ribbentrop joined in. The pact was in the bag.

Molotov's sudden change of mind was mystifying to Schulenburg. There had been barely half an hour between the end of his cool first meeting and the telephone call asking him to return to the Kremlin. What could have happened during the brief interval to have caused such a remarkable transformation? 'I assume Stalin intervened,' Schulenburg wrote at the end of his full report. But he could not say why.

The answer lay with Beaufre, on his last-ditch mission in Warsaw – or to be more precise with the French military attaché there, General Musse. During the day, Beaufre followed his instructions from General Doumenc and hammered away both at his fellow Frenchmen and at Polish military chiefs, trying to get them to find some formula by which Poland would accept Soviet military assistance, and thus save the talks. But it was proving extremely hard going.

In the face of imminent annihilation, the Poles remained calm and confident – too confident, as William Shirer recorded in his diary after a week in Warsaw. 'You ask them,' he wrote, 'as I've asked a score of officials in the Foreign Office and the army this past week, about Russia and they shrug their shoulders. Russia does not count for them.' Shirer wondered if there were not a 'terrible self-destructiveness' in the Polish character which could have been largely responsible for their nation being destroyed and partitioned by Russia, Prussia and Austria in the eighteenth century. While he could understand the historic distrust of the Poles for the Russians, 'who had treated them so badly in the past when they had ruled in Warsaw', he also understood that to survive in this world one had to make compromises. The Poles completely refused to accept this, as Beaufre quickly discovered. Like Shirer and many others, he was helpless in the face of their wilful blindness.

For the past two weeks, German armies had been concentrating on the border. The Poles were fully aware of what was going on – one activity in which they have always excelled is espionage, and by this time they had correctly identified the command posts and headquarters of the various German units – yet they appeared to remain unconcerned. They had taken no defensive measures whatever: in Warsaw, no air raid shelters had been dug, no tank traps built to protect the city against German armour. Orchestras continued to play romantic music in the open-air cafés as the citizens went on making the most of the glorious summer weather. 'One pleasant thing in Warsaw these days,' Hugh Carleton Greene of the London *Daily Telegraph* (later to become Sir Hugh Greene, Director-General of the BBC) wrote home to his mother, 'is that one would really hardly know that such a thing as war exists. These Poles are extraordinary people.'

Greene himself, the *Telegraph*'s Berlin correspondent until the previous May, when he had been expelled by the Nazis – 'an incident which I have always regarded as an honour' – had no illusions about the danger. He wrote on 21 August: 'I'm afraid it rather looks as if we are heading straight for it now. I think these ridiculous Germans have gone too far to draw back.'

Like the first of the three little pigs, however, the Poles still frolicked inside their straw house while the big bad wolf was already drawing breath outside. And this was in spite of all the warnings from their friends. Although they had said nothing to their people in Moscow, the French government had not, in fact, been deaf to Doumenc's appeals: immediately he received Doumenc's first despatch on 14 August, Foreign Minister Georges Bonnet had summoned the Polish ambassador, Juliesz Lukasiewicz, to the Quai d'Orsay for talks. He had told him what Doumenc said about the need for Polish co-operation, and reminded him of Beck's recent remarks that he would be satisfied if the Moscow negotiations succeeded and would regret their failure. Bonnet begged the ambassador to transmit the Soviet question to Colonel Beck without comment: in the event of a German invasion, would Poland permit Soviet troops to cross Polish territory?

'To say no,' warned Bonnet, 'is to lead to the rupture of negotiations, with all its consequences. The result would be catastrophe.'

Lukasiewicz had been born in Russia and was rabidly anti-Soviet. Bonnet had also once described him as 'a passionate and vehement man, who blindly serves the design of his Foreign Minister', who, Bonnet had said on more than one occasion, was a megalomaniac. The French Foreign Minister could not, therefore, have been at all optimistic about the response he would get, but nevertheless he had to try. In fact, the immediate answer from the ambassador confirmed all his fears.

'My government will never permit the Russians to occupy the territories we took from them in 1921,' the ambassador declared. 'Would you French allow the Germans into Alsace-Lorraine?'

Bonnet pointed out the vast might of the German armies assembling on the frontier. Nazi tanks could be in Warsaw in a matter of days, he said. But Lukasiewicz was unimpressed.

'On the contrary,' he boasted, 'it is the Poles who will drive straight into Germany during the first few days.' He was perfectly serious, merely echoing the fantasies of a whole generation of Polish cavalry colonels, who dreamed of leading their squadrons up Berlin's Unter den Linden, charging between the famous lime trees with sabres drawn.

On the morning of Saturday, 19 August, after receiving the latest reports from Doumenc in Moscow and Noël in Warsaw, Bonnet called the British chargé d'affaires to his office. Noël had seen Beck the previous day, and had been told by him that the Russians were 'of no military value'. Beck had been supported by the army Chief of Staff, General Stachiewicz, who had stated that he saw 'no benefit to be gained by Red Army troops operating in Poland'. He suspected that all the Russians really wanted was an excuse to occupy Polish territory. There were other considerations too.

'If Poland agreed to the passage of Russian troops,' Beck had said, 'this would lead to an imminent declaration of war on the part of Germany, as Herr Hitler would consider such a step was a further critical development in the policy of encirclement, and given his anti-Bolshevik complex he would see red and would not hesitate to precipitate the war.'

Bonnet, for so long a leading appeaser, had finally seen the error of his ways and was not prepared to accept Beck's thesis. Hitler must be stopped, whatever the cost, and this could not be achieved without the Russians. It would put the British and French governments in an almost impossible position, he told the British chargé, if they had to ask their countries to go to war for a Poland which had refused to accept the only real help that could reach them quickly in the event of a German attack. Britain and France must, therefore, exert the utmost pressure on the Poles to make them accept it. For a start, Britain could make it a condition for her guarantee to Poland, the formal treaty for which had not yet been signed.

Bonnet's suggestion was eminently sensible. In fact, it was probably the only practical lever the Allies could use to force the Poles into seeing sense – though there could be no certainty that they would not simply shrug it off with their usual arrogant bravado, claiming they needed help from no one. As it happened, it was never put to the test, for the British government refused to resort to such a 'manoeuvre', as Downing Street rather primly described it.

Although he would not apply this ultimate sanction on the Poles, there were signs that Halifax was at last beginning to take the situation more seriously. He came back to Whitehall that Saturday, albeit reluctantly, after an anguished telephone call from Sir Robert Vansittart to his house at Garrowby just before dinner the previous evening. Vansittart had been Permanent Under-Secretary at the Foreign Office until the previous autumn, when he was shunted sideways into the meaningless post of 'chief diplomatic adviser' because of his opposition to appeasement. He begged Halifax to return to London the following morning; he had received information that Hitler had definitely decided to attack Poland within two weeks. Halifax was dubious, and told Vansittart to talk to Sir Alexander Cadogan, his successor at the Foreign Office. If Cadogan thought it necessary, he would come up by the early train.

Vansittart hurried round to Cadogan's house, where he arrived 'in a state of near collapse', according to Cadogan. He had been fairly guarded on the telephone to Halifax, but now he poured out his information and his fears. He had it from a most reliable source that Hitler's attack on Poland was scheduled to begin between 25 and 28 August; Hitler himself had given these dates to the Italian government. Cadogan listened, and then agreed to call the Foreign Secretary, advising him to come to London. He remained unconvinced, however, that this was not simply one of Hitler's scare tactics. On the telephone to Halifax he said 'it was impossible to feel certain about [Vansittart's] information.'

The three men met in the Foreign Secretary's office at noon on the nineteenth, when they were joined by Horace Wilson. After listening to what Vansittart had to say, Halifax and Wilson decided not to bring the Prime Minister back from his fishing and shooting in Scotland, since he was due to return on the Monday in any case. What they would do was to send a telegram to Mussolini, urging him to use his influence to restrain Hitler, and at the same time prepare a letter for Chamberlain to send to Hitler on lines suggested earlier in the summer by Ambassador Henderson. Then, feeling he had done all that could be expected of him, Halifax had an RAF aircraft fly him back to Yorkshire so that he could get in a little more cricket and farming during what was left of the weekend.

In Warsaw, meanwhile, General Musse had taken Beaufre to meet Stachiewicz in his office at the War Ministry. They found him as charming and friendly as ever – but totally intransigent, prepared only to underline what he had said the previous day. The Polish government, he reiterated, did not trust the Russians: 'They are a dishonest people whose word is not to be relied on.' Any thought of accommodation with them was impossible, even if this meant war would come sooner rather than later.

Musse did not press the point. The truth was that he basically agreed with the Polish assessment of the situation. He had lived too long in Poland, and his affection for the country and its people blinded him to the military realities of Eastern Europe. Like so many pro-Polish observers, he was prepared to accept the Poles' own estimate of their military strength, believing their army was strong enough at least to keep the Germans at bay for some considerable time.

Beaufre was a determined and resourceful man, however, and insisted that he must at least take back to Moscow something which might allow the Allied mission to keep the talks going. It took three meetings with the Polish general staff, in which Beaufre and Musse were supported by Sir Howard Kennard, the British ambassador, and his military attaché, before they succeeded in getting a form of words which Beaufre felt would do. This did not authorise the Allied mission to negotiate on behalf of the Polish government, but it did allow it to proceed with consultations with the Soviets, provided the British and French undertook to inform the Polish government of any practical assistance the Russians were able to offer. It still left Colonel Beck free to refuse any such offer.

There could be little doubt in anyone's mind that Beck would refuse any such offer. While Beaufre and Musse were seeing Stachiewicz, Ambassador Noël was seeing Beck once more. He found him forewarned and in a foul mood. The Soviets, he declared, were merely manoeuvring for advantage. They were eager to lay responsibility for the breakdown of negotiations on Poland. If the Russians were militarily weak – as he suspected they were – what did the Poles have to gain by accepting their help? If, on the other hand, they were militarily strong, could they be trusted to evacuate their forces from Polish soil after the present crisis was over? It was a heads-I-win-tails-you-lose argument. Noël replied that the best way to call the Soviet bluff – if bluff it were – would be to accept their proposal and then see what they offered in the way of troops. But Beck would have none of this. He had no intention of allowing one Soviet soldier to set foot on Polish soil. However, instead of dismissing the French proposal out of hand, he took refuge in delaying tactics, insisting that he must consult Marshal Smigly-Rydz, as Commander-in-Chief of the Polish armed forces. It was not until the next day, therefore, that he formally rejected the Allied proposals.

Kennard and Noël hurried back to Beck's office on the evening of 20 August, to urge him to reconsider, but it was no use. 'I do not admit,' he told them, at his most haughty, 'that there can be any kind of discussion whatsoever concerning the use of part of our territory by foreign troops. We have no military agreement with the Soviet Union. We do not want one.'

As a last resort, the two ambassadors went on to appeal to Marshal Smigly-Rydz. But the Commander-in-Chief was equally adamant, and even more dramatic: 'With the Germans,' he pronounced, 'we risk losing our freedom. With the Russians, we lose our soul.'

Beaufre, already hurrying back to Moscow with his makeshift formula, knew that war could be prevented now only if the Anglo-French talks could be kept going. While there was still the threat of war on two fronts, however improbable it might seem, Hitler would surely not dare to attack. If they could go on talking long enough, it might become too late for a campaign that year, thus giving the world several months of breathing space in which to come up with other solutions. Once the Soviets knew the truth, however, the talks would be finished.

With this in mind, General Doumenc had arranged a simple code with Beaufre before he set out for Warsaw, so that he could safely keep him informed of progress. The word 'one' in a telegram would indicate that the Poles were still talking; 'two' would mean the talks had been successful; 'three' that they had failed. Beaufre had kept strictly to this foolproof arrangement. Unfortunately, others had not been so careful. Ever since that first meeting with Stachiewicz, Musse had been firing off a running barrage of telegrams to Paris and Moscow, giving full details of the discussions and emphasising Polish objections to any agreement. True, the telegrams were all in Musse's normal code, but this could have presented little difficulty to the Soviet intelligence agencies, who were naturally monitoring everything sent or received by foreign embassies.

'To anyone who knows anything about the Russian secret service,' Beaufre commented afterwards, 'it must be obvious that any telegram sent in the normal military attaché's code would be immediately deciphered. In almost any embassy in the world, the safe is not guarded at night, and a safe unguarded is an open safe.'

Musse's pessimistic and anti-Soviet messages – he had included all the Poles' most damning statements and added a few of his own, for good measure – were almost certainly on Stalin's desk even before they reached the French embassy. Their timing was disastrous, as was their effect. Stalin had been prepared to give the Allies every chance to clinch the deal, and no doubt felt he had done so with uncommon patience and generosity. There may, of course, have been more than a little self-interest in this, too – no doubt he would not have been averse to the idea of being able to recover the Soviet territories lost to Pilsudski's armies in 1920, exactly as the Poles feared. Whatever his reasons, while there was still a chance that Britain and France might succeed in forcing

Poland to accept his help, he was prepared to wait. But reading even the first of Musse's messages must have been enough to convince him that any such hope was futile.

His intelligence services, both the NKVD and the military GRU, must have informed him that Hitler had already set the date for his attack on Poland – it was hardly the best-kept secret in Europe, after all. With little more than a week to go, there was no time left to allow the Allies to go on stalling. There could no longer be certainty that the lack of a German treaty with the Soviet Union would stop Hitler invading Poland. The other side of that coin was that while the Soviet Union and the Allies were still only talking they did not have an anti-German accord. Hitler might feel he could launch his drive to the east with impunity – and once he had started, who knew where he would stop?

For Stalin, the options had expired. Between Schulenburg's two visits to the Kremlin – possibly even while he was receiving Molotov's dressing-down during the first meeting – Stalin finally took the decision to go with Hitler. It was, on the evidence available, the only way left for him to protect his country. The Soviet Union, as Molotov told Schulenburg, took its treaty obligations very seriously, and expected the other parties to do the same. Once Hitler had signed a non-aggression pact, therefore, he would stop short of the Soviet borders, no matter how successful his campaign in Poland proved to be, until the pact had been renounced. Or so Stalin believed.

20

'I HAVE THE WORLD IN MY POCKET'

Hitler barely had time to digest the welcome news that Ribbentrop could go to Moscow, before Stalin was proving he really did mean business. The mysterious obstacles to the conclusion of the trade and credit agreement – which Molotov was so insistent should be settled first – suddenly evaporated. In Berlin, Babarin called Schnurre at his home, although it was late on Saturday evening, to say he was authorised to sign immediately. Within the hour, he was making the short journey from the Unter den Linden to the Wilhelmstrasse, having paused only long enough for Schnurre to hurry to his office and organise secretaries and assistants. Schnurre's gloomy prognostications of the previous day were swept away as the Soviets showed just how fast they could move when they chose. The treaty was signed at 2 o'clock on the Sunday morning.

With the first of Molotov's conditions fulfilled, Hitler now looked all set for the major prize – indeed, earlier on the Saturday evening the Politburo had formally approved Stalin's decision to sign the pact with him. But the question of time was becoming almost as important to the German leader as the pact itself. As Weizsäcker wrote in his diary on the Sunday: 'If Ribbentrop travels to Moscow in the coming week, this means that Russia is inviting Hitler to attack Poland, and is not afraid of another 1812.'

Fully aware of this, Stalin and Molotov had to be absolutely certain that what they were doing was the best they could achieve for their country, before finally committing themselves to such an irrevocable step. Until then, they would go on keeping their options open, increasing the pressure on Hitler in the hope of squeezing even more concessions out of him. While saying that they would – eventually – sign the pact, they still refused to budge from their position on the timing: there must be a full week from the signing of the trade treaty before Ribbentrop could go to Moscow, in order to allow its full effects to make themselves felt internationally. They did not say if 'internationally' meant Britain, France and Poland in particular, but the implication was clear enough. The trade agreement might just be enough to frighten the Poles into acquiescence.

The Soviet requirement put the earliest date for Ribbentrop's visit at 27 August. This, as Stalin undoubtedly knew, was too late for Hitler, who wanted his armies to be well on their way to Warsaw by then. If he were to have any hope of signing the pact before Y-day, 26 August, Hitler would have to pull something pretty extraordinary out of the hat. The question was, what? What more, in addition to the tacit promises already made, could he do that might persuade Stalin to change his mind?

Throughout the long night from Saturday into Sunday, Hitler prowled around the Berghof, restlessly pacing the floors as he sought the answer. His ordeal was made worse by the seemingly interminable delay in receiving Schulenburg's full report, which might contain some hint or clue. The draft pact arrived first, reaching Berlin at 3.15 am. But even then, it had to be deciphered and put on the teleprinter to the Berghof and Fuschl. It was 4.30, with the dawn light already colouring the mountain peaks, before it chattered on to the machine in Hitler's study. The detailed account of Schulenburg's two meetings with Molotov, the Soviet Premier's amazing about-face, and the ambassador's vain efforts to improve on the dates, did not arrive in Berlin until 7 on the Sunday morning, by which time Hitler had retired exhausted to his bed.

The Soviet draft pact was slightly longer than Hitler's, but it was still remarkably concise for a major treaty. After a brief preamble about 'strengthening the cause of peace', there were five short articles, none more than four or five lines long. These did not, in fact, say much more than Hitler's two sentences had: the main differences were stipulations that neither side would give support to any power which attacked the other, and that the duration of the pact was to be for five years, with an automatic extension for the same period again if neither party denounced it one year before the expiry date. It would not come into force immediately it was signed, as Hitler had wanted, but would be ratified 'as soon as possible'.

That all looked simple enough. The sting came in the tail, in a postscript which had a much more steely ring to it: 'The present pact shall be valid only if a special protocol is signed simultaneously, covering the points in which the contracting parties are interested in the field of foreign policy. The protocol shall be an integral part of the pact.'

Was this the clue Hitler was seeking? He did not think so. At noon on Sunday, almost as soon as he had risen, he ordered Ribbentrop to cable Schulenburg to ask if there were any more details he could add to his report. If so, he should 'in view of the extreme urgency not do so by letter or despatch but immediately by telegram'. Schulenburg's reply barely concealed the exasperation he must have felt. No, he cabled, he had nothing essential to add: he had gone 'as far as any foreign representative can go on such an occasion' in trying to persuade Molotov to advance the dates, but had got nowhere. The only crumb of comfort he could give was that after the second interview, when taking leave of him, Molotov had said, 'That is after all a concrete step,' indicating that the Soviet government had 'accomplished a decisive action'.

Long before Schulenburg's reply arrived, Hitler had made up his mind what he was to do. The solution he arrived at during the afternoon was another of his flashes of inspiration, a typically unorthodox move, cutting across the conventions of established diplomacy. Like all such inspirations, it was startlingly simple: he would write a personal letter, direct to Stalin. After telling Ribbentrop to cable Schulenburg again, instructing him to arrange another immediate appointment, he settled down to compose it. By teatime it was finished and on the teleprinter to Berlin. At 6.35 pm, it was on its way to Moscow, with an instruction to Schulenburg to give it to Molotov on a plain sheet of paper with no letterhead. The letter read as follows:

M. Stalin, Moscow.

(1) I sincerely welcome the signing of the new German–Soviet commercial agreement as the first step in the reshaping of German–Soviet relations.

(2) To me, the conclusion of a non-aggression pact with the Soviet Union means the establishment of long-term German policy. By this, Germany resumes a political course which was beneficial to both states in past centuries. The government of the Reich is therefore resolved to accept the entire consequences of such a far-reaching change.

(3) I accept the draft of the non-aggression pact provided by your Foreign Minister, Herr Molotov, but consider it urgently necessary to clear up the questions connected with it as quickly as possible.

(4) I am convinced that the substance of the supplementary protocol desired by the Soviet Union can be cleared in the shortest possible time if a responsible German statesman can come to Moscow himself to negotiate. The government of the Reich does not see any other way in which the supplementary protocol could be cleared up and settled quickly.

(5) Tension between Germany and Poland has become intolerable. Polish behaviour towards us, a great power, is such that a crisis may arise any day. In any event, with this possibility in mind, Germany is determined to look after the interests of the Reich with all the means at her disposal.

(6) In my opinion, in view of the intentions of the two states to enter into a new relationship with each other, it is desirable not to lose any time. I therefore propose once again that you receive my Foreign Minister on Tuesday, 22 August, or at the latest on Wednesday, 23 August. The Reich Foreign Minister will have the fullest powers to draw up and sign the non-aggression pact as well as the protocol. In view of the international situation, it is impossible for the Reich Foreign Minister to stay in Moscow longer than one or two days. I should be glad to receive your early answer.

ADOLF HITLER

The next twenty-four hours was a period of excruciating suspense, which Hitler himself later described as the most agonising of his life. Several of those who were with him at the Berghof said they feared he might collapse under the strain, or suffer a nervous breakdown. His doctors waited anxiously, on stand-by in case they were needed. Throughout the night, he paced the great hall, the expression on his face so grim that none of the courtiers dared disturb him. There was only one exception: in the early hours, Eva Braun appeared, bringing a beaker of milk soup which she had personally prepared for him. He started to sip it, but immediately she left the room he put it down, and picked up an apple, belching loudly before he bit into it.

His condition was not improved when a message was finally received from Schulenburg, shortly after 3 am on Monday, 21 August, to say that he had not yet been able to fix a meeting with Molotov, and would not now be able to do so until the following morning. What was worse, at the time of sending the telegram, 11.45 pm Moscow time on Sunday, he had still not received the text of Hitler's letter. This produced a flurry of activity as Hitler had Weizsäcker, on call despite the hour, double-check the time the all-important telegram had been sent. In fact, by the time Hitler was worrying about it, it was already in the ambassador's hands, deciphered and ready for presentation, having arrived an hour after Schulenburg had sent his last message.

But Hitler could not know this. He picked up the phone and called Göring, who was sound asleep in bed at his Karinhall estate, to voice his anxieties, complain about the delays, and generally let off steam about Stalin's intractability. No doubt he also wanted to discuss their latest contingency plan, made at Göring's suggestion without reference to Ribbentrop: during the previous day, Göring had surreptitiously been in touch with the British Foreign Office, suggesting he might make a personal visit, in secret, to talk to Chamberlain on Wednesday, 23 August. Chamberlain had agreed, and arrangements had been put in hand. 'The idea,' Halifax recorded, 'was that he would land at some disused aerodrome, be picked up in a car and taken directly to Chequers [the Prime Minister's official country residence, in Buckinghamshire], where the staff would have been given *congé*.' It would have been impossible to keep such a meeting secret in London – the Field Marshal's bulk was far too conspicuous – but tucked away among the Chiltern beech woods it could be achieved. The old RAF field at Bovington, barely a dozen miles' drive from Chequers through quiet country lanes, was selected for the landing.

At the same time, the British had not given up making their own secret advances: Sir Horace Wilson was still trying to find some way of handing over Danzig to the Reich in return for nothing more than assurance from Hitler that this would finally satisfy his territorial ambitions. While Göring was arranging to fly to Britain, Wilson was busy suggesting to Ribbentrop's personal agent, Fritz Hesse, that he might fly to Germany to talk directly to Hitler.

As a last resort, therefore, if Stalin were to back out or even if he went on stalling for too long, Hitler could activate either or both of these plans in the hope that he would be able to persuade Britain, even at this late stage, to stay out of the approaching fight.

The coming of daylight on Monday, 21 August, did nothing to ease Hitler's fears, or to improve his patience. He could not bear the inactivity, relieved only by the arrival from Danzig of Forster, come for his final briefing. He had Ribbentrop send off another urgent telegram to Schulenburg, exhorting him to be sure to do everything he could. Then he went back to his pacing, until at 2 pm he finally received the news that Molotov had agreed to see Schulenburg at 3 pm Moscow time. Allowing for the two-hour difference, this meant the meeting had already taken place, and his letter had been delivered.

One relief, however, brought another torment – now he had to wait for Stalin's response. It was not until around 8.30 in the evening that the telephone rang with the answer he wanted to hear. Julius Schaub, his senior SS adjutant, lifted the receiver, listened for a moment, then announced that Ribbentrop was on the line. Hitler snatched the phone from him and pressed it to his ear. The little band of courtiers waited, not daring to move. Then, suddenly, the moment was there.

'Marvellous!' they heard him exclaim. 'I congratulate you!' Turning to them with a wolfish grin on his face, he shouted: 'Stalin has agreed! We are to fly to Moscow to conclude a pact with him!'

None of those present had ever seen their Führer so elated. Heinrich Hoffmann, hurrying to record the historic moment on film, saw him slap his knee in delight. Walther Hewel recorded that he hammered his fists on the wall in jubilation, 'uttering incoherent cries', then bursting out triumphantly: 'I have the world in my pocket!'

Hitler's mood was very quickly taken up by the others. Someone ordered champagne. Willy Kannenberg, the major-domo, appeared with bottles and glasses. Corks popped, crystal clinked, and everyone – except the man himself – drank to the Führer's great coup.

The message Ribbentrop had received at Fuschl, by telephone from Berlin in order to save time, could hardly have been better. Molotov had been 'deeply impressed' by Hitler's letter. He had given Schulenburg Stalin's answer, which the ambassador said was 'couched in very conciliatory form', at 5 pm: Ribbentrop could go to Moscow on 23 August.

Stalin had, in fact, written a personal letter to Hitler, the full text of which was following in a separate telegram. In the meantime, Molotov wanted German assent by midnight to the issuing of a short communiqué. Schulenburg thought they should agree instantly: he still found it hard to believe what was happening, and was anxious to see the Soviets commit themselves by a public announcement.

Ribbentrop, of course, was jubilant at the news from Moscow. He was already convincing himself that it was his 'very own idea' to seek a settlement with Moscow, in order, as he claimed in the memoirs he wrote while awaiting trial at Nuremberg after the war, 'to create a counter-weight to the West and because I wanted to ensure Russian neutrality in the event of a German–Polish conflict.

'Originally,' he maintained, 'I had suggested sending to Moscow someone other than myself – I had thought of Göring, for my work as ambassador in Britain, my connections with Japan, and, indeed, my entire foreign policy so far, had, I felt, given me too much of an anti-communist stamp for a mission to Moscow. But the Führer insisted on my going, because he thought I "could do this better".'

The idea of Ribbentrop ever allowing, never mind sending, Göring to take the glory in Moscow is quite preposterous, for the two men detested each other. Ribbentrop's veracity can be measured by the fact that in the next paragraph he claimed he knew nothing of Hitler's intention to attack Poland! But there can be no doubt that Hitler was delighted to send Ribbentrop. He even gave him his personal aeroplane for the flight, not only to ensure his safety and comfort but also as a visible symbol of confidence in him. Revelling in the importance of his role, Ribbentrop ordered Wiezsäcker to organise the entourage who would fly with him next day. Then, no doubt with particular relish, he telephoned Ciano in Italy.

Ciano had been trying to contact Ribbentrop all day, but the German had given him the run-around until 5.30, knowing full well that the Italians were still trying to prevent Hitler going to war. Sure enough, when he finally condescended to take the call, Ciano asked him for an urgent meeting next day at the Brenner Pass, 'to speak frankly to him, and to reaffirm our rights as Axis partners'. Ribbentrop told him he could not give him an answer right away, because he was 'waiting for an important message from Moscow'. He would phone him later in the evening. This, of course, threw Ciano and Mussolini into a complete spin, and when Ribbentrop did call at 10.30 that night, to say he could not manage the Brenner Pass, but would see Ciano at Innsbruck, since he was flying to Moscow later that day to sign a political pact, the Italians were devastated. After a swift conversation with the Duce, Ciano called off the meeting until after Ribbentrop's return from the Soviet Union.

'There is no doubt,' Ciano wrote in his diary with somewhat grudging admiration, 'the Germans have struck a master blow.'

At dinner that night, Hitler was in a happy mood, though he had not yet made a general announcement to those who had not been with him earlier. Before he did so, he wanted to see Stalin's letter. It arrived in the middle of the meal, in a teleprinter message from the Wilhelmstrasse, and was quietly handed to him at the table. He took the piece of paper and then, in the words of Albert Speer who was sitting close to him, 'He scanned it, stared into space for a moment, flushed deeply, then banged on the table so hard that the glasses rattled, and exclaimed in a voice breaking with excitement: "I have them! I have them!" Seconds later he had already regained control of himself. No one dared ask any question, and the meal continued.'

After coffee, Hitler called the men in his entourage into the great hall. Holding up the message, he told them: 'We are going to conclude a non-aggression pact with Russia. Here, read this – a telegram from Stalin.' Amid exclamations of wonder, the paper was passed from hand to hand. Stalin's letter was even more friendly than Hitler's had been. It was admirably simple and direct:

> 21 August 1939.
> To the Chancellor of the German Reich, Herr A. Hitler.
>
> I thank you for your letter. I hope that the German–Soviet non-aggression pact will bring about a decided turn for the better in the political relations between our two countries.
>
> The peoples of our countries need peaceful relations with each other. The assent of the German government to the conclusion of a non-aggression pact provides the foundation for eliminating political tension and for the re-establishment of peace and collaboration between our two countries.
>
> The Soviet government has instructed me to inform you that it agrees to Herr von Ribbentrop's arriving in Moscow on 23 August.
>
> J. STALIN.

'To see the names of Hitler and Stalin linked in friendship on a piece of paper,' recorded Speer, who had known nothing of the fevered negotiations, 'was the most staggering, the most exciting turn of events I could possibly have imagined.'

After authorising the release of a statement to the press and radio, Hitler had the cinema screen set up in the great hall, and he and his aides sat down to watch newsreel footage of Stalin reviewing one of the massive parades in Red Square. When it was over, he turned to the military adjutants for their assessment of what they had seen. They were happy to agree with his gratification that, as Speer put it, 'this military might was now neutralised'.

Hitler had every right to feel pleased with himself: he had pulled off a remarkable feat. Admittedly, the bungling and procrastination of the Allied statesmen had made a great contribution, but in the end it was still Hitler's personal achievement. What had finally swung the balance and persuaded Stalin to change his mind about the dates was almost certainly his uncanny ability to sense the psychological needs of a fellow dictator, a fellow outcast on the international scene. No other Western leader had ever written or spoken directly to Stalin, or even officially acknowledged his existence. In the world of diplomatic and governmental protocol, Stalin counted for nothing, for at that time he held no official position in government. He was not head of state, or even Prime Minister, but simply the General Secretary of the party. With his personal letter, Hitler had held out his hand to Stalin as one ruler to another. It had evidently pleased Stalin to take it.

Even at his moment of triumph, however, Hitler displayed both the shallowness of his thinking and his cynical lack of trust for the man he had just embraced. After the initial celebrations following Ribbentrop's telephone call, Hitler took Heinrich Hoffmann aside for a private chat. He had a job for him: he wanted him, as one of his oldest acquaintances, to go with the party to Moscow as his personal emissary to Stalin, to convey his good wishes and greetings to the Soviet leader.

'By sending these messages through a private individual rather than through an accredited diplomat,' he told him, 'I hope to give a personal turn to the contact with Stalin.'

The real purpose of Hoffmann's trip, however, was to take some special photographs.

'I am interested in trivialities,' Hitler told him, 'which often go unnoticed, but which sometimes give a much clearer clue to a man's character than all the reports of some silly fathead in the Foreign Ministry!'

One of the main trivialities Hitler was interested in was the shape and size of Stalin's earlobes – a physical detail which he believed would betray the presence of Jewish blood in the Soviet leader's veins. He wanted Hoffmann to make sure he took good pictures of them, so that he could see if they were 'ingrown and Jewish, or separate and Aryan'.

21

'A VERY SERIOUS QUESTION'

As arranged when their talks were adjourned on 17 August, the Anglo-French military mission met Voroshilov and his team again on Monday morning, 21 August. The Soviet marshal had apparently been excluded from the Politburo meetings which had confirmed Stalin's decision to sign with Hitler, so he did not know exactly how far things had gone in that direction. He must have been aware, however, that a Nazi–Soviet agreement was very much on the cards, for that morning *Pravda* carried a prominent report of the signing of the trade and credit treaty. The article was clearly preparing the ground for the non-aggression pact: 'This new economic and commercial agreement,' it declared, 'could turn out to be a significant step towards further improvements not only in economic but also in political relations between the Soviet Union and Germany.'

Two days earlier, *Pravda* had reprinted the lead story from the London *Daily Worker* of 7 August, under the headline 'An Attempt at a New Munich'. This claimed that a visit by British press magnate Lord Kemsley to Germany – ostensibly to arrange for an exchange of articles and features between the Nazi press and his own papers such as the *Sunday Times, Sunday Graphic, Daily Sketch* and *Western Mail* – had been the cover for 'the most far-reaching and dangerous offer to Hitler since Munich'. The central feature of the offer, according to the *Daily Worker*, was a five-power conference, from which Russia would be excluded, 'to consider ways and means of satisfying Hitler's demand for Danzig'.

'The proposal has already reached the point,' the article went on, 'where there have been secret soundings in Washington, to discover whether President Roosevelt and his Secretary of State, Mr Cordell Hull, can be lured into at least giving their blessing to the scheme.'

The Japanese were also said to be part of this plot, their job being to keep things on the boil in the Far East while Hitler deliberately heightened tension in Europe. His intention, according to the article, was to demonstrate the futility of opposing Germany. For without a pact with the Soviet Union, the Allies were powerless, physically unable to influence events in Poland.

After the war, the French communist leader Florimond Bonté stated that the Kemsley visit, along with knowledge of the clandestine meeting between Göring and the British businessmen, had been the chief factors in influencing the Soviets to seek an agreement with Germany. While this is certainly an exaggeration, there can be no doubt that the undercover dealings did have a strong influence on Stalin, as well as on Hitler, who was convinced by them that Britain would not fight. How could the Soviet leader trust a government which continued to indulge in such underhand activities while supposedly negotiating seriously with him? Admittedly, he was himself talking to the Germans, but he could always justify this as insurance, in case the Allied talks failed.

In keeping his options open until the very last moment, Stalin does seem to have been prepared to give the Allies every opportunity to succeed. The *Daily Worker* story was authorised if not actually inspired by the Soviet government; yet although it was published in London on 7 August – coincidentally the same day Göring was meeting with Charles Spencer and his colleagues – it was not reprinted in Moscow until 19 August. Was it then a warning to the Allies that time was running out, giving them one final chance to deliver the goods? Or was it a signal to Hitler, inviting him to press on? The answer is probably both, for at the time *Pravda* was instructed to print it, Beaufre was still on his way to Warsaw, demonstrating that the French at least were doing something positive about the Poles. The Allied option was still open – but only just.

The publication on the Monday of the broad hint of further developments after the signing of the trade treaty was a much clearer signal. Now, the minutes really were ticking away towards midnight for the Allies. But Drax appears to have been totally unaware of any signals at all. Such political subtleties were quite beyond his experience and Ambassador Seeds does not seem to have given him any guidance either.

When the delegates had taken their places again round the big table in the Spiridonovka, Drax opened the proceedings by saying that there were several subjects to be discussed, but first he wished to deal with the outstanding matter of his missing credentials. The relevant document, dated 15 August, had now arrived, he announced. Voroshilov asked him to read out its contents.

'The important part,' Drax explained, 'is contained in the last few lines. I would now propose to read them, unless you desire to have the whole document.'

Voroshilov, always a stickler for detail and thoroughness, said he would like to hear the whole thing.

Carefully clearing his throat, Drax began: 'I, Edward Frederick Lindley, Viscount Halifax, Knight Commander of the Most Noble Order of the Garter . . .' He paused to allow the interpreter to translate. Then, seeing the Soviet officers looking puzzled at the mention of the Garter, Drax broke off to give a brief history of this ancient order of chivalry.

'At first,' Conrad Collier recalls, 'the commissars listened with communist derision. But gradually the mood changed into one of envy of our historical tradition.'

The mood was shattered somewhat, however, when Drax came to list his own decorations, and an element of low comedy crept into the proceedings. One of his honours was that of Knight Commander of the Most Honourable Order of the Bath. Voroshilov picked on the word immediately.

'Bath?' he queried incredulously. The word seems to have been translated as 'wash-tub'. What on earth was the Order of the Wash-tub?

Unfortunately, Drax was not as knowledgeable about his own order as he was about the Garter, and he was forced to invent, revealing an unexpectedly surreal imagination.

'In the reign of one of our early kings,' he recounted, 'our knights used to travel round Europe on horseback, slaying dragons and rescuing maidens in distress. They would return home travel-stained and grimy and would at once report their adventures to the king. In cases he thought to be specially deserving, he would sometimes offer a knight a luxury that was highly prized – a bath in the royal bathroom. Hence the "Order of the Bath".'

The Soviet delegates were suitably impressed and amused, but the light note Drax's story had introduced did not last. Voroshilov, aware of Beaufre's lack of success in Warsaw, proposed that the talks be adjourned indefinitely. He and his colleagues, he said, would soon be busy with the autumn manoeuvres. When Drax and Doumenc protested, Voroshilov launched into another lecture on the facts of life.

'The intentions of the Soviet delegation were, and still are, to agree on the organisation of military co-operation by the armed forces of the three parties,' he said, and then proceeded to repeat all his statements and demands about crossing Poland and Romania. 'Soviet forces cannot co-operate with the armed forces of Britain and France if they are not allowed on to Polish and Romanian territory,' he reiterated. 'The Soviet military delegation cannot picture to itself how the governments and general staffs of Britain and France, in sending their missions to the USSR . . . could not have given them some directives on such an elementary matter . . . This can only show that there are reasons to doubt their desire to come to serious and effective co-operation with the USSR.'

And with that, the conference was adjourned.

Drax and the British delegation were despondent. But although Beaufre had returned empty-handed from Warsaw, Doumenc and the French refused to give up hope. Their determination to salvage something from the wreckage was bolstered by the long-awaited order from Paris, received on 21 August. Addressed to Doumenc, it read: 'You are authorised to sign, in the common interest and in accord with the ambassador, the best possible military agreement, subject to the approval of the French government. Daladier.' The French Cabinet had decided the situation was now too serious for any further hesitation. They must override the objections of the Poles.

Daladier claimed to have despatched the telegram on the Monday morning. But it was 10.30 at night when it arrived, owing to what Daladier described as 'some unexplained delay'. Could it have been deliberately held by the Soviet telegraph office, perhaps for Stalin to consider its implications before sending his letter to Hitler? This is certainly a possibility, especially as it was accompanied by a message from Bonnet to Ambassador Naggiar, instructing him to tell Molotov that France agreed 'in principle' to the passage of Soviet troops through Poland following any German attack.

By the time the messages reached Doumenc and Naggiar, it was too late for either of them to contact anyone that night. Barely two and a half hours later, a programme of light music on German radio was suddenly interrupted by an excited voice, announcing: 'The Reich government and the Soviet government have agreed to conclude a non-aggression pact with each other. The Reich Minister for Foreign Affairs will arrive in Moscow on Wednesday, 23 August, for the conclusion of the negotiations.'

In Moscow, Schulenburg's chauffeur, Kirstein, rushed from his room to tell the ambassador what he had heard. In Berlin, telephone lines were jammed with people calling to ask each other if they had heard the news. William Shirer, busily catching up on the events of the last ten days after his trip to Poland, missed the broadcast, but was phoned at the Adlon Hotel by Ed Murrow from London. Both were 'flabbergasted' by the news, which Murrow thought might sweep Chamberlain from office.

Georges Bonnet was still at his desk at the Quai d'Orsay in Paris when the director of the Havas news agency called him. Bonnet immediately telephoned Daladier, who had gone to bed, and woke him up to inform him. Daladier was not impressed. The report, he said, was 'just a journalist's prank'.

The official Soviet announcement was made in less flamboyant manner next day, in a typically sober statement from Tass:

Following the conclusion of the Soviet–German trade and credit agreement, the question of the improvement in political relations between Germany and the USSR has arisen.

The exchange of views which has taken place between the two governments has made apparent the desire of both parties to bring about a lessening of the political tension between them, to remove the threat of war and to conclude a non-aggression pact.

Consequently, the arrival in Moscow is envisaged during the next few days of the German Minister for Foreign Affairs, Herr von Ribbentrop, for talks along these lines.

First thing on Tuesday morning, Doumenc sent an urgent message to Voroshilov, saying the assurances they had been seeking had now arrived, and that he wanted to start negotiations again, if possible that day. There was no reply. All day Doumenc waited, but there was no word, except to say that the marshal was unavailable.

In fact, Voroshilov was not in Moscow. He had, at Stalin's suggestion, gone hunting, having left the city the night before for his preserve at Zavidova, on the Volga, some seventy miles north-west of Moscow, to shoot duck. The party, which included Nikita Khrushchev, Georgi Malenkov and Nikolai Bulganin, all future rulers of the Soviet Union, in addition to several senior Red Army officers, enjoyed marvellous sport. Voroshilov had been built up in the Soviet press as the great hunter and marksman, and Khrushchev – who always retained an element of the rude small boy in his character – was delighted to claim that he had bagged one more duck than the master shot. Voroshilov did not seem worried by this, however, and returned to the city by fast car in the late afternoon, well satisfied.

On being informed of Doumenc's request, he sent word that he would see him at 7 pm. The French general was to come alone, without Drax. He need not bring an interpreter – they would use Voroshilov's.

Sandwiched between two NKVD cars filled with armed guards, Doumenc's car swept into the Kremlin without hindrance. He was shown directly into Voroshilov's office where, as promised, they were alone, apart from one interpreter. Voroshilov seems to have liked and respected Doumenc, and did his best to let him down gently – though this did not stop him questioning the Frenchman's statements with his usual thoroughness.

Doumenc told him the French government had officially authorised him to sign a military pact which would permit the passage of Soviet troops through Poland and also, if the situation warranted it, through

Romania (though no one seems to have even asked the Romanians!).
Voroshilov was not convinced.

'I would ask General Doumenc to acquaint me with the nature of the
document he has received from his government,' he said. 'I would also
like to know if the British mission has received a reply to the same
question.'

Doumenc had to say that he had received no document as such, but
that he had received specific instructions from his government.

'And the British government?' Voroshilov demanded.

Doumenc knew – as Voroshilov almost certainly did, too – that the
British did not agree with the idea of overriding the Poles, but he
pressed on manfully.

'I do not know if Admiral Drax has received similar instructions from
his government,' he said, 'but I know that the admiral has been advised
that the conference can continue.'

'The British delegation knows about this communication?'

'I have told the admiral that the French government's reply has been
received,' Doumenc replied. 'And I am almost certain that the British
government will send the same reply.'

It was a brave try, but Voroshilov was determined to avoid any hint of
fudging. He also seems to have been keen to demonstrate to Doumenc
that he knew everything that had been going on.

'It is possible that the British mission may be agreeable to General
Doumenc pursuing these military matters,' he conceded. 'Nevertheless,
it appears to me that the British mission has played and continues to
play, if not a dominant role, at least an equal one in all our conversations.
That is why, in the absence of any reply from the British government, it
will obviously be difficult to continue the work of this conference.'

Voroshilov clearly knew that Seeds had sent a telegram to London,
referring to Doumenc's instructions from Paris, asking: 'Can we assume
that you agree?' He also clearly knew that there had been no reply. In
fact there never was one. Seeds's telegram lies in the files of the Foreign
Office with a note written on it in the hand of William Strang: 'It was not
possible to send an answer to this telegram as no decision was
taken.'

'There is also one other question which interests me,' Voroshilov
continued. 'I must ask you to excuse me, General, but it is a very serious
question which I must put to you. You have not in your reply given any
indication of the attitude of the Polish and Romanian governments. Are
they aware exactly of what is going on? Or does the reply which you have
received emanate from the French government without the knowledge
of Poland and Romania?'

Voroshilov's 'serious question' was a real stopper. There could be no
doubt left in Doumenc's mind that he really did know everything. But
having gone so far, he could not give up now.

'I do not know what conversations have taken place between governments,' he declared. 'I can only repeat what has been said to me by my own government. I would like to take this opportunity of putting the following question to you: is it, or is it not, your intention to press on with our conversations with a view to signing a military pact? I have reached that point, and time is passing.'

Voroshilov pointed out that it was hardly his fault if the representatives of Britain and France had wasted so much conference time dallying with these questions. Doumenc countered that it was possible the difficulties had not all been the Allies' own fault. But he was still desperately anxious to achieve success.

'I must say once more to you, Marshal,' he stated vigorously, 'that I, too, am prepared to work fast – indeed, as fast as possible.'

For a moment, the two men's humanity penetrated the dialectic. Voroshilov allowed something of his regard for Doumenc to show through, and Doumenc responded, as they tacitly acknowledged their roles as fellow soldiers trapped by the situation and prevented by it from achieving the result they both sought.

'I do not doubt it,' Voroshilov told Doumenc. 'In the last few days I have come to know you, and your sincerity and your genuine desire to sign a military agreement as fast as possible are apparent to me.'

'Speedily,' Doumenc added, 'and with the mutual confidence of soldiers who face a common enemy.'

But it was no use. In modern societies other than military dictatorships, the soldier must always be the servant of the politician, and even generals and marshals have to obey orders. But there are times when the yoke chafes most uncomfortably, and for Voroshilov this was one of those moments, since he was personally opposed to an alliance with Germany. Nevertheless, he had to do his duty. There had now been eleven days of discussions, and they had got nowhere. Enough was enough.

'I cannot agree to any further sessions around the conference table,' he said, 'until all official replies have been received. I do not question that the general has received an affirmative reply from his own government. But the attitudes of Poland, Romania and Great Britain are still unknown. That is why further talks can lead merely to a lot of chatter which can only be damaging politically.'

He then put his finger on the fatal flaw in Doumenc's whole strategy for trying to make him believe the Poles had submitted.

'I am quite sure that, if the Poles had given their agreement to the passage of Soviet troops, they would wish to take part in our discussions. Indeed, I am convinced that they would demand to be present, for I cannot see their general staff being willing to remain on the sidelines while questions which concern them so closely are under discussion. For this reason, I do not believe they know what is going on.'

'This may be so,' Doumenc replied. 'But I do not know and I cannot say.'

'Let us wait until everything is clear,' Voroshilov suggested.

'I can wait with pleasure, but I do not wish to wait to no purpose,' Doumenc protested. 'I must be frank with you, Marshal. It has been announced that a certain person is due to arrive here soon, and such visits do not fill me with pleasure.'

Voroshilov did not deny that Ribbentrop was coming to Moscow, but blamed the British and French for what was happening. They had had their chance of a military treaty for several years, but had done nothing.

'Last year,' he pointed out, 'when Czechoslovakia went down, we expected a signal from France and our troops were ready; but nothing happened.'

'Our troops were ready, too,' Doumenc protested.

'Then whatever happened? Here . . . the government was willing to help Czechoslovakia in accordance with our treaty obligations.'

'If the marshal had been in France,' Doumenc countered, refusing to admit to any lack of enthusiasm on the part of his country, '. . . he would have seen that everything was ready for war. If it was necessary then to create a peace front, it is just as necessary now.'

The discussion was getting nowhere, and Voroshilov decided to bring it to an end.

'The French and British representatives have drawn out the political discussions interminably,' he charged. 'For this reason one cannot exclude the possibility that during this time some political development may have taken place. Let us wait now until the situation is tidied up, until the British government's reply has been received and the attitude of Poland and Romania is clear. Then we can meet again.'

It was a forlorn prospect – even as they parted, Ribbentrop was already in the air, on the first leg of his journey to Moscow.

22

'I HAVE STRUCK THIS WEAPON FROM THE HANDS OF THOSE GENTLEMEN'

The German press on the morning of Tuesday, 22 August, was, as William Shirer put it, 'wonderful to behold'. The dailies competed with each other to give the biggest welcome to the news. The *Deutsche Allgemeine Zeitung* was a prime example: it had spent the last few years violently attacking bolshevism and the Soviet Union, now it described the promised pact as 'a natural partnership'. But for sheer, barefaced effrontery the prize, perhaps inevitably, went to Goebbels's own newspaper *Angriff* (*Attack*), which he had founded in 1927. On the front page, blazoned in big black type, appeared the headline: 'The world is faced with a towering fact: two peoples have established a common foreign policy after a long and traditional friendship which has produced the basis for mutual understanding.'

Sharing the front pages and the headlines, as if to underline the import of the pact, were stories of 'unbelievable atrocities' being committed by the Poles against their German minority.

In streets and homes, on buses and street cars, in subways and trains, the people of Germany were reading with amazement what the papers had to say. With few exceptions, they greeted the news with relief: the nightmare of encirclement, which Hitler had exploited mercilessly to extort ever-greater sacrifices from them, was now broken; the fear of a war on two fronts was dispelled. With the Russians neutralised, the British and French would surely see reason and draw back. The troop convoys rumbling incessantly eastwards could be viewed with less foreboding: the mere presence of all this military might on their frontiers would be enough to intimidate the Poles into submission. Hitler had done it again – he was about to deliver another bloodless victory.

On a bridle path in Berlin's Tiergarten, however, two horsemen meeting for an early morning ride shared very different feelings about Hitler's achievement. Erich Kordt and Admiral Wilhelm Canaris held the positions of senior counsellor in Ribbentrop's secretariat and head of the Abwehr respectively. As such, they were less gullible than most of their compatriots – though Kordt had been optimistic enough to believe that Britain and France would be successful in the Moscow negotiations, largely because of what he heard from his brother Theodore, counsellor and currently chargé d'affaires in the London embassy. Both men were only too aware of Hitler's true intentions, and therefore of what the announcement really meant.

'So the British had the pact with Russia in the bag, did they, Kordt?' Canaris greeted the younger man. 'My dear fellow, how could you let them deceive you? This Emile [Canaris's name for Hitler] is more cunning than you think – and much more cunning than your London friends.'

Kordt had no answer to this, except to acknowledge its truth. He kicked his horse into motion, alongside the admiral's. Canaris gestured towards the War Office buildings across the park in the Bendlerstrasse.

'It has started already – the rot, I mean,' he said bitterly. 'All around here, the *Silber und Goldfasane* are most impressed with what has happened. They have already begun to learn the words of the *Internationale* ready for Stalin's state visit.'

Some of the most senior of those officers with the gold and silver facings of the War Office and general staff on their uniforms were shortly to be even more impressed, when they flew south later that morning to be addressed by Hitler in the Berghof. Canaris was among them, travelling in the same aircraft that brought Ribbentrop back to Berlin.

Throughout the morning, a constant procession of gleaming black Mercedes from Hitler's motor pool shimmered through the heat haze, ferrying his most senior commanders to the Berghof. They bowled along the autobahns from Munich and Salzburg, then turned south to climb into the mountains, speeding through sleepy towns and villages to deposit their passengers at the foot of the broad steps leading up to the house.

The generals and admirals, field marshals and *Obergruppenführers* had been brought by air and rail from headquarters all over Germany. None of them was quite sure what he was to hear. They had been summoned by an order from Hitler, issued through Keitel and the OKW late on Saturday, 19 August, after he had sent his letter to Stalin.

They were to be prepared to make detailed presentations of their operational plans, down to army level, in the event of a campaign in Poland. But apart from that, there had been nothing to indicate what Hitler had in mind. The invitation had simply said they were to be there, with their plans, and that they were to dress informally, in plain clothes, so as to avoid attracting attention. 'He particularly wants the conference to remain absolutely secret,' it stressed, 'and no word of it whatever to leak out to the foreign press.' No one was to make any record of what he said.

Göring, there in his capacity as Commander-in-Chief of the Luftwaffe, had taken the informal dress instruction to extremes. According to Admiral Hermann Boehm, commander of the High Seas Fleet, he greeted his fellow commanders on the terrace wearing 'a soft-collared white shirt under a green elkskin jerkin adorned with big buttons of bright yellow leather, grey shorts and grey silk stockings that displayed his impressive calves to considerable effect. This dainty hosiery was offset by a pair of massive laced boots. To cap it all, his paunch was girded by a scarlet sword belt, richly inlaid with gold, from which dangled an ornamental dagger in an ample sheath of the same material.'

As midday approached, they put out their cigarettes and took their places in the great hall, some fifty officers seated on five rows of chairs arranged in a semi-circle: army-group and army commanders, their chiefs of staff, their navy, air force and SS equivalents. In the centre sat the three Commanders-in-Chief, Field Marshal Göring, Colonel-General von Brauchitsch, and Grand Admiral Raeder. The atmosphere was electric, with hardly anyone making a sound.

Precisely at noon, the silence was broken by the SS guards of the Leibstandarte Adolf Hitler coming to attention and presenting arms, and the assembled officers rose as Hitler appeared in the big square opening of the doorway. Acknowledging the salutes, he made his way down the three steps into the body of the room, and walked, slightly crab-like as usual, a few paces to his left. With his back to the great Gobelin tapestry, he placed his notes on the grand piano by his right hand, and started to speak.

'I have called you together,' he announced, 'to give you a picture of the political situation, in order that you may have some insight into the individual factors on which I have based my decision to act, and in order to strengthen your confidence. After this, we shall discuss military details.'

Despite the order forbidding anyone to record what he said, Canaris – tucked quietly away in a corner, as befitted the chief of the secret service – noted down every word in shorthand, to give to his fellow anti-Nazi conspirators next day. In different parts of the room at least three others, including Lieutenant-General Halder and General Admiral Boehm, also scribbled quietly. Next day, several more wrote down what they remembered. If Hitler saw any of them making notes, however, he gave no sign of it as he launched into a two-hour tirade.

The main purpose of his speech was to prepare his generals for war with Poland: to convince them that it was both just and necessary; to quell their fears of its spreading into something they could not control; and then to motivate them into tackling it with enthusiasm and determination. Naturally, he laid all the blame for the current situation on the Poles, who could if they had chosen have been Germany's accomplices in his expansionist schemes. He made no secret that his aims were expansionist. There was no need. Even though they may have quarrelled with some of his methods of achieving it, most of his audience that day believed in an extended Greater Germany. All the same, he had to be circumspect about the direction of those aims – he could hardly proclaim his plans for the Soviet Union at the very moment he was signing a pact with Stalin. To an honest man, such a problem might have been difficult to overcome. But for Hitler it was easily dealt with: all he had to do was dissemble.

'It has become clear to me,' he began, 'that a conflict with Poland had to come sooner or later. I had already decided this in the spring, but at that time I thought I would turn against the West first, in a few years' time, and only after that against the East. But one cannot always fix the order of these things. Nor can one close one's eyes to threatening situations. In the beginning, I wanted to establish an acceptable relationship with Poland, in order to fight first against the West. But this plan, which appealed to me, could not be put into effect because the essential points changed. It became obvious that in the event of a conflict with the West, Poland would attack us. Poland wants access to the sea; after our occupation of Memel there were further developments and it became clear to me that under the circumstances a conflict with Poland could start at a moment which could be inopportune for us.

'Essentially, it all depends on me,' he went on, 'on my existence, because of my political talents. Furthermore, probably no one will ever again have the confidence of the whole German people as I have. There will probably never again be a man with greater authority than I have. My existence is therefore a factor of great value. But don't forget that I could be eliminated at any moment by a criminal or a madman.'

Much the same applied to Mussolini, 'the man with the strongest nerves in Italy'. Without him, Italy's loyalty as an ally could not be counted on. There was, of course, a third fascist dictator in Europe now, but although he spoke kindly of him, Hitler had to acknowledge that Franco was not yet in a strong enough position to offer more than 'benevolent neutrality' on the part of Spain.

The difference between the new Germany and the rotten democracies was Hitler's indomitable will. There was no outstanding personality in either Britain or France, he claimed. 'Our enemies are inferior men, not men of action, not masters. They are little worms!'

But it was not only personalities that gave the Axis powers the advantage. The general political situation favoured them, too. He listed Britain's problems: rivalry with France and Italy in the Mediterranean, tension with Japan in the Far East, problems with the Mohammedan world in the Middle East, weakness still from the last war, strife with Ireland, the growing independence of South Africa, concessions having to be made to India, and at home, ailing industry. England, he said, was in the utmost peril, and a British statesman could only view the future with concern.

France's position, he said, had also deteriorated, particularly in the Mediterranean. And there were several other factors in Germany's favour: the Italian occupation of Albania had created a balance in the Balkans; Yugoslavia was 'infected with the fatal germ of decay'; Romania was vulnerable and open to attack, and was threatened by Hungary and Bulgaria; Turkey since Kemal Ataturk's death had been ruled by unsteady, weak men with petty minds.

Now, he began to warm to his subject. He paused for effect, then raised his voice for the first time: 'All these fortunate circumstances will not prevail in two or three years. No one knows how long I shall live. I am now fifty and at the height of my powers. It is best that war should come now, rather than in five years' time, when both I and Mussolini will be five years older. Therefore, the showdown had better come at once!'

These words shook the audience. The silence was broken by a sudden stirring, a gasp from the generals. Admiral Boehm marked the passage in his notes with a large exclamation point. General Halder underscored the words with a heavy line. But Hitler was only now getting into his stride.

'The creation of a Greater Germany is a great political achievement, but militarily there are doubts, since what has been achieved has come through bluff on the part of the political leaders. Now, it is necessary to test the military machine – if at all possible not in a general reckoning, but in individual actions.'

His voice continuing to rise, he launched into another attack on Poland, and on the way in which Britain had encouraged her intransigence. Again, he reminded his generals of the danger that he or Mussolini could be assassinated. Again, he described the situation with Poland as intolerable: 'We cannot face each other forever with rifles cocked.'

'The probability is still great,' he said, 'that the west will not intervene. But we must take that risk with ruthless determination, the politician just as much as the general. We are faced with the harsh alternative of striking now or of certain annihilation sooner or later. I have taken risks

– in occupying the Rhineland when the generals wanted me to pull back, in taking Austria, the Sudetenland and the rest of Czechoslovakia. I should have been stoned if I had not been proved right! Hannibal at Cannae, Frederick the Great at Leuthen, and Hindenburg and Ludendorff at Tannenberg all took chances. Now we must take risks which can only be mastered by iron nerves, iron determination.'

He began to list all his reasons for saying the Western Powers would not intervene. Neither Britain nor France, he said, was in a position to fulfil her obligations. Britain was all talk and no action, and would not take the risks of war; France, short of men and with a declining birthrate, did not want to be involved. The West had only two options in a war against Germany: a blockade, which could not be effective because of Germany's self-sufficiency and sources of supply in the East; and an attack from the Maginot Line, which he considered to be impossible. Britain and France would not violate the neutrality of Belgium, Holland or Switzerland, therefore in actual fact they could not help Poland.

'No one is counting on a long war,' he continued. 'If my general here, von Brauchitsch, had told me it would take four years to conquer Poland, I would have told him, "It cannot be done." But it is nonsense to say that England wants a long war. What we will do is hold our position in the West until we have conquered Poland, and then . . .'

He broke off, leaving the commanders to imagine what would happen next, and then turned to the big question, the one which had been occupying the thoughts of both politicians and military men since the news had broken that morning.

'The enemy had one other hope,' he told them. 'That Russia would become our enemy after the conquest of Poland. But the enemy did not reckon with my great strength of purpose. But then, our enemies are nothing but small fry – I saw this at Munich.

'I was convinced that Stalin would never accept the English offer. Only a blind optimist could believe that Stalin would be so stupid as not to see through England's intentions. Russia has no interest in preserving Poland, and Stalin knows that a war would mean the end of his regime, whether his soldiers emerged from a war victorious or vanquished.

'It was Litvinov's dismissal that decided me. It struck me like a cannonball that here was a sign of change in Moscow towards the Western Powers. I brought about the move towards Russian gradually: we started political discussions in connection with the trade treaty, then the Russians suggested a non-aggression pact. Finally, they made a more comprehensive proposal. Four days ago, I took a particular step which brought about yesterday's Russian announcement that they are ready to sign – I made personal contact with Stalin. I have arranged for Ribbentrop to fly to Moscow, immediately, to conclude the non-aggression pact the day after tomorrow.

'I have struck this weapon from the hands of those gentlemen! Now, I have Poland where I want her! We need not be afraid of a blockade: the East will supply us with grain, cattle, coal, lead and zinc.' Allowing the implications of his statement to sink in for a moment, Hitler looked around at his audience, then launched into a typical, rousing finale: 'It is a mighty aim, which demands mighty efforts. My only fear is that at the last moment some *Schweinehund* will come along with another proposal for mediation. We have made a start on the destruction of England's hegemony. Now that I have made the political preparations, the way is open for the soldiers!'

The room erupted in applause, led by Göring, who leapt to his feet, bounced up the three shallow steps to the higher level in front of the doorway, and made a brief speech thanking the Führer, and assuring him that the armed forces would do their duty.

After a lavish buffet lunch on the terrace, appropriately served with lashings of Russian caviar, Hitler's favourite delicacy, the commanders trooped back into the great hall to give presentations of their operational plans. According to Colonel Walter Warlimont, head of the OKW operations staff, Hitler 'showed himself extremely well-informed on all details, and did not hesitate to produce further suggestions of his own, without reference to the chief of the OKW [Keitel] or the head of section L [Warlimont himself], both of whom were present'. The individual commanders all took care to emphasise their confidence in his military leadership.

Hitler was delighted with the results, and followed the same pattern of giving a rousing speech, then listening to the obsequious responses of his generals, that he pursued before every important campaign right up to the Ardennes offensive at the end of 1944, his last positive move of the war. But although it pleased Hitler, this procedure infuriated Warlimont and his fellow professionals. To them, it was yet another example of the Führer's Austrian *Schlamperei*, the dilettante meddling of an untrained and disorganised mind. As a method of testing the likely effectiveness of the plans, it was 'no substitute for the well-tried and convincing method of a war game'.

With the presentation of the generals' plans completed, Hitler rose again to wrap up the conference with another speech, designed to send his commanders away fired with the conviction that he was right. He spoke for another hour, while outside the picture window dark clouds gathered over the mountains, harbingers of a summer storm.

He began quietly, saying it was impossible to prophesy with any certainty the reactions of Britain and France. They would probably impose a trade embargo, rather than a blockade, he thought, and would break off diplomatic relations, but Germans must face this with iron determination. There must be no shrinking back.

After a great deal of rhetoric describing the qualities needed for victory, Hitler turned to the practical aims of the campaign, winding himself up towards the emotional climax of his speech. 'Do not forget,' he exhorted, 'the destruction of Poland has priority. Our aim is to wipe out living forces, not to reach a certain line. Even if the Western Powers should intervene and war breaks out with them, the destruction of Poland still remains our primary objective. But it must be a quick victory, because of the season . . .

'As regards our conduct of the war – close your hearts to pity! Act brutally! Crush every living spark! Eighty million people must get what is justly theirs! Their existence must be made secure! Might is right – so we must act with the greatest harshness. You must take decisions swiftly, and always have firm faith in the German soldier. Any failures will be due solely to leaders having lost their nerve!'

The fury of his words broke over the heads of the commanders, filling the room with a charge as powerful as that in the storm clouds outside. Then, suddenly, his voice was calm and quiet again as he turned to the details of the campaign. Unemotionally, he reviewed the position of his armies on the Polish borders. He ordered the defences in Slovakia to be strengthened, while grounding her air force and guaranteeing her frontiers against attacks by Hungary. Confirming the rest of the opening moves in the campaign, he authorised simultaneous dive-bomber attacks on the bridges at Dirschau and the Polish harbour at Gdynia. Strategically, he said, what was of paramount importance was to drive wedges from the south-east and north to the Vistula and Narev rivers.

Military operations, he insisted, must not be influenced by considerations of what he might wish to do with Poland after the war. The new German frontier would be delimited according to 'sound principles'. There might be a small protectorate as a buffer state between Germany and the Soviet Union. But he took care not to enlarge upon this, or to mention the secret protocol which was to form part of the pact with Stalin.

'The wholesale destruction of Poland is the military objective,' he reminded the generals. 'Speed is the main thing. You must pursue them until they are completely annihilated. I am convinced that the German Wehrmacht is equal to all demands. I will give you the order for the start of hostilities later. It will probably be for Saturday morning.'

And with that, he picked up his notes and left the hall, beckoning to Göring, Keitel and Brauchitsch to follow him. Brauchitsch paused at the top of the steps to dismiss his fellow commanders with the confident words: 'Gentlemen – to your stations!'

In the ante-room, Hitler called over his Wehrmacht adjutant, Colonel Rudolf Schmundt, and ordered him to sniff around for reactions. He was well aware that most of the commanders, and particularly Göring, who was also in charge of economic development, had been opposed to war at that time. They were convinced Germany was not ready, knowing not only that there were desperate shortages of oil, steel and other raw materials, but also that the Wehrmacht only had enough ammunition for six weeks' fighting.

Hitler had been at pains to emphasise that he envisaged nothing more than a short, sharp campaign in Poland, a strictly limited and local conflict. There was, he stressed, no danger of its developing into anything bigger, since the British and French did not want a major war, either. But such assurances, he knew, were not enough to swing the generals completely behind him. What he believed would do so was the news of the pact with Russia.

It was not only his enemies abroad that Hitler needed to impress by signing the pact. It had a vital role to play domestically, too, in reassuring the faithful, convincing the waverers, and disarming his critics. Now, he had to know if it had worked. He need not have worried. Through the open doorway, the high good humour of most of the commanders – particularly the Luftwaffe generals Milch and Kesselring – could be clearly seen. The older men especially were completely won over: to them the idea of a deal with the Soviet Union was precisely in line with the doctrine of the great military theorist, General Hans von Seeckt, the man who had been responsible for picking up the pieces after the last war, salvaging what he could as the first chief of the new army in 1919.

General Fedor von Bock, commander of Army Group North, was heard to say he thought Hitler's speech had been 'brilliant'. Among the younger generals, Heinz Guderian, the Panzer leader and creator of the *Blitzkrieg* theory of warfare, was naturally delighted that his ideas were about to be given free rein. He and his fellow armoured commanders had already toasted the news of the pact in champagne, when they heard it on the radio the previous night.

The only drop of cold water came from Grand Admiral Raeder, who approached Hitler to remind him that a naval cadet training ship was permanently moored in the Gulf of Danzig: it would be in grave danger when the attack started. Hitler shrugged this off, being overheard to remark: 'What does it matter if the old tub goes down?' Raeder, shocked, pointed out that there were several hundred cadets on board. Hitler ignored him.

Raeder was not the only chief who was unenthusiastic. Canaris was 'utterly horrified' by what he had heard. His horror had not diminished next day, when he read out the most important passages from his notes to some of his trusted associates in the Abwehr. Hans Bernd Gisevius recalled that his voice trembled as he read, and that he 'was acutely aware that he had been witness to a monstrous scene'. But for most of those present in the Berghof that day, the Hitler magic had worked once again.

23

THE PACT IS SIGNED

Ribbentrop left Berlin late in the evening of 22 August. He thought it wiser to take the long way round, making a wide detour out over the Baltic, rather than risk flying across Poland, even though this meant breaking his journey at Königsberg, in East Prussia. In any case, he should arrive in Moscow fresher after an overnight stop than after a single, longer flight at 13,000 feet.

In fact, he would have been quite safe. Fears that the Poles might intercept the flight or even try to shoot it down were groundless, for they seemed indifferent to the dangers of Nazi–Soviet *rapprochement*. After hearing the announcement of the proposed pact, Beck informed French Ambassador Noël that he was 'quite unperturbed by this *coup de théâtre*'. He told the British embassy to send a message to the same effect to London, adding for good measure that he had 'always known the Russians were double-crossers', and that the pact would have no effect on Polish policy.

There were thirty in Ribbentrop's party, including officials, photographers and journalists. Schulenburg, surprised at the number, called it 'quite a swig out of the bottle', but said he would manage to accommodate them somehow. *Immelmann III* could not take them all, and a second Condor had to be provided from the government air pool.

Since the negotiations were now out in the open, there was no longer any need to use the economic talks as a smokescreen, and Schnurre was not even included in the party. Friedrich Gaus, the legal expert, was the senior civil servant in charge. Worried about the arrangements in Königsberg because of the short notice, Gaus asked Schulenburg's advice on how best to handle them. The ambassador told him there was a young man then in Berlin who, in addition to having a comprehensive knowledge of Moscow which might prove useful, also knew all the officials in East Prussia, having been German consul in Memel for a while before its annexation. Why not make use of him? Gaus was delighted to agree – and thus Johnnie Herwarth found himself travelling back to Moscow only five days afer he had left it for good.

The other principal members of the group – apart, that is, from Heinrich Hoffmann with his trusty camera – were Walther Hewel, Peter Kleist, head of the eastern section of the Ribbentrop Bureau, and the two Paul Schmidts – Paul Karl, director of the Foreign Ministry's press and news department, and Paul Otto, the interpreter. Paul Otto, who had been plucked from a family holiday at Norderney on the Baltic at barely two hours' notice, was puzzled by his inclusion, since Russian was not one of his languages. His instructions, which he found waiting for him on his desk in a sealed envelope, told him that on this occasion he was not going as an interpreter. Gustav Hilger, the embassy counsellor, would act as translator, while Schmidt's task would be to take notes, make detailed reports on the discussions with Stalin, and record any agreements made.

Although Ribbentrop was elated, not everyone in the party was in high spirits. Peter Kleist recalled that there was a feeling among many of them of extreme tension: 'Nobody could guarantee that the Soviets would not spring on us an Anglo-French agreement, all neatly tied up, when we arrived in Moscow.' And despite Ribbentrop's own unshakeable confidence, no one could be sure that he would not be forced into the 'long, soul-destroying negotiations' for which the Soviets were well known.

It was growing dark by the time they crossed the coast over East Prussia. As they began their descent towards land, they saw beneath them the lights of a warship – the battleship *Schleswig-Holstein*, taking her twenty-eight-centimetre (eleven-inch) guns on a 'courtesy visit' to Danzig. It was an apt reminder of the purpose of their journey. In Königsberg the delegates were driven swiftly to the Park Hotel, where they checked in at 11 pm. But for the Foreign Ministry officials there was to be no rest: Ribbentrop was far too agitated to sleep. What little composure he had left was immediately shattered by news from the Wilhelmstrasse that while he had been in the air, the Führer had spoken on the phone directly with State Secretary Ernst von Weizsäcker – the only time, in fact, that Hitler ever did so – to discuss what he should do about a message from Nevile Henderson, who had asked to see him to deliver a personal letter from Chamberlain. Hitler did not want to see Henderson, and asked Weizsäcker if an ambassador had the right to be received in the absence of the Foreign Minister. Weizsäcker, who already knew all about the letter, had persuaded Hitler to receive Henderson. He, Weizsäcker, would fly with the ambassador to the Berghof next day. Ribbentrop was furious. He phoned Weizsäcker – who had meantime gone to bed – and, as Weizsäcker recorded in his diary, 'foaming with rage, called me to account. He could indeed not change the plan for Henderson to see Hitler without him; but he tried to stir up Hitler [in a separate phone call] to treat Henderson really badly.'

Ribbentrop spent the rest of the night preparing for his meeting with the Soviet leaders. According to interpreter Schmidt, this involved 'filling many sheets of paper with notes in handwriting which grew larger and larger as the night wore on, telephoning to Berlin and Berchtesgaden, asking for the most un-get-at-able papers, and keeping the whole delegation on the run'.

In a moment of respite, Schmidt and some of the younger men took time out 'to drink a farewell toast to peace' in the bar. Others, less directly involved with Ribbentrop, occupied themselves in other ways. Johnnie Herwarth, having assured himself that all the arrangements he had made were satisfactory, spent the time seeing friends in army units stationed in the province, trying to organise a place for himself in a cavalry regiment. Hoffmann, with a reputation to maintain as a *bon viveur* – the young SS adjutants had given him the honorary title of *Reichssäufer*, Reich drunkard – settled down for the night in the bar of the nearby Deutsches Hof Hotel.

Ribbentrop's Condor landed in Moscow at precisely 1 pm, and he descended from the aircraft, wearing a long leather coat over his black jacket and striped pants, to be greeted by the small, round figure of Vladimir Potemkin, Molotov's deputy in the Soviet Foreign Ministry. Resplendent in top hat and tails, Schulenburg and Italian Ambassador Augusto Rosso, backed by most of the staff of the German embassy, also waited to welcome the great man.

The airport was decorated with swastika flags flying alongside the Soviet hammer and sickle. The Russians had had considerable difficulty in finding any at such short notice, but in the end had obtained them from the Moscow film studios, which had been using them in anti-Nazi films. The effect was marred by the fact that some had been made the wrong way round, so that the ancient Aryan good luck symbol – the left-facing swastika which had been reversed to make the Nazi emblem – appeared incongruously here and there among the crooked crosses.

A Soviet air force guard of honour presented arms, and was inspected by Ribbentrop while the band played a hastily learned version of *Deutschland über Alles*, followed by the *Internationale*. It had proved impossible to get the music for the Nazi anthem, the *Horst Wessel* song. Several of the Germans noted its omission – it was later added to the repertoire of Soviet bands, but disappeared again abruptly in June 1941.

Herwarth was met by his old friend from the embassy, Gebhardt von Walther, who greeted him with a nod. 'We watched the show in front of us,' Herwarth remembers. 'Amidst the bustle, Walther grabbed my arm and said: "Look how the Gestapo officers are shaking hands with their counterparts in the NKVD, and how they're all smiling at each other.

They're obviously delighted to be able to collaborate at last. But watch out! This will be disastrous, especially when they start exchanging files." '

Looking around at the airport, the Germans were not impressed with what they saw. Richard Schulze-Kossens – then plain Obersturmführer Richard Schulze, Ribbentrop's twenty-four-year-old SS adjutant and the youngest member of the party – recalls that most of the aircraft on view were old and that the airport itself looked uncared for, dirty and unkempt. Their impressions of Moscow itself at that time were not much better as they gazed out of the windows of the black ZIS limousines, looking very much like American Buicks, which whisked them into the city along the Leningradsky Prospekt. Ribbentrop, surrounded by an NKVD escort under the command of Colonel Nikolai Vlasik, head of Stalin's bodyguard, rode in one of Stalin's own bullet-proof cars.

'Dictators seem to delight in the magnificence of wide roads,' interpreter Schmidt reflected during the journey, regarding the surroundings on either side as 'bleak and dreary'. Schulze was fascinated, as they approached the city centre through streets cleared of traffic, by the sight of people standing in line in the baking summer heat to buy a single piece of water melon, and by the fact that everyone seemed to be wearing white canvas shoes. To Schmidt, Moscow was quite simply 'a distant planet'.

At the former Austrian legation at 6 Myortvy Peveulok, where Ribbentrop himself was to stay, there was a lavish buffet lunch waiting: smoked salmon, caviar and other delicacies, with champagne to wash it all down. Hoffmann, swiftly recovering from the night before, was astonished at the spread – he had anticipated rather meagre fare in Moscow. But Schulenburg explained that almost everything had been specially imported – even the bread came from Sweden and the butter from Denmark.

The embassy staff were mostly in high spirits. They all loved Russia and were delighted at the prospect of a non-aggression pact which they hoped would ensure peace between Germany and the Soviet Union, whatever reservations they may have had about its effects elsewhere. General Ernst Köstring, the military attaché, who had been born in Moscow, had spent much of his life in Russia, and spoke Russian as easily as German, was in particularly expansive mood.

'There have been endless rumours that Stalin is at death's door,' he warned the visitors. 'Such a sick man that he's only a figurehead . . . Don't you believe it! The man is both absolutely fit and possesses a tremendous capacity for work.' Stalin, he pointed out, was interested primarily in the Far East as a field for the expansion of Soviet influence. In the west, he merely wanted a secure border.

Ribbentrop had no time for conversation. After only a brief snack, he asked Schulenburg and Gustav Hilger, the economic counsellor at the embassy, to brief him on the latest developments in the situation, and also to tell him how things were done at Kremlin meetings. When he asked who would be there for the Soviets, the ambassador had to say that he still did not know: even at this late stage, the Soviets had not said which leader would be negotiating with them. Schulenburg thought it would probably be Molotov, but he couldn't be sure.

After a concise but thorough briefing, Schulenburg and Hilger outlined the programme they had prepared for the next few days. They advised Ribbentrop to take his time, and under no circumstances to give the impression he was in a hurry. The Soviets refused to be rushed, and it was important to be patient in negotiating with them.

Ribbentrop angrily cut them short with one of his impatient movements of the hand. He said he had to be back in Germany in twenty-four hours at the latest, and insisted that the Kremlin be informed of this immediately. Then he brought out an alternative draft of the proposed non-aggression pact, which he had drawn up on the flight from Königsberg, in collaboration with Friedrich Gaus, and asked the ambassador's opinion of it.

They had no time to discuss the document in detail, however, for the response from the Kremlin to Ribbentrop's insistence that he only had twenty-four hours was immediate and positive. Within the hour, they were on their way – just Ribbentrop, Schulenburg and Hilger – escorted again by the broad-shouldered Colonel Vlasik. The rest of the German delegation were free to pass the afternoon at their leisure, either resting or exploring the centre of Moscow with embassy wives as their guides. They wandered through the broad streets and busy squares, marvelled at the splendours of the new Metro system, but mourned the lack of cheerfulness and brightness among the people.

'Only very rarely during my walk of several hours did I see a smiling face,' wrote Paul Otto Schmidt. 'As laughter was absent from the faces, so colour seemed to me to be lacking from the clothing of the Muscovites. Occasional white head-dresses alone brought a little life into the grey of faces and clothes. Although most of the people were cleanly and neatly clad, with hardly anybody in rags, yet a melancholy grey pall seemed to hang over everyone and everything. In the case of the houses this effect was due to the fact that they had not been cleaned or painted for a long time.'

Ribbentrop had little chance to make such observations, as the big black car sped through the streets with its escort, though Schulenburg gave him a brief commentary on the historic buildings they passed on their way to Red Square. They entered the ancient fortress through the mighty Spassky Tower, and drove past the Kremlin Theatre and the gold-domed bell tower of Ivan the Great. Beyond the cathedral of the

Twelve Apostles, they turned right through a pair of ornate wrought-iron gates to stop outside the three-storey yellow stucco building of the Council of Ministers.

Stepping out of the car, Ribbentrop was greeted by a man in his forties, wearing a colonel's uniform, A. N. Poskrebyshev, head of Stalin's personal secretariat – Khrushchev called him 'Stalin's faithful dog' – who led them up a short flight of steps to the Prime Minister's office. It was, Ribbentrop himself notes, 'a long room. At the other end stood Stalin, awaiting us, and next to him Molotov. Count Schulenburg could not suppress a cry of surprise, for, although he had been in Moscow for years, he had never yet spoken to Stalin.'

Stalin, looking rather like a pre-Revolutionary landowner, was wearing what was by now his uniform: plain grey tunic jacket buttoned up to the neck, over dark, baggy trousers tucked into calf-length leather boots. The effect was slightly sloppy, but the quality of the materials was noticeably good. He was friendly and smiling and very much at ease, like a cat sure of its welcome. Only the eyes, as steady as a hypnotist's, betrayed the power of the man. Beside him, Molotov stood in his neat, dark grey suit, stiff collar and pince-nez, impassive as a Buddha.

After the preliminary exchange of courtesies, the four principals – Stalin, Molotov, Ribbentrop and Schulenburg – sat down round a table. With Molotov out from behind his schoolmasterly desk and Stalin himself in attendance, Schulenburg knew for sure that the Soviets really meant business. The treaty would be concluded now, or never.

Hilger took up his position seated just behind Ribbentrop's shoulder, and on the Soviet side N. V. Pavlov, a young interpreter who, according to Ribbentrop, 'seemed to enjoy Stalin's special trust', sat behind his two leaders. Everyone else withdrew.

Ribbentrop spoke first. The time had come, he said, for their two great countries to establish relations on a totally new footing. He had reason to believe that the Soviet Union had come to the same conclusion. In Berlin, he said, when they had read Stalin's speech at the Eighteenth Party Congress, it had seemed to them that the Soviet leader, too, had similar ideas. He spoke fulsomely, as only Ribbentrop could, on the theme of friendship between the USSR and Germany, and concluded with a neat thrust at Britain and France.

'Germany,' he said, 'demands nothing from the Russians – only peace and trade. Unlike the USSR's other Western suitors, she has not come to beg for Soviet military assistance in the event of war. She does not expect Russian blood to be spilled on her behalf. Germany is strong enough to fight her own battles, without Russian help.'

Stalin asked Molotov if he wanted to respond.

'No, no, Josef Vissarionovich,' Molotov deferred. 'You do the talking. I'm sure you'll do a better job than I.'

Stalin allowed himself to be persuaded – it was one of the rules of the game that when he asked Molotov to lead a discussion or take the chair at a meeting, Molotov would tactfully refuse. The obsession with protocol, the false delicacy of the Laurel and Hardy 'you first' routine, was intended to emphasise the fact that Molotov was Prime Minister and Foreign Minister of the Soviet Union, while Stalin was 'merely' Communist Party Secretary. Even Ribbentrop understood it perfectly.

Speaking in his usual quiet, heavily accented voice, Stalin commented approvingly on Germany's 'proud attitude' to the question of Soviet military assistance. But he added that in the event of a war between Germany and Poland, or Germany and the West, 'the interests of the Soviet Union and Germany would certainly run parallel to each other.' When he had finished, Molotov turned to the Germans with a smile of satisfaction, saying: 'Didn't I tell you he would do a better job than I?'

Then they got down to the real business of the meeting – the proposed pact. In his sessions with Gaus at Königsberg and during the flight, Ribbentrop had added a flowery and bombastic preamble to the original Soviet draft, full of high-flown references to the German–Soviet friendship. Stalin would have none of it. Smiling indulgently, he turned to Ribbentrop.

'Don't you think,' he asked, 'that we have to pay a little more attention to public opinion in our two countries? For many years now, we have been pouring buckets of shit over each other's heads, and our propaganda boys couldn't do enough in that direction. And now, all of a sudden, are we to make our peoples believe that all is forgotten and forgiven? Things don't work so fast. Public opinion in our country, and probably in Germany, too, will have to be prepared slowly for the change in our relations which this treaty is to bring about, and will have to be made familiar with it.'

The finally agreed preamble was almost identical to that proposed in Molotov's first draft:

> The government of the German Reich and the government of the Union of Soviet Socialist Republics, desirous of strengthening the cause of peace between Germany and the USSR, and proceeding from the fundamental provisions of the Treaty of Neutrality, which was concluded between Germany and the USSR in April 1926, have reached the following agreement.

The rest of the main pact presented little difficulty. Ribbentrop was delighted with the straightforward, no-nonsense approach of Stalin. He told Peter Kleist, when he returned to the embassy for dinner, that he had 'never before faced a partner across the table who had opened his ledger and given a clear and exact statement of his position, as Stalin had done'.

Hitler had, of course, accepted the Soviet draft in principle, so there were only minor details to quibble about. Article 1 was entirely straightforward:

The two contracting parties undertake to refrain from any act of violence, any aggressive action and any attack on each other, either severally or jointly with other powers.

Article 2 required only a small, but significant change of wording. The Soviet draft had read:

Should one of the contracting parties become the object of an act of violence or attack by a third power, the other contracting party shall in no manner whatever lend its support to such acts by that power.

In the final version, 'an act of violence or attack' was changed to read simply 'belligerent action'. In marked contrast to the protracted arguments with the Allies over the precise definition of 'indirect aggression', Stalin and Molotov were perfectly happy to accept such a deliberately vague phrase, which could be taken to mean almost anything Hitler chose. What was important, of course, was the way in which it could be applied to Polish 'provocations'.

Articles 3 and 4 were new additions, inserted by Ribbentrop and accepted without demur by Stalin:

The governments of the two contracting parties will in future maintain continual contact with one another for the purpose of consultation in order to exchange information on problems affecting their common interests.

Neither of the two contracting parties will join any grouping of powers whatsoever which is aimed directly or indirectly at the other party.

Naturally, in proposing this last, Ribbentrop conveniently ignored all existing treaties, especially the Anti-Comintern Pact. Stalin must have been aware of this, but evidently chose to leave any mention of it until later.

The remaining three articles were all equally simple. Article 5 provided for the settlement of any dispute or disagreement by 'friendly exchange of views or, if necessary, by the appointment of arbitration commissions'. Article 6 dealt with the duration of the pact, which was changed from the original proposal of five years to ten, with an automatic extension, if neither side denounced it, for a further five.

The final article represented another small but vitally important victory for Hitler and Ribbentrop: the pact was to come into force immediately it was signed, and not, as the Soviet draft had suggested, only after ratification.

With agreement on this, Hitler's requirements were completely satisfied. Now it was time to settle the details of Stalin's payment, to be listed in the secret protocol.

Stalin opened by confirming that he wanted clearly defined 'spheres of interest' in eastern and south-eastern Europe and the Baltic. Ribbentrop took his cue from this, and began talking about Poland. The Poles, he said, were becoming more and more aggressive. Although, naturally, Germany would do everything possible to settle the dispute peacefully, by diplomatic means, they just might cause a war. It would be a good thing, therefore, if a demarcation line were agreed, 'to exclude any German and Russian interests coming into conflict with each other'.

In no time at all, the line was fixed at the rivers Narev, Vistula and San: the fourth partition of Poland was now settled. To make quite certain that there should be no misunderstandings about the purpose of the demarcation line, Ribbentrop had had it clearly spelled out in the draft he had prepared during his flight. 'The question of whether the interests of both parties make the maintenance of an independent Polish state appear desirable and how the frontiers of this state should be drawn,' the protocol continued, 'can be definitely determined only in the course of further political developments. In any case, both governments will resolve this question by means of a friendly understanding.' Thus, wrapped in the thinnest veneer of diplomatic double-talk, the death sentence was pronounced for the Polish republic.

Stalin could be well pleased, for with that one simple clause he would take back those areas of Belorussia and the Ukraine which the Poles had grabbed from the infant USSR in 1920, and at the same time create a broad buffer zone which would keep the German armour well clear of Moscow. In fact, the German zone ended at Warsaw itself, giving the Soviet Union a considerable chunk of Poland proper.

Having disposed of Poland, Stalin turned to the two other areas of interest. The south-east presented no problems: Stalin said he wanted the Romanian province of Bessarabia, and Ribbentrop was happy to declare 'complete political *désintéressement*' in the territory. But the Baltic states were more tricky. Hitler wanted Lithuania, and proposed that the northern boundary of the German zone should be the Düna river, which would give him everything up to Riga. The remainder of Latvia, plus the whole of Estonia and Finland, would be Stalin's.

At this point, Ribbentrop discovered, as he put it, 'how hard Soviet diplomacy could be'. The British and French had offered Stalin a free hand in the whole of the Baltic states, though not in Finland. And though the addition of Finland was tempting, the loss of Lithuania was unwelcome, since it deprived him of ice-free ports – the Gulf of Riga was frozen in winter, but the Baltic coast remained clear. Stalin wanted the ports of Libau and Windau (now known as Liepaja and Ventspils), on the Baltic, which would mean redrawing the line south of Riga to include the rest of Latvia, and he was not prepared to settle for anything less.

Ribbentrop, in theory, had a completely free hand to negotiate and agree anything, but this demand was something Hitler had not foreseen. The Foreign Minister felt he had to refer back to his Führer. Stalin was not worried, and was happy to agree to an adjournment until 10 o'clock that evening. They had been talking for three hours, and it was time for a break.

Ribbentrop arrived back at the embassy in the best of spirits, 'positively bubbling over with enthusiasm about Molotov and Stalin', according to Schmidt.

'Things are going splendidly with the Russians,' he kept exclaiming. 'We shall certainly arrive at an agreement before the evening is out.'

Before sitting down to a hurried dinner, he prepared a short message for Hitler, reporting on progress so far, and asking for his agreement to giving Stalin the two Baltic ports. The message was sent at 8.05 pm, Moscow time. Ribbentrop asked for a reply 'before 8 o'clock German time', that is, within two hours. This time there would be no delays in the Soviet telegraph system: Molotov had authorised a direct telephone line between the embassy and the Wilhelmstrasse in Berlin, to be kept constantly open during the whole of the negotiations.

Herwarth was manning the phone in the embassy, and was delighted to find that he simply had to lift the receiver to find himself through to Berlin. He had volunteered for the job not only because it kept him in touch with all that was happening, but also because it gave him the opportunity – while there were no official calls to be made – to try to contact his wife. Elisabeth von Herwarth had been on holiday in Germany, taking the waters at Karlsbad. Johnnie was worried because she was due to fly back to Moscow next day, and he feared that Hitler would invade Poland immediately the pact was signed. He did not want her to be flying across Poland when the war started. Eventually, he managed to get a message to her, and she flew back safely, via Stockholm.

Hitler, waiting impatiently but no longer agonising, was pacing the terrace of the Berghof when Ribbentrop's message arrived. He reacted with great satisfaction to the news that all was going well, but was slightly puzzled by Stalin's demand for the two tiny Latvian ports, which Ribbentrop described as 'the decisive point for the final result'. He sent an orderly for an atlas, and when the man returned with an ordinary schoolbook, put on his spectacles and merely glanced cursorily at the Baltic coastline before nodding and saying the Soviet Union was welcome to the ports concerned. The message he sent back to Moscow must rank as one of the shortest in the history of diplomacy. It read, quite simply: 'Yes, agreed.'

Ribbentrop returned to the Kremlin at 10 pm. This time, in addition to Schulenburg and Hilger, he took along a much larger retinue to witness his moment of triumph. The two photographers, Hoffmann and Helmut Laux, brought up the rear in an embassy car loaded with all their equipment. The gates of the Spassky Tower swung open as the convoy approached, and NKVD men came rushing out of the darkness. Lights flared and bells shrilled. As they moved through the citadel at little more than walking pace, a bell started tolling somewhere, and continued until they drew up outside the Council of Ministers building, signalling their progress.

Stalin and Molotov waited to greet their guests like old friends. Ribbentrop announced that Hitler had agreed to the Soviet demand. 'A sudden tremor seemed to go through Stalin,' Peter Kleist recorded, 'and he did not immediately grasp the hand proffered by his partner. It was as if he had first to overcome a moment of fear. But it was over in an instant.'

While the agreed drafts of the pact and the secret protocol were taken away to be properly typed up in German and Russian and generally made ready for signature, Stalin relaxed, called for drinks, and prepared to entertain his guests. As soon as everyone had a glass, Stalin proposed the first toast.

'I know how much the German nation loves its Führer,' he declaimed. 'He is a *molodets*, a fine fellow. I should therefore like to drink his health!'

The vodka was swallowed, in the Russian manner, in one gulp. The glasses were immediately refilled. Now, it was Molotov's turn. He drank to the health of Ribbentrop. Ribbentrop proposed a toast to Stalin. Molotov proposed a toast to Schulenburg. Ribbentrop proposed a toast to the Soviet government. Molotov raised his glass to Stalin, saying that it had been Stalin who, 'through his speech of 10 March, which had been well understood in Germany, had introduced the reversal in political relations'. Ribbentrop drank 'to a favourable development of relations between Germany and the Soviet Union'. Stalin and Molotov 'drank repeatedly to the non-aggression pact, the new era of German–Russian relations, and to the German nation'. And so the night wore on.

One or two of the Germans noticed that Stalin always had his drinks poured from his own personal flask. The drink was colourless, and looked like vodka – but was it? After several drinks, greatly daring, the young Richard Schulze managed to fill his own glass from Stalin's flask. It contained water. As he drank, he was aware of Stalin watching him steadily, a faint smile on his lips. Schulze said nothing.

In between the toasts, the conversation ranged over the whole field of international relations – Japan, Italy, the Balkans, Turkey, Britain, France – as well as Soviet–German relations. Ribbentrop grandly offered to use his influence with Japan on the Soviet Union's behalf. Stalin did not say no, but wanted to be sure that the Japanese did not get the idea that any approach had originated with him: he had his own way of dealing with them.

'I know the Asiatics best,' he said bluntly. 'They want rough handling occasionally.'

Ribbentrop hastily agreed, and turned to other matters. As always, he blamed everything on the British, growing more and more vehement with every drink. It was the British who had made trouble for Germany in Turkey, where they had spent five million pounds to encourage anti-German propaganda; Stalin, smiling mischievously, said that according to his information they had spent far more than five million pounds in buying Turkish politicians. It was the British, Ribbentrop continued, who were responsible for disturbing the good relations which otherwise existed naturally between Germany and the Soviet Union.

As Ribbentrop got into his full flow, Stalin egged him on, encouraging him to go further and further by throwing in comments of his own. Molotov joined in with some choice comments on the British military mission.

'Chamberlain and Daladier went to Munich,' he rasped, 'but who do we get here? Admiral Nobody and General Inconnu!'

Stalin belittled British power, stating that England dominated the world only through the stupidity of other countries, which allowed themselves to be bluffed. Ribbentrop eagerly agreed. But when Ribbentrop sneered at the latest British warnings, saying he had proposed that Hitler should tell them that 'every hostile act, in the event of a German–Polish conflict, would be answered by a bombing attack on London', Stalin cautioned that England, 'despite her weakness, would wage war craftily and stubbornly'. He also pointed out the strength of the French army.

By now, however, there was no stopping the German Foreign Minister. He waved aside the threat from France, and returned to his obsessive attacks on Britain, even managing to lay the Anti-Comintern Pact at her door. Incredibly, he announced in all seriousness that it had never been directed against the Soviet Union, but against the Western democracies. What was more, he declared, he knew, and was able to infer from the tone of the Soviet press, that the Soviet government fully recognised this fact.

Stalin must have had a hard time keeping a straight face as he chipped in with the remark that it was not him but, 'in fact, principally the City of London and the English shopkeepers who had been frightened by the Anti-Comintern Pact'. Ribbentrop, failing to recognise the joke, seized on this enthusiastically. Emboldened, he put an arm round Stalin's shoulder, and was rewarded with a jovial bear hug.

'Do you know what they say in Berlin, where they are well known for their wit?' he asked. 'They say, "Just you wait. Josef Stalin will join the Anti-Comintern Pact himself one of these days!" '

Stalin roared with laughter, and proposed another toast. At last, the document was ready for signature. It was now almost 2 o'clock on the morning of 24 August – Ribbentrop had been in Moscow for a bare thirteen hours. Hoffmann and Laux, who had been kicking their heels in an ante-room all evening, were brought in to photograph the great event. As they set up their modern German cameras, a Soviet photographer appeared, laden down with a wooden tripod and a huge wood and brass camera in a leather case. While he assembled his antiquated equipment, the two German photographers began taking shots of the scene: Stalin standing in the background, smiling but inscrutable as ever; the big, heavily built Shkvarzev, the new Soviet ambassador-designate to Berlin, and Hilger, both hovering uneasily; Schulenburg, contriving to look like a friendly uncle at a wedding; Red Army Chief of Staff Shaposhnikov, obviously a sick man, standing with head bowed obsequiously before Stalin as he took down his orders in a small notebook, his thinning hair parted in the centre, revealing the skull beneath; Molotov taking his place at his desk, ready to sign; Ribbentrop looking fleshy and self-satisfied.

Richard Schulze was standing at the far end of the room keeping well out of the way. Suddenly, he saw Stalin nodding and smiling in his direction. He looked around, nervously, then realised that the Soviet leader was indeed looking at him, and that he was beckoning. Hesitantly, he crossed the room, wondering what he had done to be singled out. But Stalin patted him jovially on the shoulder, took his arm, and positioned him between Shaposhnikov and Ribbentrop, behind the desk. He wanted the six-foot four-inch SS man, who had had the nerve to taste his 'vodka', in the pictures.

Eventually, the Soviet photographer was ready. Molotov picked up his pen and held it poised over the paper for the first signature. The photographer stood behind his aged camera, a flash tray filled with black magnesium powder held high in one hand. Molotov signed, and with a loud bang and a cloud of dense black smoke, the flash fired and the shutters clicked. The scene was recorded for posterity.

As Molotov and Ribbentrop continued signing the documents, a woman servant dressed in white, looking for all the world like a hospital nurse, brought in champagne to celebrate the occasion, accompanied as always in Russia by snacks. The party atmosphere grew, and more toasts were proposed. Laux snapped a splendid shot of Stalin and Ribbentrop with glasses raised to each other. Stalin shook a finger at him, and said it would not be a good idea to publish the picture, in case it gave people the wrong impression of a serious occasion. Laux immediately began to take the film out of his camera, to give it to Stalin, but was stopped with a wave of the hand. There was no need for that, Stalin said – he would trust the word of a German.

Finally, it was time to leave. As they headed for the door, Stalin, serious and totally sober, took Ribbentrop by the arm.

'The Soviet government takes the new pact very seriously,' he told him. 'I can guarantee on my word of honour that the Soviet Union will not betray its partner.'

Ribbentrop and his entourage arrived back at the embassy at about 3 am. Despite the hour, the entire staff was waiting to greet him, standing in a row and applauding him as he entered. Stalin, at the same time, sped away from the Kremlin to his dacha at Kuntsevo, where Voroshilov, Khrushchev, Bulganin and Mikoyan were waiting to celebrate with him over a late supper of duck they had shot on another shooting expedition during the day.

News of the signing of the pact had already been telephoned through to Berlin, and from there to the Berghof. It was brought to Hitler, like Stalin's letter a mere three nights before, while he was at dinner. After glancing quickly at the paper, he rapped the table excitedly for silence, and then announced his success to everyone present.

A little later, when the meal was finished, he led everyone out on to the darkened terrace to view an unusual natural spectacle: a display of northern lights, the aurora borealis, not the hazy green which was quite often seen, but brilliant, bloody red, bathing not only the legendary Unterberg mountain across the valley, but also the hands and faces of all the watchers. The sky above, meanwhile, shimmered in all the colours of the rainbow. 'The last act of *Götterdämmerung* could not have been more effectively staged,' Albert Speer recalled. 'The display produced a curiously pensive mood among us.'

Hitler watched for a while, fascinated, then turned abruptly to his Luftwaffe adjutant, Captain Nikolaus von Below.

'Looks like a great deal of blood,' he said. 'This time we won't bring it off without violence.'

He might have done better to have remembered what he himself had written, fifteen years before, in *Mein Kampf*: 'The very fact of the conclusion of an alliance with Russia embodies a plan for the next war. Its outcome would be the end of Germany.'

24

'A LONG AND LASTING TREATY'

'With the Moscow pact, Hitler had crossed the Rubicon,' Ernst von Weizsäcker concluded in his memoirs. Indeed, there could be little doubt that he was now totally committed to his war, and perhaps could not escape from it even had he wanted. To Weizsäcker, who was located at the very hub, all the diplomatic frenzy was becoming meaningless. In his view: 'As a result of Hitler's frivolous game, in the last ten days of August 1939, so much unrest had been engendered in the German minority, so many frontier infringements had occurred, so many people had been carried away into central Poland, and so many other incidents had been reported, that all these things weighed heavier in the scales than the reverberating dispute of the so-called statesmen about how the original problem [the Danzig question] was to be solved. One may well ask whether the chariot had not already been rolling inexorably towards the abyss in the spring of 1939; but in the last week of August it certainly was. Hitler was now the prisoner of his own methods. He could no longer pull the horses to one side without being thrown out of the chariot. And riding on the leading horse was the devil.'

Hitler himself seemed to be well aware of this. Immediately he received confirmation that the pact was signed, he gave the preliminary order for Operation White, the invasion of Poland, to begin at 4.30 am on Saturday, 26 August. He also authorised the appointment – ostensibly by the Danzig Senate – of Gauleiter Forster as head of state in the Free City, a move which decisively removed it from all Polish or League of Nations control. But the immediate euphoria quickly gave way to doubts, for the announcement of the pact did not produce the immediate effects he had expected, either among his allies or his enemies.

Certainly, as Winston Churchill said, 'the sinister news broke upon the world like an explosion'. But the British and French did not run for cover, as Ribbentrop had always guaranteed they would. Instead, they began making sensible preparations for war. Even while Hitler was boasting to his commanders in the Berghof, Westminster City Council issued the phlegmatic announcement: 'Parents and guardians residing in Westminster are asked to bring their infants up to two years of age to one of the below-mentioned centres during the week commencing Thursday, 24 August . . . to be fitted with gas helmets.'

The British Cabinet met the same day, 22 August, for the first time after its summer break. Halifax remained as nonchalant as ever, telling his colleagues: 'The effect of the pact on Poland has been to confirm suspicions of Russia. It will certainly not make Poland more inclined to accept Russian assistance. I think that if it is true that the Soviet–German pact has been concluded, this is not of very great importance in itself. Nevertheless, the moral effect . . . will be very great.'

The Cabinet decided that Chamberlain should recall Parliament next day, to pass the Emergency Powers (Defence) Bill, which it duly did by 534 votes to 4, giving the government power to rule by decree. At the same time, it authorised a whole package of precautionary measures. These included: the call-up of 5,000 naval reservists, 24,000 RAF reservists, and the whole of the Auxiliary Air Force, including barrage balloon squadrons; mobilisation of all anti-aircraft and coastal defences; requisitioning twenty-five merchant ships for conversion into armed merchant cruisers; fitting thirty-five fishing trawlers with Asdic anti-submarine equipment; cancellation of all leave for the armed forces; activation of civil defence measures including the black-out, and the start of the evacuation of women and children from the cities. A firm statement was issued to the press, saying: 'The Cabinet had no hesitation in deciding such an event [the pact] would in no way affect their obligation to Poland, which they had repeatedly stated and which they are determined to fulfil.'

In Paris, despite Bonnet's attempts to persuade his colleagues that the Poles' stubborn refusal to help themselves relieved France of her obligations, an emergency session of the National Defence Council reached the same conclusion as the British, and issued a similar statement: 'France has no choice . . .' They called another half million men to the colours and urged Parisians to leave the city if they could. The Louvre closed, to start crating its art treasures and storing them in the basement, while back across the Channel the medieval stained-glass windows were removed from Canterbury Cathedral and buried in the countryside, and the keepers at London Zoo were equipped with guns and poisons to destroy dangerous animals in case of invasion or air attack.

After the Cabinet meeting, Chamberlain wrote a letter to Hitler stating the British position. But instead of sending it, as had been suggested by some ministers, with the tough and bilingual General Ironside, he decided it 'should be passed through ordinary diplomatic channels'. 'Any emissary would have to deal with very delicate negotiations,' he commented. 'Ironside would not be suitable.' Still clinging to the futile hope that Hitler might be won round by 'delicacy', he had the letter telegraphed to Berlin, to be delivered by Nevile Henderson. The ambassador flew down to the Berghof at 9.30 am on 23 August with Weizsäcker and Hewel, for the meeting which had so enraged Ribbentrop when he heard about it in Königsberg. Hitler was ready for Henderson, for Göring's wire-tapping service, the *Forschungsamt*, had intercepted the telegram, deciphered it, and delivered the full text to him during the night. A copy had also been sent to Moscow, for Ribbentrop – who produced it during his conversations with Stalin, only to have it dismissed with a wave of the hand and the laconic comment that he had already seen it.

The message contained in the first part of Chamberlain's letter was unequivocal: 'Your excellency will have already heard of certain measures taken by His Majesty's Government. These steps have, in the opinion of His Majesty's Government, been rendered necessary by the military movements which have been reported from Germany, and by the fact that apparently the announcement of a German–Soviet Agreement is taken in some quarters in Berlin to indicate that intervention by Great Britain on behalf of Poland is no longer a contingency that need be reckoned with. No greater mistake can be made. Whatever may prove to be the nature of the German–Soviet Agreement, it cannot alter Great Britain's obligation to Poland . . .'

Chamberlain went on to point out that the first world war might have been avoided if the British had made their position crystal clear in 1914. And now the situation was the same; the British government were 'resolved and prepared to employ . . . all the forces at their command . . .' And he added the warning that 'it would be a dangerous illusion to think that, if war once starts, it will come to an early end even if a success on any one of the several fronts on which it will be engaged should have been secured.'

Unfortunately, having given such a clear warning, Chamberlain then went on to weaken its impact by suggesting once again that there was nothing between Germany and Poland that could not be solved by negotiations – thus accepting that Germany had a case and that he would be prepared to persuade Poland if not to submit then at least to compromise. The spirit of Munich was still alive and kicking, it seemed, an impression that was strengthened by the presence in Berlin of no less than two envoys of the British Secret Intelligence Service.

The first of these envoys was Baron William de Ropp, a Baltic German who had taken British citizenship, who was putting out the familiar feelers to Hitler for a Munich-type settlement through Alfred

Rosenberg, the Nazi Party's official philosopher. The second was a flamboyant Australian flyer called Sidney Cotton, who had arrived in what he said was his own private plane, though in fact it was one of two twin-engined Lockheed 12A aircraft used by the SIS as spy-planes for photo-reconnaissance missions over Germany. Cotton and his aircraft had come to fly Göring back to England for the proposed meeting with Chamberlain and Halifax at Chequers. But by now, Hitler had withdrawn his support, considering Göring's trip 'no longer necessary'. Cotton was sent away again, empty-handed.

Henderson's approach to Hitler did nothing to reduce the impression that Britain, in a reversal of Theodore Roosevelt's old adage 'speak softly but carry a big stick', was speaking loudly but waving a white flag. With typical obsequiousness he began by saying he hoped a solution might be found to the 'difficult situation', and that 'it was understood in England that Anglo-German co-operation was necessary for the well-being of Europe'.

Hitler pounced on this sign of softness. 'You should have realised that earlier,' he declared.

When Henderson protested mildly that the British government had given its guarantees, Hitler snapped back: 'Then honour them! If you have given a blank cheque you will have to meet it.' And with that, he launched into a tirade. Having had time to prepare his act, he proceeded to put on one of his liveliest displays for the astonished British ambassador.

The measures taken by Chamberlain, Hitler warned, did not frighten him – if he heard of any further military preparations by Britain or France he would immediately order general mobilisation in Germany, where until now preparations had been confined to 'purely defensive measures'.

Hundreds of thousands of *Volksdeutsche* were being ill-treated in Poland, dragged off to concentration camps and driven from their homes, he shouted, and it was all Britain's fault. He could not allow tens of thousands of fellow Germans to be slaughtered 'for the sake of one of England's whims'. Inevitably, he announced that he had evidence which he had so far refrained from publishing. Equally inevitably, he introduced his obsession with castration: the Poles, he said, had castrated not just one German so far, but six!

On and on he went, bitterly accusing Britain of bad faith and of wanting to destroy Germany. He had been forced to build a Western Wall costing nine thousand million marks in order to protect Germany from an attack from the West. Britain had preferred to do anything rather than co-operate with Germany: she had turned to France, Turkey, Moscow, anybody.

This was Henderson's cue to raise the subject of the pact: Hitler was accusing Britain of turning to Moscow rather than to Germany, but it was Germany now who was coming to terms with the Russians. Hitler threw up his hands at this, and retorted that he had been forced into it by the Western Powers. But dealing with the Soviets was one subject on which Henderson had decided views, and he proceeded to do his best to pour cold water on Hitler's achievement. He said that he personally had never believed in a pact with the Russians. He dismissed the Anglo-French negotiations as a waste of time: the Russians, he said, had merely wanted to get rid of Chamberlain 'by procrastination, and then to profit from a war'. He would rather Germany than Britain made a pact with 'those people'.

Hitler was stung by this. 'Make no mistake,' he shouted. 'It will be a long and lasting treaty.'

'That remains to be seen,' Henderson replied. 'The Führer knows as well as I do that the Russians always make trouble.' Chamberlain, he said, had always been Germany's friend, and he had not changed.

'I shall have to judge by deeds,' was Hitler's reply. He then dismissed the ambassador, sending him to take lunch in Salzburg while he composed a written reply to Chamberlain's letter. In fact, the reply was already written, but Hitler had a tricky lunch date already fixed – with Unity Mitford, whom he was seeing for what he hoped would be the last time as her devotion was becoming an embarrassment. In any case, he wanted to make Henderson sweat a little longer. It was one of his favourite devices – he had used it a few days before on Ciano – to split his performances into two acts: the first full of fire and fury to soften up the victim; the second all calm and sweet reason. He was well satisfied with the fire and fury – no sooner had Henderson left the room than Hitler's rage magically disappeared. Turning to Weizsäcker, he 'slapped himself on the thigh, laughed, and said "Chamberlain won't survive that conversation! His Cabinet will fall this evening." '

Weizsäcker tried in vain to persuade Hitler that his actions would have precisely the opposite effect, strengthening rather than weakening Chamberlain's position and uniting Parliament behind him so long as he stood firm. But Ribbentrop's insidious persuading had done its work only too well, and Hitler remained convinced, as Weizsäcker wrote, 'that his hysterical behaviour, combined with the Moscow coup, would throw Chamberlain from the saddle', to be replaced by someone more willing to accommodate him. He refused to accept that if Chamberlain did fall, the man most likely to replace him was Winston Churchill.

When Henderson was summoned to return, two hours later, he found to his relief that Hitler 'had recovered his calm'. Hitler quietly handed over the text of his reply to Chamberlain, and watched while he read it.

The letter took note of Chamberlain's points, but stated that they 'can make no change in the determination of the Reich government to safeguard the interests of the Reich'. It repeated all the claims and complaints against Poland, and warned that 'Germany, if attacked by

England, will be found prepared and determined'. The initiative for preventing war, Hitler claimed, lay entirely with the Western Powers: 'Only after a change of spirit on the part of the responsible powers can there be any real change in the relationship between England and Germany.'

When he had finished reading it, there were tears in Henderson's eyes. 'I so much regret all this,' he sobbed.

'There are people in the British government who want war,' Hitler declared.

Henderson vigorously denied this. Chamberlain had always been a friend of Germany, he reiterated.

'What about the Minister for War?' demanded Hitler. 'I cannot imagine him as a friend of Germany.'

Henderson side-stepped the reference to Leslie Hore-Belisha, who was Jewish, and cited Chamberlain's refusal to have Churchill in the Cabinet as proof of his friendship. The hostile attitude to Germany did not represent the will of the British people, but was the work of Jews and anti-Nazis, he claimed.

Hitler acknowledged Henderson's sincerity. He did not include him personally among the enemies of Germany, he said. But his relationship with Britain had been a series of disappointments, and now the choice was reduced to understanding or war between the two countries.

'England will do well to remember that as a front-line soldier I know what war is – and that I shall utilise every means available,' he told the ambassador. 'It must surely be clear to everybody that the world war would not have been lost if I had been Chancellor at the time.'

Ribbentrop slept late on the morning of 24 August. He could afford to allow himself a slight respite, having fulfilled his purpose, and he had no further interest in Moscow for the moment. Others in the embassy were more active, notably Johnnie Herwarth.

Herwarth saw Schulenburg at 9 am – the ambassador's normal routine had been totally disrupted by the stunning series of events and he was in his office a full hour before his normal time. Carefully and deliberately using the formal title 'Herr Botschafter' ('Mr Ambassador' in the old style), which the Nazis had forbidden but which Herwarth says 'we preserved in Moscow as if it were a password symbolising our distance from Hitler's rule', the young man informed his boss that he had found a place with a cavalry regiment and wished to leave the diplomatic service at once. Schulenburg regarded him sadly.

'My dear Johnnie,' he said, 'why are you in such a rush? This war will last a long, long time, just like world war one. Even if you wait a few months, you will still have time.'

Herwarth insisted that for him time had already run out. He pressed once more for his instant release. Schulenburg sat for a moment, twiddling his thumbs, thinking hard. Then he sighed, and acknowledged the tragedy of his own success: 'Well, you may be right. I worked hard for good relations between the Soviet Union and Germany, and in one sense I have achieved my goal. But you know perfectly well I did not really achieve anything. Up to now, the brakes which keep the train of Europe from plummeting down the track have held. With this treaty, they will be released. Nothing now exists to prevent Europe from plunging into war and Germany from hurtling into the abyss.'

With that, the two men shook hands, and Herwarth took his leave, hurrying off to settle his affairs and gather his belongings before flying out with Ribbentrop's party. There was one other thing he felt he had to do, however, one foreigner to whom he had to say goodbye. Returning to his office for the last time, he called the American embassy and asked Chip Bohlen to come over right away. 'So angered and so depressed was I by now,' he says, 'that I felt no hesitation in revealing to Chip the secret contents of the Nazi–Soviet pact, presenting them as a lurid sort of going-away present. Unlike my earlier leaks, this could have no purpose beyond confronting the Western Powers as soon as possible with the result of their neglect of Hitler's actions.'

The great secret was thus broken within a few hours, and details reached Washington before Ribbentrop was back in Berlin. The knowledge, however, as Herwarth himself admitted, was of precious little use in preventing the catastrophes that were to befall Poland, Romania and the Baltic states. Ribbentrop, of course, had no inkling of the leak, and in Berlin next day issued an order that all staff in the Moscow embassy who knew anything about the protocol were to sign a solemn pledge of secrecy. They did so on 27 August – but by that time Herwarth was hundreds of miles away, serving as a captain with the 1st Cavalry Regiment, poised complete with horses on Poland's northern frontier near Mohrungen, in East Prussia. He had long believed that once war started his only chance of being able to help remove Hitler was from inside the army, 'where at least one had a weapon in one's hands'. In any case, his days as a diplomat were numbered, for he had a Jewish grandmother and was already the last non-Aryan in the Foreign Ministry.

Immelmann III took off for Germany at 1.20 pm. Ribbentrop was still on an emotional high, and issued a press statement describing the previous day as a fateful one for both nations. For once, his grandiose pronouncements were true: 'This is perhaps one of the most significant turning points in the history of our two peoples,' he proclaimed.

The original plan was for him to fly to Berchtesgaden but while they were in the air a radio message told them Hitler was on his way in another aircraft to Berlin. The triumph was too great to be celebrated in the privacy of the Berghof.

The German people, however, were more cautious in their reaction to the news. Albert Speer, who was in one of the ten cars of Hitler's motorcade from the Berghof to Salzburg, records that the populace remained unusually silent as they drove past on that beautiful, cloudless day. Hardly anyone waved. When they reached Berlin, it was 'strikingly quiet' around the Chancellery, where normally the building would have been besieged by people waiting to cheer their Führer as he drove in, alerted by the raising of his personal standard over the building.

This lack of public enthusiasm did nothing to dampen Hitler's high spirits. He greeted Ribbentrop like a conquering hero, welcoming him as 'a second Bismarck' – a ranking which clearly implied that he placed himself even higher than the Iron Chancellor. But Ribbentrop was delighted with the comparison. He beamed with pleasure as he acknowledged the plaudits of the assembled courtiers crowded into the ante-room, 'toadies and lickspittles and arrogant upstarts' as Erich Kordt, senior counsellor in Ribbentrop's secretariat, described them, 'turning the place into Belshazzar's Hall'.

Once the public welcome was over, Hitler led Ribbentrop into his study, along with Weizsäcker and Göring, to hear the details of the trip. The Foreign Minister was ecstatic in his descriptions. He had been made to feel completely at home, he said, 'just as though I were among old party comrades'. As he recounted the conversations, he proudly claimed that when Stalin had boasted: 'You will see that we have no rich men, now,' he had responded swiftly: 'Ah, but in our country we have no poor.' On the Soviet leader's personality, he told Hitler: 'Stalin is just like you, mein Führer. He is extraordinarily mild – not like a dictator at all.' In spite of this apparent mildness, however, Stalin had been a tough negotiator: in the political discussions he had not given away one inch, Ribbentrop commented with some admiration.

While Hitler listened with a certain amount of interest to what Ribbentrop had to say, he was more excited by the freshly developed pictures which Hoffmann brought in. He was pleased to see that the photographer had carried out his instructions – and that Stalin passed the earlobe test: they were clearly separate and Aryan, betraying no sign of Jewishness. He was less pleased to see that in every picture Stalin was smoking.

'The signing of the pact is a solemn act which one does not approach with a cigarette dangling from one's lips,' he scolded. He told Hoffmann to paint out the cigarettes before releasing the pictures to the press.

25

ACTION AND REACTION

If the British and French reactions were disappointing, Hitler could console himself with the belief that the two governments might need a little time to reassess their positions. In a day or two, they would surely realise the utter futility of maintaining their present line, and would then abandon Poland, leaving him to indulge in his limited war free from interference from either east or west. Meanwhile, there were enough positive reactions from other countries, especially the smaller European states, to give him satisfaction.

In Belgrade, the news of the pact was described as 'a bombshell'. 'The friends of Germany are triumphant,' the German chargé d'affaires reported, 'her opponents are amazed and perplexed. In general, the collapse of the encirclement policy is admitted and there is much talk of an impending new partition of Poland.' The Bulgarian minister in Belgrade called on the chargé and 'offered his spontaneous congratulations on the pact, which changes the world situation at one stroke', while the Bulgarian government in Sofia welcomed it 'with joy and also with great relief', describing it as 'a master stroke on the part of the Führer'. The wildly enthusiastic response, however, may have been coloured by the arrival of substantial arms deliveries from Germany, and the hope that Turkey would now be forced to behave less belligerently towards the Bulgars.

The Chinese, too, were pleased with the pact, and hoped it might lead to an improvement in Sino–German relations. These had been somewhat strained over the past two years, because they were friendly with Russia and at war with Japan, while Germany had been allied to Japan and hostile to Russia. Now, with the 'revolutionary event' in Moscow, 'a stumbling block between China and Germany had been removed.'

In Helsinki, the Finns regarded the pact as 'a skilful counter-move to the policy of the Western Powers', but were deeply suspicious that there would be a secret deal between Germany and the Soviet Union, giving the Soviets a free hand in the Baltic. After the pact had been signed,

Arne Worimaa, the Finnish minister in Berlin, called on Ernst Woermann, director of the policial department in the Wilhelmstrasse, and asked point-blank whether there had in fact been such an agreement. Woermann vigorously denied it, and went on to insist that the pact would be highly advantageous to the Baltic states and Finland. The Finns remained uneasy, however. Collaboration between Germany and the Soviet Union was the worst possible scenario for them: they would no longer be able to look to either power for protection against the other, and the Soviets were already making demands on Finnish territory which were difficult to resist.

From the other Scandinavian countries, together with Holland, Belgium, Luxembourg and Switzerland, came loud reassertions of strict neutrality. King Leopold of the Belgians broadcast an appeal to Germany and Poland to settle their differences by peaceful negotiation, and offered to mediate between them.

From Rome, Pope Pius XII also broadcast a moving appeal for peace: 'Once again a critical hour has struck for the great human family, an hour of tremendous deliberations, towards which our hearts cannot be indifferent and from which our spiritual authority, which comes to us from God to lead souls in the way of justice and peace, must not hold itself aloof. Behold us, then, all of you who in this moment are carrying a burden of so great a responsibility, in order that through our voice you may hear the voice of that Christ from Whom the world received the most exalted example of living . . .'

Across the Atlantic, Canadian Prime Minister Mackenzie King wrote a long and impassioned plea to Hitler, and news of the pact made President Roosevelt cut short his summer cruise in the presidential yacht and head for the New Jersey shore, from where he sped by train to Washington. As soon as he was back in the White House, he wrote to King Victor Emmanuel, urging him to use his influence to prevent Hitler going to war. He then wrote to Hitler himself and to President Moscicki in Warsaw, begging them to settle their differences over the conference table and not through war. Moscicki sent a dignified reply, saying he was highly appreciative of Roosevelt's 'most important and noble message' and agreeing to his proposals – but pointing out that it was not Poland who was making demands. Roosevelt immediately sent a copy of this to Hitler with a renewed appeal: 'Countless human lives can yet be saved and hope may still be restored that the nations of the modern world may even now construct a foundation for a peaceful and happier relationship if you and the government of the German Reich will agree to the pacific means of settlement accepted by the government of Poland. All the world prays that Germany, too, will accept.'

Hitler never replied to either of Roosevelt's messages, or to any of the others.

*   *   *

To both of Germany's major allies, the pact came as an unwelcome surprise. The Italians, of course, had had some warning, however late and inadequate, but to the Japanese it came as a complete bolt from the blue and was a very nasty shock indeed. 'The spirit of the Anti-Comintern Pact has been trampled underfoot!' screamed the influential Tokyo daily *Asahi Shimbun*. '[It] is reduced to a scrap of paper, and Germany has betrayed an ally.'

In Warsaw, Beck told American Ambassador Biddle that he had never seen an infuriated 'Jap' until he talked with Ambassador Professor Sakoh after the announcement of the pact. Sakoh had raged against Germany for having double-crossed Japan by not at least giving advance notice in accordance with the terms of the Anti-Comintern Pact.

For the Japanese ambassador in Berlin, General Hiroshi Oshima, the news was a particular blow, since he had developed a close personal relationship with Ribbentrop. When Ribbentrop telephoned him from the Berghof, to tell him he was going to Moscow, Oshima was shattered. He hurried round to Weizsäcker's home at midnight, his face 'rigid and grey', seeking explanations. He was afraid that the signing of the pact would enable the Soviet Union to strengthen her Far-Eastern front, and even to give real support to the Chinese in their war with the Japanese. He also felt it would give opposition politicians in Tokyo the opportunity to dispute the validity of the Anti-Comintern Pact.

Weizsäcker did his best to reassure Oshima that the Soviet pact was not a stab in the back, but he had a hard time of it. When Ribbentrop passed through Berlin on his way to Moscow, the Japanese ambassador met him at the airport and told him he had submitted his resignation. On 25 August, the Japanese government formally protested and informed Germany that the non-aggression pact had killed the possibility of a tripartite alliance between Japan, Germany and Italy, which they had been negotiating. The Japanese had seen this as an alliance of the three powers against the Soviet Union; Germany and Italy, however, had been trying unsuccessfully to persuade the Japanese to commit themselves primarily against Britain.

After three days of uncertainty and agitation in Tokyo, the government of Baron Hiranuma fell. There was a strong possibility that it would be replaced by a pro-British administration, since public confidence in Germany's friendship had been considerably shaken. Across the Yellow Sea, in Tientsin, Japanese soldiers started slapping the faces of Germans instead of Englishmen.

But from the impenetrable morass of Japanese politics the army emerged as the strongest force, and the new Prime Minister was General Abe, a sixty-four-year-old former artillery officer who had enjoyed a brilliant military career, in the course of which he had been attached for a time to a German artillery regiment and had also been military attaché in Berlin. He was a personal friend of Ambassador

Oshima, who described him as a much better Prime Minister than Hiranuma. There would inevitably be a period of political in-fighting before any clear line emerged from the new Cabinet, but the prospects for Germany were good. In fact, by the beginning of September, the Japanese ambassador in Italy was even starting to hold out the hope of some sort of settlement between Japan and the Soviet Union, to be achieved in stages, possibly even culminating in a separate non-aggression pact. This would be good news indeed for Germany since, as he put it, 'a Japan freed from the threat of Russia might be expected to modify any possible tendency on the part of the United States to interfere in Europe.'

The risk of losing Japan as an ally was one which Hitler had been prepared to take, for the Japanese had so far proved to be most unsatisfactory partners and the value of the friendship was easily outweighed by the benefits of neutralising the Soviets. The prospect of losing Italian support was more serious, but although he was slightly worried, Hitler believed he could convince Mussolini to stand firm. Ribbentrop apparently had no doubts whatever: when Weizsäcker insisted that the British would still come to the help of Poland but that Italy would leave Germany in the lurch, he stormed at him: 'I disagree with you 100 per cent. Mussolini is far too great a man to do that!' Nevertheless, Hitler moved swiftly to repair any damage caused to the relationship by the pact.

At midnight on 24 August, as soon as Ribbentrop had finished talking about his adventures in Moscow, Hitler had him telephone Ciano in Italy, to warn him that the situation was becoming critical with Poland, thus ensuring that the Italians could not claim they had not been informed. He finally got through at 1 am. Ciano was hardly surprised, but thought Ribbentrop sounded 'less decisive and overbearing' than usual. He suggested they meet. Ribbentrop immediately became evasive, and rang off.

Next morning, Hitler wrote a long personal letter to Mussolini, which he made Ribbentrop dictate over the telephone to von Mackensen, the German ambassador in Rome, with instructions to hand it to the Duce 'with the utmost speed', asking for a quick reply. In it, he apologised for having had to sign the pact without consulting his ally, and blaming Japanese procrastination, British interference, and the 'throttling' of Danzig by the Poles for creating the need for an agreement with the Soviet Union. He then tried to persuade Mussolini that the pact was mutually beneficial to Germany and Italy.

It was, he said, 'the most extensive non-aggression pact in existence', and went on: 'The pact is unconditional and includes also the obligation for consultation on all questions affecting Russia and Germany. Over and above that, however, I must tell you, Duce, that, through the agreements, the most benevolent attitude by Russia in case of any conflict is assured, and above all, *that the possibility of intervention by Romania in such a conflict no longer exists!* [Hitler's italics.]

'Even Turkey in these circumstances can only proceed to revise her previous position. But I repeat once more, *that Romania is no longer in a position to take part in any conflict against the Axis!* I believe I may say to you, Duce, that through the negotiations with Soviet Russia a completely new situation in world politics has been produced which must be regarded as the greatest possible gain for the Axis.'

Hitler's repeated emphasis on Romania sounds strange today. The Romanians, after all, were hardly the most potent military force at that time: there were grave doubts about the efficiency of an army whose officers were so vain that they regularly wore corsets and were supplied with make-up under an official contract with Max Factor. But presumably Hitler meant to impress on his friend that he would be able to pursue his aims in the Balkans without interference from that quarter.

Having dangled this carrot, Hitler went on to beg for Italy's 'understanding', warning that because of 'unendurable' and 'intolerable' provocations by the Poles, 'no one can say what the next hour may bring'. But in spite of Hitler's eloquence, Mussolini remained far from convinced. He saw only too clearly that the Soviet Union's 'benevolent attitude' gave Hitler the clear field he needed in the east, but he was less happy at the prospect of having to guard Germany's back against the military might of France and the naval and air power of Britain.

Since he had first heard of Ribbentrop's journey to Moscow, Mussolini's mood had been swinging violently between the 'furiously warlike' and abject terror that Italy was being sucked into a major war for which she was totally unprepared. He was torn by conflicting emotions. On the one hand the tunes of glory echoing through his head – coupled with the greedy hope of gaining Croatia and Dalmatia as his share of the spoils and bolstered by the fear of upsetting Hitler or being thought a coward – made him want to fight. On the other hand, encouraged by the desperate counselling of Ciano and the caution of the king, he wanted to do everything he could to prevent war, and if this were not possible, then to avoid becoming involved, at least for the time being.

On 23 August, caution had been in the ascendant. Or perhaps he had hopes of a different form of glory as the statesman who had achieved peace. In what seemed remarkably like a rerun of the Munich sell-out which he had initiated, he had Ciano present a plan to Percy Loraine, the British ambassador in Rome, in which a preliminary return of Danzig to the Reich would be followed by negotiations and a great peace conference. The proposal had been almost too much for Loraine. 'I do not know whether it was the emotion or the heat,' Ciano recorded, 'but it is a fact that Percy Loraine fainted or almost fainted in my arms. He found a place to rest in the toilet.'

Mussolini had been encouraged by the British response: Halifax had suggested that Britain might ask the Poles to return Danzig, if Hitler agreed to an international guarantee to the independence of Poland.

During the next two days, Mussolini had succeeded in totally changing his mind at least three times, but finally, when he had to reply to Hitler's letter, he was prevailed upon to see sense. He wrote that he approved completely of the pact and with all that Hitler said. Then, after beating about the bush for four paragraphs, he finally came to the real point, what he described as 'the *practical* attitude of Italy, in case of a military action'. This boiled down to the fact that Italy would do anything she could to help Germany – as long as she did not have to fight. If Hitler managed to keep the Polish campaign localised, then all would be well. But if it spread, and Britain and France entered the fray, there was nothing the Italians could do, because they were not ready for war, as they had repeatedly warned both Hitler and Ribbentrop. The Pact of Steel had envisaged war in 1942, and Mussolini's plans had been based on that assumption. In 1942, he would be ready. If Hitler wanted the Italians to fight for him before then, he would have to provide the necessary military supplies and raw materials.

Mussolini's message could not have come at a worse moment for Hitler. Friday, 25 August, had started badly and proceeded to get worse. When he rose, shortly before midday, he was greeted with the news that during the night hundreds of swastika armbands had been thrown over the wall of the Brown House, the Nazi Party headquarters in Munich, by members demonstrating their disgust at the pact with the Bolshevik devils of the Kremlin. This must have come as something of a blow to his pride as unquestioned leader of the Nazis. When Heinrich Hoffmann had raised the question at the Berghof after first learning of the Moscow visit, he had confessed to Hitler that he was slightly confused, having always believed anti-bolshevism to be one of the cornerstones of Nazi philosophy. 'How,' he had asked, 'will the party take to this volte-face?'

'The party,' Hitler had replied, grandly dismissing his objections, 'will realise that the ultimate aim of this latest gambit is to remove the eastern danger and thus facilitate, under my leadership, of course, a swifter unification of all Europe.'

Now it seemed a large proportion of the party, and in the very heartland of the faith, too, realised no such thing. There was obviously a need for more education, if not explanation.

The second disappointment that Friday morning followed fast, when Hitler sent for his press chief, Otto Dietrich, and asked him: 'Do you have the latest news and press notices from London and Paris about the repercussions of our treaty? What news do you bring me about the Cabinet crises?'

Dietrich, puzzled, had asked what crises Hitler had in mind.

'The ones in the British and French Cabinets, of course,' Hitler replied. 'No democratic government can stand up to such defeat and disgrace as have been inflicted on Chamberlain and Daladier by our Moscow treaty.'

Dietrich had to confess that he had no such news. What he did have were British and French reports of resolute speeches made by the two leaders to their respective assemblies. Hitler dismissed him and sent for Schmidt to translate.

Schmidt hurried to the study, having to push his way through the crush of party high-ups crowding the residence, among them Bormann, Goebbels, Himmler and Ribbentrop, all anxious not to miss being present for the moment of destiny when the Führer issued the final order for his armies to march eastwards, beginning the new *Drang nach Osten*. Among the clutter of brown party uniforms were those who were there because they had been ordered to attend: officials such as Weizsäcker, and officers of all three services. Around their feet a spaghetti tangle of telephone cords led to instruments placed on every available table and surface, ready to relay the great news the moment it was announced.

Closing the door on the hubbub outside, Schmidt moved swiftly to Hitler's desk and picked up the reports.

'I do not attempt to conceal from the House,' Chamberlain had told the Commons, 'that the announcement [of the pact] came to the government as a surprise, and a surprise of a very unpleasant character . . . In Berlin, the announcement has been hailed with extraordinary cynicism as a great diplomatic victory which removed any danger of war since France and ourselves would no longer be likely to fulfil our obligations to Poland. We felt it our first duty to remove any such dangerous illusion.'

Hitler listened to Schmidt's translation in silence, and then for a time sat deep in thought. Evidently, the task of separating Britain and France from Poland was going to be more difficult than he had imagined. But he still believed it could be done, that it was merely a matter of time. Sending Schmidt away, he called for his OKW adjutant, Rudolf Schmundt, and had him find out from the general staff whether and for how long he could postpone issuing the final codeword to set the attack on Poland in motion. It was due, according to the timetable, at 2 pm. The OKW agreed to a one-hour postponement, until 3 pm at the latest.

At 12.45 Hitler called Ribbentrop in and told him to summon Henderson for a meeting at 1.30. Through the sympathetic Henderson, Hitler could apply more pressure on Britain via the front door of diplomacy. While doing so, however, he characteristically decided to make use of the back door, too. He had forbidden Göring to make the trip to Chequers, but he now authorised him to send his Swedish friend,

Birger Dahlerus, to London in his place. After briefing him for two hours, Göring drove Dahlerus to the airport, where he took off in a government plane.

Hitler was just sitting down to lunch at 1.15, with nine guests round the circular table in the dining room overlooking the sunlit Chancellery gardens. As a white-jacketed SS orderly placed a dish of vegetables before him, a roll of drums from the guard of honour in the courtyard announced Nevile Henderson's arrival. Hitler rose from the table at once, excusing himself from the meal, and withdrew with Ribbentrop to the big 'public' study.

For over an hour, with Schmidt translating and taking notes, Hitler talked to Henderson 'with calm and apparent sincerity'. The only time he raised his voice was when, after reciting a long list of Polish 'provocations' – this time omitting castrations but including twenty-nine new frontier incidents and charges of shooting at civilian aircraft – he cried: 'The Macedonian conditions on our eastern frontier must be abolished!'

He complained that Chamberlain's latest speech was not calculated to change German attitudes, but that it could result in 'a bloody and incalculable war between Germany and England', which he did not want. Such a war would at best bring some profit to Germany, but none at all to England, since, unlike that of 1914–18, Germany would no longer have to fight on two fronts. Russia and Germany would never again under any circumstances take up arms against each other, and in addition the pact made Germany economically secure for the longest possible period of war.

Having pointed out the dangers to Britain, Hitler turned on the charm again. Once the Polish question had been solved, he told Henderson, he was 'prepared and determined to approach England once more with a large and comprehensive offer'.

'I am a man of great decisions,' he informed him, 'and in this case I shall also be capable of a great action. I accept the British empire and I am ready to pledge myself personally to its continued existence and to commit the power of the German Reich to this.'

This breathtaking offer came with only two conditions: that his limited colonial demands should be met – peacefully, of course, and in no great hurry – and that his obligations to Italy should not be touched. He would then be prepared to offer the British empire German assistance, 'regardless of where such assistance should be necessary' – including, by implication, in the Far East against Japan – and would even agree to reasonable arms limits. He assured Henderson that he had no interest in expansion to the west – the West Wall, which had cost thousands of millions to build, marked the final Reich frontier in that direction.

This, Hitler said, was his final offer to Britain. He would approach the British government with firm proposals immediately after the solution of the German–Polish question. Settling back in his chair, he said Schmidt would hand over a copy of what had been said later that afternoon, bringing it to the British embassy. He suggested Henderson should fly to London with it first thing next morning. As a mark of his sincerity, he would provide his own aeroplane and pilot for the trip – a gesture which he used as a mark of great favour, and which would at the same time put the recipient under some form of obligation. Then, to round off the interview, he brought out another tried and tested line, one which he was convinced could never fail: when all this was over, he said, and the Polish business was taken care of, he would return to his true loves, art and architecture. He was, he told Henderson with deep seriousness, not really a politician at all, but an artist.

Henderson's response to all this flannel and flattery was good enough to convince Hitler that it had done the trick. Indeed, Halifax agreed to Henderson's flying in *Immelmann III* to London where, according to Henderson, 'two days were spent by His Majesty's government in giving the fullest and most careful consideration to Hitler's message.'

By now, there was less than half an hour to the OKW deadline and still there was no answer from Mussolini. As Henderson left, Bernardo Attolico, the Italian ambassador, was shown in. Hitler was waiting with unconcealed impatience, and his face fell when Attolico told him he had not yet received any instructions from Rome. He sent Ribbentrop hurrying from the room to phone Ciano direct. When Ribbentrop returned, having failed to contact the Italian Foreign Minister since both he and Mussolini were spending the day at the beach near Rome, Hitler dismissed the ambassador 'with scant courtesy'.

It was now 2.45 pm, only fifteen minutes to the deadline. He shut the door on the waiting throng, closeting himself with Ribbentrop alone, to discuss the situation. There is no record of what advice Ribbentrop gave, but it is fair to assume that he had not changed his tune in any way, and that he continued to assure Hitler the British would not fight but Mussolini would. At 3 o'clock Hitler sent for General Keitel, who was with him for barely two minutes. At 3.02 Keitel emerged, and announced, before he sped away to his own office: 'Operation White!'

The attack on Poland was to begin at 4.30 next morning. The OKW issued the codeword to every service. By cable, telephone, teletype, it was passed on down the line until it had reached the unit commanders of two million troops, five armies ranged like a massive set of jaws ready to bite into Poland from north, west and south. In Prussia, East Prussia, Slovakia, ammunition was broken out, engines tested, fuel checked. The great advance towards the frontier would start rolling at 8.30 that evening.

In Berlin, Hitler's special train, *Amerika*, was brought out of its shed at Anhalt station, and made ready to take him to the front. Telegrams were sent to every Reichstag deputy, ordering them to attend an emergency session at 5 next morning. All telephone lines to France and Britain were cut.

At 5.30 pm, Coulondre, the French ambassador, arrived for an interview with Hitler. But just before he entered, a message was brought in from Otto Dietrich: the press office had just heard from London that Britain had signed a formal treaty of mutual assistance with Poland. This was most unwelcome news. Was this Britain's answer to his magnanimous offer? Hitler sat at his desk, staring at the piece of paper, brooding deeply until Coulondre was announced.

In fact, though Hitler did not realise it at the time, his 'final offer' had not yet even reached London. Poland and Britain had been negotiating since 10 August for a full treaty to replace the 'temporary assurance' of 6 April. Most of the points under negotiation had been settled by 19 August, but everything had stalled on 22 August, with news of the pact. On the morning of 25 August, Halifax suddenly informed Polish Ambassador Count Edward Raczynski that he was ready to sign. Raczynski managed to get final approval from Beck by telephone at 5 pm, and at 5.15 he and Halifax signed. There was a secret protocol added to this treat, too, which was to be significant later: the unspecified European power in the main text, against whom Britain promised to protect Poland, was named as Germany. This released Britain from the necessity of having to declare war on the Soviet Union when she invaded Poland.

Hitler got rid of Coulondre as quickly as he could, the interview lasting only half an hour. For most of that time, he was repeating mechanically what he had said to Henderson about Polish provocations, and, Schmidt noted, 'his thoughts were elsewhere.' He was still digesting the unexpected turn of events in London.

It was at this moment that Attolico returned, with Mussolini's message that Italy was not ready to fight by Germany's side. Coming on top of the Anglo-Polish news, the Duce's defection stopped Hitler in his tracks. 'The Italians are behaving just as they did in 1914,' he muttered, as Attolico left with Schmidt. Under the weight of the double blow, his nerve broke. He sent for Keitel, who hurriedly pushed his way through the crowded rooms and corridors and entered the study with Colonel Schmundt, who later recounted that he had never before seen the Führer in such a state of total confusion.

'Stop everything!' Hitler barked. 'At once. Get Brauchitsch immediately. I need time for negotiations.'

As Keitel and Schmundt left, Hitler picked up the phone and called Göring, who had disdained to join the mob in the Chancellery that day. He told him about the Anglo-Polish treaty, and said that because of it he had stopped the invasion.

'Is this temporary,' Göring asked, 'or for good?'

'No,' came the reply. 'I shall have to see whether I can eliminate British intervention.'

Göring's response was sceptical: 'Do you really think four or five days will make much difference?'

But that was precisely what Hitler did think.

Stopping the attack was more easily said than done. For a start, the army Chief of Staff, Franz Halder, and the entire operations staff of the army High Command were somewhere on the road between the War Department in Berlin's Bendlerstrasse and their new headquarters at Zossen, some twenty-five to thirty miles south of the city. Brauchitsch, the army Commander-in-Chief, was nowhere to be found at first, but after almost an hour of frantic searching was located and rushed into Hitler's presence. In the meantime, Hitler had had Keitel and Schmundt go through the long sheets of the OKW timetable, to see whether the army was already moving forward too fast to be halted.

Brauchitsch, a genuine officer of the old school, brought a breath of sanity into the proceedings. Soberly assessing the situation, he confirmed that it was not too late. What was more, he even welcomed the delay, in spite of the inevitable confusion it would create. He had always maintained that 26 August was too soon for the attack, leaving too little time for properly organised mobilisation and thus limiting the number of troops to the twenty-seven divisions that could be positioned in time.

'Give me a week to complete mobilisation as planned,' he told Hitler confidently, 'and you'll have over a hundred divisions available. Besides, this way you gain time for your political manoeuvring. I can halt the army before it hits the frontier at 0430 hours.'

For another thirty minutes, they went on trying to reach Halder, but at 7.45 pm Hitler lost patience and ordered his army liaison officer, Colonel Nikolaus von Vormann, to take a car and chase after the elusive staff, stopping them on the road if need be and handing over the order to Halder in person. At the same time, Keitel sent for the deputy chief of his operations staff, Colonel Walter Warlimont, to draft a written confirmation order.

Warlimont was relieved to think peace had been preserved, but was swiftly disillusioned the moment he arrived. 'Don't start celebrating too soon,' Schmundt greeted him. 'It's only a question of a few days' postponement.' Warlimont looked around at the chaotic scene which reflected Hitler's state of mind only too accurately. 'The picture of confusion presented by the Reich Chancellery at that moment was, for a trained staff officer, both repugnant and horrifying to a degree,' he recalled later. 'I kept asking myself whether, if war was really only round the corner, the supreme commander intended his headquarters to continue in this atmosphere of feverish activity and disorder.'

The disorder in the Chancellery was nothing compared to that on the various fronts where the German armies were already rolling towards the border. In East Prussia, the order to halt only reached General Petzel's I Corps at 9.37 pm and officers had to be rushed to the forward units to put it into effect. Further south, motorised columns of General Kleist's corps had actually reached the border, and were only stopped by a staff officer who landed his scout plane on the border itself, just ahead of them. Some Abwehr patrols clashed with Polish units, and started a little shooting, but since there had been minor skirmishes all along the frontier for several days, the Polish general staff did not realise that anything different was happening.

Alfred Naujocks, who had been waiting since 15 August, with his special detachment with their Polish uniforms and concentration camp prisoners, locked in a local school near Gleiwitz, was prevented at the last minute from staging the attack on the radio station. The sacrificial victims were granted a stay of execution, a few more days of life.

Another special detachment was less fortunate. The unit assigned to capture and hold the Jablunka railway tunnel failed to receive the order, crossed the frontier at midnight, and seized the railway station at Mosty and the entrance to the tunnel. But when the rest of the German army failed to show up next morning, they found themselves cut off and encircled by Polish troops. While Hitler ordered them to hold out as long as possible, the German authorities officially disowned them, describing them as 'an irresponsible Slovak gang'. Their commander, Lieutenant Herzner, was too brave and resourceful to take this meekly, however. He led his commando fighting back across the frontier, against great odds, and then coolly submitted an expenses claim for 55·86 Reichsmarks, to cover 3·5 days' foreign allowance and overnight accommodation, while on an 'official journey . . . with armoured vehicle'.

26

'HAVE I EVER IN MY LIFE TOLD A LIE?'

It took Hitler three days to recover his nerve. To begin with, he tried to find ways of persuading Mussolini not to desert him, demanding a list of the raw materials and supplies which the Italian claimed he had to have before he could fight. When it arrived, shortly before lunch on Saturday, 26 August, it was an impressive list – 'enough to kill a bull, if a bull could read it', Ciano noted gleefully in his diary, having specifically compiled it as something which Germany could not possibly provide. It included seven million tons of oil, six million tons of coal, two million tons of steel, one million tons of timber, impossibly large quantities of other metals, minerals and rubber, and no fewer than 150 fully equipped anti-aircraft batteries to protect the industrial quadrilateral Turin–Milan–Genoa–Savona. Ambassador Attolico tried to make it look even worse by adding, on his own initiative, a demand that everything had to be delivered before operations could begin.

Hitler discussed the situation with Keitel, Brauchitsch and Göring, who arrived at the Chancellery at noon, Göring bringing his own touch of sartorial panache by wearing all-white uniform, white shoes and socks, with a black silk cravat around his huge neck. The three advisers agreed with Hitler that there was no chance whatever of meeting Mussolini's demands in full.

In an angry mood, Hitler began drafting a reply. To Göring's horror, he offered to supply not merely the anti-aircraft batteries which Mussolini had requested, but 150 full battalions – three times the number of guns. When Göring protested, as Luftwaffe chief responsible for them, that this was totally out of the question, Hitler replied: 'I'm not concerned with actually making the deliveries, only with depriving Italy of any excuse to wriggle out of her obligations.'

But his temper soon cooled, particularly after General Milch, State Secretary in the Air Ministry, suggested that Germany might even be better off without Italy, provided the Italians made enough warlike noises to keep the British and French occupied. Her 'benevolent neutrality' would in any case deny the enemy access to the Reich through Italy, which was her only weak spot, while Germany could keep all her precious materials and supplies for her own use, and even obtain more from Italy if need be. Hitler was delighted at the idea – it was reported that he slapped his thigh yet again – and after a flurry of excuses and apologies from both sides, he wrote to Mussolini: 'In these circumstances, Duce, I understand your position, and would only ask you to achieve the pinning down of Anglo-French forces by active propaganda and suitable military demonstrations such as you have already proposed to me. As neither Britain nor France can achieve any decisive success in the West, and as Germany, because of the agreement with Russia, will have all her forces free to the east after the defeat of Poland, and as air supremacy is undoubtedly on our side, I do not shrink from solving the eastern question even at the risk of complications in the west.'

Mussolini accepted the let-out gratefully, with extravagant promises about the number of divisions he would station along his frontiers. Later that night, as the clock moved past midnight into the early hours of Sunday, 27 August, Hitler wrote his fourth letter to his friend in thirty-six hours, reassuring him and making a final request: 'Duce, the most important thing is this: if, as I have said, it comes to a major war, the issue in the east will be decided before the Western Powers can score a success. Then, this winter, or at the latest in the spring, I shall attack in the West with forces which will be at least equal to those of France and Britain. The blockade will have little effect, particularly because of the new circumstances now prevailing in the east, and also thanks to my preparations for economic self-sufficiency. Its danger will not increase but diminish with the duration of the war.

'I must now ask a great favour of you, Duce. In this difficult struggle you and your people can best help me by sending me Italian workers, both for industrial and agricultural purposes . . . In specially commending this request of mine to your generosity, I thank you for all the efforts you have made for our common cause.'

It was a brilliant solution to the problem. Italy would keep Britain and France occupied, even as a non-belligerent, and it would cost Germany nothing. At the same time, the Italians would make a positive contribution by providing labour to replace German men from factories and farms who had been drafted into the armed services. It could not have worked out better had Hitler planned it.

With the Italian question resolved to his satisfaction, Hitler had only the British and French to worry about – and he did not regard France as a major problem. He was convinced that it was in London that any decision affecting the Allies would be taken, and that whatever happened, France would follow Britain; left on her own, France would not fight.

His conviction was strengthened by a letter from the French Prime Minister, Daladier, which was delivered to him by Ambassador Robert Coulondre at 7 pm on Saturday, 26 August. It was a moving and emotional appeal, in response to Hitler's interview with Coulondre the previous afternoon, when Hitler, as was his habit, had assured the ambassador that he had no quarrel with France. But the letter contained nothing new, no concrete proposals for resolving the situation, and not enough steel to change his opinion on French resolve. Daladier completely failed to mention that he was ordering the mobilisation of another 700,000 men and that next day there would be no fewer than 2,550,000 French troops under arms. Such a warning might have had more effect than all his fine words; instead he chose to speak softly. Too softly.

'You can doubt neither my own feelings towards Germany nor France's peaceful feelings towards your nation,' Daladier wrote. No one, he claimed, had done more than himself to foster peaceful co-operation and understanding between France and Germany. Nevertheless, Hitler was mistaken if he believed that France could be deflected from honourably fulfilling her solemn promises to Poland. As for the Danzig question, this was open to solution by well-tried, diplomatic means: 'a friendly and equitable settlement' could be reached between the parties concerned.

Coulondre reinforced Daladier's letter with a passionate forty-minute speech of his own. 'I entreated him before history,' Coulondre wrote later, 'and in the name of history, not to miss this last chance. For the peace of his conscience I begged him, who has built up an empire without bloodshed, not to shed blood – the blood not only of soldiers but also of women and children – unless he first made sure that it could not be avoided. I confronted him with the terrible responsibility he would be assuming towards Western civilisation . . . I may have moved him, but I failed to deter him. His stand was taken.'

The very eloquence of the French appeals was enough to confirm Hitler's belief that they constituted nothing more than empty rhetoric, and that despite all the brave words about honour, France would not, by herself, go to war for the Poles. Indeed, when he showed Daladier's letter to Keitel, he described it as proof that France wanted to avoid war over the Corridor. And with that, he seems to have dismissed France from his calculations. He wrote a long and brilliantly contrived reply to Daladier, in which he listed all the usual grievances against Poland and asked the French Premier to put himself in Hitler's shoes by imagining an important French city, such as Marseilles, 'cut off, as a result of a gallant struggle, by a corridor occupied by a foreign power and prevented from professing allegiance to France, and the Frenchmen in it persecuted, beaten, ill-treated, even bestially murdered'. After that, there was no more contact with the French government until Coulondre delivered its ultimatum on 2 September.

The only fly now remaining in Hitler's ointment was Britain. If he could succeed in separating the British from the Poles, his triumph would be complete. He sent for a copy of the complete text of the new Anglo-Polish treaty, to study it for any possible loopholes which he could exploit. But even if he failed to achieve this aim, he no longer had any intention of being thwarted in the desire to attack and crush Poland.

Mobilisation, already begun for the cancelled invasion date, was not halted but speeded up. Troops poured eastwards in a continuous stream, not only by rail but also, William Shirer noted in Berlin, 'in moving vans, grocery trucks and every other sort of vehicle that could be scraped up'. The cancellation of the Nazi rally at Tannenberg and the party 'Day of Peace' at Nuremberg, was officially announced. So, too, was the start of rationing: 700 grams of meat per person per week, 280 grams of sugar, 110 grams of marmalade, one eighth of a pound of coffee or coffee substitute, 125 grams of soap for the next four weeks, and so on. This came as a particular blow to the German people, who heard it at the end of a hot and sultry weekend, weather which did nothing to reduce the feeling of tension in the air.

The newspapers, under the expert guidance of Joseph Goebbels, contributed to the tension. On the Saturday, the *Börsen Zeitung*'s headlines proclaimed: 'COMPLETE CHAOS IN POLAND – GERMAN FAMILIES FLEE – POLISH TROOPS PUSH TO EDGE OF GERMAN FRONTIER!' The *12-Uhr Blatt*'s read: 'THIS PLAYING WITH FIRE GOING TOO FAR – THREE GERMAN PASSENGER PLANES SHOT AT BY POLES – IN CORRIDOR MANY GERMAN FARMHOUSES IN FLAMES!' By Sunday, the claims had escalated still further. The *Völkischer Beobachter* ran banner headlines across its front page: 'WHOLE OF POLAND IN WAR FEVER! 1,500,000 MEN MOBILISED! UNINTERRUPTED TROOP TRANSPORT TOWARDS THE FRONTIER! CHAOS IN UPPER SILESIA!' All this was a skilful blend of half-truths and lies: there is no evidence of any planes being shot at, or farmhouses being deliberately burnt down at that time, but Germans were certainly fleeing for safety, and troops were on the move. However, the *Völkischer Beobachter*'s 'uninterrupted troop transport' referred only to Polish troops, who were being rushed to defend their frontiers – there was no mention of German troop movements or mobilisation. But there was a significant increase in the territory now being demanded: not only Danzig and a corridor across the Corridor, but everything in the east which Germany had lost in 1918, meaning the whole of Silesia and Posen.

Against this background, Birger Dahlerus returned to Berlin late on Saturday evening, bearing a letter from Halifax to Göring which confirmed Britain's desire to reach a peaceful settlement. Göring had already left Karinhall on his special train to travel to the Luftwaffe war headquarters at Oranienburg, and Dahlerus, in an Air Ministry staff car, caught up with it at a small station called Friedrichswalde. As the train moved off again, he handed Göring the letter. The Field Marshal tore it open with trembling fingers and tried to read it, but his English was not good enough and he thrust it back to Dahlerus to translate. When he had finished, Göring rang the bell for his aide, Lieutenant-Colonel Konrad, and ordered: 'I want the train stopped at the next station. Have a car waiting for me there.' Turning back to Dahlerus, he said: 'We are going back to Berlin. The Führer must be told about this letter.'

For once, Hitler, totally exhausted by his dealings with Mussolini and the French, to say nothing of the other events of that hectic day, had gone to bed early. Göring sent Dahlerus back to his hotel, the Esplanade, to wait until called, while he marched into the darkened Chancellery and had Hitler woken up.

After sitting alone in the lounge of the Esplanade for about fifteen minutes, Dahlerus was collected by two SS colonels, who told him: 'The Führer is asking for you.' They drove him back to the Chancellery, now ablaze with lights and filled with scurrying officials, and deposited him in the waiting room outside Hitler's study. A few minutes later, he was ushered into the presence, where he found Göring beaming with satisfaction alongside Hitler, who stood in one of his favourite poses in the centre of the room, legs apart, arms behind his back, a scowl on his face.

Hitler greeted him politely, and showed him to a couch in the corner of the study, while he himself drew up a chair to sit facing him. Göring balanced his bulk precariously on an arm of the sofa next to Dahlerus. The Swede prepared himself, ready to make his report on his meetings with Halifax, and to discuss the contents of the letter.

To Dahlerus's amazement, Hitler ignored the letter and launched instead into a twenty-minute harangue on his own and the party's early struggles and later achievements, which turned into a diatribe against the British, who had so contemptuously rejected all his overtures of friendship. When the Swede managed to get a word in, attempting to refute Hitler's bad opinion of the British character by saying that he had lived as a working man in England and could not agree, the effect was electric.

'What's that!' Hitler asked. 'You worked as a common labourer in England? Tell me about it!'

For another half hour, Hitler listened enthralled to Dahlerus's account of his days in English provincial factories, of the camaraderie of working men's clubs, of evenings spent in pubs, and of the decency and courage of the British working man. He demanded more and more information, and refused to listen to anything else.

Eventually, however, with obvious reluctance, he turned to the present situation – and immediately flew into a rage. Describing his latest proposals made to Henderson, he shouted: 'This is my last magnanimous offer to England!' He started to boast about the strength of the German Wehrmacht, his face stiffening and his gestures, according to Dahlerus, becoming very peculiar.

When Dahlerus pointed out, speaking slowly and quietly 'to avoid irritating him unnecessarily, since his mental equilibrium was patently unstable', that Germany's enemies had also strengthened their armed forces, Hitler did not answer. 'He seemed to ponder what I said,' Dahlerus wrote later, 'but then got up and, becoming very much excited and nervous, walked up and down saying, as though to himself, that Germany was irresistible and could defeat her adversaries by means of a rapid war.' Suddenly he stopped, stared into space, and began talking as if in a trance: 'If there should be a war, then I will build U-boats, build U-boats, build U-boats, build U-boats, U-boats, U-boats . . .' It was like a record that had stuck, his voice becoming more and more indistinct as it died away. Then, suddenly, a spasm shook his body. He lifted his arms in the air and began to shriek, as though addressing a huge audience, but still staccato and disjointed: 'I will build aircraft, build aircraft, aircraft . . . and I will destroy my enemies! War does not frighten me! The encirclement of Germany is impossible now. My people admire me and follow me faithfully. If there are privations ahead for the German people, then let it be now – I will be the first to starve and set my people a good example. My sufferings will spur them on to superhuman efforts.'

Dahlerus was horrified by the spectacle. He turned to see how Göring was taking it – and was equally horrified to see that the Field Marshal did not seem at all perturbed at Hitler's glassy eyes and unnatural voice.

'If there should be no butter,' Hitler shouted, 'I shall be the first to stop eating butter! My German people will loyally and gladly do the same. If the enemy can hold out for several years, I, with my power over the German people, can hold out one year longer. It is because of this that I know I am superior to all the others.'

As suddenly as it had begun, the trance evaporated. Hitler began pacing the floor again, as though regaining his senses. Turning to Dahlerus, he spoke calmly, seriously: 'Herr Dahlerus, you who knew England so well – can you give me any reason for my perpetual failure to come to an agreement with her?'

Dahlerus hesitated, then answered honestly that in his opinion the difficulty lay in the lack of confidence in Hitler and his government. At this, Hitler struck his chest with his hand.

'Idiots!' he cried. 'Have I ever in my life told a lie?'

Dahlerus did not comment on this, except to say that he was a businessman, and in business everything depended on trust. Hitler calmed down, paced some more across the rug in front of his desk, stroking his chin. Then he turned back to the Swede.

'Herr Dahlerus,' he said, 'you have heard my side. You must go at once to England and tell it to the British government. I do not think that Henderson understood me, and I really want to bring about an understanding.'

Dahlerus protested that first he must know exactly what sort of understanding Hitler had in mind. What, for example, was Hitler's precise proposal for a corridor to Danzig? Hitler smiled, and turned to Göring.

'Well,' he said, 'Henderson never asked about that.'

An atlas was found, and, with Hitler's approval, Göring outlined the territory Germany wanted, with a red pencil. Then he tore out the page and gave it to Dahlerus to put in his pocket. They then proceeded to discuss the remainder of Hitler's proposals, formulating a fresh offer which Dahlerus was to take back to London. Göring objected to committing the result to writing, and the Swede was told he must memorise the six points. These were as follows:

1. Germany wanted a pact or alliance with Britain.
2. Britain was to help Germany to obtain Danzig and the Corridor but Poland was to have a free port in Danzig, to retain the Baltic port of Gdynia and a corridor to it.
3. Germany would guarantee the new Polish frontiers.
4. Germany was to have her colonies, or their equivalent, returned to her.
5. Guarantees were to be given for the German minority in Poland.
6. Germany was to pledge herself to defend the British Empire.

Without explanation, Hitler suddenly left the room. Dahlerus supposed he had gone to the bathroom – and wished someone would ask him if he needed to. But no one ever did on these occasions. When Hitler returned, in high spirits, he said: 'Take the message to the British government.'

It was almost 5.30 am when Dahlerus left the Chancellery. Exactly twelve hours later on that beautiful summer Sunday, the Reichstag deputies, who had been cooped up in the Adlon Hotel since Friday waiting for the promised session, trooped into Hitler's presence. Four times they had been called during the previous day, and each time the order had been cancelled as Hitler had swayed backwards and forwards between peace and war. Now, they were told there was to be no immediate session of the assembly, only a secret, unofficial meeting with Hitler and various party notables.

Hitler took his place facing the deputies and Gauleiters in the great marble reception hall of the Chancellery, accompanied by Himmler, Heydrich, Goebbels, Bormann and SS Gruppenführer Karl Wolff, chief of Himmler's personal staff. His movements were jerky and disjointed, and it was obvious that he had not slept the night before. Colonel Hans Oster, chief of staff of the Abwehr, told General Halder next day that the Führer had looked exhausted, haggard and preoccupied, and that his voice was reduced to a croak.

The speech he made was unusually brief. He began by stressing the gravity of the situation but declared that he was now determined to settle the eastern question one way or another, '*so oder so*'. He told the deputies he had made an offer to Britain, through Henderson, and was still waiting for a reply. The return of Danzig and a solution of the Corridor problem was now his minimum demand. His maximum demand depended on the military situation: in other words, he would take whatever he could obtain by war, a war which he would fight, he said, 'with the most brutal and inhuman methods'. Like Frederick the Great, he was prepared to stake everything on one great gamble. The war would be hard, perhaps even hopeless, 'but as long as I live, there will be no talk of capitulation'.

He defended Mussolini, telling the deputies that Italy's attitude was in Germany's best interests. Then he turned to the question of the pact. Remembering the armbands thrown over the Brown House wall, he said he was sorry his pact with Stalin had been so widely misunderstood by the party. The Soviet Union, he explained, was no longer a Bolshevik state, but simply an authoritarian military dictatorship like their own. Because of the pact, and her own partial self-sufficiency, Germany no longer need to fear a blockade by the Western Powers.

'If any one of you believes that my actions have not been inspired by my devotion to Germany,' he challenged, 'I give him the right to shoot me down. I have made a pact with the Devil, to drive out Satan!' The applause, though it came on the proper cues, was thin.

Dahlerus was back in Berlin at 11 o'clock that night, having conferred in London with Chamberlain, Halifax, Sir Horace Wilson and Sir Alexander Cadogan, Permanent Secretary at the Foreign Office. He arrived at Göring's town residence on the Leipzigerstrasse, with the news that the British government had agreed to his returning before Henderson in order to prepare the ground and sound out German reactions before the ambassador brought the official reply to Hitler's proposals. It was, for an amateur diplomat with no status whatsoever, an extraordinary position to be in. Dahlerus had unwittingly become the fulcrum around which Anglo-German relations, and therefore possibly the peace of the entire world, revolved.

The message he brought from London was encouraging. The British were prepared to talk about a possible pact of alliance, as suggested by Hitler; they wanted Poland's frontiers to be guaranteed by the five great powers (which included Germany, of course); they proposed that Poland and Germany should start negotiations immediately about the Corridor. Göring did not consider this very favourable, but said he must talk to Hitler about it. He sent Dahlerus back to his hotel, while he drove round to the Chancellery.

At 1 am on Monday, 28 August, Göring telephoned the Swede at the Esplanade, sounding extremely happy. The Führer, he said, would accept the English standpoint. 'On condition that the note delivered tomorrow by Henderson corresponds with the report you have given us of the attitude of the British government, there is no reason to suppose that we will not be able to reach an agreement.'

However, Göring told him, the British note must contain a clear statement that the Poles had been strongly advised by Britain to establish contact with Germany immediately, and to negotiate. Hitler suspected that the Poles would try to avoid negotiations. Dahlerus dutifully passed the message on to London, through the Berlin embassy.

Hitler slept well that night, and rose feeling refreshed and reinvigorated. In keeping with the food rationing which began that day, his breakfast table was even more meagre than usual, and his staff were served with ersatz coffee and only minute portions of butter. Their leader was delighted to be setting this example to his people, as he boasted that he had knocked Britain out of the game.

His confidence now fully restored, Hitler sent for Brauchitsch. When the army Commander-in-Chief reported to him early in the afternoon, he outlined his immediate strategy, and gave his appraisal of the military situation, with which Brauchitsch agreed. Germany was in such a strong position that she was now virtually unassailable.

Very calmly and clearly, according to Brauchitsch's own account, Hitler told him he intended to force Poland into an unfavourable negotiating position, and then go all out for his maximum objective, his 'grosse Lösung', the conquest of the whole of Poland. His plan was to demand Danzig, the corridor through the Corridor, and a plebiscite in the Free City along the same lines as that which had been held in the Saar in January 1935, when over ninety per cent of the voters had opted for reunion with Germany. He thought Britain would accept this but Poland most certainly would not – which was exactly what he wanted. In this way, he would 'drive a wedge between Britain and Poland', believing that when the Poles ignored British pressure and refused to negotiate, the British would withdraw their support.

Everything, therefore, had to be directed towards convincing Britain that Germany was now being utterly reasonable, and was eager to settle the dispute round the conference table. To this end, Hitler had the

Foreign Ministry draft a set of formal proposals, sixteen in all, to be given to the British government at the right moment. These were so moderate that when Paul Schmidt came to translate them he could, as he put it, 'scarcely believe my eyes'. 'It was a real League of Nations proposal,' he noted. 'I felt I was back in Geneva.'

Hitler was now, according to his army liaison officer, Colonel von Vormann, 'in a brilliant mood'. Gone were all the hesitations and exhausted preoccupations of the past two days. Secure in the knowledge that, whatever happened, the Soviet Union would not oppose him in the east, he was now determined to go ahead, whether or not he succeeded in keeping Britain out. 'If I am pushed into it,' he told Brauchitsch, 'I shall even wage war on two fronts.'

At 3.22 pm, Brauchitsch picked up the telephone and called the general staff. Hitler had given his decision: the new date of 'Y-day', the invasion of Poland, was 1 September.

27

NO MORE CHARLIE CHAPLIN

Like their German counterparts, the great mass of the Soviet population greeted the news of the pact with relief. 'For them,' Gustav Hilger noted in the German embassy, 'a German–Soviet understanding meant the removal of the war scare which had weighed on them like a nightmare since 1933.' Stalin's fears about the effects on his people of having had 'buckets of shit' poured over them for the past six years were apparently groundless – the majority were happy to accept the new situation. It did not matter whether this was because, as Hilger claimed, the Soviet government's propaganda campaign against the Nazis had failed to instil in them a lasting hatred of Germany, or whether, as Chip Bohlen believed, the Soviet people were so docile they would accept anything Stalin told them. What did matter for them was that Stalin had done it again: he had kept the Soviet Union out of the coming European war, perhaps even prevented the war happening.

Certainly, Ivan Maisky, the Soviet ambassador in London, believed there would be no war. On 23 August, while Ribbentrop was meeting Stalin and Molotov for the first time, Maisky entertained the exiled Czech President, Edouard Beneš, to lunch at the embassy and told him: 'France and Britain have forced one Munich on Europe at *your* expense. I expect they will force another on Europe at the expense of Poland.'

Maisky shared the delight expressed by many Soviet officials at the discomfiture of the Anglo-Soviet mission, which had been left high and dry in Moscow by the success of Ribbentrop's diplomatic *Blitzkrieg*. Not since the Treaty of Rapallo in 1922 had any major treaty been concluded in such an incredibly short time. And by a striking coincidence, not only was Rapallo a treaty between Germany and the Soviet Union, but it had also been achieved as a result of the breakdown of negotiations between the Soviet Union and the Western allies. When talks for a treaty with the Allies had reached stalemate in Genoa, the Soviet representative, A. A.

Ioffe, had telephoned Baron Ago von Maltzen, head of the German Foreign Ministry's Russian section, at 1.15 am on Easter Sunday morning, 16 April; by 6.30 pm that evening, while the British and French were kicking their heels in Genoa, the treaty had been signed in Rapallo, thirty-five kilometres along the Riviera.

In 1939, the British and French were paying the price of forgetting what had happened in 1922. The French continued to hope, desperately, that something could be salvaged, and Molotov even went so far as to tell the British and French ambassadors that a non-aggression pact with Germany was not necessarily inconsistent with a mutual defence alliance with Britain and France. As soon as the situation was clearer, he said, the military talks could start again – but everything still depended on Poland agreeing to accept Soviet help.

But, as always, Molotov was only being ultra-cautious, clinging to every option until the last possible moment. On 25 August, Voroshilov saw Drax and Doumenc again and told him that in view of the pact it would be fruitless for them to continue their negotiations. That evening, their tails well and truly between their legs, the two missions left for home via Leningrad and Helsinki – from where, in marked contrast to the outward journey, Drax actually flew back to London. A member of the British embassy who went to the station in Moscow to see them off told Chip Bohlen that as the train pulled out, the two Russians who had been given the job of saying goodbye to them looked at each other and burst into laughter.

The task of educating the Soviet people to the new circumstances fell mainly, of course, on the press. The first official comment came in an *Izvestia* editorial on 24 August, which stressed the great international significance of the two agreements – the trade treaty and the pact: 'It is well understood that the establishment of peaceful and good neighbourly relations, based on broad economic ties between two such powerful states as the Soviet Union and Germany . . . cannot help but aid in the strengthening of peace . . . [The pact] brings an end to enmity in relations between Germany and the Soviet Union, that enmity which the enemies of both governments sought to foster and extend . . . Ideological differences, as well as differences in the political systems of both nations, cannot and must not stand in the way of the establishment and maintenance of good-neighbourly relations.' Thus did Stalin start selling the pact to his people.

According to Nikita Khrushchev, Stalin had a much more cynical sales pitch for him and the other members of the Politburo that day, one which was a much more accurate reflection of the *realpolitik* of his thinking. 'Of course, it's all a game to see who can fool whom,' he told them. 'I know what Hitler's up to. He thinks he's outsmarted me – but actually it's I who have outsmarted him!'

Two days later, when the Anglo-French party had finally left the country, Voroshilov gave an interview to *Izvestia*, which it printed on the front page next morning. 'The Soviet military mission,' it began, 'took the view that the USSR, having no common frontier with the aggressor, could only extend aid to France, Great Britain and Poland through the passage of its troops through Polish territory. The French and British missions did not agree with the position of the Soviet government and the Polish government openly announced that they did not require and would not accept the military aid of the USSR. These circumstances made military collaboration between the USSR and these countries impossible.'

It is interesting to note that Voroshilov, though he never mentioned Germany by name, made no attempt to hide the fact that Poland was threatened by 'the aggressor' and could expect to be invaded. What is perhaps even more interesting is that he then made no attempt to persuade Poland to come to terms with Germany or to avoid a conflict. On the contrary, he seemed to be encouraging the Poles to fight, by hinting very strongly that the Soviet Union would be ready to provide them with 'raw materials and military supplies', for which no pact of mutual assistance, still less of military intervention, was necessary: it was a purely commercial matter. As an example, he cited the fact that 'the United States and other countries' had been supplying Japan with raw materials and military supplies for the past two years, although they had no pacts with her.

He strongly denied reports in the London *Daily Herald* that he had said during the talks that in the event of a Polish–German war the Soviet Union would occupy parts of Poland, and that he had broken off the Anglo-French talks because of the pact with Germany. On the contrary, he said, the Soviet Union had signed the pact with Germany because the Anglo-French talks had failed.

To back up Voroshilov's statements, Soviet newspapers printed as many foreign press reports as they could find which justified the Soviet action and blamed the British and French. In quoting a statement by a prominent French Member of the Chamber of Deputies, Henri de Kerillis, that the Nazi–Soviet pact meant the end of the eastern front, Tass made the charge that this showed the French were upset by the pact because it disrupted their plan to bring about a Soviet–German conflict.

As usual with major policy changes in a Marxist–Leninist country, certain adjustments of language and vocabulary in the press had to be made. Almost overnight, the word 'fascist' disappeared, except when used specifically about the regimes in Italy and Spain. Where once the Nazis would have been routinely described as 'fascist hyenas', they now became simply 'the German authorities'. Most of the press fell into line immediately, though some publications whose press day came before the signing of the pact failed to register the change in time. *Krokodil*, the humorous weekly, came out on 25 August complete with anti-German cartoons. But by the next issue, Hitler and his 'gang' had ceased to be a fit subject for comedy.

In line with these changes, there were adjustments in other areas of life, too. Cinema and theatre programmes suffered a sea-change overnight. Two of the most popular movies of the time, the anti-fascist *Professor Mamlock*, a Soviet film from a play by Friedrich Wolf, and *The Oppenheim Family*, based on a novel by Lion Feuchtwanger, disappeared from screens throughout the Soviet Union on the night of 23 August, to lie in the vaults unmentioned, until 23 June, 1941, when they reappeared with equal abruptness to continue their runs as though nothing had happened.

Anti-German and anti-fascist plays vanished from theatres the same night. Even a play called *The Sailors of Cattaro* was removed, though it dealt with a naval mutiny in 1918, directed against the Austro-Hungarian monarchy – in a confused situation, the censors obviously felt they had to play safe and take no chances. In consequence, there was a sudden rash of classical revivals in the Soviet theatre: Ostrovsky and Chekhov all at once became astonishingly popular, as did the operas of Richard Wagner, which were once again performed on the stage of the Bolshoi Theatre.

For good measure, public libraries and bookshops were also purged. Anti-German literature was banished from the shelves, to join the works of Trotsky, Zinoviev, Radek and Bukharin. In the Library of Foreign Literature, émigré newspapers and magazines were replaced by Nazi journals, while the State Publishing House of the USSR decided to honour Bismarck's memory by publishing his memoirs.

Along with the press, there were other, more direct methods of informing the Soviet people, and redirecting their education or re-education. In the Park of Culture and Rest – Gorky Park – in Moscow, party members manned special booths known as 'agitation points', where they explained the new policy to citizens who queued up to be enlightened. In schools and colleges, there was an abrupt change in the teaching of history. Since 1933, German influence in the history of the Russian empire had been systematically shown as disastrous. After the pact, Eugene Tarlé, the leading expert in this field, discovered overnight that the Germans had always played a positive role in Russia's past.

Wolfgang Leonhard, who was still a student then, recalls that the victory of Alexander Nevsky over the Teutonic Knights in the Battle of Lake Peipus in April 1242, which had previously been described as the single most important event in Russian history, disappeared from the school syllabus. It no longer rated even a passing mention. In its place, students were lectured on the historical significance of Peter the Great's foreign policy, especially his support for the creation of the Prussian state in 1701 which, they were taught, 'laid the foundation stone of the close collaboration between Prussian Germany and Russia, which today, etc., etc. . . .' This was followed by instruction on the historical significance of the pact itself.

While the ordinary people of the Soviet Union, after their initial bewilderment, simply shrugged and accepted the changes either cynically or with habitual resignation, Stalin's political volte-face was harder to swallow for some of the party faithful. Inevitably, those who were hardest hit were the Austrian and German communists living in exile in Russia, refugees from the Nazi witch-hunts.

The day after the signing of the pact, Willhelm Pieck, acting Chairman of the German Communist Party, the KPD, invited several comrades to his dacha at Kuntsevo – close to Stalin's 'Nearby' dacha – to discuss the latest turn of events, which had left most of them in a state of shock. As Germans and communists, they did not know how they were expected to react. Pieck's daughter-in-law, Grete Lohde, was appalled, and said she could not help but see the pact as a betrayal.

Ernst Fischer, an Austrian communist who worked for the Comintern, did his best to explain that the pact was right for the USSR. 'The fact that Hitler has come to a temporary agreement with Moscow has not in any way altered either himself or his regime,' he argued. 'The pact will not last, but it is imperative for the Soviet Union to gain time.'

Fischer's argument convinced several of the others who worked with him at the Comintern, but somehow he failed to convince himself. Not for the first time, he began to have doubts about the true nature of Soviet communism – doubts which many other members seem to have shared. Many left the party, unable to swallow the new Stalinist line.

One who was finally disillusioned by the pact was Margarete Buber-Neumann, a tiny, highly energetic young woman who had been a loyal servant of the Comintern since 1921. Her common-law husband, Heinz Neumann, had been leader of the German Communist Party until 1932, when he was removed for political deviationism. This had been brought about by disagreement with the policies of Stalin, even at that time, towards Germany: he had been shocked when, during a discussion in 1931, Stalin had asked him, 'Don't you think that if National Socialism came to power in Germany it would occupy the West so much that the Soviet Union could develop in peace and build up socialism?'

Neumann and Margarete had been hounded out of Germany by the Gestapo, first to Spain, and then to Switzerland, from where they fled to Moscow when the Nazis demanded Neumann's extradition. They had remained faithful communists through the purges, even after they had both been arrested by the NKVD, Neumann in 1937, Margarete a year later. She was in a camp near Karaganda, in Kazakhstan, along with many other purge victims, when the news of the pact arrived. It was the final straw which broke the back of her faith. She never recovered it. But at the time, it was not wise to publicise such disillusionment. While she was discussing the pact with a group of other prisoners, one of them, a Georgian Menshevik, suddenly declared, at the top of his voice so that as many people as possible should hear him: 'The Russo-German Pact is a work of political genius; the greatest act of our great leader, Stalin. My admiration for him is unbounded.' It was a timely hint that even in the camps there were spies and informers. The others in the group fell silent.

For some German and Austrian exiles, the pact brought considerable changes in their lifestyles. Wolfgang Leonhard was then a seventeen-year-old resident of Children's Home No. 6, the special residence for children of Austrian and German émigrés. He had been living in the former merchant's mansion at 12 Kalashny Pereulok for the past three years. His mother, who had brought him to Moscow in 1935, had been arrested and sentenced to five years in the camps for 'counter-revolutionary Trotskyite activity'. During those three years, in spite of the fact that several teachers and even two of the pupils had been arrested during the purges, Wolfgang and his fellows had been treated as privileged guests of the Soviet Union. With the pact, all that was to change with remarkable speed.

The news reached them while they were all on vacation at Yeysk, on the Sea of Azov, staying in a large military academy. They were at the beach, swimming, when their political director, Igor Speransky, suddenly arrived from the town in a state of great excitement.

'Here's something really important,' he shouted breathlessly. 'I got hold of a proof copy of tomorrow morning's paper in Yeysk. We've just signed a non-aggression pact with Germany!'

'The youngsters stared at him open-mouthed,' says Leonhard. 'This was the last thing we could conceivably have expected. We had naturally been following the press closely, and we had assumed confidently that in spite of all difficulties in the negotiations, a treaty would soon be concluded with England and France against the fascist aggressors.'

'Our political director read out to us in solemn, official tones the announcement of the pact . . . and we listened dumbfounded to the words . . . This was not simply a non-aggression pact; this was a complete reversal of the whole foreign policy of the Soviet Union. What could be the meaning of "keeping each other informed" about interests in common with Hitler's government? Or not joining any group of powers formed against the interests of Hitler? It could mean only one thing – the complete abandonment of the struggle against fascist aggression in all its forms!

'We were thunderstruck. We sat there bewildered and silent. Finally Egon Dirnbacher, the youngest among us, said sadly: "Oh, what a pity.

Now we shall certainly never be allowed to see Charlie Chaplin in *The Great Dictator!*" '

The children were ordered back to Moscow immediately. By the time they arrived, their home had been closed. Furniture removers were already packing things away, and plumbers and house painters were doing the place up. All the children's personal possessions had been piled into one single storeroom.

The headmaster called them into the hall for a final meeting, and 'explained' the pact to them. The Western Powers, he told them, had tried to make use of the Soviet Union to fight for their interests, but the great Stalin had seen through their game. The immediate conclusion of the pact would allow the Soviet Union to continue to live in peace, and to build up its power. What did this mean to the Children's Home? 'In the context of the new requirements of foreign policy, we too shall have to do some reorganisation.'

The 'reorganisation' he spoke of meant the closure of the home, and the transfer of its children to the 'Spartak' Russian Children's Home – where they quickly discovered life was far less pleasant and privileged than they had been used to.

'The conclusion of a non-aggression pact with Hitlerite Germany and the closing of our Home had transformed us overnight into ordinary young citizens of the Soviet Union,' Leonhard wrote later. 'It seemed barely credible that it was only two weeks since we had been travelling to the sea in a special bus provided by the Military Academy, to be treated as honoured guests at a party given by hundreds of officers.'

Stalin was clearly determined, from the very start of the alliance, that nothing should be done which might in the slightest degree offend or upset his new partner. What started with the downgrading of a few German and Austrian children was to grow during the next two years into an obsession that would cost the Soviet people dearly.

Outside the Soviet Union, communists throughout the world were in a state of confusion. The local party leaders had received no advance warnings, and no guidance on the sudden change of course. With the Comintern itself still trying to grasp the implications of the realignment of Soviet interests, national parties were, for the moment, left to make their own assessments.

Some, like the British Communist Party under Harry Pollitt, plunged confidently into print. The London *Daily Worker* of 23 August carried a banner headline: 'Soviet's Dramatic Peace Move to Halt Aggressors'. The lead story went on: 'As realisation of the significance of this master-stroke of Soviet peace policy dawned upon the world, it was seen as a shattering blow to the policy of the "Anti-Comintern Pact" on which past aggression, particularly in Spain and in the Far East, were based; a thunderbolt for the Chamberlain Cabinet, which has for long months been sabotaging the conversations for an Anglo-Soviet Pact in the hope of reaching another "Munich" with Hitler; a demonstration before the world of the decisive power of the Soviet Union and of the results which can be achieved by a genuine stand against aggression.'

The whole of the third page of the paper was devoted to a statement by the Central Committee of the British party, backing up these views, pointing out that the pact was in line with the policy stated in Stalin's speech of 10 March, and claiming that the way was still open for an Anglo-Soviet pact.

The reaction of the French Communist Party was very similar, though its members were torn between patriotism and their allegiance to Moscow. On 25 August, their morning newspaper L'Humanité published a bold statement. 'We are in favour,' it said, 'of resistance to all acts of aggression and the communists are ready to fulfil their duties as Frenchmen in the framework of the engagements contracted by their country. They are ready to undertake all their responsibilities. If Poland is attacked, the treaty with her must come into play.'

On the same day, French communist leader Maurice Thorez proclaimed: 'If Hitler in spite of everything unleashes war, let him know that he will find before him the united people of France, with the communists in the front line, to defend the security of the country and the liberty and independence of the nations.' And two days later party spokesman Marcel Cachin published an open letter to former socialist Prime Minister Léon Blum, confirming the position and calling for a similar commitment from the French socialists. On 1 September, a formal resolution of the French Communist Party welcomed the pact but advocated aid to Poland, and a few days later, on 6 September, Thorez and his fellow communist deputies who were of military age joined their regiments with the full approval of the party.

But all this was not enough to assuage the feelings of the rest of France. The signing of the pact started a great wave of violent anti-communist sentiment throughout the country – as indeed it did throughout the world – and most newspapers began demanding a ban on the party to go with the ban on its publications, L'Humanité and the evening paper Ce Soir, which came into effect on 26 August. The party was, in fact, declared illegal on 26 September, though it was still loudly advocating war against Germany: on 19 September, Cachin had written a second open letter to Blum saying, 'We were the first to proclaim the necessity of making every sacrifice to strike down Hitlerian Nazism. We shall not cease to proclaim it. We take our orders only from the French people.'

By the beginning of October, however, when Poland's fate had been sealed, the orders were clearly coming from a different source. As Stalin backed Hitler's 'peace offensive' towards the West, Cachin and his comrades swiftly changed their tune. They berated the French government's rejection of Hitler's overtures, declaring that Soviet power could help achieve a policy of collective security which would ensure peace and the independence of France; they started making anti-war propaganda inside the armed forces and Thorez and the other prominent communists who had so bravely joined the colours less than a month before now deserted and fled to sanctuary in Moscow.

The American Communist Party were more confused than most. To begin with, the New York *Daily Worker* said nothing about the pact, while waiting either for instructions from Moscow or for the local party bosses to decide what line to take. But after a couple of days the general secretary, Earl Browder, called a press conference at which he declared that the pact was in line with 'long-declared' Soviet policy, and was an excellent example to the rest of the world. If all the powers formally declared they would not attack each other, he stated rather obviously, it would be 'a distinct contribution to the protection of the threatened peace of the world'. But, he went on, the pact had been made possible only because of the political and military preparedness of the Soviet Union, 'which is the only example, above all others, that the Nazis understand'.

'There is a great deal of newspaper comment,' he concluded, 'that this represents a change of policy of the Soviet Union, and that this is a blow against Poland, etc. All that is, of course, nonsense, although a kind of nonsense which is very valuable for Berlin.'

When the New York *Daily Worker* did publish, it was seen to be trying somewhat desperately to justify the pact, and if possible to relate it to America. After claiming that it would make it more difficult, in some unspecified way, for 'the Chamberlains and Bonnets to carry through other Munichs', it produced the conclusion that the pact gave 'greater opportunities for the people and government of the United States effectively to check Japanese aggression in the Far East, to protect the national security of the United States and the interests of the American people'. Again, it gave no explanation of just how this remarkable deduction had been reached.

During the last few days of August, as Hitler's preparations for Operation White moved steadily forward, the various communist parties all indulged in the same piece of wishful thinking: that the pact would persuade the Western Powers to enter into a 'peace front' with the Soviet Union, which might still prevent further Nazi aggression. It was an interesting inversion of Hitler's own hopes of the pact's effects on Britain and France.

The secretariat of the German Communist Party, operating clandestinely from Paris, believed that there was now more chance of preventing war, and also of rallying Germans for the overthrow of Hitler. In a statement on 25 August, the KPD said: 'The external and internal political situation created by the pact sets all anti-fascists, all peace- and freedom-loving Germans, great tasks, which can only be carried out by an intensified struggle against the Nazi dictatorship.' It called on German workers to support the Soviet peace policy and to 'place themselves at the side of all peoples which are oppressed and threatened by the Nazis'.

Of course, none of the national parties knew anything about the secret protocol to the pact, or about Stalin's expectations in Poland and the other territories assigned to him by it. Had they done so, they might perhaps have understood why he failed to give them any clear directives but was content to let them go their own ways. Heinz Neumann, former leader of the German Communist Party, remembering Stalin's earlier willingness to sacrifice Germany to the Nazis in order to take the international heat off the Soviet Union back in 1931, might have recognised the pattern. But Neumann was in a prison camp somewhere in Siberia. The existing party leaders do not seem to have suspected anything.

In order to be sure that the pact would hold, Stalin could not be seen to do or say anything which might in any way be construed as a breach of its terms or its spirit. While the Red Army was still not strong enough to repel a German invasion, he dared not risk any provocation, however slight – hence the sudden withdrawal of privileges from German and Austrian exiles and their children, and the censorship of all anti-German comment in press, radio, films, theatre or any other area of Soviet public life. But if local parties outside the Soviet Union chose, strictly on their own initiative, to make trouble, that had nothing to do with him. Hitler had himself decided that Stalin no longer controlled the Comintern – Schnurre had been instructed to say as much during the dinner party at Ewest's in July – so the Soviet leader could cheerfully disclaim all responsibility for the actions of national parties.

The French party could go stirring up trouble in the West and keeping Hitler aware of the threat from that quarter, and if the French government could be persuaded to intervene when Hitler attacked Poland, Stalin wanted them to do so as strongly as possible. They would not win, but they could make life more difficult for Hitler and slow him down, which would give Stalin desperately needed time to prepare for his own move into Poland. The German party could rally its supporters against Hitler at home, which might also help to slow things down. The Americans could perhaps help to focus their government's attention on the Japanese, which could relieve the pressure on the Soviet Union's eastern frontier. The British party was probably an irrelevance, but at least it could be relied on to go on making a noise and contributing, in however small a way, to the forces pressing Chamberlain to act resolutely against Hitler.

All this suited Stalin's purposes admirably, for everything could be achieved without any action on his part. Now that the pact had been signed, he no longer had any interest in preventing a war – indeed, in Marxist–Leninist terms a war between capitalists and fascists was something devoutly to be desired. What was more, the pact itself could be seen as a direct encouragement to Hitler to make war, as Stalin was well aware. Molotov's predecessor as Foreign Minister, Maxim Litvinov, had told the League of Nations Assembly on 14 September 1935: 'Not every pact of non-aggression is concluded with a view to strengthening general peace. While non-aggression pacts concluded by the Soviet Union include a special clause for suspending the pact in cases of aggression committed by one of the parties against any third state, we know of other pacts of non-aggression which have no such claim. This means that a state which has secured its rear or its flank by such a pact of non-aggression obtains the facility of attacking third states with impunity.' The pact with Hitler was the only one signed by the Soviet Union which did not have such an exclusion clause.

Once the second world war began, it was officially described to the Soviet people as being simply a war between the imperialists, in which they had succeeded in staying neutral thanks to the inspired genius of Stalin's foreign policy. Stalin's reasoning was neatly summed up in the first patriotic joke of the war, which became current within a few days of the start:

'Have you heard about our great new advance in aircraft production?'
'No. What is it?'
'Yesterday in Western Europe, twelve British and eight German aircraft were shot down in air battles.'
'What has that got to do with our aircraft production?'
'Why, it's obvious – we're twenty planes up!'

While the British and French missions were boarding the Red Arrow for Leningrad, Stalin and Molotov were busily weighing their pound of flesh. To their dismay, they found it was slightly short. Molotov called Schulenburg to his office to point out that, 'owing to the great haste with which the secret additional protocol had been drawn up, an obscurity had crept into the text'. What had happened was that the map they had used during Ribbentrop's visit had been too small, leading them all to believe that the river Narev, which formed part of the boundary dividing the two spheres of interest, went as far as the frontier of East Prussia. It did not, but the smaller river Pissa did, and Molotov wanted this point added to the protocol, by an exchange of letters between himself and Schulenburg.

Molotov's punctiliousness in marking out the area of Poland to be swallowed by the Soviet Union was a clear indication of where Stalin's interest lay. On the German side there was an equally revealing concern: when were the Soviet military representatives coming to Berlin? It had been agreed orally during Ribbentrop's brief stay in Moscow that there would be a full military mission in the Berlin embassy, a vital requirement if there was to be military co-operation between the Wehrmacht and the Red Army. Hitler wanted them to take up their posts without delay. It was unthinkable for him to start the Polish campaign with no responsible Soviet officials to liaise with in Berlin, and at that moment there was no one there of any importance at all. The ambassador, Alexei Merekalov, had left in mid-April and never returned – he was a Litvinov man, and therefore due to be replaced in any case; Astakhov had gone back to Moscow before the pact was signed, and seemed to be staying there. There had been no military attaché for some years.

When Schulenburg raised the question on 25 August, while seeing Molotov about the amendment to the secret protocol, the Soviet Prime Minister told him he appreciated the reasons behind Hitler's concern, and would be sending a special military representative as soon as possible. He would also appoint a new ambassador, but the problem with this was that there was no one suitable for the post. He was considering two men for lesser posts in the Berlin embassy – thirty-nine-year-old Russian Alexander Shkvarzev as counsellor and a thirty-three-year-old Georgian called Kobulov as first secretary. Schulenburg had never heard of either of them.

Shkvarzev was simply a colourless bureaucrat, one of the army of faceless men of the Foreign Commissariat. But Kobulov's nationality should have aroused Schulenburg's suspicions about him – and those suspicions would have been justified. Kobulov was in fact a junior member of the 'Georgian Mafia', one of the special agents from his own country whom Stalin used to conduct his private diplomatic ventures. He was, both in rank and function, one of Beria's lieutenants in the NKVD, and his role in Berlin would be twofold: to report directly to Stalin on events in Germany, and to set up and control an active espionage network stretching beyond Germany into Czechoslovakia and the German part of Poland, with the help of the 'journalists' of the Soviet news agency, Tass.

Despite Schulenburg's urging, Molotov refused to be hurried. Perhaps Stalin really was having a hard time finding the right people. Perhaps he simply wanted to make Hitler sweat a little longer. Either way, the result was infuriating for the Germans. Over the next four days, the messages from Berlin became more and more frantic. By the evening of 28 August, Hitler had become so impatient that at 11 pm Moscow time he made Ribbentrop personally telephone Schulenburg to tell him to apply more pressure. When the ambassador saw Molotov at 5 pm next day, he was told that the military representatives had been chosen and were ready to leave, but that he still had not found the right man to be ambassador.

Hitler had other reasons for anxiety over the Soviet position. On 25

August, the Swiss newspaper *Neue Zürcher Zeitung* had published a story headed 'Surprise from Moscow', which had been picked up by a number of other papers in different countries. The story said that the main objective of the Anglo-French negotiations with the Soviet Union had been to get a guarantee for Poland that she would not be attacked in the rear in the event of an invasion by Germany. According to the story, this guarantee had been obtained, and the Soviet Union had withdrawn some 250,000 troops from the Polish frontier as a demonstration of good faith.

Naturally, Hitler was not pleased at this development. He was relying on the threat of Russian invasion to keep Poland's forces divided between her eastern and western frontiers. He also hoped it might scare the British and French and thus, 'in the end, bring about a remarkable reduction in the readiness to help Poland'. If the report turned out to be true, he wanted the Soviets to cancel the order and move their troops back again.

Ribbentrop raised this question in his telephone conversation with Schulenburg, who told him there was not a word of truth in it: Red Army units on the Polish border were not only being kept at full strength but were also in a state of constant alert. When Schulenburg had spoken to Molotov about it, the Russian Premier had 'laughed heartily and said that of course the newspaper reports were untrue; so much nonsense was published in the press nowadays that one could not concern oneself with all of it.' But Ribbentrop would not let the matter drop. He kept on nagging about it until Molotov, with the approval of Stalin and Voroshilov, issued a strong denial to the press.

A third, and perhaps greater, source of anxiety for Hitler was waiting for the Soviet government to ratify the pact. If he attacked before this was done, and things went badly for him, the Soviet Union could rightly claim that the pact had no validity, and Stalin could attack. When the pact had still not been ratified a week after its signature, Hitler started nervously asking what were the reasons behind the delay. Molotov had assured Schulenburg that ratification was 'merely a formality', but with less than thirty-six hours to go before the attack on Poland, that formality had not been completed.

In fact, the problem was simply one of logistics. In a country the size of the Soviet Union, with its notoriously bad transport system at that time, it took several days to get all the members of the Supreme Soviet together for a special, unscheduled session. Although the extraordinary session opened on 28 August, it was not until 30 August that there was a quorum – and since 30 August was not a working day, the session proper could not begin until Thursday, 31 August.

Molotov would speak himself proposing ratification of the pact, but this was only item three on the agenda, following measures to increase agrarian taxes, and a motion by Voroshilov to reduce the call-up age from twenty-one to nineteen and extend the period of compulsory military service to three years. Only after these two issues had been decided could the assembly turn its attention to the pact. Molotov's own estimate was that this would be on the evening of Friday, 1 September – at least twelve hours after the start of Operation White. It must have seemed to Hitler that Stalin was determined to make him suffer until the very last moment.

In the event, the first two items on the agenda were disposed of remarkably quickly, and just before 4 pm on the Thursday, Molotov telephoned Schulenburg to say that he was about to introduce his motion. By 9.20 that evening, Schulenburg was able to phone Berlin with the news that, after a 'brilliant speech' by Molotov, the Supreme Soviet had ratified the treaty and that it would be published in the Soviet press next day. He asked that the German ratification – a much simpler procedure, of course, under Hitler's dictatorship – should be announced at the same time.

Molotov's speech had been exceptionally good for a man not known for the power of his oratory. He had, of course, blamed the Western Powers for the breakdown of the Anglo-French talks. They had, he said, wanted a mutual-assistance pact because it would strengthen them – but were afraid of it because it might also strengthen the Soviet Union, which was something they did not want. In the end, their fears had outweighed other considerations. 'Only in this way,' he said, 'can we understand the position of Poland, which has been acting on the instructions of Great Britain and France.'

He reminded the assembly of Stalin's 'chestnuts' declaration in the famous speech of 10 March, warning against being drawn into conflict by warmongers. 'It must be confessed,' he told them, 'that there were some short-sighted people also in our country, who, carried away by an oversimplified anti-fascist propaganda, forgot about this provocative work of our enemies.' Those enemies, it seemed, did not now include Germany. 'Only yesterday,' he continued, 'German fascists were pursuing a foreign policy hostile to us. Yes, only yesterday, we were enemies in the sphere of foreign relations. Today, however, the situation has changed, and we are enemies no longer.'

He did not claim that a general peace had been ensured by the pact, but that since the two largest states in Europe had decided 'to live in peace one with the other', the zone of possible military conflicts in Europe had been reduced: even if there were to be a war, its scale would be smaller if the Soviet Union was not involved. All those Western leaders, particularly the socialists, who wanted the Soviet Union to fight on the side of Britain against Germany were, he declared, rabid warmongers who had taken leave of their senses. 'Is it really difficult,' he concluded, 'for these gentlemen to understand the purpose of the Soviet–German non-aggression pact, on the strength of which the

USSR is not obliged to involve itself in war either on the side of Great Britain against Germany, or on the side of Germany against Great Britain? Is it really difficult to comprehend that the USSR is pursuing and will continue to pursue its own independent policy based on the interests of the peoples of the USSR and only those interests?'

Molotov did not explain just how well the pact really served the interests of the USSR. He did not mention the secret protocol. But then, he did not need to – the ratification of the pact was approved unanimously. With just seven and a quarter hours to spare, Hitler was given his free hand in the east. And Stalin was given most of those parts of the old Russian empire which had been lost after the Revolution and the Paris peace conference: as a result of a few days' bargaining, he had regained territory and strategic positions which had cost Peter the Great, 250 years before, two decades of bloody warfare. He would also have the personal satisfaction of recovering all the ground which had been lost to Poland in the war of 1920 as a result of his own disastrous interference with the Red Army's strategy.

28

HITLER'S ALIBI

Hitler's decision to attack on 1 September had left him just four days to separate Britain – and therefore France, too – from Poland. During those last four days of peace, this became his main preoccupation. Encouraged at every step by Ribbentrop, he does not seem to have doubted that he could do it. The message brought from London by Dahlerus had reinforced his confidence, but when Henderson returned with Chamberlain's official response, Hitler found this contained an unwelcome surprise.

The British ambassador arrived at the Chancellery at 10.30 pm, having driven the 400 yards from his embassy through the inky darkness of the black-out imposed that week as a rehearsal for the real thing. A silent but sympathetic crowd of Berliners and correspondents watched from the other side of the street as he was greeted by a roll of drums from the guard of honour drawn up in the courtyard, to the right of Albert Speer's monumental doorway. Henderson had landed at Tempelhof airfield two hours before, but had taken time to bath and change into his immaculate dinner suit, snatch a quick dinner and down a half-bottle of champagne, then briefly consult French Ambassador Coulondre before setting out to see Hitler. As he left the embassy, his pet dachshund waddled to the door to see him off, a fitting symbol of his attachment to Germany and things German.

Hitler and Ribbentrop greeted him warmly, for the omens were all good. Not only was Henderson as elegantly turned out as ever and looking confident and happy, but he was also wearing his customary dark red carnation in his buttonhole. The year before, during the days preceding the Munich agreement, he had deliberately stopped wearing one, telling the press that he 'considered it inappropriate at a moment of such grave crisis'. Since then, Henderson's carnation had been regarded as a visible sign of the state of Anglo-German relations. Everyone was pleased to see it being sported that night.

Hitler sat down immediately and read the translation of the British reply, which Henderson gave him at the same time as the document itself. It started well, talking about sharing Hitler's desire for friendship between Germany and Britain. It went on to accept his proposals – though they were 'stated in very general terms and would require closer definition' – as a suitable basis for discussion. It stated that the British government believed a 'reasonable solution of the differences between Germany and Poland could and should be effected by agreement between the two countries'.

So far, so good. The next paragraph was even better: there should be immediate talks between the German and Polish governments, to reach a settlement which would be guaranteed internationally by other powers. But then came the bombshell: the British government had 'already received a definite assurance from the Polish government that they are prepared to enter into discussions on this basis, and His Majesty's government hope the German government would for their part also be willing to agree to this course'.

The news that, contrary to all his predictions, Poland was prepared to negotiate seems to have taken Hitler's breath away. For the rest of the time until Henderson left at 11.45 pm, he said hardly anything, allowing the ambassador to make a lengthy speech without once interrupting him. 'It was, I think,' Henderson wrote in his memoirs, 'the only one of my interviews with Hitler at which it was I who did most of the talking.'

More immediately, in his despatch to London at 2.35 next morning, Henderson reports: 'In the end, I asked him two straight questions. Was he willing to negotiate direct with the Poles, and was he ready to discuss the question of an exchange of populations? He replied in the affirmative as regards the latter (though I have no doubt that he was thinking at the same time of a rectification of frontiers).'

For the rest, Hitler avoided giving a straight answer. He would, he said, have to give careful consideration to the whole British note. Turning to Ribbentrop, he said, 'We must summon Göring to discuss it with him.' He promised to give Henderson his reply next day.

'We took two days to formulate our answer. I'm in no hurry,' Henderson assured him.

'But I am,' Hitler responded.

When the ambassador had been shown out, still with every courtesy, Hitler took Ribbentrop into the conservatory, where Göring was already awaiting them, together with Himmler, Hess and Karl Bodenschatz, Göring's aide. In spite of the surprise he had just received, the Führer was in high spirits. He told the others the contents of the British note, saying that although it was courteously phrased, it contained nothing of real substance. Describing the rest of the interview, he launched into a brilliant impersonation of Henderson – mimicry had always been one of his talents – speaking German with a perfect rendering of the ambassador's thick English accent. It was as though he regarded this latest turn of events, despite the initial shock, as an enjoyable though not particularly serious challenge.

'Tonight, I'm going to hatch something diabolical for the Poles,' he announced with relish. 'Something they'll choke on.'

Already, a plan was beginning to take shape in his mind. He would accept the British proposals. Even the idea of an international guarantee appealed to him.

'I like it,' he chuckled. 'From now on I shall only do things on an international basis. International troops shall go in – *including Russians!*' That would certainly put paid to any possibility of the Poles agreeing.

As far as direct negotiations were concerned, he had the perfect answer for that, too. He would agree to start them immediately – on condition that a Polish plentipotentiary with full powers to negotiate arrived in Berlin within twenty-four hours. This was patently impossible, but he would be able to claim that the Poles had failed to accept his offer. And if, by some remarkable chance, they actually did manage it, it would be a simple matter to force a breakdown which could be blamed on the Poles being unreasonable. This would give the British their excuse to ditch Poland, and he could then go ahead as planned.

Göring tried to counsel caution. 'Let's drop the all-or-nothing game,' he pleaded.

Hitler's reaction was scornful. 'It's the only game I've ever played, all-or-nothing,' he replied.

With the broad idea settled, Hitler began turning his attention to the details. If he was to be successful in tricking the British and trapping the Poles, he had to move with great cunning.

'We now have to aim a document at the British, or the Poles,' he said, 'that is little less than a masterpiece of diplomacy. I want to spend tonight thinking it over, because I always get my best ideas in the small hours between five and six o'clock.'

'Mein Gott!' Göring exclaimed. 'Don't you get any sleep even now? Or have you got insomnia again?'

'The Führer replied,' Himmler recorded in his diary, 'that he often dozes from three to four o'clock in the morning and then suddenly wakes up to find the problems set out in pristine clarity before his eyes. Then he jumps up and jots down a few key words in pencil. He himself doesn't know how it happens – all that he does know is that in the wee small hours of the morning, everything that might confuse or distract disappears.'

Whether or not everything dropped neatly into place during the wee small hours no one knows. But certainly Hitler rose on the morning of 29 August with his ideas clearly defined. When he saw the army Chief of Staff, Franz Halder, in the early afternoon he gave him a swift run-down on the plan, which Halder recorded in his diary with graphic simplicity:

Basic principles: Raise a barrage of demographic and democratic demands. Plebiscite within six months, under international supervision. Those opting for Germany must remain German citizens; the same holds good for the Poles. Poles will not want Germans in their territory.
30.8 Poles in Berlin.
31.8 Blow up.
1.9 Use of force.

Hitler spent much of the remainder of the afternoon preparing the note which he presented to Henderson at 7.15 that evening in a meeting which was in stark contrast to the sweet reason of the night before. He even managed to provoke the normally suave Englishman into losing his temper and trying to outshout him at one stage.

Most of the note was taken up with the usual catalogue of recriminations against Poland, which had been given added fuel by the headlines in the lunchtime papers, screaming that at least six German nationals had been murdered by the Poles. But finally it came to the point – or rather to two points: there could be no territorial guarantees without Soviet participation, and Germany would – solely to please Britain and as a proof of the sincerity of Hitler's intentions towards her – agree to receive a Polish emissary with full powers to negotiate. But the emissary had to be in Berlin on Wednesday, 30 August – the very next day. Before he arrived, the German government would draw up proposals for an acceptable solution, and would if possible make these available to the British – the sixteen proposals which were already being prepared by the Foreign Ministry.

When Henderson protested that the time-scale had the ring of an ultimatum about it, Hitler's response was brutally blunt.

'My soldiers,' he said, 'are asking me "Yes" or "No". My army and air force are ready to strike, and have been since 25 August. They are telling me that one week has already been lost, and that they cannot afford to lose another, for fear the rainy season in Poland should be added to their enemies.'

As though to underline Hitler's threat, the ante-room outside his study was full of army officers, including Keitel and Brauchitsch, when Henderson left. Despite the shouting match, and the depressing nature of the whole interview he had just had, Henderson managed to retain a little of his sang-froid as he passed the OKW chief. 'Busy tonight, Herr Generaloberst?' he inquired, ironically. Looking down at the carnation in his buttonhole, he told Dr Otto Meissner, head of Hitler's Chancellery, who was seeing him out, that he feared he would never wear one again in Germany.

Back in the study, Hitler was congratulating himself on the success of his tactics so far. The British were reacting exactly as he wanted them to, but by now he was beginning not to care so much whether or not he succeeded in drawing their teeth. 'In two months, Poland will be finished,' he said. 'And then we shall have a great peace conference with the Western Powers.' At the dinner table that night, he was unusually loquacious, addressing the whole table on the history of German–Soviet relations, and the course of the present crisis: it did not take his guests long to realise that he was rehearsing the speech he would make to the Reichstag when the war started.

The Poles were not taken in by Hitler's moves, and Beck never even considered going to Berlin himself. He had seen what had happened to Austria and Czechoslovakia after first Austrian Chancellor Kurt von Schuschnigg and then Czech President Emil Hacha had swallowed the bait and travelled to Germany for 'discussions'. And though Henderson invited Polish Ambassador Josef Lipski to the British embassy and urged him to persuade Beck to send someone, Halifax and Chamberlain thought so little of Hitler's demand that they did not even pass it on to Warsaw.

Göring, knowing how badly Hitler's meeting with Henderson had gone, called Dahlerus away from his dinner at 10 pm and asked him to fly back to London to tell the British leaders just how magnanimous were the terms which Hitler was drawing up to present to the Poles, if they came to Berlin. The only clear-cut demand, he said, would be for the return of Danzig. Even the Corridor question would be left open, to be decided by a plebiscite held under international control. To illustrate this, he tore a page from another school atlas, and swiftly coloured in the area covered by the proposed plebiscite with a green crayon, and the area which Hitler considered purely Polish in red. He did this so carelessly that the potentially German area included the ancient Polish city of Lodz, which was some sixty miles east of the pre-1918 Prussian frontier. Carrying this map, and very little else, Dahlerus was despatched from Tempelhof airfield at 4 am. At that same moment, Henderson was delivering Halifax's acknowledgement to Hitler's message, saying that although he would give it careful consideration, it was 'of course unreasonable to expect that we can produce a Polish representative in Berlin today, and the German government must not expect this'.

All day long on 30 August, messages flashed to and fro between London and Berlin, and London and Warsaw. Henderson delivered no less than three to the Chancellery, including a personal message from Chamberlain to Hitler urging him to avoid any provocative confrontations on the Polish frontier, while waiting for the full British reply to his note. Halifax asked the Germans to stop their people in Poland causing trouble, and the Poles not to shoot any who did.

None of the messages had any effect: Hitler received Gauleiter Forster during the afternoon to give him his final instructions for action in Danzig on 1 September; the Poles' response to the British plea to keep things calm was to order full mobilisation of all their armed forces, at 4.30 pm.

Henderson saw Ribbentrop at midnight, to hand over the full reply from London. The meeting should have been at 11.20, but the message from London did not arrive in time to be deciphered by then. The result was that he arrived at the precise moment when the time limit for a Polish plenipotentiary expired, a coincidence which Ribbentrop chose to regard as deliberate.

The meeting that followed has gone down as one of the most tempestuous diplomatic exchanges in history. Neither man had had any sleep for at least thirty-six hours, and their nerves were worn to a frazzle. Ribbentrop had come straight from Hitler, and interpreter Paul Schmidt noted that 'he was obviously in a state of almost shivering excitement . . . with pale face, set lips and shining eyes' as he sat down opposite Henderson at the small table in Bismarck's former office. Within a few minutes they were both on their feet, screaming abuse at each other over the head of Schmidt, who sat tight and scribbled furiously in his notebook as they faced each other like two fighting cocks. Eventually, they cooled down sufficiently to sit again, and Henderson delivered Chamberlain's message.

It was not encouraging for the Germans. Chamberlain declared it would be 'impracticable' for the Poles to send anyone as quickly as Hitler demanded, and suggested it would be better for the German leader simply to pass his proposals to the Polish ambassador. While talks were being set up, both sides should give an undertaking to keep their armies from making any aggressive moves. Some 'temporary *modus vivendi*' might be arranged for Danzig, to avoid further incidents.

Ribbentrop barely listened as Henderson read out the note, and when the ambassador asked for the German proposals, he read them out as quickly as he could, and with a very bad grace. He may not have 'gabbled' them, as Henderson claimed, but he certainly went too quickly for the Englishman, whose grasp of the German language was far from perfect, to understand. Henderson, of course, was very tired, and was relying on being given a copy which he could take away with him. But when he requested one, Ribbentrop refused point-blank. He tossed the document contemptuously on the table, saying that it was now out of date, and in any case it was too late, since the Polish plenipotentiary had failed to arrive.

By now, the scales were beginning to drop from Henderson's eyes, and he was beginning at last to realise the truth. He had been able to get the gist of about six of the sixteen articles, but that was enough for him to recognise how mild they were. So why did Hitler not want him to see them? 'Did Ribbentrop and his master,' he asked in his record, 'not wish them to be communicated to the Polish government, lest the latter might in fact agree to negotiate? It was the only conclusion which one can draw from this episode, since it might have made all the difference to the instructions given to M. Lipski on the following day, if the Polish government had been cognisant of the official text of the German proposals. In themselves, and taken at their face value, they were not unreasonable, and might well have served as a basis for negotiation. That is why one can only assume that Ribbentrop did not wish them to be discussed, and his attitude that night was not only one of ill-manners, but also of ill-faith.'

Schmidt made a thick red mark in his notebook at the place where he had jotted down Ribbentrop's refusal, 'as a sign that in this hour the die was cast for war'. He later had confirmation from Hitler himself that both he and Henderson had been right in their reading of the situation.

'I needed an alibi,' Hitler told him, 'especially with the German people, to show them that I had done everything to maintain peace. That explains my generous offer about the settlement of the Danzig and Corridor question.'

Henderson's education was not finally complete, however. He still clung to the delusion that if the Poles could be persuaded to negotiate, the Germans would do so too, and would be forced to do so on the terms they themselves had set out. Immediately he got back to his embassy, he called the Polish ambassador and asked him to come round.

By the time Lipski arrived, at 2 am, Henderson had the full text of the German proposals. Sir George Ogilvie-Forbes, first secretary in the embassy, had telephoned Dahlerus, who was with Göring at Karinhall, to tell him about the disastrous meeting with Ribbentrop. The Swede had persuaded Göring, who had a copy of the proposals, to allow him to read them over the phone to Ogilvie-Forbes.

Henderson outlined the proposals to the Pole, and told him they were 'not unreasonable'. Lipski said nothing.

'Please take my advice and act urgently on it,' Henderson continued. 'Ring up your Foreign Minister and tell him you have heard these proposals from me. Say you would like to call on Ribbentrop with a view to communicating them to the Polish government. I urge you – do it tonight!'

'Not tonight,' Lipski replied. 'It is too late.'

Henderson continued to press him. There would be little chance of success for any negotiations conducted by Ribbentrop, he said, but there were other ways: 'Tell your government that Marshal Smigly-Rydz should meet Field Marshal Göring at once. They would get on well together. Something could be arranged.'

'I will put the suggestion to Warsaw,' Lipski said, reluctantly, 'but not tonight.'

*　　　*　　　*

At 8.30 next morning, 31 August, Henderson phoned Lipski again, to make sure he had contacted Beck, and to tell him that he had heard 'from an unquestionably accurate source that there would be war if Poland did not undertake to do something within the next two or three hours'. The 'unquestionably accurate source' was Ulrich von Hassell, former ambassador to Italy, who knew Henderson well from their early days as diplomats in Belgrade. He was acting on behalf of Weizsäcker, who was desperately trying to undermine Ribbentrop and prevent war.

Henderson was told Lipski was not available. He then called Coulondre, in the French embassy, and told him. The French ambassador hurried round to see Lipski, and to tell him he should call Beck and ask for authority to go to Hitler and Ribbentrop immediately, as a plenipotentiary.

Henderson called Lipski again shortly after 10 am. When Lipski was eventually persuaded to speak to him – he had, in fact, been on the telephone to Beck – the Pole said he was too busy to come and collect a copy of the proposals, which Dahlerus had just brought to the British embassy from Göring. So Henderson had Ogilvie-Forbes personally drive Dahlerus to the Polish embassy in his open two-seater car.

After driving across Berlin at breakneck speed, they found the embassy in a state of chaos. 'The hall was crowded with packing cases, and the staff and servants were preparing for departure,' Dahlerus wrote later. 'Lipski received us in his office, which had already been cleared of most of its furniture.'

Lipski was obviously in a bad way. Fatigue and stress were taking their toll. His face was white as a sheet, and his hands trembled as he obsessively tore up pieces of paper and screwed them into little balls. When Ogilvie-Forbes gave him Dahlerus's handwritten copy of the proposals, he stared absently at it for a minute, then muttered that he couldn't read it. All he knew, he said, was that he must remain firm and that 'even a Poland abandoned by her allies is ready to fight and die alone'.

Dahlerus offered to dictate the proposals for Lipski's secretary to type. While he was in the next room, doing so, Lipski roused himself sufficiently to tell Ogilvie-Forbes, with typical Polish bravado: 'I have no interest whatsoever in notes or any other kind of proposals from the Germans. I have a very clear understanding of the situation in Germany after five years as ambassador. I know Göring intimately and all the other leading Nazis, and I am sure of one thing: in the event of war there will be uprisings and rebellion in Germany, and the Polish army will march in triumph into Berlin.'

Colonel Beck seemed to agree with Lipski's assessment of the situation, and with the officers in the Cavalry Club in Warsaw who were drinking toasts to their forthcoming victory. At 12.40, he sent his instructions to the ambassador: he was to ask to see Ribbentrop or

Weizsäcker and tell him: 'The Polish government are examining in a favourable light the proposals of the British government, who will be receiving a formal reply on that matter in a few hours' time.' But Beck's instructions did not end there. He went on: 'Do not under any circumstances enter into any concrete discussions. If the German government make verbal or written proposals, you must explain that you do not have authority to accept such proposals, or to discuss them, and that your task is merely to pass on the above communication from your government and await further instructions.'

Inevitably, the whole telegram was copied and decoded by the Forschungsamt, the 'Research Office', set up in 1933 to control wire-tapping operations, and delivered swiftly to Göring and to Ribbentrop for Hitler. Ribbentrop flourished the intercept, typed on the light brown paper of the Forschungsamt, at Peter Kleist, his expert on Polish affairs, with a sneer: 'There you have the readiness of your famous Herr Beck to reach an understanding!'

Hitler, who had slept well and was calm and confident, was gratified to see how well the Poles were fulfilling his expectations. When Otto Meissner brought him papers to sign, he told him he was delighted that Warsaw had not taken up his proposals. But even if the Poles had taken them up, it would have made no difference at that stage. At 12.40 pm – precisely the same moment that Beck was despatching his telegram to Lipski – Hitler had issued 'Directive No. 1 for the Conduct of War'. It began:

> Now that every political possibility has been exhausted for ending by peaceful means the intolerable situation on Germany's eastern frontier I have determined on a solution by force.
> The attack on Poland is to be carried out in accordance with the preparation made for 'Operation White', with the alterations, in respect of the army, resulting from the fact that strategic deployment has by now been almost completed.
> Assignment of tasks and the operational objective remain unchanged.
> Day of attack . . . 1 September 1939
> Time of attack . . . 4.45 am
> This timing also applies for the Gdynia–Gulf of Danzig, and Dirschau Bridge operations.

The directive went on to say, at some length, that there should be no action in the West unless the British or French started something, and even then the Wehrmacht was to confine itself to purely defensive measures.

At 4 pm, the executive order to begin the invasion was confirmed to units in the field, and they began moving forward to their start positions. From that moment, the frantic efforts of the diplomats and statesmen,

British, French, Italian and German, to avert the catastrophe were totally futile.

Ribbentrop finally saw Lipski at 6.30, after keeping him waiting five hours for an appointment. It was one of the shortest diplomatic interviews on record, for Ribbentrop dismissed the Pole immediately he confirmed that he had no power to negotiate. By the time Lipski got back to his embassy, he found the telephone links with Poland had been cut. Shortly afterwards, communications with Britain and France were also stopped.

Fifty minutes after seeing Lipski, Ribbentrop received the welcome news from Schulenburg in Moscow that the pact had been ratified, and that the promised military mission, consisting of a general, a brigadier-general, a colonel and two majors, would be flying to Berlin next day, via Stockholm.

At 8 pm, Alfred Naujocks and his disguised SS men staged their attack on the radio station at Gleiwitz, fired a few pistol shots, broadcast an inflammatory 'proclamation' in Polish, and left behind the dead concentration camp victims as mute evidence. They had been carried there in trucks, already drugged unconscious by powerful injections, and shot on site in order to spill the right amount of blood. Shortly afterwards, the other frontier incidents planned by Heydrich were mounted near Kreutzburg and at Hochlinden.

At 9 pm, all German radio broadcasts were interrupted for an announcer to read out the sixteen points of Hitler's proposals, to demonstrate to the German people and to the rest of the world how reasonable they were, and how unreasonable the Poles were being in rejecting them. Naturally, the statement did not mention that the proposals had never actually been put to Poland, or that they had been set an impossible time limit for sending a representative.

The Poles responded at 11 pm with their own broadcast. It could have been their last chance to call Hitler's bluff by publicly agreeing to talk. But that was not Beck's way. Instead, the message was unequivocally bellicose: 'Words can no longer veil the aggressive plans of the new Huns. Germany is aiming at the domination of Europe, and is cancelling the rights of nations with as yet unprecedented cynicism. This impudent proposal shows clearly how necessary were the military orders [for mobilisation] given by the Polish government.'

A soft, grey blanket of mist lay across the glassy waters of Danzig harbour as dawn broke on Friday, 1 September 1939 – the exact date specified by Hitler for Operation White in his first directive back on 3 April. Through the haze, movements could be dimly made out on the shadowy bulk of the battleship *Schleswig-Holstein*, riding at anchor on her 'courtesy visit' to the Free City. The massive gun turrets swivelled smoothly around. The eleven-inch guns were levelled to fire at what, for them, was point-blank range. They were trained on the little Westerplatte peninsula across the harbour, which housed a Polish garrison of eighty-eight men. At 4.45 am precisely, with an ear-shattering roar and the flash of cordite, they opened fire.

The second world war had begun.

29

THE GREAT COUNTER-ATTACK

'By order of the Führer and Supreme Commander, the Wehrmacht has taken over the active protection of the Reich. In accordance with its instructions to check Polish aggression, troops of the German army have counter-attacked early this morning across all the German–Polish frontiers. Simultaneously, squadrons of the air force have taken off against military objectives in Poland. The navy has taken over the protection of the Baltic Sea.'

The first military communiqué of the war was a perfect example of Hitler's approach to truth, a clear warning for all who might be inclined to trust him. The fiction that it was the Poles who had started everything was promoted elsewhere, too, with great determination. A proclamation from Hitler calling on every soldier to do his duty, and claiming that Hitler had had no choice but to meet force with force, was read out by commanding officers in the field just before their units crashed over the frontiers in their 'counter-attack' at dawn. In the Foreign Ministry, Weizsäcker was ordered by Ribbentrop to send a circular to all missions in other countries telling them what to say: 'In defence against Polish attacks, German troops moved into action against Poland at dawn today. This action is not for the moment to be described as war, but merely as engagements which have been brought about by Polish attacks.'

In London, Theo Kordt, the German chargé d'affaires, was instructed to tell Halifax that reports of the bombing of Warsaw and other Polish towns were 'entirely untrue'. Kordt, as a dedicated member of the anti-Hitler conspiracy, was careful to say that it was the press office in Berlin which described the reports as untrue and Hitler who said the Poles had fired first. The information, however, was taken seriously enough by Halifax and Chamberlain to hold up their declaration of support for Poland for twenty-four hours.

Even Mussolini had to be told the same story when Hitler wrote to him that morning, releasing him from his obligations under the Axis alliance. The Poles, he said, had replied to his overtures for a peaceful settlement with 'a series of further intolerable acts of terrorism'. 'Last night,' he claimed, 'there were fourteen more cases of frontier violation, three of which were very serious.' The three he was referring to, of course, were at Gleiwitz, Kreutzburg and Hochlinden, the scenes of 'Operation Canned Goods'.

As soon as he had finished his message to Mussolini at 9.40 am, Hitler set out for the Kroll Opera House to address the Reichstag and party notables. It was a heavy, overcast morning, in keeping with the mood of the people. Those few who were on the streets were faced with the ominous sight of five heavy anti-aircraft guns which had been set up overnight along the east–west axis in the heart of the city, to augment the lighter guns which had been hoisted on to the roofs of buildings like the Adlon Hotel during the past couple of days. No one cheered as Hitler and his entourage drove past. When newsboys shouted their extras in the street, none of the workers busy on the construction of the new office building for the giant I. G. Farben chemical corporation, across the way from the Adlon, bothered to lay down his tools to buy one. The general attitude was one of apathy and disbelief.

Inside the ornate auditorium of the opera house, however, party members displayed a dutiful enthusiasm, albeit still slightly muted. William Shirer noted in his diary that 'there was far less cheering than on previous and less important occasions when the Leader had declaimed from this tribune'. As Hitler stepped briskly on to the platform at 10 am wearing for the first time a field-grey military-type uniform in place of his usual brown party tunic and black pants, he was faced by a sea of other uniforms, both party and Wehrmacht. But there were also about a hundred empty seats, the places of deputies who had already been drafted into the armed forces.

The speech was not one of Hitler's best. His voice was low and raucous as he trotted out the same fantastic farrago all over again, mechanically working himself up into a state of excitement. Shirer, listening to the speech from a studio in Broadcasting House as he relayed it live for CBS in the USA, though he sounded hesitant and unsure of himself, and strangely on the defensive, as if he was 'dazed at the fix he had got himself into and felt a little desperate about it'.

It was not until the very end of the speech that Hitler finally if unwittingly spoke the truth. 'From this moment,' he declaimed emotionally, 'my whole life shall belong more than ever to my people. I now want nothing more than to be the first soldier of the Reich. I have once more put on this uniform, which for me is the most dear and sacred of all. I shall not take it off until victory is ours – or I shall not live to see the end.'

The audience rose at last with wild shouts and 'Sieg Heils'. Goebbels shouted, 'Victory will come! There will never be another 1918!' Eva Braun covered her face with her hands and wept. 'If anything should happen to him,' she sobbed to her sister Ilse, sitting alongside her in the opera box, 'I'll die, too.' Dr Brandt, Hitler's unorthodox physician, comforted her as they left. 'Don't worry, Fräulein Braun,' he said. 'The Führer told me there will be peace again in three weeks' time.'

Eva smiled bravely, but was not reassured. Back at the Chancellery later that day she sent for Willi Kannenberg, the major-domo, and told him, 'I heard Göring say that in the Hamburg docks there are some freighters loaded with canned foods, chocolate, wine, a whole heap of delicacies. Send someone immediately to collect provisions to be sent up to the Berghof. There must be big stocks, because we'll need them for a long time.'

While German missions around the world were busily pumping out Hitler's barefaced lies, in Moscow nothing needed to be said. Stalin and Molotov did not ask. They had been kept fully informed through Schulenburg and their own chargé in Berlin, Nikolai Ivanov, of every move in the diplomatic game over the last few days. Now, they watched and waited, fascinated by Hitler's adroit manipulation of events, but still not wishing to expose their own interest in his success. When Schulenburg passed on a request for the first active measure of support at 7.30 on the morning of 1 September, the response was cautious.

The German Air Ministry wanted the Soviet radio station at Minsk to send out a continuous dash with the intermittent call-sign 'Richard Wilhelm 1.0' in the intervals between programmes. This, they said, was for 'urgent navigational tests' – a rather obvious euphemism for a radio beacon to help guide the German 'flying pencil' Dornier 17s on their bombing missions over Gdynia, Lvov, Krosno and Warsaw itself. Schulenburg was told that the Soviet government – a Russian euphemism which everyone knew meant Stalin – would order the radio station to identify itself by introducing the word 'Minsk' into broadcasts as often as possible. If there were any definite times when this would be particularly useful, the Germans simply had to ask. In any case, the station would stay on the air for an extra two hours. But Stalin would prefer not to have the call-sign broadcast, in order to avoid attracting attention.

The Luftwaffe managed very well on Minsk's normal programmes. By the end of the first day, Polish airfields were all in ruins, and the air force almost completely destroyed. The towns and cities, too, had been hard hit; Warsaw had been bombed almost continuously, with no fewer than thirteen separate air raids. The Poles were astonished at the accuracy of the German bombers in locating their targets on a day when low cloud had made visibility very poor.

Stalin's desire to keep a low profile was also in evidence in the matter of the military mission he was sending to Berlin. He had delayed its departure for two days, waiting for hostilities to begin, no doubt fearing that the arrival of a high-powered group of Soviet officers immediately before the German attack would look too much like collusion. Now, with the invasion well established and no sign of anything going wrong, it was safe to despatch them. But there was to be no announcement that they were on their way – Stalin claimed this was for security reasons – and even after their arrival nothing was to be said about a military mission. There should simply be a discreet mention in the press that a new military attaché had been appointed. To reduce the outward show still further, they would not fly straight to Berlin in a Soviet aircraft, but would go instead to neutral Stockholm. He wanted Hitler to send a German plane to collect them from there. Hitler agreed to all these conditions, but spoiled everything by ordering a full guard of honour to greet the Soviet officers at Tempelhof.

On the diplomatic side, too, Stalin had decided to avoid any obvious display of unity with Hitler by not sending a notable figure as ambassador. The faceless Alexander Shkvarzev, already nominated as counsellor of the embassy, would instead go to Berlin as full ambassador. However, he would be accompanied not only by Kobulov, who was one of Stalin's Georgian 'Mafia', but also by Vladimir Pavlov, who had until then been Molotov's private secretary and who was popularly supposed to be Stalin's illegitimate son by a Volga German woman.

While the British and French governments hesitated and vacillated, trying desperately to find some way of avoiding going to war, Stalin continued to hold back. Henderson seemed to have been taken in by German claims of Polish aggression, and telephoned Halifax to tell him that Hitler had given orders for the Poles to be driven back from the border line and for their air force along the frontier to be destroyed only after he had heard that they had attacked the radio station at Gleiwitz and had blown up the bridge over the Vistula at Dirschau. The latter piece of information was true as far as it went – but it omitted to say that the bridge had been blown because the Germans were trying to advance towards Danzig across it. The German paratroop operation to seize the bridge before it could be blown, which Hitler himself had had a hand in planning, had failed because of the early morning fog.

Henderson told Halifax he had received the information from Göring himself, and that he believed Hitler might ask to see him after the Reichstag speech, 'as a last effort to save the peace'. In fact, Halifax had already heard it two hours earlier from Dahlerus, who was also acting at Göring's behest. Henderson, his flagging faith in Hitler temporarily restored by the German version of events, even suggested that Smigly-

Rydz should come to Germany immediately, 'to discuss as soldier and plenipotentiary the whole question with Field Marshal Göring'.

The French, meanwhile, were trying to persuade Mussolini to organise another conference, another Munich. Without consulting the British, French Foreign Minister Bonnet instructed his ambassador in Warsaw, Léon Noël, to ask Beck if Poland would accept an Italian proposal for a conference. Beck's reply, considering his own nature and the state of affairs, was remarkably restrained and even dignified. 'We are in the midst of a war,' he said, 'as the result of unprovoked aggression. It is no longer a question of conferences but rather of common action which the Allies should take to resist.' The Polish ambassadors in both Paris and London had already informed their host governments that they considered the German action was a plain case of aggression and that they expected the Allies to fulfil their obligations.

In London, Count Edward Raczynski spent only a few minutes with Halifax, meeting him at 10 Downing Street in a small room on the ground floor to the left of the entrance hall, the office of the Prime Minister's private secretary, immediately before an emergency Cabinet meeting. Raczynski concluded by saying, 'The Polish government considers this to be a case of aggression under article 1 of the Anglo-Polish Treaty of Mutual Assistance.' Halifax replied, 'I have very little doubt of it.' As they stood up and went out into the hall, other ministers hurrying into the Cabinet room seemed more certain. Sir John Simon, Chancellor of the Exchequer, grasped the Polish ambassador's hand and said, 'We can shake hands now – we are all in the same boat. Britain is not in the habit of deserting her friends.'

But to Chamberlain, no doubt influenced by the messages from Berlin via Kordt and Henderson, the issue was not so clear-cut. He continued to hedge, both in the Cabinet and in the stormy session of the House of Commons that afternoon. Black-out precautions were already being observed, and Raczynski recalls that 'small, ghostly electric lamps, covered with metal shades, cast a bluish light on the paved floor of the corridors', while in the chamber itself black curtains covered the gallery windows. The House was crowded with MPs and the public galleries were packed with excited onlookers and reporters. In the diplomatic gallery every important member of the Diplomatic Corps was present – with one notable exception. Soviet Ambassador Ivan Maisky had chosen to stay away.

Those who were present heard brave words from all the leading politicians, including Chamberlain, but the Prime Minister gave little indication of any positive action.

Certainly there was no declaration that Britain was going to fight for Poland. And the messages from Chamberlain and from Daladier which were delivered to Hitler that evening merely called on him to withdraw his troops or face the consequences. In neither case was the message an ultimatum, only a warning.

To Stalin this came as no surprise. Indeed, it was exactly what he had expected. When Polish Ambassador Grzybowski had officially notified the Soviet government of the German attack and the resulting state of war between Germany and Poland, Molotov had not questioned Grzybowski's statement that the aggression was unprovoked. But he had asked him whether Poland was counting on the intervention of Britain and France, and if so, when? Grzybowski had told him he believed the Western Powers would both declare war next day. Molotov, Grzybowski later recorded, had given 'a sceptical smile' and said, 'We shall see.'

The suspicion that Britain and France would not honour their obligations did not please the Soviet leaders. Without help, the Poles were likely to be overrun by the Germans far too quickly for Soviet comfort. The prospect of the victorious German Panzer divisions sweeping right up to the Soviet frontier before the Red Army was in place was disturbing. Suppose the German generals ignored orders and kept on going? Stalin was always suspicious of the military; he believed that every general was a Bonaparte in embryo. So perhaps now was the time to do something to help stiffen Polish resistance. Earlier, Molotov had suggested to Grzybowski that the Soviet Union might help the Poles indirectly with economic aid. Next day, the Soviets offered more direct help when their ambassador in Warsaw, Sharanov, called on Beck and asked him why he had not taken up Voroshilov's broad hint to ask the Soviet Union for supplies: Poland could buy munitions and raw materials from them – presumably with the economic aid offered by Moscow.

After a violent uproar in the House of Commons on the evening of Saturday, 2 September, Chamberlain was finally forced to send an ultimatum to Hitler next morning. The French government decided to follow Britain's lead.

Ribbentrop was with Hitler at 12.45 am on 3 September when Henderson telephoned to request an interview at 9 o'clock next morning. Obviously, this was likely to be bad news. Ribbentrop turned to Schmidt, who happened to be standing near him. 'Really, you could receive the ambassador in my place,' he said. 'Just ask the English whether that will suit them, and say that the Foreign Minister is not available at 9 o'clock.'

To Schmidt's dismay, Henderson agreed to be received by him. But the meeting almost failed to take place: after going home to snatch a brief rest, Schmidt overslept and had to dash to the office in a taxi. As he was driving across the Wilhelmplatz he could see Henderson already mounting the front steps of the Foreign Ministry. He pulled up at a side door and ran up the back stairs to Ribbentrop's office. As the clock struck nine, he was standing, slightly breathless, at the Foreign Minister's desk when Henderson was announced.

The ambassador entered, looking very serious. The famous red carnation was missing from his buttonhole. He shook hands with Schmidt, but rejected the offer of a seat, and remained standing in the middle of the room.

'I regret that on the instructions of my government I have to hand you an ultimatum for the German government,' he said, his voice heavy with emotion, and then proceeded to read out the contents of the document. 'More than twenty-four hours have elapsed since an immediate reply was requested to the warning of 1 September, and since then the attacks on Poland have been intensified. If His Majesty's government has not received satisfactory assurances of the cessation of all aggressive action against Poland, and the withdrawal of German troops from that country, by 11 o'clock British Summer Time, from that time a state of war will exist between Great Britain and Germany.'

Henderson handed over the ultimatum, and took his leave, saying he was sorry to have to give such a document to Schmidt of all people, since he had always done his best to help him. Schmidt thanked him, said goodbye, then hurried over to the Chancellery, where he had to force his way through a crush of ministers and party chiefs in the ante-room before he could get into the study.

He found Hitler sitting at his desk and Ribbentrop standing by the window, staring out at the garden. Both looked up expectantly. Schmidt stopped a few feet from the desk, took a deep breath and slowly translated the ultimatum. When he finished, there was complete silence. Hitler, Schmidt recalled, 'sat immobile, gazing before him'. After what seemed an age, he turned to Ribbentrop, who was still standing by the window.

'What now?' he asked, with a savage look, clearly implying that he blamed his Foreign Minister for misleading him about Britain's probable reaction.

Ribbentrop was crushed for the moment. All he could say was, 'I assume the French will hand in a similar ultimatum within the hour.'

In fact, the French ultimatum was not delivered until midday, by which time Britain had officially been at war with Germany for an hour already. Hitler listened to Chamberlain's broadcast to the British people at 11 am. Eva Braun took a photograph of him as the fateful announcement came crackling over the air, looking thunderstruck that it should actually have come to pass.

But he soon found other matters to occupy his mind. When Coulondre arrived at the Wilhelmstrasse, Hitler and Ribbentrop were over in the Chancellery, giving a warm welcome to the new Soviet ambassador and his 'military attaché', General Purkayev. The Russians had called to present credentials and at the same time to congratulate Hitler on his successes in Poland.

In their enthusiasm to receive Stalin's envoys, Hitler and Ribbentrop kept the French ambassador waiting half an hour in the Wilhelmstrasse with Weizsäcker, who had no authority to give any answer to the French. While Coulondre waited to present his government's ultimatum demanding the immediate withdrawal of German troops from Poland, Hilter was busy telling the Russians that the campaign was going even better than he had anticipated and would all be over in a matter of weeks. However, since he was not certain of Shkvarzev's standing and therefore did not know if he was aware of the secret protocol, he did not raise the subject that was uppermost in his mind as far as the Soviet Union was concerned: when would the Red Army move into the eastern part of Poland?

The French ultimatum expired at 5 pm. Now both allies were at war with Germany. But Hitler still refused to accept that all was lost. Although the French were already almost completely mobilised, he did not believe they would do anything positive until the British, too, were ready – and in spite of the fact that ten British bomber squadrons were being deployed in France and advance units of the British Expeditionary Force were embarking for the Continent, he believed that would take weeks, or even months. If he could finish off Poland before then, there would be nothing left for the Allies to fight about, particularly with the Soviet Union occupying half the country. Surely, he reasoned, he would then be able to come to some sort of understanding with them.

With this in mind, it was obviously important to avoid any unnecessary clashes with either of the Allies and he issued orders to his troops in the West that they were not to start anything. Only at sea was any offensive action permitted against Britain, but even this was strictly limited. Hitler was furious when the submarine *U-30* torpedoed and sank the British transatlantic liner *Athenia* 200 miles west of the Hebrides en route from Liverpool to Montreal with 1,400 passengers aboard; 112 people, including twenty-eight Americans, died. At the time, there was no way of confirming who had been responsible, since all U-boats were under orders to maintain total radio silence. The German navy denied that there were any U-boats in the area, and Goebbels put out a story that the British had sunk their own ship, in order to bring the United States into the war. When the *U-30* finally returned to base on 27 September, her commander claimed he had mistaken the *Athenia* for an armed merchant cruiser on patrol, a legitimate target.

In the Soviet Union, nothing whatever was said about the Allied declarations of war. Not a word appeared in any newspaper, or was heard in any radio bulletin. The news soon leaked out, however, for the practice of jamming undesirable radio broadcasts had not been started, and many people in the Soviet Union made a habit of getting their news from the BBC, which they had learned to trust.

From this and other sources, the Soviet people, and certainly the Soviet government, also knew how fast the Germans were advancing across Poland. The Poles fought valiantly, but stood little chance against the devastating power of the forces Hitler hurled against them. Within five days, the Polish army was cut to shreds, though it continued to resist for another three weeks. During those five days, the Germans lost only 150 men killed and 700 wounded.

By a sad irony, one of the first German soldiers to fall was Weizsäcker's second son, Heinrich, a lieutenant in the infantry, who was killed at a railway crossing near Klonowo on the Tucheler Heath. Heinrich's younger brother, Richard, then a private in the same regiment, saw him hit and stayed with him through the night, until the body was taken away. Richard survived the war, although he was later wounded twice, to defend his father at the Nuremberg trials and then to follow in the family tradition of public service by becoming Mayor of Berlin, President of the Evangelical Church and, in the 1980s, President of the Federal Republic of Germany.

No matter how bravely they fought, the Poles were outnumbered, outmanoeuvred and outgunned. At times, it seemed the speed of the German advance was governed only by the ability of the supply lines to provide fuel and ammunition, and of the infantry to keep up with the armour. Richard von Weizsäcker even now remembers vividly the agonies of footslogging after tanks which were covering thirty miles and more a day with ease. In fact, the bulk of the German army still moved on foot or by horse, in spite of the legend that has grown up since that everything was Panzers. On 1 September 1939, German ground forces possessed well over half a million horses, and only four of the Wehrmacht's ninety infantry divisions were completely motorised.

The armour however, allied with superior weaponry and equipment all around, was decisive. The Germans continued to charge eastwards at a rate which alarmed Stalin. He had counted on having several weeks in which to complete the mobilisation of his forces for his invasion of Poland. Instead, before three days were out, Ribbentrop was asking him to start moving in his troops, and warning that the German army might otherwise have to cross into the Soviet zone to finish off Polish army units there.

Stalin, although keenly aware of the danger of having a victorious German army arriving on his doorstep before he had his marching boots on, was also aware of other dangers. It was not only in the military sphere but also in the political that he was not yet ready to make his move. 'It is possible that we are mistaken,' he said, 'but it seems to us that through excessive haste we might injure our cause and promote unity among our opponents.' He would 'start concrete action' when the time was right. Until then, he would understand if the Germans had to cross the demarcation line – but this would be purely temporary and would not change anything. The original plan for the partition of Poland would still stand.

30

DEATH OF A NATION

'The first soldier of the Reich' left Berlin for the front at 9 pm on Sunday, 3 September, in his special train *Amerika*. This was newly completed in August, and consisted of an engine and fifteen cars including: an armoured anti-aircraft car at each end armed with 2-cm guns and manned by a crew of twenty-six; two baggage and generator cars, one at either end of the train; Hitler's Pullman car, number 10206; a bath car; and the press chief's car with communications centre including a 700-watt short-wave radio transmitter.

Shortly afterwards, two other special trains followed: the *Atlas*, which was used by the Wehrmacht GHQ staff, and the *Heinrich*, which housed such civilian notables as Himmler – hence the train's codename – Chancellery Chief Lammers and Ribbentrop. The *Heinrich* was an amazing accumulation of cars which, according to Paul Schmidt who accompanied Ribbentrop, 'displayed the evolution of the railway coach, from ancient decorated carriages "in which Charles the Great had travelled" to Ribbentrop's newly built, streamlined saloon'. Hitler himself called it 'a crazy kind of express'.

During almost the whole of the Polish campaign, Hitler and Ribbentrop conducted their affairs from these trains, parked in sidings a little behind the battlefront, first in Pomerania and then near Ilnau in Upper Silesia. Each day, after early conferences, Hitler would set out for the front in an open car, carrying an oxhide whip and with a pistol strapped to his waist, to show himself to his men. He had his aides toss packets of cigarettes from the car, and at each stop he made a great show of inspecting kitchens and mess tents and accommodation. His interest in every detail was unflagging – but when Rudolf Schmundt, his Wehrmacht adjutant, asked him to visit the first hospital train carrying wounded, he declined. He could not do it, he said; the sight of the men's suffering would be intolerable to him.

Ribbentrop did not accompany his leader in these forays. He preferred to avoid the battlefield, and stayed behind in his saloon car, directing the Reich's foreign affairs in hour-long telephone conversations with the Wilhelmstrasse, during the course of which, Schmidt says, 'he became wildly excited. His yells resounded far across the lonely railway siding on to which we were usually shunted.' It was from this unlikely and unnecessary setting that Ribbentrop continued to press Stalin and Molotov to intervene.

At first, Stalin stayed calm and watchful, refusing to be panicked by the German successes. But when the Polish government fled from Warsaw to Brest-Litovsk on 6 September, calling on all Poles both in and out of uniform to cross the Vistula and set up a new line of defence to the east of the river, he began to realise that he might be caught out by a sudden Polish collapse. He ordered General Purkayev, the new military attaché in Berlin, to obtain the latest and fullest assessment of the military situation from OKW headquarters and then fly back to Moscow to report to him. With Hitler's immediate approval, General Jodl gave the Russian a complete briefing, and the Foreign Ministry's political department were happy to provide a German aircraft for the journey.

Even as Purkayev arrived in Moscow on 8 September, news came through that 60,000 Polish troops had been encircled near Radom, to the south of Warsaw, and that the 4th Panzer Division had smashed its way into the suburbs of Warsaw itself.

Polish Ambassador Grzybowski chose that day to take up Molotov's offer of Soviet aid. The timing was disastrous, but his government's instructions had taken two days to reach him. Molotov coldly told him that the situation had changed completely since the offer had been made, and now that Britain and France were in the war the Soviet Union could not help. He could not even allow supplies for the Poles to be sent through the Soviet Union for fear of violating her neutrality.

That evening, Ribbentrop again asked the Soviet Union to send in the Red Army. Military operations, he said, were 'progressing even beyond our expectations' and the Polish army appeared to be 'more or less in a state of dissolution'. Ribbentrop's message crossed with one from Molotov to him, sent at almost exactly the same moment, giving congratulations on the entry of German troops into Warsaw. Neutrality, it seemed, was a subjective and selective concept.

The imminent capture of the Polish capital decided Stalin that the time had come to act. At 3 o'clock on the afternoon of 9 September, Molotov told Schulenburg that the Red Army would move 'within the next few days', and this was confirmed by the Soviet staff to German military attaché General Köstring. In addition, Schulenburg noted several visible signs of impending action: large numbers of reservists aged up to forty-five were called up, particularly technicians and physicians, many foodstuffs suddenly vanished from the shops, gasoline supplies were cut, and schools were prepared as emergency hospitals. The emphasis on hospitals and doctors was a wise precaution in case things went wrong, but Stalin had no intention of getting involved in any actual fighting if he could possibly help it. His plan was to leave all that to the Germans, and to collect his share of the spoils only when they had finished. That, after all, had been his price for signing the pact. But there was a more serious implication behind the emergency provisions, and indeed behind the call-up of reservists. The Red Army was already easily big enough to cover the simple occupation of part of a defeated country, and even to deal with any resistance from the remnants of its army. Similarly, if no serious fighting was envisaged, what need was there for extra medical facilities?

The clear implication was that Stalin did not completely trust Hitler to keep his word and stop short of the Soviet frontier. If the rampaging Panzer divisions did keep right on, and did try to achieve Hitler's *Lebensraum* in the Ukraine immediately instead of in a few years' time, then the Red Army would need every extra man, and all those emergency hospital beds would be filled to overflowing.

Stalin had no strong reason to suppose Hitler would attack the Soviet Union – indeed he must have been reassured by a request on 6 September for German merchant ships to be allowed to land their cargoes at the Russian port of Murmansk, in the Barents Sea near the northernmost tips of Norway and Finland. Although well inside the Arctic Circle, Murmansk is ice-free throughout the year, and landing there would allow German ships to avoid the North Sea and the Baltic, where they were more open to attack by the British Royal Navy and the RAF. Stalin readily agreed to provide facilities for unloading and for transporting the cargoes to Germany by rail, via Leningrad. He also agreed immediately when, next day, the Germans proposed that Schnurre should travel to Moscow at the beginning of the week, to meet Foreign Trade Commissar Anastas Mikoyan, to 'get the Soviet deliveries of raw materials off to a quick start and, if possible, have them increased'. In view of this, any precautions taken to cover a possible German betrayal must be seen as little more than prudent insurance – and yet another indication of Stalin's permanently suspicious nature.

What the Soviet leader was far more concerned with at that stage was the tricky business of getting the timing for his move exactly right. It was a delicate decision requiring fine judgement in a very fluid situation. If he sent in the Red Army too soon, before the Poles had been finished, he would not only be faced with the possibility of having to fight them, he would also be laying himself open to charges of aggression. What was more, he might then find Britain and France at war with the Soviet Union, which would no longer be regarded as neutral, and this might well bring in the United States against him, too.

Equally important was the effect a premature invasion would have domestically, within the Soviet Union. Even an absolute dictator – which Stalin was not – has to sell his policies to his people if he is to survive, particularly if he is asking them to risk their lives. As it was, the rapid German victories were already giving him as many headaches in this area as in preparing his armed forces. It was difficult enough persuading the Soviet people to accept the pact in the first place, after so many years of anti-Nazi propaganda; they had barely begun reconciling themselves to the idea of Germans as their friends when they started to hear of the Wehrmacht's savage successes in Poland. Most people had vivid memories of German strength during the first world war, and the latest news rekindled all their fears and suspicions.

Ideally, Stalin needed time to convince his people – and the other members of the Politburo – that the friendship with Germany was in their best interests, that it was in fact safe to lie down with the wolf. But time was now a luxury which was denied to him. If the consequences of moving too soon were serious, those of delaying too long were potentially disastrous. The danger of allowing the Germans to advance too far would be even greater and the temptation to the German generals to attack the Soviet Union would be even stronger. But worse still was the possibility that the Poles might surrender or sign an armistice with Germany – and once that was done any action by the Red Army would in effect be the start of a new war. Since this was clearly unthinkable, Stalin would then be left without his share of the booty.

The ideal time for Stalin to move was immediately after the capture of Warsaw. Once the capital had fallen, he could claim that the Polish government had ceased to exist, and that the Red Army was being sent in to restore order. In a particularly frank and cynical conversation on 10 September, Molotov told Schulenburg that the Soviet government had planned to say that because Poland was falling apart, the Soviets had to 'come to the aid of the Ukrainians and White Russians "threatened" by Germany'. This, he said, would serve the dual purpose of making the intervention plausible to the masses without making the Soviet Union look like the aggressor.

However, Molotov was now realising that his congratulations on the fall of Warsaw had been premature. Hitler's Panzer commanders had discovered that tanks were not suited to street fighting. They had been driven back by the Poles from the suburbs of the city, and Hitler had decided to leave Warsaw to the artillery and the Luftwaffe to bombard into submission. For Stalin, this offered a welcome breathing space. Schulenburg deduced that in saying they would move within a few days, Molotov had 'promised more yesterday than the Red Army can live up to'. The Soviet Premier, while boasting that over three million men were already mobilised, told him that the military still needed possibly two or three weeks more for their preparations. Obviously, Stalin now felt that the second phase of the German campaign, tightening the noose around the defeated Polish army, which had started on 9 September with Hitler's third directive of the war, would take a little while to complete.

And a besieged city, even under heavy aerial bombardment, could hold out for a considerable period.

In addition to his concerns about the Western allies and the Soviet people, Stalin had another factor which was heavily influencing the need to play for time. At the other end of his empire, in the Far East, the Japanese problem was not yet settled. There was still the risk, albeit considerably reduced, of a war on two fronts for the Soviet Union, as well as for Germany.

The last phase of the border war with the Japanese Kwantung Army had begun at exactly the same time as Hitler wrote his personal letter to Stalin asking him to receive Ribbentrop. From then until the start of the war in Poland, the battle had raged on the Khalkin-Gol river. Throughout all the negotiations with Germany, Stalin had had the Far-Eastern situation in the back of his mind.

In fact, the build-up for the final battle had started at much the same time as Schnurre had invited Astakhov and Babarin to dinner at Ewest's in Berlin. After a particularly bloody artillery duel lasting two days, Soviet General Georgi Zhukov had succeeded in pinning down the Japanese in their trenches, while he made full use of his control of the air to cover his supply lines bringing fresh troops and *matériel* from his railheads some 750 kilometres away, and to pound the Japanese supply lines.

From the end of July, Japanese military intelligence was able to intercept Soviet wireless traffic. From this, they learned of the preparations for Zhukov's coming offensive – but they still had no idea of its scale or timing. In the crucial week from 12 to 19 August, low cloud and poor visibility prevented Japanese aerial reconnaissance planes from spotting Soviet troop concentrations, thus aiding Zhukov's own deception operations in confusing the Japanese.

In his efforts to convince the enemy that he was still thinking in purely defensive terms, Zhukov resorted to a skilful disinformation campaign: he distributed to his own troops a handbook entitled 'What the Soviet Soldier Must Know in Defence', and made sure that some of them fell into Japanese hands; he transmitted false radio reports about the construction of fortifications and backed this by numerous inquiries about the whereabouts of various pieces of non-existent engineering equipment; he had trucks and tanks, the mufflers removed from their engines, drive backwards and forwards along the front, day and night, to get the Japanese used to the constant noise of revving engines and so mask the sound of his armour massing for the attack.

The Japanese were preparing their own offensive, timed to begin on 24 August. Zhukov was aware of their plans, partly from his own on-the-ground intelligence, partly from aerial observation, and perhaps, as has been suggested by some experts, from information gathered in Tokyo by

Richard Sorge, the Soviet master spy, who is said to have supplied his controllers in Moscow with precise information on the start date.

Zhukov intended to strike first. By 19 August, he had managed to move into position some thirty-five infantry battalions and twenty cavalry squadrons, supported by a force of 346 armoured cars and 498 tanks, some of which were the forerunners of the T-34, which was to become the most successful tank of the second world war. He also had 500 warplanes. Facing him, the Japanese deployed twenty-five infantry battalions and seventeen cavalry squadrons. At last, Zhukov had the kind of superiority in men and arms that he required.

Sunday, 20 August, dawned warm and quiet, with the promise of being a beautiful day. So confident was the Japanese command that the Soviets were not ready to attack that they had allowed a number of senior officers to take weekend leave away from the front, in nearby towns and villages. The Soviets knew this. Zhukov himself said later, 'We took this important factor into consideration when we decided to launch our offensive.'

At 5.45 am, Soviet artillery opened up along the front, and half the air force, 150 bombers supported by 100 fighters, began to hit Japanese positions. At 8.15 am, they returned to repeat the dose. Half an hour later, red signal rockets all along the front announced the start of the Soviet offensive.

Day after day, the savage battle wore on. By 23 August, the Red Army had succeeded in encircling the Japanese, but still the Japanese continued to resist, and to counter-attack at every opportunity. Casualties on both sides were heavy. But Zhukov continued to display the ruthless determination that was characteristic of his generalship. At one point, the commander of a division reported to him for fresh orders after being beaten off with heavy losses when trying to storm vital Japanese fortifications. Zhukov ordered him to attack again. A short while later, Zhukov himself telephoned the divisional commander to find out what was happening.

'When will you be able to start the attack?' he demanded. The commander was doubtful. Zhukov immediately relieved him of his command.

'Hand over the receiver to your Chief of Staff,' he ordered.

When the Chief of Staff came on the line, Zhukov asked him if he could get the division back into action again. The Chief of Staff said he could, whereupon Zhukov told him he was now appointed divisional commander. But when the erstwhile Chief of Staff proved no more successful than his predecessor in launching a fresh attack, he too was relieved of command, and replaced by a man from Zhukov's own staff. Reinforced with artillery and extra air support, the division attacked again, and although it suffered enormous losses, finally succeeded in overrunning the Japanese fortifications.

The last Japanese stronghold on Mongolian soil fell to Soviet troops on 28 August, and by the morning of 31 August Soviet and Mongolian forces had retaken all the disputed territory up to their old frontier line. The Japanese had been defeated by an up-to-date, mechanised army in which artillery, tanks and aircraft had been skilfully and flexibly combined to produce a quality of firepower which the Japanese could never match. The tradition of the samurai had been found wanting, crushed by the T-26 BT and T-28 tanks and the Ilyushin fighter-bomber, just as, during the next month, the Polish cavalry were to be crushed by Hitler's war machine.

But there were those in the Kwantung Army command who were not prepared to accept this analysis, who regarded Khalkin-Gol as nothing more than a tactical set-back. Next time, they bragged, it would be different. Indeed, on 5 September, the general commanding the Kwantung Army announced that he would provide fresh reinforcements for a new offensive in the autumn which, in one mighty blow, would crush what he called this 'mouse-stirring' by the Soviets.

With such a threat still hanging in the east at the same moment that Hitler's destruction of the Poles became clear in the west, Stalin could hardly be blamed for a certain nervousness. However, help was at hand. In Moscow, acting on his own initiative since he had received no instructions, Schulenburg had a series of meeting with the Japanese ambassador, Shigenori Togo, urging him to make a settlement with the Soviet Union. In Tokyo, German Ambassador Ott made similar approaches to the Japanese government, suggesting that Germany would be ready to act as mediator. And on 9 September Ribbentrop himself joined in, telling the Japanese government how important it was to Germany that there should be a settlement between Japan and the Soviet Union.

The special pleading found a receptive audience. Unlike the Kwantung generals, the Japanese government had had enough. They had lost perhaps 55,000 men killed and wounded, against admitted Soviet losses of only 10,000, and had no wish to repeat the lesson they had learned about the growing strength of the Soviet colossus. On 13 September Ambassador Togo saw Molotov and suggested they try to find a formula which would enable the border disputes to be settled with honour. Although Molotov reacted with his customary stiffness, Stalin seized on this approach with eagerness and relief.

The official cease-fire was signed in Moscow three days later.

On 14 September, Molotov called Schulenburg to his office and, without mentioning the Japanese business, told him at 4 pm that the Red Army had miraculously 'reached a state of preparedness sooner than anticipated', so they would not have to wait the two or three weeks which he had talked about before! He asked Schulenburg to let him know as accurately as possible when the capture of Warsaw could be counted on: as soon as Warsaw fell, the Red Army would move in.

Only then did Stalin start preparing his own people for the next move, unleashing a propaganda campaign which had an oddly familiar ring to it: *Pravda, Izvestia* and Tass statements to the rest of the world denounced Polish border violations and provocations, and about Polish ill-treatment of racial minorities. The only difference between this and Hitler's campaign was that the minorities were now Ukrainians and White Russians instead of *Volksdeutsche*. The similarities did not go unnoticed outside the Soviet Union. 'Russia is showing signs of restlessness,' Ciano confided to his diary, with the comment, 'How unimaginative people are when they intend to quarrel.'

Some of the oppressed minorities in Poland were starting to play their own part that day. As German forces from East Prussia crossed the Narev river near Modlin and began their encirclement of Warsaw, and Guderian's tanks completed their 200-mile dash to Brest-Litovsk, so General List's 14th Army, which had launched its attack from Slovakia, completed the cutting-off of the Polish–Ukrainian city of Lvov. In the city, the Ukrainian population rose and started attacking Polish units.

The total dissolution of Poland could not now be far off. The first members of the Polish government had fled to Romania the night before, in fifteen civil and military aircraft which the Romanians immediately interned. The Poles included Finance Minister Kwiatkowski and the governor of the Bank of Poland. It was rumoured – though they hotly denied it – that they had brought with them the Polish gold reserves. The rest of the government, including Moscicki and Beck, hovered nervously on the other side of the frontier, ready for immediate flight.

Ribbentrop judged the moment to be right to tell Molotov that Warsaw was about to fall, and that he should keep his and Stalin's promise to send in the Red Army. At the same time, he objected to the proposed Soviet statement justifying their intervention as being necessary to protect the minorities against the Germans. Not only would it make Germany and the Soviet Union look like enemies, he said, but it was not true!

When Schulenburg delivered this message, at 6 pm on 16 September, Molotov told him Stalin was talking at that moment to his military leaders, and would give Schulenburg the day and time for the invasion later that night. He did so at 2 am, in the presence of Molotov and Voroshilov: the Red Army, he announced, would cross the Soviet border along the entire frontier from Polotsk to Kamenets-Podolsk at 6 am that morning, 17 September. After keeping Germany waiting for two whole weeks, he was now giving them barely four hours' notice – demonstrating once again how devastatingly fast he could move when he chose.

For the German military attaché, General Köstring, who had been called to the Kremlin along with Schulenburg and Hilger, it was too fast.

When Stalin said the Red Air Force would start bombing the area east of Lvov that morning, and that the German army and Luftwaffe near that area should be warned immediately in order to avoid incidents, Köstring became very agitated, and pleaded, 'almost desperately' according to Hilger, that there was simply not enough time to get word to all the troops in the field. Since the German army knew nothing of the agreement with the Soviets, clashes would be unavoidable.

Voroshilov airily brushed aside Köstring's fears. With no trace of irony, he said he was certain that the 'organisational genius of the German army would surely find time, even on such short notice, to relay the message'. Schulenburg, ever the diplomat, suggested that it might be better if, for that day at least, Soviet aircraft did not fly too close to the proposed demarcation line.

In the event, it was more by good luck than good management that there were remarkably few clashes between the two forces. The secret of the additional protocol to the pact was so secure that when the first news of the Soviet entry into Poland was received, even so high an officer as Major-General Jodl, chief of the OKW operations staff, was prompted to ask: 'Against whom?'

In a further example of the speed with which he could move, Stalin turned to the question of a joint commission to co-ordinate military activities. Ribbentrop had suggested that representatives of both powers should be sent to a point on the boundary line, possibly Bialystok, to work together. 'Agreed,' said Stalin – the Soviet commission would arrive there next day. Any military questions that needed to be dealt with at a higher level would be handled by Voroshilov and Köstring.

There was one other matter that called for agreement that night, and once again Stalin showed his smiling, affable face. He read out the proposed text of his note to the Poles, informing them of the Soviet action. Schulenburg objected to the wording, which still used the pretext of protecting the Ukrainian and White Russian minorities from the Germans as the justification for Soviet intervention. When he had spoken to Molotov about this, the Soviet Premier had conceded that it might be 'jarring to German sensibilities', but pleaded with them 'not to stumble over this piece of straw'.

The truth of the matter was probably that the wording was Stalin's own work, and Molotov did not dare to change it. Stalin agreed to do so immediately, and 'with the utmost willingness' according to Schulenburg. The result was an extraordinary piece of double-think, laying the blame entirely on the Polish government for leaving the minorities 'to their fate' by ceasing to exist. Nowhere was there a single word of sympathy. The document is so remarkable that it is worth reading in full. The style is recognisably Stalin's own:

The Polish–German war has revealed the internal bankruptcy of the

ESTONIA

Tartu●

Baltic Sea

Windau (Ventspiels)●

Riga●

LATVIA

R. Dvina

Polotsk●

Libau (Liepaja)●

Memel (Klaipeda)●

LITHUANIA

Kaunas●

Vilna●

Gdynia● Danzig

Königsberg●

East Prussia

Suwalki●

Minsk●

Stettin●

Dirschau●

R. Vistula

R. Narev

Bialystok●

Berlin●

GERMANY

Annexed to Germany

Modlin●

R. Bug

Brest-Litovsk●

USSR

Warsaw●

GOVERNMENT

POLAND

Breslau●

Radom●

Lublin●

GENERAL

Chelm●

Kiev●

Gleiwitz●

R. San

Cracow●

Teschen●

Krosno●

Lvov●

Drohobycz●

Carp

Boryslaw●

Vienna●

R. Pruth

Ruthenia

Bukovina●

Mts

Budapest●

Duna (Danube)

- - - - 1939 Frontiers
〰〰〰 Russo-German Treaty 1939
- · - · - Present frontiers

0   100 Miles
0   200 Kilometres

Polish state. During the course of ten days of military operations, Poland has lost all her industrial areas and cultural centres. Warsaw no longer exists as the capital of Poland. The Polish government has disintegrated and no longer shows any signs of life. This means that the Polish state and its government have in fact ceased to exist. Therefore the agreements concluded between the USSR and Poland have lost their validity. Left to shift for herself and bereft of leadership, Poland has become a convenient field for all kinds of hazards and unforeseen contingencies which may constitute a threat to the USSR. For these reasons, the USSR, which has hitherto remained neutral, can no longer adopt a neutral attitude towards these facts.

The Soviet government can furthermore not be indifferent to the fact that its kindred Ukrainian and Belorussian people, who live on Polish territory and who have been left to the mercy of fate, have been left defenceless.

In view of this situation, the Soviet government has directed the High Command of the Red Army to give the order to its troops to cross the Polish frontier and take under their protection the life and property of the population of Western Ukraine and Western Belorussia.

At the same time, the Soviet government intends to take all measures to extricate the Polish people from the unfortunate war into which they have been dragged by their unwise leaders, and to enable them to live a peaceful life.

This wording may have suited the Germans, but it certainly did not suit the Poles. When Molotov's deputy, Potemkin, summoned Polish Ambassador Grzybowski to the Foreign Commissariat in the early hours, just as the first Soviet units crossed the frontier, the ambassador was justifiably suspicious, and asked to be informed of the contents of the document. When told, he refused point-blank to accept it, and marched out. Arriving back at his embassy, he found a Soviet messenger had beaten him to it, and was waiting on the doorstep to hand the note over. Again, Grzybowski refused, and sent the man away. But Potemkin would not accept defeat – he had the note delivered by the Moscow Post Office, with the morning mail.

At 8.45 am, copies were delivered by messenger to all the other embassies and legations in Moscow, together with a reaffirmation of the Soviet Union's neutrality. Neither the Soviet nor the 'disintegrated' Polish government ever acknowledged the existence of a state of war.

TOP: Molotov signs the non-aggression pact. Behind him (*left to right*) are Marshal Shaposhnikov, Richard Schulze – pulled into the picture by Stalin – Ribbentrop and Stalin

BELOW: 'A second Bismarck . . .' Hitler's ecstatic reception for Ribbentrop on his return from Moscow, watched by a less enthusiastic Ernst von Weizsäcker (*right*). Liaison man Walter Hewel stands next to Hitler

ABOVE Colonel-General (later Field
Marshal) Wilhelm Keitel, chief of
the High Command of the Armed
Forces, the OKW, confers with
Hitler during a flight in *Immelmann
III*, the Führer's Condor airliner

RIGHT General (later Field Marshal)
Walter von Brauchitsch, commander-
in-chief of the German army, with
Hitler at the front

OPPOSITE PAGE:
TOP The Polish response to Hitler's
armoured Blitzkrieg – mounted
cavalry complete with lances and
swords, confidently expecting to be
charging down Berlin's Unter den
Linden

BELOW Herman Göring, wearing one
of his less flamboyant uniforms,
salutes with his field marshal's baton.
He struggled frantically to keep
Britain and France out of the war

Lieutenant-General (later Colonel-General) Franz Halder, army chief of staff, anti-Nazi and avid diarist

RIGHT Is Warsaw burning? Hitler watches the death throes of the Polish capital through an artillery periscope

Comrades-in-arms – German troops chat happily with a Red Army tank crew as they prepare for a joint victory parade in Brest-Litovsk

TOP The bloodless invasion: Red Army troops march into the Polish city, and former Lithuanian capital, Vilnius, largely ignored by the local population

BELOW David Low's famous cartoon of 20 September 1939 brilliantly sums up the Western view of the fourth partition of Poland and the pact in general

TOP 'Danzig greets its Führer!' The banner reflects the tumultuous welcome given to Hitler by the former Free City on 19 September 1939

BELOW Hauling their possessions on horse-drawn carts, Germans being 'repatriated' from Soviet-occupied territory cross the demarcation line at Hrubieszow, escorted by Soviet guards

ABOVE Erich Sommer, here wearing his Foreign Ministry dress uniform, served with the boundary commission on the demarcation line before joining Ribbentrop's office in Berlin

TOP RIGHT Finnish envoy (and later President) Juho Paasikivi and Finance Minister Väinö Tanner depart by train from Helsinki to continue negotiations with Stalin in Moscow

BELOW At every station along the line to the Soviet Union, crowds of Finns turned out to sing *A Mighty Fortress is our God*. Here Paasikivi and Tanner listen to the inhabitants of Viipuri, last stop before the frontier

Finnish 'ghost troops' near Soviet lines north of Lake Ladoga. Moving silently at speeds of 20–30 miles per hour they harassed and destroyed Red Army units in lightning raids

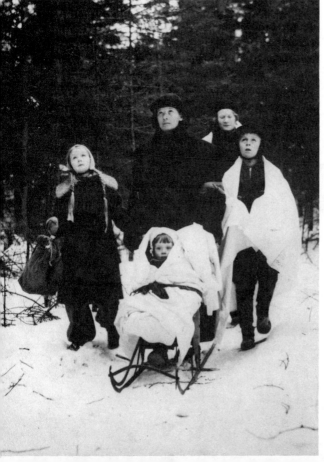

Fleeing from Soviet air attacks near Helsinki, Finnish women and children use bed sheets as improvised camouflage

31

THE FOURTH PARTITION

The fourth partition of Poland began at 5.40 am on Sunday, 17 September 1939, when some forty divisions of the Red Army crossed the border on two main fronts, one on either side of the huge Pripet marshes.

To the south, the Ukrainian front stretched down to the Carpathian mountains and was commanded by General S. K. Timoshenko, one of Stalin's most senior and most trusted officers, who was to take over the Defence Commissariat from Voroshilov within a year. Timoshenko had fought with distinction over this same territory during the war with Poland in 1920, when he led the 4th Cavalry Division. He was now in charge of the Kiev Military District, the Soviet Ukraine, and was himself a Ukrainian, born in Bessarabia, so the prospect of bringing back the western Ukraine into the Soviet fold had a special significance for him.

The northern front, the Belorussian, ran from the marshes to the Dvina river and the borders of Lithuania. This was thought to be less potentially troublesome and was under the command of Major-General M. P. Kovalev, one of Stalin's most recent promotions.

The Soviet forces on both fronts were a hastily gathered collection of cavalry, tanks and infantry supported by tachankas – horse-drawn heavy machine-gun carts. They did not need to be particularly strong, for they met little opposition: those scattered parts of the Polish army which remained in the eastern parts of the country, or which had been driven there by the Wehrmacht, were totally confused by their arrival.

The first warning of the Red Army's intervention had been given in radio bulletins, followed by leaflets dropped from aircraft calling on the Poles to receive the Soviet troops as liberators coming to defend them. When the first tanks and vehicles appeared, they were carrying white flags, and their commanders shouted to any Polish soldiers they met that they had come to help them against the Germans.

It may well be that at the outset many of the Soviet soldiers actually believed this to be the truth. Certainly, many people inside the Soviet

Union did. In Moscow, Chip Bohlen in the US embassy heard that workers in factories had leapt on their machines and cheered when they heard the news that the Red Army was going in, assuming immediately that their troops were going to fight the Germans. Evidently the workers had not had enough time to digest Stalin's new line. But they were swiftly enlightened when the party officials in each workplace explained that the Red Army was in fact moving in to take back those territories which belonged to the Soviet Union.

For the most part, the local populations in Poland greeted the Soviet troops with relief. Anything, they felt, was better than the Germans, who were not only fighting with terrible savagery, but who were also following up their front-line troops with Heydrich's SS *Einsatzgruppen*, special task forces whose job was noted by army Chief of Staff Halder as, 'Housecleaning: Jews, intelligentsia, clergy, nobility'. This bland description covered the systematic murder of everyone in those classes, with the intention of decapitating the Polish nation by depriving it of all forms of leadership, thus turning it into a servile labour force for Germany. Polish children, Hitler had decreed, were to be taught only to write their names, count up to a maximum of 500, and obey the rule: 'It is God's command that they should be obedient to Germans, honourable, industrious and brave.' The *Einsatzgruppen* went about their business with such enthusiasm that by 27 September Heydrich could claim that only three per cent of the Polish upper classes had survived.

When the Polish government had called on all Poles, civilians as well as those in the armed forces, women as well as men, to fight the German invaders with every means they could devise – women had been urged to destroy tanks by pouring petrol over them and setting them alight, for instance – Hitler seized the excuse to order total war. Every village, whether it contained military units or not, was seen as a legitimate target for attack. Everything that moved on the roads, refugee columns as well as soldiers, was mercilessly machine-gunned by fighter aircraft, or dive-bombed by the wailing Stukas.

In comparison, Soviet troops behaved impeccably during the first few days of the Soviet occupation. Everything they obtained from the local population was paid for on the spot. There was no looting, little brutality, and very little killing, except in odd spots of resistance. Some of the resistance, it must be said, came from Ukrainian nationalists who had until then been happily killing Poles and Germans as part of their struggle for a totally independent Ukraine.

Liliana Zuker-Bujanowska, then a young girl who had fled from the advancing Germans with her mother, paints a vivid picture of the first Soviet troops arriving in the little town of Chelm, just west of the river Bug, near Lublin: 'They came without firing a shot. The streets were empty for a short while, then some came out to welcome the soldiers, some even had flowers for them, others sat quietly behind closed doors and waited . . . Within a few hours, a whole Russian division with tanks and soldiers on foot poured into town. The soldiers looked tired, their coats were torn. The machine guns hung from their shoulders on their straps. Their face were dirty and harsh-looking. The noise was unbelievable. The buildings shook. Curiosity overcame fear, and children began to run into the streets to look at these enormous machines. A few soldiers stopped and talked to the children, explaining how the machinery worked and asking where they could buy watches. They wanted to buy any kind of watch, as long as it ticked.

'The next day, what we thought was a victory parade turned out to be a funeral for two soldiers killed near Chelm. The Russians dug a grave in the middle of town, covered it with red flowers, and put a red fence round it with a big red star in the middle.'

Some Polish units, especially those of the border guards, put up a spirited resistance to the Soviet advance, but eventually most realised the position was hopeless, and submitted with a grim resignation. In at least one instance, a Polish unit which found itself trapped in a wood with Germans on one side and Soviets on the other, took a vote on which way to go. The result was an overwhelming majority in favour of surrendering to the Red Army, in the belief that they would stand a better chance of surviving in Soviet hands.

Their belief was generally justified, though it did not take into account the incredible hardships involved in survival for any prisoners in the Soviet system. Initially, the Red Army received Polish units peacefully. But the 'soft' approach was short-lived. Officers and NCOs were immediately separated from their men, in order to remove all leadership, and then began the long, slow process of transferring all the prisoners out to Siberia, a journey which for most lasted all through the winter, and which many did not survive.

It is difficult to find reliable figures – they vary greatly depending on their source – but somewhere between 180,000 and 250,000 men were shipped out to the wastelands, including at least 10,000 officers and twelve generals. Many of them never returned. Some died of cold, hunger, sickness or disease. Others met a more sinister end. In 1943, when their advance into the Soviet Union had reached the Katan Forest, west of Smolensk, the Germans claimed to have discovered mass graves containing the remains of over 4,000 men. These they identified, through scraps of uniform and dog-tags, as Polish officers murdered by the NKVD on Stalin's orders. The Russians indignantly denied this, pointing the finger at the Germans, who had already committed many such massacres. But to the men in the graves, the argument was academic.

Certainly, the Soviets were at that time determined to do everything

they could to prevent any possibility of a Polish army ever being re-
formed, either in Poland or abroad. General Anders, who was captured
near the Romanian border, noticed that every village he was driven
through on his way to local Red Army headquarters was bristling with
troops, all busy digging fortifications facing north. When he questioned
a Russian major about Soviet intentions, he was bluntly told that the
troops were there to stop Poles escaping south into Romania. Another
Soviet officer told him: 'We are now good friends of the Germans, and
together we will fight international capitalism. Poland was the tool of
England, and she had to perish for that. There will never again be
another Poland. The Germans keep us fully informed about the
movement of Polish troops towards Hungary or Romania.'

Stalin was clearly enjoying his revenge – no doubt equally relished by
Timoshenko among others – for the Polish victory in 1920. It was a
revenge which came remarkably cheap: during the whole process of
occupying eastern Poland, Soviet casualties totalled only 737 killed and
1,862 wounded. Hitler, by contrast, lost 13,111 killed and missing and
27,278 wounded.

When the two victorious armies met, there were few of the incidents
which General Köstring had feared. Near Lvov, known to the Germans
as Lemberg, German troops mistook their Soviet friends for Poles, and
opened fire on them, but the mistake was realised before the clash could
develop into a full-scale engagement, and the two armies joined hands
peacefully there, as everywhere else. There was a great deal of
fraternisation, toast-drinking, and even joint military parades in which
Soviet and German tanks drove alternately, one behind the other.

On 22 September, Voroshilov and Köstring signed an agreement to
cover the military occupation of Poland, and the joint commission set up
shop in Bialystok to see that it was put into immediate operation.
German units which, being unaware of the secret protocol, had raced far
into eastern Poland, were instructed to withdraw to the four-river line.
In some cases this involved pulling back as much as 125 miles. The Red
Army thereupon moved forward to the line, which became a military
frontier pending the final political settlement.

If the entry of the Red Army into Poland signified the consummation of
the marriage between Germany and the Soviet Union, the next few days
brought the little strains and tensions often encountered by newly-weds
adjusting to each other's needs and desires. It was the Soviet Union's
turn to be annoyed first, on the very first day of the honeymoon,
17 September. In spite of the fact that Stalin had said he did not want to
issue a communiqué to the press for a few days, Ribbentrop insisted on
drafting one, and sending it Moscow for approval. Stalin did not
approve. He told Schulenburg, in Molotov's office, that the draft text

presented the facts all too frankly. However, he agreed that there should be a joint communiqué after all, and promptly took out a pencil and proceeded to compose a version in his own hand, which wrapped things up a little. When it was shown to Hitler, he was immensely impressed, describing it as brilliant and demanding to know who had written it.

Stalin was even more annoyed next day, by a report from his deputy military attaché in Berlin. It seemed that when this attaché, Colonel Michael Belyakov, had been taken by Admiral Canaris to the OKW headquarters in the Bendlerstrasse for a full briefing on the latest situation, Warlimont, head of the operations section, had shown him a map on which the future German border was drawn. This ran along the Vistula and through Warsaw, as agreed, but then included the city of Lvov and the oil-producing area of Drohobycz in the German sector. Belyakov listened 'poker-faced and without a word' as Warlimont stressed the importance of the Drohobycz area to Germany, not knowing about the secret protocol which had placed it in the Soviet zone.

Stalin was furious when he heard about this, and personally telephoned Ribbentrop to complain of what he saw as an obvious violation of the Moscow agreement. Ribbentrop did his best to placate him, then hurried across the railway siding to Hitler's train, to complain to the Führer about 'the military meddling in and upsetting his plans'. Hitler, who was still revelling in his role as a military leader, told him dismissively: 'When diplomats make mistakes in war, it's always supposed to be the fault of the soldiers.'

It was left to the ever-reliable Schulenburg to calm things down by assuring Stalin and Molotov that it was all a misunderstanding, and that what Warlimont had shown Belyakov must have been a tentative suggestion for the demarcation line which the military commission would be negotiating in detail. Neither Schulenburg nor the Soviet leaders seem to have mentioned the fact that *Izvestia* that day had published a map of Poland showing no less than two thirds of the country as Soviet.

In fact, both countries were striking postures ready for the haggling over details which they knew had to come. Ribbentrop's anger at the 'meddling' by the military may well have been brought on by the fact that the line on the map was not accidental, but an accurate representation of what he hoped to gain: he telephoned Köstring later and told him this was the settlement he wanted for the military border.

Stalin and Molotov refused point-blank. They would not consider the revised line even as a temporary measure, but insisted that the agreement of 23 August must stand. The Soviet government, Molotov explained, could not disappoint the Ukrainians, who considered the entire area up to the river San as their national territory. But to sugar the pill, he offered to let Germany have an area between East Prussia and Lithuania known as the Suwalki triangle, but excluding the forest of Augustow. The horse-trading had begun.

For the moment, Hitler was content to leave the question of political frontiers in the east to Ribbentrop. He had more pressing and more enjoyable things to occupy himself with as he continued playing the war lord, travelling to the front each day to watch the progress of his armies through binoculars, often exposing himself to great danger. On 19 September, he crossed the frontier into Danzig territory at Zoppot, where he was greeted by a jubilant Gauleiter Forster, and moved his headquarters into the luxurious and undamaged Kasino Hotel overlooking the Gulf of Danzig. After being cooped up for two whole weeks in cramped railcars which were daily turned into ovens by the baking sun, the generals, aides, secretaries and servants revelled in the fresh sea air. Taking breakfast on the hotel's broad terrace, they were entertained by the spectacle of the *Schleswig-Holstein* and another old warship, the *Schlesien*, shelling the Polish fortress of Hela, clearly visible seventeen kilometres away across the glassy waters of the Gulf.

'With their high funnels and superstructure,' Paul Schmidt recalled later, 'they made the whole scene look like some old picture of a naval engagement, especially when the Polish artillery retaliated and water spouts shot up around the ships. Our hotel was beyond the range of the Polish guns, otherwise not much would have been left of that fine building. Punctually at noon, the "naval engagement" was broken off, the ships withdrew, and the whole performance was repeated at the same time next day.' The destruction of Hela, like the other two remaining enclaves of Polish resistance, Modlin and Warsaw, was being methodically undertaken by the Germans.

From Zoppot, Hitler set out on the afternoon of 19 September to make his triumphal entry into the city of Danzig. His reception was predictably wild. Dense crowds thronged the swastika-decorated streets, packing the pavement and craning from every window and balcony along his route. Despite a directive issued on 11 September saying that for the duration of the war Hitler would receive no flowers, and that any intended for him should be given to the soldiers of the German Wehrmacht, blooms rained down from every side until the streets were close-carpeted with colour.

After reviewing parades and guards of honour, he made his way through the cheering populace to the ancient guildhall, the Artushof, a beautiful, columned building dating from the fourteenth century, the golden age of the Germanic knightly orders. But in spite of all the acclamation, Hitler was not happy. A Nazi acquaintance told William Shirer, there to report the scene for CBS, that 'the old man' was in a terrible rage, because he had counted on making the victory speech he was about to deliver in Warsaw, but had been foiled by the refusal of the Poles inside the capital city to surrender.

Shirer thought the Nazi notables surrounding Hitler as he strode imperiously up the aisle to the platform, including Himmler and Keitel, looked like 'a pack of Chicago gangsters' in their dusty field-grey uniforms, most of them needing a shave. They led the applause as Hitler wound himself into the calculated fury of his speech.

'I stand for the first time,' he began, 'on the ground which German settlers acquired five hundred years before the first white men settled in the present State of New York. For a further five hundred years this ground was, and remained, German. It will, let everybody be assured, remain German!'

Most of the speech followed the usual line of attacking Poland: 'Poland chose war, and now she has it . . . Never before in history could the saying be more exactly fulfilled, "The Lord will break them in pieces, the horse and his rider, the chariot and its rider".' He berated Britain, his face 'flaming up into a hysterical rage', according to Shirer, whenever he mentioned her. He did, however, make a slight gesture towards peace, saying, 'I have no war aims with the British and French. My sympathies are with the French *poilu* – what he is fighting for he does not know!'

For some reason – perhaps because he knew there were so many Catholics in Danzig – he abandoned his usual anti-religious stance and called on the Almighty, rather than Providence, 'who now has blessed our arms, to give other peoples comprehension of how useless this war will be . . . and to cause reflection on the blessings of peace'. His own attitude to the blessings of peace, however, seemed somewhat ambivalent, as he went on to maintain his hard-line boast: 'If this war lasts three years, the word "capitulation" will not be heard – nor will it after four, five, six or seven years!'

At no time during the speech did he make any mention of his new allies in the east, the Soviet Union. He gave Stalin no thanks for the invaluable service he had rendered. He did not even hint at the deal that had been struck. It was perhaps just as well he did not, for although he did not know it then, Stalin was about to make some very significant adjustments to that deal.

While Hitler was finishing his speech in Danzig, Stalin was making the first overt move in the game. He had a particular prize in view and was determined to win it, but had known that he could not get it in the first round. Therefore, he had built certain bargaining counters into the agreement of 23 August, for use in obtaining his prize when the time was right. Now, that time was rapidly approaching.

The prize Stalin wanted was Lithuania. In his strategy for securing all his frontiers, Lithuania was a vital component, for if it were allowed to become a German satellite, it could provide Hitler with a direct route into the Soviet Union. Estonia and Latvia were important, too, but in order to be sure of his north-west borders, he had to have all three Baltic states. The Germans, however, set great store by Lithuania, and to have demanded it during the negotiations for the pact would have been risking breakdown. So Stalin, like the oriental he often claimed to be, had had to lay his plans and bide his time, having provided himself with something to give away in exchange. That something, his bargaining counter, was central Poland.

For Stalin the Poles spelled trouble. They had always been aggressively anti-Russian, throughout history. Having a Polish population within the Soviet Union would be like having a particularly prickly burr under the saddle of a horse that was already hard to handle. The Belorussians and even the Ukrainians he could cope with. Indeed, it was a matter of pride to him to reunite these 'lost peoples' with their brothers, so that their entire nations were contained within the Soviet empire. But the partition plan agreed in the pact left the Poles split between Germany and the Soviet Union, a sure recipe for resentment and ultimately for disaster.

The alternative which had been discussed – allowing a small Polish state to exist between the two powers – could be even worse than a divided Poland, for then the Poles would have a cohesive base from which to cause trouble for both of them. What was more, establishing such a 'Congress Poland', or the equivalent of the grand duchy envisaged by Napoleon in the previous century, would mean Stalin relinquishing some of the territory he had gained, while getting nothing in return. He had therefore taken great pains during the negotiations of 23 August to ensure that he got a sizeable slice of Poland beyond the Belorussian and Ukrainian areas. Now, he said, he favoured a straight division of the country along the Pissa–Narev–Vistula–San line. This of course would mean fresh negotiations, which he wanted to start at once, in Moscow rather than Berlin, since they would have to be handled on the Soviet side by 'persons in the highest positions of authority who cannot leave the Soviet Union'. In other words, by himself.

On the German side, Hitler was quite happy to leave the negotiations to Ribbentrop, since he had other things on his mind at that time. In his suite of rooms at the Kasino Hotel he was not only playing the role of supreme military commander but also taking important steps in his civil campaign for racial purity. He summoned his constitutional and medical advisers to discuss plans for organised euthanasia, to rid Germany of most of its three quarters of a million insane or mentally ill. Although he had had this in mind for some time and had for several months been authorising mercy killings of malformed infants and those who were terminally ill and suffering unbearable pain, he now saw the disposal of mental patients as a matter of urgency: they were occupying some quarter of a million hospital beds which he needed for the military casualties in his forthcoming campaigns. So, in his airy, seaside rooms he calmly discussed with his experts the best methods of killing. Was carbon monoxide gas faster and more humane than barbiturates? He asked Dr Brandt to research the question and provide the answer.

When the subject became bogged down in discussions of the legal and ethical niceties, Hitler decided to bypass the experts in order to get things moving faster. He had an order drawn up on his own private stationery, headed with a gold-embossed eagle and the simple legend 'Adolf Hitler', which he pre-dated, significantly, to 1 September:

> Reichsleiter Bouhler and Dr Brandt, MD, are herewith given full responsibility to enlarge the powers of certain specified doctors, so that they can grant those who are by all human standards incurably ill a merciful death, after the most critical assessment possible of their medical condition.
>
> ADOLF HITLER

Despite the fancy phrasing, this was laying the foundations for other, less discriminating programmes of extermination. For the millions of people trapped in central Poland, the position of the demarcation line suddenly assumed a new and more terrifying significance.

For Hitler, the decision he had taken seemed only to raise his spirits still higher. At midnight he led a manservant carrying a silver tray of champagne-filled glasses into General Jodl's room, where a group of senior officers were celebrating Keitel's birthday. Although the room was thick with cigar smoke, for once he did not appear to mind, and he stayed for over an hour, sipping mineral water and conversing animatedly.

Ribbentrop was disappointed that Molotov would not be visiting Berlin for the final political settlement. He would have enjoyed basking in the glory of such a visit, and showing off his new Russian friend to his rivals in the Nazi Party. But he did not argue when he realised that it was Stalin who wanted it that way – and he quickly decided he would travel to Moscow again himself, rather than leave the negotiations to Schulenburg, because, as he put it: 'In view of the full powers granted me by the Führer, thus making it possible to dispense with further consultations, etc., negotiations can be brought to a speedier conclusion.' Molotov said he welcomed the idea of Ribbentrop's coming and that 27–28 September would be the best time.

Until Ribbentrop heard from Schulenburg, 25 September had been a most satisfactory day for the German Foreign Minister. He had entertained the Japanese general, Count Terauchi, to an excellent dinner in the hotel at Zoppot, and had enjoyed telling him of his conversations with Stalin in the Kremlin. Stalin, he said, had told him: 'If the Japanese want war, they can have war, but if they want a settlement, they can have that, too.' He had boasted of his personal achievement in negotiating the pact with the Soviet Union, and emphasised how beneficial it would be for Japan. He had discussed the possibility of Japanese military action against Britain in South-East Asia.

Earlier that day, Terauchi had been taken to the front, where Hitler had watched through binoculars from the roof of a sports stadium just outside Warsaw as the final artillery bombardment of the city started. It had all been most satisfactory.

And then, an hour after midnight, had come the message from Moscow: Stalin had personally told Schulenburg that in order to avoid 'anything that might in future create friction between Germany and the Soviet Union . . . he considered it wrong to leave an independent residual Poland'. He proposed that the purely Polish areas to the east of the demarcation line, including the province of Lublin and the eastern half of Warsaw province up to the river Bug, should be added to Germany's share. In return, Germany should waive her claim to Lithuania. He had gone on to say that he intended 'to take up the solution of the problem of the Baltic countries in accordance with the protocol of 23 August immediately' – specifically naming Estonia, Latvia and Lithuania, but not mentioning Finland – and that he expected the unstinting support of the German government in this.

Stalin's move threw Ribbentrop into a spin. He had barely twenty-four hours to consider the implications of the new proposals before he was due in Moscow. It was nowhere near enough for such a major item. Only that morning, Hitler had issued his fourth directive of the war, ordering that sufficient army and Luftwaffe units were to be left in the east 'to put a quick end to Polish resistance continuing behind the line of demarcation', and that the flow of refugees from the east was to be stopped immediately, apart from *Volksdeutsche* and Ukrainian activists. The directive then gave instructions for sufficient forces to be kept ready in East Prussia 'to occupy Lithuania quickly, even in the case of armed resistance'.

Once again, Stalin's timing was devastating. Both Hitler and Ribbentrop had been taken completely by surprise.

32

'IS MY SIGNATURE CLEAR ENOUGH FOR YOU?'

Hitler returned to Berlin on 26 September in a sombre mood, passing the eight-hour train journey from the Pomeranian siding to Stettin station in total silence. Ribbentrop followed in *Heinrich*; Keitel had already returned by air; the other members of the Führer's entourage were kept out of his saloon as he paced to and fro, deep in thought. The only aide in the coach was Colonel von Vormann, who sat by the telephone, sorting papers. There were no calls and no messages during the trip. And when they arrived in Berlin, there were no waiting crowds to greet the conquering hero, or to cheer him through the streets.

Dinner, served at the round table in his residence, was no more lively. It must have come as a relief to everyone when at the end of the meal Hitler rose suddenly and bade them goodnight. He did not retire to bed, however, but went to his study, where Göring was waiting with his Swedish emissary, Birger Dahlerus, to discuss with them what was uppermost in his mind: was there still a chance, now that Poland was destroyed, of a *rapprochement* with Britain?

Although he had been telling his aides and his generals ever since 5 September that he intended to attack in the west as soon as he had finished with the Poles, he still spent half the night briefing the Swedish businessman and persuading him to fly to London yet again next day, to put out peace feelers. He asked Dahlerus to find out if talks might be started using an intermediary, possibly Queen Wilhelmina of the Netherlands. The only proviso he made was that Britain must recognise that Poland was finished, and that neither Germany nor the Soviet Union would ever give up the territories they had regained.

Dahlerus had seen Ogilvie-Forbes, the former counsellor in the British embassy, in Oslo two days before and the message he had received was hopeful. The British diplomat had told him peace negotiations between the Allies and Germany were by no means out of the question. The British might well agree to talks if a formula could be found to safeguard the central European peoples.

This tied in well with the advice Hitler had received from Hans von Moltke, his former ambassador in Warsaw, and from Weizsäcker, that he might be able to settle with the West if a feasible Polish government could be established with whom he could sign a peace treaty. Moltke had suggested creating a new Polish state with twelve to fifteen million inhabitants, which could be acceptable, he thought, both to the Poles and to the West. Once such a treaty was signed, there would be no reason for the Allies not to follow suit.

Hitler still held back from going quite so far, but asked Dahlerus to tell Chamberlain and Halifax that he planned to reorganise Poland and redistribute the population – in other words to oust the Poles from their land and move in German settlers, good breeding stock who would eventually replace them entirely – though this would take fifty to a hundred years to complete. However, he thought a home might be found there for the Jews, which according to Dahlerus was one of the factors the British were concerned about.

In marked contrast to the peace proposals he sent to London with Dahlerus, Hitler called his Commanders-in-Chief to the Chancellery next day and gave them a rousing speech on his plans for an offensive in the west. The attack must be mounted as quickly as possible, he told them, since the British and French were still unprepared – they had not yet fired a shot on land and their only acts of war so far had been a disastrously inefficient raid by the RAF on naval bases at Wilhelmshaven and Brunsbüttel, an unopposed advance by the French army into a useless pocket of no-man's-land, and the sinking by the Royal Navy of one U-boat.

Hitler clearly believed he could hand out the same medicine to the British and French as he had to the Poles: Halder recorded in his diary that he had boasted he would force England down on her knees and smash France into pieces. His original plan had been to stage the attack in the west in October, but the stubborn Polish resistance in Warsaw and Modlin had made this impossible. Now, he set a new date, 12 November. His experience in the first world war, he said, had taught him that any such offensive had to be accomplished before January, when the weather closed in.

But he could achieve his plans in the West only if he could withdraw enough troops from the east in time. And before he could do that, he must not only have subdued the Poles but also have everything completely settled with the Soviet Union. Only then could he pull out his troops with complete confidence.

Whichever way he went in the West – towards peace or war –

everything depended, therefore, on reaching agreement with Stalin as quickly as possible on the ultimate fate of Poland.

Ribbentrop had flown out of Tempelhof airfield heading for Moscow a few minutes after 9 o'clock that morning, Wednesday, 27 September. His party again needed two aircraft. He and his most important aides were flying once more in Hitler's private Condor, *Immelmann III*, but the less important personnel were not given another Condor this time, but the Foreign Ministry's three-engined Junkers 52, the faithful old AMYY. Ribbentrop's SS adjutant, the young Richard Schulze, was put in charge of this plane, which took off three hours ahead of *Immelmann III*, at 6 am, because it was so much slower.

Once again, Ribbentrop demonstrated his amazing stamina by piling into work immediately he was in the air, despite the fact that he had been up most of the night conducting a series of high-powered meetings. The plane was transformed into a flying secretariat, with aides busily running to and fro carrying files and reports, and two stenographers kept fully occupied at their typewriters for the entire journey. Fortunately, weather conditions were good and the flight was smooth, so no one suffered what Andor Henke, a senior counsellor with the mission, described in his account as 'an occupational accident'.

Ribbentrop also held airborne discussions with Soviet Ambassador Shkvarzev, who was travelling with him from Berlin, and Gauleiter Forster from Danzig, who joined the party when they stopped for refuelling and a hurried one-course lunch at the Park Hotel in Königsberg, hosted by the Gauleiter of East Prussia, Erich Koch. During this meal, shortly before midday, news came through of the final capitulation of Warsaw, which everyone, Russians as well as Germans, saw as a good omen for the trip.

Unfortunately, because of a strong following wind, and because no one had allowed for Ribbentrop's stopover of an hour and a quarter in Köningsberg, the Ju-52 carrying the minions arrived over Moscow's Khodynka airfield long before the Condor. The idea had been for the faster Condor to catch up the lumbering tri-motor shortly before Moscow, so that the two aircraft would arrive at the same time, with the Condor landing first. When there was no sign of *Immelmann III*, Schulze ordered his pilot to circle. For the best part of an hour he did so, until his fuel dropped below the safety level and although Ribbentrop's plane was still nowhere near, he had to land.

On the ground, the reception committee led by Schulenburg and Potemkin took up positions. The air force guard of honour came to attention. Spotlights were switched on and newsreel cameras turned over as the aircraft came to a halt. The steps were wheeled up, the red carpet unrolled, and the band struck up *Deutschland über Alles* as the door opened. And then everything ground to a halt as the figure that emerged from the plane was seen to be not the Foreign Minister but a very tall, slim, twenty-four-year-old SS man in a grey lounge suit. After a hurried explanation from Schulze, the Ju-52 was directed to taxi away to a corner of the field, where it could wait until the Condor landed at 5.50 pm.

Despite the false start, the reception given to Ribbentrop was even more impressive than on his first visit. More swastika flags had been produced, and now even the hangars at the airport were festooned with them alongside Soviet red banners. Schulenburg, looking more aristocratic than ever in black silk top hat and black overcoat with a curly astrakhan collar, was the first to step forward to greet him, followed by Potemkin and various civil and military notables. This time, the band had the music for the *Horst Wessel* song, and played it after the *Internationale*. The guard of honour saluted him, then stood to attention while he inspected it, before treating him to a march past. And when he finally reached the gleaming black limousine, he found NKVD colonel Nikolai Vlasik, the broad-shouldered boss of Stalin's personal bodyguard who had looked after him on the last visit, waiting to serve as his honorary personal aide for the duration of his stay.

Once again, Ribbentrop and his top aides were accommodated at the old Austrian legation, where the secretariat set up again in rooms which Henke remembered from fifteen years earlier, before the Austrians moved in, as housing a club for foreign diplomats and correspondents. Those members of the party who had been there on 23 August were amused to note that the building next door, through whose windows they had seen officers of the Allied military mission kicking their heels, was now empty.

Ribbentrop did not pause for a rest, but started making telephone calls to Berlin and holding still more discussions. The news from the Wilhelmstrasse was disturbing, particularly in view of Stalin's already stated aim of gaining Lithuania. Without waiting for the new treaty to be agreed, Stalin was putting pressure on Estonia, holding Red Army manoeuvres on the border, having Soviet aircraft make extensive flights over Estonian territory, and generally threatening invasion if the Estonians did not accept a military alliance.

Talks started later that night at 10 o'clock, when Ribbentrop, Schulenburg and Hilger, accompanied by Henke and two or three other specialists, drove through the dark, empty streets to the Kremlin. The routine was exactly the same as it had been in August, with the little convoy of cars under the direction of Vlasik entering through the great Spassky gate and then making its way at walking pace through the shadows to the private entrance of Molotov's office, while a bell tolled to mark their progress. But although they had been there before, the spell of the Kremlin was still as potent. 'No matter how often,' Henke wrote later, 'there is a unique and mysterious attraction to entering the stronghold of Soviet power, with all its bizarre towers and walls. In the dark of evening and in the expectant mood in which we found ourselves, this had an extraordinarily powerful effect.'

As before, Poskrebyshev met them at the door in his colonel's uniform, and led them up the stairs and along corridors to the sparsely furnished ante-room. After a few moments, the door to the office opened and Stalin and Molotov stepped forward to greet Ribbentrop 'most cordially'. Leaving the others outside, Ribbentrop, Schulenburg and Hilger took their places at the large, green-baize-covered table and settled down to three hours of hard talking.

The tone of the conversation was friendly from start to finish – but Stalin as always dominated the proceedings, and made mincemeat out of Ribbentrop in every argument.

In reality, it was mere wishful thinking on Ribbentrop's part to imagine he had two options open to him: the first keeping to the original four-rivers line, with the boundary passing through the centre of Warsaw, the second giving Lithuania to the Soviet Union in exchange for large areas of eastern Poland, including the whole of Warsaw and the entire ethnic Polish population. But although Stalin's mind was clearly made up, Ribbentrop continued to argue over the respective merits of the two choices, agonising over which one to accept and trying at the same time to gain more territorial concessions for Germany. No matter how hard he tried, however, he was totally out of his depth in negotiating with Stalin. In the end, the only concessions he could hope to win were those which Stalin had already chosen to given him.

Stalin had an answer for everything. He explained that history had proved it was asking for trouble to split the Polish people: they had always struggled for unification when partitioned, and would certainly continue to do so, creating unrest and friction between the two powers. Therefore, he argued, to divide them now appeared to him to be 'a dubious procedure'.

If Germany were to take the entire Polish population, however, 'Polish intrigues for disturbing German–Soviet relations might possibly be eliminated.' Germany would have a free hand to deal with 'the Polish national problem'. What was more, the territories east of the Vistula which Germany would get under the second option were far more valuable agriculturally than those to the west of the river. Stalin does not seem to have mentioned the fact that there were millions of Jews now living in that area, but since he had prepared his case so carefully he must have been aware of it.

When Ribbentrop tried to get the oil-producing district of Drohobycz and Boryslaw – which had already been the source of one altercation – on the ground that the Soviet Union did not need it, since she already had rich oil reserves, while Germany had none, Stalin shot him down immediately. It was part of the Ukraine, he said, and the Ukrainian people claimed it as theirs. However, he added, if it was oil the Germans wanted, they need not worry. He would let them have the entire production, currently running at 30,000 tons a year but which he intended increasing to 500,000. In return, Germany could supply him with an equivalent value of coal and steel tubing, an excellent bargain – from Stalin's point of view.

As far as Lithuania was concerned, Germany had to remember Soviet plans for Estonia and Latvia. The Estonian Foreign Minister was already in Moscow, and was about to sign a mutual assistance pact which would allow the Soviet Union to establish naval bases on Estonian territory and to station one infantry division, one cavalry brigade, one armoured brigade and one air brigade there. Latvia would very shortly be following suit. If Lithuania were in the German zone of interest, then she might insist on Germany giving her military protection, which the world would regard as 'veiled annexation'.

There was another powerful point in favour of putting Lithuania into the Soviet camp, which both sides must have been aware of, but which they do not seem to have talked about. Stalin had taken care to see that his troops occupied Vilna, the ancient capital of Lithuania which the Poles had grabbed in 1919. Ribbentrop had personally promised the Lithuanians that Germany would restore Vilna to them, but while it was in Soviet rather than Polish or German hands this was a difficult promise to fulfil. Stalin, on the other hand, could present it to Lithuania – or keep it from her – as he chose.

The discussions rolled on until 1 am, with Ribbentrop unable to decide which option to go for – or, to be more accurate, to accept that he had no options. He then told Stalin that he needed time to think the matter over, and would give him a decision at 2 pm next day. What he really meant was that he needed to ask Hitler – and he hurried back to the old Austrian legation to draft a 1,000-word telegram to him. It was 4 am before it was finished, and rushed across Moscow to the embassy by Henke, to be put into code and telephoned through to Berlin.

When Ribbentrop returned to the Kremlin at 3 pm on the Thursday, he had still had no response from Hitler. The problem was that by the time the Foreign Ministry had decoded the message that morning, the Führer had left for Wilhelmshaven, where he was to inspect the U-boat base. So Ribbentrop had to go ahead with settling the fine details on his own initiative, assuming that the second option would be acceptable to Hitler.

This time, he took all his specialists with him, including Friedrich Gaus, the legal expert, and Karl Schnurre for the economic side. They were given two rooms near Molotov's office: the cartographers working on the maps, under the direction of Henke, were housed in the staff dining room; the typists were put into a smaller office. As the afternoon wore on, Henke shuttled busily backwards and forwards between the cartographers and typists and Molotov's room – to the intense disquiet of Molotov's own aides in the ante-room, who were clearly not used to seeing anyone other than Stalin passing freely in and out of the sanctum.

In Molotov's office, Stalin, Molotov and Ribbentrop, with Hilger and Gaus, stood round the green-baize table which was covered with maps, working out the new frontier. At first, the boundary was sketched in in great sweeps, to be refined section by section over the next few hours with painstaking thoroughness.

At 6.30 pm, the conference took a break. Stalin was giving a gala dinner for the German delegation – the invitations had been handed out already, elegantly inscribed in French on gold-edged card. This time, as a mark of the importance which the Soviet leaders attached to the occasion, the dinner was not in the usual reception rooms of the Spiridonovka, but in the Grand Palace of the Kremlin itself, with the entire Politburo in attendance. It was, for Moscow, a glittering occasion, with medals and dress uniforms being worn. In the midst of it all, Stalin stood out as a small, still figure in his usual unadorned tunic.

The German guests were met at the palace entrance by Barakov, the Soviet head of protocol who looked like Lenin's double, and conducted up the grand staircase, where Ribbentrop was surprised to see a huge painting of Tsar Alexander II with a group of peasants after the abolition of serfdom. Still starry-eyed at the treatment he was getting from the Soviet leaders, he decided hanging such a picture there 'seemed, like much else, to indicate an evolution in the course of which world revolutionary principles were giving way to a more conservative tendency'.

At the top of the stairs, they passed through the impressive congress chamber, where the Supreme Soviet met, and into a reception room richly decorated in red and gold, where the Soviet leaders were waiting for them, standing in a line on either side of Stalin and Molotov. Stalin greeted his guests, then spoke briefly to Barakov and went into the dining room with him to make a personal check on the seating arrangements – something which Hitler always did, too. When he was satisfied, the doors were thrown open, to reveal an oval room with heavily gilded walls, brightly lit by banks of electric candles in magnificent crystal chandeliers. Beneath them, the table glowed with colour from rich floral arrangements, costly porcelain and gold cutlery.

Ribbentrop took his place at the centre of the table next to Stalin and across from Molotov and the banquet began, with an army of white-clad waiters serving what Henke described as 'a repast that did full honour to the reputation of Russian hospitality. Those of our comrades who were in Moscow for the first time also learned on this occasion what a real

Russian *sakuska* is.' There were twenty-four courses, starting with sumptuous hors d'oeuvres which included lashings of caviar, and proceeding through a bewildering variety of fish and meat dishes, accompanied by non-stop supplies of vodka and Crimean champagne.

Before anyone had a chance to start eating, the traditional toasts began. Following the normal custom, Molotov proposed toasts to every guest – German and Soviet – individually. Each time, Stalin stood by the chair of the person being toasted, clinked glasses and exchanged a few words. Since there were twenty-two guests, this became something of an endurance test, particularly for the younger members such as Richard Schulze, who was last on the list. When Molotov called, 'And now to Adjutant Schulze!', and Stalin clinked glasses, he breathed a sigh of relief, thinking that was the end of it. But to his horror, Molotov, who had by now really got into the swing of the party, started a fresh round by calling, 'Now we will drink to all members of the delegations who could not attend this dinner.' And so it continued.

At first, Stalin kept egging Molotov on to make more and more speeches, more and more toasts – but when Molotov proposed the umpteenth toast to him, he roared with laughter and cried, 'If Molotov really wants to drink, no one objects – but he really shouldn't use me as an excuse!' At one point, he noticed that Hilger, who was sitting diagonally opposite him at the table, was having some sort of argument with his neighbour, Lavrenti Beria, the notorious head of the NKVD. Stalin asked what the trouble was, and Hilger explained that Beria was trying to make him drink more than he wanted to.

'Well, if you don't want to drink, no one can force you,' Stalin replied, amiably.

'Not even the chief of the NKVD himself?' Hilger asked.

'Here at this table,' Stalin said, 'even the chief of the NKVD has no more say than anyone else.'

Stalin himself was rationing his drinking carefully, in spite of all the toasts. For one thing, he had been ordered by his doctors to cut down. For another, he still had work to do later that night. Everyone else had fierce brown pepper vodka in their glasses, which Ribbentrop himself described as 'so potent it almost took your breath away'. But when the Nazi minister noticed that it seemed to be having no effect whatever on his host, and expressed his 'admiration for Russian throats compared with those of us Germans', Stalin winked at him, and disclosed that he was drinking a mild Crimean wine that was the same colour as the 'devilish vodka'.

The work that Stalin had to do after the banquet was not confined to his negotiations with Ribbentrop. At the end of the meal, he and Molotov excused themselves and sent the Germans off to the Bolshoi Theatre, to watch the first act of Tchaikovsky's *Swan Lake*. While the Germans were

away, the Soviet leaders held another negotiating meeting in Molotov's office, this time with Estonian Foreign Minister Karl Selter, who had flown into Moscow the day before to hold talks on the Soviet demand for a military alliance. By the time Ribbentrop and his party emerged from the theatre – where the Foreign Minister had been quite bowled over by the beauty of the performance and of the prima ballerina, and insisted on sending her flowers though Schulenburg warned him this practice was frowned upon in Moscow – the deal with Estonia was settled. Stalin could return to the German negotiations with a clear mind.

The final session started at midnight. Stalin and Molotov were joined by Boris Shaposhnikov, the Red Army Chief of Staff. The Germans were surprised to see that the veteran and highly respected Shaposhnikov appeared to tremble nervously before Stalin, and at one stage even dropped his pencil when Stalin called out to him. They took home tales of the terror which the Soviet ruler instilled into his subordinates, thus adding to the legends about Stalin's power – not realising that Shaposhnikov was in fact suffering from Parkinson's disease.

There had still been no response from Hitler to Ribbentrop's message, but shortly after the talks were resumed he came through on Molotov's telephone, having just returned to Berlin. With Molotov and Stalin looking on, Ribbentrop took the call at Molotov's desk. Stalin could not understand German, but he must have sensed that Hitler was agreeing to give him Lithuania only with the gravest misgivings. When Ribbentrop, through Hilger, told him that Hitler had agreed because 'I want to establish quite firm and close relations,' Stalin nodded gravely and responded, 'Hitler knows his business.'

Stalin knew his business, too, and was not taken in by the ease with which he had got his way. A little later, he was overheard to tell Molotov that by giving him Lithuania with so little argument, Hitler had in effect declared war on the Soviet Union. Stalin understood all too clearly that the only reason Hitler had done so was because he intended to take it back again as soon as the time was right.

For the moment, however, Stalin gave little indication of his suspicions, allowing only two doubtful remarks to show through the veneer of bonhomie. When Ribbentrop crowed that Russians and Germans must never again be allowed to fight each other, Stalin did not answer immediately, but pondered for a while and then said simply, 'This ought to be the case.' Ribbentrop was so surprised by this time that he asked Hilger, who was translating, to repeat it, in case he had heard it wrongly. And when Ribbentrop unwisely tried to sound him out about the possibility of turning the friendship treaty into an actual military alliance against the Western Powers, Stalin's only reply was a cryptic, 'I shall never allow Germany to become weak.'

Ribbentrop chose to interpret Stalin's second remark as meaning that he would intervene in the war if Germany looked like losing. 'I clearly remember,' he wrote later, 'Stalin uttering these words so spontaneously that they must certainly have expressed his conviction at the time. I was surprised at the great confidence in the Red Army which they appeared to express.'

Whatever Stalin's true feelings may have been, whatever doubts he may have harboured about Hitler's sincerity, he did not allow them to interfere with the business in hand. By the early hours of Friday, 29 September, the details were all settled, and the typists in the next room set to work preparing two sets of documents, one in German and one in Russian, for signature while the cartographers put the finishing touches to the definitive boundaries on the map. At 5 am, they were all completed.

There were three secret protocols, a joint declaration calling on Britain and France to end the war, and two letters of agreement drawn up by Schnurre for increased trade between Germany and the Soviet Union, in addition to the treaty itself. This was a simple document of five short clauses introduced by a preamble which must rate as one of the most cynical official statements in history:

> The government of the German Reich and the government of the USSR consider it as exclusively their task, after the disintegration of the former Polish state, to re-establish peace and order in these territories and to assure the peoples living there a peaceful life in keeping with their national character.

The secret protocols dealt with the resettlement of Germans, Ukrainians and Belorussians between the two spheres of interest, an amendment to the 23 August secret protocol to allow for the changed demarcation line, and finally a sinister undertaking that both parties would suppress any sign of Polish 'agitation' which affected the other's territory.

The map was a full-colour single sheet, measuring about five feet by three, to a scale of 1:1,000,000. The dividing line was drawn in very carefully in black ink, about one millimetre broad – too thick a line, or the slightest error, could have affected the lives of thousands of people. Stalin asked for one final adjustment in his favour near Lvov, and this was altered on the spot with a small, crescent-shaped amendment, cross-hatched in black. Satisfied, he picked up a dark blue wax crayon with a tip almost 3/16 inch wide, and signed his name on the map, a massive signature about 10 inches long with letters more than an inch high and a bold tail descending vertically some 18 inches. Smiling broadly, he turned to Henke, who had presented the map, and asked jocularly, 'Is my signature clear enough for you?' He then signed a second time, in much smaller letters alongside the amendment. Ribbentrop signed below Stalin, with a red crayon about 1/8 inch thick, a signature that was almost as bold and almost as big, measuring about 8 inches long, but entirely enclosed between the tail of Stalin's and the edge of the map. Beneath it he added the date: '28/IX/39'.

The treaty documents were signed by Molotov and Ribbentrop, watched by Stalin with obvious satisfaction, and by the rest of the German delegation who had been brought into the office to see the ceremony. Once more, there were photographs – and once more, Stalin spotted Schulze across the room and pulled him into the picture. He had obviously taken a shine to the tall young SS man, for as the meeting broke up after a final champagne toast, he took him by the arm again, shook his hand, and said, 'Next time, you must come in uniform.'

Two years later, in 1941, Schulze did exactly that.

33

'WHAT THEN IS CALLED ROBBERY?'

When Ribbentrop reported back to Hitler, his jubilation was not as wholehearted as it had been a month earlier, after the signing of the pact. This time, he had been made uncomfortably aware of the steel behind Stalin's mask of geniality. The negotiations had been tougher than any he had previously encountered anywhere in his career and he had come away with far less than he had hoped for. But he still enthused over the reception he had been given in Moscow, and told Hitler once again how he had felt very much at home, as though among 'old party comrades'. Although he said nothing, Hitler could hardly have been unaware of the irony that at home in Germany the real old party comrades looked down on Ribbentrop as a parvenu, a Johnny-come-lately who had joined the party only when the years of struggle and danger were over.

But there was one shadow which remained over the whole proceedings for Ribbentrop. He confessed in his memoirs that it had played on his mind during the entire flight home, and he raised it with Hitler as soon as he had him alone. What, he wondered, could Stalin have meant by saying he would never allow Germany to become weak? And why had he replied with 'That ought to be the case,' when Ribbentrop had eagerly asserted that their two countries should never again be allowed to fight each other?

Hitler said he interpreted Stalin's words as meaning that he believed 'that the chasm between the two philosophies was too wide to be bridged, so that a dispute was bound to arise sooner or later'. It was precisely because of this lack of trust, he claimed, that he had made the concession over Lithuania. It was meant as a demonstration of good faith, to prove 'his intention of settling questions with his eastern neighbour for good and of establishing real confidence from the very start'.

Ribbentrop had no doubt that Hitler was sincere, and that he truly believed the understanding with the Soviet Union was permanent. Stalin, however, was less gullible. Although he admired Hitler's ruthlessness, he had no illusions about his integrity and knew he would turn on the Soviet Union as soon as it suited him. In public, Stalin could scarcely refuse to support Hitler's peace appeal to Britain and France. Indeed, he even had the Comintern change its line, with the result that the French communists, for example, suddenly stopped singing their patriotic tunes and switched to an anti-war chant. Thirty-five of the forty-six communist deputies in the Assembly were arrested on 9 October for agitating against the war – most of the others escaped to Moscow. But in truth, it would have suited Stalin much better if the Western Powers had hurled their forces at Germany immediately, before Hitler had a chance to repair and replenish the Wehrmacht after the Polish campaign. A long slogging war, keeping Hitler occupied in the west, would have been the best possible defence for the Soviet Union.

As it became clear that Britain and France were not going to oblige him, and that they might even agree to a settlement, Stalin set about securing the rest of his frontiers with almost indecent haste. The eastern and western extremities of his empire were now in reasonable shape. As we have seen, he had dealt with the Far East by giving the Japanese army a thrashing it would not soon forget. In the west he had gained valuable depth by adding an extra 78,000 square miles of territory and over twelve million people to soak up the initial impact of any attack. His first priority there was to consolidate his gains as quickly as possible.

Even before the Red Army had moved in, communists in western Belorussia and the western Ukraine – the former Polish province of Galicia – had started setting up revolutionary committees and workers' militias, seizing property from private landlords and driving out local police. Within a month of the occupation, while chaos and confusion still reigned, Stalin's men staged elections for 'peoples' assemblies' which instantly proclaimed Soviet power and asked the Supreme Soviet of the USSR to 'admit' their territories into the Soviet Union. Their request was granted at an extraordinary session of the Supreme Soviet in Moscow on 3 November, two days after Hitler had formally annexed western Poland by decree.

The death agonies of Poland, however, were far from finished. The area between the new frontiers of Germany and the Soviet Union, where Stalin had given Hitler a free hand to do as he wished, were designated by Hitler as the 'Government General of Poland', to be ruled directly by Germany but not to be part of the Reich. As Governor-General he appointed Hans Frank, an intellectual gangster who had joined the Nazi Party in 1927 immediately after graduating from law school. Frank's first public pronouncement after his appointment made his attitude abundantly clear: 'The Poles shall be slaves of the German Reich,' he declared.

In addition to being responsible for liquidating the intelligentsia in his fief, Frank was also expected to extract food, supplies and forced labour for the Reich, and to accommodate, in one way or another, the millions of people who were to be poured into the Government General like waste into a sink. These fell into two categories: Jews from all parts of the Reich, and Poles from the western provinces which had been absorbed into Germany.

These unfortunate souls, whose families had often lived in the region for centuries, were to be evicted and moved east of the Vistula, to be replaced with German settlers and *Volksdeutsche*, ethnic Germans who were being moved out of the Baltic states, outlying parts of the old Poland, and the new Soviet areas. Himmler, as head of a new organisation created for the purpose, the Reich Commissariat for the Strengthening of German Nationhood, ordered the removal of 550,000 of the 650,000 Jews living in the western provinces, together with all Poles considered unfit for 'assimilation'.

Within a year, 1,200,000 Poles and 300,000 Jews had been cleared out, though only 497,000 *Volksdeutsche* had arrived to take their places. For those driven east, no housing or even shelter was provided, in spite of the fact that most of this vast movement of people took place during one of the harshest winters in living memory. The weather proved an excellent ally to the Nazis in their 'cleansing' mission: it killed more Poles and Jews than the German execution squads accounted for.

While all this was going on under the Germans, Stalin's men in the western Ukraine and western Belorussia were busy with their own housecleaning, or as Polish General Anders later described it, 'beheading the community'. The NKVD hit lists were very similar to those of the SS and the Gestapo: all members of parliament and senators, local mayors and heads of district administrations, landowners and businessmen, lawyers, priests, policemen, non-Marxist intellectuals and so on. In short, anyone who might possibly cause trouble was arrested and shipped out to the wastes of Kazakhstan or Siberia. Unlike the Nazis, however, the Soviet authorities could claim quite truthfully that their victims were not being treated any differently from their fellow citizens of the Soviet Union.

One group which was treated differently, according to Anders, comprised 'those Poles, mostly belonging to the army, who had tried to cross the frontier in civilian clothes to some neutral country, in order to join the new Polish army being organised in France under the orders of General Sikorski'. Anders charged: 'All caught by the police were deported to Russia. In spite of the fact that the official Soviet Criminal

Code punishes such a misdemeanour with one to three years' detention, these men were sentenced by a political administrative court, before which they did not even appear in person, to eight years in forced labour camps.'

After the German invasion of the Soviet Union, Anders was plucked from his Siberian prison camp and asked to form a new Polish army from fellow prisoners, to fight alongside the Red Army. One of the most difficult parts of his task was discovering how many men he had to draw on, for vast numbers had died or disappeared and no one seemed to know how many there had been to start with.

'I tried to assess the real figure of Polish citizens deported in 1939–41,' he wrote, 'but it was extremely difficult to do so. I questioned the Soviet authorities. Eventually I was directed to Fiedotov, an NKVD general who was in charge of this matter, and I had a few conversations with him. He told me in a most confidential manner that the number of Poles deported to Russia amounted to 475,000. It turned out, however, that this figure did not include all those arrested while crossing the frontier or soldiers taken prisoner in 1939. All people arrested on account of their political activities, or Ukrainians, Belorussians and Jews, indeed all Polish citizens belonging to racial minorities, were considered to be Soviet citizens. After many months of research and inquiries among our people, who were pouring from thousands of prisons and concentration camps spread out all over Russia, we were able to put the number at 1,500,000 to 1,600,000 people. Statistics obtained afterwards from Poland confirmed these figures.'

One of Stalin's prime reasons for being in such a hurry to convert the new territories into totally integrated parts of the USSR was to remove any elements which might be expected to side with the Germans in the event of an attack. There were still Ukrainians in the Romanian provinces of Bessarabia and Bukovina, and in the Carpatho-Ukraine which was now under Hungarian rule, but these were a comparatively small proportion of the whole nation, the vast majority of which was now absorbed within the USSR. Therefore, when Hitler did strike, he would not be able to bring with him sizeable detachments of Ukrainians who could be used to subvert the thirty million Soviet Ukrainians with dreams of national independence. To reduce the risks still further, Ukrainian nationalists were among the first people to be deported to the east in September and October 1939.

Logically, Stalin's next move in securing his frontiers should have been to take Bessarabia and those parts of northern Bukovina which contained Ukrainians. The area had been assigned to his sphere of interest in the original pact, though the wording had been left rather vague. This was another slice of territory which had been grabbed from the infant Soviet Union in 1918 by Romania, and so was a natural target for Stalin's ambition of restoring all the boundaries of the old Russian empire.

In 1930, some eighteen months after the Briand-Kellogg pact had ratified Allied acceptance of the Romanian annexation, he had spoken out strongly to the Sixteenth Party Congress: 'They talk about international law, about international commitments. But on the basis of what international law have the Allied gentlemen taken Bessarabia from the USSR and given it into the bondage of the Romanian boyars? . . . If this is called international law and international commitment, what then is called robbery?'

Stalin would obviously have enjoyed settling this old grievance, but Romania was supported not only by the British and French – with mutual assistance treaties that, unlike the Anglo-Polish treaty, did not specifically name Germany alone as the potential aggressor – but also by Germany and Italy, both of whom were heavily dependent on Romanian oil. And recent events in Romania had resulted in a government that was particularly hostile to the Soviet Union: on 21 September, Premier Armand Calinescu had been assassinated by members of the Romanian Nazi 'Iron Guard' for being too sympathetic to the Poles. The Romanian army had been massed on the frontier with the Soviet Union, and there could be little doubt that it would fight if the Red Army attempted to invade. Stalin wisely decided to leave Bessarabia alone for the time being.

He met with no more success in the rest of the south and south-west. Bulgaria's rulers were strongly pro-German, though the bulk of the population traditionally identified with the Russians. They rejected Soviet proposals for a treaty. The Horthy regime in Hungary, itself more or less a fascist dictatorship, also spurned Soviet advances, preferring to strengthen its political links with Nazi Germany.

A more serious failure for Stalin was with Turkey, which had been the Soviet Union's very first ally back in 1919, when Turkey had also had a young revolutionary government in place of a failed imperial court. Turkey was of considerable importance to the Soviet Union because she not only shared a long land frontier but also controlled the only entrance to the Black Sea through the Dardanelles and the Bosphorus. For twenty years, a special relationship had flourished between the two states as they had supported each other in the face of international hostility. Now, however, different political imperatives were driving them into different camps.

Turkish Foreign Minister Sükrü Saracoglu travelled to Moscow on 25 September to begin negotiations with Molotov in advance of Ribbentrop's second visit. From the first, the two sides were at cross-purposes, and their talks dragged on interminably. Saracoglu wanted a mutual assistance pact in which the Soviet Union and Turkey would each guarantee to come to the other's aid if either were attacked by another power – and that, as far as the Turks were concerned, meant Germany. For his part, Molotov was willing to sign such a pact only if Germany were specifically excluded. Stalin's orders were quite clear on this – nothing was to be done that might antagonise Hitler.

When Saracoglu refused to go along with the Soviet proposal, Molotov then demanded solid guarantees that Turkey would not permit warships of non-Black-Sea states to pass through the Bosphorus into the Black Sea. Saracoglu pointed out that any such action would be certain to rebound on Turkey, since traffic through the straits was guaranteed by international conventions. None of the great powers could afford to stand by and allow Turkey to deny their shipping passage through an international waterway.

For three weeks, the two Foreign Ministers hammered away at each other in Moscow, with neither prepared to give ground. For once, Molotov had met his match in obstinacy, and eventually they called it quits and gave up trying to reach any agreement. Saracoglu returned to Ankara without his pact; Molotov remained without his guarantees. Two days later, the Turks did sign a mutual assistance pact – but with Britain and France, not the USSR. Saracoglu, who was in any case an anti-communist and who complained bitterly of the way he had been treated in Moscow, took a certain malicious delight in telling the Soviet ambassador in Turkey that the pact had been initialled before his departure for Moscow, and that the signing of it had only been put off on account of his trip. The three agonising weeks in Moscow had been a total waste of time. The special relationship had been ended at a stroke.

In the north, Stalin's efforts met with considerably more success. He had moved quickly to calm the fears of the Baltic states immediately after the pact was announced, declaring that neither the Soviet Union nor Germany had any designs on them. He had backed this up by adding that they had not decided, either, to partition Eastern Europe. The Soviet government, he said, would adhere to a policy of neutrality and would respect the independence of the Baltic states provided – and here for the first time the wording of the Soviet text sounded a quietly ominous note – those states adopted a policy of 'favourable neutrality' towards the USSR. When asked to give an example of what his country would regard as *un*favourable neutrality, one Soviet diplomat replied that they would not take kindly to the massing of troops on the Soviet frontier. Presumably, the Soviet leaders regarded the same action on their own part in an entirely different light, for as soon as the pact with Germany was signed, they began reinforcing their army on the frontier with Estonia, the northernmost of the three Baltic states. By mid-September, there were a quarter of a million Soviet troops in position, and diplomatic circles in Moscow were openly discussing the possibility of an invasion.

The situation took a dramatic turn for the worse on 14 September, with an incident involving a Polish submarine, the *Orzel*. The *Orzel* was one of a group of three modern destroyers and two submarines which escaped from Gdynia when the Germans invaded. After cruising in the Baltic, the *Orzel* put into Tallinn to land her sick captain, and was immediately interned by the Estonians, who removed her charts and the breech-blocks from her guns, and placed armed guards aboard. Three days later, on the day the Soviets moved into Poland, the crew of the *Orzel*, with help from the Polish legation, managed to overpower the guards during the night and put to sea. The Soviets accused the Estonian government of aiding and abetting the Poles, in breach of their neutrality, and sent warships into Estonian waters to hunt for the submarine, which eventually managed, despite the lack of charts and guns, to reach England nearly a month later.

Although Molotov assured Estonian Foreign Minister Selter, 'in a friendly manner', that the Soviet action was in no way directed against Estonia, the threat posed by the presence of the Red Navy immediately off the Estonian capital could hardly be ignored. And on 22 September, Molotov stepped up the pressure, calling Selter to Moscow on the pretext of wishing to sign a trade and transit agreement which they had been discussing for some time. The basis of this was that the Soviets wanted to use Tallinn as a trans-shipment centre for their exports, and to provide repair facilities there for Soviet ships.

Not unnaturally, the Estonians were nervous of giving the Soviets such a foothold in their country. But Selter's nervousness doubled when he arrived in Moscow and was suddenly presented with a fresh demand, this time for a full military alliance, with Soviet army, air and naval bases in Estonia.

'If you do not acquiesce in our proposal,' Molotov told him, 'the Soviet Union will safeguard its security in another way, according to its own discretion, without Estonia's consent.' Estonia should not count on getting any help from either Britain or Germany, he added. Indeed, he was sure Germany would approve of his proposals.

Selter flew home to Tallinn immediately, without agreeing to anything, to consult his government. While they agonised over what action to take, Soviet troops began aggressive military exercises on the border, and violations of Estonian waters and air space by Soviet ships and aircraft intensified. On 26 September, the Estonians' nerve cracked. Selter flew back to Moscow next day, arriving shortly before Ribbentrop landed there.

In spite of having demanded a quick response, Molotov kept Selter hanging around in Moscow while he dealt with the Germans. He finally agreed to see him at 10 o'clock on the evening of 28 September, while

Ribbentrop was watching *Swan Lake* and the cartographers beavered away in the next room drawing up their maps of the new boundaries and frontiers – including those of the Baltic states.

For Stalin and Molotov, well lubricated after the gala dinner with its myriad toasts, the session with the Estonian Foreign Minister provided an extraordinary entr'acte, a tragi-comic entertainment during the interval in the day's main performance. Molotov started with a solo, in his most obdurate manner. To the horror of the Estonian delegation, he demanded that the number of Soviet troops to be stationed in Estonia under the mutual assistance agreement should be 35,000 men. Selter protested vigorously that this meant they would outnumber the entire Estonian army. For a few minutes, the argument raged backwards and forwards, until Stalin walked into the room, wearing his most benign expression. What, he asked, was the problem? He was told it was the number of troops.

'Come, come, Molotov,' he chided his sidekick gently, 'you are being rather harsh on our friends.'

To the Estonians' amazement, he suggested reducing the number by 10,000, to a mere 25,000. Molotov agreed, and so did Selter, convinced, according to Chip Bohlen, who was told the story by one of the Estonians present, that 'this understanding attitude proved that Stalin was a moderating influence'. To Bohlen and his colleagues in the American embassy, it was merely a characteristic ploy on Stalin's part. It was, however, an extremely successful ploy – the treaty was signed there and then, while Ribbentrop and his party were still at the Bolshoi. Of course, there were other factors involved in the decision, most notably the fact that the Red Army was poised to cross the Estonian frontier next day, and was stopped only by a direct telephone call from Voroshilov in the Kremlin to the commander in the field.

With the first domino toppled, the other two followed swiftly and painlessly. Latvian Foreign Minister Vilhelms Munters was invited to Moscow on 30 September, to face the same list of Soviet demands as his Estonian counterpart. Once again, Stalin and Molotov played their familiar roles of nice guy and hard man.

'I tell you frankly,' Stalin said to Munters, almost apologetically, 'a division of spheres of interest has already taken place. As far as Germany is concerned, we could occupy you whenever we wish.'

Molotov was much blunter. 'We cannot permit small states to be used against the USSR,' he declared. 'Neutral Baltic states – that is too insecure.'

As the talks continued, pressure was again applied by massing Soviet troops on the border, with the clear threat that at any time they could move in and take over the country. On 3 October, Stalin put the case as he saw it to Munters.

'You do not trust us,' he said, 'and we do not quite trust you. You believe that we wish to seize your country. We could do that now, but we do not do it.' What the USSR would prefer, he went on, was to sign a treaty such as they already had with Estonia. He explained that the USSR believed she must secure her frontiers against the Germans: he was aware that a German attack was always a possibility. Because of the pact, Germany and the USSR had become allies. 'But one cannot rely on it,' he warned. 'We must be prepared in time.'

On 5 October, the Soviet–Latvian Treaty of Mutual Assistance was signed. Under its terms, the Soviet Union was granted naval bases at Liepaja and Ventspils – the ports of Libau and Windau as they were known to the Germans, which Hitler had agreed to give to Stalin during the telephone conversation between Moscow and the Berghof – a coastal artillery base between Ventspils and Pitrags, various air bases, and the right to station 25,000 men on Latvian soil. Both in Latvia and Estonia, the entire local populations were to be evacuated from the areas of the bases.

Even before Munters had signed for Latvia, Molotov invited the Lithuanian Foreign Minister Juozas Urbsys to Moscow. Urbsys had his first meeting with Stalin and Molotov late at night on 3 October, only moments after the Soviet duo had finished talking so frankly to the Latvians. The same arguments were presented, but this time there was no need to move Soviet troops into a threatening position – the Red Army was already stationed along the old Polish–Lithuanian frontier. The only difference in the terms demanded compared with those obtained from the other two Baltic states was that Lithuania must be prepared to accept no fewer than 75,000 Soviet troops on her soil.

'It is in your own best interests to accept our proposals,' Stalin told Urbsys.

But that was not all Stalin told the Lithuanian. In spite of having promised Schulenburg that he would say nothing, he also told him about the agreement for the division of the spoils. Of particular interest to Urbsys was the fact that the new boundaries left a fairly large triangle of territory surrounding the town of Suwalki. This triangle had been allocated to Germany, to be incorporated into East Prussia. However, the demarcation line between the two spheres of interest also gave Germany a strip of Lithuanian territory on the side of the triangle.

Since this was the first Urbsys had heard of the matter, he was understandably aghast to discover that a part of his own country had been given away. What was more, it was a part which Lithuanians held especially dear, including several towns and the cities of Naumiestis and Mariampole, since many of their most prominent leaders came from there. They described it as 'the cradle of Lithuanian national rebirth'. 'Dismayed and sad', according to Molotov, Urbsys flew home at 8 o'clock next morning.

At the time, Stalin's apparent indiscretion looked simply maladroit – though Molotov claimed he had had to tell the Lithuanians 'out of loyalty to the Germans'. It was not until several months later that it could be seen as another chess piece carefully moved into position by the grand master.

With commendable openness, Molotov had told Schulenburg about Urbsys's visit in advance, though only by two or three hours. He intended, he said, to tell Urbsys that the Soviet Union planned to give Vilna back to Lithuania, but that at the same time Lithuania would have to give the strip of territory alongside the Suwalki triangle to the Germans. Molotov suggested the simplest way to accomplish this would be to have simultaneous but separate protocols between the Lithuanians and the two powers.

Schulenburg spotted the drawback in this scheme immediately. The Soviets would be seen as generous benefactors making a gift to the Lithuanians, while the Germans would be cast as robbers. He had a much better idea: the Soviet Union should give the Lithuanians Vilna in exchange for the strip adjoining Suwalki, which they could then hand over to Germany. Molotov was not keen on this, but agreed that Schulenburg should consult Ribbentrop and Hitler – he could have until noon next day to give their answer.

Schulenburg hurried back to his embassy and sent off an urgent telegram to Ribbentrop, explaining the situation and suggesting a third option: Germany should do nothing about the strip for the moment apart from signing a secret deal with the Soviets confirming that it would come to Germany when the time was right. They would then sit back and wait until the Soviet Union swallowed the whole of Lithuania, 'an idea,' as he put it drily, 'on which, I believe, the arrangement concerning Lithuania was originally based'.

Ribbentrop bought Schulenburg's suggestion and had Gaus telephone him direct at 11 am Moscow time, agreeing to it and telling him to ask Molotov to say nothing about the matter to the Lithuanians, who did not need to know at that stage. It could all be settled between Germany and the Soviet Union in a simple and secret exchange of letters between Molotov and Schulenburg. But when the ambassador telephoned the Kremlin to say this, Molotov confessed that it was too late – they had been 'forced' to tell the Lithuanians the previous evening.

Ribbentrop was somewhat put out by this unwelcome news, but when Stalin personally intervened to beg him not to insist on the cession of the strip for the moment, he decided to make the best of a bad job. Trying to claw back the point which Stalin had undoubtedly scored, he sent off a long message to the German legation in Kaunas, the Lithuanian capital, instructing the minister, Erich Zechlin, to tell Urbsys that the whole thing was a misunderstanding. 'In order to avoid complications in eastern Europe,' Zechlin was to say, Germany and the Soviet Union had

had to settle spheres of interest when signing the non-aggression pact. During the discussion of this, Ribbentrop had insisted that Vilna be restored to Lithuania, and had managed to persuade the Soviet Union to agree. But when the demarcation line had been revised for the Boundary and Friendship Treaty on 28 September, the Suwalki triangle came into the German sphere. This created 'an intricate and impractical boundary', so the idea had emerged of making a small rectification. However, Ribbentrop did not consider this to be particularly pressing.

The Lithuanians accepted this information with visible relief, and asked Zechlin to give Ribbentrop their thanks. Later that evening, after the news had been reported to the Lithuanian government, they sent another message expressing their gratitude to Ribbentrop for the Vilna settlement! In Berlin, the Lithuanian minister called on Weizsäcker to express his gratitude for the German withdrawal of their claim – Weizsäcker carefully stressed that they had only said it was 'not at the moment pressing' – and to tell him of the demands being made by the Soviet Union. He asked for German advice and help. Weizsäcker, finding himself in a now familiar cleft stick, was non-committal.

Shorn of all support, the Lithuanians realised the Soviet offer was one they could not refuse any longer. Urbsys returned to Moscow, and the treaty was signed on 10 October. On 27 October, Vilna was handed over to the Lithuanians. By then, Soviet troops were already moving into their new garrisons in all three Baltic states, but there was no attempt to take over any of the countries. That was not Stalin's way.

In Stalin's book, any move made by the Soviet Union had to have the appearance and the excuse of strict legality – even if he had to write the laws specifically for that purpose. That was why he had refused to move into western Belorussia or the western Ukraine until the Polish government had ceased to exist. That was why in both those territories 'democratic elections' had been held with such unseemly haste: he would have preferred a long time to prepare the ground, giving the Belorussians and Ukrainians time to appeal to the Soviet Union for help and thus justifying the occupation, but the speed of Hitler's *Blitzkrieg* in Poland had prevented this. In the Baltic states, however, he could afford to take a little time.

The official Soviet version of events says of the mutual assistance pacts: 'These treaties did not infringe on the sovereign rights of the Baltic states, nor did they affect their social and state system. They were based on the principals of equality, non-interference in internal affairs, and mutual respect for independence and sovereignty.'

Molotov told the Supreme Soviet on 31 October: 'We are for honest and scrupulous compliance with the concluded pacts on terms of complete reciprocity.' Reciprocity for Molotov involved taking steps to ensure that the Baltic states were completely dependent on the Soviet Union. Following the military agreements, he had immediately had trade treaties drawn up which effectively bound them to deal only with the USSR.

'In a situation where the trade of all the European nations, including neutral states, is facing immense difficulties,' he told the Supreme Soviet, 'these economic agreements of the USSR with Estonia, Latvia and Lithuania are of great positive significance to them.'

The message went out to the communists in all three countries to start holding rallies and meetings demanding the curbing of all right-wing activity and calling for even closer relations with the Soviet Union. And as if that were not enough, the writing on the wall was surely too clear for anyone to miss when the Latvian communist newspaper *Cina* proclaimed: 'The treaty has released the revolutionary dynamic forces of the people that had been held in check for twenty years. These forces have started moving and there is nothing that can stop them any more.'

The question of the Lithuanian strip of territory had been suspended for the moment, but in the meantime there was an ironic postscript to the business of the Suwalki triangle. It came on 19 October, in a letter to Schulenburg from Alexander Dörnberg, the giant, red-bearded head of protocol in the Foreign Ministry. Dörnberg said Ribbentrop was complaining bitterly about the hunting in the Suwalki region. There were supposed to be herds of fine royal red deer there in the forests of Augustow, and Ribbentrop had been particularly keen to get this area as his personal hunting preserve – apart from anything else, it would be one in the eye for Göring, his prime rival as a hunter. During the negotiations, he had made a special point of this, so much so that, according to his account, Stalin had said the region should be given to Germany specifically for him to hunt in, because of its fine stags.

Soon after he returned to Berlin, Ribbentrop had despatched Dörnberg to Suwalki, to arrange for the protection of his hunting interests. But when he arrived there, Dörnberg found there were no stags of any sort, royal or otherwise. The only time deer appeared there was when they were passing through on migration.

Ribbentrop was desolated. He sent Dörnberg to Warsaw to talk to Polish hunting and forestry experts, to find whether there were any other good game forests. The reply was disappointing – the only really good areas had all gone to the Soviet Union. The very best were in the Carpathians: one which had belonged to Baron Grödel, and had excellent shooting boxes, trails and gamekeepers of German origins, the other belonging to the Metropolitan of Lvov.

Ribbentrop wanted Schulenburg to speak to Molotov, or even to Stalin himself, and ask if one of these hunting grounds could be 'leased' to him, a fairly barefaced request for a gift. There would, he emphasised, be political advantages in such an arrangement: he would be able to keep in closer contact with his Soviet friends.

Schulenburg must have cringed at such a task, but he did his best to follow his Foreign Minister's wishes. He spoke to Molotov on 3 November, and was told Molotov would find a way of complying. A month later, he raised the matter again, and was twice promised a prompt reply. But in the end, nothing came of it, and Ribbentrop had to remain disappointed.

He did, however, have something to console him. He asked for, and got, another delivery of caviar, following one he had received at the beginning of October. 'The Minister has asked me for it,' Dörnberg wrote to Schulenburg, 'because he would like to have the caviar given to the badly wounded who can take no other nourishment. Perhaps the next courier could bring the shipment with him. It would be much appreciated here if the amount could be increased by another one-kilogram can.'

34

'THE LADIES OF ST PETERSBURG'

After his army had swept through Finnish Karelia and taken the city of Viipuri from the Swedes in 1721, Tsar Peter the Great explained in somewhat whimsical terms his reasons for undertaking the campaign. 'The ladies of St Petersburg', he wrote, 'could not sleep peacefully in their beds as long as the Finnish frontier ran so close to our capital.'

The city which Peter founded in 1703 is now called Leningrad. It is no longer the capital of Russia, having been demoted from the place of honour by Lenin himself after the 1917 Revolution. But it is still the second most important city in the Soviet Union and the Russian preoccupation with its vulnerability to attack from the north has not diminished with the passing centuries. In 1939, Stalin shared Peter's obsession that Finland represented a dangerous gap in his defences, and like Peter he was determined to do something about it.

Finland had been an independent nation – for the first time in her history – only since 1917. Like the three neighbouring Baltic states, the Finns had taken advantage of the October Revolution to break away from their Russian overlords. But unlike the Baltic states, Finland had never been an integral part of the Russian empire. The Grand Duchy of Finland had been acquired by Russia in 1809 as part of the spoils of war with Sweden. Tsar Alexander I had simply added Grand Duke of Finland to his other titles – which were already numerous enough for a man to shave himself from start to finish while reciting them aloud – and left the Finns pretty much alone.

For ninety years, under successive tsars, the Finns continued to enjoy a considerable degree of self-government. True, there was a Russian governor-general in Helsinki and permanent Russian garrisons in the country, but by and large the tsars respected Finnish autonomy and there was no serious friction between occupier and occupied until the 1890s.

In fact, life went on much as it had done under Swedish rule. Those Finns who had once profitably served the Swedish crown – and who had learned to speak only Swedish, leaving Finnish to the common herd – now discovered that their talents were equally welcome to the Romanovs in St Petersburg. Marshal Mannerheim, who was to become the greatest Finnish leader, was a good example: he joined the Nicolaevsky Cavalry School in St Petersburg, was gazetted to one of the crack Russian regiments, and rose to the rank of full general in the imperial army.

The situation changed in 1899, when Tsar Nicholas II decided to deal with the question of Finnish separatism by embarking on a comprehensive programme of Russification. For a start, the Russian language was to be introduced into the Finnish Senate, the civil service and all schools, and the small Finnish army was to be absorbed into the Imperial Russian army.

Opposition to these proposals united the country as never before. Indeed, they could almost be said to have created the nationalist movement, as indignant Finns mounted a campaign of patriotic resistance to what they saw as Russian imperialism. The idea took root, as Professor Anthony Upton puts it, 'that Russia was the implacable enemy of the Finnish nation and would always seek its subjecion'. The feeling was exacerbated in November 1914, with proposals for the complete assimilation of Finland into Russia – with the result that many young Finns joined the German army in order to fight against their oppressor.

The idea of an independent Finland, which had been discussed in purely theoretical terms for well over a century, was brought to reality by the Russian Revolution in 1917. The Finnish Parliament voted for independence and the non-socialist majority parties began to form a republican government. The socialists and other left-wing parties did not trust them, and attempted to overthrow the new republic, proclaiming a workers' government in its place. The upshot was a savage civil war between White and Red forces, lasting for three bloody months.

Though fewer in number than the Reds, the Whites were better led, with Marshal Mannerheim as their military commander, and better equipped, with weapons supplied by Germany and Sweden, who also sent volunteers to fight for the cause. The Reds were supported only by Russia, which in early 1918 was itself slipping into ever-increasing chaos.

When the Whites emerged victorious, a period of fierce repression followed which left many scars. Most of the Red leaders fled to the Soviet Union, where they formed the Finnish Communist Party under the leadership of Otto Wille Kuusinen, a poet and intellectual.

During the Russian Civil War, the new Finnish government actively supported the Western nations in their attempt to destroy the bolshevik

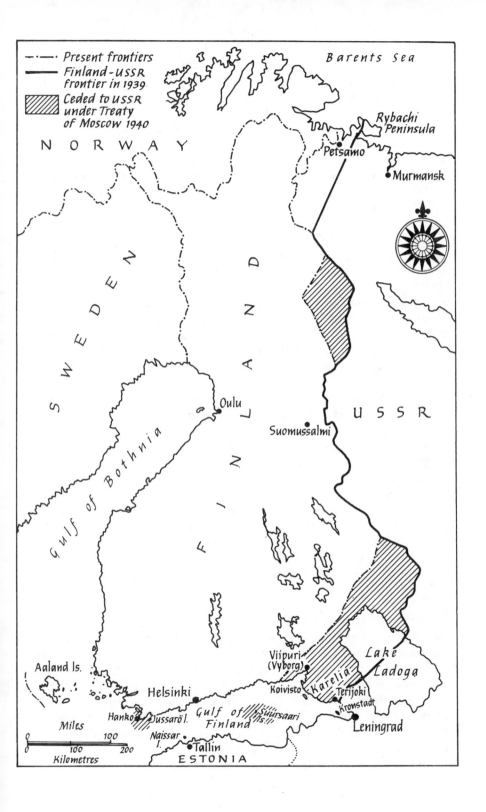

Present frontiers
Finland-USSR frontier in 1939
Ceded to USSR under Treaty of Moscow 1940

Barents Sea

Rybachi Peninsula

NORWAY

Petsamo

• Murmansk

S W E D E N

F I N L A N D

Oulu

U S S R

• Suomussalmi

Gulf of Bothnia

Aaland Is.

Viipuri (Vyborg)

Lake Ladoga

Helsinki

Koivisto

Karelia

Terijoki

Hanko
Jussarö I.
Gulf of Finland
Suursaari Is.
Kronstadt
Leningrad

Miles

Naissar I.
• Tallin
ESTONIA

0   100
0   100   200
Kilometres

regime. On occasion, they even allowed anti-Bolshevik military operations to be mounted from their territory. But with the collapse of the Allied Intervention it became necessary for Finland and the Soviet Union to regularise their diplomatic situation.

The two sides met at Tartu, in Estonia, to negotiate a peace treaty. With their Civil War and a war with Poland still raging, the Soviets were desperate to make peace with their northern neighbours – any kind of peace, as long as it guaranteed a stable frontier. Realising they held most of the cards, the Finns delighted in driving a hard bargain.

The Treaty of Tartu was most unsatisfactory from the Soviets' point of view, but they were in no position then to resist Finnish demands. Two of its most significant provisions were the legalising of the Finnish seizure of the town and district of Petsamo, with its valuable nickel deposits, only 100 kilometres from the Soviet Arctic port of Murmansk, and the redrawing of the Russo-Finnish border further down the Karelian Isthmus to a mere eighteen miles from Petrograd, as St Petersburg had then become. As the Soviet negotiators pointed out, the city had 'got itself into a quite impossible situation'. The Finns also gained possession of a number of islands in the Gulf of Finland which commanded the approaches to Petrograd and the great Russian naval base at Kronstadt.

The Soviet negotiators were most unhappy about all this. In different circumstances, they complained, if they had not been concerned solely with the question of the defence of the Soviet Union, then 'the Russian government would be obliged to demand in the most stringent fashion that not only the islands in the Gulf of Finland should be joined to Russia, but also a considerable portion of Finnish territory along the coast towards Viipuri'.

One of those Soviet negotiators was the then People's Commissar for Nationality Affairs, Josef Stalin. In 1939, he was to say very much the same thing as had been said nineteen years before – but this time the 'different circumstances' which had then been spoken of with such bitterness had arrived. This time, it was the Soviets who held the aces. Or so Stalin believed.

In the early autumn of 1939, when it was clearly only a matter of time before the three little fishes, Estonia, Latvia and Lithuania, were swallowed whole by the Soviet whale, Finland was obviously next on the menu. But Finland was no easy, bite-sized morsel. No matter what the odds against them were, the Finns were unlikely to offer themselves up without a fight. So Stalin had good reason for preferring to seek a political rather than a military solution to the security problem posed by Finland. But there were other considerations, too, which reinforced this choice.

One reason was the size and nature of the country itself. A

nineteenth-century Finnish poet, J. L. Runeberg, described his native land as 'Europe's outpost against Nature, set down amidst the ice'. As a description of Finland's harsh climate it could not be bettered. Lying between latitudes of 60° and 70° North, the country is frozen in along her Baltic coastline for the whole of the long winter months. Finland has land frontiers with three neighbours: two relatively short ones almost entirely above the Arctic Circle with Sweden and Norway, and a much longer one running from north to south with the Soviet Union, stretching over a distance approaching 1,000 miles from the Barents Sea to the Gulf of Finland.

Forests cover more than eighty per cent of the land surface, which is dotted with over 55,000 lakes. In 1939, Finland occupied about 160,000 square miles. Not only would such territory be difficult to conquer and occupy, but more to the point, as it stood, Finland provided a substantial buffer between the Soviet Union and the outside world. Would the Soviet Union be any more secure if her borders were on the Gulf of Bothnia, the long arm of the Baltic which separated most of Finland from Sweden?

A further consideration harked back to the Finnish Civil War in 1917–18. A Red government had been briefly established in Helsinki then. Otto Wille Kuusinen, formerly secretary of the Comintern and now one of Stalin's most trusted advisers, had been a member of that government. If Finland had gone communist once, why should it not happen again? And if it did, Stalin would have a reliable ally to guard his north-western flank.

Stalin started trying to find a mutually acceptable political solution with Finland as early as April 1938, shortly after Hitler marched into Austria. In the days following the *Anschluss* of Austria with the Reich, international tension had soared throughout Europe. Poland had forced Lithuania, under the direst threats, to recognise the frontier between them. Hitler had stepped up his demands for the Sudeten area of Czechoslovakia. Everywhere, there was serious talk of war for the first time since 1918.

Five days after the *Anschluss*, the Soviet Union invited Britain, France and the United States to join together in a collective security agreement 'which would aim at checking the further development of aggression and at eliminating the increased danger of a new world massacre'. Chamberlain refused point-blank, claiming that the Soviets were 'stealthily and cunningly pulling all the strings behind the scene to get us involved in a war with Germany'.

A few days after this rebuff, the then Finnish Foreign Minister Rudolf Holsti received a telephone call from the second secretary of the Soviet legation in Helsinki, Boris Yartsev.

It is not usual for lowly second secretaries to deal direct with Foreign

Ministers. Nevertheless, when Yartsev asked for a meeting Holsti agreed, not only because he was a courteous man, but also because Yartsev was a source of some interest to the Foreign Ministry. A very pale man, just under six feet in height and with reddish hair and sharp features, Yartsev had served in Helsinki for several years and was well liked in the diplomatic community. He and his wife, who worked for Intourist, the Soviet travel bureau, made a popular couple, fond of parties and always ready to socialise.

But Yartsev was something of a mystery man, for he was quite unlike the usual Soviet apparatchik in that he seemed to be under no pressure to conform. According to the then Finance Minister of Finland, Väinö Tanner, one could discuss with him 'the most delicate matters, as though he were a man who did not have to be particularly careful of what he said, unlike many people in his position'. Whatever his ostensible diplomatic rank, it was obvious that he had a degree of authority and freedom far beyond that permitted to any normal second secretary. Some in Helsinki believed at first that he was the NKVD man in the legation – but it soon became clear that he was very much more than a mere secret policeman.

Former Finnish diplomat Johann Nykopp recalls how as a young official in the Foreign Ministry in 1936, he turned to Yartsev for help with a problem concerning a number of people in the Soviet Union who, under the terms of the Treaty of Tartu, had the right to become Finnish citizens. Nykopp's efforts to sort this out were constantly being frustrated by certain officials in the Commissariat for Foreign Affairs in Moscow.

'Your people are not respecting the terms of the treaty,' Nykopp complained.

Yartsev was furious – not at Nykopp, but at the Soviet officials concerned. How dare they frustrate the workings of the treaty? 'I won't allow such a thing!' he declared.

Nykopp was astounded at the man's tone. '*I* won't allow' indeed! Ordinary Soviet diplomats simply did not talk like that.

'So, I thought,' Nykopp remembers, 'who are you? You must have powers I never suspected, to judge your own superiors.'

Yartsev gave Nykopp to understand that he had backing at the very highest level, which could only mean one thing: he must have been a member of Stalin's personal secretariat. He could only have operated with such easy confidence because he was about his master's business.

This was the man, then, who called Foreign Minister Holsti to say he had an important message from Moscow which he was required to deliver personally. Holsti made an appointment to see him on 14 April 1938.

Yartsev began by insisting that the discussions must be kept entirely secret. No word of what he had to say must be allowed to leak out, not even to Derevyanski, the Soviet minister in Helsinki. When Holsti agreed, the Russian launched into an extensive review of the general situation in Europe, and Finland's future position as envisaged by the Soviet Union. Moscow, he said significantly, was convinced that Nazi Germany was planning to attack the Soviet Union in the near future. While the main thrust of the German invasion would undoubtedly be across the Polish plains, they might also land troops in Finland and use the country as a base from which to mount an attack through the Karelian marshes towards Leningrad and Moscow.

The Soviet government's information, Yartsev continued, was that should the Finns resist German landings, the Nazis planned to foment a revolt in Finland, using the local fascists as their tool. The Finnish fascists would overthrow the Helsinki government and the Wehrmacht would be free to smash its way into the Russian heartland.

The Russians were acutely aware of the existence of a fascist group in Finland, though both they and the Germans were probably overestimating its importance. In the early thirties, indeed, the 'Lapua Movement', as the Finnish fascists called themselves, had agitated for a 'Greater Finland' which would have included not only the whole of Karelia but also the city of Leningrad itself!

Given the feasibility of the Soviet scenario, everything depended on the attitude of the Finnish government. Would they resist the Germans? Or would they co-operate with them and permit them to invade the Soviet Union from Finnish soil? If the Finns did choose to co-operate with the Germans, Yartsev warned Holsti that the USSR would have no alternative but to mount a pre-emptive strike: 'The Red Army would not remain on the border to wait for the enemy, but would advance as far as possible to meet him.'

If, on the other hand, the Finns pledged themselves to resist the Germans, then Moscow was prepared to offer Finland generous aid, both economically and militarily. On the military side, the Finns had nothing to fear from an alliance with the Soviets. The USSR was prepared to give a solemn undertaking that should the Red Army ever find it necessary to enter Finland to assist its allies, it would be withdrawn as soon as the war was over. On the economic front, Yartsev went out of his way to emphasise the advantages Finland could enjoy from close rapport with her peace-loving neighbour. He dangled a most inviting carrot in front of Holsti in the shape of a large trade agreement: his government would be willing, in the event of an alliance, to sign contracts to purchase a wide range of Finnish agricultural and industrial products.

Holsti was unimpressed. He simply did not believe his country was in peril from either internal or external forces. The government was popular and enjoyed the support of three quarters of the Diet. As for the

German threat, he assured the Russian that if the Germans should ever try to invade Finland they would be fiercely resisted – as would any other invader. In any case, he added, since 1936 Finland had established her position alongside Norway and Sweden as one of the Scandinavian neutral countries. Neutrality, as everyone knew, was now official Finnish policy.

Yartsev insisted that before the Soviet government could accept the principle of Finnish neutrality it would require guarantees. It must be convinced that Finland would not side with Germany again in any conflict with the Soviet Union.

'What do you mean by guarantees?' Holsti asked.

It was a question that was to dog all attempts at agreement over the next few months, as Yartsev had meetings not only with Holsti but also with the then Prime Minister, A. K. Cajander, and Finance Minister, Väinö Tanner. Every time, the discussions foundered on semantics. What precisely did Moscow require in the way of guarantees? When pressed, Yartsev declared, quite reasonably, that these could only be worked out in the course of negotiations between the two governments. It was now up to the Finns to make the next move.

But the Finnish government prevaricated. The matter was not discussed in the Foreign Affairs Committee of the Cabinet, and remained the knowledge of only a few senior members of the government. The truth was, no one could decide how seriously to take Yartsev. Was he a bona fide emissary from Stalin? Or was he part of some devious Russian plot? They could not understand why, if Stalin was so eager to reach an agreement, he should choose to employ such an unlikely go-between as Yartsev, instead of using normal diplomatic procedures and operating through his minister in Helsinki, Derevyanski.

But Stalin was in a hurry, and with good reason. Yartsev was Stalin's man, loyal only to him, reporting directly to him. In 1938, with the purges in the Soviet Union still taking their bloody toll of the military and political hierarchy, who else could Stalin trust but his own man?

Yartsev came to the Finns as the bearer of a secret and important message, but it was a message whose code they failed to decipher, a signal they misinterpreted. The Finns can hardly be blamed for this. They had very little experience in the field of foreign affairs: their diplomacy had barely reached the age of majority. But their failure was to have serious consequences.

In August 1938, Yartsev came back with a fresh Soviet offer. Stalin was prepared to accept Finnish assurances that they would resist any German invasion, as long as the Finns accepted Soviet military aid in the event of such an attack. In return, he offered a deal on the fortification of the Aaland Islands, something the Finns had long wanted to achieve.

The Aalands were a group of 6,500 islands strategically placed at the mouth of the Gulf of Bothnia, between Finland and Sweden. These islands had changed hands several times during the preceding centuries, passing to Russia in 1809 from Sweden, who had seized them back during the chaos of the Bolshevik Revolution in 1917. In 1921, the League of Nations placed the islands under Finnish control, but insisted they be demilitarised and granted semi-autonomous status.

In 1938, the Soviet fear was that in the event of war between Germany and the Soviet Union, the islands could be used as a base for the protection of ships carrying vital German supplies of iron ore from Sweden. For Finland, the Aalands were important for the protection of her western shore. Now, Stalin was prepared to allow Finland to fortify the islands, on two conditions. One was that the Soviets should participate in the building and send observers to supervise the work. The other was that the Finns should allow them to build a fortified air and naval base on Suursaari, one of the Finnish islands which commanded the approach to Leningrad and the Soviet Baltic Fleet's base at Kronstadt. The protection of both had become a matter of urgency for Stalin, and he was now, for the first time, prepared to do deals in order to acquire strategic bases for this purpose.

Once again, however, mutual distrust caused the talks to end in deadlock. Yartsev suggested they should be continued under cover of the official trade negotiations which were then taking place in Moscow. The Finns refused. But Stalin did not give up. In March 1939 he sent a new emissary to Helsinki: Boris Stein, then Soviet ambassador in Rome. Stein had served for some years in Helsinki and was known personally to many members of the Finnish government. No doubt Stalin hoped someone more senior than Yartsev might carry greater weight.

Stein brought fresh proposals. The Soviet Union agreed that a fortified base on Suursaari might compromise the neutrality which the Finns had gone to such lengths to establish. Therefore, the Soviets had another, less contentious offer: would Finland agree to lease to the USSR the string of islands including Suursaari? Or, if this proved unacceptable, would Finland be prepared to exchange the islands for an area of Soviet territory on the mainland? The islands measured 183 square kilometres. Stalin was willing to give a larger area in exchange, and to undertake not to fortify the islands.

In spite of advice from Marshal Mannerheim that they should negotiate seriously with the Soviets, and that it would be a mistake to send them away empty handed yet again, the Finnish government said no. Their minister in Moscow, Baron Yrjö-Koskinen, delivered their carefully worded answer on 20 March:

The Finnish government cannot negotiate regarding a matter which may in one way or another involve the cession of parts of the territory of the state to another power. This negative reply is not to be understood as meaning that the Foreign Minister would be unwilling to continue an exchange of views with the purpose of reaching a solution to the questions raised by the Soviet Union regarding guarantees to its security.

In other words, although the answer was no, there was no reason why the two sides should not continue talking.

Now, it was Stalin's turn to misinterpret the signals. The Finns' rejection of his offer fed his paranoia. It appeared that his worst fears were about to be realised: German guns on the Finnish border bombarding the city of Leningrad, which was within easy range of heavy artillery, while German and Finnish troops poured across the Karelian marshes.

Surely, the Soviet reasoning went, the Finns would refuse their proposals only if they were being encouraged to do so by another major power, with whom they were in league. And when on 28 April Ribbentrop proposed a non-aggression pact between Germany and Finland, this was seen as proof that their interpretation was correct. In Soviet eyes, the fact that Finland refused to sign such a pact with Germany on the grounds that it would compromise her neutrality simply demonstrated deceitful behaviour.

It was against this background, and with Hitler still showing no sign of softening his aggressive attitude towards the Soviet Union, that Stalin called a conference in Moscow in June 1939 to discuss the Finnish problem. Among those present were Andrei Zhdanov, the Leningrad party boss whom many considered to be Stalin's chosen successor; Admiral Nikolai G. Kuznetsov, the thirty-nine-year-old newly appointed Commissar of the Navy; Otto Kuusinen, Stalin's confidant and founder of the Finnish Communist Party; and General Kirill A. Meretskov, the forty-two-year-old commander of the Leningrad Military District. This formidable array of talent discussed the situation at length, and the conference ended with Stalin sending Meretskov away to draw up a contingency plan to deal with the military threat posed by Finland.

Meretskov delivered his plan in July. A few days later, on 29 July, Kuznetsov took Zhdanov on a short sea cruise around the Gulf of Finland. No doubt, in the heat of summer a few days spent sailing around the islands of the Baltic was a pleasant prospect, providing a welcome break from his airless office for Zhdanov. But this cruise was strictly business, for Zhdanov, in addition to his role as Leningrad party chief, was also president of the main naval soviet and therefore Kuznetsov's political boss, responsible for naval affairs in the Kremlin.

Kuznetsov wanted to give Zhdanov, who came originally from the Black Sea, a practical lesson on the geography of the waters around Leningrad and Kronstadt. He started by pointing out the nearness of the Finnish shore to Kronstadt. Anyone on that shore needed only an ordinary pair of binoculars to be able to see which Soviet ships were in port, what preparations were being made for departure, and every movement on and around them. If there were hostile forces on that shore, getting out to sea from Kronstadt would be a nightmare.

As the cruiser left its berth and nosed its way into the Gulf, Kuznetsov pointed out the many Finnish islands in their path – the islands which the Finns had refused to lease or exchange, every one a potential enemy base in time of war. He had brought along two older senior officers, L. M. Galler and N. N. Nesvitsky, both of whom had served as officers in the tsarist navy during the first world war. Galler was now commander of the Baltic Fleet. As the voyage progressed, they drew Zhdanov's attention to the proximity of Helsinki and Tallinn, formerly Russian harbours now in alien hands. And here was where minefields had been laid in 1914 by the Imperial Russian Navy, from the island of Naissar, off Estonia, to the Porkkala peninsula in Finland, to keep the German navy out. With the independence of Finland and Estonia, it would be a simple matter for an enemy operating from either country to lay mines in those waters to keep the Soviet navy in. The Baltic Fleet was the Soviet Union's strongest, but it would be totally useless if it were bottled up in Kronstadt.

As they must have known, the three naval men were preaching to the converted. In 1936, shortly after he had been appointed party boss of Leningrad, Zhdanov had made a speech which must have been ominous reading in Helsinki and the Baltic states. The fascists, Zhdanov declared, threatened the security of his city. He warned the Soviet Union's neighbours: 'It does not pay small countries to get entangled in big adventures.' If they did so, he went on, then the Soviet Union could not stand idly by – 'it would call upon the Red Army to redress the situation.'

Nevertheless, it was a highly instructive voyage for Zhdanov, and must have helped to reinforce the views he constantly propounded to Stalin. Because of his position both in the party hierarchy and in Leningrad, Zhdanov must have been the principal architect of the plan to take back the Baltic states into the Soviet orbit, and of the tougher approach to the Finns in October 1939.

It was on 5 October, the same day he signed the treaty with Latvia, that Molotov called the Finnish minister in Moscow, Baron Aarno Yrjö-Koskinen, to his office. There he gave him an invitation for the Finnish Foreign Minister, Eljas Erkko, 'or another qualified special representative of the Finnish government', to come to Moscow urgently, 'for an exchange of views on political matters of mutual interest'. Although the war between the Allies and the Germans was only a month old, it had changed everything, he said. The situation in Europe could never be the same again. He hoped Erkko would come to Moscow himself, but in any case, the Soviet government would like a positive reply within the next day or two.

Molotov did not say what the matters were that he wanted to discuss, but it did not take much imagination for the Finns to figure out what they were likely to be. Erkko told the American minister in Helsinki, Schoenfeld, that because Molotov had been especially courteous in his approach, the Soviets must have 'matters of moment on their minds'. That was the way they worked.

The invitation, in any case, did not come as any great surprise to the Finns. They had watched with growing alarm as the Soviets increased their pressure on the Baltic states, and knew their turn could not be long in coming. Obviously, they could not refuse the invitation, but, determined to demonstrate their independence, they chose to delay their reply while they sought help from elsewhere.

The first place they looked was naturally Germany, to whom they attributed Molotov's sudden friendliness after the signing of the Nazi–Soviet pact. Ironically, the Baltic states were also convinced that Stalin's 'reasonableness' over the number of troops to be stationed in their countries was due to German influence. Finnish confidence in Germany had been shaken but evidently not destroyed by the Germans' refusal to intercede with the Soviets over the Aaland Island problem two weeks before.

Even while Ribbentrop had been in Moscow signing the Boundary and Friendship Treaty, Finnish Foreign Minister Erkko had had a message relayed to him saying that Finland would never submit to the sort of demands the Soviets were imposing on Estonia. 'We would rather let it come to the worst,' he had declared.

The Germans had been non-committal both then and again on 2 October, when the Finns asked for some reassurance about the effects of the zones of influence agreed between Germany and the Soviet Union. Nevertheless, Erkko made a personal appeal to the Germans, asking if they would support Finland 'in the event of excessive Russian demands'. He played up the potential Soviet threat to Germany.

'Surely you realise,' he asked, 'that if Russia occupies the Aaland Islands or some important Finnish port, the balance of power in the Baltic will turn decisively against Germany?'

But still the Germans remained unmoved. Beginning to realise the truth at last, the Finns mobilised their frontier guards, and started looking for help elsewhere. With their traditional friend and trading partner, Great Britain, at war with Germany and therefore completely out of the game, they turned to the United States. In Washington the Finnish minister asked Secretary of State Cordell Hull if he would 'say something in some way to the Soviet government with the view of discouraging any objectionable acts by the Soviet Union'. Hull replied that he was sorry, but he could not do that. However, pressure from the

British Foreign Office and a personal letter from the Crown Prince of Sweden eventually succeeded in persuading President Roosevelt to send a message to President Kalinin of the USSR saying: 'The President expresses the earnest hope that the Soviet Union will make no demands on Finland which are incompatible with the maintenance and development of amicable and peaceful relations between the two countries, and the independence of each.'

Meanwhile, after two days of waiting, Molotov was growing impatient. On Saturday, 7 October, at 7 pm he sent for the Finnish minister and demanded to know why there had been no reply. When could he expect Erkko to arrive? In fact, Erkko's telegram was already in Moscow, where it had been held in the Soviet telegraph office since 8 o'clock that morning. It was not delivered to Yrjö-Koskinen at the Finnish legation until 11.30 pm, so it was 1 am on Sunday, 8 October, before he was able to inform Molotov officially. What he had to say was that although the Finnish government would be sending a representative, Erkko would not be coming to Moscow himself.

A newspaper proprietor by profession, very much in the Beaverbrook or Hearst mould and with a reputation for bullying his editors, Erkko had no intention of travelling to the Kremlin like a suppliant. 'The Foreign Minister's place,' he informed the foreign press corps, 'is with his government.' Instead, he would be sending a small delegation led by the Finnish minister in Stockholm, a sixty-nine-year-old State Councillor, Conservative politician and retired banker called Juho Kusti Paasikivi.

Paasikivi had many qualifications to recommend him for the job, in addition to speaking excellent Russian after studying in St Petersburg in the 1890s. But one stood out from all the others. In the course of a long and until then not particularly distinguished political career, he had had one outstanding success. It was a success with which Stalin was only too familiar: back in 1920, Paasikivi had been the leader of the Finnish delegation which had squeezed the Soviets, including Stalin himself, so mercilessly for the Treaty of Tartu.

35

NIGHT TRAIN TO MOSCOW

The Finnish government had deliberately tried to play down the importance of the Moscow talks – at least as far as the Finnish public were concerned. Not wishing to cause panic, they had kept the people more or less in the dark regarding Soviet intentions. Nevertheless, when the time came for Paasikivi and his small staff to board the train to Moscow on the evening of Monday, 9 October, the people sensed that something of profound importance to their country was in the balance.

In one of those rare moments of spontaneous national emotion, huge crowds of ordinary Finns gathered at Helsinki's modernistic red granite railway station. They crowded on to the platforms, filled the station hall, and packed the square outside. Thousands upon thousands had come to wish their unlikely hero well.

In the golden light of that northern evening, they sang patriotic songs and Luther's great hymn, *A Mighty Fortress is our God*, while the bespectacled Prime Minister, A. K. Cajander, said his farewells to the chosen emissary of his government. At the end, the crowd sang the Finnish national anthem, *Maamme* (*Our Land*). It was a scene that was to be repeated at every station where they stopped between Helsinki and the Soviet border.

Not a man given to displays of emotion – apart from pure rage at the stupidity of others – Paasikivi was nevertheless deeply moved. He stood bareheaded on the steps of his coach, then the whistle blew and he waved to the cheering crowd as the night train for Moscow slid away.

Travelling with Paasikivi were Colonel Aladar Paasonen, a former military attaché at the legation in Moscow, and Johann Nykopp, the rising young diplomat who had also served in Moscow, and who was now a departmental head in the Finnish Foreign Ministry. Both spoke Russian well. And both respected Paasikivi and understood the quirks of character that could make him such an uncomfortable colleague.

Paasikivi was a big man with pebble glasses, a square, close-cropped head, and a face that seemed to have been shaped out of wet dough. He looked like a character from one of the Grimm Brothers' fairy tales – a peasant grandfather, tough, humorous, but above all solid. He was a man of almost legendary irascibility, given to throwing inkwells and other pieces of desk furniture. Everyone who worked with Paasikivi sooner or later had to learn how to duck. And that was not all: 'If you weren't fired at least twice a week,' Johann Nykopp recalls, 'you knew you weren't doing your job properly.'

He was a staunch patriot – christened Johann August Hellsten, he had decided to Finnicise his name at the age of fifteen – and was therefore an excellent choice for the job he was now undertaking. But the Finnish government had other reasons, too, for sending him. He was a lifelong Conservative who was regarded as being utterly safe politically. He had once even advocated turning Finland into a Scandinavian-style monarchy. Coupled with the memory of his role in the 1920 negotiations at Tartu, this meant that whatever the outcome of the talks in Moscow, no one would be likely to accuse him of selling out Finland to the Bolsheviks.

A further consideration was that his active political career appeared to be over. He was, it seemed, expendable, having been put out to pasture as minister in Sweden, though this was then regarded as one of the most important Finnish diplomatic posts. Should the situation turn sour, he could be disowned with minimal political repercussions.

Conservative though he may have been in domestic politics, Paasikivi was a realist when it came to foreign affairs. His approach to the Soviet Union can perhaps best be judged from his actions when he came to power in November 1944 after Finland's defeat in the second world war – thus confounding those who in 1939 had thought he was finished. For the next twelve years, first as Prime Minister then as President of the Finnish republic, he followed what came to be known as the 'Paasikivi line'. This was laid out in the Independence Day speech he made in 1944. 'Good, trusting relations must be built up in future with our great neighbour,' he told his fellow countrymen. 'Suspicion must be banished, and friendship cemented. It is in the basic interests of the nation for Finland's foreign policy in future to be directed so that it does not clash with the interests of the Soviet Union.'

He put the matter even more bluntly to a colleague who was outraged that the USSR would not allow Finland to adopt an independent foreign policy after the war. 'We are a country of five million people living next door to two hundred million,' said Paasikivi, sucking his false tooth, as was his habit, as he spoke. 'If the situation were reversed and there were two hundred million Finns and only five million Russians, do you think we would allow them an independent foreign policy?'

Paasikivi's train arrived in Moscow the following day, the day on which the Lithuanians signed their treaty with the Soviet Union. The Soviet–Finnish talks were not due to start until Thursday, 12 October, so they had the best part of forty-eight hours to prepare themselves. The weather in Moscow was warm and dry and golden and the Finns took advantage of it to relax by walking, visiting museums and theatres. Whenever they left the legation, they were shadowed by NKVD men. Two followed Paasikivi's every move: friendly young men, he recalled, who helped him find his way about the city.

Back in Helsinki, however, the atmosphere was not so calm. German minister Blücher reported to Berlin that day that because of the fear of war with the USSR many Finns had panicked and were fleeing the city to the western part of the country in order to get as far away from the reach of the Soviet air force as possible. Finnish mobilisation was going ahead at full speed. Hospitals and schools were being evacuated and their buildings turned over to military use. The German school, Blücher said, was about to be closed. Banks were having difficulty meeting mass withdrawals. And because of persistent German refusals to become involved in the dispute between Finland and the USSR, there was a great deal of anti-German feeling: it was popularly believed that Germany had sold Finland to the Soviet Union. There had been a number of attacks on Germans, and several cases had been reported of German employees in Finnish firms being dismissed.

Poor Blücher, who had been in Finland since 1935 and had formed a deep attachment to the country and its people, was most distressed that he was unable to give any hope to those who begged him for German help. In spite of the constant flow of instructions from Berlin telling him Finland was in the Soviet sphere of interest, he continued for weeks trying to persuade Ribbentrop to give some sort of assistance to the Finns. But his appeals were all in vain. As early as 10 October, Ribbentrop sent him a curt instruction to take whatever steps were necessary to prevent former Finnish President Svinhufvud carrying out his stated intention of travelling to Berlin to try and win support for Finland.

'Germany is not concerned with Russo-Finnish problems,' Ribbentrop ordered Blücher to say. 'Germany can only recommend a direct Russo-Finnish understanding.'

Next day, Blücher was forced to telephone Berlin to ask permission for the evacuation of Germans from Finland, because of the danger of attacks on them by outraged Finns. With the war scare heightening every day, evacuation of Swedish nationals had already begun, and the Finnish government had announced its intention to leave Helsinki.

Ribbentrop gave his approval for German nationals and ethnic Germans, *Reichsdeutsche* and *Volksdeutsche*, to be evacuated if they wished. But in fact, the evacuation of Germans from Finland was the least of Hitler's concerns in the Baltic at the moment. He was much more interested in pulling the *Volksdeutsche* out of Latvia, Estonia and Lithuania, and in calming down Soviet fears caused by his plans in this direction. Stalin sent word that he was 'astonished that Germany was evidently promoting a panicky emigration of Germans from Latvia and Estonia'. Such a flight, he said 'would inevitably compromise Soviet action there'. He assured Hitler that the Soviet Union posed no threats, economically or in any other way, to Germans there.

Two days later, having heard nothing in reply from Hitler or Ribbentrop, Stalin complained that, in spite of his protest, efforts to evacuate the Germans were being increased. There were now at least ten German ships in Riga harbour, he said, German schools in Latvia and Estonia were being closed, German physicians were leaving 'in droves', and so on. He was most disturbed at such transparent lack of trust.

Ribbentrop replied at some length, saying that the emigration of *Volksdeutsche* from the Baltic states had nothing to do with any Soviet action there. Any connection between the two was purely an invention of English propaganda, trying to cause trouble between Germany and the Soviet Union. In any case, there was no question of 'panicky emigration or flight'. What was happening was a 'resettlement', which was being carried out in a perfectly calm and orderly manner, and which would probably continue for a period of months.

The reason for the exodus of *Volksdeutsche*, Ribbentrop said, was that Hitler desperately needed them to populate the farms, stores and workshops which had been vacated by the Poles and Jews forced out of the occupied areas. He expected the Soviets to agree to a similar resettlement of the Germans from the former Polish territory which they had occupied. Far from having any anti-Soviet slant, the German action in resettling the *Volksdeutsche* from the Baltic states was actually doing Stalin a favour, Ribbentrop claimed. 'It is a well-known fact,' he stated, 'that the attitude of the Latvian and Estonian population is in some instances quite hostile towards the Germans living there. This could have led to all sorts of difficulties in the future.

'The evacuation,' Ribbentrop concluded triumphantly, 'is thus a clear indication that we are taking seriously Germany's political disinterestedness in the Baltic countries, as agreed upon in Moscow.'

When Schulenburg delivered Ribbentrop's message to Molotov, the Soviet Premier expressed himself to be 'somewhat relieved', but said emphatically that his government – meaning Stalin, of course – 'saw no need for hasty resettlement'.

With the Soviet leaders obviously so jumpy about German intentions in the Baltic area, Hitler had to take extra care to avoid any danger of upsetting them over Finland. Fresh instructions were issued to all German missions that they were not to get involved in any way in offering support against the Soviet Union. Despite continuing pleas from Blücher, agonising as he watched his Finnish friends suffering, Hitler remained firm.

Promptly at 5 pm on Thursday, 12 October, Paasikivi led his small team of Paasonen, Nykopp and the Finnish minister in Moscow, Yrjö-Koskinen, into Molotov's office in the Kremlin. From there they were conducted into a conference room, where they found the Soviet delegation waiting for them, its composition showing just how seriously Stalin took the whole affair. The Soviet team included Molotov, his Deputy Foreign Minister Potemkin, the Soviet minister in Helsinki, Derevyanski, and Stalin himself, pipe in hand, wearing his usual grey tunic buttoned up to the neck, and calf-length leather boots.

Like the host at a dinner party, Stalin took his place at the top of the long conference table. The other three Russians sat on one side, with the four Finns facing them. The atmosphere was surprisingly informal and relaxed. There were no interpreters, since the Finns all spoke Russian, and, curiously for a high-powered diplomatic conference, no fixed agenda.

The proceedings opened with a rather general discussion. Molotov opened with a proposal for a mutual assistance treaty between the two countries, similar to those just signed with the Baltic states. Paasikivi rejected this on the grounds that his country was a declared neutral, like the other Scandinavian countries, Norway and Sweden. Next Molotov proposed to amend the Soviet–Finnish non-aggression pact, which had been signed in 1932, to include an additional clause saying neither party would join any alliance which might threaten the security of the other. The Finns were perfectly happy to accept this.

The preliminary skirmishing was now over. Molotov stepped back and Stalin took charge, running the conference himself from then on. He was consistently brief and to the point. Sometimes, when some particularly knotty problem came up, he would, as was his habit, rise from his seat and pace up and down, puffing on his pipe and listening carefully to all the arguments before making up his mind.

He made it clear that with the advent of the European war, the protection of Leningrad had become the immediate Soviet concern. Leningrad must be protected at all costs from any potential attack by land or sea. He therefore proposed moving the present Soviet–Finnish border northwards, up the Karelian Isthmus into Finland, a matter of some twenty-five miles, to take it well out of artillery range of Leningrad. In addition, in order to protect the city from attack by sea, he proposed that the USSR should take over all the islands in the Gulf of Finland, and lease the port of Hanko on the Finnish mainland for use as a Soviet naval base. He offered a payment of eight million Finnish marks for a thirty-year lease.

In the far north, he pointed out that the approaches to Murmansk, the

Soviet Union's only ice-free ocean port in the western part of the huge country, were also vulnerable. Here, he demanded that Finland should cede to him the Rybachi peninsula, which commanded the approaches to Murmansk.

In return for the territory to be ceded to the Soviet Union in both north and south, Stalin offered the Finns over twice as much territory alongside the centre of Finland. This would have the beneficial effect to Finland of thickening her dangerously narrow 'waist', the nightmare of Finnish military strategists since it meant an invader could swiftly divide the country in two.

The meeting ended on that note, and Paasikivi and his team returned to the legation to wire the Soviet demands to their government in Helsinki. The government's reply was uncompromising: they were not disposed to concede much, if anything at all.

The next meeting began two days later, at 4.30 pm on Saturday, 14 October, with Paasikivi reading a memorandum drafted by Colonel Paasonen, the former military attaché on his team. The colonel's argument was that, in strictly military terms, the Gulf of Finland did not pose the threat to the security of Leningrad that the Soviets seemed to believe. In view of the power of modern weaponry, the kind of naval assault which Stalin feared was no longer a practical possibility. Whoever controlled the southern – that is, the Soviet – side of the Gulf, controlled the whole Gulf.

Stalin was not impressed by this argument. If the colonel's paper had been published in the pages of some learned military journal, he said, then no doubt it could have provided the basis for a lively discussion of modern military theory. Unfortunately, he, Stalin, had to live in the real world: he had no time to waste on theories.

Paasikivi smoothly moved the whole argument on a stage further. He had been sent to Moscow by his government, he said, with the express purpose of putting Soviet minds at rest about the question of security in the Gulf. While his government had authorised him to discuss the transfer to the USSR of certain islands which lay close to the Russian shoreline, in return for some suitable compensation, his brief did not cover the Soviet request to move the frontier up the Karelian Isthmus. 'That would be quite impossible on economic grounds alone,' he declared.

'Soldiers,' Stalin replied grandly, 'never think in economic terms.'

Stalin was not a soldier – he was a bureaucrat. His days of military glory, such as they were, were long past. Yet throughout the conference he was evidently haunted by the ghosts of the Russian Civil War of twenty years before, when British warships had lurked in the Gulf of Finland and the White General Yudenich had tried to take Petrograd, the home of the Revolution. Then Stalin, having already claimed the glory for saving Tsaritsyn, the city which was later to be renamed Stalingrad, took control of the Red forces, as the special representative of the party's Central Committee, and saved Petrograd, the city which was to become Leningrad.

In June 1919, against the advice of his military experts, he had flung units of the Baltic Fleet, a few aircraft, and 800 troops from Petrograd into an assault on the two forts, Krasnaya Gorka and Seroya Loshad, which guarded the approaches to the city. 'The swift capture of Gorka,' he had written in a report at the time which did nothing to play down his part in the proceedings, 'came as a result of the rudest intervention by me and other civilians in operational matters, even to the point of countermanding orders on land and sea and imposing our own.' He had added ominously, 'I consider it my duty to announce that I shall continue to act in this way in future.' In 1939, his vision of himself as 'Stalin, the Saviour of Petrograd' kept intruding into the problems of the present.

'It is not the fault of either of us,' he told the Finns, 'that geographical circumstances are as they are. We must be able to bar entrance to the Gulf of Finland. If the channel to Leningrad did not run along your coast, we would not have the slightest occasion to bring the matter up. Your memorandum is one-sided and over-optimistic . . . It is a law of naval strategy that passage into the Gulf of Finland can be blocked by the cross-fire of batteries on both shores as far out as the mouth of the Gulf. Your memorandum supposes that an enemy cannot penetrate into the Gulf. But once a hostile fleet is in the Gulf, the Gulf can no longer be defended.

'You ask why we want Koivisto? [A Finnish island off the east coast of the Karelian Isthmus.] I'll tell you why. I asked Ribbentrop why Germany went to war with Poland. He replied, "We had to move the Polish border farther from Berlin." Before the war, the distance from Poznan to Berlin was about two hundred kilometres. Now, the border has been moved three hundred kilometres farther east. We ask that the distance from Leningrad to the line should be seventy kilometres. This is our minimum demand, and you must not think we are prepared to reduce it bit by bit. We can't move Leningrad, so the line has to move. Regarding Koivisto, you must bear in mind that if 16-inch guns were placed there they could entirely prevent movements of our fleet in the inmost extremity of the Gulf [i.e: round the port of Kronstadt]. We ask for 2,700 square kilometres and offer more than 5,500 in exchange. Does any other great power do that? No. We are the only ones who are that simple.'

In his turn, Paasikivi reiterated that he had not been authorised by his government to surrender any part of the Finnish mainland. He did not think Stalin's idea – or was it a joke? – for cutting a canal through Hanko

Neck [the strip of land behind the port of Hanko], and thus making it another island, would be taken seriously in Helsinki.

Molotov and Potemkin replied that the Finns made too much of the inviolability of their territory. After all, Russia had sold Alaska to the United States, and Spain had ceded Gibraltar to England. All the Soviet Union was now asking was to exchange territory for territory, and to lease a port for thirty years.

Following his instructions, Paasikivi based his legalistic arguments in reply to the Soviets on the Treaty of Tartu, which he himself had negotiated. But Stalin made it clear that he proposed going back two centuries earlier – to Peter the Great's conquest of Finnish Karelia in 1721.

The implications of this were not lost on Paasikivi. Nor was the fact that so far the Soviets had made no reference to the Aaland Islands. This seems to have been a deliberate tactic, designed to disarm Swedish opinion. By ignoring the question of the islands – once described as 'that pistol aimed at the heart of Sweden' – the Soviets hoped to remove Swedish concern: if Swedish interests were not at stake, why should the country eschew her long-held policy of neutrality in order to support Finland against the USSR?

At the end of this second day of the conference, Paasikivi informed Stalin that their discussions had now reached the point where he must return to Helsinki in order to obtain fresh instructions from his government. Stalin agreed, but reminded him of the urgency of the matter: the Finnish army was already mobilising, while the Soviets were reinforcing their own border troops. The situation was therefore explosive.

'This cannot go on for long without the danger of accidents,' he said.

Later that evening, the Soviets handed over a written memorandum containing their proposals. Stalin made no threats, delivered no ultimatum. He did not think it necessary to do so. He believed he made the Finns a fair offer, one they could not afford to refuse. But Paasikivi sounded a note of warning.

'We have to submit all questions of this sort to the Diet for its approval,' he explained, adding that on constitutional matters – including anything that directly concerned the territory of Finland itself – a five-sixths majority was required.

'You are sure to get ninety-nine per cent support,' Stalin replied confidently.

'And our votes into the bargain,' Molotov added, with a rare flash of humour.

Paasikivi was not so optimistic. 'The Hanko Neck concession and the cession of the area on the Isthmus are exceptionally difficult matters,' he said.

Stalin dismissed Finnish domestic problems with a wave of his hand.

'Look at Hitler,' he insisted, almost with undisguised admiration. 'The Poznan frontier was too close for him, and he took it an extra three hundred kilometres.'

Paasikivi did not care for the implication of this last remark. His country was neutral and wished to remain so. 'We want to continue in peace,' he said, 'and remain apart from all incidents.'

Stalin's reply was blunt. 'That is impossible,' he said brusquely.

Paasikivi refused to be put down, however. 'How do these proposals of yours fit in with your famous slogan, "We do not want a crumb of foreign territory, but neither do we want to cede an inch of our own territory to anyone"?' he asked.

'In Poland, we took no foreign territory,' came the reply, meaning that the Red Army had simply reoccupied land that once belonged to the tsars. 'And this is a case of exchange.'

As the Finns prepared to leave the conference room at 10 pm, Stalin said: 'We will expect you back on the twentieth or the twenty-first.'

'We'll sign the agreement on the twentieth and give you dinner the next day,' Molotov chimed in.

The Finnish negotiators left Moscow on 15 October, arriving in Helsinki the following morning. That afternoon, Paasikivi and members of the Council of State sat down to consider Molotov's demands. As usual, Paasikivi was brief and to the point. He told the members of the Council that they must offer the Soviets the sort of compromise that would satisfy most of their objectives. But the Council were deeply suspicious: they found the Soviet demands too moderate.

Obviously, they said, this was only the beginning. Later would come 'further, much more far-reaching demands'. Foreign Minister Erkko and Defence Minister Nuikkanen even refused to accept that the Soviets were genuinely concerned about the security of Leningrad or Murmansk. They believed Stalin simply wanted to return to the 1914 frontiers.

The sticking point for everyone, including the other Scandinavian countries when they were consulted, was the thought of having a Soviet military base on Finnish soil at Hanko. This was seen as a deliberate and serious threat to national sovereignty and independence, since the Soviets wanted to station no fewer than 5,000 troops there.

Only Marshal Mannerheim and to a lesser extent Finance Minister Väinö Tanner – leader of the Social Democrat Party and generally considered to be the strongest man in the Cabinet – supported Paasikivi's line. The split within the Council was such that Paasikivi refused to return to Moscow unless one of the Council members went with him. He nominated Tanner, no doubt hoping the Council would be prepared to be more realistic if he had another voice of reason backing him up.

There is no record of whether Paasikivi resorted to throwing inkwells in order to persuade the other Council members, though his rage at their stupidity must have been something to behold. Eventually, they agreed that Tanner should accompany him – but even so, Paasikivi could not have been greatly encouraged by Erkko's parting remark as they boarded the train again for Moscow, to another emotional send-off by huge crowds. Erkko advised him, in all seriousness: 'Forget that Russia is a great power.'

Back in the Kremlin again, Paasikivi must have wondered if he had done the right thing in asking Tanner along. For some reason, in response to Stalin's courteous greeting, the Finance Minister decided to make it clear he was impervious to Russian – or even Georgian – charm. Perhaps it was nerves, perhaps it was merely a desire to establish from the start that he was his own man and not Paasikivi's assistant – whatever the cause, he introduced himself with the words, 'I am a Menshevik.' Since Stalin regarded the Mensheviks, the more moderate socialists who had been the Bolsheviks' great rival in the 1917 Revolution, as the worst traitors in the Soviet state, it was hardly a remark calculated to win him over. When Tanner, whose Russian was weak, asked for permission a few minutes later to address the Soviets in German or English, Molotov replied with a curt 'Nyet!' The meeting was conducted in Russian, with Nykopp acting as interpreter for Tanner.

Paasikivi started by saying Finland was now prepared to make some concessions. These included ceding various islands in the Gulf of Finland and moving the Karelian frontier back up the Isthmus some thirteen kilometres, eight miles, though not the twenty-five miles demanded by Stalin. However, he made it clear that on Hanko the Finns had not changed their position.

Stalin was not impressed, and insisted the new concessions were not enough. The original demands, he said, had been the bare minimum required for Soviet security, and could not be bargained away. He thought the present European war could easily escalate into a world war which might last for many years. In that event, the USSR must be able to defend Leningrad from attack via the Gulf.

For two hours, both sides swapped the same old arguments with neither side giving an inch, except that the Finns did indicate they were prepared to consider a border adjustment in the north, on the Rybachi peninsula near Murmansk. Otherwise, there was nothing new, and eventually the negotiations stalled. Paasikivi and Tanner prepared to leave, to the astonishment of Molotov.

'Is it your intention to provoke a conflict?' he asked.

'We want no such thing,' Paasikivi replied firmly. 'But you seem to.'

With that they returned to the legation and drafted a telegram to Helsinki asking permission to return home.

Paasikivi's tough stand paid off. At about 9 pm, barely an hour after the Finns had walked out, Molotov's secretary telephoned them to ask if they would come back to the Kremlin for further talks that night. The resumed meeting started at 11 pm.

Again, Stalin and Molotov faced the Finns alone. Molotov had drafted a memorandum after the earlier session, in which the Soviets made certain modifications to their position. Instead of demanding the right to put a Soviet garrison of 5,000 men into Hanko, they were prepared to reduce the number to 4,000, and guarantee to remove them on 'the termination of the British–French–German war'. In addition, they were prepared to compromise on the Karelian frontier issue.

Neither Paasikivi nor Tanner thought these concessions were in themselves enough to change the mind of the government, but they agreed to report them to Helsinki nevertheless.

Early next morning, Paasikivi went to Tanner's room in the legation, after a sleepless night spent trying to find a way through the impasse. He had come to the conclusion, he told Tanner, that for the past twenty years the Finns had been living in a fool's paradise. They had chosen neutrality, but the truth was that neutrality was a luxury they could not afford with the Soviet Union as a next-door neighbour. Since they could not change the geography, they would have to change their policies.

If they refused the Soviet demands, he continued, this would lead to war – a war which Finland would inevitably lose. He proposed, therefore, to advise the Finnish government to accept Moscow's terms. It was possible that the Soviets could be persuaded to accept the island of Jussarö as a base, instead of the mainland area of Hanko. And if the Finns withdrew to a new frontier in Karelia, just short of the city of Viipuri, then perhaps the Soviets could be persuaded to accept that, too.

Paasikivi and Tanner arrived back in Helsinki on 26 October to find the Council had still failed to grasp the realities of the situation. The ministers seemed to be living in an Alice in Wonderland world, making statements which were totally at variance with the coldly pessimistic assessments of their own military advisers. Marshal Mannerheim himself bluntly forecast national disaster in the event of war with the Soviet Union. But the politicians refused to heed such warnings. Defence Minister Nuikkanen pooh-poohed his own generals. 'The military command is always too pessimistic,' he told Paasikivi airily.

To compound their stupidity, the members of the Council of State also conspired to keep the Finnish people in ignorance of the true state of affairs. Erkko even continued to preserve the fiction that in the last resort they could rely on Sweden to come to their aid. Bolstered by this false confidence, he drafted yet another set of proposals for Paasikivi to take back to Moscow. These offered a little more territory in Karelia – taking the border to thirty-seven miles from Leningrad – and some in the far north, but not enough to come close to satisfying even the latest, scaled-down Soviet demands.

'If Finland sticks to her guns,' Erkko confidently asserted, 'Russia will climb down.' It was an unfortunate choice of cliché – Mannerheim had already told him the Finnish army had only enough artillery shells to last a fortnight if war broke out.

On the Soviet side it is clear that Stalin, no doubt advised by Otto Kuusinen, his Finnish confidant, still believed the Finns would see sense in the end. Perhaps Kuusinen overestimated the political flexibility of his countrymen. In any event, the last thing Stalin wanted at this time was a war on his northern frontier. He and his advisers had analysed the Finnish position with great care, concluding that it was hopeless. They presumed the Finns must have come to the same conclusion – what other conclusion was there to be reached? Surely, their argument went, no country would contemplate its own destruction when, by coming to an agreement, it would actually gain rather than lose territory? As always with Stalin, political logic dictated his own actions, and, as always, he presumed it dictated the actions of others. Paasikivi and his party were already on their way back to Moscow when Molotov addressed the Supreme Soviet at 9 pm on 31 October. The speech was a general review of foreign affairs, but dwelt mainly upon the Finnish negotiations, its tone cool and unthreatening. Breaking the confidentiality which had been carefully maintained, at least in public, by both sides, Molotov revealed the details of Soviet demands and Finnish responses. His purpose, he said, was to deny rumours that the Soviets had demanded the city of Viipuri, the northern part of Lake Ladoga [the large lake north of Leningrad, across which part of the frontier passed] and the Aaland Islands. He advised the Finnish government to be reasonable and not to give way to 'anti-Soviet pressure and incitement from any quarter'.

Significantly, however, Molotov made no mention whatever of the Soviet demands for a base at Hanko, but spoke only of the possibility of having such a base on one of the islands. Many observers read this as meaning the Soviet Union was abandoning any claims for a base on the mainland.

One of the objects of this public speech was probably to lay the Soviet position before the Finnish public, in the hope that they would see how reasonable it was, and pressure their government into making concessions. If that was so, it had the reverse effect: Finnish opinion hardened in the face of what were seen to be Soviet threats, and this strengthened Erkko's hand to the extent that he could threaten to resign if further concessions were made.

Paasikivi and Tanner had reached Viipuri when a message was relayed to them from Erkko, telling them about Molotov's speech. They telephoned back to Helsinki for instructions. Were they to proceed to Moscow, or was the Finnish government breaking off the talks because of Molotov's speech? Erkko replied that the government had decided to leave that decision to the two representatives. Paasikivi was furious, and raged at Erkko over the phone while the train waited in the station, accusing him of evading his responsibilities. He found the Foreign Minister's threat to resign particularly distasteful, he said. Nevertheless, they decided to continue their journey, arriving in Moscow at 10.10 am on 2 November. Their next meeting with the Soviets was scheduled for 6 pm the following day.

While they waited, the atmosphere darkened ominously. For the first time, the general Soviet attitude became overtly threatening. A speech in the Supreme Soviet by Alexei Alexandrovich Kuznetsov (no relation to the Navy Commissar, Nikolai G. Kuznetsov), secretary of the Leningrad Central Committee, proposing the motion to approve Molotov's report, accused Finnish ruling circles of delaying the talks. He then went to say: 'I do not know on whom the representatives of these ruling circles are counting. It is well known to all of us that certain governments in Europe also counted on someone. They hoped for, and even obtained, guarantees, but what occurred is also well known to all of us. Is it not clear that the sole guarantee, the sole hope for the preservation of peace and for the security and independence of Finland is the Soviet Union alone?' The clear reference to Poland was unmistakable.

Next day, there was more. *Pravda* did not appear until 2.30 pm, and when it did, it carried an editorial on the front page: 'Concerning the Question of the Soviet–Finnish Negotiations'. The sub-heading read: 'The Minister of Foreign Affairs of Finland Calls for a War with the Soviet Union'. It quoted alleged remarks by Erkko – which he vigorously denied – describing the Soviet demand for frontier changes in Karelia as 'Russian imperialism which Finland could not accept and would therefore defend her territory'. Erkko's 'threats', *Pravda* stated, were 'line for line like those of the former Minister of Poland, Beck, who as is well known provoked a war with Germany'. 'The forces on whose support Mr Erkko is counting in his struggle against the Soviet Union,' the editorial continued, 'are known to us and are the same which brought on the war and are continuing their unsuccessful efforts to drag the Soviet Union into the war against Germany and its Baltic neighbours.'

The article was said to have been inspired by Andrei Zhdanov. This may well be true, but the charge of Allied provocations was one which was to be used with ever-increasing frequency by Stalin himself during the next two years.

The Finns went to the Kremlin that evening amid strong rumours that there were substantial troop movements from Moscow to Leningrad. But they said nothing about these at the meeting, nor did they make any mention of Molotov's speech or of the *Pravda* editorial. Paasikivi wisely decided that the best course was to ignore such obvious baiting. To Finnish surprise, Stalin, who had done practically all the talking for the Soviet side at every previous session, was not there. Perhaps he was expecting there to be some violent argument, in which Molotov would play the usual game of making excessive demands in order for him to walk in and make generous concessions. In any case, no explanation was given for his absence, and with the Finns refusing the quarrel, Molotov simply repeated all the old arguments. Without Stalin, he obviously did not have the authority to offer any concessions, only to make demands.

When the meeting broke up after an hour, Molotov remarked quietly, 'We civilians can see no further in this matter. Now it is the turn of the military to have their say.'

Next day, when they all met again, Stalin was back in his seat at the head of the table, doing most of the talking. He raised the question of Hanko again, but Paasikivi told him that their instructions did not allow them to discuss this at all. Untroubled, Stalin produced a chart and pointed to a group of islands which lay to the east of Hanko.

'Do you need these islands?' he asked. He would, he said, be prepared to take them for a base, in place of Hanko. In return for dropping his demand for Hanko, he would want the frontier moved a little further up the Karelian Isthmus.

Paasikivi and Tanner had to admit that this possibility had not been discussed in Helsinki. They would therefore have to cable their government for instructions. Stalin agreed to wait for the answer, and the meeting closed on a friendly note. Again, there had been no mention from either side of the threats which had been made in public.

The annual celebrations of the anniversary of the October Revolution on 7 November (calendar alterations had changed the month) created an interlude in the talks for almost a week. Because Paasikivi was unwell, Tanner attended Molotov's reception for the diplomatic corps on his own. There, he was approached by Schulenburg, who asked about the present state of negotiations. Tanner confessed that he was not optimistic about their outcome, and pointed out that it was surely not in Germany's interest to let the Soviets have things all their own way in the Gulf of Finland.

'But what can we do?' asked Schulenburg. 'We're bound. At the moment we can't do anything. Now, the Russians have the opportunity they've been waiting for.' He pointed to the drunken revellers at the party. 'We have to work with these fellows.'

One of the revellers present was Anastas Mikoyan, the Deputy Prime

Minister and Commissar for Foreign Trade, who was at the moment heavily engaged in negotiations of his own, on the economic side of the pact with Germany. He was surprised to learn of the difficulties the Finnish negotiators were encountering. It was all the fault of the Russians, he said. But the Finns need not worry. 'Stalin is a Georgian,' he told Tanner. 'I'm an Armenian . . . We understand the position of a small country very well.'

The answer from Helsinki arrived on 8 November. To Paasikivi's fury, Erkko indicated that they were to continue the talks, but at the same time made it clear that they had no room for manoeuvre. When Paasikivi read out the memorandum outlining the Finnish position at the resumed negotiations at 6 pm on 9 November, Stalin and Molotov were astonished to hear that nothing had changed. The friendly atmosphere began to evaporate. If the Finns were still not prepared to lease Hanko, 'could you perhaps let go of this?' asked Stalin, pointing to the Finnish island of Russarö on the map. Tanner and Paasikivi could only repeat that they had no authority to discuss that.

'Then it doesn't look as if anything will come of this,' Stalin replied with obvious irritation.

The Finns unrolled their own chart and pointed to the island of Suursaari, also near Hanko. They were authorised to offer the southern end of this to the Soviets. Stalin was not satisfied.

'The island would have two masters,' he replied. 'It won't do. What do you offer us on the Isthmus?'

'There is nothing new to propose,' Paasikivi responded.

'You don't even offer Ino?' Stalin demanded, surprised at such intransigence.

Tanner tried to demonstrate on the chart how well Leningrad could be defended with the Kronstadt and Krasnaya Gorka fortresses and those islands in the Gulf which the Finns were prepared to cede. But Stalin remained unimpressed.

'The Tsar had them, too, but he still needed Ino,' he said. 'On that patch of land you offer us,' he went on, indicating the area on the Isthmus that the Finns were prepared to give, 'we would sit as though on the point of a sharpened pencil.'

He tapped the sharp point of his own pencil with a stubby forefinger.

By 7 pm, it was clear that the negotiations had finally ground to a halt. The Finns rose to leave.

'*Vsevo Khoroshevo*, best of luck,' said Stalin.

There was no more talking. Except for an exchange of letters, the negotiations were finished. Now, as Molotov had said ten days earlier, it was time for the military to have their say. But for the moment, personal courtesies were still observed.

As they were leaving, the military member of the delegation, Colonel

Paasonen, turned to Molotov and asked for his help in smoothing the return journey to Helsinki.

'Can you help us?' he asked. 'We have to lose a whole day in Leningrad, because of the train connections. But it would be a great help if you could provide us with a car to take us from Leningrad to the frontier.'

Molotov did not seem to see anything strange in the colonel asking the Prime Minister of the USSR personally to provide a car, and replied, 'Yes, of course.' In fact, Paasonen's idea was to use the car journey to see what Soviet troop concentrations there were between Leningrad and the border. Molotov understood this perfectly. When the party arrived in Leningrad, they found a car waiting for them – with their old friend from the Soviet legation in Helsinki, the mysterious Boris Yartsev, standing alongside it.

'You asked for a car,' he said cheerfully. 'Well, I will accompany you to the Finnish border.'

Paasikivi and Tanner, realising the Soviet game, opted to stay in Leningrad and continue that night, by train. But Paasonen and Nykopp had little option but to go with Yartsev – who took them to the frontier by such a tortuous route along the coast that they saw absolutely nothing of any military preparations. On the way, he asked them how the negotiations were going. The Finns said it was all very difficult, and they did not know how it would all end.

'But why,' Nykopp asked him, 'are you so concerned about protecting Leningrad? After all, you have good relations with Germany.'

Yartsev did not reply, but simply smiled.

'Why are you smiling?' Nkyopp asked.

Stalin's man looked at him steadily.

'Why are you smiling, too?' he asked.

36

'A TALE OF HEROISM'

After the negotiators returned from Moscow, the Finns behaved as though the diplomatic war had been won and the possibility of a shooting war had vanished. People felt an enormous sense of relief. Reservists who had been mobilised were sent home again, on leave. Evacuees from the cities returned to their homes. Schools, which had been closed for weeks, reopened. Finnish housewives began to scrape off the strips of gummed paper which they had criss-crossed over the glass in their windows as a protection against bomb blast.

Erkko spoke soothingly of the talks being resumed at some point in time. 'There is still goodwill on both sides,' he announced. More realistically, but equally inaccurately, he told a colleague that in any case the Soviets would not invade in mid-winter.

The only voices of reason and caution came to Finland from abroad, mostly from Germany. Again and again, both officially and unofficially, the Germans advised the Finns to make 'reasonable concessions' to the Russians. 'Otherwise,' as the German military attaché in Helsinki told a Finnish general, 'nothing might remain of Finland but a tale of heroism.'

The Allies, on the other hand, were eager to stir the Finnish–Soviet pot as much as possible. Winston Churchill, then the First Lord of the Admiralty in Chamberlain's government, could not disguise his delight at the increasing tension between Germany and the Soviet Union in the Baltic and the Gulf of Finland. 'It is surely not our interest,' he wrote, 'to oppose Russian claims for naval bases in the Baltic. These bases are only needed against Germany, and in the process of taking them, a sharp antagonism of Russian and German interests becomes apparent . . . There is, indeed, a common interest between Great Britain and Russia in forbidding as large a part of the Baltic as possible to Germany.'

Stalin and Molotov did not entirely share Churchill's opinion. Molotov told Schulenburg in Moscow that he was extremely angry with the Finns, saying their stubbornness in refusing such modest Soviet demands could be explained as only 'resistance bolstered by England'. The Soviet Union, he said, had even offered to pay all the expenses involved in moving the Finnish population from areas ceded to her, including the cost of building new homes for them. It could not understand their refusal of such generosity. More and more, the Soviet line was to liken Finland to Poland, whose leaders had also been given false hopes by the British and French. A cartoon in *Komsolskaya Pravda* drove the message home with brutal force: it showed Colonel Beck saying to Polish General Sikorski, 'We will wait for M. Erkko – he is following in our footsteps.'

The failure of the negotiations to achieve the peaceful transfer of territory which he desired had far-reaching effects, even on Stalin himself. He came under considerable pressure from a strong body of opinion within the Politburo, led by Andrei Zhdanov. Lined up with Zhdanov were Admiral Kuznetsov, General Meretskov, commander of the Leningrad Military District, and Admiral Tributz, the new commander of the Baltic Fleet. No doubt Molotov, whose earliest political positions of any note had been in the Petrograd (as it then was) party, and who had been chairman of the economic council for the northern region, which included Karelia, was among those who had become convinced Stalin was being too soft with the Finns. These hard-liners thought the time for polite negotiation was over – in their view, even Stalin's initial demands had been quite inadequate in military terms. They made no bones about the fact that they wanted a return to Peter the Great's frontier with Finland, which had included the whole of the Karelian Isthmus and the city of Viipuri.

In Zhdanov's eyes, the security of Leningrad was the single most important foreign policy issue facing the USSR. If Leningrad were not made secure from any external threat, the country could be sucked into the so-called 'Second Imperialist War' because of the need to defend the city.

Stalin was a cautious man, but in the end he was won over by Zhdanov's argument – and possibly by the fear of the consequence of his not backing the judgement of his own military men. With Hitler's armies now on the new Soviet frontier, Stalin could hardly afford another purge of the Red Army, and he was uncomfortably aware that many party officials still regarded his pact with Hitler with the deepest suspicion. He still had to prove to the doubters that the pact was in the Soviet Union's interests. Since the terms of the pact's secret protocol placed Finland within the Soviet sphere of interest, he could not be seen to be giving in to the Finns. In the end, therefore, he gave Zhdanov his head – but on the strict understanding that only troops from the Leningrad Military District – under the command of Meretskov – were to be involved. In effect, he was allowing Leningrad to fight for its own security.

Meretskov called a council of war in the Kremlin, to which he invited General G. I. Kulik, Chief of the Main Artillery Directorate, and L. Z. Mekhlis, Chief of the Main Political Administration of the Red Army. In spite of their high ranks, they had only minimal military experience. Kulik was a nonentity whose claim to fame was that he had known Stalin during the days of the defence of Tsaritsyn; he was an NKVD general notorious for his brutality, incompetence and stupidity. Mekhlis was another of Stalin's creatures, a member of his secretariat and of the Orgburo. Meretskov himself was only forty-two years of age, one of the young Red Army officers whose swift rise to high rank had come as a direct result of the purges.

One of the purposes of this meeting was to pick the brains of General N. N. Voronov, Chief of Artillery of the Red Army and a soldier of genuine distinction, one of the few senior officers to survive the purges. The first questions put to him were remarkably basic: 'Have you given any thought to the number of shells that will be needed for possible combat operations on the Karelian Isthmus to the north of Lake Ladoga? What kind of artillery is needed? What can we count on?'

Voronov replied that it all depended on whether they were planning to defend or attack. 'With what forces and in what sectors?' he asked, adding, 'By the way, how much time is being allotted for the operation?'

'Between ten and twelve days,' he was told.

Voronov responded, 'I will be happy if everything can be resolved within two or three months.'

The others roared derisively at his pessimism, and General Kulik ordered him to base all his estimates on the assumption that the operation would last twelve days.

Alongside the military planning, the Soviets were making preparations for the coming takeover on the political front, too. Otto Kuusinen, the exiled Finnish communist leader, was particularly busy, no doubt rejoicing at the chance of reversing the ideological defeat he had suffered in the Finnish Civil War. Even as Paasikivi and his colleagues had left Moscow for the last time on 13 November, he had sent a courier to Stockholm with a letter for Arvo Tuominen, the current secretary general of the Finnish Communist Party, who was then running the communist underground movement in Finland from Sweden.

Kuusinen's letter ordered Tuominen to return to Moscow in order to take over as Prime Minister of the new government which the Soviets planned to set up in Terijoki, a town only six miles from the Russian border which would be the first Finnish centre to fall to the invading army. But Tuominen would have none of it. His faith had been weakened by the appalling ferocity of the purges in the Soviet Union, and the Nazi–Soviet pact had been the last straw. Unable to stomach the Stalin line any longer, he chose to follow a similar path to that which Tito was to tread some years later in Yugoslavia: he decided he was a Finn first and a communist second. He ignored the order.

A few days later, Tuominen received a direct command from Stalin himself. Again he refused, and went on to tell the Finnish Communist Party that 'the fatherland had to be defended when it was attacked. This was the progressive, justified war of which Marx spoke.' His words were listened to, and had a notable effect. Aarne Saarinen, himself a future secretary general of the party but then a young fellow traveller, recalls that when he was drafted into the army he decided, after some discussion with his wife and comrades, to answer his country's call. Most other communists did the same, and distinguished themselves as some of Finland's fiercest and most stubborn fighters. The few who refused were imprisoned immediately and shut away in camps.

Undeterred by the lack of support from the Finnish communists, the Soviets went ahead at full speed with their preparations to take what they wanted. By 23 November, the German military attaché in Moscow, General Köstring, estimated that eighteen Soviet divisions had already been deployed against Finland, four spread out along the frontier from Lake Ladoga to the Arctic Ocean, the rest concentrated on the Karelian Isthmus and to the south of Leningrad.

While the Finnish government held meeting after meeting without coming to any decision on how to deal with the situation – they claimed they were trying to find 'some method of saving Russian face' – the Russian bear continued to sharpen its claws. There was a sudden burst of reconnaissance flights over Finnish territory by Soviet planes, and the build-up of forces on the frontier continued. False reports were assiduously spread by Soviet agencies of border incidents, and of the Finns shooting down Soviet aircraft. And the Soviets mystified most observers by purchasing vast quantities of Finnish marks on the local currency market, in exchange for US dollars. By 24 November, the amount bought was reported to have reached 22 million marks, and on that day alone they spent over 200,000 dollars.

Two days later, on Sunday, 26 November, Soviet pressure escalated dramatically. In the morning, a savage attack on Prime Minister Cajander appeared in *Pravda*, describing him variously as a scarecrow, a fool, a writhing serpent, a puppet of the imperialists, and a circus clown. In the evening, Molotov summoned Finnish minister Yrjö-Koskinen to his office and gave him a note alleging that at 3.45 pm Finnish artillery had fired seven cannon shots at Soviet troops near the Russian village of Mainila on the Karelian Isthmus. These seven shots, Molotov charged, had killed three privates and a non-commissioned officer and wounded seven soldiers and two officers.

'The Soviet government,' Molotov read from the text of the note, 'is forced to put on record that the concentration of Finnish forces in the neighbourhood of Leningrad not only threatens that city but is in itself an act hostile to the Soviet Union . . . While not wishing to exaggerate the importance of this outrageous attack, the Soviet government . . . proposes that the Finnish government withdraws without delay its forces in the Karelian Isthmus . . . to a distance of twenty to twenty-five kilometres from the border, thus eliminating the possibility of fresh provocations.'

The Finnish government investigated the incident, and did not deny that seven shells had struck the village of Mainila. But they insisted that the shots had been fired from the Soviet side of the border – perhaps, they suggested, owing to an accident during Red Army firing practice. Mannerheim himself said that the shots could not have come from the Finns, since their only forces in that area were simple frontier guards, who did not have any artillery powerful enough to reach Mainila – and in any case, they had all been in church for divine service at the time the shots were fired. With a certain bravura, the Finns suggested that in order to avoid any further incidents, both sides should withdraw their forces the same distance from the frontier.

The Soviets were not amused by the Finnish reply. Molotov delivered another blast on Tuesday, 28 November. The relative positions of the two forces, he argued, were not comparable. 'The Soviet forces do not threaten any vital Finnish centre, since they are hundreds of kilometres from any of these, whereas the Finnish forces, thirty-two kilometres away from the USSR's vital centre, Leningrad, which has a population of 3,500,000, creates for the latter a direct menace. It is hardly necessary to state that there is actually no place for the Soviet troops to withdraw to, since withdrawal to a distance of twenty-five kilometres would place them in the suburbs of Leningrad, which clearly would be absurd from the point of view of the security of Leningrad.'

The Soviet Union regarded the concentration of troops near the frontier, and the incident of the seven artillery shots, as hostile acts. This was, Molotov declared, 'incompatible' with the 1934 non-aggression pact between the two countries. 'Consequently, the Soviet government considers itself obliged to declare that it considers itself as of today as being relieved of its obligations under the non-aggression pact . . . which is being systematically violated by the government of Finland.'

When it received this ominous message denouncing the pact and thereby leaving the Soviet Union free to attack, the Finnish government realised that the situation really was desperately serious. Even when the Soviets broke off diplomatic relations next day, however, Erkko and the rest of the Cabinet still could not bring themselves to accept that war was imminent. They were brought rudely to their senses at 7 o'clock on the morning of Thursday, 30 November, when Soviet guns opened up from land and sea across the borders in Karelia in the south, and around Petsamo in the extreme north. At 9.20 am a single twin-engined Red Air Force plane appeared over Helsinki and dropped five bombs on Malmi airfield. An hour later, nine more Soviet light bombers attacked the fortresses in the Bay of Helsinki, but were driven off after five minutes by anti-aircraft fire. The Winter War had begun.

On 1 December, after three heavy air raids on Helsinki, the Cajander government received a unanimous vote of confidence – and then immediately resigned, 'in order to make way for a government with which the Russians will negotiate'. The changes were not particularly striking: basically they involved only Rysto Heikki Ryti, Governor of the Bank of Finland, replacing Professor Cajander as Prime Minister, and Väinö Tanner replacing Erkko as Foreign Minister.

Tanner was obviously the man of power, but since he was considered the evil genius of the failed negotiations by the Soviets, any thought that they would be more prepared to deal with him rather than with Erkko was wishful thinking. Molotov told American Ambassador Laurence Steinhardt, who had been asked by the Finns to represent them, that he blamed Tanner entirely for the collapse of the negotiations and 'that it was impossible for the Soviet government to treat with any government headed by him'.

In fact, the appointment of Tanner was irrelevant as far as the Soviet Union was concerned. Only that afternoon a 'People's Government of Finland', under the presidency of Otto Kuusinen, had been established in Terijoki, which the Red Army had managed to 'liberate'. The Soviet Union instantly recognised this government as representing the 'Democratic Republic of Finland', and announced the formation of a 'First Finnish Corps' made up of volunteers, which would form the nucleus of the future people's army.

The first act of the new 'government' – which was given phoney legitimacy by false Soviet claims that the Ryti–Tanner government had fled Helsinki – was to appeal for the help of the Red Army in 'crushing the warmongers of the Tanner government'. It was the first time this transparent excuse for invasion had been used by the Soviet Union, though it was to become a depressingly familiar ploy in future years.

Next day, Molotov signed a pact of mutual assistance with Kuusinen. Stalin, Voroshilov and Zhdanov, Moscow Radio announced, were all present at the 'negotiations'. It was no surprise to anyone that the new pact gave the Soviets everything they had demanded in the talks with Paasikivi, including the whole of the Karelian Isthmus, Hanko and the islands in the Gulf. What was surprising was that in return the Soviet Union gave the Finnish Democratic Republic no less than 70,000 square kilometres of central Karelia – over twenty times the amount of territory being ceded by the Finns – plus 120 million Finnish marks as compensation for the railways in the Isthmus and 300 million marks for the islands and the Rybachi peninsula in the far north. At last, there was an explanation for the frantic currency deals which the Soviets had been making – they were to provide funds, in this way, for the Kuusinen government.

The new 'people's government' was not universally popular among the Central Committee in Moscow, however. The Estonian Commander-in-Chief, General Laidoner, who was in Moscow in mid-December for talks on the military garrisons being set up in his country, recalled an incident at the Kremlin dinner which had been given for him. Late in the evening, after the usual endless string of toasts, Stalin had turned to him and said, 'Now I will drink a toast that will astonish some of the guests here, and might not win the approval of all.' He had then risen and raised his glass 'to the independence and national people's government of Finland'.

Laidoner gained the distinct impression during his stay that Stalin would abandon Kuusinen without hesitation if he thought this would achieve the settlement he wanted. This, according to Laidoner, did not involve incorporating Finland into the Soviet Union, but only gaining the strategic points he needed plus 'clarifying Finnish–Soviet relations' so that Finland could not align herself with the enemies of the Soviet Union.

The scene was now set for the swift resolution of Stalin's Finnish problem. In Moscow, Deputy Foreign Commissar Potemkin boasted to French Ambassador Naggiar that the entire operation would be over in four or five days. Voroshilov personally assured Stalin that Soviet motorised columns would have no difficulty in reaching Helsinki within six days. The whole thing would be over before any other country had time to lodge a protest.

The Finns, however, had other ideas. They had no intention of lying down and allowing Stalin's men to walk over them. And they were helped in their resistance by Soviet bungling, no doubt brought on by complacency and overconfidence.

Meretsov's plan was for a rapid general advance on all fronts, with the main thrust coming from the 7th Army, which was to sweep north through the Karelian Isthmus to capture Terijoki and then Viipuri, before turning westwards towards Helsinki. It was a bold and ambitious scheme, which depended for success on well-trained, well-equipped troops with secure lines of supply. However, even by the undemanding standards of the Leningrad Military District, the organisation was little short of disastrous. Meretskov later claimed that he had only four days in which to prepare for the operation, which suggests that Stalin had not given up hope of a negotiated settlement and that the final decision to attack was not made until very late: according to Meretskov, it would have been the same day as the incident of the seven artillery shots was staged.

Whether or not one accepts Meretskov's rather lame excuse, the facts remain that the 7th Army was not up to strength and the troops were ill-trained and ill-equipped. The infantry had no submachine guns, only bolt-action Mosin rifles, and even their clothing was hopelessly inadequate for what was to be the severest weather for over a century. For once, the Russians' traditional ally, General Winter, turned against them: in the extreme cold, men, machines, even the lubricating oil for tanks and machine guns, and the hydraulic systems of the 152-mm howitzer, froze solid.

The Finnish troops, by contrast, were warmly clad and armed with quick-firing Suomi submachine guns. In the south, where Meretskov's armour might have been expected to score heavily, the Finns sat secure in the Mannerheim Line, their own version of Germany's West Wall or France's Maginot Line, a seemingly impregnable system of heavily armed fortifications. The Soviet troops dashed themselves hopelessly against this, like waves on a stout sea wall. Elsewhere, the Finns fought a brilliant defensive guerrilla war. Camouflaged in white, they swooped out of the forests, silent as ghosts on their skis, and mowed down the Russian troops, who had been neither trained to fight on skis nor equipped with camouflage gear.

Lacking armour of their own, or sufficient anti-tank weapons to stop the Red Army's, the Finns turned to inspired improvisation. The Finnish State Liquor Board, for example, provided 70,000 empty bottles, which when filled with gasoline became the first 'Molotov cocktails', to be thrown at the 'death boxes' as they contemptuously called the Soviet tanks. Soviet losses mounted, partly because as a matter of policy the Finns took few prisoners, and when they did, they often omitted to feed or house them for days on end, in Arctic weather conditions.

By mid-December, Swedish observers put Soviet losses at 25,000 dead. The Soviet dream was turning into a very nasty nightmare. The large force advancing into central Finland suddenly found itself cut off and surrounded by a Finnish counter-attack. By the end of the year, the Red Army had been driven back from Petsamo in the north, repulsed time after time in the south, and cut to shreds in the centre.

On 30 December, American minister Schoenfeld reported from Helsinki that Finnish forces had 'annihilated an entire Russian division and captured large amounts of war material' at Suomussalmi. Soviet morale was evidently so low that another division positioned alongside had ignored the 1st Division's appeal for help. Other Finnish successes reported by Schoenfeld included a large Soviet force estimated at three divisions at that moment surrounded and in danger of crushing defeat north of Lake Ladoga. Only shortage of men was stopping the Finns from completing the job.

So decisively had the Red Army been stopped in its tracks that one Soviet general observed bitterly, 'We have conquered just enough Finnish territory in which to bury our dead.'

The European war was still in its 'phoney' phase. Allied troops faced the German army from lines of trenches and fortifications reminiscent of the first world war. Only at sea was there any real action – with the British navy searching out the German surface raiders, *Scharnhorst*, *Gneisenau* and the *Graf Spee*. But in Finland a real shooting war was in progress, and international attention was concentrated there. Every country sympathised with 'brave little Finland'. The Soviet Union's only supporter was Germany. When the Finns had appealed to the League of Nations immediately after the attack, the Soviet Union had been completely isolated: in a vote taken on 14 December, there was not a single dissenting voice against expelling the USSR from the League. The American ambassador in Moscow, Laurence Steinhardt, reported Soviet dismay that there had not been even one country on the League Council which was sufficiently afraid of Soviet displeasure to use its vote to block the result, which required a unanimous decision. Hitler, of course, had pulled Germany out of the League way back in 1933, within months of taking power.

All German diplomatic missions had been instructed on the first day after the invasion that they were not to express support for Finland, or criticism of the Soviet Union in any way. For many diplomats, particularly those in the Scandinavian countries, it was a difficult order to accept, but they all obeyed it to the letter. Even poor Wipert von Blücher in Helsinki managed to avoid openly expressing his sympathies for the Finns, though he continued throughout the entire war to bombard the understanding and tolerant Weizsäcker with long memos pleading Finland's cause, begging to be allowed to do something to help her, and pointing out the damage that was being done to Germany's interests in the region.

But German support was also expressed in more tangible form than mere words. Ribbentrop agreed to bar all arms sales from Germany which might find their way to the Finns, and to stop the transit through Germany of arms from other countries bound for Finland. These came mostly from Italy, which with a fine disregard for her alliance with Germany proved to be one of Finland's most enthusiastic supporters. Indeed, Italian aircraft shipments through Germany – some of which managed to slip through before the doors were bolted – came very close to causing a serious rift between Germany and the Soviet Union. Molotov, demonstrating just how fragile the trust remained between the two unlikely friends, accused the Germans of deliberately allowing the warplanes through. Only a very swift piece of diplomatic footwork by Schulenburg managed to smooth the situation out.

Confidence in Germany was restored within days, when the Soviet naval staff asked if German ships on the regular route through the Gulf of Bothnia to northern Sweden could take fuel and food for secret replenishment at sea of Soviet submarines blockading Finland. The German naval attaché, Captain Norbert Baumbach, recommended agreement. While he did not think such supplies would do much to affect the Finnish position, he was all for putting the Soviet Union under an obligation to reciprocate with supplies for German ships or submarines in other regions, such as the Far East. Weizsäcker replied the very next day, saying that German ships would be made available within a few days, and asking for details of food requirements and the types of coupling used for fuelling Soviet submarines.

While the Soviet Union had only Germany to ask for help, the Finns could look to the whole world, in theory at least. In practice, of course, most friends always say a great deal and do very little – and that very slowly. When the Finns asked the United States for financial help to the tune of $60 million, the government hedged and finally came up with an agreement through two banks for a loan of $10 million, to be used exclusively for buying agricultural surpluses and other civilian supplies in the United States. American law and policies forbade the sale or supply of any type of war materials. Roosevelt did, however, declare a 'moral embargo' on the export of certain goods and commodities to the Soviet Union, an embargo which was not raised until 1941.

The people reacted faster than the politicians in most countries. Money was raised by public subscription in Britain and the United States – some £300,000 in Britain alone – for the Finnish Red Cross and to buy arms for Finland. Some of the British money was used to raise and equip a force of 500 volunteers, a sort of International Brigade in reverse, to fight in Finland. Applications to join came pouring in from all over the world – some even from Abyssinia. 'Anyone,' according to Max Jakobson, 'who had ever spent a skiing holiday in St Moritz was qualified.'

Shrewdly, with one eye to American support, the organisers offered command of the unit to Major Kermit Roosevelt, son of former President 'Teddy' and a cousin of the current President Franklin Delano Roosevelt. Kermit had fought in France in the first world war, had settled in England afterwards and had become a British citizen. After some hesitation, the British government allowed him to accept the command. In the event, however, only fifty of the volunteers ever reached Finland, and they were too late to be involved in any fighting.

The Allies, meanwhile, contemplated the possibility of direct and official intervention in the Finnish–Soviet war, even though they were still doing nothing on land in their own war with Germany. The French, in particular, saw it as a means of striking indirectly at Germany through her Soviet ally, who was supporting the German war economy with raw materials. Any disruption of this supply, the French reasoned, must affect Germany's ability to wage war against them. There was also the deeper motive that intervention seemed to offer a means of diverting their war away from the frontiers of France and into Scandinavia. And behind everything lay the dream of the French Right – the hope of transforming the whole European conflict into a crusade against bolshevism.

The expulsion of the Soviet Union from the League of Nations, and the universal condemnation of her actions, left the way clear for the Allies to consider a large-scale Scandinavian adventure, to be carried out under the auspices of the League. Churchill had been interested since the outbreak of the European war in blocking Germany's supplies of iron ore from Sweden. In winter, these were shipped from the Norwegian port of Narvik. As early as 16 September 1939, Churchill had advocated laying mines in Norwegian territorial waters, even though this would contravene international law, in order to prevent the ore ships hugging the Norwegian shore. They would then be forced out into the North Sea, where they could be attacked by the Royal Navy.

With the new situation in December, Churchill's small but impracticable plan was soon replaced by what the British Cabinet called the 'big plan'. This involved landing a force at Narvik, crossing the top of Norway into Sweden – it was hoped with the permission of both these neutral countries – and setting up a base at the port of Lulea at the head of the Gulf of Bothnia. From there, they would send troops into Finland. Lulea was close to the ore fields, and in fact for over half the year was the principal access for Swedish ore supplies. The effect of the operation would be to cut off supplies to Germany, open up the Baltic to Allied raids, and effectively outflank the enemy. The Norwegian and Swedish governments, to no one's surprise, rejected the British proposals.

Not to be outdone, the French came up with two schemes of their own. One proposed sending Polish forces in exile – that is to say, Poles who had found their way to the West – to Petsamo to help the Finns. Marshal Mannerheim seems to have been not unsympathetic to this idea, no doubt believing that the Poles, with their traditional hatred of the Russians, would fight well on Finland's behalf. The second French plan was to mount air strikes from British and French bases in the Middle East on the Soviet oilfields in the Caucasus. This, they felt, would reduce oil supplies not only to Soviet troops in Finland, but also to Germany. The French, who did not believe at that time that the Soviets could ever be brought into the Allied camp, had no fear of provoking war with them. The British, who still maintained the hope that Stalin would eventually turn against Hitler, were more cautious. In any event, the plan was overtaken by the fall of France.

The most direct help to Finland came, as was to be expected, from Sweden and Norway, particularly Norway, whose approach to the concept of neutrality was always less strict than Sweden's. Sweden, however, found it impossible to remain on the sidelines. Swedish military circles were strongly pro-Finnish, as was the whole population, and they continued to supply their Nordic neighbour with whatever arms they could spare, though this did not amount to a great deal. Sweden also continued to represent Finnish interests in Moscow and to offer her services as a mediator.

The Norwegians were convinced that Finland was fighting not just for herself but also for the whole future of Scandinavia, and that they were therefore honour bound to support the Finns, at least indirectly. At the same time, however, they were determined to hang on to their neutrality at all costs, and for this reason had even abstained in the League of Nations vote to expel the Soviet Union. They believed that once the Soviets had defeated and occupied Finland, northern Norway would be next on Stalin's shopping list. Mindful both of the danger they faced, and the need to preserve neutrality, the Norwegians forbade any army officers from volunteering to fight in Finland, on the grounds that they were needed at home, but did nothing to prohibit any other volunteers. By mid-December, the German minister in Oslo was reporting rumours that there were already 1,000 men waiting to go to Finland. Similarly, the Norwegian government said it would not object to volunteers from other countries assembling on its territory, as long as they arrived as civilians with normal entry visas.

Stalin became increasingly angry as defeat piled upon defeat for the forces of the Leningrad Military District. He had only been forced to go to war with Finland in order to avoid losing face after the Finns had flatly rejected his demands. Now, the Red Army's disgraceful lack of success was causing the Soviet Union to lose face to an even greater degree. He was well aware that everyone was saying much the same as Wipert von Blücher, who wrote with barely concealed delight in a private letter to Weizsäcker: 'For the past six weeks, Finland has now been the guinea pig on which the excellence of the Red Army and the appeal of bolshevism have been tested by experiment. The result is unequivocal . . . the Red Army has such shortcomings that it cannot even dispose of a small country and the Comintern does not even gain ground in a population that is more than forty per cent socialist.' Swedish explorer Sven Hedin, a hero and confidant of Hitler, wrote: 'Finnish resistance may in certain circumstances change the entire world situation.'

The dangers, as Stalin knew only too well, were not confined to the world outside the borders of the Soviet Union, but could threaten his position from inside, too. The war against Finland had been unpopular among the Soviet people from the very beginning. As it dragged on, the fear of being involved in a full-scale war, which had been diminished even if only temporarily by the non-aggression pact with Hitler, began to revive. The nervousness increased as week after week passed without a victory, food and other commodities became more and more scarce, and the number of wounded Red soldiers crowding the hospitals grew every day. The flames of dissatisfaction were fanned by letters from the front, always bringing bad news, and by the lack of official support being given to the families of soldiers.

When Schulenburg said to Molotov on 8 January that whatever happened the Finns could not expect to win in the end, and that they might now be ready to start fresh negotiations, he was interested to note that the Soviet Prime Minister did not dismiss the idea out of hand: he simply said in a gloomy tone that it was 'late, very late' and that the Finns would have been better off to have accepted the Soviet demands in the first place. But the problem was, as Schulenburg acknowledged, that the Soviet Union could not possibly agree to start negotiations while the Red Army was losing.

It was a situation Stalin was not prepared to tolerate any longer. He sent for Meretskov and told him his bungling had undermined the credibility of the Red Army. He was removed from overall command of the war, and put in charge of the 7th Army on the left wing of the Isthmus. General V. D. Grendal was brought in to take command of the right wing. General S. K. Timoshenko was made Commander-in-Chief of Soviet forces in Finland. At one stroke, Stalin had destroyed the last pretence that the Finnish campaign was the sole concern of the Leningrad Military District. One of the first victims of this abrupt change of policy was Otto Kuusinen's 'Terijoki' government. It was never heard of again – the only 'people's government' ever created by the Soviet Union that did not eventually take power.

On 15 January 1940, Soviet artillery began to pound the Mannerheim Line, with an incredible barrage of 300,000 shells a day. The bombardment lasted sixteen days until, on 1 February, the Soviets launched a massive assault, throwing some 140,000 troops into the attack. Despite the weight of the assault, however, the Finns stood firm for more than two weeks, continuing to resist everything the Soviets threw at them.

To coincide with the military attack, Stalin had opened a new diplomatic front, albeit in a typically cautious, back-stairs manner. On 19 January, Alexandra Kollontai, the Soviet minister in Stockholm, paid a call on Swedish Foreign Minister Christian Günther. Günther had been trying since the conflict started to mediate between the two sides and get talks going again. Now, Kollontai sat in his office and read out to him a telegram she had just received from Molotov.

Obviously intended to reach the ears of the Finnish government, the telegram said that 'the USSR has no objection in principle to concluding an agreement with the Ryti–Tanner government'. 'However,' it continued, 'as regards the initiation of negotiations, it will be necessary to know beforehand what concessions the Ryti–Tanner government will be prepared to make.' Molotov went on to make it clear that in view of 'the blood which has been shed, contrary to our hopes and through no fault of ours', the Soviets' original territorial demands were no longer enough to guarantee the security of their frontier. Now, because of the war, they wanted more. For the moment, however, he did not say how much more.

The Finns greeted this news cautiously. While they realised they could not hold out for ever, they were not yet ready to give up. The Finnish minister in Berlin told the German Foreign Ministry that the next two months would be the most critical for Finland. If they could get through the rest of the winter, the Finns believed they would then be able to hold out until the end of summer, since conditions in the spring, with the thawing of the lakes and marshes, would present still greater problems for the Red Army. The Soviets would have to fight for every foot of Finnish territory.

The minister did not say – but neither the Germans nor the Soviets needed reminding – that by then the Finns might not be alone. The Allies, who were already considering what they could do, would almost certainly have decided to come in alongside the Finns. The limited conflict, which Stalin still insisted was not a war, would explode into something far more serious. As Blücher had said at the very beginning: 'It can in no wise be predicted how far the conflagration in the north will extend, now that Russia has hurled the torch of war into Finnish territory.'

By the middle of February, even Ribbentrop was beginning to appreciate the dangers. He told Blücher, who had returned to Berlin for consultations, that Germany had no wish to mediate between Finland and the Soviet Union at the moment, but Blücher was to find out from Tanner, 'in a discreet way', what terms the Finns might agree to. He was also to suggest, as though it were entirely his own idea, that Tanner might ask Ribbentrop to sound out Molotov on whether he would be prepared to send someone to Berlin to talk to an acceptable Finnish representative, such as Paasikivi.

The breakthrough came for the Soviet Union on 17 February, when at long last the Red Army scored its first success. Blücher provides a graphic description of the events: 'Day after day, the Russian army command, throwing tremendous qualities of artillery ammunition, tanks and planes into the battle, hurled its shock troops against the

Mannerheim Line at Summa, along the highway leading to Viipuri from the south. The Finns fought back with their characteristic tenacity and bravery and inflicted heavy losses on the Russians. But the Finnish troops, receiving no relief, eventually were unable, because of sheer exhaustion, to hold the first line against the continuous waves of Russian reinforcements. Field Marshal Mannerheim had to make the decision to withdraw the right wing and take up new positions.'

With the tide of the war at last turning in his favour, though the breakthrough at Summa was not sufficient in itself to decide the campaign, Stalin could agree to talk without losing face. On 22 February, the same day that the Finnish withdrawal to new positions was complete, he sent details of his new demands to Helsinki through Stockholm. These now included the cession of Hanko and the whole Karelian Isthmus including the city of Viipuri, plus the north-eastern shore of Lake Ladoga – in other words, a complete return to the 1721 frontier of Peter the Great.

The Finns still hesitated, uncertain whether the various offers of help from the Allies were in fact genuine, and whether they could arrive in time. Practical Allied help depended on Norway and Sweden agreeing to permit the passage of British and French troops through their countries. On 27 February, the Finns learned that the Norwegians and Swedes had refused permission. With Stalin growing increasingly impatient and the fighting continuing, it was possible that if the Finns waited too long the Red Army would overrun the whole country. For several days they passed messages to and from Moscow via the Swedish Foreign Minister, taking care not to let the Allies know, in case they should stop preparing the help that might still be needed. But with no clear sign that the Allies were in fact going to do anything positive, they eventually came out into the open. On 6 March, the Finnish government accepted the basic Soviet terms and despatched a delegation to Moscow, by way of Stockholm, to reopen negotiations. Three days later, Britain and France sent word that they would send troops and aircraft to fight the Soviets, if the Finns asked for them. By then, it was too late.

The first meeting of the Finnish and Soviet delegations took place in Molotov's office, as before, starting at 7 pm on 8 March. The Finnish team was led by the Prime Minister, Rysto Ryti, with Paasikivi acting as diplomatic adviser. On the Soviet side were Molotov, Zhdanov and Major-General A. M. Vassilievski from the operations section of the Soviet general staff. Paasikivi was disappointed to see that Stalin was not present, concluding, correctly, that the inclusion of the hard-liner Zhdanov did not bode well. Mme Kollontai had earlier suggested to the Finns in Stockholm that if they agreed to negotiate in Moscow, 'Stalin might make a big gesture.' With Stalin absent from the table, there was no chance of any gesture at all.

Any ideas the Finns might have had that the Soviets could be persuaded to negotiate on the same terms as they had offered in October were brusquely dismissed as fantasies by Molotov. The Finns had had their chance, but since the start of the war they had proved themselves ready to act as the tool of the imperialist and anti-Soviet powers. Under the circumstances, the Soviets did not feel disposed to be generous. Indeed, they had a list of fresh demands. Besides returning to Peter the Great's frontier, Finland was now required to cede territory in the narrow waist of the country, which would therefore become even narrower and more vulnerable. In addition, the Finns were to build a rail link from the new border at Salla to the Swedish frontier at Tornio. There was to be no discussion of the draft treaty, Molotov stated: the Finns must either accept it or reject it and take the consequences.

By now, the military situation had deterioriated still further for the Finns. Viipuri was on the point of falling and more Finnish withdrawals were inevitable. The delegations met again on 11 March, when Molotov reiterated that further discussion was useless. Would the Finnish government sign the treaty or not? he demanded. Shortly after midnight, they signed. The following day, the fighting ceased.

When the Finnish President, Kyosti Kallio, ratified the treaty, he said with some bitterness, 'Let the hand wither that is forced to sign such a treaty.' A few months later his wish was fulfilled when he suffered a stroke that paralysed his right side.

37

LESSONS TO BE LEARNED

The Winter War claimed the lives of at least 24,923 Finnish soldiers, with 55,000 wounded – a staggering loss in a country with a total population of less than five million. On the Soviet side, precise figures are unobtainable: Soviet governments have always been reticent about such matters. Estimates vary from 68,000 dead to the unbelievable figure of one million quoted by Nikita S. Khrushchev many years later as part of his campaign to vilify Stalin. Mannerheim put the number at 200,000, which is probably as close as anyone can get to the truth. Certainly, however, there can be no doubt that Soviet losses in men and *matériel* were vastly greater than those of the Finns.

But the Finns lost more than men. Under the terms of the peace treaty they also lost 22,000 square miles of territory, including their second largest city, Viipuri, the Rybachi peninsula above Petsamo in the Arctic, the Baltic port of Hanko, and the whole of the Karelian Isthmus with its valuable timber industry and ten per cent of Finland's chemical, textile and metal industries. No less than twelve per cent of the population lived in the Isthmus, well over half a million people. They had to be moved out within two weeks of the signing of the treaty, and resettled elsewhere. The still snowbound roads were soon jammed with a mass of bitter and bewildered humanity, trudging north, hauling their possessions on sledges occasionally pulled by car or truck, sometimes by horse, but mostly by the people themselves. They left behind their houses, their businesses, their livelihoods – everything they could not carry with them.

In strictly strategic terms, as far as Stalin was concerned, the Winter War had been a success. It had been brief; it had not spilled over into the larger conflict, though it had threatened to do so; and above all, it had achieved its purpose. The northern approaches to Leningrad were now secure and the USSR controlled access into the Gulf of Finland. And he must have derived great personal satisfaction from having restored the frontier of Peter the Great – gradually, all the old conquests of the tsars were being reincorporated into the Soviet Union.

But as Stalin must have been only too well aware, the bill for the military and political costs of the war had not yet been presented. It was not just men and *matériel* that had been lost: the appalling series of military blunders had exposed the inadequacies of Soviet training and tactics for all the world to see. The military credibility of the Red Army as a modern fighting force had been seriously compromised, and there were those who were already considering how to take advantage of Soviet military disarray.

The German general staff studied the tactics of the Winter War with keen interest. At the end of 1939, after the early Soviet disasters, they produced an evaluation of the fighting qualities of the Red Army: 'In quantity, a gigantic military instrument. Commitment of the "mass": organisation, equipment and means of leadership unsatisfactory; principles of leadership good; leadership itself, however, too young and inexperienced; communication system, bad; transportation bad; troops not very uniform [i.e. of variable quality]; fighting qualities of the troops in a *heavy* fight, dubious.'

The report concluded by telling Hitler precisely what he wanted to hear: 'The Soviet "mass" is no match for an army with modern equipment and superior leadership.' This reinforced everything Hitler already believed about the Slavs. The *Untermenschen* would always be defeated by superior tactics, superior training. In the end, numbers were unimportant; the only thing that counted was the quality of the troops, their equipment, and their leaders.

By the end of 1939, Goebbels was recording Hitler's reactions to the events of the Winter War: 'So far as Russia is concerned, the Führer hopes she has bitten off more than she can chew in Finland. We have no need of a two-front war. So far as the West alone is concerned, we shall soon settle the issue. The Führer has decided on a great offensive as soon as the weather and circumstances allow. The whole nation awaits it.'

The nation, and in particular the armed forces, had been awaiting the great offensive in the West ever since the end of the Polish campaign. Few of them, however, were awaiting it with any great eagerness, not even Hitler himself. In early October, he had made strenuous efforts, both with public speeches and through back-door emissaries like Birger Dahlerus, who had been kept busy shuttling to and fro again, to persuade the British and French to make peace. Many senior politicians in both countries had urged their governments to accept Hitler's offer, but on 12 October Chamberlain had contemptuously rejected it. 'Past experience has shown,' he said, somewhat belatedly, 'that no reliance can be placed upon the promises of the present German government.'

Two days later, Hitler was able to enjoy a sweet revenge for this rebuff, when the British battleship HMS *Royal Oak*, pride of the fleet, was sunk by a U-boat inside the Royal Navy's safest anchorage at Scapa Flow in the Orkneys, with the loss of 833 lives. And on 16 October, the German army pushed the French back to the Maginot Line with the greatest of ease, from the one small advance they had made into no-man's-land.

On 21 October, Colonel-General Wilhelm Keitel, chief of the German High Command, delivered with great misgivings detailed plans which Hitler had ordered the general staff to prepare for 'Operation Yellow', the attack in the West. To Hitler, however, the British and French were only an unfortunate obstacle on his path. Since the Allies could not be persuaded to step aside, then they would have to be shifted by force. But that did not change his ultimate objective, which lay in the east.

Shortly afterwards, he ordered Keitel to keep Poland's road, rail and telegraphic systems in good order, since the area was to be an important military springboard. And on the same day that he received the plans for Operation Yellow, he made a long speech in the Chancellery to party notables, in which he promised them that once he had forced Britain and France to their knees, he would turn back to the east and show who was master there.

The attack in the West was initially set for 12 November, then postponed again and again. First, it was the generals' insistence that the Wehrmacht was not ready, that the regrouping, re-equipping and retraining needed after Poland were not yet complete. Then it was the weather, as the fogs and rains and finally snow descended to keep the Luftwaffe grounded and the Panzers useless.

On 23 November, Hitler assembled his senior commanders in the great hall of the Chancellery at noon for one of his long speeches, designed to fire them with enthusiasm for the coming battles. He laid out the historical background to Germany's – and his own – struggles, and expounded at some length on the need for *Lebensraum*, which lay behind everything. In 1870, he reminded his audience, Bismarck and Moltke had faced the danger of a two-front war. Moltke had been in favour of a preventive war, 'to take advantage of the slow progress of Russian mobilisation'.

Moltke, he said, had always based his plans on the offensive, never the defensive. Success was achieved only by attacking a country at a favourable moment. But the opportunities then had been lost because after Moltke's death the political and military leaders had not been tough enough. 'The military leadership,' he said meaningfully, 'always declared that it was not ready.

'For the first time in sixty-seven years, it must be made clear that we do not have a two-front war to wage. What has been desired since 1870, and considered as impossible to achieve, has come to pass. For the first time in history, we have to fight on only one front, the other front is at present free. But no one can know how long that will remain so.'

He described the quick success in Poland as 'the most glorious event in our history', with 'unexpectedly small losses of men and material', and gloated that the eastern front now only needed a few divisions to hold it, thanks to the pact with the Soviet Union. The problem now, he said, was that 'the enemy in the west lies behind his fortifications. There is no possibility of coming to grips with him. The decisive question is – how long can we endure this situation?

'Russia is at present not dangerous,' he declared. 'It is weakened by many internal conditions. Moreover, we have the treaty with Russia. Treaties, however, are kept only as long as they serve a purpose. Russia will only keep it as long as Russia considers it to be to her benefit . . . Now, Russia still has far-reaching goals, above all the strengthening of her position in the Baltic. We can oppose Russia only when we are free in the west.'

The prospects for launching the attack which would lead to freedom in the west, however, were still clouded. Hitler was determined, according to Keitel, to move 'only when there was a forecast of several days of good flying weather, so that our air force could be exploited to maximum purpose. The next dates in November came and went in the same way, and Hitler decided to wait for a lengthy period of clear, frosty weather during the winter instead. During the days that followed, Diesing, the air force meteorologist, sweated blood for every one of the daily weather forecasts he had to make either before or after the main war conferences, painfully conscious of his responsibility should his forecast prove wrong. During January 1940 Hitler realised that there seemed little further prospect of any definite period of clear and frosty weather, and he resolved to postpone his attack on the western front – which had by now virtually frozen solid – until May.'

The military planners, however, were not allowed to remain idle. While he derived a certain amount of satisfaction at the Soviet reverses in Finland, Hitler soon realised that their lack of progress posed a threat to Germany's vital iron ore supplies from northern Sweden. He quickly saw, as did Churchill in London, that a bold Allied thrust across northern Norway, under the pretext of going to the assistance of the Finns, could result in the capture of the ironfields. The Red Army, which was putting up such a poor show in Finland, would be unable to protect Germany's interests there. The only answer, it seemed, was to take matters into his own hands. On 14 December, Hitler ordered the OKW to start studying the possibility of an invasion of Norway.

*   *   *

Any doubts Hitler might have entertained about the value of Norwegian neutrality as a defence for the iron ore and its winter export route via the ice-free port of Narvik, in north-western Norway, were swept away on 16 February. On that day the British destroyer *Cossack* brushed aside both protests and Norwegian naval vessels to pursue the German ship *Altmark* into Jossing Fjord, and there board her. The *Cossack* had taken off 300 British prisoners – seamen whose ships had been sunk by the German pocket battleship *Graf Spee* before her ignominious end in Montevideo on 17 December. The deliberate violation of Norwegian neutrality had been applauded in Britain. The *Cossack*'s captain had been awarded the Victoria Cross, Britain's highest military honour. How much more would the seizure of Narvik and the iron ore deposits be applauded?

On 21 February, Hitler put infantry general Nikolaus von Falkenhorst, a fifty-five-year-old veteran of the German force which aided the White Finns in 1918, in charge of preparations for a Norwegian campaign. Eight days later Falkenhorst presented him with a complete operational plan for the occupation not only of Norway but also of Denmark, in order to provide secure lines of communication between Germany and Norway. Hitler approved of the plan. He signed a directive for the operation on 1 March.

With intelligence reports pouring in daily telling of Allied preparations to despatch troops to Narvik, Hitler pressed Falkenhorst to speed up German preparations. On 4 March, he gave him six days to complete the detailed planning, so that the invasion could begin on 17 March.

The British and French troops were ready to sail on 15 March, with the intention of landing in Norway without the consent of the Norwegian government, and then breaking off diplomatic relations with the Soviet Union immediately before joining battle with her, alongside the Finns. The Allied intervention was only prevented at the last minute by the Soviet–Finnish armistice.

'The conclusion of peace,' wrote General Alfred Jodl, chief of the OKW operations staff, in his diary on 12 March, 'deprives England, but also us, too, of any political basis for occupying Norway.' Hitler ordered the invasion, codenamed *Weserübung*, to be postponed but not abandoned. He would have to think of a new excuse, now that he could not claim to be forestalling the Allies. In London, Churchill was doing much the same. Neither had any intention of leaving Norway to the other.

By 14 March, Churchill was recommending to the British Cabinet that they could justify an occupation since under the terms of the Soviet–Finnish peace treaty 'the concessions extorted from Finland, which allow free access to Russia through Finland into Norway and Sweden, are in effect an act of aggression against us.' Two days later, Hitler decided that rumours of British invasion, to cut off Germany's ore supplies, were sufficient excuse for him to move. He fixed the new date for *Weserübung* as 9 April.

On 18 March, Hitler flew south to meet Mussolini at the Brenner Pass – the first time they had met since the Munich conference in 1938. The primary objective of the meeting, as far as Hitler was concerned, was to persuade the Italian to support him in the attack on the West, which was still being prepared. Mussolini was being as reluctant as ever, and at the beginning of January had written to Hitler roundly rebuking him for becoming too close to the Soviet Union: 'I feel that you cannot abandon the anti-Semitic and anti-Bolshevik banner which you have been flying for twenty years and for which so many of your comrades have died; you cannot renounce your gospel, in which the German people have so blindly believed ... The solution to your *Lebensraum* problem is in Russia and nowhere else; in Russia, which has the immense area of 21 million square kilometres and nine inhabitants per kilometre.'

Hitler had been furious with Mussolini for trying to give him such a lecture, and had not replied. Now, however, he wanted something, and was ready to turn on the charm again. Looking fit and full of energy, he greeted the Duce cordially amid falling snowflakes high in the Alps. They sat in Mussolini's special train and talked solidly for hours, mostly about the situation in the west and German plans for Operation Yellow. Turning to the Soviet Union, and trying to win Mussolini round, Hitler was at pains to point out that the pact had been forced on him by the British, who had wanted war. He really had had no alternative, he said, and in any case, Russia was changing drastically. There was no difference now between a tsar of 1540 and Stalin in 1940 – both were 'out and out autocrats'. The *rapprochement* between Russia and Germany had been inevitable, but what counted was that, in avoiding a war on two fronts, he was releasing sixty first-class divisions for service elsewhere.

As for his future intentions towards the Soviet Union, Hitler said nothing directly in his conversation with Mussolini. But he did make one significant remark in passing, about the *Volksdeutsche* who were being evacuated from the South Tyrol, the former Austrian province which had been given to Italy at Versailles. This decision had been bitterly resented ever since by the Austrians, who had spent nineteen years struggling to regain 'their' province. At the time of the *Anschluss* with Austria, Hitler had drawn the frontier with Italy at the Brenner Pass – where he and Mussolini were now sitting – thus accepting the Italian claim, as payment for the Duce's support. Hitler said he planned to resettle these *Volksdeutsche* in a beautiful region 'that I do not yet have, but will certainly be procuring'. The region he had in mind was the Crimea, which he publicly allocated to the South Tyroleans in 1941.

Flying south from Berlin to the Berghof four days later for the Easter weekend, Hitler underlined his ultimate aims in the east to his army adjutant, Colonel Gerhard Engel. After reading a long and detailed report prepared by General Heinz Guderian, the Panzer expert, on the low standards of Red Army equipment and training in Finland, Hitler commented: 'We shall have to destroy them, too.'

Stalin, for his part, was as conscious of the military deficiencies revealed by the Winter War as any German general. It was clear that something had to be done. The question was, what? Diagnosis is always easier than finding a cure, and in this case the problem was complicated by the fact of the Red Army's recent military success in Mongolia. At Khalkin-Gol Soviet troops had faced the Japanese Kwantung Army, a modern, formidable, well-led force, and yet there Soviet tactics and equipment had proved their superiority – albeit after a shaky start. But in Finland, where they were fighting what was essentially a citizen army, they had staggered from disaster to disaster.

While the war still raged, no long-term solutions could be sought. At the beginning of 1940 all that mattered immediately was to find ways of winning this small conflict, and Stalin achieved this by changing the commanders and pouring more men and *matériel* into the fray. As soon as the war was won, then his first priority would be to hold an inquiry into the lessons to be learned from it.

But Stalin was in a hurry. If he was to be ready to face the inevitable conflict with Hitler's Wehrmacht, he knew he could not afford to lose any time. While he was waiting for the end in Finland, there was one area at least where he could make a start – in revitalising the Soviet aircraft industry. The way he set about it, in human terms, was typical of his methods at that time.

A. S. Yakovlev was a talented young aircraft designer, who only a few months earlier had completed the designs for the first of his Yak 1 series, which was to become one of the most successful Soviet fighter planes of the second world war. On 9 January, he was working at his desk in Moscow when he received a telephone call ordering him to report to the Kremlin immediately. Dropping everything, he rushed across the city, arriving fifteen minutes later in Stalin's outer office, where he was met by Alexander Poskrebyshev, the head of Stalin's secretariat, who bustled about like some demented White Rabbit, shouting: 'They are waiting for you! Hurry!'

Inside, Yakovlev found Stalin himself, with several members of the Politburo. Stalin introduced the young designer to a stocky, fair-haired man, Alexei Ivanovich Shakurin, who he said was to be the new People's Commissar for the Aviation Industry.

'It has been decided,' said Stalin, to Yakovlev's astonishment, 'to appoint you Comrade Shakurin's deputy. You will handle the research and experimental development in aviation.'

Yakovlev's immediate reaction was to refuse the honour. He protested that he did not have the experience to cope with such a huge administrative job. Stalin brushed aside his objections. Shakurin, he said, had just been transferred from Gorky Province, where he had been secretary of the party committee: he did not have any experience of the aviation industry at all.

'I am an expert designer and not an administrator,' pleaded Yakovlev.

'That is exactly what is needed,' came the reply.

'I am still very young.'

'That is an advantage rather than a disadvantage.'

Yakovlev protested that designing was his life – he could not live without it. Stalin was unperturbed, replying that he had no intention of forcing him to abandon his design work. Yakovlev could combine his administrative duties as Deputy People's Commissar with creative work on the development of new aircraft. But Yakovlev persisted in his refusal.

'So you don't want to be Deputy People's Commissar?' Stalin asked thoughtfully.

'No, I don't, Comrade Stalin,' came the reply.

Misunderstanding the reasons for the young designer's refusal of such an offer, Stalin smiled his slow, rather tigerish smile.

'Perhaps you want the top job, instead?' he suggested.

When the horrified Yakovlev vigorously denied any such ambition, Stalin tried a different tack. As a member of the Communist Party, he pointed out, Yakovlev had no right to refuse an order. In the end, it came down to a question of party discipline.

'But that is coercion,' protested Yakovlev.

Stalin was amused. 'We are not afraid of coercion,' he declared. 'We will not stop short of coercion when it is necessary. Sometimes, coercion is useful. Without coercion, there would have been no revolution.'

On 11 January 1940, A. S. Yakovlev was officially appointed Deputy People's Commissar of the Aviation Industry for Research and Development.

At the end of March 1940, shortly after the peace treaty had been signed with the Finns, Voroshilov reported to the Central Committee of the party his own conclusions regarding the lessons to be learned from the Winter War. If he had hoped to head off criticism in this way, however, he failed. With Stalin's backing, various members of the Central Committee demanded a full-scale debate on the matter in front of the Supreme Military Council, which was to be enlarged to include not only the heads of the armed services but also senior field commanders and the heads of the country's strategic industries. Their purpose in bringing together the army and industry was to institute a total overhaul of Soviet military strategy.

The debate began on 14 April, when the enlarged Supreme Military

Council met in the Kremlin. Admiral Kuznetsov, who was of course a member of the Council, wrote later that 'the lessons of the Finnish campaign were debated vigorously'. In fact, it must have been a pretty bruising session for many of those present, with accusations of incompetence and worse being bandied about quite freely. But, significantly, when the debate turned to the subject of how command at the top should be exercised in time of war, the issue was pushed to one side.

'There were even attempts at criticising the central apparatus,' wrote Kuznetsov. 'L. Z. Mekhlis, for example, spoke of mistakes by the People's Commissar for Defence and by K. Y. Voroshilov personally. Mekhlis was sharply rebuked. After that, criticism of the highest leadership ceased entirely. It was nipped in the bud, so to speak.'

The criticism, however, had been voiced – something which could not have happened without Stalin's approval, particularly by someone like Lev Mekhlis, who was one of his associates. Mekhlis was Deputy Defence Commissar, responsible for the political commissars who had themselves come under severe criticism for their role in Finland, and had a disastrous personal record as a would-be military leader. He had also played a prominent and particularly nasty role in the purges of 1937 and 1938. Even though he had been silenced, the fact that he had spoken out at all meant the writing was on the wall for Voroshilov. Kuznetsov commented that 'it was extremely important to discuss these questions . . . The Finnish campaign had shown that organisation of military leadership at the centre left much to be desired.'

On 17 April, Stalin rose to address the Council. He argued that 'the attachment to tradition and the experience of the Civil War hindered . . . the reconstruction of the Red Army.' Army commanders must forget the past. Its techniques must exemplify modern military theory. He did not mention Voroshilov specifically, but references to the Civil War and the tradition of the past were clearly aimed in his direction.

Stalin saved his personal attack on his old friend for a more private location, at his 'Nearby' dacha at Kuntsevo, during one of the interminable, all too frequently drunken nights that his cronies had to endure. Khrushchev, who was present, recorded that 'Stalin was furious with the military and with Voroshilov.' Suddenly, in a burst of rage, Stalin leapt to his feet and began to scream at Voroshilov, blaming him for the Finnish disaster. Perhaps he had drunk even more vodka than usual, perhaps he felt he had little to lose any more, but for once Voroshilov was not prepared to be Stalin's whipping boy. He leapt to his feet, too, his face as red as a turkey cock, and shouted at Stalin: 'You have yourself to blame for all this! *You're* the one who annihilated the old guard of the army! *You* had our best generals killed!'

Stalin's angry denials were too much for Voroshilov. Khrushchev says he 'picked up a platter with a roast sucking pig on it and smashed it on the table', scattering food and supper dishes in all directions. 'It was,' says Khrushchev, 'the only time in my life I ever witnessed such an outburst.'

Voroshilov's career as Defence Commissar was over. It had, in fact, finished at the end of December, when Timoshenko had taken over the role in all but name, leaving Voroshilov as a figurehead. Now, even that was taken away from him. On 7 May, Timoshenko, the man who had finally won the Winter War, was promoted to be a Marshal of the Soviet Union, along with the chief of the general staff, Boris Shaposhnikov, and G. I. Kulik, the ex-NKVD man turned artillery expert, thus bringing the number of marshals up to the 1937 level of five. Timoshenko was appointed Defence Commissar, while Voroshilov was demoted to the post of deputy chairman of the Defence Committee, a political rather than a military body.

Ever a survivor, Voroshilov managed to secure a place for himself in Stalin's war Cabinet, but his relations with 'the Boss' were never the same again. In later years, when Stalin's intellectual abilities began to deteriorate and his paranoia increased, with the onset of his stroke, he even began to suspect Voroshilov of being a British spy! Voroshilov, however, outlived his master, becoming head of state after his death, from 1953 to 1960. He died in 1970, at the age of eighty-nine.

38

'SEALED IN BLOOD'

'The friendship of the peoples of Germany and the Soviet Union, sealed in blood, has every reason to be lasting and firm.' This was Stalin's reply to a telegram from Hitler on 21 December 1939, sending 'Best wishes for your personal well-being as well as for the prosperous future of the peoples of the friendly Soviet Union'. Neither dictator seemed to see any incongruity in an anti-Christian and an atheist exchanging Christmas greetings – indeed, why should they, when their whole relationship was so paradoxical? And so, as 1939 drew to a close, the honeymoon appeared to be still beaming on both partners in this strange alliance.

Quite apart from the momentous events in Poland, the Baltic states and Finland, there was plenty of other evidence to support this appearance of harmony. At the very beginning of the European war, for example, the Soviets had given shelter to the German liner *Bremen*, which had been caught halfway across the Atlantic from New York when Britain and France declared war. Fearful of the Allied navies – especially after the sinking of the British liner *Athenia* on the first day of hostilities – the *Bremen*'s captain, Commodore Ahrens, sensibly made for the Soviet port of Murmansk, rather than trying to get back into the Elbe estuary and his home port of Hamburg.

Soon, the great liner was joined by a whole string of other German vessels hiding from the Royal Navy, including the smaller liner *St Louis*, famous as the ship which had carried 1,128 German Jewish refugees on their futile journey across the Atlantic earlier that summer in what came to be known as the 'voyage of the damned'.

With so many German citizens cooped up in the Arctic port, Schulenburg decided he must send someone from the embassy to keep an eye on them, report their condition and look after their welfare. Since there were known to be several pregnant women on board the ships, he chose Johnnie Herwarth's wife, Pussi, who had stayed behind in

Moscow when Johnnie went off to join the army. The vivacious, attractive young woman had always been a favourite with the ambassador, and as a divorcee he was delighted to have her act as hostess at diplomatic functions and dinners, and to be his confidential secretary. The work load in the embassy had increased out of all proportion after the signing of the pact, and while the number of staff was mushrooming – it grew from thirty-five in August 1939 to 150 in the spring of 1940 – an extra pair of hands was always welcome.

To her dismay, Pussi found there were no longer any express trains running between Moscow and Murmansk. She had to take the small train, where she found herself sharing a four-berth sleeping compartment with three men, engineers returning to their work in Murmansk. The 1,000-mile journey took five days, a striking example of the state of Soviet railways at that time. In Murmansk, she found the ships anchored in line astern along the narrow fiord. Neither passengers nor crew were allowed ashore, and she had to visit them in a small boat, passing from ship to ship each day.

In the beginning, before the winter closed in, it was quite a pleasant task, and it helped – as the solicitous Schulenburg had intended it should – to keep her mind off her husband at the front in Poland. Her visits to the *St Louis* and the *Bremen* were particularly enjoyable at first. Their captains were convivial men and their ships were well stocked with luxuries from the New World. But as the weeks passed and the food and drink ran low, the ships' sojourn became an ordeal for everyone. Pussi spent more and more time seeking medical supplies for the ships' doctors, and food for all on board. She scored her greatest success when she discovered the district's winter potato stocks, buried in great outdoor 'hogs', and managed to buy enough to feed her charges.

One by one, the ships managed to slip away. The *Bremen* finally departed in December, with the help of the Soviet authorities who imposed a total clamp-down on all other movements or communications from visiting ships of other nations, until she was safely back in Hamburg on 13 December. British naval attention at that time was in any case focused on the other side of the world, where the stricken *Graf Spee* was being driven into Montevideo by the hunting warships of the Royal Navy.

One ship which Pussi was not allowed to visit in Murmansk was a mysterious vessel with its name painted out, which arrived on 27 October. In fact, this was the *City of Flint*, an American freighter which had on an earlier voyage been a witness to the sinking of the *Athenia* and which had taken on board many of the survivors. The *City of Flint* had been stopped on 9 October by the German pocket battleship *Deutschland*, while en route from New York to Liverpool and Glasgow carrying tractors, fruit, grain, leather and wax, some of which were considered contraband by the Germans.

The *Deutschland* had put a boarding party on the *City of Flint* to examine the cargo, keeping the forty-one Americans in her crew silent by a simple but effective move. The officer of the party pulled the pin from a grenade and tossed it into the sea, where it exploded. 'If any of you makes a fuss,' he told the crew, 'you'll get one of these.' The Germans then took over the ship, putting a prize crew aboard to sail her. At the same time they kept the *City of Flint*'s own crew – and that of a British ship which the *Deutschland* had earlier sunk off Jamaica – as prisoners on board. To prevent trouble, they planted a time bomb in the engine room and warned the American and British sailors against indulging in any heroics. If they attempted to overpower the German prize crew, the bomb would be detonated. Having painted out the ship's name, they then sailed north under a Danish flag.

Arriving in the Norwegian port of Tromsö, they tried to provision the ship ready to sail on, but the Norwegian authorities guessed her true nationality, and refused to allow her to leave. They took off the British prisoners, but before they could complete the formalities and hand her back to her original American crew, the Germans managed to escape with the ship and the Americans, still held captive. They made for Murmansk.

In Murmansk, the local Soviet authorities found themselves in a quandary. International law was quite clear – they were supposed to intern the Germans and hand the ship back to the Americans. While waiting for instructions from Moscow, they compromised by interning the Germans, but not releasing the ship. Stalin, however, had no doubts what they were to do. He sent orders that the Germans were to be put back aboard the ship and allowed to leave with it – friendship sealed in blood prevented him denying the Germans their prize, but prudence prevented him allowing it to stay in a Soviet port. That might lead to all manner of complications.

So, refuelled and revictualled, the *City of Flint* sailed out of Murmansk unhindered on 26 October, with the Americans still held prisoner on board. To avoid the Royal Navy, the Germans hugged the Norwegian coast, trying to stay safe by keeping inside territorial waters. But the Norwegians were not going to be caught a second time. They intercepted the ship and forced her into the Norwegian port of Haugesund, where they put international law into effect by interning the Germans and releasing the Americans, with their ship. Unharmed, and with the engine-room bomb removed, the *City of Flint* sailed away with all possible speed.

Stalin had once again demonstrated his determination not to offend Hitler, and no doubt the Soviet handling of the incident helped to ensure that Hitler did nothing to help the Finns in their struggle against the USSR. But the *City of Flint* incident had an unforeseen consequence, which eventually weighed heavily against Germany. The incident occurred at precisely the moment when President Roosevelt in the

United States was trying to convince the Congress to pass his revised neutrality laws, allowing him to do far more to aid the Allies. The idea of the Bolsheviks holding hostage American seamen and an American vessel at the behest of the Nazis was enough to sway even the most isolationist of senators. The bill was passed while the *City of Flint* was sailing home.

In addition to providing a safe refuge and handling German cargoes for overland transit, Murmansk also featured in more positive examples of collaboration between Germany and the Soviet Union. The German motor vessel *Iller* was converted into an auxiliary cruiser in the Murmansk shipyards, and Soviet shipments of timber pit props left from there for Britain – the only ships carrying vital cargoes to be allowed to sail to Britain unmolested by the German navy. The reason for this apparent lapse in German vigilance was that the timber was being exchanged by the Soviets for tin and rubber under a barter trade agreement signed on 11 October. Although the Soviets promised they would not pass on to Germany any of the commodities supplied by Britain, but would use them strictly for domestic purposes, the British supplies enabled them to release such materials from other sources to the Germans, who needed them desperately.

The German navy was most interested in the possibility of using Murmansk as a base for repairing and servicing both ships and submarines. Grand Admiral Raeder, the navy's Commander-in-Chief, hoped that 'Russian neutrality – though interpreted generously in our favour – will remain in force in relation to the Western Powers'. Some of the schemes he suggested for supplying German ships at sea would have imposed a great strain on Soviet neutrality: he wanted the Soviet navy to provide escorts for German supply ships, and even suggested that the German vessels could fly the Soviet flag at such times. If this proved too much for the Soviets to stomach, he had a beautiful scheme whereby Soviet ships, loaded with supplies of fuel, food and ammunition, could sail from Murmansk unescorted and be 'seized' by German cruisers and submarines and then 'released' after handing over their cargoes. This, he considered, would impose less strain on Soviet neutrality!

In the event, Molotov and Stalin drew the line at such dangerous practices, but had no objections to providing facilities on shore for repairs and supply bases. On 5 October 1939, Molotov told Schulenburg that they agreed to the German request for such bases, but thought Murmansk was not really suitable, since it was an important Soviet port regularly used by ships of other nations, whose crews would be able to see what was going on. The port of Teriberka, to the east of Murmansk, was much better: it was more isolated and no foreign ships were allowed there. The arrangement worked well, and was of great help to the Germans in being able to service and supply their ships and many U-boats without their having to pierce the screens of British warships, submarines and mines which waited outside every German port.

The Soviets could be just as devious as the Germans when it came to disguising the assistance the Soviet Union was giving to Germany. The British tin and rubber were good examples of this, but by no means the only ones. Trade Commissar Mikoyan, for instance, told Karl Schnurre in October that the Soviet government was perfectly agreeable to the transit of raw materials through Black Sea ports, notably Odessa, as well as Murmansk. However, he pointed out, such shipments would need to be 'camouflaged'. The Soviets were prepared to buy raw materials on behalf of Germany, and ship them to Odessa in neutral vessels, ostensibly for Soviet use. 'One way of camouflaging,' he said, 'would be to mix the contraband goods destined for Germany with other cargoes which would first be unloaded at Bulgarian or Romanian ports.'

Stalin also agreed to have German cargoes unloaded in his Far-Eastern ports of Vladivostok and Dairen, from where they could be transported overland to Europe via the Trans-Siberian Railway. This was, of course, of enormous help with vital commodities from South-East Asia and the Dutch East Indies, which would otherwise be open to seizure by the Royal Navy at any point on the long sea voyage home.

Oddly, it was the Japanese who created most difficulties for Germany in the Far East. Despite their close ties with Germany under the Anti-Comintern Pact, and their loud protestations of strict neutrality, they gave every indication of favouring the British rather than the Germans. They made no protests when Britain declared virtually everything bound for Germany to be contraband, and went to great pains to comply with British control methods. Their ships put in voluntarily for inspection at British control ports such as Haifa and Gibraltar. While insisting on 'cash and carry' for all German shipments, they allowed British firms up to three months' credit, with payment at British ports. Indeed, the Germans complained that Japan was treating the British even better than the Americans were.

The Soviets were as annoyed by the Japanese attitude as were the Germans. Mikoyan complained that the Japanese were making his arrangements with the Germans unworkable, by telling the British of every cargo that left a Japanese port for Vladivostok or Dairen consigned to the Soviet Union but destined for Germany, so that the Royal Navy could intercept them. They even, Mikoyan fumed, 'provocatively stated that goods demonstrably destined only for the Soviet Union were being purchased for Germany', which made it extremely difficult for him to buy anything on behalf of the Germans. Mikoyan himself wanted nothing more than to co-operate with Germany to the fullest extent possible in these areas.

*   *   *

Relations between Germans and Soviets were not so harmonious everywhere, however. Along the new frontier between German-controlled Poland, known as the Government General, and the Soviet Ukraine, strains soon started showing through. Although the principal line of demarcation was laid down in considerable detail in the treaty of 28 September, it was not always so easy to translate the line drawn on a map into practical reality on the ground. There was always the question of this group of houses divided by the line, this track, that stream, those trees, to be argued over by the joint boundary commission.

Another branch of the commission had the task of dealing with the thousands of people who had been caught on one side or the other of the new frontier, and now wished to move to the other. One of the young officials on the German side was Erich Sommer, a young German Balt from Latvia – who had in fact been born and raised until 1934 in Moscow, where his father had been the owner of a private foundry which provided the German Junkers aircraft factory with special equipment for military planes during the days when Germany had had to build them secretly in the Soviet Union. The young Sommer had just joined the foreign languages department of the German Foreign Ministry after graduating from Berlin University. The boundary commission was his first job, and it proved to be a formative experience for him.

Negotiations with the Soviets took place at all the major points where refugees had gathered, starting with Lvov and then working along the Bug and San rivers which marked the new boundary of the Soviet Ukraine. Sommer found the differences between the two sides staggering. On the Soviet side there were, he says, nearly 200,000 people, mostly Poles but also including several thousand Ukrainians. On the German side, wanting to cross over to the Soviets, there were less than 100, mostly communists. Not unnaturally, the Soviet officials were not particularly happy with this state of affairs, and were inclined to be obstructive.

The real source of friction on the border, however, involved Jews. German troops in the Government General took to driving groups of up to 1,000 Jews across the border at quiet spots in the woods. The Soviets did not take kindly to this, and promptly pushed them back again, fifteen kilometres or so further along. When the Germans tried to stop them, there was inevitably trouble. Colonel-General Keitel complained to Ribbentrop on behalf of the Wehrmacht, which did not like being involved in such SS activities, and before long the Soviets were complaining, too. On 20 December, Hans Frank, the Governor-General, issued an order to the SS that they were to stop immediately. 'The complaint made by the Soviet Union,' he declared, 'is to be taken absolutely seriously; disturbance of the necessary friendly relations between the Soviet Union and Germany by such actions must be avoided under any circumstances.' Friction between the two sides continued, however, and by spring there were regular complaints of Soviet border guards shooting at their German opposite numbers.

There was no shooting, however, at Brest-Litovsk, where the traffic in souls was from the east again, this time with the wholehearted consent of the Soviets. In March, 1940, Margarete Buber-Neumann, the German communist to whom the news of the Nazi–Soviet pact had been the final straw for her faith, found herself among a group of 150 former prisoners from Soviet camps who were assembled at the frontier. As prisoner number 174,475, she had been sentenced in 1938 to five years in the Kazakhstan prison camp of Karaganda as a 'socially dangerous element'. Although the pact had destroyed what was left of her faith, it had ensured her release from the gulag, under the agreement to exchange prisoners and repatriate German nationals. The question was, however, to what was she being delivered?

The prisoners had been told nothing, but for several weeks they had been fed and cared for with unusual concern in the Butyrka prison in Moscow. They had received medical attention, and new clothes, and the women had even had their hair dressed. Evidently, the Soviet authorities wanted them to look their best for whatever was to come. What was to come was for most of them a continuation of the nightmare in a different setting, and for many a sentence of death.

Still without being told where they were heading, they were taken to the bridge over the river Bug at Brest-Litovsk. Their NKVD guards crossed the bridge, and returned with several officers in the black uniforms of the SS. Margarete Buber-Neumann recalls how cordially the SS and NKVD men greeted each other, after their commanders had exchanged salutes. Now, the prisoners knew for certain what was being done with them. Some of them in her group protested – one was a Jew, another had been blamed for the death of a Nazi back in 1933, all of them were, or had been, communists, which made them criminals in Nazi Germany. Their protests were in vain: Stalin had promised them to Hitler, and Stalin always kept his promises.

They were hustled across the bridge, from one form of slavery to another. 'When we were halfway across,' Buber-Neumann recalls, 'I looked back. The NKVD officials still stood there in a group, watching us go. Behind them was Soviet Russia. Bitterly, I recalled the communist litany: Fatherland of the Toilers; Bulwark of Socialism; Haven of the Persecuted . . .' After six months in a Gestapo prison in Berlin, she spent the rest of the war in Ravensbrück concentration camp, emerging just in time to escape the advancing Red Army and reach the American lines, with the unique achievement of having survived both Stalin's and Hitler's death camps.

39

'A WIDE-OPEN DOOR TO THE EAST'

The assistance the Soviet Union was able to give Germany in Murmansk and in the transit of goods from other countries was welcome and undoubtedly of great value. But the most important area of co-operation for both sides during the period of the pact was the direct trade between them. There has long been a myth that in order to buy time and postpone the threat of invasion by the mechanised might of the Wehrmacht, Stalin was Hitler's dupe, prepared to pay any price he demanded. The reality was entirely different.

Stalin could have had no illusions about Hitler's ultimate ambitions. Neither did he have any illusions, even before the débâcle of the Red Army's performance in Finland, about the Soviet Union's ability to withstand a German attack. But before he could prepare his country, and perhaps even increase its military strength to such an extent that Hitler would be deterred from attacking, Stalin needed to buy not only time but also technology. The only people he could obtain either from were the Germans.

For his part, Hitler needed vital raw materials for his arms industry in order to build up his forces to the level necessary for attacking the Soviet Union, and food to sustain his people while the military machine was made ready. Once he had failed to keep Britain, and to a lesser extent France, out of the war, the only place he could obtain either of his needs was the Soviet Union.

By September 1939, therefore, the two leaders found themselves in the ludicrous situation where Hitler needed food and raw materials from the Soviet Union in order to attack her, while Stalin needed machinery, arms and equipment from Germany in order to be able to fight her off. The question was, who needed what most? Certainly, Stalin was perfectly well aware of Hitler's needs. And while Germany still faced the Allies in the west, he was able to drive a very hard bargain indeed.

The ink was barely dry on the non-aggression pact when Karl Schnurre began thinking about improving on the trade and credit agreement he had negotiated. On the first day of the war in Poland, he suggested he be sent to Moscow to talk directly to Mikoyan, since he knew Babarin and his trade delegation in Berlin did not have either the authority or the imagination for what he had in mind. This was what he called the open question of 'whether the Russians would be prepared, for reasons other than purely economic ones, to support the Reich by supplying raw materials'.

Schulenburg was asked to sound out the Soviet government, and on 14 and 15 September Schnurre visited Ribbentrop in his special train at Oppeln, persuaded him to accept the idea, and agreed a programme for negotiations. Ribbentrop insisted that the agreement of 19 August must not be tampered with in any way, but thought Schnurre could perhaps persuade the Soviets to speed up their deliveries. His principal task would be to try to get them 'to compensate for the loss of deliveries by sea'.

Schnurre, however, had bigger ideas. When the military and civil agencies presented him with lists of what they wanted, with a value totalling 70 million Reichsmarks, he dismissed their claims out of hand, berating them for being too faint-hearted and pessimistic. He intended, he said, to ask for 'several times' those amounts.

Schnurre knew very well that his goal would not be easy to achieve. In the end, it would depend not on economic considerations, but on political ones – and these would have to be decided 'by the highest Russian authorities'. He believed the negotiations he was about to start would be an acid test of Stalin's true attitude towards the 'new political course' on which he had embarked with the signing of the pact. Since the Soviet Union was short of the materials Germany wanted, deliveries could be made only at the expense of Soviet domestic consumption and only Stalin himself could rule on such a matter.

By the beginning of October, Schnurre had put together a list of demands to the value of 1,400 million RM for the first year alone – rather more than 'several times' the original list from the German officials. The Soviets had agreed to meet him and his negotiating team, which left for Moscow on 7 October, under the overall direction not of Schnurre, who now held the rank of minister, but of Karl Ritter, who had just been appointed ambassador on special assignment in the Wilhelm-strasse, in charge of all activities related to economic warfare. Ritter had been ministerial director of the economics department of the Foreign Ministry from 1924 to 1937, and had then spent a year as ambassador to Brazil before retiring in October 1938. Twelve months later, he had been brought back. His vast experience was of great value to Schnurre, and his rank made certain the Soviets could not complain they were being asked to deal with 'second-rate officials', as they had said of Britain's William Strang.

Together, Schnurre and Ritter made a formidable team. They were supported by a delegation of thirty-seven from government, industry and commerce, with experts from the Ministries of Transport, Food and Economics as well as the Foreign Ministry, and representatives of German state railways, the Reich grain office, companies involved in shipping, dyestuffs, chemicals, iron, steel, glass, benzene, shipbuilding, arms manufacture, export-import specialists, and the chief of transportation for the Wehrmacht.

In charge of negotiations for the Soviet Union was the People's Commissar for Foreign Trade, Anastas Ivanovich Mikoyan. Mikoyan's abilities were legendary, as were his achievements. Born in a small village in Armenia in 1895, the son of a poor carpenter, he had been educated at the same seminary as Stalin, at Tbilisi. He had then gone on to study at the Armenian Theological Academy at Echmyadzin, the religious centre of Armenia. He had started his political career while still a student, becoming a revolutionary instead of a priest.

He had risen fast in the Bolshevik world during and after the Revolution and Civil War, and had been elected to the Central Committee at the age of twenty-six. By the time he was thirty, he was made a candidate member of the Politburo – the youngest ever – and People's Commissar for Trade. At thirty-five, as head of the renamed and reorganised Commissariat of Supply, he was in charge of all trade, supply and production of consumer goods and foodstuffs in the entire Soviet Union. When he was forty-two he also became deputy chairman of the Council of People's Commissars – in other words, Deputy Prime Minister and number three in the Soviet hierarchy, after Stalin and Molotov.

One of his most celebrated achievements had been to sell off a large part of the treasures of the Hermitage Museum in Leningrad and the Museum of Modern Western Art (now the Pushkin Museum) in Moscow, to raise desperately needed hard currency for the Soviet Union. His first big deal on this was with the Armenian oil billionaire, Calouste Gulbenkian, 'Mr Five Percent'. This was followed by deals with various Americans, the biggest with the fabulously wealthy former Secretary of the US Treasury, Andrew Mellon. By 1937, Mikoyan's sales had netted $100 million, no mean figure in those days, and he had gained valuable international negotiating experience.

To find out how to improve food processing methods as well as production in the Soviet Union, he visited the United States, travelling widely and learning fast. Back home he was quick to put the new ideas he had seen into practice, shaking up the whole industry with innovations in many areas. Coming directly from his American trip was a whole range of different ice-creams – Soviets are still very proud of the range and quality they produce – and a great increase in the production of quality meat. Even today, the best pork chops are called 'Mikoyans' in the Soviet Union.

For all his great energy and ruthless efficiency, Mikoyan remained a very attractive man. Of average height, he had a good figure, with the typical black hair, hook nose and dark eyes of his race, and a full but neatly trimmed moustache. He had great charm and wit, and was very much a ladies' man. Pussi Herwarth remembers how he liked to slip his hand beneath her fur wrap when greeting her or taking his leave at receptions, to touch her bare back above her evening gown, and how he used to boast, 'I've fathered five sons and I could manage a few more!' But she was given a sharp reminder of the realities of life among the powerful when she went to fetch his coat from the cloakroom at the embassy one night, and found a large Colt revolver, fully loaded, in the pocket.

Mikoyan was a survivor – and meant to stay that way. Back in his early days he had been one of twenty-six political commissars from Baku who were captured by the other side during the Civil War. Supposedly on their way to trial, they were taken off the train and shot. Only Mikoyan lived to tell the tale; no one ever quite discovered how. One of the favourite jokes about him among party members has him caught at a friend's house when it starts raining heavily outside. Ignoring it, and without coat or umbrella, he prepares to leave. 'But you can't walk,' his friends tell him. 'It's pouring down!' 'Don't worry,' he replies cheerfully, 'I can dodge between the raindrops.'

Mikoyan took personal control of all negotiations with Schnurre and Ritter, which were centred on his large, airy office in the same block as Molotov's in the Kremlin. It soon became clear that in spite of his own efficiency and drive, the bargaining was going to be not only hard but also very slow. This, of course, was the last thing the Germans wanted, and they did their best to speed things up, but met with very little success. The Soviets were infuriatingly pernickety, checking and double-checking the tiniest detail, and negotiating every single point separately. Despite a personal appeal to Molotov by Schulenburg, after ten days of talking the only contracts that had been agreed were for some special ships worth 10 million RM and 30,000 tons of steel tubes with a value of only 3–3½ million RM – a long way from the 1,400 million RM trade which Schnurre was asking for.

While all this was dragging on, it was 22 October before Mikoyan gave even a brief idea, and then orally and not in writing, of what the Soviet Union wanted from Germany. He promised a full list within a couple of days, and said he would be sending a delegation to Berlin to conduct preliminary negotiations. By the time the delegation was ready to leave, on 24 October, there was still no sign of the list. Mikoyan said they would take it with them to Berlin – but would have no authority to settle anything.

The Soviet delegation to Berlin numbered some sixty members, headed by People's Commissar for Shipbuilding, Ivan T. Tevossyan, an Armenian like Mikoyan, who spoke some German, and General of Artillery G. K. Savchenko. On the aircraft side, the chief expert was A. S. Yakovlev, the young designer whom Stalin was to make Deputy People's Commissar seven weeks later. He was very keen to see the latest products and technology of the Messerschmitt, Dornier, Heinkel and Junkers factories. All the other Soviet experts were equally keen to see the latest things in the German arsenal – so much so that many Germans became seriously alarmed at what they considered to be nothing less than licensed spying.

As the days and the weeks passed with no sign of any contract, the Germans became more and more agitated. The only response they got from Tevossyan and his people was that they could not say exactly what they wanted, or how much, until they had seen everything there was to see, and this would inevitably take a little time. The Soviet oil experts, for instance, worked out an inspection programme that would take no less than twenty-four days. Of course, there was another, more human side to these delaying tactics: very few of the Soviet delegation ever had the chance to travel outside their own country, and they meant to make the most of every moment. As Ritter himself noted: 'Apparently Tevossyan cannot resist the general desire of his assistants to travel around Germany for a considerable length of time.'

Soon, however, the Soviets were complaining that they were not being shown the latest German military developments. At the 7 November party thrown by Ambassador Shkvarzev at the Soviet embassy to celebrate the anniversary of the October Revolution, first Shkvarzev and then Tevossyan complained bitterly to Göring that secrets were being kept back, and refused to accept his repeated – and genuine – assurances that what they were seeing was in every case the very latest equipment in use with the Wehrmacht. They brushed aside Göring's attempts to explain that Germany could not offer to sell guns, aircraft and other weapons and armaments that were still in the experimental stage, because until they were proved no one knew if they would work. In the field and in factories and workshops, the patience of senior German officers and businessmen was stretched to the limit by the Soviet attitude: some said it compared unfavourably with the Inter-Allied Disarmament Commission after the first world war!

The truth was that the Soviets had expected German military technology to be further advanced than their own. But they were astonished to discover that in many cases it was not. All this recrimination produced one interesting side-effect. While German officials, service chiefs and industrialists fumed in exasperation, the experts of the Abwehr were monitoring the reactions of the Soviet military delegation. The apparent disdain which the Soviet tank experts showed for the latest Panzer models, for instance, indicated quite clearly that they had something at least as good and probably better of their own. It was the first inkling the Germans had of the Soviet T-34, which was generally reckoned to be the best tank of the second world war. In aircraft, too, Yakovlev's dismissal of the latest Messerschmitts revealed just how advanced his own designs now were.

It was the end of November before the Soviets delivered their shopping list, and when they did, it came as a shock to the Germans. They had been expecting to be asked for a wide range of machine tools, refinery equipment, and so on. The agreements of 19 August and 28 September had both been for an exchange of industrial goods for raw materials. What the Soviets were demanding, however, was almost entirely military. It included all the very latest arms and equipment − not only those in service with the Wehrmacht but also those in development, with a total value of over a billion Reichsmarks. Schnurre's estimate for 'high-quality armament material' to be supplied to the Soviets had been only 50 million.

The list was enough to take the breath away from the German officials, and give their service chiefs heart attacks. In addition to insisting on the delivery of the very latest aircraft types such as the Messerschmitt 209 − and others which they still insisted they had not been shown, but wanted all the same − plus the latest types of mines, torpedoes, armour plating, heavy artillery, aircraft engines, a training ship, a repair vessel and a tanker, the Soviets were demanding the hulls of the partially built 10,000-ton cruisers *Seydlitz* and *Lützow*, the completed cruiser *Prinz Eugen*, and the plans for a 15-cm-gun destroyer and for the battleship *Bismarck*. Almost as an incidental, they added a complete oil refinery capable of producing high-octane aviation fuel − in return for which they promised to deliver increased quantities of gasoline to Germany. As a final turn of the screw, the Soviets demanded delivery of everything by the end of 1940, a target which was clearly impossible if Germany intended to wage any military campaigns that year.

Ritter, who had returned to Berlin to look after the Soviet delegation, leaving Schnurre to handle everything in Moscow, was aghast. He sent an urgent message to Schulenburg and Schnurre, telling them to talk to Mikoyan or Molotov, or both, pointing out that what was being proposed was turning the treaty on its head. The idea, he said, had always been for the Soviets to deliver raw materials first, which Germany would then pay for with *industrial* deliveries spread over a period of time. But since Mikoyan had so far promised only 420 million RM worth of materials − 90 million of which were due anyway under the existing credit treaty −

and had delivered virtually nothing, Germany was being asked to pledge deliveries in advance, for which the Soviets would then pay in arrears. The row threatened to kill the whole deal, as Mikoyan refused to budge. Ritter flew back to Moscow to join Schnurre in trying to persuade him to see reason, but to no avail. It was obvious to everyone that Hitler's needs were more pressing than Stalin's at the moment – or, at least, that Stalin was proving to be the bolder poker-player. No matter how much the Germans argued that the Soviets were acting contrary to both the existing treaty and to the spirit of the letters exchanged by Ribbentrop and Molotov on 28 September, Mikoyan was adamant. He wanted arms, and he wanted everything his delegation had asked for.

Hitler had personally rejected the demands for the cruisers *Seydlitz* and *Prinz Eugen*, for heavy naval and field guns, the latest mines and torpedoes, machine tools for making artillery shells, and finally the plans for the *Bismarck*. His reason for refusing to hand over the *Bismarck* plans was not that he wanted to deny the Soviets the chance of building such a powerful ship – he knew it would take them several years, by which time it would no longer matter to him – nor even that he feared the British might get hold of the secrets of its construction. His fear was that they would discover that the ship was 10,000 tons more than the limit agreed in the Anglo-German Naval Treaty signed in 1936 – a remarkable attack of scruples when he was at war with Britain!

When Mikoyan was told of Hitler's refusal, his reply revealed the strength of the Soviet hand: 'The Soviet government,' he said, deliberately using the phrase which was usually interpreted as meaning Stalin, 'considers delivery of the entire list the only satisfactory equivalent for the deliveries of raw materials, which under present conditions are not otherwise obtainable for Germany on the world market.'

Seeing the treaty on which he had staked so much slipping away, Ribbentrop was becoming more and more anxious. Ingenuously, he wired Ritter saying he was to tell Molotov 'that I am very much surprised at Mikoyan's attitude and can hardly assume that it has the approval of Stalin and Molotov'. Schnurre, in particular, found this amusing. He recalls how, a few days before, he had been sitting with Mikoyan in his office trying to sort out methods of payment for raw materials bought by the Soviet Union on Germany's behalf from other countries. When they reached an impasse, Mikoyan said he could not decide what should be done, it was a matter for Molotov – at which point Molotov himself suddenly emerged from a curtained-off archway in Mikoyan's office. After a short discussion, Molotov, in turn, said he could not decide, it was really a matter for Stalin – whereupon Stalin came out through the curtain and joined the discussion, pacing to and fro while considering the question, as was his habit, puffing on his pipe as he thought, then coming up with a decision which suited everybody. After that, any idea that Stalin and Molotov did not know everything that was going on in such an important area was patently absurd.

The arguments continued to rage for several more days, with accusations of bad faith flying in both directions, centring on the question of whether or not it had always been understood that 'industrial deliveries', as included in the previous agreements, really meant arms and military equipment. Molotov maintained that the phrase had been deliberately used as a cover, because the treaty would be published. Ribbentrop and all the Germans hotly denied this. But whatever the rights of the situation, it became more and more clear that no arms meant no deal.

Stalin entered the arena on New Year's Eve, 1939, in a three-hour session at the Kremlin. While the rest of the world celebrated the start of 1940, Stalin stonewalled, going through the fine detail of the claims and counter-claims, and appearing, as Ritter noted, 'not to be in a very friendly mood'. Nevertheless, the scale of the Soviet demands was reduced, and Stalin purported to understand Germany's difficulties. He started to lay down slightly more reasonable requirements, and it began to seem as though there might be some progress at last.

The demands, however, were still stiff enough for Hitler to have to give a new ruling, which he promptly did – agreeing to almost everything the Soviet leader wanted. Time was running out for him. If he was to launch his attack on the Western Front in May, as planned, then he had to have a settlement with the USSR. Stalin, of course, was quite happy with the delays. In any case, he had other matters on his mind as the war in Finland staggered from one disaster to another.

In January, as the Soviet offensive in Karelia got under way, Stalin had another excuse for delay – he was laid up for eight days with a severe cold. When the next conference was held in Molotov's office at 9.30 pm on 29 January, he did not take his place at the long, green-baize table, but sat in an armchair in the corner of the room, nursing the after-effects of his illness. He listened quietly as Ritter announced the German concessions on arms deliveries, which were being made, he stressed, at the expense of Germany's own armaments programme. He made no objections as the German asked for understanding on the question of delivery times, but then joined in the discussion when it reached the question of naval guns, on which he amazed the Germans with his knowledge and grasp of detail. But by the end of the meeting, after two and a half hours of hard discussion, the Soviet pressure was still being kept up. The treaty seemed as far away as ever.

In desperation, Ribbentrop wrote a personal letter, not to Mikoyan, or even to Molotov, but to Stalin. After all, it had worked for Hitler back in August, maybe it would work for him. It was, like any communication from Ribbentrop, a long letter. In it, he said nothing new and proposed no fresh solutions to the difficulties. What he did, at some length, was to remind Stalin of the terms of the treaties already existing and point out that his present actions were in direct contravention of the clauses referring to deliveries. He then dismissed this, and made an overtly emotional appeal: 'In these negotiations it really is not – and in this I believe I am in agreement with M. Stalin – a matter of an ordinary trade agreement, in which as exact and simultaneous a balancing of the mutual services as is possible is the principal thing. It is rather a question of fulfilling punctually the promise which in effect was given during the September negotiations, even if for particular reasons it was not literally mentioned in the exchange of notes – namely, the promise that the Soviet government was willing to support Germany economically during the war which had been forced upon her . . .'

The Soviets, he pointed out, had regained their Polish and Baltic territories thanks largely to the efforts of the Wehrmacht. This should be regarded as 'a not inconsiderable advance payment' against the supply of Soviet raw materials, which Germany needed in order to continue the war against France and England. His country, he said, had already agreed to make sacrifices in delivering valuable weapons in the middle of a war. He therefore begged Stalin 'to let us have the raw materials which the Soviet government can deliver to us, as rapidly as we need them, even if the German compensatory deliveries will have to be stretched over a more extended period of time than was previously requested by the Soviet government'.

When Ritter delivered the letter to the Kremlin, he was met by Molotov alone. Stalin, he said, was still not completely recovered from his illness. Molotov was as sour and obstreperous as ever, and Ritter left after reading out the letter without much hope of any improvement. Three days later, however, on 7 February, there was a message from Stalin, asking the German negotiators to call on him at the Kremlin at 1 am next morning. When they arrived, they found him smiling and friendly, all sweetness and light. Ribbentrop's letter, he said, had changed everything. The Germans could have their treaty. The Soviet Union would deliver commodities worth 420 to 430 million RM within twelve months, in addition to the 200 million RM worth agreed in the 19 August treaty. For the following six months, the Soviets would make deliveries worth 220 to 230 million RM. Germany would make deliveries to the same value over a period of fifteen months for the first part, and twelve months for the second.

Stalin, still playing his role of the reasonable man, politely asked the Germans not to ask too high prices as they had done before – 300 million RM for aircraft and 150 million RM for the cruiser *Lützow*, he quoted as examples, was really far too much. 'One should not take advantage,' he said gently, 'of the Soviet Union's good nature.'

When Stalin had finished, Mikoyan, playing a friendly role after all the hard-man tactics of the preceding four months, raised another matter which the Germans had been vainly pursuing for months. This was to station a mother ship in Murmansk for the fishing fleet, to process its catches. Without a moment's hesitation, Stalin agreed to it.

On 11 February, the new trade treaty was signed. Germany was assured of all the raw materials and grain she wanted – but the price exacted by Stalin was a heavy one. The list of war material to be given to him covered forty-two closely typed pages. At the top of the list was the cruiser formerly known as the *Lützow* (after the *Graf Spee* incident Hitler had given the name *Lützow* to the *Deutschland*, since it would have been unbearable for a ship with that name to be sunk), the hull of which was to be delivered to Leningrad after launching, for completion in the Soviet Union. The complete drawings for the *Bismarck* were to be handed over after all, together with plans for a large destroyer and complete machinery for such a ship, and full details of performance of the other two cruisers.

The aircraft list included ten Heinkel He-100s, five Messerschmitt Bf-110s, two Junkers Ju-88 twin-engined dive-bombers, two Dornier Do–215s; three Büker Bü-131s and three Bü-133s; three Fokke-Wulf Fw-58-v-13s and two Fokke-Wulf Fa-255 helicopters, plus the experimental Messerschmitt 209. All of these were regarded as test aircraft, which the Soviets could then buy in quantity or build under licence later – they vigorously denied that they intended to copy them.

On and on went the list of equipment, guns, machinery, instruments, other ships and shipbuilding gear, plus installations and plant for chemical and metallurgical processes, many of them highly secret.

In return, the Soviet Union agreed to provide an impressive list of materials including:

1,000,000 tons of feed grains and legumes
900,000 tons of petroleum
100,000 tons of cotton
500,000 tons of phosphates
100,000 tons of chromium ores
500,000 tons of iron ore
300,000 tons of scrap iron and pig iron
2,400 kg of platinum
Manganese ore, metals, lumber and numerous other raw materials.

Among the other benefits to Germany was confirmation of the right of transit to and from Romania, Iran, Afghanistan and the Far East – the last particularly important since Germany was buying large quantities of soyabeans from Manchukuo, for which the Soviets agreed to halve the freight charges on the Trans-Siberian Railway.

Schnurre summed up the agreement as meaning 'a wide-open door to the east for us', which would decisively weaken the effects of the British blockade.

Whether the sudden change of heart by Stalin was the result of Ribbentrop's letter, or whether there was some other reason behind it, is impossible to say. Soviet decisions were so often influenced by entirely separate events, as became evident within a couple of weeks of the signing of the new treaty. Suddenly, as quickly as they had started blowing hot, the Soviets started blowing cold again.

Throughout March, they became difficult, and stopped making deliveries of grain and oil, claiming Germany was in default of her deliveries of coal in exchange. The Germans were totally nonplussed by this, and on 6 April, Schulenburg saw Mikoyan and demanded the immediate resumption of deliveries. Mikoyan refused point-blank. Despite all the German promises, he charged, not a single ton of German coal had arrived to date. Soviet deliveries to Germany since August 1939, he said, were worth 66·5 million RM, while German deliveries to the Soviet Union had reached only 5·5 million. Until this situation improved, there could be no question of the Soviets sending any more. Schulenburg finally managed to persuade him to start delivering again before the end of the month, on condition that an appreciable part of German coal deliveries for the months had been made by then, but it was hard work and the goodwill and affability of a month before had entirely disappeared.

The Germans themselves were partly to blame for these difficulties. In addition to failing to supply coal, they were also stalling on arms deliveries. At the end of March, a delegation from the Soviet aircraft industry complained to Göring that after three weeks in Germany they had not managed to settle anything about deliveries. Göring, aware of what was at stake, swiftly disposed of this problem by giving his word that all the aircraft they had ordered would be delivered during April and May, and next day Hitler himself issued a decree that priority must be given to arms deliveries to the Soviet Union, even at the expense of the Wehrmacht.

On 9 April, Molotov suddenly became friendly again. He blamed the suspension of grain and oil deliveries on the 'excessive zeal of subordinate agencies'. Schulenburg noted in his report that the 'subordinate agency' was Mikoyan, who was the highest Soviet personality after Molotov himself. 'Molotov,' said Schulenburg, 'was affability itself, willingly received all our complaints and promised relief. Of his own accord, he touched upon a number of issues of interest to us and announced their settlement in a positive sense. I must honestly say that I was completely amazed at the change.'

Schulenburg's amazement was all the stronger since it was not only over the trade treaty and deliveries that there had been a sudden cooling in relations. Over the same period, there had been trouble in various other fields. Even in small things like the granting of visas the Soviets had started to make difficulties. The release of prisoners like Margarete Buber-Neumann had stopped, as had the exchange of *Volksdeutsche*, and restrictions were suddenly imposed on the use of the naval base at Teriberka, near Murmansk, which the Soviets had placed at Germany's disposal.

There had been no apparent reason for this coldness. As Schulenburg said, 'nothing had *happened.*' Now, however, just as abruptly, everything had changed back again – and the timing of the change explained it all. At the same meeting, on 9 April, at which Molotov told Schulenburg everything would be put right, he also congratulated him on Germany's invasion of Norway that day. The Soviet government, he said, understood the measures which were forced upon Germany. The British had gone much too far, completely disregarding the rights of neutral nations. 'We wish Germany complete success,' he said, 'in her defensive measures.'

The explanation of the Soviet government's strange behaviour was thta Stalin had known about the Anglo-French plans first to intervene in Finland, and then to invade Norway themselves. In his speech to the Supreme Soviet on 29 March, Molotov had drawn attention to the Allied threat: 'It is not at all the defence of small nations or the defence of the rights of the members of the League of Nations that explains the support of the British and French ruling circles for Finland against the USSR,' he said. 'The explanation of this support is that in Finland they had a ready military bridgehead for an attack on the USSR.'

Stalin was terrified of being drawn into a war with the Allies, and had determined to keep his co-operation with Germany as low and as quiet as possible, in case it was seen as jeopardising his neutrality, thus giving the Allies an excuse to go to war. That was the way Schulenburg interpreted things.

There was, however, another possible interpretation, which must have suggested itself to Stalin's paranoid mind. Was it not possible that Hitler might double-cross him, especially when the Red Army was making such a poor showing in Finland, and do a deal with the Allies to join forces against the Soviet Union in an attack through Scandinavia? As though to confirm his fears, *The Times* in London wrote about the possibility of an eventual regrouping of powers, including Germany, in the anti-Soviet front. Since *The Times* was regarded in Moscow as the mouthpiece of the British government, just as *Pravda* and *Izvestia* were organs of the Soviet party and government, Stalin took such statements very seriously.

The German invasion of Norway, forestalling the Allied plan, had laid those bogies to rest. As if to confirm at least Schulenburg's theory, *Izvestia* carried a prominent article on 11 April explaining the German action in Scandinavia, and supporting it. To the German ambassador, it read 'like one big sigh of relief'. The same could be said of the German reaction to it.

40

A NORDIC HORS D'OEUVRE

At precisely 5.20 am German summer time on 9 April 1940, the German ministers in Norway and Denmark simultaneously handed over notes from Ribbentrop to their host Foreign Ministers, informing them that their countries were being taken under German protection for the duration of the war. This, Ribbentrop explained, was entirely the fault of the British and French, who had started everything in the first place by 'unleashing this war of aggression, which they had long been preparing, against the German Reich and the German people'. 'The Reich government,' he went on, 'has resolved, from now on, to protect and definitely assure peace in the north, with all its power, against an English–French attack.'

The form of 'protection' Germany had in mind involved the immediate occupation of both countries – in their own interests, of course. And since German troops would not be setting foot on Norwegian and Danish soil as enemies, Ribbentrop expected the governments and people of both countries to 'respond with understanding to the German action, and offer no resistance to it'. Any resistance there was, he added menacingly, could only lead to unnecessary bloodshed, as the Germans would be forced to crush it.

The Danes, aware that their flat little country was completely defenceless, could only submit and watch helplessly as the German tanks and guns and troops on bicycles and horseback rolled in. The seventy-year-old King Christian had no time to flee, and decided to stay with his people. By lunchtime, it was all over: the German army had taken control of every key point and the Luftwaffe had occupied all the airfields, filling them with planes to be used against the Norwegians, should they choose to cause trouble.

The Norwegians did indeed choose to cause trouble, though they were severely hampered by having no standing army, and mobilisation notices had to be sent out by post on the morning of 9 April. Their government's immediate response to the German note had been: 'We will not submit voluntarily: the struggle is already under way.' The outraged Ribbentrop wired back telling his minister, Curt Bräuer, 'You will once more impress on the government there that Norwegian resistance is completely senseless.'

But he was too late – the mobilisation notices had been posted by the time his telegram arrived, and the king and government had already left Oslo by special train, to seek safety in the mountains. A fleet of twenty-three trucks followed, carrying secret papers from ministries and the gold from the bank of Norway. Resistance had begun.

The first German casualties of the Norwegian campaign had actually occurred the day before, when one of the German transports which had set off for the northern ports on 3 April, disguised as coal ships, had been torpedoed and sunk. This was the *Rio de Janeiro*, a slow-moving merchant vessel, which had been carrying horses and 100 men. Many were drowned, but some were rescued from the sea by the Norwegians and taken ashore for interrogation. The submarine which scored this notable hit was none other than the *Orzel*, the Polish sub which had escaped from the Germans at Gdynia and the Soviets and Estonians at Tallinn, and which was now fighting alongside the Royal Navy.

Heavier losses were inflicted on the invaders on 9 April. Approaching the Norwegian capital along the fifty-mile-long Oslo Fjord, Germany's latest heavy cruiser, the *Blücher*, was severely damaged by the 28-cm Krupp guns of the ancient fortress of Oskarsborg, and then finished off with torpedoes. The brand-new 10,000-ton ship was torn apart when her ammunition blew up, and some 1,000 men lost their lives. Among them were the Gestapo officials and administrators who were to arrest and replace the Norwegian government. The rest of the force, led by the pocket battleship *Lützow* (the renamed *Deutschland*) which had also been hit by the shore guns, turned tail and retreated ignominiously to the sea.

Further north, heading for Bergen, the cruiser *Königsberg* was also damaged by fire from shore batteries, and only just managed to limp into port, where she was sunk that afternoon by carrier-based Blackburn Skuas of the British Fleet Air Arm, the first large ship ever to be sunk by air attack. A British submarine accounted for another German cruiser, the *Karlsruhe*, just south of Kristiansand. Three more cruisers were damaged and several supply ships sunk by a fleet of sixteen British submarines which were already in the area – not to prevent the German invasion, but to protect the planned Allied landings. By an astonishing piece of fortune, Hitler had beaten the British and French to it by a mere twenty-four hours! In fact, the British had started laying mines in Norwegian waters the day before, on 8 April, and so were technically the first to violate Norway's neutrality.

But in spite of the presence of British ships in the area, the Germans still managed to occupy every one of Norway's most important towns and cities during the morning. The valiant efforts of the shore batteries in Oslo Fjord had been in vain, for the city's airfield had been left unprotected. At 7.30 am it was captured by a single Messerschmitt fighter, whose pilot was bold enough to land there. Others followed swiftly, taxiing into position to ring the strip so that troop transports could fly in safely. By noon, eight companies of infantry had landed, and 1,500 men were formed up behind a military band to march ceremoniously into the centre of the capital.

At 5.30 pm, General von Falkenhorst reported to Hitler: 'Denmark and Norway occupied ... as instructed.' Grinning broadly, Hitler passed the news to party philosopher Alfred Rosenberg, saying, 'Now Quisling can set up his government in Oslo.' Vidkun Quisling, a Nazi supporter and former government minister in Norway, had in fact already started setting up shop, but was hampered by the fact that none of the German commanders had ever heard of him. His efforts to take power in the country proved to be a total failure, even with the personal support of Hitler, but he survived just long enough for his name to become an international byword for treachery.

That evening in the Chancellery in Berlin, when Hitler and his entourage sat down to a celebratory dinner, the main course of macaroni, ham and green salad was preceded on the gold-embossed menu by an appropriate hors d'oeuvre – smörrebröd. The joyful Führer saw the occupation of Norway and Denmark itself as an hors d'oeuvre to his next great move: Operation Yellow, the assault on France and the West.

As it happened, the celebrations were slightly premature. Next day, the Royal Navy struck back at Narvik, where ten German destroyers and five troop transports had landed 2,000 mountain troops virtually unopposed. The destroyers, however, were then stuck in Narvik Fjord, for the three supply vessels which should have serviced and refuelled them had been sunk on their way from Germany. Only the tanker *Jan Wellem*, which had come from Murmansk, had arrived, and refuelling all ten destroyers from this one tanker was a slow business. Despite a blinding snowstorm on 10 April, five British destroyers managed to penetrate the fjord at dawn high water, 4 am, and attacked the German vessels. Three days later, they were joined by the first world war battleship, *Warspite*, and a whole flotilla of destroyers. All the German ships were sunk – thus accounting for no less than half the total destroyer strength of the German navy.

Hitler was devastated by this news, and by the fact that eleven plane-loads of reinforcements for the beleaguered mountain troops had been lost when the ice gave way under them on the improvised airstrip they were using on the frozen Lake Hartvig. When he heard that British troops had actually landed near both Narvik and Trondheim, his nerve cracked and he started to panic. He ordered that any town or village in which the British set foot was to be totally destroyed, without consideration for the civilian population, and that Major-General Eduard Dietl should abandon Narvik immediately and fight his way south, with his mountain troops, to Trondheim.

General Alfred Jodl, chief of the OKW operations staff and, with Keitel, Hitler's principal strategic adviser, was appalled by the Führer's loss of control. 'The hysteria is frightful,' he wrote in his diary. And he set about stiffening Hitler's resolve. In this, he was aided by his army staff officer, Colonel Bernhard von Lossberg. Hitler's order to Dietl, handwritten by Keitel, had already reached the OKW radio office in the Bendlerstrasse headquarters, but Lossberg refused to send it. Angrily, he complained to Keitel that it represented a loss of nerve 'unparalleled since the darkest days of the battle of the Marne in 1914'. When he argued that securing Narvik and the iron ore supply route was the main purpose behind the entire Norwegian campaign, Keitel turned his back on him and left the room. With Jodl's permission, Lossberg then marched off to see Brauchitsch, the Commander-in-Chief of the army, to beg him to persuade Hitler to change his mind. Brauchitsch refused.

'I have nothing to do with the Norwegian campaign,' he told Lossberg. 'Falkenhorst and Dietl are answerable to Hitler alone, and I have not the slightest intention of going of my own free will into that clip joint.'

The clip joint he was referring to, of course, was the Chancellery! However, Lossberg persuaded Brauchitsch to compose another message to Dietl, congratulating him on the capture of Narvik and saying he was sure he would defend it 'to the last man'. This was the message that was sent, while Lossberg personally tore up the Führer's order in front of Jodl and Keitel.

As the struggle for Norway wore on, with further British landings around Narvik, Hitler continued to dither and despair, and Jodl continued to prop him up. When Hitler pored over maps seeking ways of evacuation, Jodl stood over him and rapped the table with his knuckles until they showed white as he lectured him: 'My Führer, in every war there are times when the supreme commander must keep his nerve!' Hitler stopped, pulled himself together, and carefully asked, 'What would you advise?' Jodl presented him with a staff evaluation of the situation, and an order which he had already drafted telling Dietl to hold out for as long as possible. Hitler signed it without demur.

The strain was still showing when Alfred Rosenberg presented him with a bust of the emperor Frederick the Great, for his fifty-first birthday on 20 April. Hitler regarded it with tears in his eyes. 'When you see him,' he said emotionally, 'you realise how puny are the decisions we have to make compared with those confronting him. He had nothing like the military strength we command today.'

Walter Warlimont, Jodl's deputy, recorded a personal impression of Hitler in those days of doubt. Arriving in his chief's office next to Hitler's study in the Chancellery, he found the Führer 'hunched in a chair in a corner, unnoticed and staring in front of him, a picture of brooding gloom. He appeared to be waiting for some new piece of news which would save the situation and in order not to lose a moment intended to take it on the same telephone line as the chief of his operations staff. I turned away in order not to have to look at so undignified a picture.'

Hitler's fears were unfounded, however, for the British and French attempts to dislodge his forces from Norway were a catalogue of bungling inefficiency, their entire operation beset by confusion and indecision. With all the country's airfields in German hands from the first day, the Allies' hopes were always doomed. But in any case they did little to help themselves. The troops they sent were mostly inexperienced and poorly equipped – even the French Alpine troops, who should have been well suited to Norwegian conditions, had no bindings for their skis. The troops who had been landed near Narvik and Trondheim were withdrawn on 2 May.

A fresh landing was made at Narvik on 28 May, with a mixed force of British, French and Polish troops – among the latter was the former Polish ambassador to Berlin, Josef Lipski, serving as a private – but it proved to be yet another disaster. On 7, 8 and 9 June, 25,000 men were evacuated again, with heavy casualties, including the sinking of the British aircraft carrier *Glorious* and two destroyers. The Norwegian government fled to Britain.

Norway was secure for Hitler, but the celebrations were eclipsed by greater events elsewhere – three days before the evacuation of Narvik began, the evacuation of British and French troops had been completed at Dunkirk.

The occupation of Denmark had cost Hitler only twenty casualties. But Norway had proved considerably more expensive. In addition to 1,317 men killed, 1,604 wounded and 2,375 missing or lost at sea, his already small fleet had been decimated. Three cruisers and ten destroyers were lost, two heavy cruisers and one pocket battleship were severely damaged and put out of action for several months. In the summer of 1940, apart from U-boats, the German navy was virtually non-existent, comprising only one 8-inch cruiser, two light cruisers and four destroyers, a factor of considerable importance in the war against Britain.

The Norwegian campaign had one other effect which was to weigh heavily against Germany during the remainder of the war. At the beginning of May, the British people and Parliament finally lost patience with Chamberlain and his policies of appeasement. On 7 and 8 May, there was a debate on the Norwegian campaign in the house of Commons. A distinguished back-bench Conservative MP, Leo Amery, rose amid a highly charged emotional atmosphere and called to the government, using the words of Oliver Cromwell to the Long Parliament some 300 years earlier: 'You have sat too long for any good you have been doing. Depart, I say, and let us have done with you. In the name of God, go!' The veteran Liberal, Lloyd George, who had been Prime Minister during the first world war, added fuel to the pyre next day by declaring that when Chamberlain was appealing for sacrifice he should set an example himself by sacrificing his seals of office.

Chamberlain wriggled for a further two days. When it became inescapable that he would have to go he did his best to install the faithful Halifax in his place – anything to forestall Winston Churchill and his supporters – but was finally forced to bow to the inevitable. In the early evening of 10 May 1940, King George VI, who would also have preferred Halifax, reluctantly sent for Churchill and asked him to form a new government.

41

'THE GREATEST WAR LORD OF ALL TIMES'

Hitler had set 10 May as the date for Operation Yellow, the attack on Holland and Belgium, two days earlier, after hearing that the Dutch were starting a full-scale mobilisation, with all service leave cancelled, civilians being evacuated from key areas and road blocks being set up in frontier areas. It was the fifth change of date in a week, and the twenty-ninth postponement since October. But the delays had not been time wasted. Though the Allies had steadily built up the strength of their forces until, on paper at least, they were superior to the Germans, there had been a fundamental change in the German plan during that time. It was a change that was to prove decisive.

Hitler was now totally confident. Despite continuing pleas from Göring for yet more time to prepare the Luftwaffe, he declared adamantly, 'Not a day longer!' He instructed his secretaries and the rest of his entourage to be ready for a journey on 9 May – but said nothing of where they were going. The tight security was designed not only to maintain secrecy about the start and direction of the offensive, but also to protect his person, following an abortive assassination attempt by a bomb which had exploded just after he left the annual gathering of his old comrades in the Munich Bürgerbräukeller on 9 November 1939. The journey to his field headquarters on 9 May consequently developed into a bizarre mystery tour.

The party was first taken by car to the airport, where *Immelmann III* was ready for take-off. But instead of stopping there, the convoy swept on to the small railway station at Finkenkrug, just outside Berlin. There, the Führer's special train collected them and steamed off to the north. When some members of the group asked Hitler, 'Are we going to Norway?' he said yes. The word was passed that they were bound for Kiel, where they would board a plane for Oslo. At Hanover, the train halted, for Hitler to receive a weather report from the Luftwaffe's chief meteorologist, Diesing; at last the news was good – Friday, 10 May, would be a fine day. Hitler, pleased, resolved to give Diesing a gold watch as a reward. Then he confirmed the order to attack at dawn, and retired to bed, earlier than usual. He found it impossible to sleep, however, and was still awake and worrying about the possibility of early morning fog when the train changed direction near Uelzen in the middle of the night and headed south at full speed. It arrived at Euskirchen, a small town some fifty kilometres west of Bonn, at 4.25 am.

Within five minutes, Hitler was out of the train and in his armoured Mercedes heading south on the fifteen-kilometre drive to his new field headquarters, codenamed *Felsennest*, 'Rocky Nest', or 'Eyrie', a converted anti-aircraft artillery site which had been blasted out of a wooded mountain top at Rodert, near Münstereifel, forty-five kilometres by road from the Belgian border. As he arrived dawn was breaking. He checked his watch, angrily – 'I was filled with rage,' he said later: dawn had come fifteen minutes earlier than he had been told. But although it offended his passion for detail, this small aberration was of no consequence. Even as he inspected the bare concrete bunker that was to be his home for the next few weeks, its furnishings minimal, its soundproofing so poor that Keitel, who was given the cell next to his, would be able to hear him turning the pages of a newspaper, the air was filled with the roar of engines as wave after wave of Luftwaffe bombers and their fighter escorts swept overhead. They were on their way to attack more than seventy airfields in Belgium, Holland and northern France, destroying between 300 and 400 planes on the ground and so ensuring air superiority for Hitler for the vital next two weeks.

Some of the planes carried paratroops – a Soviet invention which Hitler had been quick to adopt for the Wehrmacht – to be dropped in Holland at strategic points inland where they would seize and hold vital bridges and communications. The Dutch and Belgians had received advance warnings from both their own and German intelligence – Colonel Hans Oster, Canaris's deputy in the Abwehr and a fellow member of the anti-Hitler resistance, had personally told the Dutch military attaché in Berlin the date and time of the attack, and air reconnaissance had spotted lines of tanks and trucks stretching no less than seventy-five miles back into Germany from the border. But for some reason both they and the Allies chose to ignore them all. The result was that when the paratroops landed and the tanks roared across the frontiers of Holland, Belgium and Luxembourg, the defenders were caught napping. Hitler, amazingly, had achieved the vital element of surprise once again. Once again, it soon became clear that he was about to score another quick and easy victory in the Low Countries.

Luxembourg could offer very little resistance, and was gobbled up by the rapacious Wehrmacht in almost as little time as it took for the German tanks and trucks to drive across the little duchy.

In Holland, the Dutch troops did what they could, but it proved to be very little against vastly superior armaments and numbers. The Dutch army fell back almost immediately. Plans to halt or at least to slow down the invaders by blowing bridges, opening dykes and flooding great areas of the country were thwarted by the German paratroops. On the first day, Queen Wilhelmina sent her daughter, Crown Princess Juliana, and her two little granddaughters to England on the British destroyer *Codrington*. Two days later she was forced to follow, with her government, on another British destroyer. On 14 May the Germans were in control of the whole country as the port of Rotterdam surrendered. Next day, all fighting in Holland ceased.

The occupation of Holland was important, but the real key to Hitler's plan lay in Belgium, and here his armies met with an even more striking success. The fortifications of the Maginot Line meant that the only way Hitler could advance into France was by going round it, through neutral Belgium. The Belgians, of course, were as aware of this as everyone else. On their frontier with Germany, to protect the city of Liège and the approach to Brussels, they had built their own fortress: Eben Emael, a great mass of concrete and steel which was reputed to be the most powerful fort in the world.

Hitler had taken a great personal interest in planning the capture of Fort Eben Emael. He had spent many hours with a scale model of it in the Chancellery, and had come up with a typically unconventional idea: the fort had a vast flat roof; forty-one gliders filled with shock troops and engineers were to land on the roof, and capture the fort from there. In the event, thirty-two of the gliders failed to make their target, but nine succeeded, carrying eighty-five men who leapt out and attacked the gunports with grenades and flamethrowers, shattered the casements with explosives and blew up the ventilating system. Within an hour, those eighty-five men had neutralised 1,000 defenders whom they had trapped inside their impregnable fortress.

With Eben Emael knocked out, the invaders quickly managed to secure bridges over the Albert Canal and the broad river Meuse. The door was open for the advance into central Belgium. Hitler literally hugged himself for joy when he heard of this – but there was even better news to follow: the British and French were advancing at full speed from France into Belgium to meet his armies. 'When the news came that the enemy was advancing along the whole front,' he recalled later, 'I could have wept for joy! They'd fallen right into my trap! It was a crafty move on our part to strike towards Liège – we had to make them believe we were remaining faithful to the old Schlieffen Plan.'

The Schlieffen Plan was what the Germans had used when they attacked France in August 1914. It involved a great sweep across Belgium to the coast then turning south and advancing on north-west

France on a broad front. It was the natural, indeed the obvious way of attacking France. The Maginot Line may have been a wonderful defence for the eastern frontiers of France, but since it did not continue to the Channel but stopped as soon as it reached the frontier with Belgium, it made the invasion of Belgium quite inevitable.

The Allies, of course, were prepared for this, and had already drawn up their own plans to counter it. Anticipating that the Germans would gather in strength in Holland and the northern half of Belgium, they were ready to rush north to meet them head on before they had time to turn and begin their advance southwards. On 10 and 11 May they did just that. Hitler was delighted, because the main and most important thrust of his attack was elsewhere – through the mountains and forests of the Ardennes and directly into north-eastern France through Sedan, to the south of the advancing French and British armies.

The French had barely bothered to guard this sector, leaving only reserve divisions around Sedan. They, like everyone else, knew that the Ardennes were impassable for tanks, being a region of thick forest, steep hills, and narrow, twisting lanes. It was a tank commander's nightmare: deep gullies and ravines carved out by fast-flowing and often unfordable streams formed natural anti-tank obstacles; small, hump-backed bridges, many set with explosive demolition charges, made perfect tank traps. One blown bridge, one immobilised tank or supply vehicle could block the way, bringing chaos to the whole invasion force. The tank is a vehicle designed for fast operations across flat, open ground. In confined spaces it is clumsy and difficult to manoeuvre. There was no way whole divisions of tanks could be driven safely through the Ardennes.

Unfortunately for the French, there were two men who had refused to believe this – General Erich von Manstein and Adolf Hitler. In the face of almost total opposition from the other generals, Hitler had in February changed their conventional plan of attack for a daring scheme devised by Manstein and himself to drive powerful Panzer divisions through the woods and forests until they emerged on the flat plains beyond, in perfect tank territory.

The execution of the new plan was put into the more than capable hands of Colonel-General Gerd von Runstedt, who had already proved his skill with armour in Poland. His Army Group A included three crack Panzer corps, seven divisions which had been tuned to perfection during the preceding few months. Commanding the XIX Panzer Corps on the vital left flank, the most southerly, was General Heinz Guderian, 'Hurrying Heinz' as he was known, creator of the theory of *Blitzkrieg* and one of the most brilliant commanders of tanks in the history of warfare.

The German army planners had allowed nine days for the Panzers to cross the Ardennes and reach the river Meuse. Guderian said he could do it in four. In the event, he reached it in only two. There were no breakdowns, no blockages, and no blown bridges. Vehicle preparation and maintenance was impeccable and teams of mechanics rode with each column ready to deal with any emergency on the spot. Specialists from the crack Brandenburger Regiment, the Abwehr's special service unit, went ahead of the rest of the force in civilian Volkswagen cars, disguised as tourists. They sought out demolition charges on bridges and in narrow cuttings along the winding roads and dismantled them; engineers dealt with more serious obstacles. The tanks followed shortly afterwards, rolling through Luxembourg without opposition, and into south-east Belgium, their drivers threading their unwieldy vehicles through the 'impassable' forests by sheer nerve and driving skill.

At 1500 hours on Monday, 13 May, the first German soldiers crossed the Meuse and established a bridgehead. At dawn next day, Guderian's tanks started pouring across. By 15 May, his way was clear and he swept on across France, ignoring orders to halt, first from Rundstedt and then from Hitler himself – who had once again temporarily lost his nerve, unable to believe his good fortune.

For mile after mile, Guderian's tanks sped on, still unopposed, racing towards the coast, over open roads to the rear of the Allied armies. When they ran out of fuel they simply stopped at roadside filling stations and used the pumps – without paying, of course. From time to time, some stopped for their crews to milk cows in the fields. The other divisions in Army Group A – the most northerly led by the recently appointed General Erwin Rommel, who had previously only commanded Hitler's bodyguard – were also powering their way west. The Allied armies, including the whole of the British Expeditionary Force, were cut off from their supply lines in the south as the trap snapped shut.

At 7.30 am on Wednesday, 15 May, Winston Churchill was awakened in his bed at Admiralty House in London by a telephone call from Paul Reynaud, who had taken over from Daladier as French Prime Minister six weeks before. The still somnolent Churchill was brought rapidly to his senses by Reynaud's opening words.

'We have been defeated,' he said agitatedly, in English.

Stunned, Churchill did not reply for a moment.

'We are beaten,' Reynaud reiterated. 'We have lost the battle.'

In vain, Churchill tried to persuade Reynaud that all was not lost, that experience showed the Germans would have to stop for supplies after a few days, and could then be hit by a counter-attack. But the French Premier only repeated what he had first said: 'We are defeated. We have lost the battle.'

What Renaud said was true. Although the fighting continued until mid-June, the issue was already decided. In five incredible days, Hitler had taken Holland and Luxembourg, broken into Belgium, and ensnared the British and French armies. For several days, Hitler himself refused to believe it was really true, and continued to agonise over every detail of the campaign. By 20 May, however, even he had to accept that he had achieved his aim, when Brauchitsch telephoned him with the news that Guderian's tanks had reached the Channel, at Noyelles, near Abbeville. They had covered 200 miles in ten days, in a giant, deadly, sickle cut.

'The Führer is beside himself with joy,' Jodl wrote in his diary that night. 'Talks in words of highest appreciation of the German army and its leadership. Is working on the peace treaty, which shall express the tenor: return of territory robbed from the German people over the last 400 years . . .'.

Hitler could hardly wait to draw up the details of the peace treaty he intended to impose on France, through which he would repay all the shame inflicted on Germany in 1918. To ensure that the moment would not lose one jot of its poignancy, he would insist that it be signed in the same railway carriage, at the same spot in the Forest of Compiègne, as the Armistice of 1918. That would dispose of the French. As for the British, they could have a negotiated peace 'as soon as they return our colonies to us'.

Next day, however, 21 May, the remnants of the British army, under General Lord Gort, valiantly attempted to break through the German encirclement, as they had been ordered to do. Gort could muster only two tank battalions, with a grand total of sixteen tanks, but he struck the Germans at Arras with such force that Rommel claimed he was being attacked by five armoured divisions. By evening, however, the tiny British force was exhausted and compelled to fall back. Next day, a French attack also failed, and on 24 May another French attempt in the south was completely ineffectual. The German line was now so firmly established along the Somme that it was unbreakable.

At this point, Hitler's nerves again got the better of him. When Rundstedt halted his Panzers, in spite of protests from some of the commanders on the ground and many of the general staff, Hitler supported his decision. He considered, as did Rundstedt, that the exhausted men and machines needed time to regroup before beginning the final assault on the Allied forces. The British had already started falling back on Dunkirk, the only Channel port left open to them since Guderian had taken Boulogne the day before, but they could well turn and fight when their backs were to the sea.

Many people later believed Hitler had stopped deliberately in order to allow the British army to withdraw through Dunkirk, in the hope that he would then be able to reach a separate peace with them. The facts do not bear this out. Hitler allowed his armies to halt because he genuinely believed they needed time before the final battle against tough opponents. Neither he nor any of his generals fully appreciated the scale of the defeat they had already inflicted on the Allies. It seemed, quite simply, too good to be true. Hitler had no doubts that they would eventually be victorious, for he believed there was no escape for the

380,000 men caught inside his net. But he thought he could finish them off at his own pace – or rather, at Göring's, for the fat Field Marshal had persuaded him that the Luftwaffe could complete the annihilation of the Allied armies from the air.

'This is a special job for the Luftwaffe!' he cried enthusiastically when he heard that the trap had finally been sprung. And when he had persuaded Hitler to leave everything to him, keeping German troops and armour well back out of the way of his bombs, he was exultant. 'We've done it!' he told General Milch, his Chief of Staff. 'The Luftwaffe is to wipe out the British on the beaches. I have managed to talk the Führer into halting the army.'

Hitler had several other reasons for stopping his forces. One was to avoid damaging any more property than was necessary in the Flemish part of Belgium, since he regarded the Flemings as being basically Germanic. But the most important of his other reasons was purely military. He was concerned with pressing on with the next stage of his strategic plan, 'Operation Red', the battle for France, and was therefore wary of committing the tanks he would need for this to the swampy low ground of Flanders.

On 24 May, shortly after issuing the halt order to his forces around Dunkirk, he issued his directive for Operation Red. In this, he said that the Luftwaffe's present task was to break the remaining resistance of the encircled enemy, and prevent any British forces escaping across the Channel. Jodl questioned the protests from some of his staff by telling them: 'The war is won. It just has to be ended. There is no point sacrificing a single tank if we can do it much more cheaply with the Luftwaffe.'

It was not until 26 May that anyone on the German side realised that the British really were withdrawing through Dunkirk. That morning, aerial reconnaissance planes spotted thirteen warships and nine troop transports in Dunkirk harbour. But even then, Hitler permitted his armour to make only limited advances, preferring to bring up artillery to supplement the air attacks. And in any case, the tank crews were now resting and overhauling their vehicles, and could not leap back into action immediately.

Göring, too, was still totally confident that his planes could keep the British pinned down. He flew into *Felsennest* in a light aircraft and boasted ebulliently of their successes: 'Only fishing boats are getting through. Let's hope the Tommies can swim!'

The 'fishing boats' and other small craft – yachts, motor cruisers, paddle steamers, pleasure boats and working boats, almost anything that could float, a total of 861 assorted vessels – were to fling Göring's contemptuous words back in his teeth over the next nine days as they chugged back and forth across the sea, laden to the gunwales with British and French soldiers plucked from the beaches under the noses of the Germans. After the disasters in Norway, there was no German navy to stop them. For some of the time, bad weather prevented the Luftwaffe from flying, and when they did, they received a shock – the RAF Spitfires and Hurricanes, flying from British bases that were in many cases nearer than the Luftwaffe's in Germany, quickly established air superiority. Between 27 and 30 May, the RAF shot down 179 German aircraft for the loss of only twenty-nine. Although Churchill himself had warned Parliament to prepare for 'hard and heavy tidings', and had expected hardly more than 20,000 men to be saved, 'Operation Dynamo' as the evacuation was named brought out no fewer than 224,585 British and 112,546 French and Belgian troops. But many thousands were left behind, along with all the transport and heavy arms and equipment. Between 10,000 and 15,000 men lay dead on the beaches, around the harbour and in the streets of the blazing town. Some 25,000 French troops had not managed to get away and were taken prisoner.

Churchill stood up in the House of Commons in London on 4 June, the day the Germans broke into Dunkirk, and made one of his most memorable speeches: 'We shall fight on the beaches, we shall fight on the landing grounds, we shall fight in the fields and in the streets, we shall fight in the hills; we shall never surrender.' They were brave words, but for all their defiance they could not mask the fact, admitted by Churchill, that what had happened in France and Belgium was 'a colossal military disaster'.

Hitler chose to ignore Churchill's determination, convinced that Britain would have no option but to seek peace terms after he had disposed of France – which he proposed to do immediately. Belgium had surrendered on 28 May, and now that the British had gone he was free to turn his entire fighting strength, some 136 divisions, against the forty-nine tattered divisions still left of the French army.

The French soldiers fought hard, but they could not hope to hold the advancing Wehrmacht. The Germans broke through their defences after two days and swept down on France, fanning out in all directions. The French leaders panicked. Defeat turned into total collapse. The government fled, first to Tours and then to Bordeaux, abandoning Paris and declaring it an open city to prevent its destruction. German troops entered it without opposition on 14 June, and marched victoriously through the Arc de Triomphe and down the Champs-Élysées. General Bock, commander of Army Group B, flew into Paris airport unhindered to take the salute, then paid a visit to Napoleon's tomb and took lunch at the Ritz before doing a little shopping in the city's luxury stores.

Meanwhile, Mussolini had entered the war on 10 June, desperately anxious that it would all be over before he had a chance to claim either glory or spoils. His forces only managed to advance a few hundred yards along the Riviera into Menton, however, before they were halted by

French troops whom they outnumbered by three to one. In the United States, Roosevelt spoke scathingly of the Italian attack. In a speech at the University of Virginia in Charlottesville, he said, 'On this tenth day of June, 1940, the hand that held the dagger struck it into the back of his neighbour.'

To the German army, the Italian intervention was a total irrelevance. They were still swarming across France as fast as they could go. On 14 June, German troops opened a new front by launching a frontal attack on the Maginot Line near Saarbrücken, overcoming the supposedly impregnable defences with flamethrowers and explosives. Three days later, Guderian also penetrated the Maginot Line close to its beginning near Switzerland, attacking it from the rear after surprising Hitler with a report that he was at Pontarlier, a town just north of Lake Geneva. Hitler queried this, wiring back the correction, 'You probably mean Pontaillier-sur-Saône.'

'No mistake,' Guderian responded. 'I am myself on the Swiss frontier.'

That same day, 17 June 1940, the French sued for peace. Hitler received the news of France's capitulation in the small Belgian village of Brûly-de-Pesche, which he had taken over as his new headquarters on 5 June, at the start of Operation Red. When he heard the request for an armistice, his secretary, Christa Schröder, recalled, 'He was literally shaken by frantic exuberance.' He slapped his thigh, in the now-familiar gesture of joy, and jerked up his knee in a movement that was caught on film by Hitler's official cameraman, Walter Frentz, and later converted by Canadian director John Grierson into a ludicrous jig by looping the original eight frames to create an endless repetition.

There was nothing ludicrous in the occasion for those who were present, however. Calling for a toast, Keitel raised his glass of champagne to Hitler as 'the greatest war lord of all times'. At that particular moment, there could be few people in the entire world willing to deny him such an accolade. He had earned it with an unprecedented run of successes.

Many of those successes, moreover, were due to personal decisions which he had taken despite stubborn opposition from his generals. They had claimed his plan of campaign for Norway was unworkable, since the invasion flew in the face of every accepted law of naval warfare. They had resisted his decision to strike at France through the Ardennes – indeed, when Manstein had tried to push through the same idea he had been relieved of his post as Rundstedt's Chief of Staff and relegated to commanding a reserve corps in the east. That both operations had been so brilliantly successful had been due to Hitler's own imagination and determination.

He had personally dreamed up the daring plan for the coup against Fort Eben Emael. He had continued to astonish everyone not only with his encyclopaedic knowledge of armament systems and equipment – his near photographic memory recorded every tiny statistic in the manuals which were his constant bedtime reading – but also with his uncanny ability to pick out their strengths and weaknesses. He had thought up the idea of fitting the Stuka dive-bombers with the screaming sirens which so powerfully heightened the terror they struck into their victims. In defiance of the experts, he had insisted on equipping tanks with the long cannons which outgunned their rivals. He had demonstrated beyond all doubt his uncanny command of the psychology of his opponents, with only one notable exception: he never did manage to understand the British. But in June 1940 even that did not matter, for he had driven them from the continent of Europe.

All this clearly vindicated his belief in his powers of judgement: among all his triumphs in 1939 and 1940, one of the most significant for the future was the conquest of his own generals. After the defeat of France, even they were prepared to acknowledge his 'genius'.

Stalin, too, was uncomfortably aware of Hitler's achievements. He had been perfectly justified in anticipating a long and gruelling war of attrition in the West, giving him time to build up his own strength while Hitler, even if he succeeded in defeating the Allies, would have been seriously weakened. The rout of Poland had been a foregone conclusion, though three weeks had been an unnervingly short time to achieve it. But for Hitler to have taken little more than two months to conquer Denmark, Norway, Luxembourg, Holland, Belgium and France, and force the British to scuttle back to their island, was nothing short of alarming. What is more, the Wehrmacht's effortless achievement contrasted most disagreeably with the laborious struggles of the Red Army against lesser forces in Finland.

Thanks to the pact, Hitler had been able to deploy almost the entire German army in the West, leaving a mere seven divisions to guard his eastern frontiers. 'Seven divisions,' as Keitel told the Military Tribunal at Nuremberg after the war, 'from East Prussia to the Carpathians, two of which were transferred to the West during the campaign but later on were transported back again.' But even so, on 10 May he had been able to field only 136 divisions against 137 French and British, plus 34 Dutch and Belgians; his Luftwaffe had had barely 1,000 more aircraft than the Allies' 2,800; some 2,700 German tanks and armoured vehicles had faced 3,200 British and French, and some of the French tanks were more powerful than any of the German. Defeating these numerically superior forces had cost Hitler a mere 27,074 dead, against 135,000 on the Allied side. For that relatively small cost, he had gained the resources of the whole of Western Europe, which he would be able to utilise in preparing for the assault on the Soviet Union. It was indeed a fearsome accomplishment.

On 17 June 1940, Molotov called Schulenburg into the Kremlin and gave him 'the warmest congratulations of the Soviet government on the splendid success of the German Wehrmacht'. He then went on to tell the ambassador about Soviet action in the Baltic states. Stalin was wasting no time in moving to strengthen his defences.

42

'TWO HUNTING DOGS AFTER THE SAME BONE'

The success of Hitler's lightning war in the West meant Stalin had to move faster than he had intended in order to complete the consolidation of his frontiers. Knowing the Wehrmacht would soon be free to be turned against him, he no longer had time for the classic ploy of gradually undermining the governments of the countries he needed – Lithuania, Latvia and Estonia. He could not afford to wait several months for his own men to take power and then invite the Red Army in to protect them before begging for incorporation into the Soviet Union, as the Belorussians and the Ukrainians in Galicia had done. Nor could he continue to await a favourable moment before doing something about recovering the province of Bessarabia from Romania.

Molotov had signalled the Soviet Union's intentions towards Bessarabia in his speech to the Supreme Soviet on 29 March. Then, however, he had been at pains to keep the threat veiled. He pointed out that Romania was the only one of the Soviet Union's immediate neighbours with whom she did not have a non-aggression pact. 'The reason for this,' he said, 'is the unresolved question of Bessarabia, whose seizure by Romania has never been recognised by the Soviet Union, although she has never raised the question of recovering Bessarabia by force of arms.' He concluded his remarks by stating that 'there are no grounds for any worsening of Soviet–Romanian relations'.

By the time Guderian's tanks hit the English Channel on 20 May, however, the situation had changed completely. Border incidents were being staged at the rate of two or three a week, and the Red Army was already moving in force towards the Romanian frontier. The entire rail network in the Soviet western Ukraine, especially in the Lvov–Kiev area, had been taken over for troop transports. Molotov claimed these movements were purely defensive measures – a phrase that by now was becoming depressingly familiar – aimed against Italian plans to grab territory in the Balkans.

The Bessarabian move was the most delicate of all those on Stalin's list. The Romanians were traditionally aligned with the British and French, and the Allied guarantee for Romania's territorial integrity, given at the same time as that to Poland, was still in force. King Carol II and his government were violently anti-communist and pathologically afraid of a Soviet attack. They responded instantly to the Soviet build-up by mobilising their own forces and pouring them into Bessarabia.

King Carol had sworn that if the Soviets attacked his country not only would his army fight back but the Romanians, aided by the British, would immediately destroy their entire oil industry. There could be little doubt that he meant it, and little chance that anyone would be able to do anything to stop it happening – though the German minister in Bucharest, Wilhelm Fabricius, devised a daring plan for special German commando units to sail into Romania from Vienna on Danube passenger boats. He even considered the idea of fomenting a revolution, but Baron Manfred von Killinger, inspector of German diplomatic missions in the Balkans, dismissed this out of hand. 'The primitive Romanian people,' he told Ribbentrop, 'consisting for the most part of peasants of whom fifty per cent are illiterate, could not be used for such an undertaking in the prevailing conditions. They obey orders as soldiers without question, including the destruction of the oil wells.'

However, although the Romanians' hatred of the Soviet Union was stronger than ever, they were swiftly drawing closer to Germany. The relationship improved markedly with every German success, and by 1940 they had become important trading partners. In addition to providing large quantities of grain, meat and timber, they were the Reich's largest suppliers of oil, with 1·2 million tons a year. This was considerably more even than the Germans were obtaining from the Soviet Union, accounting for well over half their total imports of petroleum products. The arrangement was especially attractive to the Germans, since they were paying for the oil not in hard currency but with the arms they had captured from Poland. For the Romanians, Prime Minister Tatarescu explained to Fabricius that the arms were 'necessary to strengthen Romania's political position with respect to Russia'.

With such a situation, Stalin could achieve his purpose only with Hitler's help. The balance sheet between them was more or less even at that time – Hitler had paid for Soviet acquiescence in the Polish campaign by allowing Stalin his 'promenade into Poland'; Stalin had paid for the rest of the provisions of the pact by giving Hitler a clear run in the West. Now, it was Hitler's turn again – and in any case, it was obviously in his interest to avoid a Soviet invasion which could cost him more than half his oil.

After his victories in the West, the Romanians were begging for Hitler's friendship, and for his protection against attack, either from the Allies wishing to cut off the oil, or from the Soviets. On 28 May, they signed a new petroleum agreement. On 1 June, Ribbentrop, in a message from the special train *Heinrich*, gave the first indication of the price Germany required for the friendship the Romanians so earnestly desired. How far were they prepared to go, he asked, in accepting the 'revisionist' claims of their neighbours, especially the Soviet Union in the Bessarabian question? Clutching desperately at any straw, the Romanians acknowledged that they 'would have to satisfy certain revisionist claims'. They agreed to start talks with the Soviets.

While the acquisition of Bessarabia was proceeding, albeit cautiously, Stalin could afford to act more decisively in the Baltic. In fact, he could scarcely afford not to. As seen from the Kremlin, the Baltic states offered Hitler a most convenient springboard for an attack on the Soviet Union. What was worse, ideologically they looked to Berlin rather than to Moscow, in spite of having effectively become client states of the Soviet Union. True, there were now sizeable Soviet garrisons in all three countries, but those troops were there to hold down the population during what Stalin had hoped would be the gradual process of Sovietisation, rather than to protect the frontier with Germany. The Baltic states were beginning to look like the weak link in his defensive chain.

Lithuania was chosen for the start of the operation. On 25 May, Molotov called in the Lithuanian minister in Moscow and complained of 'provocative acts' involving the disappearance of Soviet soldiers from their bases in Lithuania. In fact, the disappearances were simply the result of the soldier's traditional fondness, in any country, for booze and girls. A handful of Red Army men had gone absent without leave, or had deserted, in order to enjoy the delights of the local bars and brothels. Most of them returned to their units after a few days, but one soldier, Butaev by name, committed suicide when arrested by the Lithuanian police – probably because he was terrified of facing punishment at the hands of a Soviet military tribunal. Marshal Timoshenko, when he subsequently met Lithuanian Prime Minister Antanas Merkys in Moscow, showed scant sympathy for Butaev – the man was a scoundrel, he said.

Soviet press and radio reported the incidents prominently, using strong language and suggesting that 'these disappearances have been arranged with the support of the Lithuanian government'. Veteran Kremlin watchers in Moscow were quick to read the signs. Schulenburg noted that the reports 'caused a sensational stir in political and diplomatic circles here. It is believed that the present demands could be the first move towards energetic Soviet action against Lithuania and possibly also against the other Baltic states.' Their suspicions were strengthened during the first two weeks in June, as the Soviets staged a series of incidents on the borders of all three states, and started acquiring large amounts of their currencies, just as they had done with Finland.

The border troubles came to a climax on 15 June, when Soviet troops attacked a Latvian frontier post, killing two of the guards and a woman, seriously wounding another woman and a child, and taking prisoner ten guards and a number of civilians before burning down the building. The same day, the Soviet navy blockaded Estonian and Latvian ports, and just after lunch two Estonian airliners were attacked by Soviet fighters, one of them crashing into the sea just north of Tallinn. At 3 o'clock that afternoon, Soviet troops marched into Lithuania, unopposed, following the rejection of every offer made to solve the problems by the Lithuanians.

In the middle of the night in Moscow, the head of the foreign department of the NKVD, Vladimir Georgievich Dekanozov, summoned several officials to his office in Dzerzhinsky Square. The most important among them was Andrei Vyshinsky, like Dekanozov a Deputy Foreign Commissar of the Soviet Union. This Polish-born lawyer had been chief prosecutor at all the great trials during the thirties, including those of the purges, when his cry 'Shoot them, like the mad dogs they are!' had echoed through the courtrooms like a recurring refrain.

Dekanozov, a minute, bird-like man barely five feet tall, with a little, beak-like nose and dark eyes, his scant black hair slicked back across his head, was a man of immense power. He was another of Stalin's Georgian Mafia, coming from the same area as Stalin himself, though he was twenty-two years younger than the Party Secretary. He was nicknamed 'the hangman of Baku', for the countless death sentences he had doled out in the early twenties in the Caucasus, where he had first made his name as a very young man in suppressing dissension and organising the incorporation of the then independent republics of Georgia, Armenia and Azerbaidzhan into the Soviet Union. It seemed he had now been given the same job in the Baltic states, and was resolved to approach it with the same ruthless determination.

When everyone was gathered in his office, Dekanozov told them they had been selected for a diplomatic mission to the Baltic states. He would lead the group going to Lithuania, Vyshinsky that to Latvia, and Andrei Zhdanov, who was not present at the meeting, that to Estonia, the state bordering his Leningrad stronghold. He then produced from his desk a bundle of red diplomatic passports, which he distributed before making a short speech.

'At the decision of the Politburo and at the request of Comrade Stalin,' he began, 'the security problem along our north-west frontier is now to be solved.' He went on to accuse 'the bourgeois governments of the three Baltic states . . . on the instructions of the stock exchanges of Paris and London . . . [of doing] everything possible to sabotage the treaties they signed with the Soviet Union.' In the face of 'unbelievable provocations' against Soviet military personnel, the USSR had been forced to send in the three groups to – as he put it – 'create conditions' in which the Red Army would be able to defend 'the north-western frontiers of our socialist motherland'. In case anyone had any doubts about the purpose of the operation, Dekanozov concluded by saying that 'if the workers of Latvia and the other Baltic states should express the wish that the new governments should be called "Soviet" and "Socialist", Comrade Stalin has said he will have no objections to such demands.'

A few hours later, Soviet bombers flew Dekanozov to Kaunas and Vyshinsky to Riga. Zhdanov arrived in Tallinn on 19 June by armoured train from Leningrad. Taking no chances, he was driven from the station to the Soviet legation, and thence to the Estonian presidential palace, in an armoured car escorted by two tanks. All three commissars carried in their briefcases typewritten lists of the men chosen by Moscow to form the new Baltic governments.

In each country the approach was identical. 'You may be sure,' Zhdanov told a man called Vares, who had been selected to be Prime Minister of the provisional Cabinet in Estonia, 'that everything will be done in accordance with democratic parliamentary rules and regulations. We are not Germans. We will ask your President, Pats, to form a new government. Because the existing Cabinet is not in a position to solve the existing problems, the President will order new elections and we will support the new government.' Vyshinsky and Dekanozov said much the same to their charges.

There was a slight legal hiccup before Dekanozov's chosen Lithuanian collaborators could be appointed. The Lithuanian President, Antanas Smetona, had fled to Germany, crossing the open frontier unceremoniously by wading across a stream with his trousers rolled up around his knees. He had not, however, resigned from office, and so remained President, creating a small constitutional problem for Dekanozov: under the Lithuanian constitution, only the President had the power to appoint a government. Dekanozov hesitated, but not for long. He soon got round the little difficulty by declaring that in leaving the country Smetona had resigned. He then appointed his own acting President, an obscure left-wing journalist called Justas Paleckis, and forced Prime Minister Merkys to resign, replacing him with a writer and linguist, Professor Vincas Kreve-Mickevicius.

Kreve recalled how Dekanozov sent for him in the middle of the night to offer him the post, coupled with that of Foreign Minister. When Kreve protested at the Soviet demand, 'in order to keep Lithuania out of the war', to post more troops to the bases acquired nine months earlier, saying his country was neutral and that Germany would in any case only attack if the Soviet Union approved, Dekanozov treated him to a lengthy historical–political lecture.

'Our friendship with Germany,' he said, 'can be compared with that of two hunting dogs both after the same bone. Rest assured, Comrade Stalin and I personally wish Lithuania the very best. We do not suffer from the Russian disease of patriotic chauvinism. We love and respect the Lithuanian people, the fate of whom is similar to that of the Georgian people.' For centuries, he continued, the Lithuanians had defended themselves against German expansionism. Surely they more than anyone must recognise the fact that Germany's territorial ambitions were boundless. Surely they more than anyone must realise that the USSR could not afford to gamble on Germany's peaceful intentions: Moscow had to take sensible precautions. 'Today, [the Germans] have no choice but to be our friends. But tomorrow, they could become our worst enemies, and then their first step would be the occupation of Lithuania, this important strategic point.

'It is therefore a matter of the greatest importance for us to have a government in Lithuania that has the trust of the people and does not bend to German demands. By doing that, we want to protect ourselves, and indirectly Lithuania. As soon as the danger is past, we will withdraw our troops immediately, and you can carry on living as you are today.'

Kreve did his best to keep his country out of the Soviet clutches. He even flew to Moscow to confront Molotov himself, but only received another lecture for his pains. Molotov pointed out that the second world war would deliver the whole of Europe into the hands of the USSR, just as the first world war had been responsible for giving the Bolsheviks Russia. The third world war, he said, 'which was inevitable', would complete the story by delivering the rest of the world to the communist cause. In the end, there was nothing Kreve could do but accept the situation, and form a new Lithuanian government acceptable to the Soviets, just as Latvia had done on 20 June and Estonia on 22 June.

The expected elections took place in all three countries on 14 July. In spite of the fact that only between ten and thirty per cent of the populations voted in each case, the so-called 'List of the Working Class' was elected almost unanimously, claiming no less than 99·2 per cent support. On 21 July, the newly elected deputies in all three countries proclaimed themselves to be Soviet Socialist governments, and asked to be incorporated into the USSR. The Supreme Soviet, meeting in Moscow, granted their requests on 3 August. The Red Army started moving in in force on 1 August. By 6 August, the operation was complete.

*　　　*　　　*

The Baltic states had been swallowed whole; all that remained for the Soviet Union was the more lengthy process of digestion. This had begun at the end of June with the arrival from Moscow of formerly exiled communist leaders and Soviet 'instructors' to start the bloody business of purging and liquidating bourgeois business, and removing leading personnel from the army, police, ministries and administrative bodies. The first wave of deportations to Siberia began even before the elections, on 11 July. From then until the German invasion in June 1941, the classic campaign of Sovietisation continued unabated, with the aim of transforming intellectual, economic and political life.

First, the local universities and schools were purged of anti-Soviet or nationalistic elements. Where necessary, new syllabuses were imposed in which the correct party line was stressed. Books were vetted and libraries cleansed of those considered unsuitable. At the same time, the dead hand of Sovietisation was felt in the economy. Businesses were nationalised, and all bank accounts above a certain amount were frozen. All land, with the exception of smallholdings, was nationalised and incorporated into state land reserves.

Finally, Lavrenti Beria, head of the NKVD since 1938, Dekanozov's immediate boss and another of Stalin's most trusted Georgian Mafia lieutenants, was given the task of purging the remainder of the population. He began by recruiting thousands of local volunteers for the NKVD, then turning them loose on their fellow citizens. The aim was to identify and then banish any potential leaders of opposition to the new regime – intellectuals, writers, teachers, trade union leaders, these were the targets. Lists of names were built up in NKVD files. Beria's men moved swiftly: whole families were arrested, piled into cattle trucks and sent to labour camps or exile in the wilds of Siberia or Central Asia.

The purges continued right up to the German invasion. Only a week before the start of 'Barbarossa', on the night of 14–15 June 1941, some 60,000 Estonians, 34,000 Latvians and 38,000 Lithuanians were deported, carrying only their hand luggage as they were herded away. The Soviet plan, halted in 1941 by 'Barbarossa', was for no less than one third of the entire population of Lithuania, and equally substantial proportions of the peoples of Latvia and Estonia, to be sent to Siberia, Kazakhstan, and other penal areas as far away from the western borders as possible. As it was, approximately four per cent of the Estonian population and two per cent of those of Latvia and Lithuania found their way to the gulags. They were replaced in their countries by Russians who, like the *Volksdeutsche* in the Polish provinces occupied by Germany, took over their homes and their jobs as if the original inhabitants had never existed.

During all that time, in spite of agonised warnings from Karl Schnurre that German economic interests were being severely damaged by the Soviet occupation of the Baltic states, and completely disregarding

U S S R

R. Pruth

Ruthenia

R. Dniester

Cernauti

Herta

Northern
Bukovina

B E S S A R A B I A

M O L D A V I A

Batta

Jassy

Kishinev

R. Pruth

R U M A N I A

R. Sereth

Brasov

Ploesti

Bucharest

Galatz

Black

Sea

Constanza

R. Danube

Southern
Dobrudja

Varna

BULGARIA

/// Ceded by Rumania to USSR, 1940
||| Ceded by Rumania to Bulgaria

0 _____ 50 Miles
0 _____ 100 km

hundreds of years of German involvement and influence in the Baltic, Hitler made no move whatever to help the people. The only concern he or any of his senior officials showed was for evacuating those *Volksdeutsche* who had remained in the Baltic states, and for protection of or compensation for German property there. As far as he was concerned, the situation was purely temporary, and would soon be put right again.

Ribbentrop was more concerned with the Lithuanian Tip, the strip of land which he had argued over so volubly before. When the Red Army moved into Lithuania, it 'accidentally' occupied the strip at the same time as the rest of the country. Ribbentrop protested loudly to Stalin and Molotov, who calmly agreed that a mistake had been made, but firmly resisted all suggestions that they order the Red Army to withdraw. Stalin asked, as a personal favour, for the Germans to allow the strip to remain as part of Lithuania – he knew well how important it was to the Lithuanians themselves – pointing out that the population of the area included only 7·3 per cent Germans, as opposed to 82·3 per cent Lithuanians. Since the area had no great strategic importance – it was generally believed the Germans wanted it only because it ran alongside Göring's private hunting reserve – Hitler gave in to the Soviet demand. It was agreed that the Soviet Union would pay compensation for the land, but it took until January 1941 before the price was finally agreed at 7,500,000 gold dollars, in gold and non-ferrous metals.

The blatant overstepping of the agreed terms of the pact over the Lithuanian Tip shook Hitler's belief in Stalin's good faith. There could be no doubt that the occupation of the land had not been an oversight but a deliberate act. It was, to be sure, a relatively small matter, and Stalin had handled it with considerable charm. But it was still a breach of trust. What was to follow came as an even more unpleasant warning that the Soviet leader was prepared to push Germany to the limit.

Events in Romania had remained fairly quiet during most of June, though there was steady Soviet pressure from the presence of some thirty divisions of troops on the borders. The surprise came on 23 June, when Molotov informed Schulenburg that the Soviet Union was not prepared to wait any longer for the Romanians to come to heel, and that she wanted not only Bessarabia, but also the neighbouring province of Bukovina, which had never been mentioned before.

Coming on the very day when Hitler paid a secret visit to Paris, a city he had always dreamed of seeing, the Soviet news must have added a certain bitter flavour to the heady taste of success. Molotov had told Schulenburg he would wait until 25 June before presenting his demands to Romania, in order to give the Germans time to let him know their feelings on the matter. He need hardly have bothered, for he and Stalin must have known perfectly well that as long as the oilfields around

Ploesti were kept safe, Hitler would give them anything they asked for, simply to keep the peace. All the Soviets had to do was to keep threatening to attack.

Schulenburg presented Hitler's reply at 9 pm on 25 June. It was that Germany would of course support the Soviet government in pressing its claims, though there were certain points they were not altogether happy about. It would make things easier if the Soviets were to drop Bukovina from their claim, since it had never belonged even to tsarist Russia: it had been an Austrian crown province, and therefore was 'packed' with Germans – more so than Bessarabia, which itself had some 100,000 *Volksdeutsche*. Molotov was unmoved. Bukovina, a small, heavily wooded area in the foothills of the Carpathian mountains on the borders of the Ukraine, was, he said, 'the last remnant still missing from a unified Ukraine', and for that reason it must be dealt with at the same time as Bessarabia. Of course, he added, the Soviet Union would take care of all German interests in the area. But they were determined to send in the Red Army if there was any further delay.

Next day, Molotov told Schulenburg that the Soviet government had considered the German response, and was prepared to limit its demands in Bukovina to just the northern half of the province. At 10 o'clock that night, he called in the Romanian minister and presented the demands, in a twenty-four-hour ultimatum.

During those twenty-four hours, the German minister in Bucharest, Fabricius, worked like a madman to persuade the Romanians to settle on the Soviet terms. He even showed the Romanian Foreign Minister newsreel film of recent battles, to demonstrate the full horror of modern war. King Carol, who had assumed dictatorial powers five days before, 'to guide the moral and material life of the nation', was furious with both the Soviets and the Germans, who had let him down. Hitler, he shouted, had given his word when he had seen him at the Berghof on 24 November 1938 that he would support Romania. How could he now expect him to cede one third of his country without a fight?

Ribbentrop sent instructions to Fabricius to blame everything on the British. It was they who were inciting the Soviet Union to threaten Romania. It was they who wanted to cause a war between them: the new British ambassador in Moscow, Sir Stafford Cripps, had openly encouraged the Soviet government to take action in the Balkans – as Molotov had promptly informed Germany. Finally, Ribbentrop told Fabricius he 'would have no objections' to his pointing out that Romania had got herself into this mess by accepting the British guarantee. Romania could expect no help from Germany. Indeed, the Germans considered, as the Romanians must 'upon sober and realistic reflection', that the Soviet claim was well founded, and they therefore had to advise the Romanians to yield.

After a nerve-racking few hours, during which the Germans also had to persuade Hungary and Bulgaria not to attack Romania in pursuit of their own claims on chunks of her territory like jackals tearing at a lion's kill, King Carol capitulated. On 28 June, the Red Army moved into the two provinces. Stalin had finally obtained his complete pound of flesh from the pact – and perhaps a few ounces over.

43

'A LONG AND DANGEROUS MISSION'

With the new frontiers of the Soviet Union firmly established in the north, south and west, Stalin had gained some 286,000 square miles of territory and well over twenty million people. His borders had advanced hundreds of miles, creating valuable buffer zones to soak up the impact of any German attack. But the security of the Soviet Union depended on other factors, too, equally important if not more so. Apart from the leadership of Stalin himself, the most notable of these were military efficiency and industrial performance. He approached both areas with typical ruthlessness and determination.

The reorganisation of the Red Army had been started after the Winter War, with the sacking of Voroshilov as Defence Commissar and his replacement by Timoshenko on 7 May. Three days later, the urgency of the task facing the new commissar was revealed all too clearly as the Wehrmacht smashed its way into the Western countries with terrifying power. There was obviously no time to be lost, and Timoshenko, with Stalin's backing, started at once. In the thirteen months that remained before those German troops were unleashed against the Soviet Union, he subjected the Red Army commanders to an unprecedented shake-up. The incompetent were weeded out; many were demoted; some were shot.

Among those arrested and summarily executed was the chief of the GRU, Soviet Military Intelligence, Lieutenant-General of Aviation Ivan Iosifovich Proskurov, who was charged with the responsibility for poor intelligence during the Winter War. Rumour had it, however, that his real 'crime' was openly speaking against the Nazi–Soviet pact. He was replaced by Lieutenant-General F. I. Golikov, an appointment which was to be of great significance, particularly in the first half of 1941, since Golikov would be responsible for collating and presenting all intelligence reports to Stalin.

Timoshenko's order No. 120, issued on 16 May 1940, was diagnostic in intent. It identified many of the organisational failures of the Finnish war: inadequate preparation and training of the troops, failure of discipline, lack of enterprise shown by front-line commanders, lack of co-operation between different branches of the armed forces resulting in massive casualties in the field, shortcomings in communications, supply and transport – the Military Council's diagnosis was not so very different from that made by the German general staff for Hitler.

Order No. 160, also issued on 16 May, was intended to be therapeutic. It proposed cures for some of the ills of the Soviet military machine. A new and strenuous training programme was devised; in future all troops must be in a state of 'complete combat readiness'. A new and ferocious disciplinary code was drawn up. Under it, unconditional obedience was demanded of every Soviet soldier. The authority of the officer – though still officially known only as a 'commander' – was re-established, along with saluting, medals and insignia of rank. Some of the old ranks like those of admiral and general, which had long been abolished in favour of more ideologically acceptable but infinitely more cumbersome titles such as 'army commander first, second or third grade', were restored and additional ranks created, like that of colonel-general, borrowed from the Germans.* In brief, Trotsky's vision of an army inspired solely by revolutionary ideals was abandoned – to be replaced, ironically, by the concept of a professional fighting force, professionally officered, which had been advocated by Marshal Tukhachevsky, one of the major victims of Stalin's purges.

Timoshenko even went so far as to tackle the sensitive problem of political interference in the field. The Red Army was hag-ridden by political commissars: he succeeded in limiting their power, while skilfully managing to avoid a head-on clash with the party. In future, the commissar would stick to the task of political indoctrination and leave military decision-making to the officer in charge. Since Stalin's own military reputation had been established by overriding the military commanders at Tsaritsyn and Petrograd, this must have been a particularly tricky issue for Timoshenko to tackle, and his success a considerable achievement.

But there was another, equally tricky area where the new Defence Commissar also triumphed. He brought back, as though from the dead, some 4,000 officers who had been disgraced and imprisoned or exiled during the purges. Colonel K. K. Rokossovsky, the former tsarist cavalry sergeant who was later to become a Marshal of the Soviet Union, was the most celebrated of these revenants. In June 1940 he was rescued from the limbo to which he had been consigned on a trumped-up and never proved charge of 'anti-Soviet conspiracy', to become one of the

---

* We have used the new ranks throughout this book, in order to avoid confusion.

479 new major-generals of the Red Army, and take command of one of the newly constituted mechanised corps.

A typical story is that of Alexander V. Gorbatov, whose experiences cast an interesting light on those desperate days when Timoshenko was trying to resurrect an army. Gorbatov, a man of seemingly impeccable political pedigree, had joined the Red Army in 1919, the same year that he joined the party. He fought with distinction in the Civil War and was awarded the Order of the Red Banner for the part he played in the Polish war. He rose through the ranks until, in 1936, he was promoted to command of the 2nd Cavalry Division. At 2 am on 22 October 1938, he was suddenly arrested, taken to the NKVD headquarters at the Lubyanka, and tortured in order to make him confess to his 'crimes'. He refused to confess to anything, but was still sentenced to fifteen years in a labour camp plus five years' internal exile. He was sent to the Kolyma gulag in Siberia.

More than two years later, he was with a work party in a Siberian forest when he was informed by a minor official that his case was under review. On 5 March 1941, he was released in Moscow – but only after he had signed a document promising he would remain silent about his imprisonment. The euphemism he was to use, like all similar military men, was that he had been away 'on a long and dangerous mission'. Two days later, he was ordered to report to Timoshenko's office.

'I am pleased to see you alive,' the marshal greeted him. 'I have already given the order that you should be reinstated in the army and that you should receive back pay in your old rank for the full thirty months [that you have been away].'

Timoshenko then asked whether Gorbatov was ready to return to duty with the cavalry, or would he prefer a change? Some different arm of the service? Gorbatov opted for the infantry, and was sent to the 25th Rifle Corps as deputy commander until he got used to 'all the innovations'. Shortly afterwards, he was promoted to the rank of lieutenant-general and put in command of the 3rd Army in the Mtensk area.

Not all Timoshenko's reorganisation proved to be as simple as reinstating men like Gorbatov. Too many of the old guard had been shot, or had died in the camps. Consequently, there were still huge gaps left by the purges, and while it was all very well to promote younger men – indeed, because of the decimation of senior ranks it was vitally necessary to do so – Gorbatov must have echoed the thoughts of many senior officers, including Timoshenko himself, when he wondered how these newly appointed commanders with no experience of battle would handle operations in a real war. 'Yesterday's battalion commander would be head of a division,' Gorbatov wrote later, 'yesterday's regimental commander of a corps; in charge of an army, or a whole front, there would be at best a former divisional commander or his deputy.'

Gorbatov for one had no illusions that war with Germany was coming. And when it did, the German generals would all have had some two years' battle experience.

Timoshenko's problems did not stop at divisional or corps commanders. The purges had done nothing to encourage independence of thought in the Supreme Military Council. Senior officers who had survived the terror were understandably cautious about publicly risking their careers, and possibly their lives, in questioning the strongly held beliefs of their political masters – even when those beliefs were clearly misconceived. And as for those who had just been promoted to the most senior ranks – 'the good comrades, the yes-men, the lickspittles', as Ernst Fischer calls them – they had no intention of being controversial, either. As a result, despite all the good intentions, there was within the Red Army a consensus of mediocrity, fear and misapprehension.

Because of their military failures in the Winter War, Soviet leaders allowed themselves to become fixated by their few successes. S. S. Biriuzov, later a Marshal of the Soviet Union but then a young and recently promoted commander of a rifle division, later wrote: 'The storming of the Mannerheim Line was regarded as a model of operational and tactical art. Troops were taught to overcome the enemy's protracted defence by a gradual accumulation of forces and a patient "gnawing through" of breaches in the enemy's fortifications . . . We ceased to deal seriously with mobile combat and with the struggle against highly mechanised units of great firepower.' In other words, they ignored the existence of German Panzer divisions. They also ignored 'combat-in-depth tactics . . . [involving] large-scale troop concentrations, strikes by tanks, cavalry and mechanised units on the enemy's rear, and large-scale airborne operations'. And yet these were the very tactics the Soviet army had pioneered in the early thirties. It was the Wehrmacht which had borrowed Soviet tactical ideas worked out by men like Tukhachevsky, Uborevich and Yakir – all army commanders who had been executed.

When Hitler sent his armoured divisions smashing through the Ardennes and his paratroops into Holland, his tactics, as Biriuzov pointed out, 'were exactly the same as those we had to deal with in 1941: massive aerial attacks, tank breakthroughs, pincer movements and encirclements. And, of course, there was nothing like this on the Karelian Isthmus in the winter of 1939–40.' Yet, right up to the German invasion of the Soviet Union, 'the spirit of battles for the Mannerheim Line continued to hover over [Soviet] tactics and combat training.'

In just the same way, it must be said, the Allied commanders in France and Belgium were trapped by their experiences in the first world war. But the Soviet leadership seemed unable to learn from the disasters that overtook the Allies in the Battle of France, and continued to go to considerable pains to absorb the lessons from the Finnish war. Unfortunately, these proved to be the wrong lessons for the war they were about to fight. In Marshal Biriuzov's words, 'We had to retrain ourselves under enemy fire, paying a high price for the experience and knowledge.'

Hitler, meanwhile, seemed to think he had no lessons to learn at all – success after success had made him supremely confident. While Stalin was busily building up the Red Army, Hitler was actually reducing the size of the Wehrmacht. In the second week in June he ordered the field army to be reduced in strength immediately by thirty-five divisions, from a grand total of 155 divisions down to 120, though twenty of those which were to be disbanded could be reconstituted quickly if the need arose.

The main reason for this reduction in the armed services was to release manpower for use in industry: it is an unavoidable predicament of any nation at war that at the very time it needs the highest production from its industries to supply its armed forces, all the extra manpower needed by those industries has been sucked into the armed forces. In a long war, this becomes a serious problem, unless incredibly high stocks have been built up in advance. Hitler had not had time to build up those stocks – it had taken every bit of the Reich's resources simply to create the Wehrmacht in only six years. He was not equipped, therefore, to fight a long war, only a series of short ones. The *Blitzkrieg*, both in theory and practice, was ideally suited to this situation, and up to the summer of 1940 had proved itself hugely successful. After each episode of lightning war, large numbers of troops could be released to work in the factories and thus provide the material needed for the next.

Such was Hitler's confidence in 1940, however, that a high proportion of men going back into industry found themselves producing consumer goods, as peacetime production was restarted in many areas.

Stalin could not afford such complacency: the Soviet Union had too great a backlog to make up. While Timoshenko was trying to reshape and revitalise the Soviet war machine, Stalin set about harnessing the Soviet Union's huge labour force to supply and service it, with a whole series of new labour laws.

For many years, the week in the Soviet Union had consisted of only six days, partly in an attempt to do away with the traditional Sunday. The old names were discarded, and replaced by numbers: days one, two, three, four and five were working days, day six was rest day, and then came the next day one, and so on. Ever since 1932, a seven-hour working day had been the norm under the constitution. Now, all that was to change. Not only was the working day to be extended to eight hours, but the working week was extended to seven days, with no day off.

Strict discipline was introduced into the workplace. It became a crime for any worker to be more than twenty minutes late for work, unless he or she could produce a doctor's certificate. Absenteeism, of course, was totally forbidden. The law was strictly enforced, and across the USSR there were tens of thousands of cases of office and factory workers being sentenced to several months in prison, or to a term of what was called 'forced labour'. This was a particularly galling form of punishment, in which the convicted worker was required to continue with his or her regular job, but with a cut in salary of twenty-five per cent, or in some cases by as much as fifty per cent. The average length of forced labour sentences was between three and six months. Penalties against theft, 'hooliganism' – an all-embracing term which could be used for any form of dissent or behaviour that could be called anti-social – refusal to obey the orders of foremen and managers, and all cases of 'disorderly conduct' in the office or factory, were savagely increased.

Managers and chief engineers, those at the very top of the managerial ladder, were as vulnerable under the harsh new regime as were the workers on the factory floor. If the plant or department they were responsible for regularly failed to meet production quotas or consistently produced goods that were not up to specification, they faced gaol sentences. The well-publicised fate of one unfortunate Moscow factory manager must have sent shivers down many a Soviet managerial spine: found guilty of consistently producing sub-standard electric motors, he was sentenced to six years in prison.

There was more to the re-organisation of Soviet industry than merely imposing a new set of draconian labour laws. Much thought was given to the recruitment of what were described as fresh 'state labour reserves'. By a decree promulgated on 2 October 1940, between 800,000 and a million youths from the ages of fourteen to seventeen were conscripted into various trade, railway and industrial schools. There, those with high potential underwent intensive two-year study courses to train them as metallurgists, industrial chemists, railway engineers or whatever. For the less talented, those considered more suitable for general occupations such as coalmining or building, there were six-month courses. All training was free of charge, as was all accommodation, clothing, food, books, and equipment. The pupils were to be 'maintained by the state during the period of their studies'.

American journalist John Scott reported seeing lines of youths in uniform being marched through the streets between the dormitories and their various schools. While there may have been some dissent at this conscription of the young, to many parents it seemed a great opportunity for their sons to get away from the collective farm and learn a valuable trade at no cost to themselves.

In order to pay for all this, and to discourage parents from attempting to opt out of the system, the Soviet government decreed that anyone wanting to keep their children on at normal high school must pay about 200 roubles a month for their tuition. This was directly contrary to the 1936 Soviet Constitution, which guaranteed free education for all – but the Constitution was not amended – it was, according to Scott, 'simply edited'.

By the end of 1940, Stalin had succeeded in mobilising the entire people of the Soviet Union, outside the armed forces themselves, into a vast industrial army, and had placed the whole of Soviet industry on a war footing, though standards of efficiency still left a great deal to be desired. But even with his new frontiers, most of his industrial centres were still vulnerable to air attack, since they were largely concentrated in the European side of his great empire. So, starting in early 1940, he made strenuous efforts to transfer various key industries to the east, beyond the Ural mountains, out of the range of German bombers.

This strategy soon ran into the problem which has always afflicted the Soviet Union – the inadequacy of the transport system in a country so vast and climatically inhospitable. In spite of considerable investment in new railways and technical improvements to track and traffic handling, the situation improved only marginally.

It was also hampered by the fact that there were massive industrial complexes near Leningrad and Moscow, and in the Ukraine, which it was simply not practical to move because they were already close to transportation systems, particularly waterways like the great rivers such as the Volga and the Don, and to their sources of essential raw materials and fuels, none of which could be moved. The Donbas coalfields in the Ukraine, for example, the most productive in the USSR, were surrounded by plants and factories. Although many new oilfields and coalfields had been opened up in the lands beyond the Urals, it would be some time before they came into full production, and even then it was doubtful if they would ever equal the output of the Ukraine or Baku – though even these established areas of production were having their problems at that time.

The huge amounts of oil which Stalin had promised to supply to Hitler – in return, of course, not only for arms but also for the equipment, expertise and machine tools necessary to modernise his industry – made it increasingly difficult for the Soviet oil industry to supply the immediate national needs, never mind producing a surplus for strategic stockpiling. In 1939, Soviet oil production had been at least thirteen per cent below the target set by the Five Year Plan. During the first six months of 1940, it fell still further, to below two million tons a month.

Industria, the official journal of the Oil Commissariat, in an editorial on 6 May 1940, blamed – among other things – an acute shortage of spare parts for oilfield machinery, including trucks. In the Emba fields in Kazakhstan, production that year, according to the *Kazakhstanskaga Pravda* of 27 November 1940, was 'considerably less than for the first ten months of last year'. The paper blamed frequent transport breakdowns for the failure to meet production quotas: less than half the local fleet of 347 trucks were in working order. The rest were sitting idle, waiting, inevitably, for replacement parts. An additional concern was that much of their oil had to be stored in open lakes because they could not afford to build metal tanks; this situation led to serious losses through theft.

Every oilfield blamed the aftermath of the Winter War for many of these problems. But the shortage of spare parts was largely due to the fact that so many factories which normally produced parts for the oil industry had now been turned over to full-time arms production – another example of the vicious spiral in which Stalin found himself trapped.

One way of relieving the pressure on the oilfields was, of course, to save fuel wherever possible. An intensive campaign to this effect was mounted throughout the Soviet Union. *Pravda* was constantly inveighing against those who wasted fuel, particularly those industrial plants which 'constantly burn more than their planned and allotted amount of liquid fuels and lubricants'.

As a result of this pressure, many trucks and tractors – John Scott gives a figure of 100,000 – were converted from petrol or diesel oil to burning peat or charcoal. Stationary engines fired by petrol or diesel were replaced by wood, coal, peat or carbide burners. On the streets of Moscow, carbide gas generators became a common sight, while in the countryside greater use was made of water and wind power.

While Stalin struggled to make Soviet industry more efficient and to bring it up to date, he gave Mikoyan, as Commissar for Foreign Trade, a different task: to find new markets abroad for Soviet exports. Mikoyan was remarkably successful. During 1940 and the early part of 1941, he negotiated trade agreements with – in alphabetical order – Afghanistan, Belgium, China, Denmark, Finland, Greece, Hungary, Iran, Norway, Romania, Slovakia, Sweden, Switzerland and Thailand. Of course, in the case of Belgium, Denmark and Norway, which had all been overrun by the Germans, Mikoyan simply negotiated direct with Gustav Hilger in the German embassy in Moscow. But to reach amicable agreements with Finland and Romania, both of whom could be expected to harbour certain resentments against the Soviet Union, was a considerable achievement in the circumstances.

In essence, all these trade agreements took much the same form as those with Germany – and with exactly the same purpose. They all involved the exchange of Soviet raw materials – petroleum products, grain, fodder, cotton, lumber, minerals, and so on – for foreign manufactured goods – anything from machine tools to ball bearings, rolling stock to military equipment. Everything was destined for use by or for the Red Army.

In order to support this massive export drive, the Soviet people were forced to accept serious shortages of even the basic necessities of life, including food and clothing. And because certain foodstuffs were not available in sufficient quantity, the government deliberately raised prices by anything up to twenty-five per cent, and in some cases by as much as seventy five per cent. Food rationing was also introduced, even in Moscow. No one was permitted to buy at any one time more than 2½lb of bread, ¼lb of butter, ¼lb of cheese, 1lb of meat, 1lb of sausage, five eggs, 1lb of sugar, or one can of preserves – if they could be found. In the larger cities, such as Moscow, Leningrad or Kiev, there was nothing to stop anyone going from store to store buying the same amount of food each time – provided they could afford to buy the goods at their inflated prices. In the rest of the country, each person was allowed to buy food only from a specific store, which kept a record of their purchases.

The shortages varied from place to place, the situation tending to be easier in those areas where an important industry was sited. When John Scott got permission to visit Baku in April 1941, for example, in order to write a story, he found the stores there well stocked with food and consumer goods, and the oilfield workers living in comparative luxury. But oil was, of course, a strategically vital industry: it was worth Stalin's while bribing the workers with a few goodies if it produced steadily rising production figures.

In 1940, the Soviet government spent 56 billion roubles on defence, more than twice as much as in 1938, and over twenty-five per cent of all industrial investment. As a result, the defence industry developed at three times the rate of all other industries. During the time between the signing of the pact and the Nazi invasion, the value of the Soviet Union's material resources was nearly doubled, an impressive achievement, even allowing for the low starting figure. Much of this went into reserve, in one of two ways.

The Commissariat for State Reserves was, as its title suggests, responsible for stockpiling such essential supplies as food, fuel, ferrous metals and so on. Its activities are very revealing of Stalin's state of mind and maybe of his intentions at that time.

Ever since the fall of France, the commissariat's agents had been active everywhere, walking into the warehouses and storage buildings of any enterprise and earmarking large quantities of strategic war materials – machines, spare parts and equipment of all kinds – to be taken away for 'state reserves'. 'Several acquaintances of mine who worked in factories near Moscow,' wrote Scott, 'complained bitterly of the arbitrary power of the commissariat . . . which continuously and systematically filched raw materials and needed tools and equipment from the plant.' These items were then shipped off to dumps, usually situated in the Urals or western Siberia. By 1 January 1941, the reserves held in this way were considerable. General food stocks alone – at a time of great deprivation for most of the population – amounted to 6,162,000 tons, sufficient to last the armed forces from four to six months in the event of war.

In addition to these state reserves, there were also the so-called 'mobilisation reserves', stocks or strategic raw materials such as non-ferrous and rare metals, which were necessary for various industrial processes. Unlike the state reserves, these were stored in the west of the country, close to the industries which would use them. But when the Red Army general staff, led by Marshal Shaposhnikov, approached Stalin with plans to move the mobilisation reserves to safer positions beyond the Volga, he refused. Indeed, he insisted that the reserves be left where they were or even, in some cases, actually moved westwards, closer to the German border, where they would be immediately vulnerable to any attack. It was an inexplicable decision.

General Khrulev, Chief of Supply and later Quartermaster-General of the Red Army, blamed one of Stalin's most unpleasant lieutenants, Lev Mekhlis, for encouraging him in his madness. Mekhlis, an ex-editor of *Pravda* and, as Chief of the Main Political Administration of the Red Army one of the men who had so badly advised General Meretskov on the initial planning of the Winter War, was appointed in September 1940 to head the new Commissariat of State Control – another manifestation of Stalin's state of mind. There were already three organisations, the NKVD, the Party Control Commission and the Soviet Control Commission, which kept an eye on the controllers, or, in Scott's words, 'to check up on those who checked up on those who did the work'. Mekhlis was loyal only to Stalin. If he did support his master against the general staff, then it is unlikely that he had any more machiavellian purpose than to score brownie points.

Stalin's strange refusal to move the mobilisation reserves to safety was not part of some grand strategic plan. The only possible explanations are either that he was afraid Hitler might consider such a move as a provocative act, or, more likely, that it was simple paranoia. A prime example of this at the time was the fact that he refused to allow the Red Army to control its own ammunition dumps, placing them instead under the authority of the NKVD. He did not trust the army, or the general staff. In fact, he trusted nobody, but ruled by a combination of terror and internal division, making sure that no department or institution or grouping within the Soviet Union would ever possess the physical means to threaten his power, no matter what it might cost his country.

In the event, it was to cost his country very dear, for it was against this background of fear and suspicion that he and his associates had to prepare for the attack which everyone knew must come eventually. What Stalin did not know – and in any case would have refused to believe – was that by the end of July 1940 Hitler had already started the countdown.

44

OTTO, FRITZ AND
SEA LION

Hitler started thinking seriously about the Soviet Union as early as Sunday, 2 June, while the British were still evacuating their battered and beaten army from Dunkirk. In the process of discussing Operation Red, the battle for France, with General von Rundstedt and his Chief of Staff at Charleville, he told them: 'Now that England will presumably be willing to come to a sensible peace arrangement, I shall at last have my hands free for the real major task, the conflict with bolshevism.' Then, referring to the German people, he added with a smile: 'The only problem is how shall I break it to my child?' His chief worry, it seemed, was not defeating the Red Army, but 'having to call the German people to arms once more'.

Throughout June, as he waited confidently for France to collapse and Britain to acknowledge his victory, he pondered the problems of launching his great crusade. For the moment, time seemed to be entirely on his side, allowing him to savour the sweetness of success as he prepared to sign the armistice with France. The hated railway carriage in which the armistice of 1918 had been forced on Germany was dragged out of the museum which had housed it ever since. German army sappers knocked down the wall of the building to drag it through the hole and position it on the exact spot in the forest at Compiègne which it had occupied then, among the elms, oaks, cypresses and pines in the circular clearing.

It was there, exactly twelve hours before the ceremony, that a minor Foreign Ministry official, Erich Tuch, was an accidental witness to a bizarre scene. Strolling through the trees on that mild summer evening, he suddenly became aware that he was not alone. 'Ahead of me,' Tuch told his friends when he returned to Berlin, 'scarcely twenty paces away, the Führer turns up at the bend in the path. He doesn't notice me; he's walking along with head high, eyes fixedly to the front. Now, he raises his hand in salute; stops, and smiles graciously in all directions.

' "Has he gone crazy?" I think. "Whom is he saluting there? Whom is that gracious smile for?" I creep cautiously after him. More nodding and waving to right and left. The 1918 parlour car gleams through the trees. No sentry anywhere near. With head high, Hitler approaches the monstrosity, mounts the steps with dignity, and turns the newly polished knob. In a flash, I see it – he's rehearsing his act. I peer out slyly from behind a tree. Damn, the door seems to be sticking. He shakes at it savagely. "Get back there, on the double!" I think. What fun! Sure enough, he turns round, climbs down, and starts the scene over. Salutes, nods, the gracious smile of the victor. Then the dictator of Germany disappears inside the car.'

Next day, Hitler's appearance naturally went without a hitch. He led his entourage into the clearing, crossed to the great granite block which stood in the centre and read, as though for the first time, the inscription carved into it in French: 'Here on the eleventh of November 1918 succumbed the criminal pride of the German empire – vanquished by the free peoples which it tried to enslave.'

William Shirer, there to report the occasion for CBS Radio, recorded the scene in his diary: 'He steps off the monument and contrives to make even this gesture a masterpiece of contempt. He glances back at it, contemptuous, angry – angry, you almost feel, because he cannot wipe out the awful, provoking letters with one sweep of his high Prussian boot. He glances slowly around the clearing, and now, as his eyes meet ours, you grasp the depth of his hatred. But there is triumph there, too – revengeful, triumphant hate. Suddenly, as though his face were not giving quite complete expression to his feelings, he throws his whole body into harmony with his mood. He swiftly snaps his hands on his hips, arches his shoulders, plants his feet wide apart. It is a magnificent gesture of defiance, of burning contempt for this place now and all that it has stood for in the twenty-two years since it witnessed the humbling of the German empire.'

Evidently, Hitler's rehearsals had paid off. The 'act', as Erich Tuch had described it, was perfect. He entered the railway car, as he had done the previous evening, to await the arrival of the French delegation. After greeting them, he stayed only long enough to hear the preamble to the armistice read out, then departed. He had no intention of sitting there while the French marred his moment of glory by arguing. When the negotiations were complete and the peace treaty signed, he had the railway coach shipped to Berlin and the French monument dynamited out of existence.

For the next few days, while still turning over in his mind the options open to him for future action, he treated himself to a short holiday. On 23 June he took a Sunday outing to Paris, accompanied not by his military chiefs but by three artists: the sculptor Arno Breker, and two architects, Albert Speer and Hermann Giessler. All three had been provided with field-grey uniforms for the occasion. Arriving at Le Bourget at 5.30 am, the party boarded three large Mercedes sedans and roared off for a three-hour whirlwind tour of the city. Hitler acted as guide: although he had never been there, he had spent many hours poring over books and plans and pictures; his photographic memory had locked in every detail. By 9 am the sightseeing was over, and they headed back to the airport, leaving behind a number of Parisians who had been understandably shocked to find themselves suddenly face to face with Hitler. 'The Devil!' a newspaper seller had cried. 'It's him! It's him!' a fat market woman had screamed in terror. But on the heights of Montmartre, the worshippers entering the Sacré Cœur for mass had passed him by in dignified silence, ignoring his presence.

'It was the dream of my life to be permitted to see Paris,' he told Speer. 'I cannot say how happy I am to have that dream fulfilled today.'

Speer was surprised. 'For a moment, I felt something like pity for him,' he wrote later. 'Three hours in Paris, the one and only time he was to see it, made him happy when he stood at the height of his triumphs.'

That night, back in Brûly-de-Pesche – which he had personally given the romantic codename *Wolfsschlucht*, 'Wolf's Gorge' – Hitler sent for Speer. The architect found him sitting alone at the table in the small living room of the peasant house he was occupying on the village's single street. Hitler came to the point immediately. 'Draw up a decree in my name ordering full-scale resumption of work on the Berlin buildings,' he told Speer. 'Wasn't Paris beautiful? But Berlin must be made far more beautiful. In the past, I often considered whether we would not have to destroy Paris. But when we are finished with Berlin, Paris will be only a shadow. So why should we destroy it?'

The decree was duly issued. 'Berlin is to be given the style commensurate with the grandeur of our victory,' Hitler declared. 'I regard the accomplishment of these supremely vital tasks for the Reich as the greatest step in the preservation of our victory.' While Stalin, who in September 1939 had admired photographs of Speer's models for the new Berlin, was concentrating all his resources and manpower on war preparation, Hitler was content to divert German effort into his grandiose building schemes. In spite of all the shortages which Germany faced, he insisted that the Berlin buildings be pushed forward at full speed, and even widened the programme, which had originally included only Nuremberg, Munich and Linz in addition to Berlin: in the autumn of 1940, he added, by personal decrees, another twenty-seven 're-construction cities'. The horrified Speer estimated that the cost of party buildings alone in those cities would be between 22 and 25 billion marks. Even as late as April 1941, Göring assigned no less than 84,000 tons of precious iron and steel a year to the projects, and contracts worth

30 million marks were awarded to granite companies in Norway, Finland, Italy, Belgium, Sweden and Holland. Incredibly, a special transport fleet was created, with shipyards set up in Wismar and Berlin to build a thousand boats with a cargo capacity of 500 tons each. The reconstruction programme was to be complete, Hitler decreed, by 1950, and nothing must be allowed to stand in its way.

At 1 am on 25 June, buglers of the 1st Guards Company took up positions at each end of the village street in Brûly-de-Pesche. Seated at the plain deal table in his peasant's house, with Speer, his adjutants and personal staff plus two old friends from the first world war, his former sergeant Max Amann and fellow infantryman Ernst Schmidt, Hitler ordered the lights to be switched off and the window opened. The silence in the little room was broken only by the whispered commentary of a radio set, turned down low. Occasional flickers of heat lightning pierced the darkness from a thunderstorm brewing somewhere in the distance. Someone, no doubt overcome by emotion, blew his nose. At 1.35 am, the time set for the armistice to take effect, the buglers sounded the cease-fire. When the echoes of the last pure notes had faded there was a moment's stillness, then Hitler murmured softly, as though to himself, 'The burden of responsibility . . .' His voice died away, then came again, more firmly. 'Now switch on the light.'

Next day, Speer flew back to Berlin, to start work again. When he approached Hitler to take his leave, he found him pacing to and fro on the gravel path outside the house, deep in conversation with Generals Keitel and Jodl. As Speer drew close, he caught a few words of what Hitler was saying: 'Now we have shown what we are capable of. Believe me, Keitel, a campaign against Russia would be like a child's game in a sandbox by comparison.'

Earlier that day, Hitler had received the news that the Soviets, who had of course already moved into the Baltic states and grabbed the Lithuanian tip, intended occupying not only Bessarabia but also Bukovina. When he first heard of this, he flew into a rage and insisted it was completely outside the agreement laid down in the secret protocol of the pact. He made Ribbentrop show him a copy of the protocol, only to find that while Bessarabia was indeed the only place specifically named in the south-east, clause 3 did give Stalin a free hand throughout the rest of the region. There was nothing he could do, except register a protest.

Ribbentrop, covering himself frantically, pointed out that Hitler had only himself to blame. Everything agreed in Moscow had been in line with the general instructions he had been given before his departure, and in fact Hitler had even given him a special directive on this particular matter. He had personally told the Foreign Minister 'to declare German disinterestedness in the territories of south-eastern

Europe, even, if necessary, as far as Constantinople and the Straits'. Ribbentrop commented that he had not had to go that far.

But Hitler was scarcely mollified. Although he could say nothing in public, he described the Soviet moves to his adjutants as 'the first Russian attacks on Western Europe'. 'This is Russia trying to safeguard her flanks,' he told them, adding that it was to be taken very seriously indeed. That he himself took it seriously was very soon demonstrated. A week before France had finally fallen, he had had the army general staff start planning the transfer of troops to the east. Initially, this was to involve only fifteen divisions, but on 25 June he ordered the number to be increased to twenty-four, six of which were to be Panzer and three motorised infantry.

All the formations being moved to the east were to be under the command of General Georg von Küchler, 'for special military tasks'. Army Chief of Staff Halder told Küchler that for the time being their job was simply 'to demonstrate the presence of the German army' in the east, and that they were to take care they did not 'openly reveal a hostile attitude'. The arrival of these twenty-five divisions was to be presented as part of the normal redisposition of troops after the completion of a campaign. As further camouflage, the intelligence services were ordered to put out the story through all available channels that the divisions being withdrawn from France were intended for an attack on British positions in the Middle East.

At the same time, Hitler ordered the transformation of the entire army into an even more mobile, harder-hitting force. The units that were to be disbanded in order to return men to industry consisted of twenty-two under-equipped infantry divisions. The fighting strength of the army was therefore not significantly reduced. The remaining 120 divisions were all to be combat-ready, fully equipped in the light of the experience gained in both east and west on mobile warfare. The number of Panzer divisions was to be increased from ten to twenty, and these were to be given heavier tanks. The age of the fighting troops was to be kept, as far as possible, below thirty.

This tougher, streamlined army was not intended for use against Britain. Its whole style was suitable for a fast-moving land war, to be fought across vast, dusty plains, not for a campaign in a verdant island which it could not even reach.

On 28 June, the restless Führer moved to yet another new headquarters, this time deep in the Black Forest on the Kniebis mountain near Freudenstadt. The installation was codenamed *Tannenberg*, 'Pine Mountain' – though in view of the decision Hitler was pondering the name could have had a deeper significance – Tannenberg, in East Prussia, was where Field Marshal Hindenburg had decisively beaten the Russian army in 1914. It was a dismal encampment, shadowed by dense pine trees, the half-buried concrete bunkers and blockhouses running with damp and barely habitable. For most of the eight days Hitler spent there, it rained, the dripping trees adding to its gloomy atmosphere.

While he worked on the great victory speech which he intended to deliver to the Reichstag on 8 July, he continue to turn over in his mind the military dilemma which faced him. Should he wait until Britain pulled out of the war before he launched his attack on the Soviet Union? And what should he do if Britain refused to submit? Should he try to knock her out physically, which would mean an invasion? Or should he go for the Soviets immediately, before the British had time to pull themselves together again, rearm and be ready to strike at his back the moment he was occupied in the east?

He discussed the situation with Ribbentrop, whose view was that Britain was already defeated, and all that remained to be done was to make her admit it. He also discussed it with his Wehrmacht adjutant, Schmundt, and with General Jodl, who was cautious on the subject of attacking the Soviet Union. Nevertheless, Jodl instructed Bernhard von Lossberg, the OKW colonel who had refused to send Hitler's panicky message to Narvik during the Norwegian campaign, to start drafting a plan. Lossberg called the plan 'Fritz', after his son.

While Lossberg was working on 'Fritz', on behalf of the supreme command of all the armed forces, the army High Command, under Brauchitsch and Halder, was enthusiastically drawing up its own plan, to be co-ordinated with the deployment of troops, which they called 'Otto'. 'Otto' and 'Fritz' went along totally independently for several weeks, the two sets of planners each unaware of what the other was doing. At that point, Hitler had not asked Brauchitsch to do anything, but it did not take much foresight to know that sooner or later he would, and Brauchitsch wanted to be ready.

Meanwhile, there was the small question of Britain still to be dealt with. On 30 June, Halder called on Weizsäcker, at the Foreign Ministry in Berlin, and warned him that they 'must keep a weather eye on the east', though Britain would have to be disposed of first. 'Britain will probably need a display of force,' he said, 'before she gives in and allows us a free hand for the east.'

It was with this in mind that on 2 June Hitler authorised the start of planning for a possible invasion of the British Isles, to be called 'Operation Sea Lion'. At this stage, it was nothing more than a tentative idea, which Hitler allowed to be floated only to keep the service chiefs happy. He was convinced it would never need to go any further. Next day, however, he received a powerful signal that Britain had no intention of pulling out of the war, when the Royal Navy attacked and destroyed the French fleet in harbour at Mers-el-Kebir, Algeria, killing some 1,200 French sailors.

Hitler had said the ships would be interned in French-retained territory and would take no further part in the war, but Churchill dared not trust the Nazi dictator's word. 'It is impossible for us now to allow your fine ships to fall into the power of our German or Italian enemies,' he told the French, offering them a choice of sailing either to Britain to join forces with the Royal Navy, or to the French West Indies where they would stay neutral, out of German reach, or of scuttling their ships where they lay. When the French refused all three options, the British struck, displaying a ruthless determination which came as a shock to the Führer.

This set-back to Hitler's hopes upset all his calculations. Although he went ahead with his triumphal return to Berlin on 6 July, a day he declared a public holiday to celebrate his victories, he postponed the speech he had planned to make in the Reichstag on 8 July, and after a brief meeting with Italian Foreign Minister Ciano, travelled south to Munich and then to the Berghof. The British insistence on fighting on came as a bitter disappointment to him, and called for serious thought.

The conclusion he came to was that the answer to the British problem lay not in the west, but in the east. He called his Commanders-in-Chief to the Berghof on 13 July. 'The Führer,' Halder wrote in his diary that evening, 'is obsessed with the question why England does not yet want to take the road to peace. He sees, just as we do, the answer to this question in the fact that England is still setting her hope in Russia.'

Despite having just seen captured documents showing that Britain and France had planned as far back as April to mount air raids on the Soviet oil installations in the Caucasus with the object of cutting Germany's supplies, Hitler suspected that Churchill was making a secret deal with Stalin. In fact, Stalin was going to extraordinary lengths to show his friendship for Germany, even passing over full reports of conversations with Britain's ambassador in Moscow, Stafford Cripps, in which Cripps warned him that Hitler intended to attack the Soviet Union. But still Hitler believed Stalin intended to double-cross him and join forces with the Allies. Only the hope of this, he reasoned, could make Britain continue to resist his advances. Once the Soviet Union had been dealt with, there would be no more trouble from Britain – therefore, worries about Britain should not prevent Germany attacking the Soviet Union.

At the same time, there was always the possibility that if he kept up the direct pressure on Britain, she might see reason in any case. So, on 16 July, with marked lack of determination he took 'Sea Lion' one step further by issuing a directive for the preparation – but not yet the execution – of a landing. Everything was to be ready by mid-August, and everything was to be done ostentatiously. A thousand heavy barges were to be taken from Germany's inland waterways and a further 900 from Holland and Belgium. They were to be assembled on the French coast, in full view of the British. The fact that this would cripple the German transport system and bring large sections of the economy to a grinding halt was apparently less important than putting on a sufficient show of strength. No doubt Hitler believed he would soon be able to return all the barges safely to their normal work.

His deliberations completed, Hitler returned to Berlin on 18 July. Next day he delivered his promised speech to the Reichstag, in the Kroll Opera House – an eminently suitable setting for such a theatrical occasion, and for the notable performance he gave to his eager audience. The auditorium was packed, with generals and admirals in the dress circle, Reichstag deputies in the orchestra stalls, and diplomats in the theatre boxes. Every nook was crammed with flowers, and medals glittered on hundreds of gold-braided dress uniforms. Outshining everyone in this respect was Göring, who had designed himself a brand-new outfit for this day, a dazzling creation in pale sky blue – prompting his own officers to grumble that he had chosen to stop wearing Luftwaffe uniform.

Göring undoubtedly knew what they did not – that he was to be promoted that day from field marshal to the specially created rank of Reichsmarschall of the Greater German Reich, and presented with the Grand Cross of the Iron Cross, the only one to be awarded by Hitler during the entire war. Göring's elevation was necessary to keep him ahead of the other commanders, for Hitler also created no fewer than twelve new field marshals during his speech: Brauchitsch, Keitel, Rundstedt, Bock, Leeb, List, Kluge, Witzleben and Reichenau from the army, and Milch, Kesselring and Sperrle from the Luftwaffe. Such wholesale and unnecessary largesse was in marked contrast to both the Kaiser's promotions during 1914–18, when he created only five field marshals during the whole war, and Stalin's in the Soviet Union, where five marshals were also thought to be sufficient.

The speech Hitler made that day was to be the last of his great orations to the Reichstag, and possibly the finest. William Shirer, who watched it all from the gallery, bore witness in his diary that night to a masterly performance: 'The Hitler we saw in the Reichstag tonight was the conqueror, and conscious of it, and yet so wonderful an actor, so magnificent a handler of the German mind, that he mixed superbly the full confidence of the conqueror with the humbleness which always goes down so well with the masses when they know a man is on top. His voice was lower tonight; he rarely shouted as he usually does; and he did not once cry out hysterically as I've seen him do so often from this rostrum.'

It was a long speech, but the real point of it came at the end: after a vituperative personal attack on British political leaders in general and Churchill in particular, he made Britain one last offer. 'In this hour, I feel it to be my duty before my own conscience,' he declared solemnly, 'to appeal once more to reason and common sense in Great Britain as much as elsewhere. I consider myself in a position to make this appeal since I am not the vanquished begging favours, but the victor speaking in the name of reason. I see no reason why this war must go on.'

The response from Britain to this appeal to reason was a very loud raspberry, and the stepping-up of bombing raids on the Reich.

Two days after his Reichstag speech, on 21 July, Hitler summoned Brauchitsch, Grand Admiral Raeder and the Luftwaffe Chief of Staff, General Hans Jeschonnek, to the Chancellery for a conference. He began by discussing plans for 'Sea Lion', insisting that the main thrust of the invasion had to be completed by 15 September. When Raeder pointed out that the navy simply did not have the means to ship the proposed forty divisions across the Channel, Hitler ordered him to report back within a week on the prospects.

'If the preparations cannot definitely be completed by the beginning of September,' he told him, 'it will prove necessary to consider other plans.'

The other plans he had in mind were for an early invasion of the Soviet Union. To his surprise, when he broached the subject to Brauchitsch, immediately after Raeder had left to start his investigation into the feasibility of 'Sea Lion', the new Field Marshal reacted to the idea enthusiastically. The usually cautious Commander-in-Chief, whose pessimistic attitude had so infuriated Hitler during the earlier campaigns in Poland and the West, was transformed into a raging optimist. Backed by the studies his staff had been making since the beginning of the month for just such a moment as this, he launched into a full-scale proposal for attacking the Soviet Union that same autumn.

Brauchitsch expressed the military aims of the campaign as: 'the defeat of the Russian army or the capture of at least as much Russian territory as necessary to prevent enemy air attacks on Berlin and the Silesian industrial areas'. He reckoned that since the Soviets had only fifty to seventy-five good divisions, they could be beaten during the autumn by eighty to a hundred German divisions, which could be concentrated ready for the attack in between four and six weeks.

Brauchitsch's ideas for the political aims were very similar to the terms of the Treaty of Brest-Litovsk, when Russia had been knocked out of the first world war in 1918 – the lingering results of which had only just been reversed by Stalin. There was to be a 'Ukrainian empire' and a federation of Baltic states which would act as a 'thorn in the flesh' of the Soviet Union. Belorussia and Finland would form part of a chain of German vassal states providing a buffer from the White Sea to the Black Sea.

Hitler liked the sound of Brauchitsch's proposals, but doubted whether the attack in the east could really be mounted in such a short time. For once, it was the army generals who were advocating what seemed like lunatic boldness, and Hitler himself who was being cautious, a complete reversal of the roles each had played during the past year. He questioned Brauchitsch hard, then sent him away to do more thinking, and to draw up detailed plans for a war with the Soviet Union. While Brauchitsch and Halder did so, Hitler turned to the OKW, asking Keitel and Jodl to study the proposition and give their views.

While he was waiting for the navy, the army and the OKW to come up with their reports, Hitler again took time off to drive south, first to Weimar and then on to the Wagner festival at Bayreuth, where he watched a performance of *Götterdämmerung* and met his old school chum August Kubizek for the last time.

Fortified by his annual infusion of Wagner he then returned to Berlin for two days, where Raeder again tried to persuade him to call off or at least postpone 'Sea Lion'. Hitler sent him away, telling him to report on the situation again in a few days. That evening, as he prepared to leave once more, this time for the Berghof, he was shown an intercepted telegram from the pro-Soviet Yugoslav ambassador in Moscow, Milan Gavrilovic, to his government in Belgrade, reporting on conversations he had had with the British, French and Turkish ambassadors, and with Molotov. These conversations had all taken place in a burst of activity between 14 and 18 July. Their content provided a spur to Hitler's decisions concerning both Britain and the Soviet Union.

While Sir Stafford Cripps had stressed that Britain would resolutely carry on the war to the end, he had claimed that the fall of France had made the Soviet Union afraid of Germany. Pointing out that Molotov, during two weeks' leave he had recently taken, had refused three requests for an interview with Schulenburg but had seen him twice, Cripps had claimed that the Soviets feared a surprise German attack, and were playing for time, though they did not believe Germany could be ready for a war that winter.

The Turkish ambassador, Haydar Aktay, had spoken of his conviction that Germany was trying to provoke trouble between his country and the Soviet Union, 'since she had the greatest interest in involving the Soviet Union in a long war'. He had then talked about the strength of the Red Army. Its mechanisation, he said, was much further advanced than any-one outside realised, it already comprised 180 divisionss, which were much more powerfully organised than any other army at that time, and 'apparently, all this was directed against Germany, while Japan was only a secondary consideration.' Aktay believed war between Germany and the Soviet Union was a foregone conclusion. 'The Soviet Union,' he had said, 'was consolidating its positions at the expense of Germany in order to be strong enough if it should be attacked by Germany.'

But it was the Yugoslav ambassador's talk with Molotov that gave

Hitler most cause for concern. At the end of a 'very friendly' fifty minutes, the conversation had turned to Hitler's racial theories, particularly his stated belief of the inferiority of the Slavs, as declared in *Mein Kampf.*

'They [the Germans] will not achieve everything that has been written for them in *Mein Kampf*,' Molotov had said 'with deep conviction'. He had gone on to say that, like Yugoslavia, the Soviet Union – 'the Ukraine, that is' – had once been occupied by the Germans. 'But,' he had added with some emphasis, 'our army was also in Berlin once, and the Germans know that very well.'

With these phrases echoing in his head, Hitler left Berlin and headed south again, arriving at the Berghof in time for lunch on 26 July. As always, the OKW headquarters packed up their belongings and followed, in their special trains, settling in various rail sidings in the Berchtesgaden area. Walter Warlimont's Section L, the operations section, was in its special train *Atlas* in Bad Reichenhall station on 29 July when Jodl arrived to speak to the senior officers.

'We all imagined,' Warlimont wrote later, 'that, although we had not done very much, this unusual visitation must be concerned with some special recognition following our victory in the West.' At the same time that his chief, Keitel, had been made a field marshal, Jodl had been promoted to full general straight from major-general, so Warlimont's assumption was a reasonable one. It proved, however, to be totally wrong.

'Four of us were present,' he recorded, 'sitting at individual tables in the restaurant car. Instead of what we expected, Jodl went round ensuring that all doors and windows were closed, and then, without any preamble, disclosed to us that Hitler had decided to rid the world "once and for all" of the danger of bolshevism by a surprise attack on Soviet Russia to be carried out at the earliest possible moment, i.e. in May 1941.'

Jodl had just come from the Berghof, where he and Keitel had presented Hitler with a memorandum saying that 'the time and space factors alone' made an autumn attack 'totally impracticable'. Jodl had spread out railway maps on the red marble table in the Berghof's great hall, to prove his point, and Hitler had accepted the facts. He had then ordered that top priority was to be given to expanding the rail capacity in the east.

Jodl did not tell the officers of Section L about the narrow escape they had had from the potential disaster of an autumn attack. But he dealt with the hail of questions they showered upon him clearly and confidently. 'Two of his answers stand out in my memory,' Warlimont wrote. 'First, when he repeated Hitler's view and probably his own also, that the collision with bolshevism was bound to come and that it was better therefore to have this campaign now, when we were at the height of our military power, than to have to call the German people to arms once more in the years to come; secondly, when he said that at the latest by the autumn of 1941 the full strength of the Luftwaffe, brought to a new pitch of efficiency by further victories in the east, would once more be available for employment against England.

'At the end of an hour of bitter argument it became clear what we had to do – produce a draft of a preparatory order for the immediate transport, movement and accommodation of the bulk of the army and air force to the occupied areas of western Poland (where communications incidentally were poor). Under the heading "Build-up in the East" [*Aufbau Ost*] this order was included in the records of the prosecution at Nuremberg as the first document dealing with "aggression" against Soviet Russia.'

On the last day of July, the chiefs of the OKW, army and navy met Hitler in the great hall of the Berghof at 11.30 am. Grand Admiral Raeder, who had flown down from Berlin that morning, opened the proceedings by giving his situation report and proposals concerning 'Sea Lion'. Although he did his best to assure Hitler that the navy would be ready, as ordered, by 13 September, he spent most of his time trying to persuade him to postpone the whole thing until the spring. Hitler listened patiently as the admiral trotted out an impressive list of reasons, then overruled him. However, he did promise him that the invasion would go ahead only if the Luftwaffe succeeded in defeating the RAF.

When Raeder had left the meeting to return to Berlin, Hitler told the field marshals and generals who remained that although he was satisfied with what the navy was accomplishing, he was extremely sceptical about the technical feasibility of an invasion. As always, he was worried about bad weather, and in addition was conscious of British naval supremacy – neither of which he could do anything about. He saw no reason, he said, to risk so much for so little: the war as such was won, and could be decided by his U-boats and the Luftwaffe, though this would take from one to two years.

With obvious relish, he turned to what was really on his mind: the invasion not of Britain, but of the Soviet Union. To convince his listeners, he began by outlining his reasons in terms which he knew they would understand. The great fear of any German military man was a war on two fronts, therefore Hitler had to dispose of this major objection if he was to carry the military with him. He did it with consummate skill, developing his argument that the only way of ending the war with Britain was by knocking out the Soviet Union.

'England's last hope,' he told them, 'is Russia and America. If hope of Russia is eliminated, then America, too, is eliminated, because the elimination of Russia will lead to an enormous increase in the importance of Japan in the Far East. Russia is the far eastern sword of

TOP Soviet casualties frozen stiff by the bitter cold await burial by the Finns

BELOW The trade agreement in operation: Soviet oil being transferred to German rail tankers at Przemysl during 1940

TOP The fall of Oslo: German troops invade the Norwegian capital on bicycles

BELOW Good news from the Western front: in his headquarters Brûly-de-Pesche, 'Wolfsschlucht', Hitler hears that his panzers have reached the English Channel

The situation elsewhere was more difficult: the harbour at Narvik after the British attack

TOP The famous jig: watched by Walter Hewel and his adjutants, Hitler stamps his foot with glee on learning that France has capitulated – a movement turned into a ludicrous dance by looping the film

BELOW The tiny figure of Ambassador Vladimir Dekanozov, leaving the Reich chancellery after presenting his credentials to Hitler on 19 December 1940, is dwarfed by his Foreign Ministry protocol department escorts, specially chosen because of their height

Ribbentrop greets Molotov on his arrival in Berlin, 12 November 1940. Gustav Hilger, showing
the effects of his heavy cold, translates

Soviet Trade Commissar, Deputy Prime Minister and later President, Anastas Mikoyan was the Soviet regime's greatest survivor – he occupied posts at the highest level for 55 years, was a member of the Central Committee for 54, and of the Politburo for 40

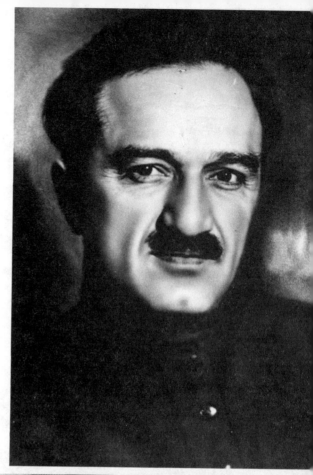

Japanese Foreign Minister Yosuke Matsuoka waves to well-drilled cheering crowds from the chancellery balcony on 28 March 1941, backed by Hitler and Japanese Ambassador Oshima. But Hitler did not tell him about Barbarossa

ABOVE RIGHT Marshal Semen K.
Timoshenko succeeded Voroshilov as
Defence Commissar

ABOVE LEFT General (later Marshal)
Georgi K. Zhukov, greatest general
and most decorated man in Soviet
history, tried desperately to convince
Stalin of the coming attack

Watched by an approving Field
Marshal Keitel, Hitler greets Finnish
Marshal Carl Gustav Mannerheim,
who led the Finns against the Soviet
Union as 'comrades in arms' of the
Germans, seeking revenge for the
Winter War

The final word, amid the ruins of Berlin's Unter den Linden in 1945

England and America against Japan.' Once Japan no longer had to worry about the Soviet Union, he reasoned, she would pose such a threat to the United States in the Pacific area that the Americans would have their hands so full they would be unable to help the British.

'Something has happened in London,' he said. 'The English were entirely down; now they are up again.' He blamed the Soviet Union for this, claiming that intercepted messages showed the Soviets were encouraging the British to fight on, because they themselves had been frightened by the speed of developments in the West. 'Russia need never say more to England,' he continued, 'than that she does not want Germany to be great; then the English hope like a drowning man that things will be completely different in six to eight months. Should Russia be smashed, however, then England's last hope is extinguished. Germany is then master of Europe and the Balkans.'

His decision, therefore, was to dispose of the Soviet Union as soon as possible. He confirmed that the time for this – both the earliest and the latest he could undertake it – was spring 1941. 'The quicker we smash Russia the better,' he declared. 'The operation only makes sense if we smash the state heavily in one blow. Simply winning a certain amount of territory will not do.'

It would have been preferable to have gone that same year, but unfortunately it was now too late to be able to complete the campaign in a single operation, and it was too dangerous to take a break for the winter. If they started in spring 1941, in May, there would be five clear months of summer in which to finish the job.

The aim of the operation, he said, was the annihilation of Russia's vital energy. The method would be by a huge two-pronged advance converging on Moscow through Kiev in the south and the Baltic states in the north, with a separate operation against the oilfields around Baku. He ordered the army to be built up to 180 divisions, with 120 of these to be assembled in the east, forty of which were to be made up of battle-hardened men. He would explain this huge build-up to Stalin as troops being prepared and held in areas which were safe from British air attack, for use in Spain, North Africa and Britain.

By 1.45 am, Brauchitsch and Halder were aboard their Ju-52 aircraft at Salzburg, ready to fly back to their headquarters, which was then stationed at Fontainebleau, near Paris. Keitel and Jodl had returned to their train to brief their planning staff in the greatest secrecy. The conference was over. The preparations for the invasion of the Soviet Union were under way.

45

'I WILL NOT LET MYSELF BE OVERRUN BY THE RUSSIANS'

'The purpose of the campaign is to strike the Russian armed forces and to make Russia incapable of entering the war as an opponent of Germany in the foreseeable future.' This was the opening statement of the army's draft plan 'Otto', drawn up at the beginning of August 1940 by General Erich Marcks. Like most of the generals of the OKH, the army High Command, Marcks refused to accept that Hitler's aim was not simply to defend Germany against a Soviet intervention while he was dealing with the recalcitrant British.

Bernhard von Lossberg, working on his study for 'Fritz' for the supreme command of the armed forces, the OKW, knew better. He was aware that Hitler's true intention was to destroy the Soviet state for ever and take over its European lands as German *Lebensraum*. He explained this in some detail to his cousin, a young officer whom he had summoned from his regiment 'for a heart-to-heart talk'. The young man whose advice he was seeking knew a great deal about the Soviet Union, for he was none other than Hans 'Johnnie' von Herwarth, Schulenburg's former aide in the Moscow embassy. When Herwarth heard what was in Hitler's mind he was horrified – not only by the enormity of such cold-blooded aggression but also at the absurdity of the notion that it could ever be successful.

Stressing that everything he said was in the strictest secrecy, since only a very limited number of high-ranking officers on the general staff had been permitted to know anything about it, Lossberg explained that Hitler believed this was his best and probably his only chance of destroying the Soviet Union and the whole communist system. The Soviets were getting stronger every day, but he thought they would collapse within six weeks both militarily and politically if he hit them soon enough and hard enough.

'All Soviet territory up to the "A–A line", i.e. the north–south line between Archangel and Astrakhan, was to be occupied in order to secure the necessary *Lebensraum* and raw materials for the German people,' Herwarth recorded later. 'Hitler was convinced that this area could be secured by mobile troops alone. After securing this area, these forces would then be replaced by German military settlements similar to the old Austrian military colonies that had held that country's frontier against the Ottoman Turks for centuries. Lossberg wanted my opinion on all this.

'I told him that he would have the greatest difficulty in reaching the A–A line at all. Even if our army could get that far the Russians would still have a sufficiently broad industrial base behind the A–A line to enable them to continue waging modern warfare against us. I reminded Lossberg of [the military attaché in Moscow] General Köstring's frequently stated view that the USSR was incapable of a major offensive campaign but eminently capable of waging a sustained defensive war. Further, I argued that the notion of reaching the A–A line within six weeks was absurd, given the problems of provisioning an army at such distances and in so hostile a climate.

'Lossberg agreed with everything I said but had to admit there was nothing he could do about it, since Hitler considered himself to be his own best general.'

Lossberg completed his study for 'Fritz' four weeks later. It was an excellent piece of detailed staff work in spite of his personal reservations, and formed the basis of Hitler's final invasion plans in 1941. Its opening statement was in marked contrast to the OKH 'Otto' plan: 'The aim of a campaign against Soviet Russia is to destroy the mass of the Soviet army in western Russia, to prevent the withdrawal of battleworthy elements into the depth of Russia, and then, having cut western Russia off from the seas, to advance to a line which will place the most important part of Russia in our hands and on which it will be easy to form a shield against Asiatic Russia.'

Herwarth, meanwhile, took advantage of being away from his regiment to wangle himself a trip to Moscow, to see his wife. On the way, he was able to see for himself the military build-up which was already starting in Poland. In Moscow, he had long conversations with Schulenburg and Köstring, telling them what he had seen in Poland and also what Lossberg had told him in Berlin, 'on the grounds that as ambassador and military attaché they ought to have full knowledge of everything that was occurring'.

'They were flabbergasted at my report of a possible attack on Russia,' he says. 'Both wavered between viewing these preparations as an exercise in contingency planning or as one more lever by which Hitler could press the Russians to increase their deliveries of grain, manganese, and other raw materials. Neither of them could believe that Hitler would do so foolish a thing as to destroy himself by attacking the Soviet Union. By that time, everyone in the embassy had read Caulaincourt's famous book on Napoleon's campaign in Russia, which had just been newly published in a German translation. Was Hitler really intending to repeat Napoleon's mistakes? Our experts found it unthinkable.'

The fact that none of the experts took his intentions seriously was, to Hitler, the best possible form of security. While ensuring that the planning and preparations went on steadily throughout the autumn of 1940, he also took care never to give specific directions which would reveal his final purpose to those he did not completely trust. To a large extent, the camouflage he created was intended to deceive his own officers as much as his enemies outside.

On 14 August, the newly created field marshals assembled at the Chancellery in Berlin to receive their diamond-studded batons from the hands of their Führer. At the celebration lunch which he gave them after the ceremony, Hitler made a speech outlining his strategic thinking, as he wished them to see it. He told them he still hoped the conflict with Britain could be settled by the Luftwaffe alone, and that the army would be used only 'if we were absolutely forced to'. He accepted that bad weather might prevent the Luftwaffe achieving his purpose immediately, in which case he would put off the decision about 'Sea Lion' until May 1941.

But he said nothing about invading the Soviet Union in that same month. He repeated his conclusion that Britain was refusing to make peace because of the hopes she placed in America and the Soviet Union, and that she was trying to set the Soviets and Germans at each other's throats. 'But Germany is militarily far superior to Russia,' he declared. 'The films of Russian warfare in Finland contain quite ludicrous scenes.' There were, he said, two danger areas which could spark off a clash with the Soviet Union: Finland and Romania.

'Russia,' he said, 'has once shown an inclination to overstep the agreements made with us. However, she remains loyal at present. But should she reveal the intention of conquering Finland or attacking Romania, we shall be forced to strike. Furthermore, we need Romania's oil. Therefore, Germany must keep fully armed. By the spring there will be 180 divisions.'

While he was being cagey with his new field marshals, Hitler was more revealing to others. That same day, Göring told the chief of the economics and armaments branch of the OKW, General Georg Thomas, that the Führer wanted Soviet orders to be delivered punctually only until spring 1941. After that he had no interest in satisfying Soviet demands, though new contracts were still to be accepted. Meanwhile, Thomas and his office were to make a detailed survey of Soviet industry, transportation systems and oil production centres. This was needed not only as a guide for targets to be attacked, but also to provide information for the administration of the conquered territory.

The day after the baton presentations, 'Operation Eagle', otherwise known as the Battle of Britain, began in earnest. Göring sent wave after wave of bombers and fighters across the Channel, confidently expecting them to crush Britain's air defences and leave her helpless. By 15 September, the battle of the air was over. On that day, the RAF shot down some sixty German planes for the loss of twenty-six British, a ratio which reflected the overall results. During the summer, the Luftwaffe lost a total of 1,733 aircraft of all types, against British losses of 915. The German air force never completely recovered from this set-back, as both Britain and the Soviet Union were each already producing more aircraft than Germany, and the gap continued to widen over the next four years.

The immediate consequence of the Luftwaffe's failure – Hitler's first ever major defeat in battle – was the cancellation of 'Sea Lion'. On 17 September, it was postponed 'indefinitely', and two days later Hitler ordered the invasion fleet to be dispersed and the barges and fishing boats returned to their normal work. Although the night bombing raids and the U-boat war on Britain continued, for the remainder of 1940 he could concentrate his attention on his plans in the east.

As summer wore into autumn, sizeable cracks began appearing in the friendship between Germany and the Soviet Union, though both sides did their best to hide the growing tensions and disagreements. Molotov claimed, in a speech to the Supreme Soviet on 1 August, that the prospect of an increase in German power did not worry the Soviet leaders, since 'the friendly relations between Germany and the Soviet Union are based on the fundamental interests of both countries'. 'Our relations with Germany, which were radically changed nearly a year ago,' he said, 'remain entirely as laid down in the Soviet–German agreement.' Nevertheless, he evidently felt he had to remind Hitler that the Soviet government had strictly observed the terms of the pact, giving him the assurance of security in the east.

'Far from reducing the significance of the Soviet–German non-aggression pact,' Molotov added, 'events in Europe have, on the contrary, emphasised the importance of its existence and further development.' He went on to add that Berlin should not forget that the 'magnificent success' of the German army was owed in large part to the Soviet Union. He did not say that during the whole of June, while he had been congratulating Hitler on that 'magnificent success', neither *Pravda* nor *Izvestia* had carried a single leading article on the war in the West. Nor did he mention that Soviet hopes for Britain's survival were manifested in those newspapers in increasingly appreciative comments on the achievements of the RAF against the Luftwaffe.

The trade treaty was now operating perfectly – from the Soviet side. A week before Molotov's speech, Schnurre had reviewed progress in a detailed memorandum. 'It should be recognised,' he wrote, 'that especially in the last two months the Soviet government has made considerable efforts in transportation and production to accomplish deliveries of raw materials urgently needed by us.' Soviet deliveries to date had reached a value of 160 million Reichsmarks, and were accelerating all the time, with another 450 million RM worth already contracted for. What was more, in certain commodities, such as copper, nickel and tin, the Soviets had already delivered the entire amounts promised for the whole year, and were ready to provide large quantities of non-ferrous metals and raw materials which they had bought from other countries.

On the other side of the balance sheet, German deliveries had reached only 82 million RM, including a deposit of 25 million RM for the unfinished cruiser, the ex-*Lützow*, which had been towed to Leningrad at the beginning of May. Schnurre foresaw complications because of the imbalance, though he pointed out that it was largely because of the 'very difficult negotiating procedure and the general slowness of the Russian agents' that German deliveries were falling short to a much greater extent than had been provided for in the agreement.

By the end of September, the position had worsened considerably, and Mikoyan was threatening to stop all Soviet deliveries unless the Germans did something to improve things. By this time, Schnurre had already started negotiations for the second year's operation of the trade treaty, and Mikoyan was entering his haggling mode, knowing that with grain deliveries running at over a million tons a year, and with the Soviets alone having a good grain harvest, the Germans were completely at his mercy for their daily bread as well as for oil and raw materials for their arms industry.

Schnurre found himself in a serious dilemma. If the German factories were to fulfil the arms programme set out by Hitler for the Wehrmacht, there would be nothing to spare to give the Soviets. What was more, Göring had given orders that there should be no shipments to the Soviet Union which would directly or indirectly strengthen Russia's war potential. The matter had to be referred to Hitler himself, since deliveries could be made only at the expense of Germany's own armaments production – but this would suffer at least as badly, and possibly much more seriously, if the Soviets stopped their deliveries of vital raw materials.

Another factor in the impossible equation was the Soviet Union's role as a supply route, Germany's only way around the British blockade. 'Our sole economic connection with Iran, Afghanistan, Manchukuo, China, Japan and, beyond that, with South America,' Schnurre pointed out, 'is the route across Russia, which is being used to an increasing extent for German raw material imports (soyabeans from Manchukuo).'

Adding to the problems was the fact that Mikoyan, 'presumably reacting to the changed German attitude', had cancelled all long-range projects in the treaty. 'This means,' Schnurre wrote, 'that they do not want to have processes, installations and capital goods deliverable over a long-tem period, but to restrict themselves to goods which will benefit their economy, especially their military rearmament, within the next eight to ten months.'

Göring supported Schnurre's view that it would be disastrous for Soviet deliveries to be stopped, and that he must therefore be allowed to negotiate the best deal he could get. Hitler gave his consent. It must have come as a blow to him to see such clear evidence of Soviet suspicion and distrust, particularly since a period of eight to ten months coincided exactly with his planned date for the attack. But there was really no alternative. After preliminary talks in Berlin, Schnurre set off for Moscow on 28 October at the head of a large delegation to open the bidding. Negotiations stretched on for the rest of the year, with Soviet goodwill fluctuating, as always, according to the current political climate. It was 10 January 1941 before the agreement was finally signed – and if all went according to plan, the whole war would be finished before eight to ten months from then.

Hitler had told his generals that the most likely areas of conflict with the Soviets were the two extreme wings of the interface, Finland and Romania. This proved to be an accurate forecast: a whole sequence of quarrels over those two countries threatened to disrupt the pact and spoil his planned timetable during the late summer and early autumn.

The situation in and around Romania proved to be particularly volatile after the cession of Bessarabia and Bukovina to the Soviet Union. Continuing reports of Soviet troops being concentrated in the new regions of the USSR made Hitler extremely nervous. He was afraid Stalin might decide to move in on the oilfields which were so vital to Germany, or that he might not be satisfied with the two provinces and push on through Romania to the Dardanelles, the narrow straits which controlled the only entrance to the Black Sea. 'I will not let myself be overrun by the Russians,' he told Ribbentrop, determinedly. He ordered the first army divisions posted to the east to be placed in south-eastern Poland with the specific intention of showing Stalin they were poised to move into Romania the moment the Red Army showed any sign of threatening the oilfields.

The threat to the stability of the area did not come from the Soviet Union alone, however. Taking advantage of the situation – and perhaps afraid that if they did not act swiftly it would be too late for them to act at all – Bulgaria and Hungary also pressed their claims to large slices of Romania. Although King Carol had by now announced his allegiance to Hitler and the Axis, the German Führer made no move to prevent the two predators taking what they wanted. Instead, he used the danger of Soviet intervention to put pressure on the three states to settle their differences by direct negotiation, making it clear that he expected Romania to accept Hungary's demand for the mountain province of Transylvania and Bulgaria's for the Black Sea province of Dobruja. It appeared, both at the time and later, that Hitler and Stalin were acting in concert, but in reality the Soviet troop movements which frightened all the participants so badly were intended by Stalin as a demonstration of his independence of Germany.

The Bulgarians, whose claim was in fact supported by Stalin as well as Hitler, met a Romanian delegation on a Danube steamer, and reached agreement after some three weeks of negotiation. The Hungarian settlement was more difficult, and imposed a very serious strain on German–Soviet relations, coming close to destroying the pact.

Hitler and Mussolini finally called the Romanians and Hungarians to Vienna, where Ribbentrop and Italian Foreign Minister Ciano imposed a settlement on them in the elegant surroundings of the Belvedere Palace. On 30 August, eight men gathered round the circular table in the Golden Chamber, a little round room richly ornamented with baroque gilding, for the result of the arbitration. Paul Schmidt, who was interpreting and assisting Ribbentrop, spread out the map of Transylvania on the table, with the demarcation line already drawn on it. The Hungarians were not particularly happy – they had possessed the whole of the province before the first world war, and had demanded all of it now. Ribbentrop and Ciano had allotted them about two thirds. But their dismay was nothing compared with the Romanians'. Foreign Minister Manoilescu took one look at the new boundary line and immediately passed out in a dead faint across the table. Medical help was summoned, 'doctors, massage, camphorated oil', according to Ciano, who went on, 'Finally he comes to, but shows the shock very much.'

When he had recovered sufficiently, the payment to Romania for capitulating was announced. 'With effect from today,' Schmidt read out from the treaty document, 'Germany and Italy undertake to guarantee the inviolability of Romanian territory.'

Stalin and Molotov were furious at the Vienna Award, and at the guarantee – since the only country against which it could be directed was the Soviet Union. Their exclusion from the negotiations smacked of Munich all over again. They had not even been consulted. When Schulenburg called on Molotov, to tell him about the decisions reached in Vienna, the Soviet Premier received him very coldly. He had already heard about everything, he said, from the press and radio, despite the fact that article III of the non-aggression pact provided for prior consultation. Instead of this, he had been presented with a *fait accompli*, in direct violation both of the pact and of assurances by the German government.

The row rumbled on for several weeks, amid accusations of bad faith on both sides, with charge and counter-charge being flung backwards and forwards. Molotov sarcastically suggested that article III could be scrapped or renegotiated if Germany found it inconvenient – implying fairly heavily that this also applied to the whole pact.

During those weeks, there were other developments in Romania which disturbed the German–Soviet relationship still further. On 6 September, King Carol was forced to abdicate, ostensibly in favour of his son, but in reality to hand over complete dictatorial powers to General Ion Antonescu. Two weeks later, Antonescu asked Hitler to send him German troops, under the guise of a military mission to help train the Romanian army. Hitler responded immediately by authorising the despatch of a motorised division, augmented by tanks, and backed up by Luftwaffe squadrons.

'Their *real tasks*,' Field Marshal Keitel wrote on Hitler's behalf, 'which must not become apparent either to the Romanians or to our own troops, are: (a) to protect the oil fields from seizure by a third power and from destruction; (b) to enable the Romanian army to carry out definite tasks in accordance with an effective plan developed in favour of German interests; (c) in case a war with the Soviet Union is forced upon us, to prepare for the commitment of German and Romanian forces from the direction of Romania.'

Hitler had been able to turn Soviet amitions in the area to his own advantage, considerably strengthening his position in south-eastern Europe. To all intents and purposes, Romania had become a German satellite under military occupation, a most valuable launch pad for an invasion of the Ukraine. The Hungarians, once they had recovered from their initial indignation at not getting everything they had demanded, showed their gratitude for what they had received by moving steadily closer to Germany. Bulgaria, with a Slav population and Germanic rulers, was traditionally torn between allegiance to Russia and allegiance to Germany, but while Stalin was offering a friendship and mutual assistance pact, Hitler was giving more tangible benefits in the way of arms supplies and military advisers. By October there were more than 30,000 German military 'tourists' in Bulgaria.

*   *   *

Hitler had now extended his line for an assault on the Soviet Union as far south as the Black Sea. At the other end of Europe, meanwhile, he was in the process of reaching out beyond the Arctic Circle to the White Sea, as he consolidated Germany's relationship with Finland, using the Finns' resentment and fear of the Soviet Union to draw them into his camp.

Friction grew over the Petsamo nickel mines in northern Finland, close to the Soviet border. They were leased to British and Canadian mining companies, but both Finland and the USSR wanted to gain control themselves over the output of the mines. This quickly developed into an acrimonious squabble between the two powers which dragged on into 1941 and was never settled. But this was essentially a dispute over trade and resources, even though it did symbolise the struggle for economic dominance over Finland. Alarm bells started ringing more loudly in Moscow on 21 September, when Molotov discovered that the Germans had persuaded the Finns to allow their troops to cross Finland to get to northern Norway.

Under the terms of the pact, Germany was obliged to give the Soviets advance notice of any such arrangement. Ribbentrop did fulfil this obligation – but only just. He gave Schulenburg strict instructions five days before that he was to tell Molotov on the afternoon of 21 September, 'verbally and casually, preferably while engaged on another errand', that the troops were due to land in Finland next morning.

The agreement with Finland was supposed to be for the transit of one anti-aircraft battalion, which was said to be for defence against attacks by the RAF. In fact, Hitler had ordered the northern fjords of Norway to be fortified for use as bases against the Soviet Union, should the Soviets invade northern Finland and try to take Petsamo by force. On 6 September he had sent word to Stalin that the German navy no longer needed the base near Murmansk, now that it could use bases in Norway, and thanked the Soviets for their valuable assistance. Grand Admiral Raeder was told to express the German navy's gratitude in a personal letter to Admiral Kuznetsov.

Molotov was not put off by such effusions. He was understandably suspicious that the German–Finnish agreement might simply be a convenient cover for the stationing of troops in Finland itself – which was, of course, in the Soviet sphere of interest as defined in the pact. He demanded more information, including sight of the agreement itself, 'together with any secret protocols', but the Germans managed to evade his questions and never gave him a straight answer. Above all, they never told him that they were paying for the privilege by giving the Finns large quantities of arms.

The relationship was also being soured at this time by events in Lithuania, which contributed to the general growth of tension. Stalin's seizure of the Lithuanian Tip still rankled with Hitler, and even more so with Ribbentrop. The question of compensation was far from being settled. Now, the Germans were getting a little of their own back in Memel. When Hitler annexed the area in March 1939, he had placated the Lithuanians a little by guaranteeing them free port facilities in the town. Now that Lithuania had become part of the USSR, he decided to end the arrangement – the Soviet Union had other ports and plainly did not need such concessions. Molotov, of course, did not agree, and protested vigorously, but to no avail. Hitler was determined to deny Stalin any bases of operations outside the newly Sovietised Baltic states.

The Soviets were more successful at the other end of their long frontier, where the inclusion of Bessarabia and Bukovina into the USSR had taken them on to the Danube river and delta. Hitler had hoped to prevent Stalin taking a hand in controlling the waterway and the region, but eventually had to submit, albeit with a very bad grace. However, he was soon finding ways of turning Stalin's interest in the region to his own advantage, and for the moment he was glad of anything that would keep the Balkans calm.

Even as the situation in the Balkans was appearing to settle down, however, Hitler had another unpleasant surprise in store for Stalin which revived his fears for the Far East. On 27 September, at 1.15 pm, three men sat at a long table in the vast Hall of the Ambassadors in Hitler's Chancellery, to sign another pact from which the Soviet Union was excluded. The men were Ribbentrop, Italian Foreign Minister Ciano and the Japanese ambassador, Saburo Kurusu. What they were signing was the Tripartite Pact, a political and military alliance between their three countries which revived and strengthened the defunct Anti-Comintern Pact.

The new pact called for the three powers 'to assist one another with all political, economic and military means if one of the three is attacked by a power not at present involved in the European war or in the Japanese–Chinese conflict'. Although clause 5 stated that the treaty 'in no way affects the political status at present existing between each of the three powers and Soviet Russia', Stalin and Molotov were justifiably upset at the implication that they could expect Japan to attack them in the Far East in the event of any conflict with Germany.

They were also angry that once again Ribbentrop had left it until the very last minute to inform them of the impending treaty. They found it hard to accept his assurances that the new pact was aimed not against the Soviet Union but solely against America, with the intention of keeping her out of the war. They were right to be dubious – Ribbentrop had told Ciano in Rome when first suggesting a new military alliance with Japan that it was directed against both.

Relations were still strained in early October. Molotov kept on asking awkward questions about German activities in Finland and Romania and quoting sections of the non-aggression pact verbatim at Werner von Tippelskirch, who was acting as chargé d'affaires in Moscow during Schulenburg's absence on home leave. There was a growing danger that things would come to a head before Hitler was ready. It was obviously necessary to forestall this, and to allay Soviet fears for as long as possible. The best and quickest way, Hitler believed, was by personal contact, cutting out the diplomatic middlemen whom he so despised. Ribbentrop suggested a summit meeting between Hitler and Stalin, to be held in Berlin as soon as possible. But Hitler quickly pointed out that Stalin would never agree to leave Moscow, and he himself was not prepared to go there. They decided, therefore, to invite Molotov to come to Berlin.

Hitler dictated a long letter, which the Foreign Minister then sent off under his own signature addressed personally to Stalin. Most of its nineteen pages were spent reviewing and superficially analysing the events of the past year, blaming everything that had happened – including German actions in Finland and Romania – on the British, who were even then doing their best to cause trouble between Germany and the Soviet Union. Finally, after explaining the Tripartite Pact as being anti-British and anti-American, and claiming that Ribbentrop was working tirelessly to improve relations between the Soviet Union and Japan, it came to the point: a proposal that the three signatories and the Soviet Union should carve up the world between themselves, for all time. In essence, this was an invitation to join the Tripartite Pact in a full-scale alliance.

Schulenburg, who had taken the letter with him when he returned from leave, reported on 17 October that he had handed it to Molotov, who had said he could not deny that he owed Ribbentrop a visit to Berlin, but could not give an answer until he had studied the letter's contents. Ribbentrop was furious with the ambassador, and wired back immediately demanding to know why he had given the letter to Molotov, and not to Stalin in person, and why it had taken four days. Schulenburg replied that in the first place he had got back to Moscow only on 15 October, because his plane had been delayed, and that it had then been necessary to translate the letter into Russian, very carefully, before delivering it. It had, he reminded Ribbentrop, been a very long letter, as well as a very important one. As to giving it to Molotov, the Soviet Premier would have been deeply offended at being bypassed, which would not have been helpful in future dealings, and in any case, he was sure Stalin would not have agreed to see him.

Huffily, Ribbentrop accepted the explanations, but told Schulenburg to deliver Stalin's answer as quickly as possible, as he would be away for a few days – actually, in his train following Hitler on a 4,000-mile round trip through France to meet the French and Spanish leaders in fruitless attempts to persuade them both to join the war against Britain.

Molotov gave Schulenburg Stalin's reply in the early hours of 22 October, in a sealed envelope, but with an open copy. While despatching Hilger by air to deliver the original letter by hand, Schulenburg wired a translation of the copy. The form and style, to say nothing of the tongue-in-cheek irony of its opening, left no doubt that it was written by Stalin himself:

My Dear Herr von Ribbentrop:

I have received your letter. I thank you sincerely for your confidence, as well as for the instructive analysis of recent events which is contained in your letter . . . M. Molotov acknowledges that he is under obligation to pay you a return visit in Berlin. He hereby accepts your invitation.

It remains for us to agree on the date of arrival in Berlin. The time from 10th to the 12th of November is most convenient for M. Molotov. If it is also agreeable to the German government, the question may be considered as settled . . . As to joint deliberation on some issues with Japanese and Italian participation, I am of the opinion (without being opposed to this idea in principle) that this question would have to be submitted to a previous examination.

Yours, etc.
J. STALIN

46

THE HAMMER GOES TO HITLER

Molotov hated the idea of flying. And since this was to be the first time in his fifty years that he had set foot outside the Soviet Union – an interesting achievement for the Foreign Minister of one of the world's great powers – there would be anxieties enough without needlessly adding more. It was also the first time any Soviet Prime Minister had travelled abroad on official business, so everyone was concerned to reduce the physical dangers involved to a minimum. His journey to Berlin therefore started from Moscow's Belorussia railway station, in a train made up of special European-style coaches to accommodate the sixty-plus aides in his party (no less than sixteen of whom were security men), three personal servants and one a doctor.

Since Schulenburg and Hilger were also accompanying him, the staff of the German embassy were among those who gathered to see him off, late in the evening of Sunday, 10 November 1940. Most of them had come straight from a reception at the Japanese embassy, where they had been startled to see all five Marshals of the Soviet Union. The mystery of why this powerful quintet, so rarely seen together, had attended such an unimportant diplomatic function was explained when they suddenly appeared at the station – they had been killing time by enjoying free drinks and Japanese hospitality before going on to wish Molotov well on his historic mission. Their appearance there underlined the importance Stalin attached to the trip – but Stalin himself did not join them.

By one of those small ironies which dot the course of history, at almost the same moment as Molotov set out from Moscow to try to save the Soviet Union's alliance with Nazi Germany, the one man who might perhaps have been able to prevent its happening in the first place, Neville Chamberlain, died at his home in Hampshire, England. Meanwhile, the man who had unwittingly done most to promote the

Nazi–Soviet pact, former Polish Foreign Minister Josef Beck, in exile in Romania, had learned that he, too, was terminally ill with cancer.

Molotov's journey passed uneventfully, the only incident to disturb the peace of the travellers coming during the next night, when the train reached the German side of the new border between Soviet Belorussia and the Polish Government General, at Eydtkuhnen. Here, the broad-gauge Soviet rail track gave way to the narrower European standard – the Soviet engineers had wasted no time in extending their own track to the edge of the newly acquired territory. It was normally necessary to change trains there, not only the wheels but also the bodies of the Soviet coaches being too wide for the Western European rail system. Molotov's train, however, was made up of specially designed European-sized rolling stock, so that only the undercarriage needed changing and the passengers could stay in their own compartments for the whole trip. Indeed, the undercarriages had already been changed at the Soviet side of the border. But the German officials would have none of this. They had a German train already prepared and waiting, and insisted that everyone, including Molotov, move over to it.

The Soviet train chief refused. There was an altercation. One coach was uncoupled and shunted to a siding where a measuring frame was installed to check wagon sizes. There, to the Germans' delight, one of the little balls hanging from the frame just brushed the roof. They insisted that proved the Soviet train was too large, but still the Soviets refused to budge. In the end a compromise was reached – the German coaches were attached to the Soviet train, and the whole thing moved off into the night again.

Valentin Berezhkov, a young Soviet interpreter with Molotov's party, had his own ideas about the Germans' motives. 'The German carriages were very comfortable with one-berth compartments,' he says, 'an excellent bar and restaurant and salons fitted with radios. There were even vases of fresh roses in the compartments. Obviously, it was not concern for our comfort that made the Germans so stubborn in insisting that we should change trains. Undoubtedly their carriages were not only equipped with a fine bar, but with a fine lot of bugging apparatus, too.' Perhaps this was one of the reasons why none of the Soviets would eat in the German restaurant car until they had radioed back to Moscow for permission.

Security was tight all the way. On both sides, the track was guarded over the whole length of the journey by armed soldiers posted at short intervals. On board, arrangements were under the personal supervision of V. N. Merkulov, Vice-Commissar of the Interior and head of the NKGB, the state security section of the NKVD. The seriousness with which he took his job surfaced when Gustav Hilger, having forgotten the name of the new frontier town and not realising that their train was intended by the Soviets to go right through, innocently asked him where they should change. Merkulov replied, 'We shall change trains at such a place as will be designated by the Chairman of the Council of People's Commissars.' Hilger argued, in vain, that it did not depend on any decision of Molotov's, but simply on where one gauge ended and the other began, but Merkulov refused to divulge this vital secret and Hilger had to wait until he could read the name of the station for himself.

The train arrived at Berlin's Anhalter station five minutes behind schedule at 11.05 on the morning of Tuesday, 12 November. It was a cold, dank day, with a fine drizzle falling from an overcast sky. Inside, the station was decorated with evergreens, cascades of flowers illuminated by hidden spotlights, and flags of the two nations cleverly draped so that it was almost impossible to see the hammer and sickle on the Soviet red flag, while the Nazi swastika was clearly visible everywhere.

Although all senior officials of state and party had been ordered to attend, Ribbentrop was upset that neither Goebbels nor Rosenberg, nor any of the other top Nazi ideologists, could be persuaded to appear. The welcoming party did include, however, Field Marshal Keitel, Heinrich Himmler, Labour Minister Robert Ley, press chief Otto Dietrich, and former Chancellor Franz von Papen, now German ambassador to Turkey, along with various generals and minor ministers.

Ribbentrop had them all carefully lined up along the platform, ready to be introduced to the Soviet Premier and Foreign Minister when he stepped out of the train on to the thick red carpet. But all was thrown into confusion when the train driver missed his mark and stopped several metres beyond the painted white line. This left the door from which Molotov was to emerge facing the middle of the line-up, instead of the beginning, where Ribbentrop and Keitel were standing. As the military band struck up a very fast version of the Soviet national anthem, the *Internationale*, they had to scuttle along the carpet to receive their guest.

Molotov, short, stocky, his spectacles perched carefully above his close-clipped moustache, looked like some minor clerk or book-keeper in his grey suit, grey overcoat and grey Homburg hat, amidst the uniforms worn by all the Germans. But he returned Ribbentrop's broad smile of welcome, and although he recognised very few names among those he was introduced to as they passed along the line, he greeted each one with a firm handshake, raising his hat well clear of his head every time. He spent longest with Himmler, the two staring into each other's fish-cold eyes as though seeking some hidden message.

Ribbentrop then led Molotov into the Anhalter station's *Fürsten-zimmer*, the 'princes' room' where distinguished guests had been received by the sovereign in the Kaisers' times. They spent a few moments there discussing the schedule before leaving by a side door to where a guard of honour from the Berlin garrison was drawn up ready for inspection. Paul Schmidt had mischievously suggested to Ribbentrop that it could be dangerous to have the *Internationale* played in public, since there would be many spectators who remembered it from years gone by, who might join in and sing the German version. Ribbentrop, of course, had not seen the joke, and as a result the communist anthem was rushed through again as quickly as possible, while *Deutschland über Alles* and the *Horst Wessel* song were given the full treatment. Nevertheless, Valentin Berezhkov for one took great satisfaction in seeing German generals and high Nazi officials standing to attention for the communist hymn. He also claimed to have seen workers in a tall brick building to the right of the station, which he took to be 'some sort of factory', waving red handkerchiefs and scarves from the windows.

The handshakings and inspections completed, the party climbed into a fleet of open black Mercedes limousines, for the drive through the city. Erich Sommer, the young German Balt who had been working with the joint border commissions in the east, had been recalled to Berlin to act as a guide and interpreter for the lesser members of the Soviet delegation. He asked his charges if any of them wished to go sightseeing while in Berlin, or on a shopping spree using the special vouchers available to diplomats. No doubt conscious of the presence of Merkulov and his sixteen security guards, they all refused, politely but firmly, and made their way to the waiting cars like a line of convent schoolgirls only allowed out under supervision. Sommer thought even their clothes looked like school uniforms: they all wore identical dark blue, badly fitting, off-the-peg suits, plain silver-grey neckties, and cheap felt hats. The hats were the oddest part, in Sommer's eyes. He thought the Soviet men were obviously not used to wearing Western headgear, since some had them on the side of the head like Cossack caps, some wore them stuck on the back of the head, and others had them jammed down very low over the eyes. Weizsäcker viewed the visitors more seriously than Sommer – he thought they would make good gangster types for a film, and was depressed to think that a nation of 130 million should be represented by such a shabby crew.

As the long procession made its way through the cold, damp streets, escorted by steel-helmeted motor-cycle outriders, observers were all struck by the absence of crowds or decorations. There were not even any flags along the route, and the few people who were out remained silent as the Soviets passed. Hitler had not seen fit to order any cheering demonstrators, or fanfares. Without such orders, the people of Berlin chose to stay away, though they had been given plenty of notice, since the newspapers had been writing about Molotov's visit for days. The day before, in fact, the party paper *Völkischer Beobachter* had devoted virtually the whole of its front page to the event, with a four-column headline underlined in red, a photograph and biography of Molotov in the first column, an editorial on Soviet–German relations, and a summary of press comment in the rest of Europe. But on 12 November, even the

'Via Spontana', as Foreign Ministry wags like Schmidt called the Wilhemstrasse during organised demonstrations, was virtually deserted.

Molotov and his delegation were accommodated in the beautiful Schloss Bellevue, a former Hohenzollern royal palace in the Tiergarten, surrounded by acres of trees and lawns and approached through a long avenue of limes, now used as a government guest house. The Soviet delegates were overawed by the opulence of the recently refurbished building. 'We were amazed at the ostentation of the rooms,' Berezhkov noted. 'Everywhere we could smell the delicate scent of roses coming from the bouquets which stood in tall porcelain vases in every corner. The walls were decorated with tapestries and paintings in heavy gilt frames. There were statuettes and vases of the finest porcelain standing all around in exquisitely carved cabinets . . . The furniture was antique and the servants and waiters were garbed in gold-braided livery.' But the elegant surroundings and expert service were not enough to calm all Soviet fears – they insisted that all crockery must be boiled before food was served on it, to protect Russian stomachs against Nazi germs.

With Molotov ready and waiting in the wings, the scene was now set for a series of dialogues which could revive or finally destroy the uneasy and unnatural friendship between Hitler's Germany and Stalin's Soviet Union. It was still just possible, in spite of everything Hitler had said and done since July, that Stalin could find some new way of buying him off, diverting him from an attack, even if only for the time being.

Hitler had as yet made no open commitment, and could therefore change his mind with no great loss of face. His real intentions were known only to a tiny few: the generals and field marshals of the OKH, the army High Command, were still being led to believe that his first priority was the defeat of Britain and that their ideas for 'Otto' were more in the nature of contingency planning; Raeder and the navy had not even been told that much, for all discussions about a possible attack in the east had taken place at Führer conferences only after the Grand Admiral had left. Only a handful of men, mainly in the OKW, were aware of what he was after, and even fewer of them knew that the prime objectives of his talks with Molotov were to discover how much Stalin and the Soviets suspected and what they were doing about it, and if possible to lull them into a false sense of security.

That very day, 12 November, Hitler had issued his directive No. 18, dealing with 'Strategy in the Immediate Future'. In drafting it, Walter Warlimont, in the OKW operations section, had originally put 'Sea Lion' at the head, giving it first priority for the spring of 1941. Jodl, his boss and Hitler's closest military adviser, moved it from the beginning to the end, knowing what Hitler wanted.

In addition to the plans being prepared in both OKH and OKW, 'preparations for the east' were going ahead by now in various other ways. A few days before, Hitler had told Göring, as economic supremo, to make sure all contracts for the Soviet Union were punctiliously fulfilled for the moment, to keep Stalin quiet. He had then authorised the start of high-altitude photographic reconnaissance flights deep into Soviet air space by Luftwaffe intelligence. And even as Molotov arrived in Berlin, at OKH headquarters in Fontainebleau, General Halder and his staff were conducting war games in which the Wehrmacht was pitted against the Red Army, to test out their operational plan.

The first item on the agenda for Molotov was a meeting with Ribbentrop in the Foreign Minister's new office. He had recently moved out of Bismarck's historic room at 76 Wilhemstrasse, where he had never felt at ease under the shadow of so much tradition and such an illustrious predecessor, and crossed the street to the former presidential palace, which had been allocated to him as his official residence. Most of the old building had been reconstructed twice – Hitler had made the mistake of criticising the almost complete first version while being shown round it by Ribbentrop, who immediately ordered everything to be torn down and started again, incorporating more grandiose features which he thought would appeal to the Führer. Before Hitler saw it next time, Speer begged him to keep his mouth shut, despite the architectural horrors which had been perpetrated, to prevent Ribbentrop starting yet again and going even more over the top.

Somehow, Ribbentrop had managed to furnish his personal office with a reasonable amount of restraint, and it was, according to Schmidt, 'fairly comfortable'. At noon, he welcomed Molotov to the room with an effusiveness that quite startled Schmidt, who was there to take notes. Recalling the last foreign visitor to the room, Schmidt recorded that 'Ciano would probably have rubbed his eyes if Ribbentrop had smiled at him in the friendly way he did at the Soviet Foreign Minister'. Accompanying Molotov was his deputy, Vladimir Dekanozov, who, having finished with the Baltic states, had come to Berlin as his principal aide. Vladimir Pavlov, from the Soviet embassy, was there to act as his interpreter. Interpreting for Ribbentrop was Gustav Hilger. Poor Hilger was suffering from flu but carried on manfully throughout the entire visit, despite constant headaches and nausea, and nose bleeds from time to time. The six men took their seats round a circular table and Ribbentrop launched into a high-flown speech of welcome.

Molotov sat listening sphinx-like to the flowery phrases and sweeping generalities. Only occasionally, Schmidt noted, did he respond to the German's oily smirks, 'when a rather frosty smile glided over his intelligent, chess-player's face'. At his side, Dekanozov sat crouched in his chair, his short legs barely touching the floor, listening with rapt attention and a completely expressionless face.

On and on Ribbentrop droned, drifting airily through yet another survey of the current state of the war before getting even remotely near the point. He stressed that 'no power on earth could alter the fact that the beginning of the end has now arrived for the British Empire. England is beaten, and it is only a matter of time before she admits her defeat.' Whatever happened, he promised, Britain would definitely beg for peace in the coming year. Only bad weather had prevented Germany from finishing the job already. Britain was depending on America, but her hopes would be in vain: Germany and Italy 'would never again allow an Anglo-Saxon to land on the continent of Europe', and the German navy would prevent any US aid crossing the Atlantic.

Boasting of German strength and successes to date, Ribbentrop crowed that the Axis powers were no longer considering how they might win the war, but rather how quickly they could end a war which was already won. With this in mind, they had looked around for friends who had the same interests as themselves, and out of this had come the Tripartite Pact. Already, a number of other countries had declared their solidarity with its ideas. Of supreme importance, the three signatories had all declared that the new pact would in no way disturb their relations with the Soviet Union.

Having raised the subject of Japan, Ribbentrop quickly started to expand on it. He was keen, he said, to promote friendship between the Soviet Union and Japan, remembering that Stalin himself had told him in Moscow that he would welcome any such moves. Japan was no longer looking to the north or east for her *Lebensraum*, but to the south, away from the Soviet Union. Ribbentrop claimed that this was largely due to his influence.

'Japan has already turned her face to the south,' he announced, his own face assuming the statesmanlike expression which Schmidt said he reserved for great occasions, 'and will be occupied for centuries in consolidating her territorial gains. For her *Lebensraum* Germany, too, will seek expansion in a southerly direction, that is, in Central Africa, in the territories of the former German colonies. With regard to Russia, German has set boundaries to her spheres of interest.'

This talk of the south was to be a running theme for both Ribbentrop and Hitler during the whole of Molotov's visit, as Hitler tried to divert Stalin's attention away from the west. In addition to the rather naive idea that this might prevent Stalin realising what was going on on his western frontiers, Hitler may well have been considering the vague possibility of some sort of trade-off: the thought that he might be able to persuade the Soviet leader to give him part or even all of the Ukraine and the Crimea in return for German complicity in obtaining other lands in the south. In any case, Ribbentrop told Molotov, Hitler wanted to establish new spheres of interest for Germany, Italy, Japan and the Soviet Union. They should, he believed, all be looking south. The Soviet Union should be looking in that direction for the natural outlet to the open sea that was so important to her.

Molotov was not impressed by Ribbentrop's vapid grandiloquence. He wanted facts, not the 'great concepts', as Ribbentrop described them. Cutting across the German's verbosity he demanded, coolly, 'Which sea are you talking about?'

Ribbentrop was thrown. For the moment, all he could do was to launch another spate of generalisations about 'Britain's insane policy', the reward there had been for both the Soviet Union and Germany in the West as a result of the non-aggression pact, and of how 'both partners had together done some good business'. Finally he worked his way round to the answer Molotov had demanded, and the 'good business' that could accrue from fresh agreements.

'The question now,' he said, 'is . . . whether in the long run the most advantageous access to the sea for Russia could not be found in the direction of the Persian Gulf and the Arabian Sea, and whether at the same time certain other aspirations of Russia in this part of Asia – in which Germany is completely disinterested – could not also be realised.' This heavy hint about India – which Ribbentrop reinforced by talking about 'the new ordering of affairs in the British Empire' – drew no response whatever from Molotov, who retained what Schmidt described as his 'impenetrable expression'. He was not interested in German promises of handing over prizes which had not yet been won.

Ribbentrop followed up with another such promise, this time of a new agreement governing the Dardanelles and controlling all access to the Black Sea, with special privileges for the Soviet Union, forcing Turkey if need be to come to heel. He then turned to the big issue – the possibility of the Soviet Union's joining the Tripartite Pact and collaborating with the other three partners to carve up the rest of the world between them. Of course, he was not actually making any concrete proposals yet, he added, merely a summary of the ideas which he and Hitler had had in mind when Ribbentrop wrote his letter to Stalin. But if these ideas seemed feasible to the Soviet government, then Ribbentrop would be quite prepared to come to Moscow himself to discuss them with Stalin. He could even bring the Italian and Japanese Foreign Ministers with him, if the Soviet leaders wished.

Probably the greatest obstacle to the Soviet Union's joining any pact alongside the Japanese at that time was the war which was still raging between Japan and China. In an obvious attempt to minimise this, Ribbentrop artlessly mentioned that he would be prepared to offer his services as a mediator – though he had to admit that he had not yet offered to do so, and nobody had asked him, either.

Molotov acknowledged that it would be a good thing for everybody if the Chinese and Japanese could reach some agreement. He also agreed that discussion of the other great matters would be interesting. But before he could consider any suggestion of joining the Tripartite Pact there were a number of questions that needed answering. The treaty gave Germany and Italy 'leadership in establishing a new order in Europe', and Japan leadership in 'Greater East Asia'. What exactly, Molotov wanted to know, did 'Greater East Asia' mean? This, he said, was quite vague for anyone who had not been a party to the treaty.

Ribbentrop agreed that it was indeed vague, but confessed that it had not been defined in any detail to him, either. It had only been suggested at the last minute, and the negotiations had all 'proceeded very rapidly'. But he could say that it had nothing to do with the spheres of influence vital to the Soviet Union.

This did not even remotely satisfy Molotov. 'Spheres of influence must all be more properly defined,' he said drily, particularly those between Germany and the Soviet Union. These had now been rendered 'obsolete and meaningless' by recent events, with the exception, he added ominously, of the Finnish question, which he would discuss in detail later. 'A permanent solution will take some time,' he concluded. 'First we want to reach an understanding with Germany, and only then with Japan and Italy – after we have received precise information regarding the significance, the nature and the aims of the Tripartite Pact.'

On that warning note, the meeting broke up. Molotov, Dekanozov and Pavlov were driven to the Schloss Bellevue for lunch with the rest of the Soviet party in the dark oak-panelled dining room, where they were served with discreet efficiency by white-gloved waiters, under the direction, according to Berezhkov, 'of a tall, grey-haired *maître d'hôtel* whose chest was adorned by a gold chain and huge medal and who silently conducted the proceedings with nothing more than a barely noticeable gesture or look'.

Immediately they had finished, the Soviet delegates rose from the table and marched out to the waiting cars which were to take them to the Chancellery for Molotov's first meeting with Hitler. This time, it was a larger party, for Molotov was taking with him not only Dekanozov and Pavlov but also his various experts and advisers. Valentin Berezhkov joined Pavlov to assist with the interpreting and note-taking. It was therefore a long line of limousines which swept out of the Tiergarten, shepherded by motor-cycle outriders on to the Charlottenburger Chaussee, past the Brandenburg Gate and into Wilhelmstrasse. By now, there were more people on the streets. Near the Chancellery they even made quite a decent crowd, filling the pavement. But they stayed silent, staring curiously at the small red flag with its hammer and sickle emblem on the front of the leading car, and at the small man who called himself 'The Hammer', sitting inside it.

In the courtyard of the Chancellery, Molotov was greeted by Otto Meissner, state secretary in charge of the presidential office, an old-style civil servant who had held the same position under former President Hindenburg. He led the Soviet party through the great bronze doors and along the processional route through the building, specially created by Speer on Hitler's instructions to impress visitors on occasions such as this. Every few yards tall, black-uniformed guards snapped out their right arms in the Nazi salute like automatons. Finally, they arrived in the circular marble hall, outside Hitler's study, in the centre of which had been placed a table laid with hors d'oeuvres, canapés and soft drinks. The Soviet experts and advisers were to wait here, in the company of German officials and specialists, including Erich Sommer and Johnnie von Herwarth, who had been recalled from his regiment yet again to act as an aide to Schulenburg. In place of his army uniform, he had been kitted out with the new black dress uniform and cap designed by Ribbentrop for Foreign Ministry staff and dilomats.

Molotov's entry to Hitler's study was staged with well-rehearsed theatricality. Two immensely tall, blond SS men in immaculate, tight-fitting black uniforms threw open the ceiling-high doors with a single, smooth movement then, with their backs pressed to the door jambs on either side, raised their arms in a salute which formed an arch over the heads of the visitors as they passed through. Inside, Hitler was seated at the great desk at the far end of the room. Berezhkov recalls that 'he observed us silently for a moment, then, with a sudden movement, stood and walked to the centre of the room with small, rapid steps. Here he stopped and raised his arm in the Nazi salute, bending his palm unnaturally. Still without a word, he came up close and shook each one of us by the hand. His palm was cold and moist to the touch, and his feverish eyes seems to bore through you like gimlets.'

The SS men silently swung the doors shut behind the Soviets. After a few words of welcome, Hitler led his guests to the lounge area of the study. As he did so, Ribbentrop entered through a curtained-off opening in the far corner, followed by Hilger and Schmidt. Hitler suggested Molotov should sit on a sofa, its back to the wall, while he took an armchair facing him across the low, circular coffee table. Hilger sat on Hitler's right, and then came Ribbentrop and Schmidt. Dekanozov sat on Molotov's right, Berezhkov on his left, and Pavlov in the armchair between him and Hitler. Hilger thought the Führer's approach to his guests was surprisingly gracious and friendly. He began, as usual, with a long monologue, speaking without notes, his speech flowing smoothly, reminding Berezhkov of 'an actor who knew his lines well', with regular carefully spaced pauses for the interpreters.

For an hour, he poured out generalities which were just as vague as those mouthed by Ribbentrop before lunch, but even more grandiloquent. Molotov listened politely, from time to time expressing his agreement with the fine sentiments Hitler was expressing. Most of the time, in fact, Hitler was simply trying to reassure the Soviet Premier that his country had nothing to fear from Germany, that the interests of the two nations could be satisfied without conflict. He spoke at some length of the benefits, both past and future, of friendship between the two greatest peoples in Europe, and of his hopes for peaceful collaboration to their mutual advantage, stretching far into the future, even beyond the life-span of the present leaders.

Britain was finished, he insisted. He was only waiting for atmospheric conditions to improve, allowing him to deliver the great and final blow. While preparing for this, he was also clarifying the political issues which would be important both during and after this final showdown.

Anticipating the complaints which Ribbentrop must have warned him to expect, he bemoaned the fact that the war with Britain had forced him to do many things which no one could have foreseen – including advancing into far-distant territories in which he was not really interested either politically or economically. However, the war had shown up the importance of other requirements, such as 'certain sources of raw materials which were considered by Germany as most vital and absolutely indispensable'. In these cases, he was determined to protect German interests at all costs.

Because of this, he went on, there were probably instances where Molotov thought Germany had overstepped the mark of the agreements reached in Moscow. But, he pointed out, the Soviets had also departed from the agreements in Poland and in Lithuania, where he had not wanted to make concessions but had done so in order to meet them halfway, and to eliminate potential sources of friction.

He had no political interest in the Balkans, and would withdraw his troops from Romania immediately there was peace. He did not like having to keep them there, in any case, hundreds of kilometres from their supply centres, but it was a case of military necessity, as was stopping the British getting a foothold in Greece and establishing air and naval bases at Salonika.

Molotov listened calmly as Hitler repeated his arguments again and again, then innocently asked why he considered Salonika a threat. It was so close to the Romanian oilfields, Hitler replied.

Now it was Molotov's turn. Adopting the schoolmasterly manner so well known to many observers in Moscow, he proceeded to examine Hitler with a series of probing and insistent questions. In what Schmidt described as a tone of gentle remonstrance he said Hitler had made general statements, to which he could, in general, agree. But he did not want generalities. He wanted detail, and very specific detail. That was what he had come to Berlin for.

First, however, he had a short lecture of his own to deliver. Stressing that everything he was about to say was completely in line with the views of Stalin, who had given him precise instructions on every point before he left Moscow, he reminded Hitler of all the benefits he had obtained from the pact. He had been able to wage war so successfully over the past year because his rear had been totally secure. He had gained considerable economic advantages in Poland. Hitler had spoken of the Lithuanian question, but he had obtained valuable territory in the east, around Lublin, in a fair exchange for his part of Lithuania. And in any case, this had removed a potential source of friction.

Then he started throwing the awkward questions. What about Finland? Did Hitler consider the 1939 agreement was still in force concerning Finland? What exactly was the significance of the Tripartite Pact? What was the meaning in it of 'the new order in Europe and Asia'? What role did he expect the Soviet Union to play in it? What exactly were the boundaries of the so-called Greater East Asian sphere? Where did Germany stand regarding Romania, Bulgaria and Turkey in connection with the safeguarding of Soviet interests in the Balkans and the Black Sea?

No one had ever spoken to Hitler like this before. Schmidt, who had seen the Führer's temper flare on other occasions, half expected him to leap up and march out, or to say there was no point in continuing the discussions. Instead, he stayed 'meekly polite' and answered almost apologetically, while Ribbentrop sat staring at him, his arms folded across his chest, or drumming his fingers lightly on the table.

'The Tripartite Pact,' he explained, 'is intended to regulate relationships in Europe according to the natural interests of the European countries themselves. That is why Germany is now approaching the Soviet Union, so that she can express her views on the areas which are of interest to her. In no case will a settlement be made without Soviet Russian co-operation. This applies not only to Europe, but also to Asia, where Russia herself will co-operate in defining the Greater East Asian sphere and where she will designate her own claims. Here, Germany will play the role of a mediator – in no circumstances will Russia be presented with a *fait accompli*.'

As far as Soviet interest in the Balkans and the Black Sea were concerned, he went on, he had not contacted the Soviet Union before, because he had not foreseen any problems in the German–Soviet relationship. It was, rather, the relationship between Germany, Italy and France which had been his main worry, and he had not felt able to approach the Soviet Union until that had been satisfactorily dealt with. He said he considered their conversation represented the first concrete step towards a comprehensive collaboration in Europe and the Far East. As a reminder of earlier claims that the Tripartite Pact was aimed at the United States, he added that all the partners were concerned with opposing any attempts by America to make capital out of the affairs of Europe. 'The United States,' he concluded, 'has no business in either Europe, Africa or Asia.'

Molotov agreed with everything Hitler had said about Britain and the

United States. He also said that he thought Soviet participation in the new pact seemed 'entirely acceptable in principle – provided we are to be treated as an equal partner and not merely as a dummy'. But he returned again to his demand for detail. 'First, the aims and objects of the pact must be more closely defined,' he reiterated, 'and I must be more precisely informed about the boundaries of the Greater East Asian sphere.'

The meeting had lasted nearly three hours, and it was now dark outside. This gave Hitler the perfect excuse to avoid answering any more questions.

'I fear we must break off this discussion,' he said, rising from his armchair. 'Otherwise, we shall get caught by the air-raid warning.'

Promising Molotov he would deal with his questions in detail next day, he joined him in posing for German and Soviet photographers, then saw him out of the study.

47

UNINVITED GUESTS

Later that evening, Ribbentrop held a reception for Molotov at the Kaiserhof Hotel, just along the Wilhelmstrasse from the Foreign Ministry. The security precautions were the most elaborate ever seen in Berlin, with the entire area sealed off by the SD, who were terrified there would be an assassination attempt on the Soviet Premier. With the aid of the Gestapo, all politically suspect persons were screened, and Russian émigrés were removed from the city and sent to stay in distant hotels, at government expense. Molotov's own security men, under Merkulov, worked closely with Heydrich's SD and Müller's Gestapo, under the overall control of Himmler. Every side door and tradesmen's entrance to the hotel was hermetically sealed and guarded.

Everyone who was anybody in Berlin was there, with one notable exception – Hitler did not attend. His two deputies, Göring and Hess, did, however, Göring making up for the Führer's absence by his size and splendour – according to Berezhkov, he was wearing a uniform of silver-thread fabric, his chest covered from shoulder to waist in medals and other decorations, and his fingers jammed with rings sparkling with precious stones.

The dinner was served at a huge, horseshoe-shaped table. Having experienced ceremonial dinners in the Kremlin, Ribbentrop was determined to put on a show which would stand comparison, but not all the Soviet guests appreciated his efforts. Erich Sommer found himself seated next to Merkulov, the NKGB boss, who was determined to play the role of humble proletarian, demanding that the waiter remove the six elegant wine glasses arrayed on the table before him, leaving him with just one, from which to drink toasts. The fish course consisted of a splendid lobster, which he refused to touch, calling it a sea monster. He laughingly enjoyed watching Sommer attack his sea monster with the special pincers and fork provided, studying the process closely and then offering the young man his to eat, too. Sommer thanked him, but declined – the animals really were very large. When the toasts began,

Merkulov pretended not to hear Molotov propose the health of Hitler, and pointedly did not touch his glass of champagne.

There were only two speeches, by Ribbentrop and Molotov. Ribbentrop's was typically flowery, full of his global ideas involving the Soviet Union signing the Tripartite Pact and joining the war against Britain. When Molotov rose to reply, he apologised for not having had time to read Ribbentrop's speech, though he had been given a copy earlier in the day. This absolved him from having to relate his own speech to it, and he proceeded to ignore everything the Nazi Foreign Minister had said. After the banquet, when he was asked for the text of his speech for publication, he smiled and said it had been improvised on the spot, therefore he did not have a copy. And in any case, he added, still smiling, it had not been meant for the general public, so it would perhaps be best if it were not released. Ribbentrop had no option but to agree – and was therefore prevented from issuing his own speech, which was undoubtedly what Molotov had wanted to achieve.

To everyone's relief, the RAF did not bomb Berlin that night, despite Hitler's fears, so the visitors were able to return to their quarters peacefully through the blacked-out streets, and to sleep soundly in their beds.

Next morning before lunch, Molotov called on Göring and then on Hess. With Göring, at his Air Ministry office at 10 am, the discussion was about the state of trade between Germany and the Soviet Union. Molotov wanted answers again: why were German deliveries falling so badly behind schedule? Göring turned on all the jovial charm for which he was renowned, and refused to be ruffled, as Hitler and Ribbentrop had been by the Soviet leader's hard line. As a result, the atmosphere stayed friendly, though neither man gave an inch. The problem, Göring explained, was entirely of the Soviets' own making: their orders were concentrated in a very narrow range of commodities, chiefly machine tools and armaments, which were in unusually great demand in Germany itself. Molotov countered by saying that surely Germany now had greatly increased resources after occupying so many foreign territories, and so should have no difficulty filling Soviet orders.

Göring had a ready answer to that, too. Only a few days before, he had been complaining to Hitler that the new lands were proving to be a strain on Germany, that economically they were more of a burden than a benefit. He then returned to the attack by complaining about the amount of technical aid being asked for by the Soviet Union. Some of this, he said, amounted to demands for industrial secrets. The encounter ended in a draw.

The meeting with Hess immediately afterwards had nothing to do with negotiations or agreements, but was simply a fact-finding exercise for the Soviet Premier. He asked Hess to explain the organisational structure of the Nazi state, and where he fitted in as Deputy Führer. The two men amicably compared notes on the relationship between party and state in their two countries. It must have been an enjoyable, almost recreational interlude for Molotov among the tough talking and manoeuvring of his other sessions.

At 2 pm, Hitler entertained Molotov and nine leading members of his party, including Merkulov, Deputy Foreign Commissar Dekanozov, Industry Commissar Tevossyan, and the aircraft designer Yakovlev, to lunch in his private dining room in the residence. On the German side there were twelve guests in addition to Hitler himself, the principal ones including Ribbentrop, Bormann, Goebbels, Ley, Keitel and Schulenburg. Hitler and Molotov sat side by side in the centre of the long table, with Hilger alongside Molotov to translate, and Ribbentrop immediately opposite, flanked by Ambassador Shkvarzev and Dekanozov.

The luncheon was a quiet, low-key affair, with no speeches and little drinking. After the splendours of the official banquet the night before, Hitler's menu was so simple it was almost stark. The plain white card, edged in black and with a small Nazi eagle embossed in gold at the top, carried only the date and three words: '*Kraftbrühe, Fasan, Obstsalat*', beef tea, pheasant, fruit salad. When this frugal meal was over, Hitler led Molotov, Ribbentrop, Dekanozov and the interpreters to his study to resume the talks he had broken off so abruptly the evening before.

By now Hitler had recovered from the shock of being outfaced on his own ground, and this time was determined to give nothing away. Molotov, however, had reported back to Stalin overnight and had been given fresh instructions, and it was he who drew first blood – on the delicate subject of a possible Soviet occupation of Finland. When Hitler asked what he had meant by saying the terms of the pact were now fulfilled with the exception of Finland, Molotov referred him to the pact itself, and in particular to the secret protocol which defined the two spheres of influence. Finland, of course, was clearly named as being in the Soviet sphere.

Stung, Hitler retorted that there was nothing in the protocol about the Soviet Union occupying Finland. 'When it comes to actually taking possession,' he said, 'we ourselves have always adhered strictly to the secret protocol – which is more than can be said for Russia. Come what may, Germany has never occupied any territory in the Russian sphere.'

He went on to cite Lithuania as an example of Soviet greed. The Lublin district of Poland was by no means fair compensation to Germany for the loss of Lithuania, but he had seen that it was in the Soviet Union's interest, and so had agreed to the change. In Bukovina, too, he had given in to Soviet demands, though strictly speaking the pact had named only Bessarabia in that region.

Now, he said, Molotov was talking about Finland in the same way.

Germany had no political interest there. This had been proved during the Winter War, when she had been meticulous in fulfilling her obligations to provide 'benevolent neutrality' and had done the Soviets many favours, several of which he proceeded to list. But Germany needed Finnish nickel and lumber while Hitler's war with Britain was still on, and he did not want any danger of new conflicts in the Baltic, one of the few seas still open to his shipping.

He rejected the charge that German troops were occupying Finland. As the Soviet government had already been informed, they were simply being transported to Norway – though because of the length of the journey the trains did have to stop two or three times in Finnish territory. As soon as the contingent was in place, there would be no more. Although Germany had no political interest in Finland, he repeated, Germany's economic interest in the country was at least as great as it was in Romania. He expected Soviet consideration of this, especially in view of the understanding he had shown to Soviet interest in Lithuania and Bukovina.

Molotov responded by pointing out that the boundaries between Germany and the Soviet Union had been fixed by the pact, as had the issues concerning the Baltic states, Romania, Finland and Poland. As for the revisions involving Lithuania and the Lublin district, the Soviet Union would not have insisted on this, if Germany had really objected. And in any case, he insisted, Germany had received fair compensation.

Hitler tried to argue this point, but Molotov merely moved on to the Lithuanian strip, on which he said the Soviet government was still waiting for an answer from Germany. Then he dropped another bombshell: while the Soviet Union had so far been content to confine her demands in Bukovina to the northern part of the province, she still wanted the south, as well. Hitler, he said, knew this, and yet had guaranteed the whole of Romania, completely disregarding Soviet wishes.

For several minutes, they debated fiercely, with Hitler becoming more heated as he repeated his arguments over and over, while Molotov calmly blocked every point. Hitler held out the promise of great things to come for both countries if they continued to work together – and provided the Soviet Union kept out of those territories which were of interest to Germany for the duration of the war. 'The more Germany and Russia succeed in fighting back to back against the outside world,' he cried, 'the greater will be our successes, and the more we face each other breast to breast the smaller they will be! In the first case, there is no power on earth which could oppose our two countries!'

Molotov remained unmoved. While he agreed with what Hitler had said, adding that the Soviet leaders, and Stalin in particular, thought it both possible and expedient to strengthen relations between the two countries, he brought everything back to earth with a bump by insisting that there were still things that had to be sorted out. Finland was one of them.

'If Germany and the Soviet Union have a good understanding,' he went on, 'the Finnish question can be solved without war. But there must be no German troops in Finland and no political demonstrations there against the Soviet government.'

'I need not deal with your second point,' Hitler replied, 'since that has nothing to do with us. In any case, demonstrations can be staged very easily, and it is very difficult afterwards to find out who were the real instigators. But as regards the German troops, I can give you an assurance that when we have reached general agreement on the whole question, there will be no more German troops appearing in Finland.'

'When I spoke of demonstrations,' Molotov replied tartly, 'I was referring to the sending of Finnish delegations to Germany, and the reception of leading Finns in Berlin.' What was more, he continued, the presence of German troops had made the Finns bold, and they were bringing out anti-Soviet slogans, such as 'No true Finn approves the last Soviet–Finnish peace treaty.'

'The Soviet government,' he concluded, 'considers it its duty to settle the Finnish question once and for all. No new agreements are needed for that. The existing German–Soviet agreement assigned Finland to the Soviet sphere of influence.'

Hitler was now losing his temper at such intransigence. 'We do not want war in the Baltic,' he snapped. 'We urgently need Finland as a supplier of nickel and lumber. We have no political interest in Finland – unlike Russia, we have occupied no Finnish territory. The transit of German troops will be finished within the next few days, and we shall not send any more. The decisive question for Germany is whether Russia intends going to war against Finland.'

Molotov side-stepped the question neatly.

'Everything will be all right,' he said, 'if the Finnish government gives up its ambiguous attitude towards the USSR, and if agitation against us among the population, like bringing out slogans such as I have mentioned, ceases.'

'Next time,' Hitler warned, 'Sweden might intervene in a Russo–Finnish war.'

On and on the argument ran. Nothing Hitler could say seemed to make any impression on Molotov, who was now settling comfortably into the immovable, indestructible posture that had earned him the nickname 'Stone-Ass'. When Hitler repeated that there must be no war in Finland, because this would have far-reaching repercussions, Molotov obdurately replied, 'Then you are departing from our agreement of last year.' When Hitler spoke of the dangers of Allied intervention in any war in the Baltic, he said he could not understand what Germany was afraid of: Hitler had not objected last year, when the international situation was worse for Germany than it was now.

As the discussion became more tense, Ribbentrop kept trying to intervene, to say something that might relax the two protagonists. But he could not bring himself actually to interrupt Hitler, so kept rising from his chair to attract the Führer's attention. Eventually, Hitler acknowledged him and indicated with a wave of his hand that he could speak.

'Please permit me, my Führer, to express a thought on this matter,' he began.

Hitler nodded, and according to Berezhkov took a large handkerchief from his pocket and wiped it across his upper lip as Ribbentrop proceeded: 'There is actually no reason at all for making an issue of the Finnish question. Perhaps it was merely a misunderstanding.' He went on to summarise the position as he saw it, suggesting that when the transit of the German troops had finished, there would be no more problems with the Finns. 'If one considers matters realistically,' he concluded, 'there are no differences between Germany and Russia.'

This breathtaking assertion gave Hitler the excuse to break off the discussion of Finland, and turn to what he described as more important problems. These turned out to be plans for dividing up the 'bankrupt estate' of the British empire, in which he invited the Soviet Union to join with Germany, France, Italy and Japan, in sharing out the spoils.

After sitting through yet more verbose generalisations, Molotov commented that he had been following Hitler's arguments with interest, and added with more than a touch of asperity that he agreed with everything he had understood. But first, they must be clear about German–Soviet collaboration. They could bring in Italy and Japan later.

This set Hitler off on another flight of fancy, outlining his hopes for creating a world coalition of interested powers, stretching from East Asia to North Africa. He had, he claimed, already found a formula which satisfied everybody in the West. Now, it was time to sort out the East. This, he said, included not only the Greater East Asian sphere but also 'a purely Asiatic area oriented towards the south, that Germany even now recognises as Russia's sphere of influence'.

His clumsy attempt to divert Soviet interest southwards met with no more success than Ribbentrop's efforts in the same direction the day before. Molotov was simply not interested. He wanted, he said, to talk first about matters closer to Europe, and raised the subjects of Turkey, the Danube and Romania.

On Romania, he immediately brought up again the German guarantee. 'The Soviet government has already explained its position twice,' he rasped. 'If I may express myself so bluntly, we are of the opinion that the guarantee is aimed against the Soviet Union. Therefore, the question arises of revoking the guarantee.'

'For a certain time, it is necessary,' Hitler replied. 'Its removal is therefore impossible.'

Molotov was displeased by the answer. Anything which affected Soviet interests in the Black Sea – which he described as 'England's historic gateway for attack on the Soviet Union', referring back both to the Crimean War and the Intervention of 1918–19 – was of serious concern to the USSR. 'What would Germany say,' he asked, 'if the Soviet Union gave Bulgaria . . . a guarantee under exactly the same conditions as Germany and Italy have given Romania?' In other words, how would Germany react if the USSR took Bulgaria into her political orbit?

Hitler hedged. 'If you want to give a guarantee under the same conditions as we did to Romania', he replied, 'I must first ask you if the Bulgarians themselves have asked for such a guarantee. I do not know of any such request.' In any case, he went on, Molotov was asking his questions of the wrong person. Italy had important strategic interests in the Aegean and the Black Sea. Molotov should therefore consult Mussolini.

But Molotov refused to be side-tracked. The Soviet Union, he said, wanted a guarantee against an attack on the Black Sea through the Straits 'not only on paper but also in reality'. He believed he could reach direct agreement with Turkey, the other country adjoining the Straits, but would still need Bulgaria. He was prepared to guarantee Bulgaria an outlet to the Aegean Sea. So, once again, he was asking Hitler, 'as the one who decided the entire German policy', what he thought.

Irritated, Hitler replied that Germany was 'only interested in the matter secondarily. As a great Danubian power, we are interested only in the Danube river, and not in the passage to the Black Sea.' Then, in a flash of petulance, he dismissed the whole thing: 'If by any chance we were looking for sources of friction with Russia, we would not need the Straits for that.' And, badly rattled, he started talking about the great share-out of the British Empire once again, proposing that all the Foreign Ministers should meet in Moscow, after the ground had been prepared through diplomatic channels.

When Molotov failed yet again to rise to this bait, Hitler decided he had had enough. They had been talking now for three hours, and he had failed to make any headway at all. Using the possibility of British air raids as an excuse once again, he rose from his chair and said it would be best to end the meeting now. In any case, he said, they had probably discussed the main issues sufficiently. The question of safeguarding Soviet interests as a Black Sea power would have to be examined another time, as would the Soviets' wishes regarding their future position in the world.

It was left to Molotov to draw the final line under the meeting. Ominously, he told Hitler that their talks had raised a number of important and new questions for the Soviet Union. 'The Soviet Union,' he warned, 'as a great power, cannot remain aloof from the great issues in Europe and Asia.' He was obviously determined to leave Hitler in no doubt whatsoever that the Soviet Union could not be bought off.

Despite the sour atmosphere at the talks, Molotov went ahead that evening with the reception and dinner he had planned at the Soviet embassy. Göring, never one to miss out on a feast, was there again, as were Hess and, of course, Ribbentrop, leading a good turn-out of top personalities and officials. But Hitler did not attend. He stayed in the Chancellery, sulking over his failure either to hypnotise or bully Molotov into compliance.

The old palace which housed the embassy on the Unter den Linden had changed little since tsarist days, the only noticeable difference being a bust of Lenin in the entrance hall. The building itself was quite splendid, though the furnishings and decoration in its magnificent rooms were looking somewhat faded: the golden tassels on the heavy red velvet curtains were rather tarnished, the rococo furniture was a little chipped and the monumental mirrors were all slightly grey. But the banqueting table, laid in a huge marble hall, was adorned with fresh carnations and gleaming antique silver. A dinner service of fine china, which had been kept in store at the embassy for longer than anyone cared to remember, had been brought out to add its rich colours to the scene, sparkling in the light of great crystal chandeliers.

The food and drink were as sumptuous as at any Kremlin celebration. There was Crimean champagne for the start of the reception, and the dinner itself included all the best Russian produce, with lashings of caviar and vodka. 'No capitalist or plutocratic – to use the word then current in the Third Reich – table could have been more richly spread,' wrote Paul Schmidt. 'Everything had been most tastefully arranged. The Russians proved perfect hosts, so that in spite of language difficulties it was a very good party.'

Before it had finished, however, the dinner was brought to an abrupt halt by the arrival of unwelcome gatecrashers – the RAF. 'We had heard of the conference beforehand,' Churchill wrote later, 'and though not invited to join the discussion did not wish to be entirely left out of the proceedings.' Molotov had made a short speech, proposing a toast to Hitler, and Ribbentrop had just risen to reply when the air-raid sirens sounded. Trying to appear nonchalant, he said sarcastically, 'Our British friends are complaining that they have not been invited to the party. But we shall not let their fireworks interfere with us in any way. We shall continue in the air-raid shelter.'

The embassy, in fact, did not possess its own shelter. Everyone headed for the doors as fast as they could, with Göring and Hess leading the way: once they had dived into their limousines and been driven off at high speed, the other guests poured out of the building and hurried to find protection elsewhere. Ribbentrop took Molotov to his own shelter, beneath his new residence just around the corner. The others scattered in various directions: some guests found their way to the underground railway station at the Brandenburg Gate; most of the Soviet delegates were driven at top speed back to the Schloss Bellevue, where the cellars had been converted into luxurious bunkers with paintings and tapestries on the walls and waiters serving drinks; others found themselves cut off before they could reach their chosen destinations.

Paul Schmidt, hurrying along the street on foot to join Ribbentrop and Molotov in order to record what was said, had only got as far as the Adlon Hotel before the bombs started to fall. As the anti-aircraft guns across the street opened up with an ear-shattering salvo, he dived inside, along with several colleagues and, as William Shirer, who had been standing in the Adlon's doorway, put it, 'a stray Russian or two', who had missed the turn at the corner of the street. They spent a far more convivial two hours than they would have done in the Foreign Minister's bunker, where Ribbentrop and Molotov – by courtesy of the RAF – were face to face. Only Hilger, now looking at death's door with flu but still soldiering manfully on, was available to interpret and take notes of the impromptu discussions.

At 9.45 pm, to the muffled background of guns and bombs, Ribbentrop began his final attempt to stave off the rupture in German–Soviet relations which by now was looking more and more certain. But from his opening words it was obvious that he had learned absolutely nothing from the previous three sessions with the unmovable Soviet Premier. Time after time, Molotov had demonstrated that he was interested only in precise and detailed proposals. Fine words and airy concepts, no matter how grand, left him completely cold. And yet that was precisely what Ribbentrop proceeded to serve up, without even varying the recipe by the inclusion of one new ingredient. Molotov, trapped in the underground bunker with him, was forced to sit and listen for two and a quarter hours to a dreary rehash of empty phrases.

In all the seemingly endless flow of words which poured from Ribbentrop during that time, there was not a single new idea. The closest he came to anything fresh was when he suddenly drew from his pocket a draft which he had already prepared for an agreement admitting the Soviet Union to the Tripartite Pact. Even this, however, was vague and imprecise, skirting round all the issues to which Molotov had already demanded detailed answers.

The three main articles in the proposed agreement spoke of the signatories 'expressing their willingness to extend their collaboration to nations in other parts of the world which are inclined to direct their efforts along the same course as theirs'; undertaking to 'respect each other's natural spheres of interest' and 'constantly to consult each other in an amicable way' over problems arising from overlapping areas; not to join or support any alliance directed against one of the others; and to co-operate economically.

The agreement was to be for an initial period of ten years. It would, of course, have secret protocols 'in a form still to be determined, establishing the focal points in the territorial aspirations of the four countries'. These 'focal points' brought up once again the German efforts to redirect Soviet ambitions to the south, away from Europe and in the direction of the Indian Ocean.

Molotov, when pressed to reply, did not even mention the draft agreement. He also ignored Ribbentrop's repeated offer to mediate between the Soviet Union and Japan, pointing out that relations between them had 'always been fraught with difficulties and reverses' but that the Japanese, even before their recent change of government, had already suggested a non-aggression treaty. He went on to make it clear that this subject was far too complex and delicate for Ribbentrop to handle.

He also brushed aside Ribbentrop's suggestion that Germany could help to get a new agreement on the Dardanelles, and pointedly turned to the Balkans. The Soviet Union, he insisted, had an interest not only in Turkey but also in Bulgaria, and in Romania and Hungary. Suddenly, he was asking awkward questions again. What did Germany intend doing about Yugoslavia and Greece? About Poland? Did the German government regard the secret protocol concerning Poland as being still in force? What about Swedish neutrality? Did Germany still believe this was important to both herself and the Soviet Union?

This was not what Ribbentrop had wanted to hear at all. He had done his best to steer the conversation away from both the Balkans and the Baltic, but Molotov could not be steered. There was even worse to come. The Soviet Union was interested in the exits from the Baltic, as well as the Black Sea, Molotov stated, and wanted discussions about this, too. There was no point, however, in discussing Finland – he had already said everything there was to be said to Hitler.

As a final professorial touch, Molotov asked Ribbentrop to comment on all these questions. Ribbentrop did his best, but it was clear he was floundering. Like a drowning man, he sought desperately for something to cling to – and found it in Britain. Or at least, he thought he had. Blaming Britain for everything that was happening, especially in the Baltic, the Balkans and the Black Sea, he found his way on to what seemed to be the firm ground of the dissolution of the British Empire. Inviting the Soviet Union, once more, to participate in this, he ended with a confident flourish by reminding Molotov that he had not yet answered his question about whether the Soviet Union was interested in obtaining an outlet to the Indian Ocean.

Molotov's response must surely rank among the most cutting in the history of diplomacy. The Germans, he said, were assuming that the war against Britain had already been won. If therefore, as Hitler had said earlier, Germany was waging a life and death struggle against England, he could only construe this as meaning that Germany was fighting 'for life' and England 'for death'. And when Ribbentrop, completely missing the heavy sarcasm, continued to reiterate that Britain was indeed finished, Molotov wearily delivered his final thrust.

'If that is so,' he said, 'then why are we in this shelter, and whose are those bombs which are falling?'

Next morning, at 11 o'clock, Molotov and most of his advisers – with the exception of those such as Yakovlev and Tevossyan who stayed behind to place further orders for machinery, arms and aircraft – left Berlin and headed home again. They had been in the city for exactly forty-eight hours. At the Anhalter station, the only leading Nazi to see them off was Ribbentrop.

48

BARBAROSSA

Hitler had told his new field marshals he would be forced to strike if the Soviet Union showed any sign of wanting to invade either Finland or Romania. Since Molotov had made it perfectly clear that Stalin wanted both Finland and a large part of Romania, and would not be put off or diverted, it seemed the chips were now down. Still smarting from the indignity of having been argued with, lectured at and answered back in his own study, the Führer was faced with the harsh reality of having to carry out his threats, unless Stalin overrode his Premier's statements.

At the daily war conference in the Reich Chancellery at noon on the day Molotov left, the atmosphere was grim. Keitel's adjutant, Ottomar Hansen, later described it as 'funereal'. One of Hitler's own adjutants recorded: '[The Führer] says he had never expected much from it all. The discussions have shown, he says, which way the Russians' plans are lying. Molotov has let the cat out of the bag. He (the Führer) is vastly relieved, this won't even have to remain a *mariage de convenance*.'

To all but a select few in his inner circle, however, Hitler maintained a pretence that the talks had been successful. Newspaper reports stated that agreement had been reached on all major issues, and Weizsäcker was told to circulate a memorandum to all missions overseas giving the same reassuring illusion. The discussions, Weizsäcker's memorandum stated, 'took place in an atmosphere of mutual confidence', and had served to co-ordinate Soviet policy with that of the Tripartite Pact. 'This result,' it went on, 'clearly proves that all conjectures regarding alleged German–Russian conflicts are in the realms of fantasy and that all speculations of the foe as to a disturbance in the German–Russian relationship of trust and friendship are based on self-deception.'

In Moscow, Stalin too seemed determined to put on a brave face, avoiding any hint to the public that everything was not as smooth as it might be. Wolfgang Leonhard, the young German émigré student, noted: 'There was not the slightest inkling to be found in the Soviet press of a deterioration of relations. Every report in the foreign press which might do the least damage to our relations with Germany was immediately and emphatically denied. Great importance was attached to Molotov's journey to Berlin . . . *Pravda* published a picture of a session in the negotiations, at which Molotov and Hitler were seen together.'

At the Bolshoi, rehearsals were going ahead at full speed for a remarkable production intended to underline the happy state of German–Soviet relations. Stalin had personally ordered a production of Wagner's opera *Die Walküre* (*The Valkyries*); Dmitri Shostakovich, the Soviet composer, said it was because Stalin wanted 'to give Hitler a big hug to loud musical accompaniment' – certainly Wagner was Hitler's favourite composer and *Die Walküre* was his noisiest work. But who was to direct the opera? The Soviet cultural authorities had to find someone well-known enough to impress the Germans. They settled on Sergei Eisenstein, the celebrated film director noted for movies like *Battleship Potemkin*, who was available at the time since his latest film, *The Great Ferghana Canal*, had been aborted. Eisenstein was not enthusiastic about this new project: he loathed Wagner. But he realised that he could not reject an order from the General Secretary of the Communist Party, particularly if he wanted to continue directing films in the future.

In the eyes of the Soviet authorities, Eisenstein was ideal for the job. Not only was he half German, but his father was even a converted Jew. The political significance of this seems to have escaped the director himself, until he invited his friend Alexander Tyshler to design the sets. Tyshler was a Jew and much more streetwise than Eisenstein. 'Don't you realise,' he said, 'they won't let you use my name on the posters? The production will have to be *Judenfrei.*'

The failure of Molotov's talks was not allowed to interfere with the production, which opened on 21 November to a very mixed and generally incredulous reception. The director had made his feelings about Wagner and Germany very plain in his work. Ernst Fischer, the Austrian journalist working for the Comintern, thought it 'a wild parody of Wagner's opera, the view-halloo of the Valkyries like ululations of *Heil Hitler,* every kind of cinematic trick and flashback exploited so as to make the transition from the sublime to the ridiculous as precisely as possible'.

Walter Schmid, the young man who had accompanied Schnurre to the famous dinner at Ewest's, says it was 'very interesting, very Asiatic – nothing Germanic at all. The people on the stage moved like little, frightened dwarfs; it wasn't the great Germanic piece. It was quite extraordinary – there were things that had never been done on stage before: two scenes taking place simultaneously, intercutting between them like a film, trees moving, and so on, things you would never dream of doing in an opera house.'

Some of the other attachés in the embassy wanted to make an official protest against Eisenstein's 'Jewish insolence' in 'desecrating Richard Wagner'. And Ernst Fischer felt the whole production was designed to arouse the same hatred of the Germans as had the director's 1938 film *Alexander Nevsky*, a patriotic epic which told of the heroic defence of Mother Russia against the German hordes in the twelfth century, in which the invading Teutonic knights were spectacularly drowned in the waters of Lake Peipus, swallowed up amidst the breaking ice. Naturally, this film was among those consigned to the vaults for the duration of the Nazi–Soviet pact.

Soviet officialdom was still doing its best to keep up the show of friendship wherever possible, though for the most part this never got beyond the stage of fine talk. Schmid was put in charge of cultural relations for the embassy, with the brief to promote exchanges of artists and scientists, but none of the proposals came to anything. The only German artist or performer who was actually invited to Moscow was a conductor, Leo Blech – but he was a Jew and was barred by the Nazis from accepting.

However, when a German opera house decided to mount a production of Glinka's opera about Tsar Ivan Suzarin – in the final scene of which Polish prisoners are seen crossing Red Square after the defeat of Poland by Russian forces – the Soviets went to great trouble to provide Schmid with the score he had been instructed to obtain. What he took to be delaying tactics proved to be the time needed for students of Moscow Conservatory to copy all the parts out by hand, since there were no printed versions available.

Behind the façade, however, Stalin was thinking very hard about the situation. On the economic front, he was prepared to continue the friendship – whatever it cost, he had to have German tools and technology. He ordered Mikoyan to take the brakes off the negotiations he was holding with Schnurre: the amount of grain being offered was suddenly increased from 1·5 to 2·5 million tons, and other problems suddenly evaporated. But politically, it seemed he had reached the point of no return.

Partly as a result of Molotov's Berlin visit, Stalin had begun to realise that Germany might not be as all-powerful, as all-conquering, as everyone thought. The prospect of joining the Axis – which is what signing the Tripartite Pact amounted to – seemed less necessary and less inviting than it had done. For all Hitler's big talk, he had not succeeded in defeating Britain, or even in bringing her to her knees. 'Sea Lion' had had to be called off; the Battle of Britain had been lost; the RAF were hitting Berlin and other German cities every night.

As for the other partners, the Italians, who had invaded Greece at the end of November against Hitler's wishes, were being routed by the Greeks and driven ignominiously back through Albania. Their actions had given the British an excuse to put forces into northern Greece and

Crete, and so far the Axis powers had been able to do nothing about it. In the North African desert, too, the Italians, after a small initial success, were being smashed by the British. There was obviously no need for Stalin to fear the Italians as potential enemies, nor any advantage in having them as allies.

On the Far-Eastern front, the Japanese were posing no threat, either. In fact, quite independently of Hitler, they had proposed a non-aggression pact of their own with the Soviet Union.

Since this was a vitally important moment, however, the decision could not be taken instantly. Stalin's deliberations lasted ten days, during which time he examined every scrap of evidence and talked to every expert. Alexander Yakovlev, who arrived back from Berlin during that time, was one of them.

'Upon my return to Moscow,' he writes, 'I was summoned to the Kremlin virtually from the railway station . . . Stalin, as before, was very keen to know whether the Germans were deceiving us in their sales of air equipment. I reported that now, as a result of this third trip, I could say quite definitely that the Germans had shown us the real level of their aviation technology. And that the models of this technology purchased by us – Messerschmitt 109s, Heinkel 100s, Junkers 88s, Dornier 215s, and others – were representative of the present state of Germany's aircraft industry . . . I said that it was my firm belief that, rendered myopic by their successes in subjugating Europe, the Germans never let the thought enter their heads that the Russians could give as good as they received . . . Late that night, before letting me go home, Stalin said: "Organise the study of the German aircraft by our people. Compare them with our latest. Learn to overcome them." '

The first indication of the way Stalin's thoughts were running came on 20 November, when he announced that he wished to replace Shkvarzev, the engineer who had been his ambassador in Berlin since the pact was signed, who had already travelled back to Moscow with Molotov. In his place, he intended to send none other than Vladimir Dekanozov, the Deputy Foreign Minister, member of the Georgian Mafia with a direct line to himself, and highly experienced intelligence officer and spy master. Short of sending either Molotov or NKVD chief Lavrenti Beria, it would have been impossible to find a more heavyweight appointment in either the diplomatic or intelligence fields. Obviously, it was now more important to have someone in Berlin who could handle politics and espionage, rather than someone who could understand German industry and technology.

While Stalin was deliberating, Hitler was moving fast to consolidate and strengthen his position. The special trains rolled south from Berlin again the day after Molotov left, carrying Hitler to his beloved Berghof, Ribbentrop to Fuschl, and the OKW to their usual railway sidings.

At the Berghof, Hitler spent two days of quiet preparation before embarking on a hectic programme of persuasion and coercion. On 18 November, he saw Spanish Foreign Minister Serrano Suñer, Italian Foreign Minister Ciano, and King Boris of Bulgaria. To the Spaniard he proposed a joint operation against Gibraltar, which would draw Spain into the war against Britain. To Ciano, he delivered a scathing condemnation of Mussolini's misadventure against the Greeks, complaining that it had undermined the credibility of the entire Axis alliance and given the British the excuse to move into Greece and start building air bases within 500 kilometres of the Romanian oilfields. If necessary, he said, he would send German troops through Hungary and Bulgaria to dislodge the British, but this would not be possible until after the winter. In any case, the Germans would need the co-operation of Yugoslavia, and Italy would have to pay for this. He suggested Germany and Italy guarantee Yugoslavia's own frontiers and promise her part of Greece, around Salonika. Mussolini himself, as Hitler well knew, had designs not only on Salonika but also on Yugoslavia.

Ciano, who had not managed to get a word in during Hitler's tirade, hurriedly agreed with this proposal. He even had some good news: as it happened, the Yugoslavs themselves had already made approaches to Italy for an alliance. Hitler was delighted. His mood changed completely, becoming, as Ciano recorded in his diary, 'warm and cordial, at times almost friendly. The idea of an alliance with Yugoslavia excited him to the point that while his pessimism at first appeared too black, now his optimism seems too rosy.'

The interview with King Boris was friendly from the start. Normally, Hitler did not like kings and princes, feeling ill at ease in their company. But Boris was a lively individual, with a very sharp business brain and a passion for donning engineer's overalls and driving his own royal train. He assured Hitler that he had no intention of accepting any Soviet guarantee, and that when the time was right he would accede to the Tripartite Pact, though for the moment it was necessary for him to move with great care, to avoid upsetting Stalin. He was perfectly amenable to allowing German troops to cross his territory on their way to Greece, or anywhere else.

Next day, after a brief meeting at the Berghof with another monarch, Leopold, King of the Belgians, Hitler travelled to Vienna, where on 20 November he met Hungarian Prime Minister Count Teleki and Foreign Minister Count Czaky. That day, Hungary signed the Tripartite Pact. Two days later, back in Berlin, Hitler received the Romanian dictator, General Antonescu, who immediately impressed him with his strength of purpose, soldierly bearing and total agreement with the Nazi cause. Next day, Antonescu too signed the pact, adding Romania to Hitler's growing band of official allies. The day after, 24 November, Slovakia joined, while in Yugoslavia the Foreign Minister accepted an invitation to travel in secret to Berlin for talks on his country's joining, too. In a remarkable four-day period, while waiting for Stalin's reply to the proposal that the Soviet Union should join, Hitler had increased the number of signatories from three to six, with a further two expressing their willingness to sign in due course.

Stalin's answer arrived on 26 November. It was a perfect illustration of the way his mind was working. He could not risk provoking a show-down with Hitler for the moment – neither the Soviet economy nor the Red Army was anywhere near strong enough, yet. Therefore, he could not openly reject Hitler's offer of a share in the Tripartite Pact. At the same time, however, he had to start showing he was not afraid of Germany, posting a warning that the Soviet Union was no push-over and could no longer be bought off cheaply.

So, when Molotov called Schulenburg to his office late on 25 November, he first told him, with Dekanozov looking on impassively, that Stalin had decided to accept Ribbentrop's proposals for Soviet accession to the pact. He then went on to read out the Soviet terms for joining, a list of conditions which was not only impossible but was clearly meant to be. All German troops were to be withdrawn from Finland immediately, and the country handed over to the Soviet Union. Bulgaria was to become a Soviet satellite through a mutual assistance pact, and was to provide military and naval bases for the protection of the Dardanelles and the Bosphorus – so setting off down the road already trodden by the Baltic states. Also in the region of the Straits, Turkey was to be forced, if necessary by joint military action, to agree to Soviet bases on her territory. The area south of Batum and Baku in the general direction of the Persian Gulf was to be recognised as a Soviet interest – in other words, the Soviet Union was to get the Arab and Iranian oilfields. Japan was to renounce her rights to oil and coal in northern Sakhalin, the island off the Siberian coast which had long been a source of contention. Nowhere was there any mention of moves towards the Indian Ocean, nor of sharing out the remains of the bankrupt British Empire.

Hitler understood Stalin's message only too well: by presenting such a list he was signalling that the honeymoon, if not the entire marriage, was over. There would be no more gifts for Hitler: anything he wanted from now on would have to be paid for, or fought for. 'Stalin is clever and cunning,' Hitler told Halder shortly afterwards. 'He demands more and more. He is a cold-blooded blackmailer.' He ordered Ribbentrop not to make any reply. In fact, although the trade talks which Schnurre was holding still went ahead, and economic co-operation – which both partners needed – continued for several more months, there were no political conversations of any importance between Germany and the Soviet Union from that moment until June 1941. Any doubts Hitler may have had about launching an attack in the spring had been finally dispelled. He ordered the army High Command to present its plan.

The German army's war games finished at the beginning of December, and on 5 December, at 3 pm, Brauchitsch and Halder brought the results, in the shape of their draft plan 'Otto', to the Chancellery. For four hours, while a blizzard raged outside the windows, they discussed their ideas and proposals with Hitler, and with Keitel and Jodl, who had already shown Hitler the OKW's operational plan 'Fritz', as prepared by Lossberg.

In general, the two plans had a great deal in common and Hitler approved of most of the ideas expressed in them. However, the linchpin of the army's plan was a powerful drive for Moscow, which was not only the political heart of the Soviet Union but also the hub of its communications systems and the centre of its arms industry. To Halder and Brauchitsch, the capture of Moscow was all-important and would bring about the collapse of the entire Soviet Union.

Hitler did not agree: 'Moscow is not all that important,' he said. What was important was to destroy the Soviet 'life force'. When Brauchitsch protested, he silenced him with the retort: 'Only completely ossified brains, absorbed in the ideas of past centuries, could see any worthwhile objective in taking the capital.' While the army chiefs quite naturally considered the campaign in purely military terms, Hitler's objectives were political. He was concerned with the destruction of bolshevism, and the way to achieve that was to wipe out its breeding grounds, the two cities whose very names glorified the revolution, Leningrad and Stalingrad.

Following the lines suggested by Lossberg, Hitler wanted two great thrusts: one in the north to encircle the Soviet armies in the Baltic states, culminating in the destruction of Leningrad; the other south of the Pripet marshes, to encircle and liquidate the Soviet armies in the Ukraine and open the way for a drive towards Stalingrad. This, he believed, would not take long – 'We shall be in Leningrad in three weeks,' he said. Once he had achieved these objectives, and liberated the Ukrainians and Balts from Stalin's grip, he could decide what to do about Moscow: whether to advance on the city directly, or to bypass it and cut it off from the rear.

He did not press these ideas very strongly, however, but gave instructions for preparation to proceed at full swing on the basis of the planning already carried out. During the build-up for the great campaign in the east, the Wehrmacht could be used to deal with what he saw as the minor problems of removing the British from Gibraltar and Greece, if that should still prove necessary, and rescuing Italy from the results of Mussolini's follies. He did not intend to mount a full-scale occupation of Greece. Any units used there in March could easily be released in time to move back through Yugoslavia, Bulgaria and Romania to take part in the attack on the Soviet Union in May. Meanwhile, 'Sea Lion' was to be abandoned – he now considered an invasion of Britain to be no longer possible.

Hitler waited restlessly while Warlimont's section L of the OKW finalised the draft plans into a directive for him to sign. On 8 December, he received Italian Ambassador Alfieri, who brought confirmation that the Italians had indeed suffered a major disaster in Greece, and would definitely need German help there. He issued a directive five days later, under the codename 'Marita', for a short, sharp campaign in Greece to start in March.

On 10 December, he gave a rousing speech to the workers at the Rheinmetall-Borsig armaments factory in Berlin, which was widely reported in all the papers next day, with photographs of the Führer in full rhetorical flight amid a bower of guns. In this speech, he introduced the first note of his preparation of the German people for the great attack in the east. After fulminating against Britain as usual, he began speaking of the inequalities of the distribution of wealth and resources between nations. Complaining that it was unfair for Germans to have to live at a density of 360 persons per square mile, while other unspecified countries were so thinly populated, he cried: 'We must solve these problems and therefore we shall solve them!'

Next day he left by train for Munich, where he spent two days at his apartment. For once, Ribbentrop stayed behind, though only temporarily, to receive Dekanozov, who had been in Berlin for several days already and who was waiting impatiently to present his credentials to Hitler. He had brought with him a signed photograph of Stalin, which Ribbentrop had asked for during his second visit to Moscow, and which he had told Schulenburg to remind Molotov about before he came to Berlin. Although Molotov had promised to bring it with him, it had not materialised until now. Ribbentrop accepted the gift with the delight of a movie fan getting an autographed picture of his favourite star. He promised Dekanozov a meeting with Hitler on 19 December, then hurried off to his train to head south to Fuschl, to be near his Führer, who had moved on yet again to the Berghof.

After three days among the snow-covered mountains, Hitler was back in Berlin on 17 December, where Jodl was waiting with the completed draft of the new directive. He was annoyed to see that this followed the OKH plan for concentrating the main assault on Moscow, and ordered it to be changed immediately to his own preference for primary attacks in the Baltic and the Ukraine. He was particularly insistent on the northern thrust to drive the Soviets out of the Baltic states and capture Leningrad.

'So with a stroke of the pen,' Warlimont wrote later in disgust, 'a new concept of the main lines of the campaign against Russia was substituted for that which the OKH had worked out as a result of months of painstaking examination and cross-checking from all angles by the best military brains available . . . Thus was produced the patched-up document which set the Wehrmacht off on the fateful road to the east. It was consecrated next day by Hitler's signature.'

The eleven-page document, which Jodl presented next day retyped on the special large-print 'Führer typewriter', was confined to nine copies, to be issued under the strictest security to the Commanders-in-Chief and the OKW only. In addition to the alterations Hitler had demanded to the plan, he had made one more significant change: the operation was to be known not as 'Fritz' or 'Otto', but as 'Barbarossa', the name of the legendary Holy Roman Emperor Frederick I, who had united the German states for the first time and marched them east on a great crusade in 1190. But although 'Barbarossa' undoubtedly had a better ring to it than 'Otto' or 'Fritz', it was in some ways an unfortunate choice, and an odd one for someone as superstitious and concerned with omens as Hitler was: the Emperor Barbarossa never made it to the Holy Land, but drowned in a river on the way, as every German schoolboy knew.

It was not this, however, which made Brauchitsch, Halder and the other generals in the OKH, as well as Grand Admiral Raeder for the navy and Göring for the Luftwaffe, uneasy and unenthusiastic about the great campaign. They were still uncomfortably aware that Britain was not yet defeated, and that they were being faced with the two-front war which every one of them dreaded. They had all argued with Hitler about it. To them the dangers were so obvious that they could not believe he was really serious. Brauchitsch even asked Major Engel, Hitler's army adjutant, 'to establish whether Hitler really intended to resort to force or was only bluffing'. It was a question Stalin was still asking six months later, no doubt for many of the same reasons which prompted the German military chiefs' disbelief. But Hitler had no doubts, and his directive No. 21, dated 18 December 1940, left no room for uncertainty. It began simply and uncompromisingly:

> The German Wehrmacht must be prepared *to crush Soviet Russia in a quick campaign* (Operation Barbarossa) even before the conclusion of the war against England.
>
> For this purpose the *Army* will have to employ all available units, with the reservation that the occupied territories must be secured against surprises.
>
> For the *Luftwaffe* it will be a matter of releasing such strong forces for the eastern campaign in support of the Army that a quick completion of the ground operations can be counted on and that damage to eastern German territory by enemy air attacks will be as slight as possible.

At the same time, the directive continued, 'offensive operations against England, particularly her supply lines, must not be permitted to break down.' To that end, 'the main effort of the *Navy* will remain unequivocally directed against England even during an eastern campaign.'

Preparations for the assault on the USSR were to be completed by 15 May 1941. But secrecy was to be preserved at all costs: the Soviets must not perceive German intentions. The attack, when it came, must be swift and daring, aiming to destroy the Red Army in the west. Soviet units must be cut off and prevented from fleeing into the vastness of Russian territory. The aim of the whole operation was to conquer Russia as far as a line drawn from the Volga in the south to Archangel in the north.

Once the Red Air force was destroyed, the Luftwaffe would then be free to turn its attention to bombing the remaining Soviet industrial centres in the Urals.

Under the heading 'Probable Allies and their Tasks', the roles of Romania and Finland were clearly defined:

The High Command will in due time arrange and determine in what form the armed forces of the two countries will be placed under German command at the time of their intervention.

It will be the task of *Romania* to support with selected forces the attack of the German southern wing, at least in its beginnings; to pin the enemy down where German forces are not committed; and otherwise to render auxiliary service in the rear area.

Finland will cover the concentration of the German *North Group* (parts of the XXI Group) withdrawn from Norway and will operate jointly with it.

Their task was to take the Soviet base at Hanko, protect Petsamo and its ore mines, and then launch an attack to cut the Murmansk railway, thus isolating the port. In addition, the main body of the Finnish army would concentrate on pinning down Russian forces in the Lake Ladoga area.

As far as the grand strategy was concerned, the main German attack would be directed north of the Pripet marshes and would involve two army groups, one driving from Warsaw through Belorussia, the other from East Prussia through the Baltic states towards Leningrad and Kronstadt. Only when the two objectives had been taken would the attack wheel south towards Moscow. South of the Pripet marshes another army group would aim for Kiev and the economically important area of the Donets basin. Romanian forces would cross the lower Pruth and form one arm of a pincer movement through the Ukraine.

In order to preserve secrecy, the directive concluded:

All orders to be issued by the Commanders-in-Chief on the basis of this directive must clearly indicate that they are *precautionary measures* for the possibility that Russia should change her present attitude towards us. The number of officers assigned to the preparatory work at an early date is to be kept as small as possible; additional personnel should be briefed as late as possible and only to the extent required for the activity of each individual. Otherwise, through the discovery of our preparations . . . there is danger that the most serious political and military disadvantages may arise.

The directive was signed 'Adolf Hitler'.

49

'THE WHOLE WORLD
WILL HOLD ITS BREATH'

With the 'Barbarossa' directive issued, the preparations for the great attack began in earnest. For Hitler, there could be no turning back now – though most of his generals and field marshals still refused to believe the decision was final. Even six weeks later, on 31 January, when they issued their deployment directive to the army, Brauchitsch and Halder continued to hedge, perhaps hoping vainly that their opening sentence might turn out to be true: 'In case Russia should change her present attitude towards Germany, all preparations are to be taken as precautionary measures to make it possible to defeat the Soviet Union in a quick campaign even before the end of the war against Britain.'

Hitler spent Christmas in his train visiting his troops in the West – Christmas dinner was eaten in the dining car at Calais – then headed for the snow-covered Berghof for his traditional New Year celebration. His entourage were all struck by his air of calm confidence – reflected in his seasonal greetings card, which showed a photograph of the ancient Greek statue known as the Winged Victory of Samothrace which had been taken from the Louvre in Paris and installed in his private study in Berlin. A frieze of German bombers and fighters was printed above the photograph, with the caption, 'Our Winged Victory'.

Because it was New Year's Eve, he allowed himself one glass of champagne and at midnight had the big picture window in the Great Hall lowered while he stood, glass raised, staring out towards the east, past the Emperor Barbarossa's mythical resting place to the distant, unseen, Carpathian mountains, the Ukraine, and the vast Soviet lands beyond.

Already, he was persuading himself that he had no alternative but to attack in the east, and to do it as quickly as possible. There were three principal reasons behind this. The first he had given to Jodl on 17 December, while making his alterations to the draft directive. 'We must solve all Continental European problems in 1941,' he said, 'since from 1942 on, the United States will be in a position to intervene.' His fear in this instance was well founded: Franklin Delano Roosevelt had been elected for an unprecedented third term as US President on 5 November, and although he had promised the 'fathers and mothers' of America 'Your boys are not going to be sent into any foreign wars,' he had continued with massive rearmament.

On the very same day that Hitler spoke to Jodl, 17 December, Roosevelt had for the first time publicly advocated direct arms aid to Britain, repeating the call on 29 December: 'The people of Europe who are defending themselves do not ask us to do their fighting. They ask us for the implements of war, the tanks, the guns, the freighters, which will enable them to fight for their liberty and our security.' On 6 January he outlined what came to be called the Lend-Lease programme: 'For what we send abroad, we shall be repaid within a reasonable time following the close of hostilities, in similar materials, or at our option, in other goods of many kinds.' From there it was only a matter of time before America entered the war.

Hitler's second reason was his old dictum that Britain was relying on the Soviets to come to her rescue and that only by knocking out the Soviet Union, 'England's last hope', could the British be persuaded to see sense and come to terms.

The third reason had a more familiar ring: it was the pre-emptive strike, the preventive war intended to stop a Soviet attack on Germany, just as in 1939 it had been necessary to stop a Polish invasion. This argument may have been needed to persuade the German people once again that they were not aggressors but victims fighting for their lives, but such is the human capacity for self-delusion that many of the generals and even Hitler himself came to believe it, creating a myth which still lingers today.

In 1945, trapped in the bunker beneath the Chancellery while the Red Army advanced on Berlin through the shattered remains of the Third Reich, Hitler dictated his own justification to Martin Bormann:

'During the war, I had no more difficult decision to make than the attack upon Russia. I had always said we must avoid a two-front war at all costs, and what is more, no one will doubt that I more than anyone had reflected on Napoleon's Russian experience. Then why this war against Russia? And why at the time I chose?

'We had lost hope of being able to end the war by a successful invasion on English soil. For this country, ruled by stupid leaders, had refused to acknowledge our supremacy in Europe and would not conclude a peace without victory with us as long as there was a great power on the Continent which in principle confronted the Reich as an opponent. Consequently, the war would have to go on endlessly, and moreover, with increasingly active participation from the Americans.

The importance of the American potential, the continuous rearmament, the nearness of the English coast, all meant that rationally we should not allow ourselves to be drawn into a long-lasting war. For time – it is always a matter of time! – would of necessity be working against us more and more. In order to persuade the English to surrender, in order to compel them to make peace, we therefore had to remove their hope of confronting us on the Continent with an enemy of our own class, that is, the Red Army. We had no choice: for us it was an inescapable compulsion to remove the Russian piece from the European chessboard. But there was also a second, equally valid reason, which would have been sufficient: the enormous danger that Russia was to us by the very fact of her existence. It would inevitably be fatal for us if she were to attack us some day.

'Our only chance of defeating Russia lay in anticipating her . . . We must not offer the Red Army any advantage of terrain, make our autobahns available to her for the deployment of her motorised formations, allow her the use of our railroad network to move men and *matériel*. If we seized the initiative, we could defeat her on her own territory, in her swamps and moors, but not on the soil of such a civilised country as ours. That would have given them a springboard for the onslaught upon Europe.

'Why 1941? . . . Because we could allow ourselves as little delay as possible, since our enemies in the West were steadily increasing their fighting power. What is more, Stalin himself was by no means remaining inactive. Time was working against us on both fronts. The question, therefore, is not "Why as early as 22 June 1941?" but "Why not earlier?" . . . In the course of the final weeks I was obsessed with the fear that Stalin might forestall me.'

Hitler went on to talk about Germany's economic dependence on Soviet deliveries, and the opportunities this gave Stalin for blackmail. But at the time, he was himself concerned with squeezing every last drop of oil, every last grain of wheat, every last ounce of ore out of Stalin before making his move. In truth, it was Hitler who was doing the blackmailing in January 1941, and Stalin who was paying. Schnurre had completed the economic negotiations with Mikoyan before Christmas, and was ready to sign, but Hitler held him on a short leash while he extracted still more concessions. On 2 January, Molotov doubled his last offer of compensation for the Lithuanian Tip, and five days later Stalin personally agreed to increased deliveries of copper, tin, nickel, tungsten and molybdenum.

On 10 January, a whole complex of treaties was signed in Moscow: the trade deal; compensation of 7·5 million gold dollars for the Lithuanian Tip (on Schnurre's return to Berlin, Ribbentrop eagerly asked to see the gold, and was most disappointed when it was explained that this was a paper transaction which halved the German trade deficit);

agreement on the new boundary between Lithuania and Germany; a lump sum payment for private German property in the Baltic states; and agreements covering the resettlement of Germans from those countries.

A jubilant circular from the Wilhelmstrasse to all embassies and legations described the package as settling all the questions pending between Germany and the Soviet Union. Economically, it claimed, the trade deal meant the final collapse of the English blockade, and the refuting of 'the malicious expectations which our enemies expressed upon conclusion of the first economic agreement that Soviet promises would exist only on paper'. 'The Soviet Union,' it went on, 'has delivered everything that she promised. In many fields she has delivered even more than had originally been agreed upon. In the organisation of the huge shipments, the Soviet Union has performed in a really admirable manner.'

The decks were thus cleared and ready for action. On 7 to 9 January, Hitler had held a council of war at the Berghof with the OKW and the operational chiefs of all three services, in which he outlined his global plans. For the final session, which turned into yet another long speech reviewing the current situation and setting out the grand strategy for the future, Ribbentrop joined the military leaders. After running through the position of Britain, France, Spain, the Balkans and Italy, Hitler came to the Soviet Union. His words were in marked contrast to the Foreign Ministry's circular.

'Stalin, Russia's master, is a clever fellow,' he told the conference. 'He will not take an open stand against Germany, but it must be expected that he will increasingly create problems in situations which are difficult for Germany. He will not hesitate to tear up every written treaty if it suits his purpose. He is driven by the *Drang nach Westen*. Also, he is well aware that after a complete German victory Russia's position would become very precarious.'

Hitler went on to present the defeat of the Soviet Union as the answer to everything. If it did not force Britain to capitulate, it would release the full power of the German forces to finish her off. In addition, it would keep America out of the war in Europe by allowing the Japanese to turn the full power of their forces against her in the Pacific. He had always believed, he said, in destroying the enemy's most important positions in order to advance another step. Therefore, 'Russia must be smashed,' and soon.

'Even though the Russian armed forces are a clay colossus without a head, their future development cannot be predicted with any certainty,' he continued. 'Since Russia has to be beaten in any case, it is better to do it now, while they have no leaders and are poorly equipped, and while they have problems with the development of their armament industry.'

He repeated the strategic objectives which he had outlined in his

'Barbarossa' directive, dismissing the vast distances involved as being 'no greater than those which have already been mastered by the Wehrmacht' and even added a new goal – the oilfields of Baku, on the Caspian Sea. His fantasies flowered as he built up to the climax of his speech, concluding with the promise: 'The gigantic territory of Russia conceals immeasurable riches. Germany must dominate it economically and politically, without annexing it physically. Thus we will have everything we could possibly need to wage war in the future even against whole continents, if need be. We shall be invincible. When we fight this campaign, let Europe hold its breath!'

In Moscow, Stalin was also conferring with his marshals and generals. But what he had to say to them was very different from the arrogant confidence of Hitler's call to arms. Stalin, too, was assessing the state of his forces following extensive war games, but unlike Hitler, he could find no cause for satisfaction in his conclusions.

Senior military commanders had gathered in Moscow from all over the Soviet Union for the annual conference of the Main Military Soviet, to be held during the last week in December 1940. Normally, the chief purpose of this conference was to enable them to report on the state of military and political training in their districts. This time, however, the conference was to go far beyond its traditional objectives. In addition to the commanders of military districts, their chiefs of staff and members of their military district councils, invitations had also been given to commanders of armies, divisions and corps.

The whole week from 23 to 29 December had been set aside for the conference itself. Afterwards, there were to be strategic war games played on charts. 'It was,' declared General M. I. Kazakov, with almost English understatement, 'to be a rather unusual conference.' For a start, its importance was demonstrated by the interest shown by Stalin himself, the defence establishment, and the Politburo. There were members of the Politburo present throughout the entire conference; Zhdanov in particular was there almost all the time.

The first part of the conference was the normal review of military and political preparations during 1940, and an examination of the problems affecting combat training. The second part was devoted to extensive discussions on the latest theories of both offensive and defensive operations. There were five major reports, the most important of which was 'Character of the Modern Offensive Operation', by General Georgi K. Zhukov, the victor of Khalkin-Gol, the battle against the Japanese in Manchuria, now commander of the Kiev Special Military District, who had been responsible for the smooth occupation of Bessarabia and northern Bukovina.

Some generals, like the Jewish Colonel-General Shtern, who had fought against the Japanese with Zhukov in Manchuria, and Lieutenant-

General Romanenko, the commander of the 1st Mechanised Corps, criticised Zhukov on the grounds that his ideas were already out of date. Although the use of armour figured prominently in Zhukov's proposals, simply providing masses of tanks, Romanenko pointed out, did not constitute 'armoured forces' in the modern sense. He pleaded for the creation of complete 'armoured armies'. Zhukov brushed this aside and, after considerable discussion, the conference accepted his broad theories, and occupied itself with working out the details.

On New Year's Eve, divisional and corps commanders were dismissed and allowed to return to their own headquarters. The top generals who remained were due to start a large-scale war game shortly afterwards, but instead were suddenly summoned to the Kremlin to see Stalin. 'He greeted us with a faint nod,' Zhukov recalled later, 'and perfunctorily motioned us to take seats around the table.'

Stalin began by sternly reprimanding Defence Commissar Timoshenko for not clearing with him the speech he had made at the conclusion of the conference, thus putting him firmly in his place in front of the generals. But Timoshenko was not so easily put down. He vigorously protested that he had sent a draft of his speech to Stalin's office, and since he had heard nothing he had presumed the speech had been approved. Stalin changed the subject, moving on to the real purpose of the meeting.

'When is your war game due to start?' he asked.

Having been told it had now been put off until next day, he ordered that the commanders involved should not leave as soon as the game was over – he intended being present at the *post mortem*.

'Who is playing the Blue side,' he asked, 'and who the Red?'

Timoshenko told him Zhukov and Colonel-General F. I. Kuznetsov, commander of the Baltic Military District, had been nominated for the 'Blues', the attackers. The 'Reds' – the defending Soviets – would be commanded by Colonel-General D. G. Pavlov, the top armoured specialist sometimes – erroneously – known as 'the Soviet Guderian', who had recently been appointed commander of the Special Western Military District, supported by General V. Y. Klimovsky, of the same military district.

The following day, in an operations room in the general staff headquarters, the two sides began fighting out the first of the 'operational–strategic games' on the huge charts. Timoshenko supervised everything and acted as umpire. The scenario was based on the premise that a German army had launched an attack on the western frontier of the USSR. The game was played in a calm, almost clinical atmosphere. Each front had up to eighty divisions at its disposal, deployed between East Prussia and the Pripet marshes. 'Both adversaries and all participants were given sufficient time to make decisions and to work out the basic operational documents,' General Kazakov wrote, referring to such items as order of battle and so on. 'I myself had occasion to act in the capacity of Chief of Staff of an army and, subsequently, as commander of a cavalry-mechanised group made up of two corps of cavalry and one motorised corps.'

To general consternation, Zhukov mounted three powerful concentric attacks with his 'Western' forces, wiped out most of the concentrations of the 'Reds' and smashed his way deep into Russia.

In the second game, the contestants changed sides, with Zhukov and Kuznetsov now commanding the defending 'Reds', and the Pavlov team attacking. The theatre of operations this time was in the south-west of the Soviet Union. This time, the results were not so clear cut.

According to precedent, the initial analysis of the games should have been made by Timoshenko himself as Commissar for Defence, or by General K. A. Meretskov, recently appointed Chief of Staff of the Red Army. Instead, Timoshenko invited the two commanders themselves, Zhukov and Pavlov, to criticise their own and each other's performances. Perhaps he intended by this to allow the officers of the operations department more time to process the results of two particularly complex games. Whatever his purpose, however, the result was a humiliation for Meretskov.

On the morning of 13 January, Stalin suddenly telephoned Timoshenko at general staff headquarters and summoned everyone to the Kremlin, where he and the eleven members of the Main Military Council, plus the Politburo and various members of the government, were waiting to learn the results and the conclusions to be drawn from them. As the processing was far from complete, it was left to Meretskov to attempt a summation, relying entirely on his memory.

One of the other generals present at the meeting, A. I. Yeremenko, commander of the North Caucasus Military District, declared later that 'no general would have been able to present an exhaustive analysis of a complex war game' without adequate preparation. Certainly Meretskov was not prepared for the grilling he got from Stalin, nor was he able to recall every move and detail of the two games. Consequently he fumbled and bumbled, embarrassing his fellow officers. When Stalin began to question him in detail, Meretskov – as he frequently did – lost his head and panicked. He told Stalin what he thought the tyrant wanted to hear – that the 'Reds', that is, the Soviets, had won the first game, even though it was clear that the ratio of forces was not in their favour.

When it came to the second game, Stalin acidly demanded: 'Well, who finally won? Was it the "Reds" again?' Meretskov tried to avoid giving a direct answer. Stalin exploded. 'The members of the Politburo . . . want to know which of the opponents in the war games turned out to be the winner!' he shouted. But no intelligible answer was forthcoming from the unfortunate Chief of Staff.

At the end of this fiasco, Stalin took the floor. He was in devastating form. 'It may be,' he declared, 'that for propaganda purposes our regulations should say that a Soviet division can rout a fascist German division, and that in an attack one and a half of our divisions can break through the defences of one enemy division. But among this group of people assembled here, within the circle of present front and army commanders, we have got to discuss practical possibilities.' He then threw the discussion open and invited the other officers to air their views.

After scathing criticism by the aviation commanders on the short-comings of their service's structure and training methods, the ineffable Marshal Kulik, the NKVD's military chief, and like Meretskov one of Stalin's favourites, took the floor, and managed to make an idiot of himself on the subject of the mechanisation of the Red Army. Sounding like some Soviet Colonel Blimp, Kulik insisted that mechanisation was unnecessary. When he had fought in Spain in 1939, he said, infantry supplied by horse-drawn transport had proved more than adequate in inhospitable terrain. If they were good enough to fight Franco, they were good enough for Hitler.

Lieutenant-General Ya. N. Fedorenko, head of the Armoured Forces Administration, immediately took issue with this, but Kulik went on insisting that tanks were of no use. 'The artillery will shoot all your tanks to pieces, why produce them?' he shouted. As a first-class row started to erupt, with Kulik crumbling under the attack not only of other officers but also of members of the Politburo, Stalin intervened. Irritated, he turned to Timoshenko. 'As long as there is such confusion in the army on motorisation and mechanisation, you will never get any mechanisation or motorisation at all.'

Timoshenko would not have this. There was no confusion in the army about the need for mechanisation, he insisted – the only confusion was in Marshal Kulik's mind.

'Well, let's hear what the district commanders have to say,' said Stalin, and he proceeded to ask each in turn how many tank corps he needed in his particular theatre of operations. It was quickly clear that they were unanimous in wanting wholesale mechanisation.

'Everybody,' reported Kazakov, 'noticed that the members of the Politburo received these requests with satisfaction. It was then explained to us why the process of equipping our troops with tanks had proceeded at such a slow pace. We were told that in the last few years the Central Committee and the government had literally forced on the leadership of the People's Commissariat for Defence their views that it was necessary to create large mechanised and tank units, but that the Commissariat for Defence had allegedly shown a strange timidity about adopting them.'

This was a clear attack on Voroshilov, who had fallen from favour because his master held him responsible for the Finnish débâcle. But the attack on the Defence Commissariat boomeranged: many of the officers present in the Kremlin believed that if Stalin had seen errors in the way the army was being equipped, then he should have corrected them. 'We knew,' Kazakov wrote, 'that Stalin himself had taken part in the adoption by the Main Military Council of the erroneous decision of 21 November 1939, on the basis of which the tank corps had been dissolved. And, of course, it was with his knowledge that people like Kulik reached high positions in the army.'

Stalin was not deterred by this. Now, it was Kulik's turn to feel the lash of his anger. 'Kulik defends the massed 18,000-man division with horse-drawn transport,' he charged. 'He has spoken against the mechanisation of the army. The government is pressing on with the mechanisation of the army, it is bringing the motor to the army, but Kulik is against the motor. This is just about the same as if he had spoken out against the tractor and the combine harvester, defending the wooden plough and the economic independence of the village. If the government had adopted Kulik's position at the time of collectivisation, we would still find ourselves with individual peasant farms and wooden ploughs!'

In his final speech to the conference, Stalin spoke of the impending war and the danger of having to fight on two fronts: in the west with Nazi Germany and in the east with imperialist Japan. He made no attempt to predict the date of this war, but he did say that it would be a war of movement, of huge armies. In such a war, he said, supply would be the key to victory – supplies of ammunition, armament, fuel, foodstuffs. 'He spoke,' wrote General A. I. Yeremenko later, 'of the necessity of stockpiling food and termed wise the decision of the government of tsarist Russia to stockpile hardtack [dry biscuits] . . . which is light in weight and can be stored for a long time. "Tea and hardtack," he said earnestly, "already constitute a meal." '

The meeting broke up in some disarray. Shaposhnikov, at sixty-eight the elder statesman of the general staff, 'sat there gloomily . . . only the sad expression in his big, intelligent eyes and the faint twitching of his large head betrayed the "Old Man's" tenseness.'

Some good things did emerge from the conference. The Red Army gained more tanks and more mechanised transport, which was welcome. Meretskov was fired as Chief of the General Staff, and replaced by Zhukov, which was also welcome in certain quarters. But Kulik retained his command until he was demoted in the fall of 1941, and again in 1943. Various other high-level changes were made in the commanders of military districts.

With Stalin's blessing, and under the control of Timoshenko, Zhukov immediately set about speeding up the improvements in the military system which they had already begun, cutting bureaucracy, weeding out imcompetent commanders and generally gearing up for the fight which was so obviously looming on the horizon. But when the new training plan was issued to the Red Army five days after Stalin's meeting with his generals, there was no mention whatever of the likelihood of war.

Throughout January and into February, the twin danger zones of the Balkans and the Baltic continued to vex both Hitler and Stalin, as they manoeuvred for advantage. Romania's allegiance was already settled – Antonescu had opted for alliance with Germany, and his position was strengthened on 20 January by a *coup d'état* mounted by the Nazi-backed Iron Guards. Yugoslavia remained uncertain, and both powers continued to woo her. Bulgaria and Finland became the flashpoints, where the two dictators tested each other's nerves.

Bulgaria was swarming with German 'tourists', wearing plain clothes and driving Volkswagens, busily surveying roads and bridges and assessing rail and river capacities. But as yet, King Boris had not openly sided with Hitler and German troops had not officially started to move into and through his country. Stalin was aware of the situation, however, and proceeded to issue warnings, pointing out that Bulgaria was in the Soviet Union's 'security zone'. Hitler ignored them, and pushed on with his war preparations.

In Finland, too, he continued the steady development of relations, though with a little more caution, especially when Stalin threatened to use force to take control of the Petsamo nickel mines. The canny Finns, wishing only to regain the territory they had lost, chose to regard themselves not as allies of Germany but, when the time came, as 'comrades in arms', which suited Hitler well enough, though Stalin failed to appreciate their logic.

As his war machine gathered momentum, Hitler's confidence grew. When he entertained Mussolini at the Berghof for two days of talks on 19 and 20 January, he said nothing to condemn the Duce's ill-considered ventures in Greece or his failures in North Africa. Instead, he offered German military help in both theatres. He spoke scathingly of the Soviet Union, knowing this would accord with Mussolini's own views. Ciano noted in his diary that he was in a very anti-Russian mood. 'I don't see any great danger coming from *America*,' he said, 'even if she should enter the war. The much greater danger is the gigantic block of Russia. Though we have very favourable political and economic agreements with Russia, I prefer to rely on the powerful means at my disposal.'

He did not, however, say anything about the use of those 'powerful means' in 'Barbarossa': he did not trust the Italians to keep anything secret for five minutes. In any case, he did not want to give them any opportunity to join in, having no intention of sharing the spoils of war with an ally whose help he could well do without.

Hitler's certainty of the Wehrmacht's ability to smash the Red Army was not shared by all his generals. Certainly in the OKW Jodl told Walimont, in response to a query as to whether the Führer was still firm in his intention to carry out Operation 'Barbarossa': 'The Russian colossus will be proved to be a pig's bladder; prick it and it will burst.' But others, notably Halder, Brauchitsch and the army group commanders, had their doubts. The anticipated ease of the victories posed its own problems: the speed of the advance was likely to create enormous supply difficulties. The Soviet rail system was unlikely to be of any use in the early part of the campaign – even if the Soviets did not destroy the track as they retreated. The difference in gauge would prevent German locomotives and rolling stock from using it until it had all been relaid. The German armies would therefore have to rely entirely on motor transport over inadequate Soviet roads to keep them supplied with fuel, ammunition, spares and food over an expected distance of more than 600 miles. General Thomas, the OKW's economic chief, produced the chilling news on 28 January that there was a deficiency of almost fifty per cent in tyre requirements, and that stocks of fuel oil were sufficient only for the concentration of the forces and two months' fighting. And Field Marshals von Leeb, von Bock and von Rundstedt, meeting Halder and Brauchitsch on 31 January to discuss 'Barbarossa' for the first time, all had serious misgivings about the strategic situation.

Brauchitsch, no doubt remembering earlier occasions when he had taken unwelcome information to Hitler, was loath to report this to him; it was left to the lean, austere Bock to raise the subject during an audience two days later. As tactfully as he could, Bock told the Führer that although he had no doubt the German armies could and would defeat the Red Army if the Soviets chose to give battle, he was by no means certain that they could be forced either to stand and fight, or to make peace when they had lost.

Hitler did not explode. Instead, he calmly said he was confident that the loss of Leningrad, Moscow and the Ukraine would make them give up. And if they did not, then German motorised forces would have to drive on, past Moscow to Ekaterinburg. 'In any event,' he went on, 'I am happy that our war production is equal to any demand. We have such an abundance of material that we have had to convert back some of our war plants [to civilian production]. The armed forces now have more manpower than at the beginning of the war, and our economy is in an excellent condition.' Any possibility of dissuading him from proceeding with 'Barbarossa' was dismissed out of hand. 'I shall fight,' he declared. 'I am convinced that our attack will flatten them like a hailstorm.'

None of the generals tried to press their doubts and misgivings on Hitler any further. On 3 February, at noon, they all attended a conference with him in the Chancellery, to discuss the army's operational directive for the campaign in the east. Halder, who had the task of presenting the plan, said nothing to dissuade Hitler. On the contrary, he gave him reassuring news about intelligence assessments of Soviet strength: it was believed there would be only 155 Soviet divisions facing more or less the same number of German, who were 'far superior in quality'. And though they estimated Soviet tank strength at about 10,000, compared with the German total of 3,500, the Soviet tanks were believed to be mostly old and obsolete models.

In this area, Halder was a little more cautious: 'Even so, surprises cannot be ruled out,' he warned. Had he but known, there were indeed some surprises to come, for although total Soviet production of the superb new T-34 medium tank and the KV heavy tank during the whole of 1940 had amounted to only 115 and 234 respectively, during the first six months of 1941 the Soviet factories produced over 1,000 T-34s and 393 KVs. What was more, the estimated number of Red Army divisions on the Soviet western front had to be amended to 247 in April, and when fighting started at least 360 were identified.

Hitler readily agreed with the poor impression Halder had of Soviet arms and production, however. He treated the generals to a ten-minute statistical lecture on Soviet tank production since 1928, rattling off figures and specifications from memory. Unfortunately, the manuals and reports he had memorised were all either faulty or out of date. His figures proved conclusively how thinly armoured and poorly equipped all the Soviet tanks were; in reality, the new models were so strong that no German anti-tank gun was effective against them.

Lack of good, accurate intelligence was a constant problem for the Germans in their planning against the Soviets. 'It would be easier for an Arab in flowing burnous to walk unnoticed through Berlin, than for a foreign agent to pass through Russia!' General Köstring, the military attaché in Moscow, told Abwehr chief Admiral Canaris. And since any Soviet citizen who showed any sign of dissent soon found himself in the gulags, the opportunities for recruiting local agents were few and far between. With reliable information so scarce, the intelligence assessors tended always to belittle Soviet abilities, in line with Nazi ideology which branded all Slavs as *Untermenschen*, inferior beings incapable of great achievement. Most of the information that reached Hitler, therefore, tended to be wildly optimistic – especially since he was inclined to fly into a rage when presented with anything he regarded as negative thinking – thus fuelling his appetite and ambitions still further.

Nothing he heard from Halder or anyone else on 3 February did anything to dent his beliefs. His only worry, it seemed, was that the generals would not be bold or daring enough. He reminded them that it was important to wipe out large sections of the enemy, and not just make them run. He wanted great pincer movements to encircle and cut off the Soviet forces, so that they could be utterly destroyed. He intended to follow every part of the army's preparations in detail and to be personally involved in all decisions. He wanted copies of the maps used for the planning, and situation maps showing the deployment of both German and Soviet forces, each month until the attack was launched. His enthusiasm was greater than ever, and he ended the conference on an even higher note than he had sounded on 9 January: 'When Barbarossa starts, the whole *world* will hold its breath and say nothing.'

50

'WE WILL STAY FRIENDS WITH YOU, WHATEVER HAPPENS'

With only fourteen weeks left until the planned start date for 'Barbarossa' and the movement of the first wave of troops to the east building up steadily, Hitler needed to make sure of his flanks without delay. This, of course, is a basic requirement for any military campaign, but for Hitler the two extremes of his enormous front had an extra importance as the sources of his most vital supplies – nickel and iron ore from Finland and Sweden, and above all oil from Romania.

Finland and the Baltic were reasonably secure already, and he could regard them with a certain amount of confidence. Sweden would remain neutral and continue to supply ore either across the Baltic, which meant the Soviet fleet would need to be dealt with, or through Norway via Narvik. The Finns could be relied on to defend themselves vigorously if they were attacked, with the help of the increasingly large quantities of arms Hitler had been pumping in and of the German troops who were already in the country, 'in transit'. The Petsamo nickel mines would be swiftly taken by a German task force from northern Norway the moment 'Barbarossa' began. The north, therefore, seemed to present no real problems.

At the southern end of the front, however, Romania was still looking vulnerable – and without Romanian oil, the Wehrmacht would not be able to move, let alone fight. Apart from a relatively short Black Sea coastline, Romania was surrounded by potential enemies: the Soviet Union in the north and north-east, Hungary in the north-west, Yugoslavia in the west and Bulgaria in the south. The Soviets, Hitler knew, had powerful forces deployed in Bessarabia and Bukovina, along Romania's northern frontier. Of the other three countries, only Hungary was Germany's ally, and she was separated from the Ploesti oilfields by the Transylvanian Alps. Stalin was making efforts to woo both the Yugoslavs and the Bulgarians. If he succeeded in winning them over to his side, and carrying out his stated wish to offer Bulgaria the same sort of 'mutual assistance' as he had given to the Baltic states, then he would hold Romania helpless in the palm of his hand, ready to be crushed from three sides.

Now, there was an added complication: Mussolini's disastrous attack on Greece, through Albania, had forced Britain to move in, in order to counter the increased threat to the approaches to North Africa and the Suez Canal. Having already thrashed the Italians in North Africa itself, the British were able to start pulling out some 60,000 men, including two Australian divisions and one New Zealand, and shipping them to Greece. They were in the process of setting up bases which would not only give them control of the eastern Mediterranean – including the entrance to the Black Sea – but would also put their bombers within easy range of the Romanian oilfields.

Hitler had already decided he must intervene, despite Mussolini's initial reluctance to humble himself by accepting help. He took over the conduct of the North African campaign from the demoralised Italians, sending an armoured corps of two Panzer divisions, plus one light infantry division, to rescue them. On 6 February, he named General Erwin Rommel as commander of the Afrika Korps, despatching him to Tripoli so quickly that he did not even have time to pack his bags. As soon as the weather was good enough, Hitler proposed to send his troops, which were already in Romania, into Greece to subdue the Greeks and drive out the British, before they could get themselves really established.

Hitler made no attempt to hide the build-up – indeed, he even went out of his way to publicise it. On 22 February, Schulenburg was told that he and the members of the embassy, together with 'any available trusted persons', were to start spreading the word in Moscow that there were now 680,000 German troops in Romania, ready for action; that these included 'an unusually high percentage of technical troops with the most up-to-date military equipment, especially armoured units'; and that 'behind these troops there are inexhaustible reserves in Germany, including the permanent units stationed on the German–Yugoslav border'. Schulenburg was to tell everybody – not only the Soviet government but also all the other diplomatic missions – that these troops were 'more than sufficient to meet any eventuality in the Balkans from any side whatsoever'.

To get to Greece, the Germans had to cross either Bulgaria or Yugoslavia – another reason why Hitler had to win the tussle with Stalin for control of these two countries. The Bulgarians, like most other nations at that time, did not rate Soviet chances very high in a war with

Germany. Determined to be with the winners from the outset, they soon succumbed to Hitler's blandishments.

By the end of January, the Bulgarian general staff had had two series of meetings with Field Marshal List for the OKW, and had agreed the details for allowing German troops in. But they were extremely nervous of the Soviet reaction and asked that nothing be announced until the very last minute. Hence, although agreement for Bulgaria's joining the Tripartite Pact was settled by 8 February, they did not sign for another three weeks, when the Germans were ready to move. Hitler was himself nervous of possible Soviet intervention, since Stalin and Molotov had been vehement in declaring Bulgaria to be part of the Soviet security zone. So Schulenburg was instructed to wait until the evening of 28 February before informing Molotov that Bulgaria was signing the pact next day, and until the evening of 1 March before following up with the news that German troops would be marching in next morning.

To everyone's surprise and relief, Stalin, while complaining bitterly, took no action whatever. He issued no ultimatum to stop or reverse the event. He did not try to carry out reprisals by stopping or even delaying supplies to Germany. Instead, he actually stepped up his deliveries, in a desperate effort to avoid offending Hitler in any way. From the beginning of March onwards, Stalin, who had sneered and railed at the Allied appeasers two years before, became himself the arch appeaser. And the result of this policy was exactly the same as the result of Chamberlain's equally misguided efforts at Bad Godesberg and Munich: Hitler's appetite grew with each concession, his own confidence with every sign of weakness on the part of his adversary.

Yugoslavia proved a more difficult nut for Hitler to crack. Despite their deep internal divisions, the Yugoslavs were united in their desire to stay independent. For week after week, they resisted the efforts of both Hitler and Stalin to persuade them to attach themselves to one or the other side. By mid-February, Hitler was resorting to threats in his efforts to draw Yugoslavia into his orbit, but still they resisted.

The heir to the throne in Yugoslavia, King Peter, had not yet come of age, and the country was ruled by his uncle, Prince Paul, as regent. Paul was himself pro-German, but had to move carefully because public opinion was heavily weighted towards the Soviets. On 4 March, Hitler had him brought to the Berghof in great secrecy and offered him part of Greece, including Salonika, as a bribe. But there was no agreement, and ten days later he was back to issuing even stronger threats. Finally, on Tuesday, 25 March, the Yugoslavs succumbed. The Premier and Foreign Minister were smuggled out of Belgrade to avoid the wrath of their own countrymen, slipped over the frontier in a plain car, and whisked off to Vienna, where they signed the pact and met Hitler at the Imperial Hotel, where he promised to give them Salonika, to guarantee their sovereignty and frontiers, and not to send German troops through their country. They departed for home again swearing to repay Hitler's kindness and understanding with feelings of loyalty and devotion towards Germany.

It seemed as though Hitler had won yet another trick from Stalin, since the Soviets had been outspoken in warning the Yugoslavs not to sign. He was in high spirits as he hosted a birthday dinner for Walther Hewel, Ribbentrop's liaison man in his entourage and a personal friend who had been in Landsberg prison with him back in 1923–4. Throughout the evening he joked and teased Hewel about the fact that at thirty-seven he was not yet married, signing the menu as a souvenir, 'To the peacock, from a well-wisher, Adolf Hitler'.

Before he left Vienna, he was visited by a 'Frau Wolf' – his sister Paula, using his nickname as a pseudonym to cover her true identity and so avoid the unwelcome glare of reflected glory in the military hospital where she worked as a medical secretary. 'Sometimes,' she told him, 'when I am in the mountains I see a little chapel and go in and pray for you.' Hitler, deeply moved, replied, 'You know, I am absolutely convinced that the Lord is holding his protective hand over me.'

Hitler's triumph over Yugoslavia, however, was short-lived. The very next night there was a *coup d'état* in Belgrade. Paul and his government were overthrown in a popular uprising led by senior army and air force officers. The seventeen-year-old King Peter, who escaped from his uncle's minders by climbing out of a window and sliding down a drain pipe, announced that he had ascended the throne. The new government was led by the air force chief, General Dusan Simovic, who immediately refused to ratify the Tripartite Pact, and offered instead to sign a simple non-aggression pact with Germany, thus avoiding either alliance or dependence and completely ruling out all possibility of allowing German troops to cross the country. The Yugoslav people were delighted. There were wild scenes on the streets of Belgrade. Crowds demonstrated outside the German legation and destroyed the German tourist office, and the unfortunate Swedish minister, who was mistaken for a German, was attacked and beaten unconscious. Worse still, from the German point of view, Union Jacks, distributed by the British legation, were appearing everywhere, along with the Stars and Stripes of America, and many of the crowds were singing the *Red Flag*.

When Hitler received news of the coup at noon on 27 March, in a telegram saying the former government ministers had been arrested, he thought at first it was a joke. When he realised it was true, he flew into one of the most violent rages of his life. Screaming that he had been personally insulted, he sent for Ribbentrop, Göring, the army and Luftwaffe commanders, and for the Hungarian and Bulgarian envoys. Then he stormed through the Chancellery to the conference room where Keitel, Jodl and the adjutants were waiting for the daily briefing.

He brandished the telegram at them, 'bursting out spontaneously', as Keitel himself recalled, 'that he had no intention of standing for that: now he would smash Yugoslavia for once and for all; never mind what the new government might tell him, he had been disgracefully betrayed, and a declaration of loyalty now would only be a feint, a ploy to win time.' He intended, he declared, to order immediate attacks on Yugoslavia from the north and east.

He brushed aside Keitel's protests that they could not mount such attacks now because they were locked into the carefully planned timetable for 'Barbarossa' with the railways operating to maximum capacity, that Field Marshal List's army in Bulgaria was not strong enough for the job, and that they could not rely on the Hungarians for help. 'Some solution will have to be found,' he stormed. 'I intend to make a clean sweep in the Balkans – it is time people got to know me better. Siberia has always been a state prone to *Putsch*, so I am going to clean her up.'

For anyone who wanted to get to know Hitler better, his actions now provided a most revealing insight into his true character. It seemed his personal spite, his desire to punish a small nation which had dared to slight him, took precedence over the great crusade in the east. Yugoslavia must be made an example to all small states, a dire warning not to cross him. As the military chiefs hurried in from their various offices around Berlin, they were treated to a diatribe against Yugoslavia, especially the Serbs and Slovenes. Brauchitsch and Halder were among the last to arrive, along with Ribbentrop, who had been called from a meeting with Japanese Foreign Minister Yosuke Matsuoka, who had arrived on an official visit the previous evening and was due to meet Hitler at 4 o'clock that afternoon.

When they were all gathered, Hitler told them he was determined to smash Yugoslavia both militarily and as a state. The moment was right, he said, both for political and military reasons – it would have been much worse if the coup had taken place during 'Barbarossa'. There would be no ultimatum, no diplomatic approach – Ribbentrop, according to Keitel, was not allowed even to open his mouth – Hitler did not wish to hear any promises. 'The Yugoslavs,' he spat, 'would swear black is white. Of course they will say they have no warlike intentions, and when we march into Greece they will stab us in the back!'

Hungary, Bulgaria and Italy would be called on to help. He had already spoken to the Hungarian minister for fifteen minutes while the conference was assembling, and broke off halfway through to talk to the Bulgarian envoy for five minutes. Later that day he would send a message direct to Mussolini. They would all be paid for their co-operation with pieces of the dismembered corpse of Yugoslavia – the Adriatic coast for Italy, the Banat region north of Belgrade and the port of Fiume (Rijeka) for Hungary, Macedonia for Bulgaria. The attack must start as soon as possible. 'Politically,' he declared, 'it is especially important that the blow against Yugoslavia be carried out with merciless severity, and that the military destruction be carried out in a *Blitzkrieg* operation.'

The mood of the meeting became one of exhileration as he poured out a stream of orders. Amazingly, he already had a complete plan formulated in his mind covering all the German forces and those of her three allies. It was vital, he said, to strike with sufficient strength right at the beginning. Extra troops could be taken from the concentration echelons for 'Barbarossa' to make sure of this. The Luftwaffe was to wipe out the Yugoslav air force on the ground and then totally destroy Belgrade with wave after wave of bombers.

Preparations were to start immediately, he ordered. He wanted the OKW's operational plan that same night – and he got it, from Jodl, who had worked non-stop with Warlimont and the army staff, at 4 o'clock next morning in a document which he issued as directive No. 25, starting: 'The military putsch in Yugoslavia has changed the political situation in the Balkans. Even if Yugoslavia should at first give declarations of loyalty, she is to be regarded as an enemy and therefore is to be destroyed as quickly as possible.'

Because of this new operation, 'Barbarossa' would have to be postponed for up to four weeks, he said. In the event, the delay was to be five weeks – five weeks which were to prove fatal to the great attack, when the icy Russian winter froze the Germans into immobility on the very outskirts of Moscow. But in fact, it was not entirely time wasted: that spring was exceptionally wet in central Europe, and the boggy ground, flooded dykes and swollen rivers meant Hitler's Panzers could not operate until early June in any case, when everything dried out again.

The welcome given to Japanese Foreign Minister Matsuoka on his arrival in Berlin made a striking contrast with that given to Molotov four months earlier. If there had ever been any doubts about the ersatz nature of Hitler's supposed friendship with the Soviet Union, the difference between the two receptions dispelled them in a most obvious way. While the hammer and sickle had been carefully obscured on the flags at the Anhalter station in November, the rising sun of Japan's emblem was displayed not only in the flags intertwined with those of Germany and Italy at the end of the track, but also in a huge wreath of yellow chrysanthemums at the station entrance.

Where the streets had been deserted for Molotov, hundreds of thousands of people – the Nazi papers claimed a figure of a million – had been released from their jobs and marched to prearranged spots on the pavements throughout the afternoon. Military bands were stationed at intervals along the route, and at other points martial music was relayed through loudspeakers. Bundles of paper flags were tossed out of trucks passing along the lines, for the people to wave. There were flagstaffs jutting from the rooftops every five feet along the way, with others, supporting Japanese, German and occasionally Italian flags, between each pair of lamp posts, all the way from the station to the Schloss Bellevue, where the Japanese party were to stay.

When Matsuoka arrived at the Chancellery next day for his meeting with Hitler at 4 pm, there were more crowds – 150,000 marshalled in the Wilhelmplatz alone – and for his departure on 30 March, Goebbels's newspaper *Der Angriff* ordered them to make another appearance: 'The Berlin population will take their places along the given route towards 16 hours to say farewell.'

On his way to Berlin, Matsuoka had stopped off in Moscow. He had intended to make only a courtesy call on Molotov, but the Soviets had invited him to meet Stalin, too. He had spent some thirty minutes talking to Molotov and then a further hour with Stalin, lecturing him for most of the time on Japanese ideology and claiming that although their ancestors had many years ago rejected the idea of political or economic communism, the Japanese people were 'moral communists'. He had floated the idea of a trade treaty and a non-aggression pact between Japan and Germany, and had also done his best to encourage Stalin to join the Tripartite Pact, but had received little encouragement.

In Berlin, Hitler and Ribbentrop both did their best to persuade the Japanese to go to war against Britain in the Far East, urging them to attack Singapore immediately, and to prepare for war against the United States as soon as possible. To Matsuoka's surprise, Ribbentrop – who had always tried to push Japan into closer friendship with the Soviet Union – was suddenly advising caution in this area. Both Ribbentrop and Hitler spoke scathingly about the Soviets, dropping a series of heavy hints that there might be trouble before long. But neither said anything whatsoever about 'Barbarossa'. Hitler had specifically forbidden any mention of it to the Japanese at any level, in spite of pleas from Halder and Grand Admiral Raeder that Matsuoka should be told, so that Japan could be prepared to join in, at least to provide a diversion, at best to force Stalin to fight on two fronts. But Hitler had no intention of sharing the glory or the spoils of what he saw as another easy victim, and in this he was backed up by the OKW. Warlimont recorded that the attitude in OKW headquarters was summed up in the phrase coined there: 'We don't need anyone just to strip the corpses!'

So Matsuoka went on his way, first to Rome, then briefly back to Berlin on 4 and 5 April before departing for home again via Moscow, blissfully unaware of Hitler's true intentions towards the Soviet Union.

By the time Matsuoka arrived back in Berlin from Rome on 4 April, Hitler's preparations both for the campaign in the Balkans and for 'Barbarossa' had moved forward decisively. Since Hitler's outburst on

27 March, completely new plans had been prepared for 'Marita', the operation to drive the British out of Greece, to include a simultaneous attack on Yugoslavia. By any standards, this was an almost incredible feat of general staff work, as Keitel noted in his memoirs: 'When one bears in mind that all our previous plans for the attack on Russia, the campaign in Greece and aid for Italy were just dropped for the time being and new dispositions, troop movements, redistributions, the agreements with Hungary about the operations, the transit of German troops and the organisation of the whole supply system had to be improvised from scratch, and despite all this the invasion of Yugoslavia – coupled with an air strike on Belgrade – followed only nine days later, the achievement of the operations staffs of the High Command, the War Office and the air force can only be termed an outstanding performance, of which admittedly the lion's share was borne by the army general staff.'

The attack was to begin at dawn on Palm Sunday, 6 April. It was another test of Stalin's nerve, and Hitler was once again in an agony of suspense as the days passed. Would Stalin intervene? Would he take the opportunity to invade Romania and cut off Germany's oil supplies? On 31 March, in a desperate and rather transparent effort to frighten Germany off, the Yugoslav military attaché told the German embassy that the Soviet authorities (he did not specify exactly who) 'had summoned him and offered to deliver war material to Yugoslavia', though he said he had turned the offer down. There was also a report, which was sharply denied in *Pravda* on 1 April, that the Soviet government had sent the new regime in Belgrade a telegram of congratulations after the putsch.

Hitler did not take either of these reports seriously, though he still sent word to Antonescu in Romania 'suggesting' that border defences should be strengthened and the oilfields protected 'both against air raids and against the dropping of demolition teams by parachute at night'. On 5 April, the Romanians reported that the Soviets had increased their aerial photographic reconnaissance flights over Romania, that at least sixty Soviet aircraft had suddenly arrived at the Bessarabian airfield of Leofa, and that the Red Army had established a new paratroop school at Kiev.

This was worrying enough, but it was not all. That morning Hitler had heard, both from Göring's Forschungsamt and from Schulenburg in Moscow, that the Yugoslavs were negotiating for a friendship and non-aggression pact with the Soviet Union. Molotov had sent for Schulenburg late the previous evening, and had told him the pact would probably be signed within the next twenty-four hours. When Schulenburg protested about this, Molotov replied that Yugoslavia had already signed the Tripartite Pact with Germany, so why could she not sign something less far-reaching with the Soviet Union?

The pact was signed in the early hours of Sunday, 6 April. At 5.30

that morning, the German armies crashed across the frontiers of both Greece and Yugoslavia, and Luftwaffe planes began their bombing missions against Yugoslav air bases, railways and the undefended city of Belgrade. This was a moment of truth for Stalin. Halder noted in his diary review of that day: 'Disposition of the Russian forces gives food for thought. If one discounts the much-advertised idea that the Russians want peace and would not attack on their own account, one cannot help admitting that their troop dispositions are such as to enable them to pass to the offensive on shortest notice. This might become extremely unpleasant for us.'

In fact, Stalin did nothing. It may have been that he was hoping the Germans would get bogged down for several months in the difficult terrain of Yugoslavia, thus losing the opportunity of invading the Soviet Union that year before winter set in, and giving him desperately needed breathing space, at least until the spring of 1942. Or it may simply have been that Hitler had called his bluff. Either way, he did nothing and said nothing, as the Germans proceeded to astonish everybody once more by the speed of their progress. Advance units of one Panzer division reached Skopje, the capital of Macedonia, as early as 7 April, having fought their way through sixty miles of difficult and hostile terrain in thirty-two hours.

Schulenburg finally managed to inform Molotov officially of the attack at 4 in the afternoon – the Soviet Premier always spent Sundays at his dacha out of Moscow and had not been contactable until then. Molotov did not even mention the Soviet pact with Yugoslavia, but confined himself to repeating several times that 'it was extremely deplorable that an extension of the war had thus proved inevitable after all'. And when Dekanozov called on Weizsäcker on 8 April – he was never received by Ribbentrop these days – it was only to discuss minor matters. He did ask Weizsäcker if he could tell him anything about the military situation in the Balkans, and was surprised to learn that not only had the Germans taken Skopje but that in one place they had already reached the Aegean Sea. But to the State Secretary's great surprise, 'he did not make one word of criticism of our intervention in Yugoslavia.'

Stalin and his military chiefs could only look on in horrified trepidation at the latest demonstration of German power and efficiency as the German armies smashed on through Yugoslavia and Greece. The Hungarians and Italians hurriedly joined them on 10 April, when the scale of their success was clear. On 12 April, less than a week after the start of the campaign, the German XLVI Panzer Corps stormed into Belgrade – or what was left of it after more than 500 almost non-stop bombing raids had reduced it to rubble and killed over 17,000 civilians in an operation which Hitler had significantly codenamed 'Punishment'. On 13 April, Easter Sunday, the city fell.

Stalin's hopes of seeing Hitler bogged down in the Balkans were finally extinguished that same day, when the British started preparing to pull out of Greece after the Germans had broken through their defence lines and taken their strongpoints. And to complete the picture of German invincibility, news arrived from North Africa that after a week of continuous advances through Libya, Rommel had surrounded the British and Commonwealth forces in Tobruk, and was at the Egyptian border. There really did seem to be no chance of anybody being able to halt the Nazi war machine.

In Moscow, Matsuoka was about to leave for home after a week of total frustration. Day after day, he had tried to persuade Stalin and Molotov to agree to a treaty which would leave Japan free to fight Britain and the United States without having to worry about her back. The Soviet leaders had been at their most intractable. They had resisted every effort by the Japanese Foreign Minister to reach a compromise on the issues which divided them, constantly demanding impossible conditions. American and British journalists in Moscow had already reported that his visit had been a complete failure.

Suddenly, Stalin called Matsuoka back to the Kremlin on the evening of 12 April. Making a show of having been forced to concede by Matsuoka's tough negotiating – 'You are choking me!' he exclaimed, making the appropriate throttling gesture with his hands – he withdrew the Soviet demands and suggested they sign a full-scale neutrality pact. When the Japanese Foreign Minister asked how this would affect the Tripartite Pact, and Stalin's attitude towards it, Stalin answered that he was 'a convinced adherent of the Axis, and an opponent of England and America'.

The treaty was signed at 2 pm next day, 13 April, startling all the observers who had written off any possibility of success. But there was an even more remarkable episode still to come, later that afternoon at the station when Matsuoka was leaving on the Trans-Siberian Railway. The departure had been put back for one hour, because of the signing ceremony, after which there had been a celebration party at which Stalin himself had carried plates of delicacies to the Japanese delegates. There had also been many toasts, with the vodka flowing freely, as a result of which it soon became obvious that Matsuoka, who did not hold his liquor well, was drunk. Stalin, of course, was not – he was sticking to his usual tipples of water and wine, reserving his hard drinking for the private, all-night sessions at his dacha.

'The treaty has been made,' Matsuoka said, turning boozily to Stalin. 'I do not lie. If I lie, my head shall be yours. If you lie, be sure I shall come for your head.'

'My head is important to my country,' Stalin replied drily. 'So is yours to your country. Let's take care to keep both our heads on our shoulders.'

Later in the afternoon, Stalin told the Japanese Foreign Minister, 'You are an Asiatic. So am I.'

'We are all Asiatics,' declared Matsuoka. 'Let's drink to Asiatics.'

It was in this frame of mind that Matsuoka left for the Jaroslavl station, where almost the entire press and Diplomatic Corps were assembled. To everyone's absolute amazement, both Stalin and Molotov suddenly appeared on the platform, an unheard-of event, particularly for Stalin, who never saw off any visiting dignitaries, and certainly not mere Foreign Ministers. Yet here he was, approaching Matsuoka in what Schulenburg described as 'a remarkably friendly manner', embracing him and wishing him a pleasant journey.

Some of those present wondered whether Stalin might be drunk, as well as Matsuoka, since his left eye seemed to be half closed, he groped for the right words, and he appeared to look much older than usual. In retrospect, however, it is clear that he knew precisely what he was doing, and that he had deliberately staged the scene at the station in order to attract the maximum attention.

'The European problem,' he was heard to say loudly to Matsuoka, 'can be solved in a natural way if Japan and the Soviets co-operate.'

'Not only the European problem,' the Japanese replied expansively. 'Asia can be solved, too.'

'The whole world can be settled!' Stalin cried.

Before the train pulled out, Stalin looked around and publicly called for Schulenburg. Spotting him standing nearby, he marched up to him, threw an arm around his shoulders and proclaimed, 'We must remain friends and you must now do everything to that end.' A few minutes later, seeing Colonel Hans Krebs, the acting military attaché who was standing in for General Köstring who was on sick leave in Germany, he first made sure he was a German, then took his right hand, pressed it strongly between both of his, and said loudly, 'We will stay friends with you, whatever happens.'

Hitler had taken to his special train again on 10 April, to be as near the fighting as possible. He spent most of April sitting in a railway siding at Mönichkirchen, near Graz, at one end of a 3,000-metre-long tunnel through the Alps, directing 'Marita' from there via the OKW's faultless radio communications system, his only other contact with the fighting being the rough-cuts of newsreel films, shown twice weekly in the nearby Mönichkirchener Hof Hotel which the OKW had commandeered. The newsreels were without a soundtrack, and the commentary had to be read out from a script by one of the adjutants.

His ministers and other functionaries had to travel there to see him, as did Hungary's dictator, Admiral Horthy – and a young Luftwaffe lieutenant, Franz von Werra, 'the one who got away', the only German prisoner of war to escape from the British, leaping from a train in

Canada and getting out through the United States. Other personal callers included King Boris of Bulgaria, anxious like Horthy to discuss his country's share of Yugoslavia and Greece, and Italian Foreign Minister Ciano, who arrived on 20 April to congratulate the Führer on his fifty-second birthday. So, too, did Grand Admiral Raeder, who kept on asking if Hitler had told Matsuoka about 'Barbarossa', as he had urged him to. Hitler admitted that he had only hinted at it – but he was surprisingly positive in his reaction to the Russo-Japanese pact: it would, he said, allow the Japanese to concentrate all their energies on attacking Singapore and helping to knock out the British, rather than Vladivostok, where they were not needed.

In fact, to the great relief of his staff, their stay in the cramped confines of the train lasted only two weeks, until 25 April, for the operation against Yugoslavia ended on 17 April with the unconditional surrender of the Serbian army, and the Greek campaign was all but settled. The swastika was flying over the Acropolis in Athens on 27 April, and by the end of the month the last British and Commonwealth troops had left the Peloponnese; their only remaining foothold was in Crete, and before he returned to Berlin Hitler signed directive No. 28, 'Operation Mercury', to deal with this by a massed paratroop attack.

There was now little chance that anyone or anything could persuade Hitler to call off 'Barbarossa'. The last person to try was probably Schulenburg, who had returned to Berlin on 14 April, the day after Stalin had embraced him at the Jaroslavl railway station. Schulenburg had been trying to get back to Germany since the beginning of the year, primarily so that he could inspect the final stages of the restoration of Burg Falkenberg, the ruined castle he had bought in the Oberpfalz, but his requests for leave were constantly deferred. Hitler and Ribbentrop needed him to stay at his post. The work on the castle was now complete, but although he was officially home on leave, he was given little chance of enjoying it, or of planning the furnishing. The real purpose of his trip was to see Hitler, present the Foreign Ministry's arguments on why there should be no war with the Soviet Union, and convince him of Stalin's peaceful intentions.

After kicking his heels in Berlin for several days, staying at the Adlon with Gebhardt von Walther, who had taken Johnnie Herwarth's place as his secretary, he was finally granted an audience on 28 April, immediately after Hitler had returned from the Balkan campaign. The night before, Schulenburg had dinner at Karl Schnurre's house with Schnurre and the Herwarths – Johnnie was in Berlin attending an army course for military interpreters and Pussi had travelled back with Schulenburg since she was expecting her first baby as a result of her husband's last visit to Moscow. Schnurre was pessimistic about the ambassador's chances of influencing Hitler: he remembered how Hitler had grilled him about the Soviet Union for an hour and a half when he had returned from signing the last economic agreements in January. Hitler had wanted to know everything about Moscow, Stalin and the Soviet regime, but had categorically denied that he was even considering an attack – a denial which they all knew was a blatant lie.

Next day, Schulenburg and Walther left the Adlon at 5 pm for the Chancellery. Pussi Herwarth saw them off, and Schulenburg asked her to wait in the hotel lobby until they returned, still hoping that he could achieve the miracle which had eluded everyone else by persuading Hitler to see reason. Before he left Moscow, he had written a long memorandum for Ribbentrop to give Hitler, explaining the situation in the Soviet Union and setting out clearly and forcefully all the arguments against war. Although Ribbentrop had toned down the memorandum, to Schulenburg the arguments were so powerful that he believed Hitler must acknowledge them – though he anticipated a long and difficult meeting while they were discussed. In the event, the meeting lasted exactly thirty minutes.

Hitler received them coolly but courteously in his study. Schulenburg's memorandum lay on the table before him, but he gave no indication whatever that he had even looked at it. Instead, he asked whether the ambassador would be back in Moscow for the May Day celebrations, talked about the Soviet–Japanese pact, and asked what kind of devil had possessed the Russians to sign a friendship pact with Yugoslavia. He went on at some length about Britain, whom he blamed for everything, as usual, and brushed aside Schulenburg's assurances that Stalin had no intention of joining up with the British: if Britain and France had been unable to win him round in 1939, when they were still strong, Schulenburg argued, they were certainly not going to be able to do so now, 'when France had been destroyed and Britain badly battered'.

Schulenburg insisted that Hitler could rely on Stalin to honour his commitments and not to attack Germany. All Stalin's recent actions, Schulenburg said, arose solely from his fears for the Soviet Union's security, and were therefore defensive rather than offensive. He was convinced that Stalin was even prepared to make further economic concessions, pointing out that he had hinted strongly to Schnurre that if the Germans applied in due time, 'Russia could supply us with up to five million tons of grain next year'. But Hitler did not wish to hear such things. 'Russian deliveries are limited by transportation conditions,' he responded dismissively. When Schulenburg pointed out that transport difficulties could easily be overcome by use of Soviet ports, Hitler abruptly ended the discussion by standing and putting the unread memorandum into the drawer of his desk. Shaking hands with them both, he said, 'Thank you, that was extremely interesting.' As they reached the door, he called out, 'Oh, one more thing: I do not intend a war against Russia.'

'The die has been cast,' Schulenburg told Gustav Hilger at the airport as he arrived back in Moscow. 'War has been decided!' In the privacy of the car as they drove to the embassy, he described his meeting with Hitler, and what had been said. When Hilger asked how this squared with his statement that Hitler had decided on war, Schulenburg shrugged his shoulders in resignation. 'Well,' he replied, 'he deliberately lied to me.'

That same day, 30 April, after conferring with Jodl, Hitler fixed the new date for 'Barbarossa': it was to begin in seven and a half weeks' time, at dawn on Sunday, 22 June 1941. And with that settled, he took time off to drive out to Ribbentrop's villa in the Berlin suburb of Dahlem, to help celebrate his Foreign Minister's forty-eighth birthday.

51

'THE BLIND TOOL OF GERMANY'

April had been a depressing month in Moscow, with icy winds, lowering skies and dirty piles of winter snow lingering in the cobbled streets. 'Spring,' complained *Pravda*, 'has stayed somewhere in the south.' But 1 May dawned bright and clear, with the first warm sunshine of the year. Moscow was *en fête* for the annual holiday and the traditional May Day parade through Red Square, with red flags, banners bearing revolutionary slogans, and photographs of Lenin and the present Politburo members hanging everywhere.

Onlookers gathering in the square to watch the parade saw the various dignitaries taking their places on the saluting base on the top of the highly polished red marble box that was Lenin's mausoleum. All the usual faces were present – Stalin, Voroshilov, Molotov, Mikoyan, Kalinin and so on. But among them could be seen someone new – Ambassador Dekanozov. And he was conspicuously placed next to Stalin himself, at his right hand.

Any change in the order of precedence among the party hierarchy on occasions such as this was seen by Muscovites and knowledgeable foreign observers alike as reflecting real changes in political status within the Kremlin's magic circle. The fact that a mere ambassador was thus favoured could only signify the overwhelming importance attached by Stalin to the diplomatic post the man now occupied. Schulenburg, sitting in the box reserved for members of the Diplomatic Corps, immediately recognised this as a clear signal of Stalin's complete confidence in Dekanozov, and a significant gesture of friendship towards Germany.

The parade that followed, however, was just as clearly a warning, a demonstration of Soviet strength. As the bells in the Spassky Tower opposite the fantastically coloured domes of St Basil's Cathedral started to clang the hour, Marshal Timoshenko rode into Red Square on a handsome chestnut stallion. Following him came squadrons of the latest Soviet tanks and armoured cars, and then some 50,000 troops, including naval units, civilian home guards and women's sanitary units, as well as regular infantry. Before the last of the procession had crossed the square, nearly 300 Soviet air force planes flew in formation overhead. All the while, a 500-piece military band played rousing marches. Schulenburg noted that an unusually large number of generals and admirals of the Red Army and Red Fleet took part in the review. When Timoshenko had completed his ride across the square, he dismounted and joined the other leaders on top of Lenin's tomb, taking his place next to Stalin, on his left, so that the Soviet dictator was flanked by the twin symbols of his dual message, diplomacy and defence.

It was Timoshenko, however, who made the May Day speech at the parade. The section dealing with the international situation summed up Stalin's attitude perfectly:

'The government of the Soviet Union firmly and consistently carries forward the wise foreign policy of Stalin, the policy of peace among the peoples and the guarantee for the security of our fatherland. In this, it meets with the sympathies of the peoples of the countries waging war. The Soviet Union stands outside the war and fights against its extension. That is the purpose of the neutrality pact with our eastern neighbour, Japan, as well as of other international acts of the Soviet government. We are for peace and for the consolidation of friendly and good-neighbourly relations with all countries which are seeking to establish the same relations with the Soviet Union. The Bolshevik Party and the Soviet government take account of the fact... that the international situation is very heated and harbours all sorts of surprises. That is why the entire Soviet people, the Red Army, and the navy must be in readiness to fight.'

In Germany, May Day, although still celebrated as the day of labour and treated as a public holiday, was no longer the occasion it used to be. Gone were the compulsory marches by workers and employers in every city. In Berlin, the hundreds of thousands who used to gather in the Olympic Stadium, the Tempelhof or the Lustgarten for an address by Hitler were left to their own devices. The only speech by a Nazi leader was made by Rudolph Hess, the Deputy Führer, in the Messerschmitt plane factory at Augsburg, and broadcast throughout the Reich. Its tone was markedly different from Timoshenko's: 'I call upon you in the name of the Führer to greater achievements in the production battle of German factories for the year 1941–2. From now on until next May I am sure our production will not decrease. We are near a military decision in this war and the German worker will aid in its realisation.'

The 'German workers' exhorted by Hess now included more than two million men from the occupied countries, forced to labour on Germany's behalf in order to feed themselves and their families. In addition, millions of prisoners were employed on construction and repairing bomb damage, thus freeing Germans for armaments manufacture and for military service. Millions more were released by the employment of young people for a year's compulsory labour service. But with the Wehrmacht increasing in size every day, there was still a chronic shortage of labour, and workers in Germany, just as in the Soviet Union, were not allowed to leave their jobs.

There can be few better examples of Stalin's twin aims of placating Hitler and preparing his own people than the events surrounding the speech he made at a grand banquet in the Kremlin on 5 May for several hundred graduates of sixteen military academies and nine university military faculties. The guests included members of the government and many high-ranking officers of the armed services, but no foreigners of any description. No text was ever issued, and no one took notes at the time, so there is no official version of what Stalin said in his forty-minute speech, apart from a brief report in *Pravda* on 6 May quoting him as saying: 'In the current complicated international situation, we must be prepared for any surprises.' A statement that was, to say the least, somewhat ambiguous.

Shortly afterwards, however, the Moscow correspondent of the German news agency DNB, a man called Schüle, was approached by an officer who had been present and who was prepared to leak the contents of Stalin's secret speech to him. According to the anonymous Soviet officer: 'Stalin devoted more than two thirds of his speech to a precise and completely dispassionate comparison between the German and Soviet war potential. In his well-known quiet manner of speaking, without any emotion of any kind, he gave his listeners a detailed demonstration of the strength and equipment of the German army, navy and Luftwaffe, by means of some figures, and just as clearly indicated the achievements of the German war and armaments industry, from time to time comparing them with corresponding data on the Soviet war potential.' Stalin's conclusion, the officer said, was that the Red Army was no match for the Wehrmacht, that the Soviets must take this into account and that they must press on with all their strength to complete their preparations for the defence of their country. The impression he was said to have left was that he was obviously trying to prepare his audience for a new compromise with Germany.

Seen in this light, the *Pravda* report could also refer to the possibility of new concessions and some sort of new deal. But was that what Stalin had really said? Later, during the war, Hilger talked to many captured officers who had been at the banquet. Their version of what Stalin had said was quite different from that which had been so carefully fed to the Germans through the DNB man. When 'a high-ranking general had proposed a toast to the peace policy of the Soviet Union, Stalin had replied, 'The slogan "long live the peace policy of the Soviet Union" is now outdated. It's about time to end this old nonsense.' And when someone else toasted the friendship with Germany, Stalin was said to have replied that the Soviet people should stop praising the German army to the skies. .

Other sources give Stalin's speech as following this line much more closely than the leaked version. 'Our glorious Red Army,' he is reported as saying, 'must be prepared to fight fascist Germany at any moment.' Needless to say, the Soviet government would try 'by all means at its disposal to delay a German attack . . . at least until the autumn'. By then it would be too late for that year. Autumn rains and the onset of winter would reduce the mobility of any invading army. If this strategy succeeded, if Germany could be kept at bay for the whole of 1941, then 'almost inevitably' there would be a war in 1942. But that war would be fought in circumstances much more favourable to the USSR. For one thing, the Red Army would be better trained and equipped. It would be in a position to take the initiative. Indeed, to forestall a German attack, the USSR might have to strike first.

From the Soviet domestic point of view, it did not matter what Stalin actually said. The gist of his speech – that the country was in imminent danger from Germany – was all over Moscow within twenty-four hours, and Muscovites drew their own conclusions. Their worst fears must have seemed confirmed when they read in *Pravda* on 6 May, along with the brief and ambiguous report of his speech, the much more surprising news that he had replaced Molotov as Chairman of the Council of People's Commissars, the Soviet Prime Minister, thus becoming head of the government as well as the party. After nearly two decades of wielding power behind the scenes, through the medium of the Communist Party, Stalin had now decided to move centre stage. With one eye to the historical significance of the post, he chose to take over the position first occupied by Lenin, thus becoming Lenin's successor in name as well as in fact. Henceforth, Molotov would be Deputy Chairman, while retaining his position as Foreign Commissar.

Of course, in terms of real political power the 'promotion' of Stalin was meaningless. He already held near absolute power, ruling the USSR as surely as Peter the Great or Nicholas I had ruled Russia. Instead, the move must be seen as a piece of political theatre: the stage trap door sprang open and up jumped the Demon King to take charge of the proceedings. It was a signal to the Soviet people that the international situation had grown so dangerous that the USSR could no longer be left in the hands of lesser men: only the great Stalin himself could be trusted to lead the country through the treacherous quicksands that lay ahead.

The signal to the outside world was very similar, though it was perhaps even more important. Certainly, Molotov's deputy, Vyshinsky, and the senior officials of the Foreign Commissariat thought so – they told the new ambassador of Vichy France, Gaston Bergery, that Stalin's appointment was 'the greatest historical event in the Soviet Union since its inception'. Schulenburg, while not going as far as that, reported that it 'constituted an event of extraordinary importance'. He rejected all suggestions that it had been brought about by domestic problems in the Soviet Union. To him, it was Stalin's response to the deterioration of relations with Germany, for which he blamed Molotov's obstinacy. He pointed out that the decision had followed Stalin's discussions with Dekanozov on May Day, and with his generals at the officers' graduation ceremony. Stalin was reacting to the size and speed of the German successes in Yugoslavia and Greece, which had made him realise how urgent it was to change his diplomatic course and seek to end the estrangement with Hitler which had followed Molotov's visit to Berlin.

'In my opinion,' Schulenburg reported to Ribbentrop, 'it may be assumed with certainty that Stalin has set himself a foreign policy goal of overwhelming importance for the Soviet Union, which he hopes to attain by his personal efforts. I firmly believe that, in an international situation which he considers serious, Stalin has set himself the goal of preserving the Soviet Union from a conflict with Germany.'

Within the first week of assuming office, Stalin made several moves which were clear signals of good faith and good intention towards Germany. On 8 May, he issued through Tass a strong denial of reports of Soviet troop concentrations on the western borders. That same night, Milan Gavrilovic, the Yugoslav minister, was called to the Foreign Commissariat where Vyshinsky informed him 'with genuine regret' that diplomatic relations between their two countries must now cease. Gavrilovic was hardly surprised at the news – he had been expecting it for some time. But this was not the usual cold, official dismissal of an embassy or legation. Vyshinsky went on to say that no member of the Yugoslav delegation need return to his country if he did not wish to do so. They could all remain in the Soviet Union as private citizens, where they would be shown every consideration. In truth, the Soviets found themselves in a rather embarrassing position regarding Yugoslavia: having encouraged the coup a month before, and signed a friendship pact, they had then been forced to stand back and watch as Hitler had destroyed the country in less than two weeks. Now, Yugoslavia no longer existed as a nation, therefore the friendship pact was no longer valid and to continue to recognise it would be an unfriendly act towards Germany, which could offend Hitler.

The Belgian and Norwegian ministers were not treated with the same courtesy and consideration as the Yugoslav. On the morning of 9 May a brown envelope of the kind used to deliver rent bills was handed in to the Norwegian legation from Burobin, the Soviet department which

dealt with accommodation for foreign firms and missions. It was opened
by a secretary, Ivor Lande. Inside, he found a terse note informing the
legation that since Norway was no longer a sovereign state, formal
diplomatic relations must now be considered at an end. The Belgian
legation received a similar communication. From now on anything concerning either Belgium or Norway would be dealt with by the German
embassy. Three weeks later, Greece was cast off in a similar manner.

For the same reason that he had severed his relations with Germany's
conquered territories, Stalin was happy to grant recognition to Hitler's
friends. He had already sent an envoy to Vichy France with the rank of
full ambassador: Alexander Bogolomov had presented his credentials to
Marshal Pétain on 24 April, and the Vichy ambassador to Moscow had
been received on 6 May. On 12 May, Stalin officially recognised the
pro-German government in Iraq, led by the nationalist Rashid Ali Al-
Gailani, which had been set up in Baghdad on 3 April. Once part of the
Turkish empire, Iraq had become a British mandate at the end of the
first world war and had achieved independence only in 1932. But
independent or not, the country had been bound to Britain by a military
alliance and agreements with powerful British oil interests – an
arrangement which offended the sensibilities of Iraqi nationalists. The
country was therefore ripe for destabilisation, and Berlin had been
encouraging the pan-Arab movement since before the war. Stalin's
gesture now was remarkable for the fact that he had previously shown
little interest in Iraq and had never before recognised her diplomatic
existence. In the event, it was to prove a rather futile gesture, since the
Rashid Ali government collapsed on 30 May, when British troops
reached Baghdad.

Further confirmation of Stalin's desire to placate his dangerous ally
came from another source three days after the recognition of Iraq. Franz
von Papen, one-time Chancellor of Germany and a former intelligence
agent, had been German ambassador to Turkey since April 1939, a
demanding post which he had handled with great skill. Turkey was
determined not to commit herself finally to Germany, the Soviet Union
or Britain, but to remain friendly with all three. On 15 May, one of his
secret agents succeeded in intercepting a despatch from the Turkish
ambassador in Moscow to his Foreign Ministry. Quoting conversations
he had had with the British and American ambassadors and with Arkady
Sobolev, the General Secretary of the Soviet Foreign Commissariat, the
Turkish ambassador said it was generally accepted that Stalin had
gravely miscalculated in the Balkans, and that the scale of the German
victory had terrified him. Stalin, he said, 'who now feels as though his
tender feet had plunged into ice water', was prepared to go to any
lengths to appease Hitler. 'In my opinion,' he wrote, 'Stalin is about to
become the blind tool of Germany.'

*   *   *

The belief that Stalin would do almost anything to placate Hitler was borne out by the punctiliousness with which deliveries of raw materials were made. Schnurre reported on 15 May that these were well up to schedule, and reiterated that it would be possible to obtain even more. The transit route through Siberia was still operating well, with the Soviets even laying on special trains to carry an extra 2,000 tons of raw rubber during April. Indeed, they were so eager to keep up the flow that they were constantly complaining of German delays in offloading and returning Soviet rail trucks, which were piling up at the border.

Further evidence came with the Soviet reaction to increasingly blatant violations of Soviet air space by German spy planes. On 22 April the Soviets protested that between 27 March and 18 April there had been no fewer than eighty such flights, and that when one aircraft had made an emergency landing near Rovno in the Ukraine, it was found to be carrying cameras and maps of sensitive areas of the Soviet Union. Several rolls of exposed film left no doubt whatever of the purpose of the flights, some of which had penetrated over 100 miles inside the frontiers.

The Soviets had protested several times about such flights, though the Soviet assistant military attaché in Berlin had told Göring that the Defence Commissariat had given orders to border troops not to fire on German planes flying over Soviet territory, 'so long as such flights do not occur frequently'. It was an act of remarkable forbearance for a country which was always extremely touchy about its boundaries.

The immediate response from the Germans to the Soviet protest was totally cynical – Jodl drew up a list of 'deliberate provocations' by Soviet aircraft over German territory, claiming eight incidents on 17 April alone. There was then complete silence for a whole month, during which the flights continued and the Soviets said nothing. On 17 May, Tippelskirch, first secretary of the German embassy in Moscow, was instructed to say that 'the seventy-one cases mentioned of border violations by Germans are being investigated' – but that this would take some time as every aircrew involved would have to be questioned individually. In the meantime, he was to arrange for the early return of the plane which had landed at Rovno.

Astonishingly, Stalin accepted this reply and did nothing about it, or about the further 180 spy flights which were reported before the end of May, as the Luftwaffe completed its survey of every airfield and military base in the western USSR. By the time 'Barbarossa' was ready, each one had been targeted for instant destruction on the first day of the invasion.

The OKW chiefs were puzzled and even a little worried by the Soviets' 'soft and indulgent attitude'. Abwehr chief Canaris noted in his diary that Jodl told him, only half in jest, 'If these chaps keep on being so accommodating and take offence at nothing, then *you* will have to stage an incident to start the war!'

*   *   *

Stalin's nervousness had been increased at this time by the strange behaviour of Rudolf Hess, still officially Hitler's deputy and chosen successor in the party. On the evening of 10 May, like some airborne Parsifal, Hess had flown to Britain in a specially equipped Messerschmitt from the factory where he had made the May Day speech. His self-imposed mission was to persuade the British to make peace with Germany before the start of Hitler's crusade against bolshevism. He hoped to use the Duke of Hamilton, to whom he carried a letter of introduction, to make a direct appeal to King George VI. By using the Duke as intermediary to the King, he hoped to go over the head of Churchill, the man whom he regarded as the arch warmonger. Hess's plane crashed, but he parachuted to safety near the village of Eaglesham not far from Glasgow, where a startled farmer and his wife found him and called the local police. While waiting, they courteously gave him tea, keeping a shotgun handy in case of trouble.

Hess's half-baked peace flight confused the British, who did not know how to react and so failed to make much propaganda out of the capture of such an illustrious prisoner. It enraged Hitler – Karl Schnurre, who was at the Berghof when the news arrived, recalls that everyone in the house cowered fearfully as he stormed from room to room in a wild fury. The Führer saw Hess's escapade as an act of treachery and publicly declared it to be the result of insanity. But to Stalin, it confirmed his worst fears. In the Kremlin it was greeted with profound suspicion. Nikita Khrushchev voiced the view of the entire Politburo when he told Stalin: 'I think Hess must actually be on a secret mission from Hitler to negotiate with the English about cutting short the war in the West to free Hitler's hand for a push east.'

'Yes, that's it,' replied Stalin. 'You understand correctly.'

Stalin had always half expected such a scenario. It was clear to him that Hess and Churchill together were trying to unite the capitalist and fascist worlds, so that they could make common cause in a crusade against the USSR. He had always believed this was in Churchill's mind: was not the man one of the architects of the Intervention of 1918, when armies of no fewer than eleven foreign powers, including Britain and the USA, had invaded Russia? Had not Churchill then declared himself an implacable enemy of bolshevism?

The distrust engendered by Hess's flight made Stalin doubly suspicious of Britain's true intentions, and doubly determined to avoid giving Hitler any excuse for joining forces with Britain against the Soviet Union. He chose therefore to ignore the persistent rumours that were sweeping Moscow, such as reports that Schulenburg was depressed and worried and had returned from Berlin only to complete the packing he had already started, and that the families of most of the embassy staff had already left for home, while those who remained were going soon.

Schulenburg was more worried than Stalin about such rumours, and moved to protect himself against their effects on Berlin. 'Everything that my colleagues here are going around saying and reporting to their governments is complete nonsense,' he cabled the Wilhelmstrasse. 'I do not believe that I am "especially depressed" and I have not thought of "packing up my private belongings in boxes" either. My very costly rugs are lying in their old place, the pictures of my parents and other relatives are hanging on the walls as before and in my residence nothing has changed, as every visitor can see for himself.'

To Stalin, the rumours were obviously spread by the British, as provocations intended to create discord between Germany and the Soviet Union, a view reinforced by the fact that since mid-April British Ambassador Cripps had not only been openly asserting that Hitler was about to attack, but also naming 22 June as the day – a fortuitous assumption by British intelligence, since Hitler had not then finally fixed that as the date. Other rumour-mongers, some of them Germans, were setting the date as early as 20 May.

Like Stalin, the political department of the German Foreign Ministry also tried to pass the rumours off as British troublemaking. When Schulenburg complained that it was impossible to counteract these stories while every visitor to Moscow not only spread them but also kept confirming them by citing facts, the response from Berlin was that they were without any foundation and were therefore regarded as 'a renewed attempt on the part of England to poison the wells'. It was, Schulenburg was told, 'very desirable to quash these rumours', and to this end he was to inform everybody that while the Soviets were building up 'substantial Russian troop concentrations near the border, this was without military justification, since on the German side, only such forces are posted at the border as are absolutely necessary as rear cover for the Balkan operations'. He was also to spread the word that German troop movements from east to west were reaching 'considerable proportions' during the first half of May.

Schulenburg did his best to obey these instructions, but the results were neatly summed up by one of the series of Stalin–Hitler jokes going the rounds in Moscow. Stalin to Hitler: 'What are all your troops doing on the Soviet border?' Hitler: 'They're on vacation. What are all your troops doing there?' Stalin: 'They're there to see that yours stay on vacation!'

One of the stories 'without any foundation' was that 12,000 German troops had arrived in Finland, complete with tanks and artillery. This was published in *Pravda* on 30 April, and attracted the attention of many people in Moscow, including John Scott, the American journalist. Scott found it curious that the presence of German divisions in Finland should be mentioned in the organ of the Central Committee of the Soviet Communist Party. In his view, it was not so much a news item as an internal political measure, a veiled warning. He decided to follow up the story, and approached officials in the German embassy, who told him that the troops were 'going through to Narvik, as provided for by a well-known Finnish–German agreement'. Curious, he inquired why they needed tanks and artillery in Lapland. 'To hunt polar bears,' was the sardonic reply.

While continuing to placate Hitler with every means at his disposal, Stalin was also concerned to go on warning him, as tactfully as possible, that the Soviet Union would defend herself if attacked. Until mid-May, he did not take too much trouble to hide the steadily increasing build-up of his forces in the west, allowing British, German and other military attachés to travel through the areas where they were concentrating. The attachés reported seeing train after train heading west loaded with troops, tanks and mechanised equipment. They also noted that 1,000 people a day were being called up for military service in Moscow alone, and that in early May the youngest age-group was called up six months early. Alexander Kollontai, the Soviet minister in Sweden, was allowed to say that never in history had more powerful Russian forces been massed in the west – the general consensus in the international intelligence community was that well over sixty per cent of the Red Army was already massed in the west, and more were arriving all the time. Another secret that was not too well kept was that factories around Moscow were being transferred to the safety of the lands beyond the Urals.

Stalin was undoubtedly aware from agents of the GRU, his military intelligence agency, that German intelligence consistently under-estimated Soviet military strengths. Johnnie Herwarth, who spent January and February of 1941 on secondment to the Luftwaffe High Command's Reconnaissance Division, was particularly struck by the number of assessment papers which had been written by Germans who had either been born in the Soviet Union or who had lived there and been expelled, and who therefore had an interest in belittling everything Soviet. Under normal battle conditions, such a situation would have been very desirable for the Soviet Union: to be underestimated by your enemy is to gain an important psychological and even tactical advantage. But in the spring of 1941, the circumstances were very different.

When the man Herwarth had been working for, Colonel Engineer Dietrich Schwencke, travelled to the Soviet Union in April 1941 to see for himself what was going on, he was at first shown very little. Suddenly, however, he and his party of two other officers and eight representatives of German industries were taken to see a number of important and highly revealing plants – during the month of April they were shown round four aircraft body factories, three engine factories and a light metalworking plant, all of which were working flat out on the very latest Soviet aircraft. The German experts were most impressed – the factories they saw were the biggest and most modern in Europe, and more were being built. The aircraft they were producing were simple but tough, and far superior to those in service with the Soviet air force, on which German intelligence assessments were based.

The abrupt change in the Soviet willingness to show their hand had two causes. One, of course, was the shock of Germany's staggering success in the Balkans. The other was the man who occupied the next office to Schwencke in the Air Ministry back in Berlin – Lieutenant Harro Schulze-Boysen, a leading member of the GRU's *Rote Kapelle* (Red Orchestra) spy network. Johnnie Herwarth discovered after the war that Schwencke's first messages from Moscow had all landed on the desk of Schulze-Boysen, who had immediately copied them to Centre, the GRU headquarters in Moscow, where they were seen by the highest GRU officers. 'Though he had not yet been shown much,' Herwarth says, 'Schwencke's reports had been reasonably positive. The Soviets concluded that if he had been this positive on the basis of such slim evidence, he should be permitted to see everything, in the hope that he would emphasise yet more firmly the Soviet strength.'

At the end of their tour, the German experts were treated to a farewell dinner, at which a leading Soviet aircraft designer, Artem Mikoyan, youngest brother of the Trade Commissar and co-designer of the MiG fighters, told them: 'Now you have seen the mighty technology of the Soviet fatherland. We shall valiantly ward off any attack, whatever quarter it comes from!' It would be hard to imagine Stalin's message being put more clearly.

As it happened, this aspect of Stalin's strategy for deterring Hitler backfired, perhaps because it was already too late. The more Hitler learned now about the growing strength of the Soviet Union, the more he realised that he could not afford to delay too long. He said later that Schwencke's report on the Soviet air force and aircraft industry had finally convinced him of the need to attack at once.

Whether or not he succeeded in stalling Hitler, Stalin still needed to speed up the preparation of the Soviet people for the coming war. Throughout May, there was a constant series of civil defence exercises throughout the Soviet Union. The leading role in these was taken by an organisation called the Osoaviakhim League, a kind of cross between an army, navy and air cadet force and the ARP, with strong connections with the Soviet armed forces. Its full title translates as 'The Society for the Promotion of Defence Against Air Attack and Chemical Warfare'. After the summer of 1940 and the fall of France, the League grew in size until it boasted nearly twelve million volunteer members, many of them children. They took part in the numerous black-outs and practice alerts which were held in every large city from Kiev to Alma Ata.

On 15 and 16 May 1941, a particularly large-scale civil defence exercise was staged at Ramenskoye, a town some twenty kilometres east of Moscow. This involved some 20,000 civilians and was based on a scenario which assumed the worst: four groups of enemy paratroops were said to have been dropped in the area and a number of the neighbouring villages were supposed to be under artillery bombardment; incendiary bombs were supposed to have been dropped on the surrounding countryside and forest, starting a number of fires; and to cap it all, Ramenskoye itself was assumed to have suffered a gas attack.

In Mosow at about this time, whole districts were blacked out during exercises while rescue squads practised the evacuation of all women and children. American journalist John Scott described one such exercise in which he played an unwilling part: 'I came down from our apartment, intending to go downtown. At the bottom of the stairs I was stopped by a grotesque figure dressed in heavy rubber overalls, boots, gauntlets and gas mask. This apparition was both mute and dumb. Not only could I not tell who it was, but it was impossible to say whether it was man or woman – though I found out afterwards it was the scrubwoman who washed down the stairs.

'For twenty minutes I stood and watched while super-realistic air-raid manoeuvres went on. Our apartment house had been "hit" by an HE [high-explosive] bomb and a gas bomb. The former had demolished one wing of the building, the latter had contaminated one half of the courtyard and the wall of the central wing of the building.

'A first aid unit arrived, wearing gas masks and oilcloth suits. They went to the demolished wing, took the first dozen people they found, threw them down on stretchers, bandaged them arbitrarily, smeared Ts on their foreheads to show that they had been inoculated against tetanus, and rushed them off to a base hospital, well wrapped up in blankets.

'A decontamination unit drove up and spread chemical neutralisers on part of the courtyard and wall which had been contaminated by the gas bomb. In the meantime, the fire brigade had put out the fire and the demolition squad was clearing up the mess. This whole performance was organised and carried out by volunteer Osoaviakhim members.'

In their desire to be as realistic as possible, local authorities sometimes overstepped the bounds of good sense. In Baku, for example, they had aircraft fly over the city dropping dummy bombs. One of them fell on the central square, doing considerable damage. Several genuine fires were started and had to be extinguished by the local air-raid wardens and fire department. All damage was made good by special emergency crews. According to the local newspaper, *Bakinski Rabochi* (*Baku Worker*), the entire population of the city spent that evening and the rest of the night in air-raid shelters. During the exercises in Kiev, one section of the city was completely evacuated and all able-bodied men mobilised to round up 'enemy parachutists'.

It was not only the urban population which was being organised for war: even in small rural communities, peasants were being mobilised to face an enemy attack. Regular officers gave lectures on what to do in the event of enemy paratroops landing behind the lines – round them up and kill them – or in the face of a large enemy advance – destroy everything that could be of value to the invader. In addition, they instructed people on the basic principles of guerrilla warfare.

The members of the Osoaviakhim League played their part in these mass war games, too. Having been trained in the basic military skills of markmanship, grenade-throwing, map-reading and so on, they were responsible for passing on their expertise to the rest of the population. In order to demonstrate how seriously the authorities took these exercises – and no doubt to ensure maximum co-operation from the public – a number of regiments of NKVD troops were deployed to back up the work of the League.

After twenty-one months of promoting the idea of friendship with the Nazis, the Soviet arts and media suddenly began – albeit gently at first – to sound warning notes. Eisenstein's film *Alexander Nevsky* was revived at a special performance in the Kremlin and awarded a Stalin Prize, which was reported in *Pravda* and *Izvestia*. Early in May, Eisenstein gave *Life* correspondent Erskine Caldwell and his wife, photographer Margaret Bourke-White, a private showing, and told them: 'We think that it will not be much longer before *Alexander Nevsky* will be shown in public cinemas again.'

At about the same time, the writer Ilya Ehrenburg received a surprise telephone call in his Moscow apartment. It was from a member of Stalin's personal secretariat, who told him to dial a certain number, because 'Comrade Stalin wants to talk to you.' It turned out that all Stalin wanted – on the surface at least – was a literary chat about the novel Ehrenburg was working on, *The Fall of Paris*, based on his experiences in the French capital when the Germans marched in in 1940. Ehrenburg was writing the book in three parts. The first part had been passed by the censors with only minor amendments – the word 'fascism' had to be taken out so that the slogan 'Down with Fascism!' for example, became 'Down with the reactionaries!' But the second part had run into trouble. Four days before Stalin's telephone call, he was told that the censors were not prepared to pass it in its present form.

Stalin told Ehrenburg he had read the first part, and found it interesting. He offered to lend him a manuscript translation of André Simon's book, *J'Accuse: The Men Who Betrayed France*. Ehrenburg thanked him, but said that he had already read it. Stalin then asked whether he intended to denounce the German fascists in his book.

Ehrenburg replied that the last part of the novel, on which he was now working, dealt with the war, the invasion of France by the Nazis, and the first weeks of occupation. He added that he was afraid it would not be passed by the censors. Stalin was amused. 'Just go on writing,' he said. 'You and I will try to push the third part through.'

By this time, of course, Ehrenburg had realised that his novel was not Stalin's prime consideration. If he had really been concerned about the book alone, all he had to do was order the censor to pass it – no minor official was going to question the judgement of the General Secretary of the party. It was clear to Ehrenburg that Stalin no longer cared whether *The Fall of Paris* upset the Germans. What he wanted was to make use of Ehrenburg: as the recently returned man from the mysterious West, as the carrier of first-hand news about the Nazis, Ehrenburg was an object of interest to every Soviet intellectual. People would be eager to listen to him. Therefore, he would make an ideal unofficial mouthpiece, to carry Stalin's message of warning to certain sections of the Soviet community.

When Ehrenburg hung up the receiver in his apartment, his wife and daughter immediately clamoured to know what Stalin had said. Ehrenburg, who had already decoded Stalin's message, replied: 'There'll be a war soon.'

A few days later, Ehrenburg set out on the road, touring round Kharkov, Kiev and Leningrad, seeing old friends and giving lectures. When he lectured at the House of Culture in Vyborg – the former city of Viipuri, taken from the Finns after the Winter War – he was bombarded with questions. But they were not of a literary nature: what the audience wanted were answers to questions such as, 'Is it true that the Germans are preparing to violate the non-aggression pact, or is the rumour just a British provocation?' Ehrenburg did his best to answer.

In return for his services, Ehrenburg enjoyed the advantages of Stalin's patronage. Almost overnight, *The Fall of Paris*, swiftly cleared by the censors, became a hot literary property. Suddenly editors from all over the Soviet Union were telephoning him for permission to publish extracts, and a little while later he was even invited to join the presidium of the prestigious Writers' Club.

On 17 May, Stalin clamped down on the sightseeing trips of foreign military attachés – some, particularly the Finns, had been travelling too enthusiastically. No doubt he considered they had seen enough by then, and summer manoeuvres were due to start in early June for the Red Army. Next day, on 18 May, a new exhibition opened at the historical museum in Moscow which was perceived as having great significance, both internally and internationally. This was the '1812 Fatherland War Exhibition' – about the defeat of Napoleon's invasion. 'Napoleon's army having penetrated into Russia,' *Pravda* said in its review, 'increasingly broke down, whilst the Russian became stronger. The exhibition shows how the war gradually turned into the people's struggle for national independence . . . and how bravely the Russian troops fought under Kutuzov.'

Two days later, *Pravda* carried another pointed article, describing the huge cost of military expenditure in Britain, the USA and Germany. And on 21 May, *Komsomolskaya Pravda*, the newspaper of the communist youth movement, published an article describing in clear and uncoded language the effects of Nazi conquest. 'The peoples of Europe,' it declared, 'have been made into colonial slaves.' And why had this happened? Because the conquered nations had not been militarily prepared to face the Nazi hordes. This was the first anti-Nazi piece to appear in the Soviet press since the signing of the pact. It provided readers with both a warning and some modicum of comfort. The sacrifices made by ordinary citizens over the past two years had not been in vain. The Red Army, it implied – reassuringly if falsely – was ready to defend the Soviet Union.

Four days later, *Pravda* published a vituperative piece by its senior political commentator, Andrei Zaslavski, denouncing a report which had appeared in the Finnish newspaper *Helsinki Salomat*. The report, which had very possibly been planted by the Soviets themselves to give Stalin the opportunity of refuting its claims in public, asserted that he had agreed to cede the Ukraine to Germany and was also prepared to offer German business concerns further economic concessions in the Soviet Union. Such stories, Zaslavski indignantly stated, were childish fantasy: they belonged to the world of Edward Lear. As May ended, therefore, the party itself was signalling loud and clear, both to Hitler and to the Soviet people, that Stalin had at last decided to draw the line.

52

'THE GREATEST DECEPTION OPERATION IN MILITARY HISTORY'

While Stalin, like some nervous animal threatened by a ferocious adversary, alternated between displays of brave strength and abject submission, Hitler was concerned only with his own plans. Having set the date for the start of 'Barbarossa', he completely ignored both Stalin's warning signals and his desperate efforts to buy Germany off. So confident was he now that he spent much of his time pondering exactly what he would do with the remnants of the Soviet Union once he had won.

As far back as the beginning of March, his ideas had been outlined in a draft directive, drawn up for him by Jodl:

The forthcoming campaign is more than a mere armed conflict; it is a collision between two different ideologies. In view of the size of the area involved, this war will not be ended merely by the defeat of the enemy's armed forces. The entire area must be split up into different states, each with its own government with which we can then conclude peace.

The formation of these governments requires great political ability and must rest upon well-thought-out principles.

Any large-scale revolution gives rise to events which cannot subsequently be expunged. The socialist ideal can no longer be wiped out in the Russia of today. From the internal point of view, the formation of new states and governments must inevitably be based on this principle. The Bolshevik–Jewish intelligentsia must be eliminated as having been the "oppressor" of the people up to now. The old bourgeois and aristocratic intelligentsia, in so far as it still exists among the émigrés, does not come into the picture either. It would be rejected by the Russian people and is basically anti-German. This applies particularly in the ex-Baltic states.

In addition, we must do everything possible to avoid allowing a nationalist Russia to appear in place of a Bolshevik Russia, for history shows that this will also again become anti-German. Our object is to construct as soon as possible, using the minimum military effort, socialist mini-states which will be dependent on us. This task is so difficult it cannot be entrusted to the army.

Hitler made various comments on this, to be incorporated into the final version. The army was to operate in as shallow an area as possible, and there were to be no military governments set up in the rear of the battle zones. Instead, the SS and special Reich Commissioners would be responsible for the organisation of the new states and their political machinery. Himmler's *Einsatzgruppen* would deal with 'all Bolshevik leaders and commissars', who were to be liquidated immediately, without trial or court-martial.

'We have to set up de-Stalinised republics,' Hitler told Halder shortly afterwards. 'The intelligentsia appointed by Stalin must be destroyed. The Russian empire's command machinery must be smashed. In the whole of Russia, it will be necessary to use the most naked brute force. The ideological ties are not yet strong enough to hold the Russian people together. Once the officials are disposed of, the nation will burst apart.'

On 30 March, he expanded on these ideas to a gathering of some 250 of his most senior commanders and their staff officers. For most of them, it was the first they had heard officially of 'Barbarossa'. Few were happy at what they were told. Seated in long rows in order of rank and seniority, on small gilt chairs specially brought in from Goebbels's Propaganda Ministry, their hostility filled the air of the packed conference room at the Ebertstrasse end of the Chancellery's great hall as Hitler addressed them in what Walter Warlimont described as 'forceful terms'. 'They sat there before him,' Warlimont recorded, 'in stubborn silence, a silence broken only twice – when the assembly rose first as he entered through a door in the rear and went up to the rostrum, and later when he departed the same way. Otherwise, not a word was spoken, but by him.'

Halder claimed later that the generals were outraged at being told that the war would have to be conducted 'with unprecedented, unmerciful and unrelenting harshness', and that they would 'have to rid themselves of obsolete ideologies', ignoring the niceties of international law by liquidating all commissars. 'Russia has not participated in the Hague Convention,' Hitler declared, 'and therefore has no rights under it.' But at the time, no voice was raised in protest as he told them: 'I know that the necessity for such means of waging war is beyond the comprehension of you generals but . . . I insist absolutely that my orders are carried out.'

A written directive confirming these orders was issued five weeks later, on 6 May. After describing what commissars actually were, and how to identify them by the red star embroidered on their sleeves along with a gold hammer and sickle, it went on:

> Political authorities and leaders (commissars) constitute a special menace to the security of the troops and the pacification of the conquered territory.
>
> If such persons are captured by the troops or otherwise apprehended, they will be brought before an officer who has disciplinary powers of punishment. The latter will summon two military witnesses (officer or NCO rank) and establish that the person captured or apprehended is a political personality or leader (commissar). If adequate proof of his political position is forthcoming, the officer will forthwith order his execution and ensure that it is carried out.

But it was not only commissars and the lesser local party officials known as politruks who were to be dealt with in this way. Any Russian who was suspected of criminal acts was to be brought before an officer, who would decide there and then whether or not the offender was to be shot. However, Germans who committed offences against enemy civilians were not necessarily to be disciplined, 'even where the deed is at the same time a military crime or offence'. Courts-martial of German soldiers would be necessary only where 'maintenance of discipline or security of the forces call for such a measure'. And any sentences imposed would be confirmed only if they were 'in accordance with the political intentions of the High Command'.

Halder himself inserted an extra refinement to the orders, in a clause reading:

> Immediate collective punishments will be enforced against towns and villages from which ambushes or treacherous attacks on the Wehrmacht are made, on the orders of an officer of not less than battalion commander's rank, if circumstances do not permit the rapid arrest of the individual perpetrators.

While Himmler was given the task of cleaning out the occupied areas of the Soviet Union, with the guarantee that there was to be no interference from anyone as his SS special action groups went about their grisly business unchecked, the job of setting up and administering the new states went to Alfred Rosenberg, the Nazi Party philosopher. Rosenberg, who was himself half Russian, having been born in Estonia to a Baltic-German father and a Latvian-Russian mother, was the head of the party's Foreign Political Section and its supposed expert on

Russian affairs. He was also a former editor of the party newspaper, *Völkischer Beobachter*, and the author of the book which, after *Mein Kampf*, was the official party gospel, *The Myth of the Twentieth Century* – a book which Hitler had never bothered to read. He was generally regarded with utter contempt by Hitler – which shows only too clearly the Führer's attitude to the job he gave him.

Rosenberg was named head of a Political Office for the East on 31 March, the day after Hitler had spoken to his generals. He learned of his appointment only on 2 April – the delay providing another indication of its low importance rating – but managed to deliver a lengthy memorandum outlining his proposals on the same day. These included separatist states for Belorussia, the Ukraine, the Cossack lands, the Caucasus and even Turkestan, far beyond the Archangel–Astrakhan line which the 'Barbarossa' plan laid down as the limit of German occupation. The vast area of the Baltic states and the former Polish provinces was to be reserved for colonisation by Aryans from Germany, Scandinavia, Holland and England: the Russian inhabitants were to be moved out to the east.

On 20 April, Hitler's birthday, the name of Rosenberg's office was changed to the Central Department for the Treatment of Eastern Questions, and he was ordered to produce a far more detailed scheme for the new regions. He delivered this on 9 May. It was based on an ingenious legalistic device: making use of the Soviet constitution of 5 December 1936, which gave the sixteen republics of the USSR the individual right to secede.

But Hitler was no longer interested in such niceties. His attitude towards the conquered territories of the Soviet Union had changed considerably since the end of March, perhaps as a reaction to Stalin's perfidy in signing a pact with the Yugoslavs, perhaps simply as a result of his own psychological build-up for 'Barbarossa'. He no longer wanted the separate states to be legitimised – the *Reichskommissariats* were to be purely a temporary measure, paving the way for full-scale German colonisation.

Hitler was already moving away from his original thought of dividing the Soviet Union into a number of weak socialist states, and towards a new policy which gave the Russians no sovereignty whatever. He told Goebbels later that he intended to rule Russia as the British ruled India. Under this policy the Baltic states, the Crimea, the Baku region, the German Volga republic and the Kola peninsula were to be annexed immediately into Germany. Leningrad was to be razed to the ground, and the area given to Finland. Romania was to be rewarded with the return of the whole of Bessarabia plus a strip of new territory including Odessa.

In addition to being excluded from all security matters in the new eastern territories, Rosenberg was also given no say in their economic exploitation. This was to be the preserve of Göring. Briefly, all the food produced in the fertile black-earth regions in the south was to be sent to Germany, and not to the Soviet industrial cities. The inhabitants of those cities would simply be left to starve, or to find their way to Siberia. In the directive of 23 May 1941, Göring left no doubts of his intentions:

> The German administration in these territories may well attempt to mitigate the consequences of the famine which will undoubtedly take place and to accelerate the return to primitive agricultural conditions. However, these measures will not avert famine. Any attempt to save the population there from death by starvation by importing surpluses from the black-earth region would be at the expense of supplies to Europe. It would reduce Germany's staying power in the war, and would undermine Germany's and Europe's power to resist the blockade. This must be clearly and absolutely understood.

By mid-May it was time to start the process of bringing in Germany's allies. This, of course, had to be done with the utmost care in order to avoid security leaks. Italy, for instance, was not to be told anything at all until the invasion was actually under way. When Ribbentrop hurried to Rome on 14 May to reassure Mussolini after Hess had flown to Britain, they had a long conversation at the Palazzo Venezia and discussed almost every aspect of the war. But when the subject of the Soviet Union came up, Ribbentrop assured the Duce that everything was in order, relations between the two countries were 'very correct', and he did not think Stalin would try anything against Germany. If he did, however, he would be destroyed within three months. When Hitler met Mussolini in the Brenner Pass on 2 June, the Soviet Union was not even mentioned.

Japan, too, was kept in the dark, and of Germany's other friends, Hitler told the OKW that the only countries he would consider allowing to take part in 'Barbarossa' were those 'which were either neighbours of Russia and therefore in a position to assist the German advance, or had some account of their own to settle with the Soviets'. That, of course, meant only Finland and Romania to start with. Later on, he might consider including Hungary and Slovakia. Sweden could have a part to play early on, though only by providing indirect support, such as allowing German troops to cross her territory to reach Finland from Norway.

Schnurre was sent to Finland, to talk to the government there on 20 May and persuade them to send a military mission from their general staff to meet the OKW chiefs at Salzburg and agree upon joint plans, which they were happy to do. Hitler dealt with the Romanians himself, inviting General Antonescu to visit him at the Führer Building in Munich – though not until 11 June. Antonescu was delighted to agree to join in the attack right from the start. In both cases, the allies were fed the fiction of a preventive war, forced on an unwilling Germany by the threat of aggression from Soviet forces concentrated provocatively on her frontiers.

A clash was possible by early summer, Jodl warned the Finnish delegation on 25 May, and therefore the Finns should agree upon the basis for co-operation. They would not be saddled with heavy burdens, but simply told what Germany would like, and left to make up their own minds what they would do. 'The course of this potential war can be predicted with certainty,' he went on. 'After losing a certain area through the participation of many small states in an anti-Bolshevik crusade, and in particular through the superiority of the German Wehrmacht, Russia will be unable to go on fighting. The collapse will come fastest in the north, and the Baltic will soon be in our hands. After the Russian catastrophe, Germany will be Europe's leading and unassailable power. She will then be able to reduce her army in favour of air and naval armaments, to defeat England, which still pins her hopes on Russia.'

The Finns needed little persuasion to join in the destruction of the Soviet Union. At the meeting the broad outlines of co-operation were agreed, with the fine details settled in talks with the army High Command immediately afterwards. The Finns said they needed nine days for mobilisation, but would have to proceed very cautiously and in great secrecy – if the Soviets found out, they could strike at Finland before the mobilisation was complete. German troops would start moving on 5 June, the first units arriving in Finland on 8 June, and German armour between 10 and 15 June.

The Finns were therefore totally committed to fighting alongside Germany – but even so, Hitler ordered that they were to be told only as much about the German plans as they needed to know for their local operations. The need for secrecy was growing more vital with every passing day.

The military preparations in the east and south-east, meanwhile, were proceeding steadily. Only the airborne invasion of Crete on 20 May looked like creating any possible hiccups, particularly when the British troops put up stiffer resistance than had been expected, tying down aircraft needed for 'Barbarossa'. By 22 May, Halder was worrying about being able to get them back in time, and even suggesting 'Barbarossa' might have to be postponed, as British warships bombarded the airfield at Heraklion. But by the end of the month it was all over. The last British troops had been pulled out, the all-conquering Wehrmacht had notched up yet another remarkable ten-day victory, and Hitler was able to confirm that 22 June still stood as the start date for his great adventure.

After the fall of France, there had been a mere handful of German troops in the east – seven divisions at the most. By the end of the year, this number had risen to thirty-four divisions. But from February onwards, the build-up leapt forward on a massive scale. By 14 March, 2,500 trainloads of men and equipment making up the first phase of the deployment had been moved east. Over the next ten weeks no fewer than 17,000 special trains carried the second, third and fourth echelons. By the end of April, with the second phase complete, the number of divisions had risen to 103, with a further seventeen making up the third echelon on 20 May. By the beginning of June, with most of the formations from the Balkans back in place, there were 129 divisions, only twenty short of Hitler's final target, standing ready for the short move into their start positions.

The Luftwaffe's aircraft, of course, did not need to fly east until the last possible moment. But airfields and ground support organisations had to be prepared in advance, and on a scale large enough to cope with nearly two thirds of the entire Luftwaffe strength: 2,770 aircraft out of a total of 4,300. Concealing these preparations from Soviet aerial reconnaissance, and from spies and agents on the ground, was difficult but vital, for not only were the aircraft to be spread thinly over a front stretching for 1,800 miles, but they were also faced with an estimated Soviet strength of between 8,000 and 10,000 aircraft. Although these were thought to be mainly inferior or obsolete types, their sheer numerical superiority could prove to be a great problem. The only way the Luftwaffe could be sure of knocking out the Soviet air force was to do it at the very beginning, if possible on the ground, making use of all the reconnaissance flights and aerial photographs they had taken of Soviet airfields. This, of course, depended entirely on achieving the element of surprise.

The enormous size of the Red Army posed similar problems. Every fresh intelligence report confirmed the fact that the attacking troops would face considerably larger Soviet forces, so here, too, surprise was not just desirable but essential. With such massive troop movements, and the presence of over three million men under arms, concealment was virtually impossible. What had to be done, therefore, was to conceal not their presence but their purpose, through a vast deception.

Hitler understood this completely. He ordered the deception operation for 'Barbarossa' at the same time as he made the very first announcement of his intention to attack the Soviet Union, on 31 July 1940. After outlining his aims to Keitel, Jodl, Brauchitsch and Halder at the Berghof, he went on to specify that the build-up in the east should be passed off as training and preparation for attacks on Gibraltar, North Africa and England, in areas that were out of range of British air attacks. General Köstring, the military attaché in Moscow, was instructed to feed this story to the Soviets, and to assure them there was nothing for them to worry about.

As the plans matured, every possible means was used to create a huge double-bluff, by presenting 'Barbarossa' itself as 'the greatest deception operation in military history', aimed not at the Soviet Union but at Britain. The idea that everything that happened in the east was directed towards either preparation or deception for the invasion of Britain remained the principal cover story right up to the end. In order to strengthen the fiction, Hitler deliberately deceived his own commanders, even at the highest levels, for as long as he was able.

In August 1940, he told Grand Admiral Raeder – who had not been let into the secret of his eastern ambitions – that the movement of troops to the east was a large-scale camouflage measure for 'Sea Lion'. At that stage, 'Sea Lion' itself was still supposed to be genuine – but when it was finally abandoned after the Battle of Britain, Raeder was ordered to keep it going as a deception measure until the beginning of the Russian campaign. All training and preparations were to be kept at full strength, particularly during spring 1941 – though it would not, of course, be necessary to reassemble the river barges on the coast: even if the operation were for real they would not be needed until the summer.

On 6 February 1941, in his directive No. 23, 'Guidelines for the Conduct of War Against the English War Economy', Hitler ordered: 'Until the start of regrouping for "Barbarossa", we should strive to step up progressively aerial and naval operations, not only to inflict the greatest possible damage on England, but also to simulate the appearance of an impending attack on the British Isles this year.'

Nine days later, on 15 February, he formalised his ideas in a written order, signed by Field Marshal Keitel. There were only fifteen copies made and it was headed 'Matter for Chiefs.' It began:

Guidelines for Deception of the Enemy
The aim of the deception is *to conceal* the preparation of *Operation* BARBAROSSA. This essential goal is the guiding principle for all the measures aimed at keeping the enemy misinformed. It is a matter of maintaining uncertainty about our intentions during the first period, that is, until the middle of April. In the ensuing second period, the misdirecting measures meant for BARBAROSSA itself must not be seen as any more than misdirection and *diversion for the invasion of England.*

In the beginning of the deception operation it was important to give the impression that all the preparations were for a coming invasion of England. Troop movements connected with 'Barbarossa' were to be explained as the normal rotation of military units between west and east, or as the relocation of reserves which had been built up for the invasion of Yugoslavia, or as providing a necessary defensive cover against the USSR.

Later, of course, such explanations would begin to sound increasingly threadbare. At that point all troop movements in the east were to be explained as part of a grand deception plan, a cover-up for the final preparations for the invasion of England. Everyone had a role to play – even the troops in the field, though they did not know it. They were told that their presence on the Russian border was designed to confuse the English, to draw their attention eastwards, while a small but powerful German force prepared for a sudden cross-Channel attack. Hitler and the High Command were banking on such stories finding their way back home and there being picked up by enemy agents and passed on to London and Moscow.

In order to preserve the illusion, the Abwehr – under Admiral Canaris – was ordered to carry out a vast disinformation campaign aimed at convincing neutral diplomats that the invasion of England was imminent. To add a touch of authenticity, English interpreters were to be attached to various German military units; special maps of Britain were to be printed and issued to senior ranks; certain strategic areas of the Channel coast and the coast of Norway were to be closed to civilians, as if they were intended as deployment areas for an invasion force.

Everything was to be done to convince British – as well as Soviet – intelligence that Hitler's next move would be in the West: the invasion of England.

The German deception planners do not seem to have had the imaginative flair of the British and Americans who later carried out such coups as floating a body off Spain with a briefcase chained to its wrist containing supposed orders for the invasion of Sardinia and Greece as a cloak for the landings in Sicily, flying an actor disguised as Field Marshal Bernard Montgomery to Gibraltar to inspect troops under the eyes of known German spies, or creating a phantom American army in East Anglia with thousands of plywood 'aircraft' and inflatable 'tanks', commanded by a genuine and highly visible General George S. Patton. But much of their work was highly ingenious, thorough and very intricate. In late March, for instance, they activated 'Operation Harpoon South' in Norway, to help strengthen the belief that 'Sea Lion' was still about to happen. What is particularly interesting about 'Harpoon' is that it was itself a deception operation for 'Sea Lion', involving a fake invasion attempt on the east coast of Scotland. The idea was that invasion troops would embark on ten transport ships in southern Norway, in broad daylight, but would disembark again at night, in secrecy. The transports would then sail, escorted by four cruisers, and head for Scotland, turning back and dispersing under cover of darkness. Details were allowed to leak through agents in Norway, presumably in the belief that such elaborate deception operations must mean that 'Sea Lion' itself was genuine.

A second and bigger operation, codenamed 'Shark', was ordered on 24 April. This called for military activities stretching from Scandinavia to Brittany, all giving the inescapable impression that they were preparations for an invasion of Britain, to be launched from the coast between Rotterdam and Cherbourg.

A month afterwards, on 22 May, the entire deception operation was stepped up, to coincide with the start of the final phase of the timetable for 'Barbarossa'. In particular, the story was to be spread that units in the east were there only as rear cover against Russia during the invasion of Britain, or as a 'feint assembly of forces'. Elaborate plans were worked out for the rapid movement of large forces to the west, and orders were given (to be rescinded later) to as many units as possible to prepare to travel. There were frequent entrainment exercises in the east, while in the west troops were assembled at ports and given detailed orders, some of which were allowed to fall into the hands of enemy agents. While the Luftwaffe made ostentatious and intensive air reconnaissance of possible landing sites in England, handbooks were printed on the British way of life, ready for distribution to invading troops. In Berlin, several dummy ministries were set up to take charge of administration of a conquered Britain – though, for the most part, these remained as names only.

Some of the methods used to foster the illusion that the main fighting strength of the Wehrmacht was in the west while those units in the east were mainly inefficient garrison troops had a decidedly theatrical ring to them. Paratroop officers supposedly on leave in Berlin talked noisily about the pleasures of living in France; Panzer commanders puffed Dutch cigars in public to give onlookers the idea that they were stationed in Holland. A senior officer, apparently the worse for drink, accidentally let slip the date of the invasion of Britain, while making an appointment for the following day. Next day, he failed to keep the appointment – giving the impression that he had been arrested for his criminal act.

On German radio, the popular forces request programmes every Sunday were brought into the act, broadcasting phoney messages among the real ones. These messages purported to come from paratroop units, armoured regiments, crack SS regiments – all assault troops who would inevitably be in the first wave of any invasion force, and all of whom were supposedly stationed in France and the Low Countries while messages from garrison troops invariably came from the eastern frontier:

Three happy paratroops on the Channel coast send greetings to Nurse Kaethe at Reserve Hospital II in Potsdam.

Reserve Hospital Berlin–Wilmersdorf thanks an armoured division's artillery regiment for 100 bottles of Bordeaux wine.

Members of the Leibstandarte [Hitler's SS Lifeguards] send their wounded commander three bottles of Hennessy and wish him a quick recovery.

Sergeant S. on garrison duty in East Prussia sends greeting to his sick mother in Kiel . . .

Such messages, of course, were intended mainly for the British and Soviet monitoring services.

Although the deception operation as a whole was in the hands of the OKW, under the control of Canaris, Goebbels joined in enthusiastically with the Propaganda Ministry. 'I am having an invasion of England theme written,' he wrote in his diary, 'new fanfare composed, English-speakers brought in, setting up propaganda companies for England, etc. . . . The coming weeks will be very nerve-racking. But they will provide further proof of the supreme skill of our propaganda. The other civilian ministers have no idea what is going on. They are working towards the apparent goal of England. I am eager to see how long it will be until things really take off.'

At the beginning of June, he called a meeting of specially selected senior staff. 'Gentlemen,' he told them, 'I know that some of you think that we are already going to fight Russia. But I must tell you today that we are going to fight England. The invasion is imminent. Please adapt your work accordingly.'

To Goebbels, the airborne invasion of Crete was a godsend. With Hitler's full approval, he wrote a major article for *Völkischer Beobachter*, headed 'Crete as an Example'. Much of it was concerned with describing the technical details of the operation, and praising the troops and the Luftwaffe. But the heart of the piece was a warning to Britain.

'If the British today are excitedly discussing the fall of Crete,' he wrote, 'all you have to do is substitute England for Crete, and then you will know why they are so frantic. If the Churchill clique in England doesn't discuss the theme of invasion publicly, it is not because they do not fear an invasion, but precisely because they do fear it . . . The Führer himself has coined the phrase that there are no more islands . . .'

The article was published on 13 June, in the Berlin edition of the paper – which was then 'seized' at 3 am and withdrawn from circulation 'at the request of the Wehrmacht', as soon as copies were known to have reached the foreign correspondents and embassies in the city. Goebbels then placed himself in public 'disgrace', to complete the illusion that he had committed a grave indiscretion.

The article worked like a bombshell, he wrote in his diary next day. 'Everything goes without a hitch. I am very happy about it. The big sensation is under way. English broadcasts are already claiming that our troop movements against Russia are sheer bluff, to conceal our plans for an invasion of England.' Next day, he was still congratulating himself, and no doubt blowing up the effects of his article out of all proportion. 'At home, people regret my apparent *faux pas*,' he gloated, 'pity me or try to show their friendship despite everything, while abroad there is feverish conjecture. We stage-managed it perfectly. Only one cable got through to the USA, but that is enough to bring the affair to the attention of the entire world. We know from tapped telephone conversations between foreign journalists working in Berlin that all of them fell for the decoy.'

While the 'greatest deception' ploy was pursued right through until June, Hitler also specified a second line which was to be followed at the same time. The two were not incompatible, and indeed there were several areas where they complemented each other beautifully. This second line was that some at least of the troops in the east were there as protection against the Soviet Union. As early as 6 September 1940, he directed the Abwehr to feed information to Soviet intelligence in such a way that the Soviets would 'draw the conclusion that we can protect our interests – especially in the Balkans – with strong forces against Russian incursion at any time'.

This, as we have seen, was the explanation fed to the German commanders. The 'Barbarossa' directive itself laid down that 'All orders to be issued to Commanders-in-Chief on the basis of this directive must clearly indicate that they are *precautionary measures* against the possibility that Russia should change her present attitude to us.' It was also the fiction that was fed to all Germany's allies, right up to the very last moments.

When Stalin began building up his forces in the border areas during the spring of 1941, in response to German strength there, he played right into Hitler's hands. Hitler was able to point to the growing 'threat' from the Red Army to justify his own 'defensive measures'. To lend added credence, he ordered that field fortifications were to be constructed, both near the border and in rear areas, though this was not to interfere with training for 'Barbarossa'. It was important, he laid down, that those defensive fortifications near the border should not be haphazard, but should be positioned in the most likely places for any real Soviet attack. At the same time, in order to help in misleading the Soviets, defences were to be built in those areas where the main centres of the German attack were going to be. The local Polish population was to be conscripted as labourers. They were certain to spread rumours of what they saw, which would mean that the information that the Germans were preparing for defence in depth would soon reach British and Soviet ears.

This line of deception was particularly valuable in implying that

Germany would react only to Soviet moves. According to Warlimont, it 'certainly caused confusion in the German ranks and convinced many senior officers that Hitler's decision to invade Russia was made in the spring of 1941 only under the threat of a Soviet attack on Germany'. Stalin's determination not to do anything that might be regarded as provocative demonstrates just how successfully it confused him, too. It was largely responsible for persuading him that Hitler was about to make fresh demands on him during the summer of 1941, and that he could therefore expect to receive some sort of ultimatum on which he could negotiate, before any attack.

This expectation was strengthened by rumours, assiduously spread by Canaris, Goebbels and the Foreign Ministry. To ensure that the rumours reached beyond Germany, they were firmly planted in Goebbels's Auslandpress Klub and Ribbentrop's Ausland Klub, which were frequented by foreign press men, neutral diplomats, senior state officials and army officers. One of the most plausible of these rumours named the actual conditions that Hitler was to demand of Stalin in his ultimatum, most notably that he wanted German control over the grain-producing Ukraine. Indeed, Goebbels was responsible for circulating the claim that Hitler wanted a ninety-nine-year lease of the Ukraine.

Göring backed this up in mid-June by telling his old friend Birger Dahlerus, in a five-hour session in Berlin, that he had personally drafted a list of demands to ensure the steady supplies of food and oil which Germany needed from the Soviet Union in order to continue the fight against Britain. These included demobilisation of the Red Army, the establishment of a separate government in the Ukraine, control of the Baku oilfields, and a guaranteed outlet to the Pacific. Dahlerus was led to believe that these would be presented to Stalin in the near future, in the shape of an ultimatum. Dahlerus, always notoriously indiscreet, hurried off to Stockholm and told the British minister and the American embassy. So convincing was this information that when it reached the State Department in Washington, Sumner Welles told Lord Halifax – who was now British ambassador to the USA – that this was part of Hitler's pressure tactics, and that he thought Stalin would agree to almost everything, except Soviet demobilisation.

Other officially started rumours were designed to strengthen the impression that negotiations were still possible between Germany and the Soviet Union, and that all would soon be well between them. In Rome the state radio broadcast a story that they had already signed a full-scale military alliance. And Ribbentrop is believed to have been responsible for the rumour that swept Berlin at the end of May that Stalin himself was about to arrive in an armoured train for talks with Hitler in Berlin or Königsberg. This story was supported by various arrangements that were made in Berlin. The management of the Schloss Bellevue was told at the end of May to prepare for a visit by

Soviet dignitaries and the Anhalter railway station was closed to the public at the beginning of June while decorations with red banners and a huge electric red star were tried out. In both cases, the staff were given strict orders not to talk about what was going on – with the inevitable and desired result that they all talked like mad and the story spread swiftly throughout the city.

Ruth Andreas-Friedrich, the young woman who had noted Hitler's rehearsals for the French armistice, recorded the effect in her diary for Sunday, 15 June:

' "Have you heard?" my milkman says, confidentially. "Stalin is coming to Berlin. Two hundred women have been put to work sewing flags."

' "You don't say!" I am astonished. "Two hundred women? Really to sew flags?"

' "Absolutely for sure. I heard it from an absolutely reliable source."

'. . . As I go home with my purchases, I meet a neighbour on the stairs. "Heil Hitler!" he says smartly. "Have you heard the latest? Stalin is arriving in the next few days, by special armoured train." He measures me with a glance of triumph. "Heil Hitler!" he repeats smartly, and marches on iron heels down the stairs.

' "Stalin is coming . . . Stalin is on the way," the rumour runs like wildfire through the town.'

Other rumours were started at lower levels, one source being a member of the Wehrmacht staff disguised as a porter in the Berlin fruit and vegetable market, meeting place for hundreds of shopkeepers and merchants. Another useful starting point was the newspaper distribution centre, where newsagents collected their supplies every morning. These stories were generally simple and direct, talking of improved deliveries of grain from the Soviet Union, the possibility of Stalin taking a four-week rest cure at Baden-Baden, the stopping of all leave in the West, and the 'fact' that there were to be no more through trains to the West.

Such rumour-mongering may seem pointless and insignificant. But in fact it had an extremely important part to play in the deception campaign as a whole, helping to create confusion and 'noise' – the swamping of genuine intelligence information with a mass of disinformation, distortions and half-truths. With hindsight, it is always easy to pick out the true information, but at the time it can be virtually impossible, and the more successful an enemy is at creating 'noise', the more difficult it becomes. Stalin received the correct information that 'Barbarossa' would start on 22 June for instance – but he was also given other dates ranging from 6 April right through May and up to 15 June – and as each one proved wrong, it became less likely that he would accept the true version for what it was. Werner Wächter, a senior official at the Propaganda Ministry, later explained Goebbels's technique in admirably simple language. The preparations for 'Barbarossa', he said, were accompanied by so many rumours, 'all of which were equally credible, that in the end there wasn't a bugger left who had any idea what was really going on'.

Certainly, that comment seems to have been true for Stalin and his intelligence chiefs as the hour for the attack drew steadily closer.

53

'I HAVE SURE INFORMATION'

There was no shortage of genuine and often accurate warnings of Hitler's intentions – some historical analysts have since identified and documented at least eighty-four. With all the rumours and German-inspired 'noise' and disinformation, it must have seemed to Stalin that the whole world was crying wolf as messages flooded in from friend and foe alike. They came, indeed, from all quarters: from Soviet spy rings in Western Europe and Japan; from Soviet embassies and consulates in many different countries; from naval and military field intelligence; from the Poles, Czechs, Yugoslavs, Swedes, Americans and British; even from Germans.

From Tokyo on 2 May, Richard Sorge, the master spy working for the GRU, Soviet Military Intelligence, radioed:

1. Hitler is fully determined to make war upon and destroy the USSR, in order to acquire the European area of the USSR as a raw materials and grain base.
2. The critical dates for the presumed initiation of hostilities:
   (a) the completion of the destruction of Yugoslavia
   (b) completion of the spring sowing
   (c) completion of the talks between Germany and Turkey.
3. The decision about the hostilities will be taken by Hitler in May.

Sorge, born in Baku to a German father and Russian mother, had grown up in Germany and was a journalist by profession. He had been recruited by the GRU in 1929, and had been active in Japan since 1933, following a period as head of a spy network in Shanghai. A man of magnetic personality, a *bon viveur* and inveterate womaniser, Sorge had quickly made his mark among Tokyo's foreign community. As a 'loyal' Nazi – he joined the party in 1934 – and Japanese correspondent for the prestigious newspaper the *Frankfurter Zeitung*, he found himself welcome in the German embassy, and soon became a boon drinking companion of the ambassador, Major-General Eugen Ott, from whom he obtained much of his information.

Sorge sent his first news about the impending German attack to Moscow on 5 March 1941, in the form of microfilm of a series of telegrams from Ribbentrop to Ott. The date of the invasion was then given as some time in May.

In April, following a drinking session with the German military attaché, Colonel Max Kretschmer, he was able to inform Centre in Moscow: 'The decision on peace or war depends solely on Hitler's will, and is quite irrespective of the Russian attitude.' More drinking sessions with German military men enabled him to update his intelligence during May: the attack would now begin on 20 June, or possibly two or three days later; in any case, the military preparations for the invasion were complete. An estimated 170–190 German divisions, he reported, were massed on the eastern front. He was even able to inform Moscow that Hitler would issue no ultimatum or declaration of war, but would strike at the USSR without warning. The German High Command calculated, he said, that the Red Army would rapidly disintegrate in the face of their *Blitzkrieg* tactics, and the Soviet regime would fall within two months – an accurate account of Hitler's own predictions.

On 15 June, Sorge acquired additional information which enabled him to pinpoint the start date for 'Barbarossa'. He radioed Moscow that the attack would definitely begin on 22 June.

The second major Soviet spy network to report was the *Rote Kapelle*, the 'Red Orchestra', based in France and the Low Countries and run by a Polish Jew, Leopold Trepper, codenamed 'Le Grand Chef'. Part of this network operated from Berlin, where it was led by Luftwaffe Lieutenant Harro Schulze-Boysen, the man who had reported on the German mission to Soviet aircraft factories.

In January 1941, shortly after Hitler had issued the 'Barbarossa' directive, Schulze-Boysen had sent his GRU director precise information about the plan. The invasion, he reported, would begin with a massive aerial bombardment of Leningrad, Kiev and Vyborg (Viipuri). He was also able to supply information about the number of divisions Hitler was prepared to commit to his grand design.

In February, Trepper followed up with details of the German divisions which were being withdrawn from France and Belgium and sent to the east. In May, he gave his contact in the Soviet embassy in Vichy, the military attaché General Susloparov, further information about German plans, including the original date: 15 May. Later, he reported that this had been postponed, because of the Balkan campaign.

On 21 June, Trepper learned from Schulze-Boysen and another of his agents that the German invasion would start next day. He rushed to Vichy to pass the news to Susloparov, whose response was off-putting to say the least.

'You're completely mistaken,' the general declared. 'Only today I met with the Japanese military attaché, who has just arrived from Berlin. He assures me that Germany is not preparing for war. We can depend on him.'

Why a Soviet general should take the word of a military attaché from one of Germany's allies was beyond Trepper.

Stalin's attitude to intelligence reports predicting war was made clear by April 1941. Another GRU agent, a vice-president of the Skoda armaments firm in Czechoslovakia named Skvor, reported through Berlin with details of the massive movement of troops to the east. He also gave the significant information that Skoda had been ordered by Göring to stop delivering arms to the Soviet Union under the economic treaty, because war had been scheduled for the second half of June. When this report was passed to Stalin on 17 April, he wrote on it in red ink: 'This information is an English provocation. Find out who is making this provocation and punish him.' A GRU major was promptly sent to Berlin under cover as a Tass correspondent to carry out the order.

There is no record of whether the major succeeded in his mission, but it is doubtful if he would have received a great deal of co-operation from the 'Red Orchestra' or from the Soviet embassy. The embassy itself had been sending similar reports since the beginning of the year, starting with an anonymous letter that reached Major-General Tupikov, the military attaché, on 25 December, giving a full and accurate summary of the 'Barbarossa' directive. A few weeks later, in mid-February, the embassy received another gift, this time from a German printer, in the form of a German–Russian phrase book which his firm was producing in large numbers for the army. It contained sentences such as: 'Where is the kolkhoz chairman?', 'Are you a communist?', 'What is the name of the secretary of the district committee of the party?', 'Hands up or I shoot!' 'Surrender!'

On 14 March, Tupikov sent Moscow a statement he had obtained from a German major: 'We are changing our plan completely. We are going east, against the USSR. We will seize the USSR's grain, coal and oil. Then we will be invincible and we can go to war against England and America.' Within the week, Tupikov was reporting that Germany would invade between 15 May and 15 June.

Being committed to the idea that Britain and America were intent on creating war between Germany and the Soviet Union, Stalin automatically regarded any warning received from either as a deliberate provocation. This was naturally frustrating for the English-speaking nations, but they had to try, nevertheless, to convince him of the truth.

For America, the most important warnings came from two very different sources: an amateur intelligence gatherer, the US commercial attaché in Berlin, Sam E. Woods, and the highly professional code-breakers of the US Army's Signal Intelligence Service. They were all passed on to the Soviet ambassador in Washington by the Under-Secretary of State, Sumner Welles, who was specifically assigned to this task by President Roosevelt and Secretary of State Cordell Hull.

Sam Edison Woods was an amiable and unassuming Texan, a man of commendable discretion with a talent for friendship. He was not a career diplomat, but a qualified engineer who had been a businessman and also a college teacher for many years, before joining the State Department in 1928 at the relatively ancient age of thirty-six. He became a commercial attaché in Prague first, and then in Berlin, where he made friends with a number of well-placed people, including Johnnie Herwarth during one of his sojourns in the capital. From those friends, and one in particular, Woods received a steady flow of vital information from mid-1940 onwards.

'Sam Woods,' wrote William Shirer, 'a genial extrovert whose grasp of world politics and history was not striking, seems to those of us who knew him and liked him the last man in the American embassy in Berlin likely to have come by such crucial intelligence.' Nevertheless, he undoubtedly did come by it, and he passed it all on to Washington, where Welles in turn passed it to Soviet Ambassador Umansky.

Exactly who gave Woods the information – usually in the shape of handwritten notes passed over in the darkness of various Berlin cinemas, where they met for safety – remains something of a mystery. Woods never revealed the identity of his informant, either at the time or after the war, when the man might have been in danger from embittered countrymen. It has been asserted that the special friend was none other than Johnnie Herwarth, but Herwarth himself, while acknowledging that he had 'a number of far-reaching conversations', denies it. 'Granted that I had done the Americans a favour by my earlier revelations to Bohlen, and that my reports to Woods may also have been useful, I cannot flatter myself that I played the cloak-and-dagger role assigned to me after the event.' In any case, for most of the time when Woods was meeting his mysterious friend in darkened movie houses, Herwarth was with his regiment in France or Poland.

As early as August 1940, Woods was told that 'Sea Lion' was no more than a blind. In January, he was able to send to Washington a long and accurate report giving details of Germany's military and economic plans for the Soviet Union.

When Hull and Welles were satisfied of the authenticity of Woods's information, they took it to Roosevelt, who declared that the Soviets must be informed at the highest level. This was fine, but the problem, as always, was how to do it. The normal course of events would have been for the US ambassador in Moscow to pass the intelligence direct to the appropriate authorities. But when Laurence Steinhardt was consulted, he pointed out that it would be fruitless for him to hand such intelligence to Molotov or Vyshinsky direct – because they simply would not believe it. They would see it as yet another Anglo-American provocation.

On 20 March, therefore, Welles took the initiative himself. At an official meeting with Ambassador Umanski on a quite different matter, Welles took him aside and, off the record, told him what the US government had learned. 'Mr Umansky turned very white,' Welles wrote later. 'He was silent for a moment, then merely said: "I fully realise the gravity of the message you have given me. My government will be grateful for your confidence and I will inform it immediately of our conversation." '

Naturally, Welles could not tell Umansky the source of this information. Still less could he tell him anything about America's other prime source of information at that time – 'Magic', the breaking of the Japanese diplomatic ciphers. All he could do was pass it on, and hope. From intercepted and deciphered radio messages between Ambasador Oshima in Berlin and the Japanese Foreign Ministry, the Americans were able to obtain repeated confirmation of the coming invasion. On 4 June, for instance, Oshima reported to Tokyo following meetings with Hitler and Ribbentrop: 'Both men tell me that in every probability war with Russia cannot be avoided.' A few days later, he advised: 'For the time being I think it would be a good idea for you, in some inconspicuous manner, to postpone the departure of Japanese citizens for Europe via Siberia. You will understand why.'

The British had first tried to warn Stalin of the danger he was in from Hitler on 25 June 1940, when Churchill wrote a personal letter to him. He was convinced, he said, that Germany wanted to engulf the whole of Europe, including the Soviet Union, and suggested that Britain and the Soviet Union should get together for mutual self-protection. No doubt remembering the British failure to respond to his calls for collective security in the spring and early summer of 1939, Stalin swept such suggestions aside contemptuously, saying he did not believe German military successes threatened the Soviet Union in any way. He then proceeded to give the Germans a full written account of Churchill's proposals, and of everything that had been said during his meeting with the new British ambassador in Moscow, Sir Stafford Cripps.

Churchill's warning in the summer of 1940 was not based on any hard evidence. Indeed, as Churchill himself wrote later: 'Up till the end of March [1941] I was not convinced that Hitler was resolved on mortal combat with Russia nor how near it was. Our intelligence reports revealed in much detail the extensive German troop movements towards and into the Balkan states . . . But none of these necessarily involved the invasion of Russia and all were readily explainable by German interests and policy [in that area].' As if to justify Stalin's own suspicions of Britain's motives, Churchill goes on: 'That Germany should at that stage, and before leaving the Balkan scene, open another major war with Russia seemed to me to be too good to be true.'

Churchill, together with all the British intelligence assessors and Foreign Office experts, was almost completely taken in by the German deception smokescreen. Not even the increasingly regular decrypts of intercepted German radio traffic using the supposedly impregnable Enigma ciphers could provide clear and unmistakable proof, since everything that was revealed was open to other interpretations. It is small wonder, therefore, that Stalin, too, was unconvinced.

The picture changed for the British Prime Minister, at least, on 27 March, the day of the coup in Belgrade. The Enigma decrypts then revealed that the movement of Panzer divisions from Romania to Poland, which had been ordered only the day before, after Yugoslavia had joined the Tripartite Pact, had been cancelled. Churchill commented later that this news 'illuminated the whole scene in a lightning flash. The sudden movement to Cracow of so much armour needed in the Balkan sphere could only mean Hitler's intention to invade Russia in May. This seemed to me henceforward certainly his major purpose. The fact that the Belgrade revolution had required their return to Romania involved perhaps a delay from May to June.'

Having confirmed this conclusion with his Foreign Minister, Anthony Eden, he set about trying to persuade Stalin. On 3 April he sent him a message, via Cripps: 'I have sure information from a trusted agent that when the Germans thought they had got Yugoslavia in the net, that is to say after 20 March, they began to move three out of the five Panzer divisions from Romania to southern Poland. The moment they heard of the Serbian revolution this movement was countermanded. Your Excellency will readily appreciate the significance of these facts.'

Churchill's instructions to Cripps was that he should deliver this message to Stalin in person and immediately. For a variety of reasons, which made Churchill furious when he found out, Cripps did not deliver it until 19 April, more than two weeks later. One of the reasons was that Cripps, although he was personally convinced that Germany would attack, knew that Stalin would regard the message as a provocation. Vyshinsky, to whom Cripps handed the letter, did not acknowledge it until three days later, when he said he had given it to Stalin. Stalin never acknowledged it.

During his first wartime visit to Moscow on 15 August 1942, Churchill reminded Stalin of the letter, and to jog his memory even showed him a copy of the original. Stalin shrugged. He remembered it.

'I did not need warnings,' he said. 'I knew the war would come, but I thought I might gain another six months or so.'

Stalin's reply to Churchill was not entirely honest, though in 1942 it was convenient. In fact, his reception of the message is a perfect illustration of the difficulty encountered by the British in trying to persuade him to recognise the truth as it was, rather than the truth as he saw it. In spite of the difficulties, and of the obvious lack of trust, Churchill persevered from then until the start of 'Barbarossa'. Between mid-April and mid-June, Eden saw Soviet Ambassador Ivan Maisky no fewer than five times. Each time he warned him about the continuing German military build-up along the Soviet frontier – though he was careful not to say that both the British Foreign Office and the intelligence chiefs remained unconvinced right up until early June that it was not simply a ploy to intimidate the Soviet Union into granting even greater concessions. In fact, virtually the whole diplomatic world was reluctant to believe that Hitler would be mad enough to attack the Soviet Union, when he could probably get almost everything he wanted without actually going to war.

Churchill's attempts to warn Stalin were not confined to purely diplomatic channels, however. In his efforts to penetrate the barriers of suspicion and fear, he also used an altogether more unorthodox means of communication. Once he became convinced that Hitler really did mean to attack the Soviet Union – after 27 March – he turned to his intelligence service, ordering Victor Cavendish-Bentinck, chairman of the Joint Intelligence Committee, which was responsible for the co-ordination, assessment and direction of all British intelligence, to devise a method whereby material could be filtered through to the USSR in such a way that the British Enigma sources would not be compromised, nor Soviet suspicions aroused. It was important, Churchill stressed, that this material must not be seen to have originated with the British at all, but from some other, less contaminated, source.

Cavendish-Bentinck passed the problem over to Lieutenant-Colonel Claude Dansey, Vice-Chief of the Secret Intelligence Service. It was the kind of problem Dansey was by nature and experience peculiarly well equipped to solve. The *éminence grise* of British intelligence for the past ten years, Dansey had been working in the shady world of international intelligence and espionage since 1900. He was a notoriously devious operator – those who worked for him spoke in awe of his ability to think in nine different ways at the same time – and had high-level contacts in every country in the Western world.

Dansey quickly came up with a solution. It so happened that he had an agent in place who was ideally situated to help, albeit unwittingly: Alexander Allan Foote, a beefy Yorkshireman nearing his thirty-seventh birthday, a former corn-merchant, who had joined the RAF when his business failed, hoping to satisfy at last his taste for adventure. He had been headhunted by Dansey while serving in the RAF as an aircraft fitter, and became one of his numerous freelance agents, working for the 'Z Organisation', Dansey's own 'private' espionage organisation, which had no official connection with the SIS. After a remarkable period in Spain during the Civil War, he had infiltrated the GRU's European network, and was now working as radio operator and second-in-command of an important spy ring in Switzerland – a country which, as far as intelligence matters were concerned, Dansey regarded as his own personal fief.

The Soviet spy ring, one of the most successful of all times, has since come to be known as the 'Lucy Ring', after the codename of one of its central characters, Rudolf Rössler, an émigré German anti-fascist publisher who had settled in Lucerne – hence his codename: 'Lucy' = Lucerne. Rössler was not in fact a spy at all, but a brilliant analyst with a card-index mind who worked for a Swiss intelligence agency, the Bureau Ha. At the same time, he was also involved with the Soviet spy network run from Geneva by Sandor Rado, a Hungarian communist and an agent of long standing, and Allan Foote. Rado supplied Moscow with a steady flow of industrial, military and political intelligence from various sources, including a Franco-Swiss ring run by a Swiss journalist, Otto Pünter, and another small Soviet ring which operated from the International Labour Organisation office in Geneva, under the control of a German ILO employee called Rachel Dübendorfer.

In addition to controlling Allan Foote, and therefore all the Lucy Ring's communications to Moscow, Dansey also had direct links with the Pünter network, the Bureau Ha and Swiss intelligence, and Czech intelligence – which supplied the Swiss with much of their best information. He also controlled Rachel Dübendorfer, who had turned to the British for desperately needed money. Thus, via all these sources, Dansey was able to filter Enigma intelligence into one of the most trusted Soviet spy rings. Rössler, 'Lucy' himself, evaluated and authenticated the material, which was then transmitted to Moscow by Foote, its source totally disguised.

It was no coincidence, therefore, that in April 1941, while Churchill's message to Stalin was still lying undelivered on Cripps's desk in Moscow, the Lucy Ring informed Centre that Hitler would attack the Soviet Union in mid-June. They gave the date at first as 15 June, which they amended a few days later to 22 June. Right up to that date – and in fact for a further two years, until the Red Army had finally turned the tide against the Wehrmacht – Lucy continued to provide Moscow with exact details of the German order of battle and their every objective. But it was not until after 22 June that Stalin was prepared to accept any of it.

By 10 June, Enigma decrypts left no remaining doubts that the German build-up was in earnest and that this was no bluff on Hitler's part. While still passing intelligence through Switzerland, Churchill felt he had to continue with the direct approach. Since the previous four warnings through Maisky seemed to have had no effect and had not even been acknowledged, something more explicit was clearly needed. Sir Alexander Cadogan, the Permanent Under-Secretary of the Foreign Office, summoned the Soviet ambassador and told him he had important news for him.

'Please take a sheet of paper,' he instructed him, 'and put down what I tell you.'

Maisky took pencil and paper and, like an obedient schoolboy, wrote down at Cadogan's dictation a detailed account of German troop deployments in the region of the Soviet frontier. Cadogan gave dates and times of movements, the number and name of each division, its armaments, and where it had been positioned. When Maisky had finished writing, Cadogan rose to his feet and said: 'The Prime Minister asks you urgently to communicate all these data to the Soviet government.' Impressed, Maisky hurried back to the embassy to encipher a message to Moscow.

But the only response the British ever received was in the form of a Tass statement – generally believed to have been written by Stalin himself – which was broadcast on Moscow Radio on the evening of 13 June, and published to the world next day. As a mark of good faith, Molotov even called in Schulenburg before the broadcast and gave him an advance copy of the text.

The statement complained of widespread rumours of 'an impending war' between the USSR and Germany and blamed them on Cripps – who had just been recalled to London for consultations on the abject failure of his mission. After outlining the stories, the Tass statement went on to deny them, point by point: 'Despite the obvious absurdity of these rumours, responsible circles in Moscow have thought it necessary, in view of the persistent spreading of these rumours, to authorise Tass to state that they are clumsily concocted propaganda measures by forces hostile to the Soviet Union and Germany, which are interested in a further extension and intensification of the war.'

Germany, it seemed, had made no demands on the USSR. Indeed, she was abiding 'by the provisions of the Soviet–German non-aggression pact as steadfastly as the Soviet Union'. Rumours that Germany intended to break the pact and launch an attack against the Soviet Union were completely without foundation. As for the USSR, she, too, had every intention of abiding by the terms of the pact. Rumours that the Soviet Union was preparing for a war with Germany were 'false and provocative'.

This last-ditch attempt by Stalin to appease Hitler had no effect on the

German leader whatsoever. On the day the statement was published, he was far too busy in the Parliament Chamber of the old Chancellery, with the final briefing of his senior commanders. From 11 am till 6.30 pm, the generals and field marshals and admirals were made to give him final details of their plans and objectives. They were each given different times to arrive, and allocated different doors by which to enter the Chancellery, to conceal the fact that a great conference was taking place.

At 2 pm they broke for lunch, at which Hitler made what Halder described as 'a comprehensive political speech', explaining yet again his supposed reasons for his 'preventive war' against the Soviet Union, and stressing that the collapse of the Soviets would force Britain to give up the struggle. He also reminded the commanders that the war must be conducted with the utmost brutality, creating 'an unprecedented terror'.

The atmosphere of the conference was one of confidence, almost of eager anticipation. Everything was completely in order. The great timetable for the final deployment, which had been triggered on 22 May, was proceeding exactly on schedule. The machinery of Armageddon was rolling forward on well-oiled wheels.

54

'YOU CAN'T BELIEVE EVERYTHING YOU READ IN INTELLIGENCE REPORTS'

The Kremlin's hostile attitude to reports of German activities in the frontier zones was not likely to encourage any Soviet commander to venture his unsolicited opinion as to German intentions. Nevertheless, this did not prevent most frontier commanders from passing on their unwelcome intelligence – even if they had little hope of Moscow taking it seriously. Consequently, the intelligence from Britain, the USA, the world of diplomacy and the spy networks was augmented by disturbing reports from all along the frontier.

Stalin grew unnerved and irritated by these reports, according to Admiral Kuznetsov, the Navy Commissar, who said 'he brushed facts and arguments aside more and more abruptly.' But still they continued to come. Since mid-May, border commanders had been reporting increasing German aerial activity over their lines. On 2 June, the Main Directorate of Border Troops reported that they had identified eighty to eighty-five infantry divisions, seven armoured divisions, sixty-five artillery divisions and various other units being concentrated by the Germans near the Soviet frontier.

On 4 June, General Dimitri G. Pavlov, commander of the Western Special Military District with headquarters at Minsk in Belorussia, passed on a report from his intelligence section which made gloomy reading. Ever since 25 May, they had been noticing increased military activity amongst the German troops facing them; now, it was clear that they had been reinforced. Pavlov's intelligence had identified the recent arrivals as two SS Panzer divisions and two to three infantry divisions. At the same time, they were aware that the Germans had evacuated all local civilians from the border area. But perhaps the most disturbing news was that the Germans were already recruiting officials for posts in the future government of western Russia. All the signs pointed clearly to war. The report concluded, rather forlornly: 'The information on the intensive preparations . . . and on strengthened troop concentrations in the zone opposite the Western Military District is trustworthy.'

Leningrad Military District was responsible for the security of the Finnish frontier from the Baltic to the Arctic Ocean. It reported concentrations of German and Finnish troops in the far north, opposite the ports of Murmansk and Kandalaksha, on either side of the Kola peninsula. German troops, the intelligence section there reported, were being brought in by rail from northern Norway and by ship to the Finnish port of Oulu, at the head of the Gulf of Bothnia. The news from the Karelian Isthmus frontier at the southern end of the military district was equally alarming. Soviet border guards there reported increasing military activity, including the construction of a large number of towers on the Finnish side of the frontier.

Soviet officials in Leningrad noticed that when German ships put into the port now, they did not unload their cargoes but, after a visit from German consular officials, invariably turned round and sailed home again. The behaviour of the consular officials themselves was also perplexing to local tailors: the Germans, it seemed, had suddenly cancelled their orders for suits and overcoats.

Down in the Ukraine, Colonel I. I. Fedyuninsky took command of the 5th Rifle Corps of the Kiev Special Military District in April. His headquarters were in Kovel, some 133 kilometres south-east of Brest-Litovsk, 460 kilometres west of Kiev and just 60 kilometres from the frontier. On arrival at his new command, he discovered a tense situation, since the local border guards had for some time been observing sizeable troop movements on the German side of the frontier. Fediuninski reported this to the military district headquarters in Kiev, but was told that everything was 'proceeding in accordance with the non-aggression pact', and warned that 'any reports about the aggressive designs of the Hitlerites were considered provocations'.

Meanwhile, sinister rumours continued to circulate among the local population in the area, who were mostly either Poles or Ukrainian nationalists, both of whom loathed their new Soviet masters. Fedyuninsky wrote later that they said: 'You just wait. The war will begin soon. The Germans will show you!'

In Brest-Litovsk, the rumours had the effect of stimulating local trade. Shops began running short of the necessities of life as people hastened to stock up with such items as flour, sugar, kerosene and soap.

The Brest tailors and shoemakers continued to do a roaring trade, taking orders for overcoats, suits, shoes and boots from their Red Army customers. But once they had got the orders and pocketed the deposits, they did not rush to complete the work: they reasoned that if the Germans did attack, the Red Army personnel would be in no position to demand the goods they had ordered, which could then be resold to the victorious Germans.

All this, and more, was faithfully reported to Moscow, but without any apparent effect. Admittedly, on 5 June, sixty-six-year-old M. I. Kalinin, the President of the USSR, made a speech at the Military Academy in Moscow in the course of which he said: 'The Germans are preparing to attack us, but we are ready. The sooner they come, the better: we will wring their necks.' But not only was Kalinin wrong, he was also completely out of step with Stalin and the rest of the Politburo.

When the draft for a new set of instructions to the Red Army's political workers was circulated to the party hierarchy for comment on 3 June, Georgi M. Malenkov, then head of the Central Committee's Cadre Administration, a man described by Roy Medvedev as 'the instrument of Stalin pure and simple', exploded. The instructions, emphasising the need for the armed forces to remain vigilant, ready for war at any moment, were totally contrary to his master's policy. Malenkov was scathing in his condemnation. 'The document,' he declared, 'is formulated in primitive terms as though we were going to war tomorrow.' Forewarned by Malenkov, Stalin rejected the offending draft out of hand. The instructions were never issued.

The same deliberate blindness was much in evidence elsewhere, too. When Zhukov was appointed Chief of the General Staff in Moscow, he was replaced as commander of the Kiev Military District by Colonel-General M. P. Kirponos. A close friend of Timoshenko, Kirponos had been lucky in his career. He had been commandant of the infantry commanders' school in Kazan from 1934 to 1939 and so had been forgotten in the purges which had eliminated so many of his contemporaries. Promoted to divisional commander in the Finnish war, less than a year later he was now in charge of one of the largest and most important military districts in the Soviet Union.

'It is quite possible that Kirponos ranks at present amongst our most prominent generals,' his gruff, beetle-browed Chief of Staff Lieutenant-General M. A. Purkayev once remarked, 'but his military talents . . . are not striking.' Certainly, Kirponos's chief talent seems to have been for surviving. Yet he was no fool. As he listened to the information which his chief intelligence officer, Colonel G. I. Bondarev, brought him day after day, he became more and more worried. Eventually, on 10 June, he called a full meeting of his military council.

Colonel Bondarev began the proceedings with a summation of their present knowledge of German troop movements in their sector. After some discussion, Purkayev, who had not spoken until that point, suddenly demanded that Moscow should be advised of the urgent need to improve the transport facilities of the whole command. 'There are no tractors,' he said. 'Many divisions are not fully equipped with transport; there is nothing on which to deliver ammunition; and there is also a shortage of manpower . . . if something should happen now, the corps would be unable to move out a considerable part of its artillery.'

Everyone looked to Kirponos. But the general was not prepared to risk his neck by informing Stalin of something he did not want to know and which in any case was contrary to official policy. 'You and I ought to understand,' he told the meeting, 'that the party and government leaders and Comrade Stalin personally, while taking every possible step to strengthen the country's defence capacity, are preoccupied with one thought: to prevent an outbreak of war with Germany, which the British and French governments so obstinately wish to provoke. To build up the manpower of our divisions and corps to full strength, to supply them with the tractors and trucks they lack . . . would require partial mobilisation. It would be impossible to hide this from German intelligence.'

The political commissar, Vashugin, naturally backed up Kirponos strongly. However, as a compromise, a decision was made to move some units closer to the frontier. No sooner had this begun than a blistering telegram arrived from Zhukov in Moscow:

Report on what grounds you ordered the units . . . to occupy the forward zone. Such actions can immediately provoke the Germans to armed conflict and are fraught with all kinds of consequences. Cancel the order immediately and report who, specifically, issued that arbitrary order.

Zhukov was obviously acting under orders himself when he sent his telegram to Kirponos. He claimed in his memoirs that he and Timoshenko already realised that it was no longer a question of if the Germans would attack but when and where. They finally decided, he wrote, that things could not be allowed to drift any further. On Friday, 13 June, Timoshenko telephoned Stalin and asked permission to alert and deploy Soviet border forces, as a preventive measure.

'We will think it over,' Stalin replied.

The following day, Timoshenko annd Zhukov went to see Stalin in person. Once again, they impressed on him the growing concern of the frontier commanders: their troops must be put on combat readiness as soon as possible, they said. But Stalin still hesitated.

'You propose carrying out mobilisations, alerting the troops and moving them to the western borders?' he wailed. 'That means war! Do you understand that or not?'

Eventually, he demanded to know how many Soviet divisions were already stationed in the border areas.

'149,' was the reply.

'Well, isn't that enough?' demanded Stalin. 'According to our information, the Germans do not have so many.'

Zhukov did his best to explain that the German divisions were all up to full strength, at 14–16,000 men each, combat-ready and fully equipped. The Soviet divisions, on the other hand, were at best only at half strength and lacking much of their equipment. But Stalin was not disposed to listen to their arguments.

'You can't believe everything you read in intelligence reports,' he declared dismissively.

The commissar and his chief of staff left Stalin's office in gloomy mood, but they were determined to do something to prepare the defence of their country. Although Stalin had expressly forbidden them to move troops up to the frontier without his permission, he had said nothing against holding tactical exercises in border areas. So they encouraged their military district commanders to conduct a series of troop manoeuvres – and if these should happen to take place near suitable deployment areas, and railheads, so much the better.

All the military districts co-operated willingly. But ironically, the very success of this scheme almost proved fatal. Since the beginning of the year, the Soviet artillery had not practised range firing, and was therefore unprepared for real warfare. Aware of this, most of the district commanders decided to send part of their artillery to the ranges. As a result, many corps found themselves without most of their guns when the Germans attacked.

Admiral Kuznetsov, the Naval Commissar, found himself in exactly the same situation as Timoshenko. At a conference in the Kremlin on 13 June, Kuznetsov gave Stalin the latest naval intelligence about German ship movements. Soviet fleet commanders, he said, were by now convinced that the Germans were preparing a major offensive against the Soviet Union from the Barents Sea to the Bosphorus. He also pointed out that the Germans had stopped work on the cruiser which they had sold to the Soviets and which was being fitted out in the Leningrad shipyard with the aid of German technicians. It was the second time Kuznetsov had complained about German dilatoriness on that score. The first time had been in February. Then, Stalin had listened attentively and asked to be kept informed of developments. But now, Kuznetsov had the impression he was just not interested. 'Is that all?' Stalin asked, when the admiral finished.

It was obvious that Stalin was under great pressure. He was known to be becoming more and more irascible when anyone came to him with reports of the ever-growing German threat. Nevertheless, the following day, after a session with Molotov, Kuznetsov once again brought up the subject of suspicious German naval movements. He even produced a graph of German merchant ship traffic, which showed that German ships were leaving Soviet ports even if they were not yet completely loaded. By 21 June, he said, there would not be a single German cargo vessel in any Soviet port. Like Stalin, Molotov waved aside the evidence. 'Only a fool would attack us,' he said.

During the next seven days, Kuznetsov kept in constant touch with Timoshenko. He had already decided to follow the Defence Commissar's example and encouraged the Baltic, Northern and Black Sea Fleets to conduct a series of training exercises designed to bring them up to combat readiness. What he did not know was that the naval war had in effect already begun on 15 June, for on that day Hitler had given authority for German warships in the Baltic to start the 'annihilation of Russian submarines without any trace, including their crews' in waters to the south of the Aaland Islands. The assumption was that this could be achieved without serious risk of premature trouble, since it was normal practice for submarines to maintain radio silence while on patrol, and any loss would not be known for several days. Any incident that did become known could be passed off as an attack on a presumed British boat.

Even allowing for all the 'noise', false rumours and deliberate deception and disinformation created by Germany, there was obviously enough genuine intelligence from so many different sources by June that it still seems incredible that Stalin refused to recognise the truth. One of the major reasons was undoubtedly the way in which the intelligence was assessed and presented to him.

The man responsible for this was the director of the GRU and Deputy Chief of the General Staff, Lieutenant-General Filipp Ivanovich Golikov, who handled all intelligence about the war. Golikov was only about forty years of age when he was appointed to run the GRU by Stalin in June 1940. In view of the importance of the post, his loyalty and obedience must have been beyond question. A small, stocky man with a broad, friendly peasant face and a large, round, shaven head which always seemed too large for any cap, his political pedigree was impeccable. He was in many ways a typical military apparatchik, having joined the Red Army and the party in 1918. During the twenties and thirties his career had blossomed. In 1935, while still only in his middle thirties, he had risen to command a division and then, thanks to the disappearance of so many senior officers during the purges, had come promotion to corps commander. In 1939, he was given command of the 6th Army during the occupation of Poland – a politically sensitive military post, before being given command of the GRU.

The GRU was, in fact, a highly efficient organisation. 'Along with the collection and analysis of extensive data,' Golikov himself told Soviet historian A. M. Nekrich in 1964, three years after he had been promoted to marshal after completing a glittering career, 'the Intelligence Directorate exhaustively studied international information, the foreign press, the comments of public opinion, the military–political and military–technical literature of Germany and other countries. Soviet military intelligence had trustworthy and tested sources for obtaining secret information in a whole series of countries, including Germany itself.'

If the sources and the organisation and its director were all good, one may ask, why was the Soviet Union so unprepared for the German invasion?

'The trouble was,' Zhukov later declared, 'Golikov was directly responsible to Stalin and made no reports to anyone else, not even the Chief of Staff [Zhukov himself] or the Commissar for Defence, Marshal Timoshenko.'

Golikov was Stalin's man, and Stalin read only the intelligence reports and analyses prepared by Golikov's directorate. He did not, as Churchill frequently did, ever take time out to examine the occasional piece of intelligence material in its original state, so that he could judge for himself its significance and reliability. Moreover, Stalin depended on Golikov to sort out the reports, to divide them into sheep and goats, classifying them into 'reliable sources' and 'doubtful sources'. No one knows the criteria which Golikov employed in this categorisation, but some idea can be gained from a note he sent to various GRU agents on 20 March 1941. 'All documents claiming war is imminent,' he instructed his networks, 'must be regarded as forgeries from British or even German sources.'

According to Leopold Trepper, 'Le Grand Chef' of the Red Orchestra and a recipient of one of these notes, Golikov used to scribble in the margin of important reports from such agents as Schulze-Boysen, Sorge, and Trepper himself, the words 'double agent' or 'British source' – thus confirming Stalin's suspicion of any information that did not accord with his own view of reality.

Why should Golikov act like this? The obvious, and probably correct, answer is that Stalin wanted it that way, that Golikov was merely obeying orders and exhibiting what may be described as the Russian three U's syndrome: *ugadat, ugodit, utselet*. This can best be translated as: 'sniff out, suck up, survive.' Or to put it another way, find out what the boss wants, and give it to him regardless.

The person who actually took the intelligence reports from Golikov to Stalin was a man called Gnedich. He told a meeting in Moscow in 1966 that for two vital years, beginning in 1940, he 'delivered to Stalin and Molotov the reports of the information services. All of them passed through my hands.' This suggests that Gnedich was either a member of Golikov's staff or, as is more likely, of Stalin's own secretariat.

It was not that Stalin did not bother to read those reports which predicted an imminent German attack – indeed, there is considerable evidence that he studied them carefully – but he deliberately chose to ignore them. According to Gnedich: 'His policy was to take no defensive measures.' It did not matter, therefore, what Churchill or Sorge or Trepper or Lucy might send him; Stalin had no intention of making any use of it.

'Stalin,' declared Gnedich, 'took over the government not to prepare for the country's defence, but to reach agreement with Hitler.' He still believed, it seemed, that somehow Hitler could be fobbed off with more concessions, which would enable him to step up the war against Britain. The truth was, he had no alternative: there was nothing else he could do, for, in the words of Nikita Khrushchev, he had 'lost all confidence in the ability of the Red Army to put up a fight'. And he had every reason for his pessimism – for he himself had brought about the sad state of his armed forces by the military purges of 1937–8.

Stalin's intention in destroying the Red Army had been not only to remove a potential source of internal opposition, but also to create a new, politically more amenable institution in its place. From the ashes of the old would spring up a new army, sensitive to the demands of the party and its leader. But the plan had failed. The Finnish débâcle, if it proved anything, demonstrated that the new Stalinist military blueprint simply did not work. He had had to go back to the drawing board, and time was running out: it is impossible to create an army overnight. In 1941, Stalin was left with a Humpty Dumpty army, broken and disorientated, with an officer corps living in terror of their lives. It is no wonder that he had lost all confidence in it, and was prepared to do anything to buy more time. And in such a situation, it is perhaps small wonder that he should refuse to recognise what he did not wish to see.

The crowning irony to the eighty-four unheeded warnings of imminent German attack surely lies with Leopold Trepper's experience with his Soviet contacts in France. 'Le Grand Chef' had warned the Soviet military attaché in Vichy, General Susloparov, that according to his sources, 22 June was to be the start date for 'Barbarossa'. Although Susloparov was sceptical, he duly agreed to transmit Trepper's news to Moscow. The GRU's reply was delivered personally by the Soviet air attaché, Wolosiuk, when he returned to Vichy from a spell of home leave. Just before he left Moscow, Golikov had called him into his office to give him a personal message to pass on to Trepper.

'You can tell Otto [Trepper's codename] that I have passed on the information on the imminence of the German attack to the big boss. The big boss is amazed that a man like Otto, an old militant and an intelligence man, has allowed himself to be intoxicated by English propaganda. You can tell him that the big boss is completely convinced that the war with Germany will not start before 1944.'

The message was delivered to Trepper when Wolosiuk arrived back in Vichy – on Monday, 23 June.

55

'PUSHING OPEN THE
DOOR TO A DARK ROOM'

Three days after his last great conference with his military commanders at the Chancellery on 14 June, Hitler confirmed that 'Barbarossa' was to start at dawn on Sunday, 22 June, following the shortest night of the year. Out of a total strength of 3,800,000 men in Germany's field armies, 3,200,000 were now in their assembly areas in the east, ready to move forward to their start positions. All that was needed to trigger off the greatest invasion in history was the codeword: 'Dortmund'.

Through military channels, Hitler informed Romania, Finland, Hungary and Slovakia of his decision. He said nothing to the Italians – he had long since come to the conclusion that Italian security was so poor he could only tell them things he wanted his enemies to hear. In any case, he did not want to give Mussolini the chance to take part in the operation, partly because the Italians' military record was so bad they were more likely to be a liability than a help, and partly because he did not wish to share the proceeds with them. At the same time, he took the final step in safeguarding his southern flank by drawing up a treaty of friendship with Turkey, to ensure that the Turks kept out of the fight.

The German embassy in Moscow was not told officially, but Schulenburg was well aware of what was going on. The letters he wrote regularly to Pussi Herwarth show his mounting despair as the final weeks passed. On 20 May, he said everything was very quiet, with nothing to do, and he feared this was the calm before the storm. By 24 May, he was writing that he expected 'the affair which interests us' to come by the end of June, and commenting on how strange it seemed, after all the hectic activity of the previous two years, to have no German delegations of any sort in Moscow. 'The diplomatic pouch only takes a few minutes,' he wrote. 'There is nothing to do but swim and play tennis.' By 28 May, he was reporting that Moscow was full of rumours, both positive and negative.

Schulenburg's last letter from Moscow was sent on 17 June. 'This is probably the last courier by which I can write to you from here,' he told her. 'I will therefore report to you as much as possible. We still don't know anything, but the famous rumours are reaching Himalayan heights. The Soviet government published a communiqué five days ago, in which it claimed that the USSR would never attack Germany and that one should not expect an attack by Germany on the USSR. All the rumours collapsed. Everyone believed the communiqué had been issued with our agreement. But then there was no response from Germany. We don't know if the Soviet communiqué was even published in Germany! This caused the diplomatic corps to lose the little composure it still had! Yesterday, today and tomorrow the English and Italian women and children, as well as the Hungarians, departed or will depart. The Americans are staying put. But Steinhardt [the ambassador] has rented a dacha "somewhere" for his office, "just in case of emergency". He has also bought a bus for some incomprehensible reason and stocked up on petrol . . . Miyakarda [a Japanese official] spent a long time with Hilger yesterday, questioning him about the possibility of a German–Soviet clash. He could not believe we knew nothing about it . . . As you can see, dear Pussi, there is much going on here. But we are watching developments calmly.'

That same day, Schulenburg received orders from the Wilhelmstrasse to take steps to secure his secret files. He was also told that Berlin 'would have no objection to the inconspicuous departure of women and children'. He arranged for those remaining to start leaving immediately. The Soviet authorities raised no objections – in keeping with Stalin's policy of appeasement they even eased the normal exit formalities, and Hilger reported that Soviet frontier officials were more polite than ever to the German travellers.

Back in Berlin, however, Soviet Ambassador Dekanozov gave Hitler one of his worst frights when he suddenly asked to see Weizsäcker, on 18 June. The Chancellery was thrown into a state of near panic. Had Stalin woken up at last to what was going on? Was he about to deliver an ultimatum? Was he going to spoil everything by making some grand gesture of conciliation, some new offer that would be too good to refuse? Hitler and Ribbentrop went into a huddle with Hewel and Engel, Hitler's army adjutant, as they discussed the possibilities, and what they could do to forestall Stalin. They decided the Führer and his Foreign Minister would have to disappear from the capital, so they could not be reached. They might go to Ribbentrop's estate at Sonnenburg, or to Göring's Karinhall, or to Luftwaffe headquarters at Wildpark, outside Potsdam; even the Berghof was considered, despite its distance. In the end, they settled for the simple solution of using their special trains, and these were brought out of their sheds and prepared for a journey to nowhere, with the locomotives under steam at the station, ready to depart at a moment's notice.

As it happened, the trains were not needed. When Dekanozov called on Weizsäcker at 6 pm, he only wanted to discuss minor routine matters, and after a pleasant social chat left without even raising the subject of Soviet–German relations. Weizsäcker had found himself in something of a quandary, torn between the wish to warn Dekanozov and his professional duty to remain silent. 'Now that Hitler was waiting to pounce like a tiger,' he wrote in his memoirs, 'in this state of virtual war, I could only talk to Dekanozov in an unconcerned manner. If I had committed a political indiscretion in conversation with him, it would no longer have held up the disaster. At most, it would have put the Russian front on the alert and cost the lives of German soldiers.'

Hitler was told about Dekanozov's lack of concern while he was in the middle of dictating his proclamation to the troops, which was to be read out by the officers of every front-line unit before the attack began. But the news did little to lessen the tension, which was by now starting to take its toll on him. During the last few days, his mood alternated between nervousness and depression. His insomnia became markedly worse. Even after sitting up until 3 or 4 o'clock every night, wearing out Ribbentrop, Hewel, Himmler, Ley and his court circle with endless discussions, he could get to sleep only with the aid of sedatives. But his confidence and his resolve never faltered: his anxiety was solely that something might happen to upset his plans.

Most of Hitler's nerves came simply from impatience. On the day he had left the Berghof for Berlin, 11 June, he had sent his Wehrmacht adjutant, Rudolf Schmundt, to Rastenburg in East Prussia, to check that his new headquarters for the eastern campaign was ready for him to move into immediately 'Barbarossa' began. The headquarters, which he named 'Wolfschanze', 'Wolf's Lair', was a collection of wooden huts and concrete bunkers, set in a swamp in the middle of a dreary pine forest some eight kilometres outside Rastenburg. It was a damp and dismal spot, plagued by swarms of mosquitoes which were to make life hell for his staff, but he did not seem to mind. 'No doubt some government department found the land was cheapest here,' he joked. In any case, he only intended to stay there for about four weeks, since he expected the war against the Soviet Union to be over within two months at the outside. 'We have only to kick in the door,' he told Jodl, 'and the whole rotten structure will come crashing down.'

In the event, he was to occupy 'Wolfschanze' intermittently until 20 November 1944, and almost met his death there on 20 July of that year, when Colonel Claus von Stauffenberg exploded a bomb under his conference table, the last of a series of unsuccessful assassination attempts by a group of anti-Nazi officers. But that was still far in the distant future. In mid-June 1941, Hitler did not doubt that 'Wolfschanze' would be the base from which he was about to conduct his greatest triumph. 'This whole headquarters will one day become a historic monument,' he told Jodl, 'because here is where we founded a new world order.'

Hitler's certainty was echoed by all the leading lights in the Nazi Party. On 19 June, Alfred Rosenberg demanded that as soon as 'Barbarossa' started he should be given the Soviet embassy building at 63 Unter den Linden and the Soviet trade mission at 11 Lietzenburgerstrasse, to house his new Ministry for the East. He also asked for all the officials in the Soviet section of the Foreign Ministry, plus the staff of the Moscow embassy and all German consulates in the Soviet Union, to be transferred to his ministry, since they would no longer be needed when the Soviet Union ceased to exist as a separate state. Rosenberg's demands met with a frosty reception from Ribbentrop, but the Foreign Minister's refusal did little to dampen his enthusiasm.

Rosenberg's keenness was shared by others with vested interests in the destruction of the USSR. General Biskupsky, leader of the White Russian emigrants in Germany, had already had an Orthodox church service held to celebrate the coming events, and had begun setting up a Russian government from amongst his fellow immigrants. The Lithuanians, too, were eagerly anticipating their country's release from the communist yoke, and Kazys Skirpa, the former Lithuanian minister in Berlin, also called on the Foreign Ministry on 19 June to talk about the restoration of independence. There was already what amounted to a government-in-exile in Berlin, led by former Prime Minister Galvanaukas, which was ready and waiting. There were also, Skirpa pointed out, numerous armed partisan bands in Lithuania, which had been providing valuable intelligence to the German Abwehr, and which were ready and willing to take up the fight against the Russians as soon as the moment came.

That same day, Hitler sent for Hans Frank, his Governor-General in occupied Poland, and broke the news to him for the first time. 'We are facing a war with the Soviet Union,' he told him, and then, as Frank reacted with alarm, explained that German attack units would shortly be passing through Poland, but that there would be no fighting there. He went on to tell Frank that his territory would no longer have to be used as the Reich's dumping ground for Jews and undesirables. There would be no need for Frank to establish any more ghettos, since in due course all the Jews would be moved on to the east, to the area of what he called White Ruthenia, around Minsk. He promised a relieved Frank, who had always objected loudly to having to accommodate the Jews, that in future his area would serve only as a sort of giant transit camp.

Most Red Army officers deliberately closed their eyes to the looming catastrophe. Blindly they obeyed orders, telling themselves that whatever happened, 'the Boss knew best'. Such was the fear that Stalin's purges had wrought in the Red Army. When Rear-Admiral Golovko, commander of the Northern Fleet, asked his anti-aircraft battery commanders why they had not opened fire on a German reconnaissance plane which had flown low directly over the naval base at Polyarnyi on 17 June, obviously taking photographs, they replied that they had refrained for fear of 'causing confusion in some way'. It was an attitude that was common among all the Soviet forces.

On 17 and 18 June, Soviet border guard detachments in Belorussia succeeded in rounding up several groups of German saboteurs with orders to destroy railway lines and blow up bridges. If successful, they would have isolated the important railhead of Minsk from the western frontier, and paralysed Soviet army movements in much of the region. From the interrogation of the saboteurs, the NKVD learned that the Germans were expected to attack on 21–22 June. Stalin was informed but, as with so much else, chose to ignore the information, like a frightened child who hides his head under the blankets.

The date was confirmed on the evening of 18 June, further down the frontier in the Ukraine, when border guards picked up a German deserter. The guards telephoned Colonel I. I. Fedyuninsky, the recently appointed commander of the 5th Rifle Corps of the Kiev Special Military District, who immediately drove to the unit headquarters where the deserter was being questioned. The German, Fedyuninsky recalled later, 'was a young, tall, rather ungainly fellow, with big red hands which trembled perceptibly. I allowed him to sit down. He sank on to a stool in the middle of the room.' Fedyuninsky questioned him through an interpreter, and was told that he had struck an officer while drunk and, knowing he could be shot for this offence, had fled across the border. He had, he said, always sympathised with the Russians: his father was a life-long communist. He then repeated what he had already told the border troops' commander: the Germans were planning to attack all along the Soviet frontier, starting, he said, at 4 am on Sunday, 22 June. Seeing the colonel's scepticism, he declared: 'Colonel, sir, at 5 am on 22 June you can have me shot, if it turns out that I have lied to you.'

When he got back to his headquarters, Fedyuninsky immediately telephoned the commander of the 5th Army, Major-General M. I. Potapov, who was not impressed with his news.

'We should not believe provocations,' the general told him in a calm basso voice. 'A German fearing for his skin could babble anything.'

Fedyuninsky, who had already reported on German activity across the frontier, begged the general to allow him to move two rifle regiments closer to the border, but was told, 'You are sounding the alarm for no reason.' However, he persevered, pointing out that the Germans were hardly likely to notice the additional presence of two rifle regiments under cover of the trees in the forest, eight kilometres from the border. The general finally agreed. In doing so, he was deliberately ignoring Moscow's specific orders, for as reports of increased German activity multiplied and were passed back to the Kremlin by anxious commanders, the answer they received was always the same: 'Don't panic. Keep calm. The Boss knows all about it.'

Stalin himself appeared to be keeping perfectly calm, and most senior politicians were following his example. On 19 June, the Leningrad party boss and chief of the Main Naval Soviet, Andrei Zhdanov, left for his annual summer holiday with his wife and family at the Black Sea resort of Sochi, where Stalin also had a villa. It was a reassuring move for the general population: surely Zhdanov, of all people, the man still regarded as Stalin's heir, would not be allowed to take a vacation if there were any real danger of war.

In Moscow itself, the public knew nothing of the alarms on the frontier. Nothing appeared in *Pravda* or *Izvestia* to suggest that the Germans were gathering ready to strike, or even to hint that the international situation for the Soviet Union was other than hopeful. While the press in the entire outside world – with the exception of Germany and her satellites – was dominated by speculation on the imminence of war, or the possibility of fresh negotiations and concessions, editorials in Soviet newspapers during June dealt with such subjects as 'Preparing for Harvest', 'Mastering New Equipment' and at least twice with 'The Importance of More Fodder for Cattle on Collective Farms'.

The privileged few who were allowed to see newspapers and journals from abroad were instructed to ignore what they read. One of the young Wolfgang Leonhard's fellow students asked Walter Ulbricht, the future leader of communist East Germany, after a lecture, 'Comrade Ulbricht, foreign newspapers are carrying more and more frequent reports of the danger of a German attack on the Soviet Union. It is true that these reports are categorically denied in the Soviet press, but would it perhaps be possible to hear something in more detail on the subject?' Ulbricht simply repeated the official denial, and concluded, 'These are nothing but rumours spread with the intention of provoking trouble. There will be no war.'

Radio programmes were as proscribed as the newspapers, consisting mostly of concerts, poetry readings, lectures, and some sport. Current affairs coverage extended to little more than a weekly report on the war situation in the West and lectures on such subjects as the Battle of the Somme, in the first world war.

Not surprisingly, the average Muscovite was more concerned about the weather than the international situation. The month had started badly, with snow on 2 June, heavy rain on 7 June, and bitter cold –

temperatures in the first few days were the lowest for the time of year since 1881. By 11 June, however, the thermometer had reached 17°C, climbing to a hopeful 21°C the following day, and by the second half of the month seemed to be settling into the normal summer pattern. The good news was that the long-range forecast predicted much warmer weather in July, August and September. What the ordinary Soviet citizen failed to realise was that this was even better news for the Germans, who had been watching the early rains with some concern. By 20 June, Halder was able to record in his diary, with some relief, that the weather in the east was now 'favourable' with 'rivers partly below normal'.

Moscow was looking at its best by then. The gilded onion domes glittered in the sun and children played happily in the Alexandrov Gardens beneath the Kremlin walls, amid a profusion of lilac and chestnut-tree blossom. The schools had closed for the summer vacation on Friday, 13 June, and the following day the Moscow city council announced the reopening of Soviet Square, off Gorky Street, which had been closed to the public for restoration work. The gardens had been planted with linden trees and even some palms, plus 500 rose bushes, some of which were already in bloom. The remainder, it was promised, would flower in July and August. The fountain in the centre of the square was working again, and would be floodlit every evening until 11 pm.

For the average Muscovite, life was even slightly improved because more food and clothing were available: with the extra production targets forced on the people to meet Stalin's commitments to Germany, some goods and materials inevitably spilled out on to the domestic market. Elderly Muscovites today still fondly recall the 'consumer summer' immediately before the German invasion – though this did not seem to have penetrated the whole of the state supply mechanism. An inspector for the Trade Commissariat reported on the shortage of fresh vegetables in the official greengrocery shops in the city. The entire stock of one shop he visited consisted of ten bunches of radishes and twenty cucumbers – though at a nearby unofficial street market all kinds of farm produce was on offer in profusion.

Life went on as normal in sport and leisure, as though there were no threat from outside. Moscow Dynamo, the leading soccer team, lost its unbeaten record; over 500 oarsmen competed in races on the Moscow river near Gorky Park; sailing dinghies raced on a local reservoir; twenty-seven vehicles, ranging from small Kim 10 saloon cars to ZIS 5 heavy trucks, took part in a motor rally, racing through the countryside around Mosow on a 44·5 kilometre course that heavy overnight rains had turned into rivers of mud.

In the park where the All-Union Agricultural Exhibition was being held, the circus played through the month, from 11 June – anyone who bought a free ticket for the circus got into the exhibition free. Star of the show was 'Charlie, the almost human monkey' – who turned out to be a clown in a monkey skin. Nearby in the park, a grand fencing competition involving teams from seven Soviet cities was held from 15–20 June.

The Moscow theatre scene was as lively as usual. Opera lovers could enjoy Verdi's *La Traviata* and Gounod's *Romeo and Juliet* at the Bolshoi during the month, alternating with ballet programmes, and a new production of *Rigoletto* opened on 19 June. A Russian translation of Molière's *Tartuffe* was playing at the Gorky Theatre, while the Moscow Arts Theatre offered Chekhov's *The Three Sisters* and a dramatisation of *Anna Karenina*, and promised a new production of Sheridan's *School for Scandal* later in the season.

The programmes displayed a curious lack of German influence. Wagner seems to have been banished again, and the only German writers represented on the Soviet theatre scene were Schiller, whose *Mary Stuart* – a British subject, in fact – was playing at the Leningrad District Theatre, and Rudolf Friml, whose *Rose Marie* – which was set, of course, in Canada – was packing them in at the Operetta Theatre.

On 18 June, one quarter of *Izvestia* – a whole page – was devoted to articles celebrating the anniversary of the death of the famous writer, Maxim Gorky. In the same edition, a government advertisement called on all Soviet citizens to collect glass jars and bottles for re-use. If they were undamaged and clean, the price offered for one-litre jars was one rouble, while bottles fetched fifty kopeks. Giant fifteen-litre bottles were worth as much as six roubles each. Other advertisements featured a new eau de cologne, 'Zhiguli', and a face cream, 'Nochnoy', which could be obtained in all Moscow shops, and 'Ugrim', a cream guaranteed to clear up pimples and blackheads.

But of the likelihood of war, there was still no mention.

Eight hundred thousand copies of Hitler's proclamation to the troops on the eastern front were issued secretly to the armed services on the evening of 20 June, in a leaflet comprising four closely printed pages which Halder described as 'a long-winded manifesto'. The leaflets were to be rushed to the front and distributed to every company and platoon – a considerable feat of logistics – to be read out to the men by their officers on the night of 21 June, before the attack. Security was so tight during printing and distribution – both of which took an incredibly short time – that no hint of the leaflet or its contents was leaked to the Soviets or anyone else. The proclamation, in fact, was way above the head of the average soldier, consisting mainly of a review of German foreign policy since 1939, and the political reasons why Hitler felt he had to attack the Soviet Union.

'Weighed down for many months by grave anxieties, compelled to keep silent,' Hitler began, 'I can at last speak openly to you, my soldiers.'

He went on to claim that the German people had never wished any harm to the Russians, 'but for two decades the Jewish–Bolshevik rulers of Moscow have endeavoured to set not only Germany but all Europe alight.' He described Soviet attempts at subversion, and charged them with creating tension by a massive build-up of forces along the German frontier. 'You, my soldiers,' he said in an astonishing piece of blatant distortion, 'know for yourselves that until a few weeks ago there was not one single German Panzer or mechanised division on our eastern frontier.'

The proclamation ended:

At this moment, soldiers of the eastern front, an assembly of strength on a size and scale such as the world has never seen is now complete . . . When this, the biggest front line in history now begins its advance, it does so not just to provide the means of ending this great war for all time, or to defend those countries now concerned, but for the salvation of our entire European civilisation and culture.

German soldiers! You are about to join battle, a hard and crucial battle. The destiny of Europe, the future of the German Reich, the existence of our nation, now lie in your hands alone.

May the Lord God help us all in this struggle.

With his proclamation on its way to the front, Hitler ordered Jodl to issue the codeword: 'Dortmund'. It was flashed eastward by radio, and that night, under cover of darkness, the mighty juggernaut began moving steadily forward.

In the Chancellery, Hitler sat with his inner circle, talking the night away. He told Hewel that he had spent that morning going over every minute detail yet again, and had found no loopholes. There was no possibility, he said, of the enemy being able to get the better of Germany. But he wished he were ten weeks on, since there must always be an element of risk in any new campaign.

'I feel,' he said quietly, 'as if I am pushing open the door to a dark room, never seen before, without knowing what lies behind the door.'

56

'SURELY WE HAVE NOT DESERVED THAT'

Saturday, 21 June, was oppressively hot and close in Berlin. For those in the know, the heat and humidity added almost unbearably to the tension, which was increased still further when Valentin Berezhkov, first secretary in the Soviet embassy, telephoned the Foreign Ministry halfway through the morning and asked for an urgent appointment for Dekanozov to see Ribbentrop. Rattled, Ribbentrop ordered his office to say he was out of Berlin and would not be back until evening. Berezhkov asked to speak to Weizsäcker, but was told that the State Secretary, too, was unavailable – indeed, it seemed that all the high-ranking officials of the Foreign Ministry were either on holiday or out of town.

At about noon, Berezhkov did manage to raise Ernst Woermann, head of the political department at the Wilhelmstrasse, but all Woermann did was confirm the situation. 'There seems to be an important conference going on at the Führer's headquarters,' he explained rather lamely, 'so I expect they are all there. If you have any urgent business, tell me and I'll try and get in touch with the leadership.' Berezhkov said he could not do that: the embassy had a note which was to be handed only to the minister himself. The instructions from Moscow were quite specific. Would Woermann please inform Ribbentrop of this?

Woermann, of course, did so immediately he had put down the phone, calling Ribbentrop at the Chancellery, where he was closeted with Hitler. The news did nothing to calm either man's nerves – the last thing Hitler wanted now was to have his hand forced in any way by the Soviets. This time, there was no question of actually leaving Berlin, so Ribbentrop ordered his office to answer any further calls from the embassy by saying that as soon as he returned to the city that evening he would let Dekanozov know when he could see him.

At regular intervals throughout the day, Berezhkov – who was almost alone in the embassy since most of the staff had taken the day off to enjoy the sunshine in the Potsdam parks, or to go swimming in Berlin's lakes, the Wannsee and the Nikolassee – called the Foreign Ministry, spurred on by increasingly impatient messages from Moscow. But the answer remained the same, except that at 3.45 Ribbentrop gave a revised order to his staff – they were now to say they had not yet been informed as to when he would return, but that Dekanozov would be told immediately he did.

While Ribbentrop played his game of hide and seek with the Soviets, the deadline for any cancellation or alteration to the order for 'Barbarossa', 1.30 pm, passed in silence. There could be no turning back now: it was too late to stop the war machine.

Hitler spent the afternoon composing another proclamation, this time to the German people as a whole, which was to be read out over the radio by Goebbels at 5.30 next morning, and selecting suitable musical phrases for use as fanfares. He settled on a few bars of the *Horst Wessel* song to introduce the first proclamation, but had more difficulty deciding the right music to precede the announcement of victory in the east.

He also wrote long letters to Mussolini and Admiral Horthy, the Regent of Hungary, at last telling them what was happening, and laying all the blame on the Soviet Union. Claiming he had clear evidence that the Soviets were about to attack Germany, he told Mussolini he had decided 'to put an end to the hypocritical performance of the Kremlin'.

Most of the long letter to the Duce was the usual mixture of half-truths, wishful thinking and outright lies. Even the ending, though it was undoubtedly from the heart, contained a major distortion of the truth: 'Since I struggled through to this decision, I feel spiritually free again. The partnership with the Soviet Union, in spite of the complete sincerity of my efforts to bring about a final conciliation, was nevertheless often very irksome to me, for in some way or other it seemed to me to be a break with my whole origin, my concepts, and my former obligations. I am happy now to be relieved of these mental agonies.'

In between dictating these letters and checking the final drafts of the long memorandum to be presented to the Soviets in lieu of a declaration of war, the Führer managed to find time to talk to Albert Speer and Grand Admiral Raeder about his plans to build a great new naval base near Trondheim, in Norway. Along with the base would be state-owned shipyards and docks, and a brand-new city for a quarter of a million people, to be incorporated into the Greater German Reich. Not even the invasion of the Soviet Union, it seemed, was allowed to interfere with the progress of his grandiose schemes for the future.

Hitler had a second and more pressing reason to speak to Raeder. The evening before, he had received a report that a U-boat commander in the Atlantic had attempted to attack the US battleship *Texas*, which he had encountered some ten miles inside the blockade zone announced by Germany. Although Hitler had at first agreed that the U-boat commander had acted correctly, he had changed his mind on reflection, and had telephoned the naval High Command to order that no further attacks were to be made on US ships. Raeder tried to argue with Hitler, but the Führer was adamant. This was the second incident involving an American vessel within the last few days – another U-boat had sunk the freighter *Robin Moore* outside the blockade zone, claiming it had been carrying contraband goods for Britain. With so much at stake in the east, Hitler was terrified of doing anything which might bring the United States into the war. As far as he was concerned the timing of these two incidents could not have been worse, and he angrily forbade any attacks on US ships or aircraft, anywhere.

While Berezhkov kept trying to make an appointment for Dekanozov to see Ribbentrop, in Moscow Schulenburg was summoned to the Kremlin, to see Molotov. This sounded ominous – since the disaster of his visit to Berlin, Molotov had kept his distance, leaving contacts with the Germans to his deputy, Vyshinsky, and lower officials. Now, out of the blue, he suddenly wanted to see Schulenburg himself, at 9.30 that evening.

To Schulenburg's relief, Molotov still did not appear to realise the true gravity of the situation. The purpose of the meeting, it seemed, was to hand over a note protesting at the continuing flights by German aircraft over Soviet territory. Such blatant violations of Soviet air space could well have formed the basis for an ultimatum, and with any other nation than Germany, the Soviets would undoubtedly have delivered one. But all Molotov did in his note was to say he was sure the German government would put a stop to the flights.

Having completed the formal business by delivering this surprisingly mild admonishment, Molotov turned to the true reason for the meeting, talking about the rumours of war, and the general state of Soviet–German relations. He could not understand, he said, why the German government was giving the impression it was in some way dissatisfied with the Soviet government. Why, he wondered plaintively, had the Germans made no reponse to the Tass communiqué of 13 June? Could the dissatisfaction be the result of the Yugoslav question? He would be grateful if the ambassador could enlighten him. He was, in fact, asking what Hitler wanted from the Soviet Union, opening the door for fresh negotiations.

Poor Schulenburg, unhappy at being put into such a spot, could only stall. He had no information that would explain anything, he said. Molotov persevered, though still only gently. He had been told, he continued, that not only the businessmen but also all the women and children from the embassy had left the country. This made him wonder whether there might not be something in the rumours, after all. Schulenburg, unable any longer to hide his embarrassment, tried to justify the departures as simply the normal summer vacation trips home. Clutching at straws he added – truthfully, since several wives and secretaries had not yet been able to leave, because of the short notice – that not *all* the women had gone. At this, Molotov gave up, with what Hilger described as 'a resigned shrug of his shoulders'.

In Berlin, two hours after Schulenburg's meeting with Molotov, Dekanozov was at last admitted to the Foreign Office – though not to see Ribbentrop. Weizsäcker was delegated to receive him at 9.30 pm. The urgent message he had to deliver turned out to be the exactly the same note about overflights that Molotov had given Schulenburg. Dekanozov's instructions from Moscow were that he should invite the Germans to make the demands which Stalin was so certain would be coming. But Weizsäcker cut short any discussion by insisting that he had a long list of Soviet violations of German air space, and that it should therefore be Germany that was making the protest. He sent Dekanozov away, telling him a reply would be made later.

While Molotov was seeing Schulenburg, Defence Commissar Timoshenko, together with Chief of Staff Zhukov and Zhukov's deputy, Lieutenant-General Vatutin, were on their way to see Stalin, to press him to take the invasion threat more seriously. Zhukov had already telephoned Stalin with news of a second deserter, a German sergeant-major who had crossed the lines earlier that evening and surrendered to Soviet border guards. He had told them that German troops had now begun moving up to their start positions and that the attack had been ordered for the coming morning.

Timoshenko, Zhukov and Vatutin were shown straight into Stalin's oak-panelled office on the first floor, where they found him alone, pacing the carpet beneath the portraits of Marx, Engels and Lenin, clearly worried. He did not waste time on greetings, but came straight to the point.

'Perhaps the German generals have sent this deserter to provoke a conflict?' he suggested.

The three Red Army men disagreed. They insisted that a border alert was necessary. As Stalin considered their demand for action, various members of the Politburo arrived for a meeting. Stalin appealed to them: 'What are we to do?' he asked. No one replied. Timoshenko took the initiative. He had no doubts on the matter – 'A directive must be given immediately, to alert all the troops of border districts,' he stated. As it happened Zhukov just chanced to have the draft of a directive in his pocket.

'Read it out!' snapped Stalin.

Zhukov did so. But Stalin could not bring himself to accept the document. 'It's too soon to give such a directive,' he said. 'Perhaps the questions can still be settled peacefully. We must give a short directive stating that an attack may begin with provocative actions by the German forces. The troops in the border districts must not be incited by any provocation, in order to avoid complications.'

Zhukov and Vatutin hurriedly retired to the next room, to prepare a new draft along lines acceptable to Stalin. When they returned, and read it out to him, he insisted on making further amendments, watering down the orders still more, before handing it over to Timoshenko and Zhukov to sign, as Defence Commissar and Chief of Staff. Vatutin took the signed document to general staff headquarters, and saw that it was transmitted to each military district. It was 12.30 am on Sunday, 22 June, by the time the transmissions were complete – barely 135 minutes before the attack was due to begin. The directive was too late to be any use, but in any case it never reached most operational echelons. Before it could be passed to them, German sabotage units had cut the cable communication lines from all Soviet frontier military district head-quarters to their forward units.

Thus, no one warned most of the frontier units. No one warned the railway staff, either. At midnight the Moscow–Berlin express rumbled across the bridge over the river Bug at Brest-Litovsk, from the Soviet Union into German-occupied Poland. Shortly afterwards, a long freight train loaded with grain followed, the last ransom payment from Stalin to Hitler.

At 12.30 am, Zhukov telephoned Stalin again, with fresh news. A third deserter, a communist labourer from Berlin called Alfred Liskov, who had been serving with the 222nd Infantry Regiment in the 74th Infantry Division on the river Pruth in Romania, had left his unit and swum across the river at 9 pm to warn the Soviets, after hearing the order to attack read out by his commanding officer. Zhukov told Stalin of this, and of the general staff's belief that the Germans were indeed moving up to the frontier.

Stalin reacted calmly. He asked if the alert directive had been received by all military districts – and ordered that Liskov should be shot, 'for his disinformation'. Fortunately for Liskov, his interrogation was still proceeding when the Germans attacked, whereupon he immediately became a communist hero. No further mention was made of the firing squad.

After dismissing Zhukov, Stalin left his office, and walked down the long, red-carpeted corridor to the lift, which he took to the ground floor. His armoured limousine and security motorcade, under the command of the huge figure of General Vlasik, sped out of the Kremlin by the Borovitsky Gate and roared through the sleeping streets of Moscow, bearing him home to his *Blizhny* dacha at Kuntsevo, twenty miles away. There he stretched out on his sofa, and was fast asleep a good two hours earlier than usual.

In Berlin, Hitler also went to bed early. He had taken a short drive through Berlin after dinner, before settling down with Goebbels to go through the text of the proclamation for the last time, and then to spend a whole hour choosing fanfares. Goebbels noted in his diary that Hitler looked completely exhausted when he returned from his drive, but that this changed as the time for the attack approached. No doubt, the adrenalin was beginning to build up. 'The Führer seems to lose his fear as the decisive moment approaches,' Goebbels wrote. 'It is always the same with him. He relaxes visibly. All the exhaustion seems to drop away.'

When he had finished with Goebbels, Hitler called Albert Speer into the salon, and had a record put on, to play a few bars from a Liszt prelude. 'You'll hear that often in the near future,' he told the young architect, 'because it's going to be our victory fanfare for the Russian campaign . . . How do you like it? We'll be getting our granite and marble from there in any quantities you want.'

At 2.30 am, Hitler bade goodnight to his entourage, and retired to bed, leaving them with a suitably portentous statement: 'Before three months have passed, we shall witness a collapse in Russia, the like of which has never been seen in history!'

At 3 am, the German embassy in Moscow received orders from Ribbentrop to destroy its secret files and ciphers, and to put its radio set out of commission. Schulenburg was told to ask for an immediate meeting with Molotov, and was given a memorandum to hand over. He was not to enter into any discussion, but was to remind Molotov that the Soviet government was responsible for the safety of all embassy personnel.

Shortly after 3 am, Vice-Admiral F. S. Oktyabrsky, commander of the Soviet Black Sea Fleet, telephoned the Naval Commissariat to report German air attacks on his warships in Sevastopol harbour. Almost simultaneously, from the other extreme of the Soviet frontier, Vice-Admiral V. F. Tributz, commander of the Baltic Fleet, reported German air and torpedo-boat attacks in the Gulf of Riga.

Knowing that Stalin usually worked in the Kremlin until 5 am, Admiral Kuznetsov, the Naval Commissar, called his office with this disturbing news. Loginev, the duty officer, answered. He told Kuznetsov Stalin was not there, and said he did not know his whereabouts – the very existence of the Kuntsevo dacha was a secret to all but a few of Stalin's associates, and no doubt his office was instructed never to mention it. Even at a moment such as this, Stalin ostensibly vanished when he left the Kremlin.

'I have an exceedingly important message which I must relay immediately to Comrade Stalin in person,' the Admiral declared.

'I cannot help you in any way,' Loginev replied, and hung up.

Kuznetsov tried reaching Stalin at various phone numbers, but failed completely. Once again, he phoned Loginev.

'Inform Comrade Stalin that German planes are bombing Sevastopol,' he ordered. 'This is war!'

A few moments later, Kuznetsov's phone rang. It was not Stalin, however, but Malenkov, in a state of some irritation. 'Do you know what you are saying?' he demanded.

Kuznetsov's message never reached the sleeping dictator.

At 3.30 am, the Chief of Staff of the Western Military District in Minsk, Major-General V. Y. Klimovsky, reported to Timoshenko and Zhukov that German aircraft were now bombing towns and cities in Belorussia. At 3.33 am, Lieutenant-General M. A. Purkayev, Chief of Staff in the Kiev Military District, came on the line to report German air strikes on strategic towns and cities in the Ukraine. At 3.40 am, it was the turn of the commander of the Baltic Military District, General F. I. Kuznetsov, with news of air raids on Kaunas and Vilnius, in Lithuania. There could no longer be any doubt that this was the prelude to invasion. Timoshenko ordered Zhukov to inform Stalin.

Unlike Admiral Kuznetsov, Zhukov had the number of the Kuntsevo dacha. Having established, to his surprise, that Stalin had left the Kremlin, he dialled it and waited. For what seemed a long time, the phone rang and rang. Eventually, someone lifted the receiver and a sleepy voice answered. Zhukov demanded to talk to Stalin.

'Who is speaking?' asked the voice of General Vlasik.

'Chief of the General Staff, Zhukov. I demand to be connected urgently with Comrade Stalin.'

'What? Now?' replied the security chief. 'Comrade Stalin is asleep.'

'Then wake him immediately. Tell him the Germans are bombing our towns.'

There was a long silence, while Vlasik contemplated the prospect of waking the General Secretary of the Communist Party when he had had only about an hour's sleep. Finally, he told Zhukov to hang on. About three minutes later, Stalin picked up the receiver. Zhukov reported the situation and requested permission to order the troops to fight. Stalin was silent. The only thing Zhukov could hear, he wrote later, was the sound of Stalin breathing heavily.

'Do you understand me?' Zhukov asked.

Still there was silence. At last, Stalin asked, 'Where is the Commissar of Defence?'

'Talking with the Kiev Military District on the HF [the top-security radio-telephone system],' Zhukov replied.

'Go to the Kremlin with Timoshenko. Tell Poskrebyshev to summon all Politburo members.'

At 4 am, Vice-Admiral Oktyabrsky was able to report that the German air attack on Sevastopol had been beaten off. There was no damage to the fleet, but bombs had been dropped on the city itself.

At 4.10 am, Moscow time, Western and Baltic Military Districts reported the start of large-scale German offensives in their sectors. Stalin, meanwhile, was speeding back to the city in his motorcade, and the other members of the Politburo were being hastily roused from their beds.

At 4.30 am, Timoshenko and Zhukov arrived in Stalin's office again, where they found him sitting at the long, green-baize table, cradling his unlit pipe in his hand, his face white with strain. Still hoping against hope that the German invasion was only a political gambit, he reasoned that if it were war, surely there would have been a formal declaration, international negotiations, meetings of Foreign Ministers, at the very least. Hitler would not just have attacked, like some brigand. He ordered that someone phone the German embassy, to find out what was happening. The phone call revealed that Schulenburg was himself asking for a meeting with Molotov.

In Berlin, a few minutes later, the young interpreter Erich Sommer picked up the phone in the protocol department at the Wilhelmstrasse, and dialled the number of the Soviet embassy. It was answered almost immediately by Valentin Berezhkov, who was still at his desk. Sommer, his throat tightening with nerves at the importance of his task, informed Berezhkov that Ribbentrop wished to see the Soviet ambassador in half an hour's time. An official car would be at the embassy to collect him in fifteen minutes.

Sommer noticed that at the other end of the line, Berezhkov caught his breath for a moment, before he asked if this was the meeting with the German Foreign Minister which he had been trying to fix the previous day. Sommer, truthfully, replied that he knew nothing of that. All he knew was that Ribbentrop wanted to see Dekanozov at once. Berezhkov's voice shook as he confirmed that the ambassador would be ready.

Sommer put down the phone and glanced at his wristwatch. It was almost 3 am, Berlin time. The protocol timetable, which he had been given, showed that the meeting with Dekanozov had been scheduled for 3.30 am until 4. Afterwards came a list of all the friendly foreign missions, starting with Alfieri of Italy, who was allotted ten minutes, with the others following at five-minute intervals until 7.10, with a break in the middle for a press conference at 6. There was a busy four hours ahead.

Dawn was breaking as Sommer and his superior in the protocol department, Dr Hans Strack, collected Dekanozov and Berezhkov in the official Mercedes. They sat in the jump seats, wearing their black dress uniforms with high SS-type caps, facing the two Soviet diplomats, who sat side by side, trying to hide their nervousness. As they passed through the Brandenburg Gate, Dekanozov pointed to the lightening sky over the Tiergarten.

'It promises to be a glorious day,' he said.

Sommer translated for Strack, who replied, ambiguously, 'We hope so, Mr Ambassador.'

Arriving at the green-painted gate of the Foreign Ministry, they found the entrance ablaze with lights. Photographers, film cameramen and reporters, sent by Goebbels to preserve the occasion for posterity, swarmed around them as they stepped out of the car and passed between the two stone sphinxes flanking shallow steps, carpeted in vivid red in the entrance hall. Uniformed SS adjutants stood to attention and raised their arms in stiff Nazi salutes, while their chief led the way through the glass-panelled doors to the office which had been Bismarck's, and which Ribbentrop had deserted in favour of his new building across the street.

Tonight, however, Ribbentrop had returned to the historic room, and was waiting for Dekanozov, standing beside Bismarck's ornate antique desk, with its marble-top. He was wearing his grey-green official uniform, the flush of excitement on his face hidden by his perpetual artificial suntan. By his side stood Paul Schmidt. Away from them, in a small group, three or four other officials stood in one corner of the great office. As the tiny Dekanozov advanced towards him, Ribbentrop took a few steps forward and greeted him silently, with a formal handshake.

Dekanozov, with Berezhkov translating, started to read out the note from Moscow, which he had brought with him. Ribbentrop, stony-faced, held up his hand to stop him.

'That is not the question now,' he said. 'The Soviet government's hostile attitude to Germany and the serious threat represented by Russian troop concentrations on Germany's eastern frontier have compelled the Reich to take military counter-measures. As from this morning, the relevant counter-measures have been taken in the military sphere.'

With that, he signalled to Schmidt, who stepped forward and began to read out a many-paged document. After a general preamble accusing the Soviet Union of enmity to Germany, and of breaking the terms of both the non-aggression pact and the friendship treaty, the note proceeded to list a number of grievances and border incidents stretching back over the whole twenty-two months of the pact. These, plus the overflying of German territory, the note declared, were 'unambiguous proof' that the Soviet Union was about 'to stab Germany in the back during her battle for her very existence'.

Berezhkov had started translating for Dekanozov, whispering into his ear as Schmidt read. But after the preamble, when the note began listing incidents and the dates of alleged frontier violations, the ambassador could see where it was leading, and waved him to stop. Berezhkov, at a loss, stood in silence, running the fingers of his right hand through his thick dark hair. Sommer, standing two steps behind them, watched in fascination as the back of Dekanozov's bald head gradually became lobster-red, and his hands, which were straight down by his sides, clenched tightly.

The reading of the note took some twenty minutes of the thirty which had been allotted for the interview. While it continued, Ribbentrop stood leaning against Bismarck's desk, looking, to Sommer, as though a heavy load had been lifted from his shoulders. When it was finished, he nodded his approval, and Schmidt handed the bulky document to Dekanozov, who stood there, shocked, repeating over and over in Russian, 'I deeply regret this . . . I deeply regret this.'

Pompously, Ribbentrop proclaimed that he, too, regretted that all his efforts to reach an understanding with the Soviet Union had proved unsuccessful. But Dekanozov had regained his composure, and was not prepared to accept this final iniquity.

'It is entirely due to the non-co-operative attitude adopted by the German government,' he snapped. 'Under the circumstances, there is nothing more for me to do but make the necessary arrangements with your *chef de protocole* for the transport home of my mission.' With that, he gave a curt bow, and departed.

By a sad irony, the scene with Dekanozov, which marked the final demise of Bismarck's eastern policy of maintaining good relations with Russia, was the last official act ever to take place in the Iron Chancellor's old office. Ribbentrop never used the room again.

There were no photographers and no bright lights when Schulenburg, accompanied by Hilger, drove into the Kremlin to meet Molotov at the same time as Ribbentrop's scene was being played out in Berlin. The ancient fortress was abuzz with activity, however, as Politburo members hurried in from their town houses and apartments. Although he had himself driven out to Kuntsevo, as usual, Stalin had forbidden the other leading members of the government to leave the city: he wanted them there to hear the political, economic and possibly territorial demands which he was sure Hitler was about to make.

Molotov received the ambassador at once, looking tired and worn. He listened in silence as Schulenburg read out the telegram from Berlin. It was a compressed version of the lengthy note which was at that moment being given to Dekanozov, and contained exactly the same feeble alibi of the intolerable build-up of Soviet troops on the border forcing the Reich to take military 'counter-measures'. Again, there was no mention of war as such.

When he had finished, there were several seconds of deep silence, while Molotov visibly struggled to control the deep emotions he was feeling. Then he asked: 'Is this supposed to be a declaration of war?'

Schulenburg, deeply distressed, said nothing, but expressed his feelings with a huge, helpless shrug.

'The message I have just been given,' Molotov said, his voice rising now, 'could not mean anything but a declaration of war, since German troops have already crossed the Soviet border and Soviet cities, like Odessa, Kiev and Minsk, have been bombed by German aircraft for an hour and a half.'

Now, Molotov's anger spilled over, and he no longer tried to contain it. The German action, he shouted, was a breach of confidence unprecedented in history. Without any cause, Germany had attacked a country with which it had a pact of non-aggression and friendship. The reasons given in the note were an empty pretext – it was sheer nonsense to speak of Soviet troop concentrations on the German border. Any Soviet troops that were there were simply taking part in the usual summer manoeuvres. If the German government was offended by them, a note to the Soviet government would have been enough to have it remove those troops. Instead, the German government was unleashing a war, with all its terrible consequences.

'Surely,' Molotov concluded bleakly, 'we have not deserved that.'

Schulenburg could only reply that he was under orders from his government to say nothing more. He only wanted to add a request that he and his staff be allowed to leave the Soviet Union, under the rules of international law. Molotov replied, tersely, that they would be treated strictly on the basis of reciprocity.

The meeting was ended. The two Germans took their leave of Molotov in silence but, unlike Dekanozov and Ribbentrop in Berlin, they parted with a handshake.

By the time Molotov got back to the Politburo meeting, there had been more news from the frontiers, none of it good. After a heavy artillery barrage, German troops were already advancing from the west and north-west, along a front stretching from the Ukraine to the Baltic. It can have come as no surprise, therefore, when Molotov announced: 'The German government has declared war on us.'

Stalin sank back in his seat, like a man who has just seen his last hope expire. For some time, he did not speak. There was a long pause, then Zhukov decided to get things moving. He pointed out that now was the time for the frontier districts to strike back at the invaders with all their forces. Whatever else, they must hold up the German advance.

'Annihilate,' Timoshenko interposed. 'Not hold up.'

Stalin roused himself, wearily. 'Issue a directive,' he said.

The directive – Defence Commissar's directive No. 2 – was issued at 7.15 am on 22 June. Considering that the Soviet Union had already been under attack for four hours by then, it was a curious document. While it ordered Soviet troops to fight back with all the means at their disposal, destroying the enemy where they had violated the frontier, Soviet troops were forbidden to cross the frontier line themselves. There was to be no hot pursuit. Only the air force was allowed to attack German airfields and troop concentrations up to 150 kilometres behind the border – but by that time, the Soviet air force had been all but destroyed.

Nowhere in the directive was there any acknowledgement that Germany and the Soviet Union were at war. Stalin was still not prepared to admit that this was a real war, and not some great political ploy by Hitler. Indeed, on his orders the Soviet Foreign Commissariat remained in full radio contact with the Wilhelmstrasse throughout 22 June, and at noon Stalin even contacted the Japanese government in Tokyo, asking it to mediate between Germany and the Soviet Union on the political and military differences between them.

Throughout the morning, there was no announcement to the Soviet people. In Moscow and all the cities away from the western frontier, the morning of 22 June started like any other Sunday. The only intimation the people had was a brief statement on the early radio, among the music and the daily callisthenics programmes, that Molotov would broadcast to the nation at midday.

'This is Moscow calling. You will now hear a speech from the Deputy Chairman of the Council of People's Commissars of the USSR and the Foreign Commissar of the USSR, Vyacheslav Mikhailovich Molotov' – the introduction at 12.15 pm gave no hint of what was to follow. There was a brief pause, then Molotov's voice was heard, grave, solemn, slightly halting as he controlled his stammer.

'Citizens, men and women of the Soviet Union!' he began. 'The Soviet government and its head, Comrade Stalin, have authorised me to make the following statement: This morning, at four o'clock, without any claims having been presented to the Soviet Union, without a declaration of war, German troops attacked our country . . .'

It was not a long speech – in fact, some listeners have said it was the shortest they had ever heard in the Soviet Union – nor was it an inspiring one. Molotov was no orator, no Churchill; he spoke in a flat, expressionless voice, like a man reading a railway timetable. But the content of his speech was the most devastating news the Soviet people had heard since the October Revolution in 1917. He listed the places where the German bombs had fallen, complained that hostile attacks by air and artillery fire had also come from Finnish and Romanian territory, and repeated the charges he had earlier made to Schulenburg. 'The entire responsibility for this predatory onslaught on the Soviet Union therefore falls clearly and unequivocally on the German fascist rulers!' he declared – suddenly restoring the word 'fascist' to the Russian vocabulary after an absence of exactly twenty-two months – before concluding: 'The government appeals to all of you, men and women, citizens of the Soviet Union, to rally as never before around our glorious Bolshevik Party, around the Soviet government, around our great leader, Comrade Stalin. Our cause is just. Our enemy shall be defeated. Victory will be ours!'

After 669 days, one of the most unlikely alliances in history was at an end.

Epilogue

'THERE ARE NO INVINCIBLE ARMIES'

There is a legend that Stalin suffered a nervous collapse on hearing of the German invasion and hid himself away to wring his hands in a drunken stupor, wailing: 'All that Lenin created we have lost for ever!' This story was fostered by Nikita Khrushchev in 1956, as part of his campaign to shatter the icon of Stalin, which was still casting its huge shadow across party and people. But Khrushchev was far from Moscow at the time of 'Barbarossa', in Kiev. Those who were in the Kremlin, such as Colonel-General (later Marshal) N. N. Voronov, commander of Soviet anti-aircraft defences, tell a different story, recalling that Stalin was working furiously in his office during the days following the invasion, though he seemed nervy and low-spirited and attended command meetings only erratically.

It would have been understandable had Stalin collapsed. The shock of the attack must have been immense to a man whose dialectic reasoning proved 'Barbarossa' was not a rational possibility. His pact with Hitler had begun as something both dictators needed – indeed, for the first year Hitler's need had been the greater, allowing Stalin to drive hard bargains in both political and economic negotiations. But Stalin clearly failed to realise that after the German victories in the West, the balance had swung the other way.

As more and more territory and resources came under his control, Hitler had become less and less dependent on Soviet supplies of grain, oil and raw materials. In any case, the high payment Stalin was exacting – much of it in the shape of armaments which would be turned against Germany – was increasingly unwelcome. The longer Hitler waited, the stronger Stalin would become, until he reached the point where he could choose to stop providing supplies, and at the same time cut Germany's lifeline to the Far East.

By the time of Molotov's disastrous visit to Berlin in November 1940, where his intransigence showed all too clearly that Stalin still thought he could call the tune, Hitler's confidence in the invincibility of the Wehrmacht was such that he was convinced he could take all he needed from the Soviets by force. What was more, he was eager to do so: impatient to resume his crusade against bolshevism, to smash the Soviet state for ever, and to realise his dream of taking over and colonising the Ukraine with its rich agricultural lands and industrial and mineral wealth. He had already rescinded his earlier order that deliveries to the Soviet Union were to take precedence over the requirements of the German armed forces; with the decision taken to launch 'Barbarossa', he ordered that deliveries were to stop altogether, in spite of the fact that this meant falling deeper and deeper into the red, which might arouse Stalin's suspicions.

Stalin, however, remained deliberately blind. It may be that he was simply unable to contemplate such an appalling prospect, and therefore persuaded himself it could never happen. It may be that, as he claimed, he did not believe Hitler could mount an invasion before 1942: the sheer immensity of the Soviet Union surely ruling out a *Blitzkrieg*, for no military commander in his right mind could imagine conquering those vast spaces in a short campaign. It would still take many more months – and many more deliveries of strategic raw materials – for even the Germans to build up the necessary resources and reserves for a full-scale, major war.

On that basis, it was logical to expect that Hitler would start making greater demands on the Soviet Union for the supplies he needed. And since Stalin was always a prisoner of his own logic, it was easy for him to delude himself into seeing the massive German build-up as a threat designed to extort blackmail payments, rather than genuine preparations for an immediate invasion.

Stalin was not alone in this delusion. During the final week before 'Barbarossa', several Western newspapers, notably *The Times* and the *Manchester Guardian* in Britain and the *Svenska Dagbladet* in Sweden, carried reports that Hitler had presented the Soviet Union with a list of demands which Stalin was at the moment considering. The precise nature of these supposed demands varied slightly from paper to paper, but they all agreed on a number of fundamental points: German insistence on the demobilisation of the Soviet western armies (some reports said of the whole Red Army); German control of the Ukraine's agricultural production; the establishment of an autonomous Ukrainian state under German control; the German take-over of Soviet shipyards in the Baltic; and lastly the right for Germany to set up war industries in Soviet territory beyond the reach of British bombers. According to the *Svenska Dagbladet*, betting in Budapest on the chance of a war between Germany and the Soviet Union by the end of June, which only a few

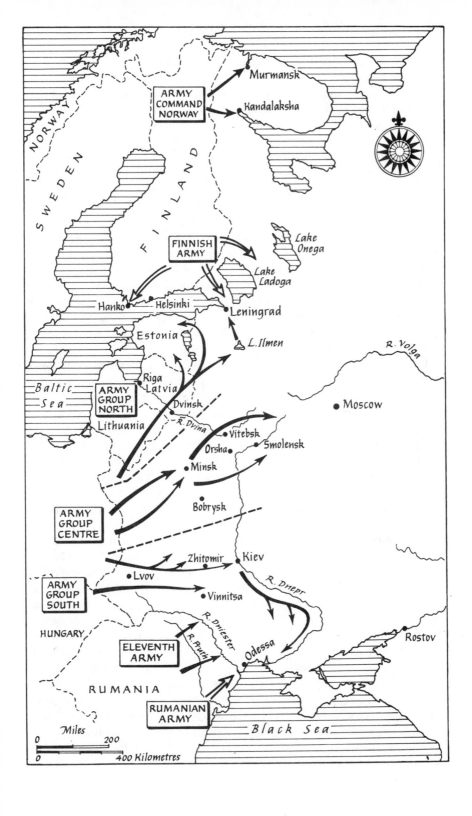

NORWAY

SWEDEN

FINLAND

ARMY
COMMAND
NORWAY

● Murmansk

● Kandalaksha

FINNISH
ARMY

Lake
Onega

Lake
Ladoga

Hanko ● ─ Helsinki

● Leningrad

Estonia

△ L. Ilmen

R. Volga

Baltic
Sea

Riga
Latvia

ARMY
GROUP
NORTH

● Dvinsk

● Moscow

Lithuania

R. Dvina

● Vitebsk

Orsha ●

● Smolensk

● Minsk

ARMY
GROUP
CENTRE

● Bobrysk

Zhitomir

● Kiev

ARMY
GROUP
SOUTH

● Lvov

● Vinnitsa

R. Dnepr.

HUNGARY

R. Dniester

● Rostov

ELEVENTH
ARMY

R. Pruth

● Odessa

RUMANIA

RUMANIAN
ARMY

Black Sea

Miles

0   200

0   400 Kilometres

days earlier had been running at odds of 5–1 on, had now dropped to even money.

These reports may well have been part of the German deception operation, intended to lull Stalin into a false sense of security by seeming to make indirect proposals through the international press – a practice which Stalin himself was known to use regularly. What is equally possible, however, is that they could have been Soviet plants, following that same practice, designed to let Hitler know the sort of proposals Stalin was prepared to consider and thus encouraging him to make his demands. If that was the case, they either show the extraordinary lengths to which Stalin was prepared to go to avoid war, or they represented an attempt to draw the Germans into lengthy negotiations, never intended to succeed, which could be strung out until it was too late for an attack to be launched in 1941. In this way, Stalin would buy time and postpone the inevitable invasion at least until late spring or early summer 1942, by which time the Red Army would be better prepared. There is no firm evidence to show whether the press stories originated in Moscow or Berlin, but their nature and style is certainly consistent with Stalin's methods on many other occasions.

Whatever the truth may be, there can be no doubt that Hitler's sudden blow came as a complete surprise to the Soviet leader. His stubborn refusal to accept that Hitler might attack that summer had not only kept the frontier defences in a state of pitiful unreadiness but had also prevented the establishment of any effective High Command organisation, or the appointment of a supreme commander. For eleven days, Stalin remained out of sight to all but his closest associates, even his name conspicuously absent from directives and reports which ascribed everything to 'the Soviet government', 'the Central Committee', and 'Sovnarkom', the Council of People's Commissars, of which he was now chairman.

By the end of those eleven days, in early July, the situation was little short of disastrous. Brest-Litovsk was in German hands, so were Minsk, the capital of Belorussia, Riga, capital of Latvia, and the whole of Lithuania; near Minsk, no fewer than four Soviet armies were encircled between Novogradok and Bialystok; in the south, Lvov had fallen and 7,000 Jews in the city had been murdered by German SS *Einsatzgruppen* units; the Finns, who had officially joined the war on 25 June, were advancing down the Karelian Isthmus towards Leningrad, while in the far north German troops had reached the Litsa river, only thirty-five miles west of Murmansk. Jubilation reigned at German general headquarters: General Halder, the Chief of Staff, wrote in his diary on 3 July: 'It's no exaggeration to say that the campaign in Russia has been won in two weeks.' The OKW operations chief, General Jodl, noted that the German armies had advanced one third of the way to both Moscow and Leningrad in just one week, and could expect to be in both cities in another fortnight, or even sooner.

Hitler was as confident as his military commanders, ordering that Moscow was to be flattened and its site flooded with a huge reservoir, its name expunged for ever, while Leningrad was also to be razed and the site given to Finland. He told Schulenburg, who had been safely repatriated from the Soviet Union with all his staff: 'By 15 August we shall be in Moscow. By 1 October the Russian war will be over.'

At 6.30 that morning, 3 July, Stalin broke his silence. There had been no pre-publicity, no announcement, no warning to the public. After completing his usual night's work, he sat in front of a microphone in his office in the Kremlin, and spoke to his people in a nationwide broadcast. At intervals throughout the day, the speech was read again by announcers, booming out through loudspeakers in the streets and squares of cities, towns and villages. At the same time, the text was posted on fences and walls, so that by nightfall everyone would know what their leader had said.

Unlike Hitler, Stalin was no orator. He distrusted the easy emotions whipped up by people with such dangerous talents, and his political career was noteworthy for his steadfast refusal to indulge in facile speech-making. As a result, when he did choose to speak, the public listened, knowing that whatever he had to say must be important. What he had to say on the morning of 3 July was probably the most important statement of his entire life, and the Soviet people hung on his every word.

On one level, Stalin's performance was unimpressive, even laughable: he was obviously unused to the microphone and ill at ease on the radio; he spoke slowly and unemotionally in his thick Georgian accent, the speech punctuated by pauses during which he could be heard drinking water from a glass. Ernst Fischer, the Austrian Comintern official, noted that 'Stalin analysed the situation and issued his directive as though discussing production tasks rather than a catastrophic war.' But it was exactly right for that moment. What mattered most was that Stalin, the man of steel, was speaking directly to each and every Soviet citizen in their hour of need. The leader was at his post. 'He's pulled us to our feet,' was the comment heard everywhere. 'We can hold our heads up again.'

'Comrades, citizens, brothers and sisters, fighting men of our army and navy,' he began, dramatically. 'I am speaking to you, my friends!' It was an unusual and personal form of address, one he had never used before and would never use again. He then went on to admit that so far the German army had enjoyed considerable success, but the people must not imagine that this army could not be defeated. 'History shows,' he reminded his listeners, 'that there are no invincible armies, and never have been. Napoleon's army was considered invincible, but it was beaten successively by Russian, English and German armies.' The same was true of Kaiser Wilhelm's army in 1914, which was finally smashed in France.

Like Molotov in his broadcast on 22 June, Stalin defended the pact with Germany: 'Had not a serious mistake been made? Of course not. No peace-loving country could have rejected such a pact with another country, even if rogues like Hitler and Ribbentrop were at its head.' What had been gained from the pact? 'We secured for our country peace for a year and a half and the opportunity of preparing our forces to repulse fascist Germany should she risk an attack . . .' True, he said, Germany had gained a temporary advantage, and this was why he was calling on the Soviet people to give their total, wholehearted support to the Red Army. He made little mention of the party – this was 'a patriotic war' for all Russians. What could his countrymen do to bring about victory? They must work as never before in the factories and on the collective farms; they must form home-guard units to defend plants and power stations; they must organise effective civil defence against German air raids; and they must beware the deserters, the panic-mongers, the rumour merchants, all who would disrupt the war effort.

Where the Germans were advancing, nothing must be allowed to fall into their hands; 'not a single locomotive, not a single rail car, a single pound of grain or gallon of fuel. Collective farmers must drive off all their cattle and turn over their grain to the safe keeping of state authorities. Anything which cannot be removed, including even non-ferrous metals, must be destroyed. Nothing must be left to the enemy. And in those areas which he has already occupied, guerrilla units must be formed. Their task will be to blow up bridges, roads, stores, set fire to the forests, disrupt communications and so on. Conditions must be made unbearable for the enemy.'

This was not just a war between two armies, Stalin went on, it was a war of 'the entire Soviet people against the German fascist forces'. And it was a war in which the Soviet Union did not stand alone: they were not without allies, for both Great Britain and the USA had made offers of military aid. Calling on everyone 'to rally around the party of Lenin–Stalin and around the Soviet government, and to give selfless support to the Red Army and the Red Navy,' Stalin ended with the exhortation: 'Forward to victory!'

The victory which Stalin called for took a long time and great sacrifice to achieve. Just as the twenty-two months of the pact had been a monstrous chess game between the two dictators, with whole countries as the pieces, so the war became a duel to the death between the two men, using their armed forces as weapons, as each assumed personal control of his country's operations and strategy. Hitler had proclaimed himself Supreme Commander when he established the OKW in February 1938; on 19 December 1941, he also took over from Brauchitsch as

Commander-in-Chief of the army. Stalin consolidated his own position in three stages – becoming chairman of the newly created State Defence Committee, a body with overriding powers in all military, civil and economic matters, on 30 June; Chairman of the *Stavka*, a combined GHQ and high command, on 10 July; and taking over from Timoshenko as Defence Commissar on 19 July. On 8 August, he was officially named as Supreme Commander of the Soviet Union – a title which later became transmuted into the one word 'Generalissimo'.

The two war lords both had a great deal to learn and both made huge mistakes and miscalculations, for which millions of their subjects paid with their lives from the very start. Stalin had misinterpreted Hitler's intentions, exposing his people to the power and savagery of the German attack without adequate preparation or protection. Hitler for his part had underestimated the size of the task he had given his armies, both in terms of the immense spaces of the Soviet Union and of the determination and toughness of the Soviet people.

Hitler had also seriously underestimated the severity of the Russian climate, or rather, his arrogant certainty that the campaign would be over in a few weeks – 'You have only to kick in the door and the whole rotten structure will come crashing down' – had led him to disregard the need to provide his soldiers with adequate protection against the Russian winter. He had tempted providence by launching his invasion on the very anniversary of Napoleon's ill-fated attack in 1812, without taking heed of the disasters which befell the French *Grande Armée*. Napoleon actually took Moscow before the weather forced him to withdraw. Hitler's armies reached the suburbs in the autumn of 1941, and on 16 October the city was evacuated in a great panic. But Stalin stayed put in the Kremlin, and was saved by three great Russian generals: General Mud, General Winter and finally General Zhukov.

The mud brought the first German advance to a halt in late October, when the autumn rains turned the dirt roads and indeed the whole countryside into a quagmire, bogging down men and machines and preventing supplies reaching the tanks and other tracked vehicles which could traverse the sodden terrain. With the frosts of November, the ground hardened again, and the assault on Moscow could be continued. But by then the Red Army had been able to bring up reserves and reinforcements, and to prepare the city's defences in depth.

By the time the Wehrmacht was ready to start hurling itself at Moscow again, winter was closing in. Without adequate clothing, the German troops began freezing to death. Soon, General Guderian was losing up to 1,200 men a day to frostbite, and any wounded who were not carried into cover within minutes had no hope of survival. Guns and equipment jammed as the lubricating oils froze solid. Fires had to be lit under tanks to thaw out their engines, turrets and tracks in temperatures which according to German sources plummeted to an awesome −52°C

– though the Soviets dismissively say they were no worse than the 'normal' 30–40° below zero.

On 6 December, their latest assault battered to a freezing standstill by grimly determined defenders less than fifteen miles from the Kremlin itself, the Germans suddenly found themselves facing a third and even more fearsome enemy when Zhukov unleashed his great counter-attack. For five and a half months, the Wehrmacht had rampaged through the Soviet Union, killing and capturing and destroying. They had taken well over two million prisoners, more than half a million at Kiev alone, and inflicted hundreds of thousands of casualties. Although they were themselves almost exhausted they were entitled to expect that the Red Army must be at its last gasp. And yet, suddenly, they found themselves facing powerful new armies, well equipped, warmly clad, tougher even than the elite SS Panzer troops. To the reserves he had dredged up from new conscripts and the remnants of the western armies, Zhukov had been able to add massive reinforcements from the Far East, battle-hardened Siberian troops to whom the Moscow temperatures seemed like a mild spring day. Japan, still smarting from the defeats inflicted upon them by Zhukov himself with these very troops, and bound by the treaty they had signed with Stalin on 13 April 1941, had decided not to enter the war against the Soviet Union, but to attack America instead. Master spy Richard Sorge, in his last coup before he was discovered and arrested in September, had informed Moscow that they had nothing to fear from the Japanese that year. Stalin had promptly transferred half the entire strength of the Far Eastern Command to the defence of Moscow, some ten rifle divisions, plus 1,000 tanks and 1,000 aircraft. Zhukov was therefore able to hit the Germans with three fresh armies made up of over a million men, including some of the toughest fighters in the world. Within three weeks he had driven the enemy back nearly a hundred miles.

'The miracle of Moscow' was Hitler's first major defeat, but the war was far from over. It was to take Stalin two years before he finally learned how to destroy Hitler's Wehrmacht, and another one and a half years after that to complete the process. In truth, however, it is doubtful whether Hitler ever had the resources to accomplish his plan. He had counted on only a short campaign, but found himself trapped in a long and bloody conflict. The riches he had sought in the Ukraine and the rest of European Russia eluded him, for in addition to Stalin's scorched-earth policy, with crops, mines and railways destroyed and dams blown, the Soviets physically moved whole industries out of the combat areas even faster than the German Panzers advanced. Between July and November 1941, a total of 1,523 complete installations, 1,360 of which were major facilities directly involved in armament production, were dismantled, transported to safety east of the Urals on the equivalent of a million and a half freight cars, and reassembled. Ten million workers were shipped out to man them. By the end of the year, the factories which Hitler had hoped to capture and turn to his own use were back in production and sending heavy tanks and other weapons to the front to join in the fight against him.

For the whole of 1942, the struggle swayed to and fro, with victories and defeats for both sides. The next major turning point came at Stalingrad, where the Red Army inflicted a second crushing defeat on the Germans in January 1943, but it was not until the Battle of the Kursk Salient, in July and August of that year, that Stalin finally gained the upper hand. Kursk, the greatest land battle in history, with some 6,300 tanks and over two million men engaged in an area only fifty miles in length and fifteen miles deep, was also the most decisive of the second world war. In the cauldron of Kursk, Hitler's Panzer strength was so badly smashed that recovery was impossible and his ultimate defeat inevitable.

Stalin had learned how to win – but the cost had been truly terrible. By the time his troops raised the red flag over the ruins of Berlin on 1 May 1945, over twenty million Soviet citizens had been killed – the equivalent of nine lives lost every minute of the war, 587 every hour, and 14,000 every single day. There were countless villages where not one man came back from the war. And for the Germans, the losses were proportionately almost as heavy. There are no precise figures available for German deaths related specifically to the eastern front; estimates vary from the Soviet figure of over ten million to more conservative Western figures of around five million dead and missing. For both nations, the result was a tragedy.

Hitler may have won the chess game leading from the signing of the non-aggression pact to the launch of 'Barbarossa'. But it was Stalin who emerged victorious at the end of the war as the most powerful politician in the world, while the Nazi dictator committed suicide in his bunker beneath the devastated remains of the Chancellery on 30 April 1945. And it was Stalin who determined that neither he nor his country would ever be caught unprepared again, and who extended his empire to set up a solid wall of buffer states to protect his western frontiers, behind what Winston Churchill described as 'an iron curtain' from the Baltic to the Black Sea.

Stalin died in 1953 in his villa in Kuntsevo. But the bitter experience of the Great Fatherland War continues to cast a vast shadow over Soviet foreign policies: the legacy of the broken pact is with us still.

SOURCE NOTES

Detailed information concerning the books referred to in shortened form in these notes will be found in the Bibliography. The full names of correspondents and those interviewed are given in the list on p. 666. The following abbreviations are used to identify documents and records consulted:

BA: Documents in Bundesarchiv (Federal German Archives) at Koblenz (Civil) and Freiburg (Military)
CAB: British Cabinet Papers
CCA: Reports of Selected Committee on Communist Aggression, House of Representatives. US Government Printing Office, Washington
DBFP: Documents on British Foreign Foreign Policy. HMSO
DDI: Documenti Diplomatici Italiani, Italian Foreign Ministry, Rome
DGFP: Documents on German Foreign Policy, Series D, Volumes IV—XII. HMSO
DMREW: Documents and Materials Relating to the Eve of the Second World War. Foreign Languages Publishing House, Moscow
FBB: Documents Diplomatiques, 1938–9, The Development of Finnish–Soviet Relations in the Autumn of 1939 (Finnish Blue Book), Finnish Ministry of Foreign Affairs. Harrap
FRUS: Foreign Relations of the United States, Diplomatic Papers, 1939, Vols I and II. US State Department, Washington
FYB: Documents Diplomatiques, 1938–9 (French Yellow Book)
HALD: Halder Diaries. Imperial War Museum
HWD: Hitler War Directives 1939–45. Sidgwick & Jackson
ID: Istoria Diplomatii (History of Diplomacy), Moscow
IMT: Trials of War Criminals before the Nuremberg International Military Tribunals. US Government Printing Office, Washington
JOD: Jodl Diaries. Imperial War Museum
MK: Hitler *Mein Kampf*
NCA: Nazi Conspiracy and Aggression. Office of the US Chief of Counsel for the Prosecution of Axis Criminality. 8 vols. US Government Printing Office, Washington
OKW: Kriegstagebuch des Oberkommando der Wehrmacht. Bernard & Graaf, Frankfurt-am-Main
PSR: Documents on Polish–Soviet Relations, 1939–45. General Sikorski Historical Institute, London.
PWB: Documents Diplomatiques, 1938–9, Official Documents concerning Polish–German and Polish–Soviet Relations (Polish White Book). Polish Ministry for Foreign Affairs

PROLOGUE: 'The biggest front line in history'
Stalin leaving office: Zhukov
Descriptions of office and dacha: Djilas;
  Alliluyeva, *Twenty Letters to a Friend*
Evening of 21 June: Erickson, *Road to Stalingrad*

Bullfrogs: Carell
'Soldiers of the eastern front . . .': Baynes
Invasion force details: HALD
'Like a lightning flash': Churchill, *Their Finest Hour*

'The last warnings . . .': Zhukov
'Soviet ambassador Ivan Maisky': Maisky, *Memoirs of a Soviet Ambassador*
Sunday picnic: Berezhkov
'Still Stalin brushed the warnings aside': Zhukov
'Chaos and confusion': Erickson, *Road to Stalingrad*; Carell
Germans had destroyed some 1,200 Soviet aircraft: Erickson, *Road to Stalingrad*; HALD
Official Soviet figures: Sipols, *The Road to Victory*; Israelyan
'Stalin was so afraid of war': Khrushchev

CHAPTER 1: *'The road of the Teutonic knights'*
Teutons and Slavs: Schreiber; Cecil
'1,800,000 ethnic Germans': Cecil
Separate peace treaties: WheelerBennett
'If land was desired in Europe', etc.: MK
Details of purges: Erickson, *Soviet High Command*; Grey, *The First Fifty Years*; Ulam; Medvedev, *Let History Judge*
Polish–Soviet war: Erickson, *Soviet High Command*; Grey; Hosking; Kennan; Kusnierz; Rothstein and Dutt; Ulam, *Expansion and Coexistence*; Watts
German–Soviet trade: DGFP
KPD to vote for Nazis: Nollau
'Shoot your communists': Hilger
Litvinov gaoled in London, etc.: Grey
Occupation of Rhineland to be aborted: JOD; IMT
Hitler to Ciano: DGFP

CHAPTER 2: *'My poor friend, what have you done?'*
'His eyes were fabulous . . .': Keitel
'From the bottom of my heart . . .': IMT
'Should things go ill with the Führer': François-Poncet
'A greasy, shifty-eyed, paunchy . . .': Shirer, *The Nightmare Years*
Ribbentrop background: Schwarz; Ribbentrop
'I prayed fervently': Ribbentrop
Ribbentrop was so besotted: Schmid (interview); Sommer (interview)
'The meal proceeded . . .': Churchill, *The Gathering Storm*
'It can be fairly said of Neville Chamberlain . . .': Strang, *Home and Abroad*
'You have only to look at the map . . .': Feiling
'As always, he spoke his thoughts out loud . . .': Keitel
'It is my unshakeable resolve . . .': Keitel; JOD
'It would be difficult to exclude other powers . . .': Henderson
'The Soviets had started massing troops, etc.': DMREW
'On 21 September, Litvinov addressed the Assembly . . .': DMREW
'It is indeed astonishing . . .': Churchill, *The Gathering Storm*
'The last of his territorial ambitions . . .': CAB; DBFP
'I feel certain you can get . . .': DGFP
'They were to evacuate . . .': DGFP; DBFP
'The Soviet offer was in effect ignored': Churchill, *The Gathering Storm*
'My poor friend . . .': Coulondre

CHAPTER 3: *'The one and only Colonel Beck'*
'The softening-up process': DGFP
Ribbentrop's proposals to Lipski: DGFP; PWB
Polish foreign policy: Mackiewicz; Cienciala
'Other, more serious shortcomings . . .': Raczynski (interview); Mackiewicz
'The one and only Colonel Beck': Cooper
Beck's background: Harley; Mackiewicz; Raczynski; Syrop
'An army of 170 men . . .': Syrop
'I am a strong man . . .': Syrop
'Germany's hors d'oeuvre . . .': Cienciala
'The dead dictator's successors': Mackiewicz; Raczynski (interview)
'To forestall German intrigues': PWB
Berghof details: Speer
Beck's meeting with Hitler: DGFP; PWB; Beck; Ribbentrop
Jews in Poland: Gilbert, *The Holocaust*
'One of Ribbentrop's prime characteristics . . .': Schmidt
Ribbentrop–Beck meeting: DGFP; PWB; Beck; Ribbentrop
Beck's meeting in Warsaw: PWB; Beck; Cienciala
'A possible compromise solution': DGFP

CHAPTER 4: *'A new era in German–Soviet relations'*
Crystal Night: NCA; IMT
Hitler's new Chancellery: Speer
Merekalov calls on Wiehl: DGFP
German–Soviet trade: Beloff
Göring's secret lecture, shortages of materials, etc.: Christie papers, Churchill College, Cambridge
'Early in October 1938 . . .': DGFP
Schnurre called a meeting: DGFP; Schnurre (interview)
Hitler's new year receptiion: FRUS; Irving, *The War Path*
Mussolini's meeting with Chamberlain: DGFP; Gibson; DDI; Halifax; Birkenhead; DBFP

CHAPTER 5: *'Chestnuts out of the fire'*
'Towards the Soviets . . .': DGFP; Goralski
'Merekalov was told . . .': DGFP
Schnurre details: Schnurre (interview); Schmid (interview)
Banquet in old Brühl Palace: Kleist
Ribbentrop's speech: PWB
Ribbentrop–Beck meeting: DGFP; PWB
'Already in a thoroughly bad mood . . .': Kleist
'Schnurre protested vigorously . . .': Schnurre (interview)
'Sudden, urgent business . . .': DGFP
Schulenburg letter to Weizsäcker: DGFP
'He no longer had any faith . . .': Cienciala
'Stalin was undoubtedly upset . . .': Kleist
'On 27 January, an article appeared . . .': *News Chronicle, Pravda*
Hitler's speech on 30 January: Baynes
'On 20 February, Halifax dined . . .': Maisky, *Who Helped Hitler?*; DBFP
'. . . was a natural phenomenon . . .': DGFP
Stalin's speech: Rubinstein; ID: Rothstein
'He was told that German troops . . .': DGFP
Hacha collapse and injection: Keitel; Heston
'Children! Kiss me!': Zoller
'We reached the outskirts of Prague . . .': Keitel

Discussions on indirect aggression: Strang, *Home and Abroad*; DBFP

CHAPTER 9: *'The biggest bribe in history'*
'I have a message . . .': DGFP
'Schnurre was astonished . . .': Schnurre (interview)
A. J. Cummings article: Maisky; *News Chronicle* 11 July 1939
'Safeguarding World Peace': Feiling
'From Berlin Ambassador Henderson. . .': Henderson
'A discreet invitation . . .': DGFP
Wilson–Wohlthat meeting: DGFP
'By a supreme irony . . .': Macleod
Chamberlain–Halifax–Ironside meeting: Macleod; DBFP; CAB
'Two days later, he was singing . . .': CAB
Ironside visit to Warsaw: Macleod; DBFP
'Wohlthat had returned . . .': DGFP
Dahlerus–Halifax meeting: Dahlerus
'This will not cause me very great anxiety': CAB
Moscow parade: *Pravda*, Albrecht von der Schulenburg (interview)
Schulenburg conversation with Merekalov: DBFP; Hilger
Strang's letter to Sargent: Strang, *Home and Abroad*; DBFP
'The biggest bribe in history: *News Chronicle*; *Daily Express*; DGFP
'I do not see any harm . . .': *Hansard*
Halifax to Seeds: DBFP
'Seeds and Strang were horrified. . .': Strang; DBFP
'When Ribbentrop telephoned from Fuschl . . .': DGFP

CHAPTER 10: *Dinner at Ewest's*
Navy Day parades and speeches: *Pravda*; *Izvestia*; *Daily Worker*
Molotov–Seeds–Naggiar meeting: DBFP; FYB; Strang, *Home and Abroad*
Ironside–Belisha meeting: Macleod
'To help with this difficult decision . . .': CAB
Maisky's visit to Foreign Office: Maisky, *Who Helped Hitler?*
Hitler in Bayreuth: Speer; Kubizek; Irving, *The War Path*
Astakhov invitation for two Germans: DGFP
Ribbentrop's report on Italians: DGFP; Ribbentrop
Schloss Fuschl: Schwarz; Schnurre (interview)
Ribbentrop's instructions to Schnurre: Schnurre (interview)
The dinner party at Ewest's: Schnurre (interview); Schmid (interview); DGFP

CHAPTER 11: *'A quick failure, or a slow one?'*
Gripenberg–Butler meeting: Gripenberg
Drax background, briefing, meeting with Sinclair: Drax
'Across the Channel . . .'; DGFP
Weizsäcker's report to Ribbentrop at Saarbrücken: DGFP; Weizsäcker
Detailed instructions to Schulenburg: DGFP
Danzig situation: DGFP
Greiser's note: PWB

'In the House of Commons that afternoon . . .': *Hansard*; Maisky, *Who Helped Hitler?*
'They were all narrow specialists . . .' Maisky, *Who Helped Hitler?*
Dirksen's report to Berlin: DGFP
Soviet All-Union Agricultural Exhibition: *Daily Worker*
Meetings in the Tiergarten: Schnurre (interview); DGFP
Annual air exercises: DBFP
Henderson's visit to Bayreuth and letter to Halifax: Henderson
FPC discussion of military mission to Moscow: CAB
Molotov's reaction: Strang; DBFP
'It was yet another rainy day . . .': Drax

CHAPTER 12: *'From the Baltic to the Black Sea'*
'The attitude in Berlin . . .': DGFP; Schnurre (interview)
Astakhov–Ribbentrop meeting: DGFP; Weizsäcker
Schnurre–Astakhov meeting: DGFP; Schnurre (interview)
'I shall not be replying . . .': DBFP
Churchill speech: *Hansard*
Wilson–Dirksen meeting: DGFP
Hitler and Kubizek: Kubizek
'At 8.30 that evening . . .': DGFP; Hilger
Hitler's apartment: P. Hoffmann
Hitler's meeting with Keitel and Lossberg: Lossberg; OKW
'Early on Friday, 4 August . . .': Drax
Luncheon in Soviet embassy: Maisky, *Who Helped Hitler?*
Daladier instructions to Doumenc: FYB; Beaufre
Chamberlain meeting with Drax and Sinclair: Drax
Halifax's briefing to businessmen: Dahlerus

CHAPTER 13: *Slow Boat to Moscow*
Strang returns to London: Strang, *Home and Abroad*; Roberts (interview)
Descriptions of British officers: Beaufre
'The French were not encouraged . . .': Beaufre
'The only other member . . .': Collier (interview)
Arrival in Leningrad: Beaufre; Collier (interview)
Arrival in Moscow: DGFP; Collier (interview)
Schulenburg's reports to Berlin: DGFP
Introductions in Kremlin and Defence Commissariat: DBFP; Drax
Voroshilov background: Medvedev, *All Stalin's Men*; Grey, *The First Fifty Years*
Spiridonovka Palace and banquet: Beaufre; Collier (interview); Drax

CHAPTER 14: *Military Secrets in a Smoke-Filled Room*
'The first session of the military talks . . .': Drax; Beaufre; Collier (interview)
Security arrangements: Drax
'They'll divide any figure . . .': Collier (interview)
'Back in London that same day . . .': Macleod
'The Soviet figures were an impressive proof . . .': Collier (interview)
Soviet scenarios: DBFP
'Yesterday, I asked General Doumenc . . .': Beaufre

'The three men met in the Foreign Secretary's
  office . . .': Halifax; Cadogan
'In Warsaw, meanwhile . . .': Beaufre
Noël's meeting with Beck: FYB; Bonnet
'Kennard and Noël hurried back . . .': FYB;
  DBFP: Bonnet
Musse's telegrams to Moscow: Beaufre
'The Soviet Union . . . took its treaty obligations
  . . .': DGFP

CHAPTER 20:'I have the world in my pocket'
'Babarin called Schnurre at his home . . .':
  Schnurre (interview); DGFP
'If Ribbentrop travels to Moscow . . . ': Weizsäcker
'Throughout the long night . . .': IMT (Gaus)
Arrival of draft pact: DGFP
Hitler's letter: DGFP
Hitler's anxiety, Eva Braun and milk, etc.: IMT
  (Gaus); Kordt
Hitler's telephone call to Göring: IMT (Gaus)
Göring's approach to British Foreign Office:
  Halifax; FO 800.317
Wilson's approach to Hesse: Hesse; DGFP
Hitler receiving Stalin's agreement: H. Hoffmann;
  BA (Hewel diaries)
'The message Ribbentrop had received . . .':
  GFP; Ribbentrop
Ribbentrop–Ciano telephone conversation:
  Ribbentrop; Gibson; DGFP; DDI
'At dinner that night . . .': Speer; Hoffmann; IMT
  (Gaus)
Stalin letter: DGFP
'Hitler took Heinrich Hoffmann aside . . .':
  Hoffmann

CHAPTER 21: 'A very serious question'
Florimond Bonté's statement: Beloff
Drax's credentials, Order of the Bath: Drax;
  Collier (interview); Beaufre
'The intentions of the Soviet delegation . . .';
  DBFP; Drax
Delayed French telegram: Bonnet; FYB
German radio announcement: Shirer, The
  Nightmare Years
Schulenburg's chauffeur: DGFP
'Just a journalist's prank': Bonnet
Official Soviet announcement: DGFP
Doumenc's message to Voroshilov, and meeting:
  Beaufre; DMREW; FYB; DGFP; FO 800.317
Voroshilov out hunting: Khrushchev

CHAPTER 22: 'I have struck this weapon from the
hands of those gentlemen'
German press: Shirer, Berlin Diary
'In streets and homes . . .': Schmidt
Canaris–Kordt meeting: Kordt
Hitler's order of 19 August: OKW
Göring's dress: IMT; Boehm
Hitler's speech, 22 August: DGFP; HALD; IMT
  (Boehm); BA (Canaris diary)
Pact toasted in champagne: Guderian
'The only drop of cold water . . .': Raeder
Canaris 'utterly horrified': Gisevius

CHAPTER 23: The Pact is Signed
Ribbentrop's departure: DGFP; Herwarth
  (interview); Schulze-Kossens (interview)
'This coup de théâtre': FYB

'Russians were double-crossers': DBFP
'Quite a swig out of the bottle': DGFP
'Gaus asked Schulenburg's advice': Herwarth
  (interview)
Schmidt's instructions: Schmidt
'Nobody could guarantee . . . ': Kleist
Arrival in Königsberg: Hoffmann; Kleist;
  Herwarth (interview)
Hitler–Weizsäcker conversation: Weizsäcker
'Ribbentrop spent the rest of the night . . .':
  Schmidt
'In moments of respite . . .': Schmidt; Herwarth
  (interview); Schulze–Kossens (interview); H.
  Hoffmann
Ribbentrop's arrival in Moscow: DGFP; Schmidt;
  Kleist; Herwarth (interview); Schulze–Kossens
  (interview)
Lavish buffet lunch: Hoffmann–Köstring convers-
  ation: Hoffmann
Ribbentrop's briefing: Hilger; Kleist
'Only very rarely during my walk . . .': Schmidt
'Schulenburg gave him a brief commentary . . .':
  Ribbentrop; Kleist
Arrival in Kremlin: Ribbentrop; Hilger
'Germany demands nothing . . .': DGFP;
  Ribbentrop
Ribbentrop–Stalin–Molotov meeting: DGFP;
  Ribbentrop; Hilger; Kleist
'Ribbentrop arrived back . . .': Schmidt
Messages for Hitler: DGFP; Herwarth (plus
  interview)
'Hitler, waiting impatiently . . .': Speer
'Yes, agreed': DGFP
'Ribbentrop returned to the Kremlin at 10 pm':
  Kleist; Hoffmann
'I know how much the German nation . . .':
  DGFP: Ribbentrop
Stalin's personal flask: Schulze–Kossens
  (interview)
Conversation between toasts: DGFP; Schmidt
'Josef Stalin will join the Anti-Comintern Pact':
  Ribbentrop; DGFP
Photographing the great event: H. Hoffmann
Stalin and Schulze: Schulze–Kossens (interview)
Ribbentrop's arrival back at embassy: Kleist
'Stalin . . . sped away from the Kremlin . . .':
  Khrushchev
Hitler receives news: Speer

CHAPTER 24: 'A long and lasting treaty'
'With the Moscow pact . . .' and 'As a result of
  Hitler's frivolous game . . .': Weizsäcker
Preliminary order for Operation White: OKW
Appointment of Forster: DGFP
'The sinister news broke upon the world . . .':
  Churchill, The Gathering Storm
'The effect of the pact . . .': CAB
Package of precautionary measures: CAB
Emergency session of French National Defence
  Council: FYB; Bonnet
Chamberlain letter to Hitler: DBFP; DGFP;
  Henderson
Decision against sending Ironside: CAB
Stalin 'had already seen it': DGFP
Two envoys of British SIS: DGFP
Henderson meeting with Hitler: DGFP;
  Henderson; Weizsäcker
'Chamberlain won't survive . . .': Weizsäcker

Henderson–Ribbentrop 'tempestuous exchange':
  Henderson; Ribbentrop; Schmidt; DGFP;
  DBFP
'I needed an alibi . . .': Schmidt
Henderson–Lipski meeting and telephone calls:
  Henderson; DBFP
Ogilvie-Forbes telephones Dahlerus, drives him to
  see Lipski: Dahlerus
Beck's instructions to Lipski: PWB; PSR
Forschungsamt intercept: Kleist
Directive No. 1: DGFP
Executive order confirmed: HALD
Ribbentrop finally sees Lipski: DGFP
Gleiwitz attack: IMT (Naujocks)
Polish broadcast, 'Words can no longer veil . . .':
  PWB

CHAPTER 29: The Great Counter-Attack
'To meet force with force': Baynes
'In defence against Polish attacks . . .': DGFP
Kordt's instructions: DGFP
Halifax and Chamberlain take information
  seriously: CAB
'Last night there were fourteen more cases . . .':
  DGFP
Hitler at Kroll Opera House: Shirer, Berlin Diary
'Eva Braun covered her face . . .': Gun
Minsk radio station broadcasts identifica-tion:
  DGFP
Low profile on Soviet military mission: DGFP
Shkvarzev to be ambassador: DGFP
Henderson telephones Halifax: Henderson;
  DBFP; Dahlerus
'We are in the midst of a war . . .': FYB; Bonnet
Raczynski sees Halifax at 10 Downing Street:
  Raczynski (plus interview)
Chamberlain's speech in House of Commons:
  Hansard; Raczynski
Grzybowski–Molotov meeting: PWB; Beloff;
  Documents on Polish–Soviet Relations
Near mutiny in Cabinet and violent uproar in
  House: CAB; Hansard; Churchill, The Gathering
  Storm
'Really you could receive the ambassador . . .':
  Schmidt
Henderson–Schmidt meeting: Henderson;
  Schmidt; DBFP
'What now?': Schmidt
Hitler welcomes Shkvarzev: DGFP; Weizsäcker
'Hitler was furious . . .': DGFP
Death of Heinrich von Weizsäcker: Weizsäcker;
  President Richard von Weizsäcker (interview)
'It is possible that we are mistaken . . .': DGFP

CHAPTER 30: Death of a Nation
Special train Amerika: P. Hoffmann
Special train Heinrich: Schmidt
'During almost the whole of the Polish campaign
  . . .': Schmidt
Polish government calls on all Poles: PWB
Jodl gives Purkayev complete briefing: Warlimont
Grzybowski takes up Molotov's offer of aid: PWB
Ribbentrop again asks Soviet Union to send in Red
  Army: DGFP
Molotov tells Schulenburg 'within the next few
  days': DGFP
German request to use Murmansk: DGFP

Proposal that Schnurre should travel to Moscow:
  Schnurre (interview); DGFP
Battle raging on Khalkin-Gol: Erickson, The Road
  to Stalingrad; Zhukov; Mackintosh; Hosking
Schulenburg–Togo meetings and Ribbentrop's
  intervention: DGFP
Molotov tells Schulenburg Red Army ready:
  DGFP
Polish government flees: Greene (interview and
  despatches); DGFP
Ribbentrop objects, and Molotov tells
  Schulenburg Red Army will cross Polish
  borders at 6 am: DGFP
Köstring's fears: Hilger; DGFP
Schulenburg objects to wording: Hilger; DGFP
Stalin's note to Poles: DGFP; FRUS: Beloff
Grzybowski refuses to accept note: FRUS;
  Grzybowksi (to Bohlen); Raczynski (plus
  interview)

CHAPTER 31: The Fourth Partition
Red Army crosses Polish border: Erickson The
  Road to Stalingrad; Mackintosh
Leaflets and white flags: Anders
Soviet workers cheer: Bohlen
Heydrich's Einsatzgruppen: HALD; IMT
Soviet troops enter town of Chelm: Zuker–
  Bujanowska
Polish unit votes on which way to go:
  Andrezejewski (interview)
Red Army digging fortifications: Anders
Casualty figures: Goralski
Voroshilov and Köstring sign agreement: DGFP
Belyakov shown German map: Warlimont
Stalin complains: DGFP
'When diplomats make mistakes in war . . .':
  Warlimont
Stalin offers Germany the Suwalki triangle: DGFP
Scene at Kasino Hotel, Zoppot: Schmidt; Kleist
'A pack of Chicago gangsters': Shirer, Berlin Diary
Hitler's Danzig speech: DGFP; Hitler's Speeches
Stalin favours a straight division: DGFP
Plans for organised euthanasia: IMT (Brandt)
Hitler joins Keitel's birthday celebration: Keitel
  (original ms)
Ribbentrop decides to go to Moscow himself:
  DGFP; Ribbentrop
Ribbentrop entertains Terauchi: DGFP
Stalin proposes Germany should waive claims to
  Lithuania: DGFP

CHAPTER 32: 'Is my signature clear enough for you?'
Hitler passes train journey in silence: Vormann
Hitler briefs Dahlerus yet again: Dahlerus
Advice received from Moltke: DGFP
Hitler's speech to generals on offensive in West:
  DGFP; HALD
Ribbentrop's flight to Moscow: Schulze-Kossens
  (interview); DGFP
Arrival in Moscow: Schulze-Kossens (interview)
'Ribbentrop did not pause . . .': Schnurre
  (interview); DGFP
Opening talks: Hilger; Ribbentrop; DGFP
'This time he took all his specialists with him . . .':
  Schnurre (interview); Hilger
Gala dinner in Kremlin: Ribbentrop; Hilger;
  Schnurre (interview); Schulze-Kossens
  (interview)

CHAPTER 53: 'I have sure information'
Sorge's message from Tokyo, 2 May: Deakin;
    Erickson, *The Road to Stalingrad*
'Red Orchestra': Trepper
'This information is an English provocation . . .':
    Whaley
German–Russian phrase book: Berezhkov; Bialer
Tupikov sends statement to Moscow, 14 March:
    Zhukov
Information passed to Soviet ambassador in
    Washington: Welles
'Sam Woods, a genial extrovert . . .': Shirer, *The
    Rise and Fall of the Third Reich*
Herwarth denies being Woods's informant:
    Herwarth
Oshima's reports to Tokyo: Boyd
Churchill's personal letter to Stalin: Churchill,
    Their Finest Hour; DBFP
Churchill and experts taken in by German
    smokescreen: Woodward; Hinsley
Picture changes for Churchill: Churchill, *Their
    Finest Hour*
'I have sure information . . .': DBFP
Churchill furious at Cripps's delay: Churchill,
    Their Finest Hour; Woodward
Eden sees Maisky five times: DBFP; Woodward
Dansey and the Lucy Ring: Read and Fisher,
    Operation Lucy
Cadogan–Maisky meeting: Maisky, *Memoirs of a
    Soviet Ambassador*; Dilks
Moscow Radio broadcast: DGFP; *Pravda*
Hitler's final briefing of senior commanders:
    HALD; Warlimont

*CHAPTER 54: 'You can't believe everything you read
in intelligence reports'*
Stalin unnerved and irritated: Kuznetsov
Pavlov's report, 4 June: Erickson, *The Road to
    Stalingrad*; Nekrich
Tense situation in the Ukraine: Fediuninsky (in
    Bialer)
Kalinin's speech: Erickson
New set of intructions to Red Army's political
    workers: Scott
Malenkov's reaction: Medvedev, *Let History Judge*
Kirponos calls meeting of his military council:
    Purkayev (in Bialer); Bagramian (in Bialer);
    Zhukov
Timoshenko and Zhukov press Stalin to deploy
    troops: Zhukov
Start of manoeuvres, artillery goes to ranges:
    Zhukov
Kuznetsov gives Stalin naval intelligence:
    Kuznetsov
'Only a fool would attack us': Kuznetsov
'Annihilation of Russian submarines . . .': DGFP
Golikov and the GRU: Nekrich
'. . . Golikov was directly responsible to Stalin . . .':
    Zhukov
'All documents claiming war is imminent must be
    regarded as forgeries': Nekrich
Golikov scribbling in margins of reports: Trepper
Gnedich's statement to meeting in 1966: Petrov
Trepper's warning, and Golikov's reply: Trepper

CHAPTER 55: 'Pushing open the door to a dark room'
Hitler informs Romania, Finland, Hungary and
    Slovakia: Weizsäcker

Treaty of friendship with Turkey: DGFP
Schulenburg's letters to Pussi Herwarth: Frau von
    Herwarth (interview)
Schulenburg receives orders to secure files, etc.:
    DGFP
Arranges for remaining women and children to
    leave: Hilger
Dekanozov asks to see Weizsäcker: Weizsäcker;
    BA (Hewel diaries)
Hitler and Ribbentrop panic: BA (Hewel diaries);
    Sommer (plus interview)
'Now that Hitler was waiting to pounce . . .':
    Weizsäcker
Tension taking its toll on Hitler: BA (Hewel
    diaries)
'Wolfschanze' description: P. Hoffmann; JOD
'We have only to kick in the door . . .': JOD
Rosenberg demands Soviet embassy building:
    DGFP; Sommer
Skirpa calls on Foreign Ministry: DGFP
Hitler breaks news to Frank: DGFP
Golovko asks why batteries did not open fire:
    Nekrich
Interrogation of saboteurs: Nekrich
German deserter picked up and interrogated:
    Fediuninski (in Bialer)
Zhdanov leaves for annual holiday: *Pravda*, 19 June
    1941
Student questions Ulbricht: Leonhard
Moscow weather, etc.: *Pravda*
'Consumer summer': Scott
Hitler's proclamation issued: Taylor; HALD
Text of proclamation: *Hitler's Speeches*
Codeword 'Dortmund' issued: JOD; HALD
'I feel as if I am pushing open the door . . .': BA
    (Hewel diaries)

CHAPTER 56: 'Surely we have not deserved that'
Berezhkov asks for urgent appointment: Berezhkov
Ribbentrop's order to say he was out of Berlin:
    DGFP
Soviet embassy staff take day off: Berezhkov
Hitler composing another proclamation and
    choosing fanfares: Taylor
Hitler's letters to Mussolini and Horthy: DGFP
Hitler talks about plans for new naval base: Speer
Hitler forbids attacks on US ships: Raeder; DGFP
Schulenburg summoned to Kremlin: Hilger;
    DGFP
Dekanozov–Weizsäcker meeting: Weizsäcker;
    DGFP
Timoshenko, Zhukov and Vatutin tell Stalin about
    second deserter: Zhukov
Zhukov and Vatutin draft directive: Zhukov
Transmission of directive: Erickson
Last trains cross bridge at Brest–Litovsk:
    Herwarth
Zhukov telephones Stalin about third deserter:
    Zhukov
Stalin orders Liskov to be shot: Erickson, *The Road
    to Stalingrad*
'The Führer seems to lose his fear . . . ': Taylor
Hitler calls Speer into salon: Speer
Schulenburg receives instructions at 3 am: Hilger;
    DGFP
Fleet commanders report air and torpedo-boat
    attacks: Kuznetsov
Klimovsky reports bombing in Belorussia: Zhukov

Zhukov telephones Stalin, and meeting in Stalin's office: Zhukov
Sommer telephones Soviet embassy, collects Dekanozov and Berezhkov: Sommer; Berezhkov
Ribbentrop–Dekanozov meeting: DGFP; Sommer; Berezhkov; Schmidt
Molotov–Schulenburg meeting: DGFP; Hilger
Stalin receives news, issues directive No. 2: Zhukov
Stalin contacts Japanese government: HALD
Molotov's broadcast: Leonhard; Cassidy

EPILOGUE: 'There are no invincible armies'
'All that Lenin created . . . ': Khrushchev
Stalin 'nervy and low-spirited': Voronov

For eleven days, Stalin remained out of sight: Erickson, *The Road to Stalingrad*
Situation little short of disastrous: Erickson; Clark; Carell; Israelyan
Jubilation at German general head-quarters: JOD
'By 15 August, we shall be in Moscow': Hilger
Stalin's speech: Cassidy; Scott; Fischer
The miracle of Moscow: Israelyan; Erickson; Clark; Carell; Novosti Press Agency; Werth; Zhukov
Sorge's last coup: Deakin
Movement of industries to east: Erickson, *The Road to Stalingrad*; Werth
Battle of Kursk: Erickson, *The Road to Stalingrad*
Soviet casualty figures: Novosti Press Agency

INTERVIEWS AND CORRESPONDENCE

Dr Christopher Andrew
Professor B. Andrzejewski
Mr Andrei Antonovksi
Frau Margarete BuberNeumann
Air Marshal Sir Conrad Collier
Mr Roman Czerniawski
Mr Norman Dewhurst
Mr Virgil Dijmarescu
Heinrich Graf von Einsiedel
Professor John Erickson
Dr Ingeborg Fleischhauer
Herr Hugo Geiger
Sir Hugh Greene
Dr Heinz Haushofer
Frau Elisabeth von Herwarth
Herr Hans von Herwarth
Professor Leonard L. Heston
Professor Geoffrey Hosking
Dr Max Jakobson
Dr E. Keipert
Lord Lauderdale (Patrick Maitland)
Mr Lasse Lehtinen
Professor Wolfgang Leonhard
Sir Fitzroy Maclean

Dr Zhores Medvedev
Herr Hubert Meyer
Professor Alexander M. Nekrich
Mr Alexei Nikiforov
Mr Johann Nykopp
Mr B. Panov
Mrs Lana Peters (Svetlana Stalin/ Alliluyeva)
Count Edward Raczynski
Sir Frank Roberts
Mr Arne Saarinen
Mr Kazimierz Sabbat
Dr Walter Schmid
Dr Karl Schnurre
Albrecht Graf von der Schulenburg
Herr Richard Schulze-Kossens
Mr Henry Shapiro
Dr Erich F. Sommer
Mr Edmund Stevens
Dr Martti Turtola
Professor Anthony Upton
Professor Michael Voslensky
President Richard von Weizsäcker

BIBLIOGRAPHY

The following books have been consulted by the authors in the writing of this book. Unless otherwise stated, publication was in London.

ABRAMSKY, C. (ed.), *Essays in Honour of E. H. Carr* ('The Initiation of the Negotiations Leading to the Nazi–Soviet Pact: A Historical Problem', D. C. Watt) Macmillan, 1974

ABYZOV, VLADIMIR, *The Final Assault*, Novosti, Moscow, 1985

ALEXANDROV, VICTOR, *The Kremlin, Nerve-Centre of Russian History*, George Allen & Unwin, 1963

ALLILUYEVA, SVETLANA, *Only One Year*, Hutchinson, 1969
Twenty Letters to a Friend, Hutchinson, 1967

AMORT, R., and JEDLICKA, I. M., *The Canaris File*, Wingate, 1974

ANDERS, LIEUTENANT-GENERAL W., *An Army in Exile*, Macmillan, 1949

ANDREAS-FRIEDRICH, RUTH, *Berlin Underground, 1939–1945*, Latimer House, 1948

ANON, *A Short History of the Bulgarian Communist Party*, Sofia Press, Sofia, 1977

ANON, *The Crime of Katyn, Facts and Documents*, Polish Cultural Foundation, 1965

ANON, *The Obersalzberg and the Third Reich*, Plenk Verlag, Berchtesgaden, 1982

ANTONOV-OUSEYENKO, ANTON, *The Time of Stalin, Portrait of a Tyranny*, Harper & Row, New York, 1981

BACON, WALTER, *Finland*, Hale, 1970

BARBUSSE, HENRI, *Stalin: A New World Seen Through One Man*, Macmillan, New York, 1935

BAYNES, N. H. (ed), *Hitler's Speeches, 1922–39, 2 vols*, OUP, 1942

BEAUFRE, ANDRÉ, *1940: The Fall of France*, Cassell, 1968

BECK, JOSEF, *Dernier Rapport*, La Baconnière, Brussels, 1951

BEDELL SMITH, WALTER, *Moscow Mission 1946–1949*, Heinemann, 1950

BELOFF, MAX, *The Foreign Policy of Soviet Russia*, Vol Two, *1936–1941*, Oxford, 1949

BEREZHKOV, VALENTIN, *History in the Making*, Progress Publishers, Moscow, 1983

BIALER, S., *Stalin and His Generals*, Souvenir Press, 1969

BIELENBERG, CHRISTABEL, *The Past is Myself*, Chatto & Windus, 1968

BIRKENHEAD, LORD, *Halifax*, Hamish Hamilton, 1965

BOHLEN, CHARLES E., *Witness to History, 1929–1969*, Weidenfeld & Nicolson, 1973

BONNET, GEORGES, *Fin d'une Europe*, Geneva, 1948

BOURKE-WHITE, MARGARET, *Shooting the Russian War*, Simon & Schuster, New York, 1942

BOYD, CARL, *Magic and the Japanese Ambassador to Berlin*, Paper for Northern Great Plains History Conference, Eau Claire, Wisconsin, 1986

BUBER, MARGARETE, *Under Two Dictators*, Gollancz, 1949

BUBER-NEUMANN, MARGARETE, *Von Potsdam nach Moskau — Stationens eines Irrweges*, Hohenheim, Cologne, 1981

BULLOCK, ALAN, *Hitler: A Study in Tyranny*, Pelican, 1962

BURCKHARDT, CARL J., *Meine Danziger Mission, 1937–1939*, Munich, 1960

BUTLER, J. R. M. (editor), *Grand Strategy, Vols I–III*, HMSO, 1956–1964

BUTSON, T. G., *The Tsar's Lieutenant: The Soviet Marshal*, Praeger, 1984

CALDWELL, ERSKINE, *All Out on the Road to Smolensk*, Duell, Sloan and Pearce, New York, 1942

CALIC, ÈDOUARD, *Unmasked: Two Confidential Interviews with Hitler in 1931*, Chatto & Windus, 1971

CARELL, PAUL, *Hitler's War on Russia*, Harrap, 1964

CASSIDY, HENRY C., *Moscow Dateline*, Houghton Mifflin, Boston, 1943

CECIL, ROBERT, *Hitler's Decision to Invade Russia, 1941*, Davis-Poynter, 1975

CHANEY, OTTO PRESTON, JR., *Zhukov*, David & Charles, Newton Abbot, 1972

CHAPMAN, GUY, *Why France Collapsed*, Cassell, 1968

CHURCHILL, WINSTON S., *The Second World War*. Vol. I: *The Gathering Storm*, Vol. II: *Their Finest Hour*, Vol. III: *The Grand Alliance*, Penguin, 1985

CIENCIALA, ANNA M., *Poland and the Western Powers*, Routledge & Kegan Paul, 1968

CLARK, ALAN, *Barbarossa*, Hutchinson, 1965

COATES, W. P. and Z. K., *The Soviet–Finnish Campaign*, Eldon Press, 1942

COHEN, STEPHEN (ed.), *An End to Silence* (from Roy Medvedev's underground magazine, *Political Diary*), W. W. Norton, New York, 1982

COLLIER, RICHARD, *1940 — The World in Flames*, Hamish Hamilton, 1979

COLVILLE, JOHN, *The Fringes of Power, Downing Street Diaries, 1939–1955*, Hodder & Stoughton, 1985

COLVIN, IAN, *The Chamberlain Cabinet*, Gollancz, 1971

CONQUEST, ROBERT, *The Great Terror: Stalin's Purge of the Thirties*, Macmillan, 1968

COOKE, RONALD C., and NESBIT, ROY CONGERS, *Target: Hitler's Oil*, Kimber, 1985

COOPER, DIANA, *Autobiography*, Michael Russell, 1979

COULONDRE, ROBERT, *De Staline à Hitler*, Paris, 1950

CRUIKSHANK, CHARLES, *Deception in World War II*, OUP, 1979

DAHLERUS, BIRGER, *The Last Attempt*, Hutchinson, 1948

DALADIER, EDOUARD, *The Defence of France*, Hutchinson, 1939

DEAKIN, F. W., and STORRY, G. R., *The Case of Richard Sorge*, Chatto & Windus, 1966

DEIGHTON, LEN, *Blitzkrieg*, Jonathan Cape, 1979

DELBARS, YVES, *The Real Stalin*, George Allen & Unwin, 1953

DEUTSCHER, ISAAC, *Stalin. A Political Biography*, OUP, 1949

DIETRICH, OTTO, *The Hitler I Knew*, Methuen, 1957

DILKS, DAVID, (ed.), *Diaries of Sir Alexander Cadogan 1938–1945*, Cassell, 1971

DJILAS, MILOVAN, *Conversations with Stalin*, Penguin, 1963

DOBSON, CHRISTOPHER and MILLER, JOHN, *The Day We Almost Bombed Moscow: Allied War in Russia 1918–1920*, Hodder & Stoughton, 1986

DOLLMANN, EUGEN, *The Interpreter*, Hutchinson, 1967

DONNELLY, DESMOND, *Struggle for the World*, Collins, 1965

DOUGLAS, CLARK, *Three Days to Catastrophe*, Hammond, 1966

DRAX, ADMIRAL SIR REGINALD PLUNKETT-ERNLE-ERLE-, *Mission to Moscow, August 1939*, Privately, 1966

DREA, EDWARD J., *Nomohan: Japanese–Soviet Tactical Combat. 1939*, Combat Studies Institute, Leavenworth Papers, January 1981

EDEN, ANTHONY, *Facing the Dictators*, Cassell, 1962

The Reckoning, Cassell, 1965

EDMONDS, H. J., *Norman Dewhurst, MC*, Privately, Brussels, 1968
EHRENBURG, ILYA, *Eve of War*, MacGibbon & Kee, 1963
EINZIG, PAUL, *In the Centre of Things*, Hutchinson, 1960
EISENSTEIN, SERGEI M., *Immoral Memories*, Peter Owen, 1985
ENGEL, GERHARD, *Heeresadjutant bei Hitler 1938–1943*, Deutsche Verlags-Anstalt, Stuttgart, 1974
ERICKSON, J., *The Road to Stalingrad* Weidenfeld & Nicolson, 1975
    The Soviet High Command, Macmillan, 1962
    'Reflections on Securing the Soviet Far Eastern Frontier: 1932–1945', *Interplay*, August–September 1969
EUGLE, E., and PAANEN, L., *The Winter War*, Sidgwick & Jackson, 1973
FEILING, KEITH, *The Life of Neville Chamberlain*, Macmillan, 1946
FEST, JOACHIM C., *Hitler*, Harcourt Brace Jovanovich, New York, 1974
    The Face of the Third Reich, Weidenfeld & Nicolson, 1970
FISCHER, ERNST, *An Opposing Man*, Allen Lane, 1974
FLANNERY, HARRY W., *Assignment to Berlin*, Michael Joseph, 1942
FLEISHER, WILFRID, *Volcano Isle*, Jonathan Cape, 1942
FOOTE, ALEXANDER, *Handbook for Spies*, Museum Press, 1949, 1953
FRANÇOIS-PONCET, ANDRÉ, *The Fateful Years*, Gollancz, 1949
FRANKEL, ANDREW, *The Eagle's Nest*, Plenk Verlag, Berchtesgaden, 1983
GAFENCU, GRIGOIRE, *The Last Days of Europe*, Frederick Muller, 1947
GALANTE, PIERRE, *Hitler Lives — and the Generals Die*, Sidgwick & Jackson, 1982
GARLINSKI, JÓZEF, *The Swiss Corridor*, J. M. Dent, 1981
GIBSON, HUGH (ed.), *The Ciano Diaries, 1939–1943*, Doubleday, New York, 1946
GILBERT, MARTIN, *Finest Hour*, Heinemann, 1983
    The Holocaust, The Jewish Tragedy, Collins, 1986
    Winston Churchill, The Wilderness Years, Macmillan, 1981
GISEVIUS, HANS BERND, *To the Bitter End*, Cape, 1948
GORALSKI, ROBERT, *World War II Almanac, 1931–1945*, Hamish Hamilton, 1981
GORBATOV, ALEKSANDR V., *Years Off My Life*, Constable, 1964
GORODETSKY, G., *Stafford Cripps' Mission to Moscow, 1940–42*, Cambridge U.P., 1984
GREW, JOSEPH C., *Ten Years in Japan*, Hammond, Hammond, 1945
GREY, IAN, *Stalin, Man of History*, Weidenfeld & Nicolson, 1979
    The First Fifty Years. Soviet Russia, 1917–1967, Hodder & Stoughton, 1967
GRIGORENKO, PETRO G., *Memoirs*, Harvill, 1983
GRIPENBERG, G. A. (trs. Albin T. Anderson), *Finland and the Great Powers*, Univ. of Nebraska Press, Lincoln, 1965
GUDERIAN, HEINZ, *Panzer Leader*, Ballantine Books, New York
GUN, NERIN E., *Eva Braun, Hitler's Mistress*, Frewin, 1968
HALDER, COLONEL-GENERAL FRANZ, *Kriegstagebuch*, Kohlhammer, Stuttgart, 1963
    Hitler als Feldherr, Münchener Dom-Verlag, Munich, 1949
HALIFAX, LORD, *Fulness of Days*, Collins, 1957
HARLEY, J. H. (based on Polish by Conrad Wrzos), *The Authentic Biography of Colonel Beck*, Hutchinson, 1939
HARRIMAN, W. A., and ABEL, E., *Special Envoy to Churchill and Stalin, 1941–1946*, Random House, New York, 1975
HASLAM, J., *The Soviet Union and the Struggle for Collective Security in Europe, 1933–1939*, Macmillan, 1984
HAUNER, MILAN, *Hitler. A Chronology of His Life and Time*, Macmillan, 1983
HAYASHI, SABURO (with ALVIN D. COOX), *Kogun, The Japanese Army in the Pacific War*, Marine Corps Association, Quantico, Va., 1959
HEIBER, HELMUT, *Goebbels*, Robert Hale, 1972
HENDERSON, SIR NEVILE, *Failure of a Mission*, Hodder & Stoughton, 1940
HERWARTH, HANS VON (with FREDERICH STARR), *Against Two Evils*, Collins, 1981

HESSE, FRITZ, *Das Spiel um Deutschland*, List, Munich, 1953
Hitler and the English, Wingate, 1954
HESTON, LEONARD and RENATO, *The Medical Case Book of Adolf Hitler*, Kimber, 1979
HILGER, GUSTAV (with ALFRED G. MEYER), *The Incompatible Allies: A Memoir-History of German–Soviet Relations, 1918–1941* Macmillan, New York, 1953
HILL, LEONIDAS E. (ed.) *Die Weizsäcker Papiere, 1933–1950*, Berlin, 1974
HINSLEY, F. H. with THOMAS, E. E., RANSOM, C. F. G., and KNIGHT, R. C., *British Intelligence in the Second World War*, Vol. 1, HMSO, 1979
HITLER, ADOLF, *Mein Kampf*, Hutchinson, 1969
Hitler's Secret Conversations, Signet, New York, 1961
The Testament of Adolf Hitler. The Hitler–Bormann Documents, Cassell, 1961
HOFFMANN, HEINRICH, *Hitler Was My Friend*, Burke, 1955
HOFFMANN, PETER, *Hitler's Personal Security*, MIT, Boston, 1979
HÖHNE, HEINZ (trs. R. Barry), *The Order of the Death's Head: The Story of Hitler's SS*, Secker & Warburg, 1969
HOSKING, G., *A History of the Soviet Union*, Fontana, 1985
HYDE, H. MONTGOMERY, *Stalin*, Rupert Hart-Davis, 1971
INFIELD, GLENN B., *Hitler's Secret Life*, Hamlyn, 1980
IRVING, DAVID, *Hitler's War, 1939–1942*, Macmillan, 1983
The War Path, Michael Joseph, 1978
ISRAELYAN, V. L., *The Diplomatic History of the Great Fatherland War*, Moscow, 1959
JAKOBSON, MAX, *The Diplomacy of the Winter War*, Harvard UP, Boston, 1961
JEDRZEJEWICZ, WACLAW (ed.), *Diplomat in Paris: 1931–1939 – Papers & Memoirs of Juliusz Lukasiewicz*, Columbia UP, New York, 1970
JONES, F. C., *Japan's New Order in East Asia. Its Rise and Fall*, OUP, 1954
Manchuria Since 1931, Royal Institute of International Affairs, 1949
JONES, R. V., *Most Secret War*, Hamish Hamilton, 1978
JONGE, ALEX DE, *Stalin and the Shaping of the Soviet Union*, Collins, 1986
The Weimar Chronicle. Prelude to Hitler, Paddington Press, 1978
KAZAKOV, GENERAL M. I., *Nad Kartoi Bylykh Srazhenii*, Voenizdat, Moscow, 1965
KEITEL, WILHELM, *Memoirs*, Kimber, 1965
KENNAN, GEORGE F., *Soviet Foreign Policy 1917–1941*, Robert E. Krieger, Princeton, 1960
KHRUSHCHEV, NIKITA S., (Trs. and edited by Strobe Talbott), *Khrushchev Remembers*, André Deutsch, 1971
KIRBY, D. G., *Finland in the Twentieth Century*, C. Hurst & Co., 1979
KIRKPATRICK, LYMAN B. JR, *Captains Without Eyes. Intelligence Failures in World War II*, Macmillan, New York
KLEIST, PETER, *European Tragedy*, Times Press/Anthony Gibbs & Phillips, Isle of Man, 1965
KORDT, ERICH, *Nicht aus den Akten: Die Wilhelmstrasse in Frieden und Krieg*, Stuttgart, 1950
KRAVCHENKO, VICTOR, *I Chose Freedom*, Robert Hale, 1947
KROSBY, HANS PETER, *Finland, Germany and the Soviet Union, 1940–41: The Petsamo Dispute*, Univ. of Wisconsin, Madison, 1968
KRYLOV, IVAN, *Soviet Staff Officer*, Falcon Press, 1951
KUBIZEK, AUGUST, *The Young Hitler I Knew*, Houghton, Mifflin, Boston, 1955
KUSNIERZ, B. N., *Stalin and the Poles*, Hollis & Carter, 1949
KUUSINEN, AINO, *Before and After Stalin*, Michael Joseph, 1974
KUZNETSOV, N. G., 'In Charge of the Navy' (from *Stalin and His Generals*, ed. Seweryn Bialer), Souvenir Press, 1969
LEACH, BARRY A., *German Strategy Against Russia, 1939–1941*, OUP, 1973
LEHMAN, JEAN-PIERRE, *The Roots of Modern Japan*, Macmillan, 1982

LENSEN, GEORGE ALEXANDER, *The Strange Neutrality. Soviet–Japanese Relations During the Second World War 1941–1945*, Diplomatic Press, Tallahassee, Fla., 1972
LEONHARD, WOLFGANG, *Child of the Revolution*, Collins, 1957
LEWIN, RONALD, *Hitler's Mistakes*, Leo Cooper, 1984
Ultra Goes to War, Hutchinson, 1978
LITVINOV, MAXIM, *Notes for a Journal*, André Deutsch, 1955
LITYNSKI, ZYGMUNT, *I Was One of Them*, Cape, 1941
LOSSBERG, BERNHARD VON, *Im Wehrmachtführungsstab*, Nölke, Hamburg, 1947
LUKACS, JOHN, *The Last European War*, Routledge & Kegan Paul, 1977
LYONS, GRAHAM (ed.), *The Russian Version of the Second World War*, Leo Cooper, 1976
MACKENZIE, A., *The History of Transylvania*, Unified Printers & Publishers, 1983
MACKIEWICZ, STANISLAW, *Colonel Beck and His Policy*, Eyre & Spottiswoode, 1944
MACKINTOSH, M., *Juggernaut. A History of the Soviet Armed Forces*, Secker & Warburg, 1967
MACLEAN, FITZROY, *Eastern Approaches*, Cape, 1949
MACLEOD, COLONEL R., and KELLY, DENIS (eds.), *The Ironside Diaries, 1937–1940*, Constable, 1962
MAISKY, IVAN, *Memoirs of a Soviet Ambassador*, Hutchinson, 1967
Who Helped Hitler?, Hutchinson, 1964
MANCHESTER, WILLIAM, *The Arms of Krupp*, Michael Joseph, 1969
MANVELL, ROGER, and FRAENKEL, HEINRICH, *Hitler, the Man and the Myth*, Granada, 1978
MEDVEDEV, ROY, *All Stalin's Men*, Blackwell, Oxford, 1983
Let History Judge, Alfred A. Knopf, New York, 1971
Khrushchev, Blackwell, Oxford, 1982
On Stalin and Stalinism, OUP, 1979
MERSON, ALLAN, *Communist Resistance in Nazi Germany*, Lawrence & Wishart, 1985
MORAVEC, FRANTISEK, *Master of Spies*, Bodley Head, 1975
MORLEY, JAMES W. (ed.), *The Fateful Choice: Japan's Road to the Pacific War*, Columbia UP, New York, 1980
MOSLEY, LEONARD, *On Borrowed Time*, Weidenfeld & Nicolson, 1969
NEKRICH, A. M., *1941, 22 Iyunia*, Nauka, Moscow, 1965
NOLLAU, GÜNTHER, *International Communism and World Revolution*, Hollis & Carter, 1961
NOWAK, JAN, *Courier from Warsaw*, Collins/Harvill, 1982
OTETEA, ANDREI, *The History of the Romanian People*, Scientific Publishing House, Bucharest, 1970
OVSYANY, IGOR, *The Origins of Word War Two*, Novosti, Moscow, 1984
PAASIKIVI, JUHO KUSTI, *Am Rande einer Supermacht, Behauptung durch Diplomatie*, Hosten Verlag, Hamburg, 1966
PARKINSON, ROGER, *Peace for Our Time*, Hart-Davis, 1971
PAYNE, ROBERT, *The Rise and Fall of Stalin*, W. H. Allen, 1966
PETROV, VLADIMIR, *June 22, 1941. Soviet Historians and the German Invasion*, Univ. of S. Carolina, 1968
RACZYNSKI, COUNT EDWARD, *In Allied London*, Weidenfeld & Nicolson, 1962
RADO, SANDOR, *Sous le Pseudonym Dora (Dora Jelenti)*, Julliard, Paris, 1972
RAEDER, ERICH, *My Life*, US Naval Institute, Annapolis, 1960
READ, ANTHONY, and FISHER, DAVID, *Colonel Z*, Hodder & Stoughton, 1984
Operation Lucy, Hodder & Stoughton, 1980
REISCHAUER, EDWIN O., *The Japanese*, Harvard UP, 1977
REITLINGER, GERALD, *The House Built on Sand*, Weidenfeld & Nicolson, 1960
RIBBENTROP, JOACHIM VON, *Zwischen London und Moskau: Erinnerungen und letzte Aufzeichnungen*, Stuttgart, 1955

RICH, NORMAN, *Hitler's War Aims: Ideology, the Nazi State and the Course of Expansion*, Norton, New York, 1973
Hitler's War Aims: The Establishment of the New Order, Norton, New York, 1974
RINGS, WERNER, *Life with the Enemy*, Weidenfeld & Nicolson, 1982
ROKOSSOVSKY, K., *A Soldier's Duty*, Progress Publishers, Moscow, 1970
ROOS, H., *A History of Modern Poland*, Eyre & Spottiswoode, 1962
ROSSI, A., *The Russo–German Alliance*, Chapman & Hall, 1950
ROTHSTEIN, ANDREW, and DUTT, CLEMENS (eds.), *History of the Communist Party of the Soviet Union*, Foreign Languages Publishing House, Moscow
RUBINSTEIN, ALVIN Z. (ed.), *The Foreign Policy of the Soviet Union. The Search for Security 1934–41*, New York, undated
RUSSELL, WILLIAM, *Berlin Embassy*, Michael Joseph, 1942
RYABOV, VASILI, *The Great Victory*, Novosti, Moscow, 1985
SALISBURY, HARRISON E., *A Journey for Our Times*, Harper & Row, New York, 1983
The Siege of Leningrad, Secker & Warburg, 1969
SCHAPIRO, LEONARD, *The Government and Politics of the Soviet Union*, Vintage Books, 1978
SCHMIDT, PAUL, *Hitler's Interpreter*, Heinemann, 1951
SCHRAMM, PERCY ERNST, *Hitler: The Man and the Military Leader*, Allen Lane, 1972
SCHREIBER, H., *Teuton and Slav*, 1965
SCHWARZ, PAUL, *This Man Ribbentrop*, Julian Messner, New York, 1943
SCOTT, JOHN, *Duel for Europe*, Houghton Mifflin, Boston, 1942
SEATON, ALBERT, *The Russo–German War 1941–45*, Arthur Barker, 1971
Stalin as Warlord, Batsford, 1976
SEVOSTYANOV, PAVEL, *Before the Nazi Invasion*, Progress, Moscow, 1984
SEYMOUR, CHARLES (ed.), *The Intimate Paper of Colonel House*, Houghton Mifflin, Boston, 1926
SHACHTMAN, TOM, *The Phony War 1939–1940*, Harper & Row, New York, 1982
SHIRER, WILLIAM, *Berlin Diary*, Bonanza Books, New York, 1984
The Nightmare Years, 1930–1940, Little, Brown, Boston, 1984
The Rise and Fall of the Third Reich, Secker & Warburg, 1960
The Collapse of the Third Republic, Literary Guild, 1966
SHOSTAKOVICH, DMITRI, *Testimony*, Hamish Hamilton, 1979
SIPOLS, V. J., *Secret Diplomacy. Bourgeois Latvia in the Anti-Soviet Plans of the Imperialist Powers, 1919–1940*, Riga
The Road to Victory, Progress, Moscow, 1985
SMITH, HOWARD K., *Last Train from Berlin*, Cresset Press, 1942
SOMMER, ERICH F., *Das Memorandum*, Herbig, Munich, 1981
SOUVARINE, BORIS, *Stalin: A Critical Survey of Bolshevism*, Longmans, Green, New York, 1939
SPEER, ALBERT, *Inside the Third Reich*, Weidenfeld & Nicolson, 1970
STALIN, J. V., *The Great Patriotic War of the Soviet Union*, International Publishers, New York, 1948
STERN, J. P., *Hitler. The Führer and the People*, Fontana, 1975
STONE, NORMAN, *Hitler*, Hodder & Stoughton, 1980
STORRY, RICHARD, *A History of Modern Japan*, Penguin Books, 1960
Japan and the Decline of the West in Asia 1894–1943, Macmillan, 1979
STRANG, LORD, *The Moscow Negotiations 1939*, Leeds UP, 1968
Home and Abroad, André Deutsch, 1956
STYPULKOWSKI, Z., *Invitation to Moscow*, Thames & Hudson, 1951
SUKHANOV, N. N., *The Russian Revolution, 1917*, OUP, 1955
SUVOROV, VIKTOR, *Soviet Military Intelligence*, Hamish Hamilton, 1984
SYROP, KONRAD, *Poland in Perspective*, Robert Hale, 1982
SZEMBEK, JAN, *Journal, 1933–1939*, Léon Noel, Paris, 1952

TANNER, V., *The Winter War*, Stanford UP, 1957
TARULIS, ALBERT N., *Soviet Policy Toward the Baltic States, 1918–1944*, Univ. of Notre Dame Press, 1959
TAYLOR, A. J. P., *The Origins of the Second World War*, Penguin, 1961
The Second World War, Hamish Hamilton, 1975
TAYLOR, FRED (ed.), *The Goebbels Diaries 1939–41*, Hamish Hamilton, 1982
THAYER, CHARLES, *Diplomat*, Harper, New York, 1959
T'HOMI, ABRAHAM, *The Dream and the Awakening*, Gareth Powell Associates, Sydney, 1977
TOKAEV, G., *Comrade X*, Harris Press, 1956
TOLAND, JOHN, *Adolf Hitler*, Doubleday, New York, 1976
The Rising Sun. The Decline and Fall of the Japanese Empire, 1936–1945, Cassell, 1970
TROTSKY, LEON, *My Life*, Grosset & Dunlap, New York, 1960
Stalin: An Appraisal of the Man and his Influence, Harper, New York, 1941
TUOMINEN, ARVO, *The Bells of the Kremlin*, Univ. Press of New England, 1983
ULAM, ADAM B., *Expansion and Coexistence. Soviet Foreign Policy, 1917–73*, Praeger Publishers, New York, 1974
Stalin, the Man and his Era, Allen Lane, 1974
UPTON, A. F., *Finland 1939–40*, Davis-Poynter, 1974
Finland in Crisis, 1940–1941, Faber & Faber, 1964
The Communist Parties of Scandinavia and Finland, Weidenfeld & Nicolson, 1973
URBAN, GARRI S., *Tovarisch, I am not Dead*, Weidenfeld & Nicolson, 1980
VANSITTART, LORD, *The Mist Procession*, Hutchinson, 1958
VARDYS, V. STANLEY (ed.), *Lithuania Under the Soviets 1940–1965: Aggression Soviet Style 1939–1940*, Frederick Praeger, New York, 1965
VIGOR, P. H., *Soviet Blitzkrieg Theory*, Macmillan, 1983
VOLKOV, FYDOR, *Secrets from Whitehall and Downing Street*, Progress Publishers, Moscow, 1980
VORMANN, NIKOLAUS VON, *Der Feldzug in Polen, 1939*, Weissenburg, 1958
VORONOV, N. N., *Na Sluzhbe Voennoi*, Moscow, 1963
WALLER, BRUCE, *Bismarck at the Crossroads*, Athlone Press, 1974
WARLIMONT, WALTER, *Inside Hitler's Headquarters, 1939–45*, Weidenfeld & Nicolson, 1964
WATT, DONALD CAMERON, *Too Serious a Business*, Temple Smith, 1975
WATTS, RICHARD M., *Bitter Glory: Poland and its Fate, 1918 to 1939*, Simon & Schuster, New York, 1979
WEINBERG, GERHARD L., *World in the Balance*, Univ. of New England, 1981
WEIZSÄCKER, ERNST VON, *Memoirs*, Gollancz, 1951
WELAND, JAMES EDWIN, *The Japanese Army in Manchuria*, Ann Arbor, Michigan. Dissertation, University of Arizona, 1977
WELLES, SUMNER, *A Time for Decision*, Harper, New York, 1944
WERTH, ALEXANDER, *Russia at War*, E. P. Dutton, New York, 1964
WHALEY, BARTON, *Codeword Barbarossa*, MIT, Boston, 1974
WHEATLEY, RONALD, *Operation Sea Lion*, OUP, 1958
WHEELER-BENNETT, JOHN W., *The Nemesis of Power: The German Army in Politics, 1914–1945*, Macmillan, 1953
WISKEMANN, ELIZABETH, *Europe of the Dictators 1919–1945*, Fontana, 1966
WOODWARD, LLEWELLYN, *British Foreign Policy in the Second World War*, HMSO, 1962
WUORINEN, JOHN H., *A History of Finland*, Columbia, New York, 1965
YAKOVLEV, A., *Purpose of My Life. Notes of an Aircraft Designer*. Progress, Moscow, 1974
YEREMENKO, MARSHAL G. K., *Vospominaniya i Razmyshleniya*, Novosti, Moscow, 1970
YOUNG, KATSU, *The Japanese Army and the Soviet Union 1939–1941*, Univ. of Washington, 1958

ZARIK, O., *German Odyssey*, London, 1941

ZHUKOV, GEORGI I., *Memoirs*, Cape, 1970

ZOLLER, ALBERT, *Douze ans auprès d'Hitler* (Memoirs of Christa Schröder), Julliard, Paris, 1949

ZUKER-BUJANOWSKA, LILIANA, *Liliana's Journal, Warsaw 1939–1945*, Piatkus, 1981

Index